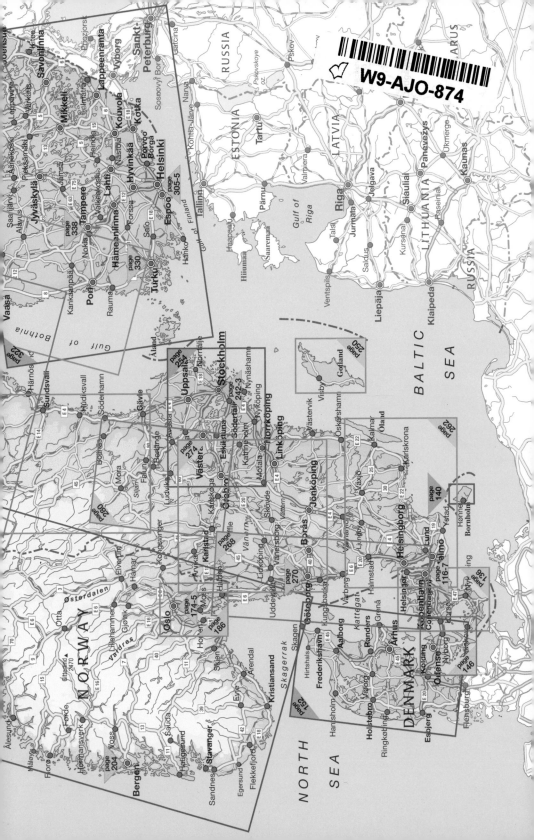

INSIGHT GUIDES
SCANDINAVIA

APA PUBLICATIONS L
Part of the Langenscheidt Publishing Group

※ INSIGHT GUIDE

SCANDINAVIA

Editorial

Project Editor
Siân Lezard
Series Manager
Rachel Lawrence
Publishing Manager
Rachel Fox
Art Director
Steven Lawrence
Senior Picture Researcher
Tom Smyth

Distribution

UK & Ireland
Dorling Kindersley Ltd (a Penguin Group company)
80 Strand, London, WC2R 0RL
customerservice@dk.com

United States
Ingram Publisher Services
1 Ingram Boulevard, PO Box 3006,
La Vergne, TN 37086-1986
customer.service@ingrampublisher
services.com

Australia
Universal Publishers
PO Box 307
St Leonards NSW 1590
sales@universalpublishers.com.au

New Zealand
Brown Knows Publications
11 Artesia Close, Shamrock Park
Auckland, New Zealand 2016
sales@brownknows.co.nz

Worldwide
**Apa Publications GmbH & Co.
Verlag KG (Singapore branch)**
7030 Ang Mo Kio Avenue 5
08-65 Northstar @ AMK
Singapore 569880
apasin@signet.com.sg

Printing

CTPS-China

©2012 Apa Publications UK Ltd
All Rights Reserved

First Edition 2001
Second Edition 2012
Reprinted 2012

ABOUT THIS BOOK

The first Insight Guide pioneered the use of creative full-colour photography in travel guides in 1970. Since then, we have expanded our range to cater for our readers' need not only for reliable information about their chosen destination but also for a genuine understanding of the culture and workings of that destination.

Now, when the internet can supply inexhaustible (but not always reli-able) facts, our books marry text and pictures to provide those much more elusive qualities: knowledge and dis-cernment. To achieve this, we rely heavily on the authority of locally based writers and photographers.

How to use this book

Insight Guide: Scandinavia is care-fully structured to convey an under-standing of the countries of Denmark, Norway, Sweden and Fin-land and their cultures as well as to guide readers through their sights and activities:

◆ The **Best of Scandinavia** section at the beginning of the book gives you a snapshot of the highlights in each country, helping you prioritise where to go and what to do.
◆ The **Features** section, indicated by a pink bar at the top of each page, helps you understand the region by looking at its historical and cultural development; this is followed by illuminating essays on the Danes, the Norwegians, the Swedes and the Finns. In addition, we look at Scandinavia's artistic and cultural achievements and a range of other subjects, from the popularity of Nordic cuisine to exploring the great outdoors.
◆ The main **Places** section, indi-cated by a blue bar, is a complete guide to all the sights and areas

worth visiting. Places of special interest are coordinated by number with the maps.

◆ The **Travel Tips** section, with an orange bar, provides a handy point of reference both to help you plan your trip and give you guidance once you're there. For each country we provide an A–Z of useful information, from Activities to Visas, and a selection of the best hotels and restaurants.

The contributors

Insight Guide: Scandinavia was commissioned by **Siân Lezard** and edited by **Cathy Muscat**. The book builds on the solid foundations laid by the late **Doreen Taylor-Wilkie**, editor of the original Insight Guides to each of the four countries.

This edition was updated by **Fran Parnell** (Denmark and Sweden) and **Joan Gannij** (Finland and Norway).

Fran Parnell's passion for Scandinavia began while studying Anglo-Saxon, Norse and Celtic at Cambridge University. Since then, she has travelled regularly in the region, writing travel guides to Iceland, Sweden, Denmark and Scandinavia, between climbing glaciers, cross-country skiing, and fulfilling her ambition to run a marathon in each Scandinavian capital. She loves Iron Age and Viking history, has a passion for long-distance wilderness walking, and this summer is looking forward to bear-watching in Finland's Karelia.

When Joan Gannij relocated to Amsterdam from the US, she planned to discover the southern climes of Spain, Italy and Portugal. Instead she headed radically north on her first assignments, first to Finland and then to Norway, developing her expertise in Nordic culture over the past decades. "As a child, the music of Grieg was constantly on the record player, so answering to the call of the North was simply a matter of time."

The photos are a key element of Insight's appeal, and although they are the work of several photographers, special thanks go to **Glyn Genin** (Norway), **Julian Love** (Sweden) and **Gregory Wrona** (Finland).

Thanks also go to **Neil Titman** for proofreading the book and **Helen Peters** for compiling the index.

Map Legend

—––·–	International Boundary
––––	Province Boundary
–·–·–	National Park/Reserve
– – –	Ferry Route
⊖	Border Crossing
✈ ✦	Airport: International/ Regional
🚌	Bus Station
Ⓣ Ⓜ Ⓣ	Metro/Tunnelbanan
Ⓢ	S-Tog (S-Train)
Ⓙ	Lokaltåg (Suburban Rail)
✉	Post Office
❶	Tourist Information
∴	Archaeological Site
✝ ✝ ✝	Church/Ruins
✝	Monastery
☾	Mosque
✡	Synagogue
∩	Cave
🯄	Statue/Monument
★	Place of Interest
⌐	Beach
⊼	Lighthouse
🏰 ⌂	Castle (ruins)
✳	Viewpoint
🏠	Mansion/Stately Home

The main places of interest in the Places section are coordinated by number with a full-colour map (eg ❶), and a symbol at the top of every right-hand page tells you where to find the map.

Contents

LEFT: Danish style.

Maps

Inside front cover:
Scandinavia. **Inside back
cover:** Stockholm Transport
and Oslo T-bane.

Travel Tips

THE BEST OF SCANDINAVIA: TOP ATTRACTIONS

Whether you want to see the Northern Lights, take a Finnish sauna, go island-hopping off the coast of Denmark, explore Norway's fjords or see brown bears in Sweden, we'll point you in the right direction

△ Norway's breathtaking **fjords** are an experience not to be missed. The Hurtigruten coastal steamships make 34 ports of call, heading way up north from Bergen to the North Cape and Kirkenes. *See page 220.*

▷ **Northern Lights**. The eerie aurora borealis billows like smoke and streaks like silent fireworks across the winter skies in Greenland and Arctic Scandinavia. Experience them in Tromsø, "Gateway to the Arctic", and Norway's far north. *See pages 25 and 378.*

Feel the therapeutic benefits of **a real smoke sauna** in rural Finland, followed by a brave leap into the lake or sea. *See pages 318 and 335.*

△ **Vigeland Sculpture Park**, Oslo. An open-air sculpture park filled with huge, arresting figures, many writhing and tumbling, in Vigeland's fantastic vision of humanity. A favourite with Oslo inhabitants. *See page 182.*

▷ **Turku**, Finland's oldest city and medieval capital, the "cradle of Finnish culture" brims with history and vitality. *See page 329.*

△ **Helsinki**. Discover great works by the masters of Finnish art at the Ateneum, one among many great museums in the capital, then head for the galleries and boutiques of the design district. *See pages 308 and 315.*

△ **Bergen**. Norway's most beautiful city sits on a craggy shoreline surrounded by hills, and makes an ideal base for a fjord holiday. A highlight of any visit is a summer concert at Troldhaugen, the former villa of composer Edvard Grieg. *See pages 203 and 207.*

▷ **Åland Islands**. Explore this lush collection of islands off the west coast of Finland by bike. *See page 327.*

△ **Medieval Trondheim**. Norway's ancient capital and its third-largest city is steeped in history and atmosphere. *See page 223.*

▽ **Porvoo** in winter, with its low wooden houses set against the snow, their chimneys expelling smoke, exudes a fairytale atmosphere. An elegant town, with a gorgeous riverside setting and a rich cultural heritage. *See page 324.*

△ **Stockholm.** Europe's first Green Capital floats on 14 islands: visit Gamla Stan, a medieval maze of alleyways and enchanting architecture, and Södermalm's bohemian shops and bars. *See pages 245 and 253.*

▽ **Bohuslän Coast**. Sun-worshippers flock to the sandy beaches of Bohuslän in summer, or take to sailing boats and kayaks to explore thousands of offshore islands, skerries, rocks and reefs. *See page 271.*

△ **Frederiksborg Slot**, Hillerød. Scandinavia's largest Renaissance castle, built across three islands in the middle of a lake, comes straight from the pages of a children's storybook. *See page 137.*

▽ **Orsa Björnpark**, Sweden. Old honeypaws, the King of the Forest, is a shy creature in the wild: this park offers a great chance to see brown bears and their cubs up close. *See page 281.*

△ **Icefjord**, Disko Bay, Greenland. Countless icebergs calve from Greenland's most productive glacier and float out to sea in a glinting parade at this Unesco World Heritage site, near Ilulissat. *See page 160.*

△ **Bornholm**. A well-kept Danish secret, the island of Bornholm is the sunniest place in Scandinavia. Hire a bicycle and explore its rugged coastline and unique medieval round churches. *See page 140.*

△ **Viking Ship Museum**, Roskilde. State-of-the-art ships and superb seafaring knowledge swept the Vikings to success: this excellent museum contains five original Viking vessels, and lets visitors row a reconstruction around the fjord. *See page 138.*

▽ **Inlandsbanan**. This historic railway runs from Sweden's heartland right into the Arctic Circle, stopping at tiny stations for meals, and to shoo reindeer off the tracks. *See page 286.*

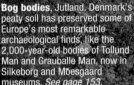

Bog bodies, Jutland. Denmark's peaty soil has preserved some of Europe's most remarkable archaeological finds, like the 2,000-year-old bodies of Tollund Man and Grauballe Man, now in Silkeborg and Moesgaard museums. *See page 153.*

▽ **Kungsleden Trail**. Sweden's most famous long-distance walking path wends its way through the mountains of Lapland, through dark forests and broad green valleys scattered with Alpine flowers. *See pages 76 and 399.*

▽ **Visby**, Gotland. Turreted walls encircle this medieval Hanseatic trading town, full of crooked houses, cobbled streets and rose-covered ruins. In August, troubadours and jousting knights bring the past to life during the Medeltidsveckan festival. *See page 265.*

THE BEST OF SCANDINAVIA: EDITOR'S CHOICE

Stunning scenic journeys, the best museums, festivals, family fun and unique attractions... here, at a glance, are our recommendations for a memorable visit to Scandinavia, plus some money-saving tips

BEST JOURNEYS

Here's your chance to experience the sheer beauty of Scandinavia.

● **Hurtigruten (Norway)** The world-famous postal boat sails up Norway's fjord-lined coast, stopping in at 34 picturesque ports along its 12-day route. *See page 220.*

● **Göta Kanal (Sweden)** Cross the country in the most leisurely manner possible, along Sweden's 19th-century engineering masterpiece, the Göta Kanal. *See page 277.*

● **Karelian Circle Trek (Finland)** Pull on your walking boots and launch yourself into the wilderness – this 1,000km (620-mile) trail takes in four stunning

national parks. *See page 77.*

● **Hærvejen (Denmark)** Cycle through Denmark's peaceful countryside on this bicycle path, which stretches from Germany to Viborg in central Jutland. *See page 78.*

● **Flåmsbana (Norway)** The mountain railway journey from Myrdal to Flåm packs the most dramatic scenery – ravines, rivers and toppling waterfalls – into its 20km (12-mile) route. This is part of the "Norway in a Nutshell" trip that adopts a variety of forms of transport to experience Norway's exhilarating natural beauty. *See pages 215 and 386.*

OUTDOOR ADVENTURE

● **Husky safaris, reindeer-sledging and snowmobiling (Finland)** Explore Lapland's icy wastes in classic fashion, driven along by a team of huskies or reindeer, or hop on a skidoo. *See pages 81 and 354.*

● **Cycling (Denmark)** Flat countryside and fabulous bike paths make Denmark a cycling dream. Try Bornholm island for a taste of two-wheeled freedom. *See page 78.*

● **Cross-country skiing (Oslo, Norway)** The Oslomarka area has an incredible 2,500km (1,500 miles) of cross-country skiing trails. *See page 185.*

● **Sailing (Sweden)** Experience the joy of sailing the Stockholm archipelago on a full-day sailing adventure in a historic schooner or a modern luxury yacht. *See pages 255, 258, 400.*

● **Bear-watching (Finland)** Get up close and be mesmerised by Finland's brown bears in their natural habitat. *See page 349.*

● **Hiking (Norway)** Scandinavia offers plenty of exceptional hiking, but there's something magical about the vast Jotunheimen National Park. *See page 212.*

LEFT: the railway from Myrdal to Flåm winds through magnificent mountain scenery.
ABOVE: sledging through Lapland's snowy terrain.

BEST MUSEUMS

● **Vasa Museum (Stockholm, Sweden)**
Carvings of cherubs and mermaids festoon this spectacular 17th-century warship. *See page 250.*

● **Viking Ship Museum (Oslo, Norway)**
On display are splendid Viking longships unearthed in southern Norway. *See page 185.*

● **Skansen (Stockholm, Sweden)**
Over 150 traditional Swedish buildings at the world's oldest open-air museum. *See page 249.*

● **Louisiana (Humlebæk, Denmark)**
This huge modern-art gallery contains an impressive collection, including works by Giacometti and Andy Warhol. *See page 137.*

● **Alvar Aalto Museum (Jyväskylä, Finland)**
Discover Finland's best-loved designer and architect. *See page 337.*

● **National Gallery (Oslo, Norway)**
Among the paintings here is Edvard Munch's *The Scream. See page 181.*

FINEST FOOD TRADITIONS

Scandinavia is a gastronomic treat, with fresh seafood in abundance.

● **Crayfish parties**
In July and August, crayfish parties are the speciality to celebrate the long days in Finland and Sweden.

● **Artistic sandwiches**
Smørrebrød in Denmark, *smörgåsbord* in Sweden and *voileipäpöytä* in Finland – all wonderfully pretty hot-and-cold buffet dishes.

● **Pickled herring**
An acquired taste, but one that will always bring back fond memories of Scandinavia.

● **Cloudberries**
Picked and devoured in Scandinavian forests in late summer and early autumn.

● **New Nordic cuisine**
The rise of this type of food, led by Copenhagen's pioneering restaurant, Noma, has put Scandinavia's capitals firmly on the culinary map.

ABOVE: crayfish parties are held to celebrate the summer, with lots of singing and drinking of schnapps. **LEFT:** experience the Swedish way of life, preserved at Skansen in Stockholm. **BELOW:** you can pose with reindeer at the North Cape, where they graze in summer on the plateau.

ONLY IN SCANDINAVIA

● **Sami culture**
The nomadic Sami still base their calendar and culture around ancient reindeer-herding traditions. *See page 80.*

● **Lumilinna (Kemi, Finland)**
Each year, the marvellous Snow Castle is fashioned from blocks of snow and ice. *See page 345.*

● **Scandinavian style**
From Saab cars and Arne Jacobsen chairs to Marimekko textiles and Nokia mobile phones, the success of Nordic design is a global phenomenon. *See page 90.*

● **Christiania (Copenhagen)**
A fascinating social experiment, the "Free City" is open to curious visitors. *See page 128.*

● **Father Christmas**
Several places in Scandinavia claim Santa Claus as their own. Joulupukin Pajakylä in Lapland allegedly has the real thing. *See page 353.*

● **Stave churches (Norway)**
Two of the most striking of these ancient wooden churches are at Urnes and the Heddal in Telemark. *See pages 215 and 195.*

12

SCANDINAVIA FOR FAMILIES

● **Legoland (Billund, Denmark)**
Win eternal admiration by taking your children to Legoland, with waterpark, rides and the marvellous Miniland, created from 20 million bricks. *See page 153.*

● **Tivoli (Copenhagen, Denmark)**
Utterly delightful theme park and gardens, right in the heart of the capital city. Fountains and fairground rides as well as jugglers and acrobats make this a fun family day out for everyone. *See page 120.*

● **Moomin World (Finland)**
A theme park for smaller children based on the Moomin books by Tove Jansson. The blue-coloured Moomin House is the main attraction. *See page 331.*

● **Glasriket (Småland, Sweden)**
For something a little different, let your children paint, engrave and even blow their own glass at a traditional glassworks. *See page 264.*

● **Egeskov Slot (Funen, Denmark)**
One of Denmark's most famous historic sights. This well-preserved fairytale castle has a gardenful of endearing attractions, including one of the world's biggest permanent mazes. *See page 147.*

● **Norwegian Museum of Cultural History (Oslo, Norway)**
The Folk Museum on Bygdøy peninsula offers something for children of all ages. Horse and wagon rides, livestock, folk dancing and music and a playground, all in a charming historic setting. *See page 185.*

● **Frogner Park (Oslo, Norway)**
Oslo is a very family-friendly city, with outdoor pools, an adventure playground and the Vigeland sculpture park. *See page 182.*

ABOVE: celebrating Midsummer with a bonfire on the beach, in West Jutland, Denmark. **LEFT:** Copenhagen's *Little Mermaid*. **BELOW LEFT:** all aboard the Legoland train, in Billund, East Jutland, Denmark.

BEST FESTIVALS

● **Midsummer**
Celebrated with bonfires, parties and great gusto across Scandinavia on the nearest weekend to 23 June.

● **Savolinna Opera Festival (Finland)**
International artists perform at Olavinlinna castle, on Lake Pihlajavesi, in July at Finland's most famous cultural festival.

● **Holmenkollen Ski Festival (Norway)**
Oslo's Holmenkollen ski jump is the focus of this traditional sports event, held annually in March.

● **Horsens Middle Ages Festival (Denmark)**
Medieval history is brought to life in late August at this lively festival, with music, dancing and theatrical performances.

● **Dalhalla Summer Music (Sweden)**
There's something to appeal to everyone at this cavernous open-air arena, set in the depths of an abandoned limestone quarry near Rättvik. Its summer-long music programme encompasses opera, jazz, pop and rock.

● **Roskilde (Denmark)**
Northern Europe's largest annual music festival, held over four days in early July, features world-famous rock and pop bands.

● **Bergen International Festival (Norway)**
Norway's answer to the Edinburgh festival; from late May to early June artists and musicians flock to Bergen from all over the world to perform in this, the loveliest of Norway's cities. Ibsen and Grieg are, of course, focal points.

BEST IN SCANDINAVIAN DESIGN

● **Oslo Opera House (Norway)**
This striking building in white granite and glass sitting on the waterfront is one of the Oslo's top attractions. *See page 179.*

● **Carl Larsson's house (Sundborn, Sweden)**
The artist's beautiful riverside cottage is a

humbling example of love, family life and Swedish design working in perfect harmony. *See page 281.*

● **Finnish *Jugendstil* (Finland)**
The National Romantics

used art and architecture to express independence from Russian rule: you can admire their beautiful Art Nouveau buildings in Helsinki's Katajanokka area. *See page 312.*

● **Designmuseum Danmark (Copenhagen, Denmark)**
Ceramics, furniture, textiles, prints and posters – the best in Danish design is here. *See page 125.*

● **Central Railway Station (Helsinki, Finland)**
Designed by Eliel Saarinen, it links two of Helsinki's most prevalent styles: National Romanticism and Functionalism. *See page 308.*

● **Lysøen (Norway)**
The residence of violin virtuoso Ole Bull, on an island outside Bergen, is a daring blend of styles that never fails to wow visitors. *See page 207.*

ABOVE: Päijänne Lakes; the popular view of Finland, with its endless lakes and forests. **LEFT:** Oslo Opera House sits dramatically on the waterfront.

NATURAL WONDERS

● **Stockholm archipelago (Sweden)**
Right on the city's doorstep lie 24,000 islets and skerries, a sight that gave author August Strindberg "goose pimples of sheer delight". *See page 255.*

● **Preikestolen (Norway)**
Featured in every tourist brochure on Norway, majestic Pulpit Rock has unbeatable fjord views. *See page 196.*

● **Jostedalsbreen Glacier (Sognefjord, Norway)**

Europe's largest glacier. *See page 214.*

● **Lake Päijänne (Finland)**
33,000 islands are yours to explore in Finland's Lakeland. *See page 336.*

● **Cliffs of Møn (Denmark)**
Hunt for fossils along the edges of Denmark's most famous landscape, the shining white chalk cliffs of Møn. *See page 139.*

● **Ruska (Lapland)**
The dazzling electric colours of nature as seen during *Ruska* (Indian summer) in late August in Lapland. *See page 351.*

MONEY-SAVING TIPS

● **Tourist Cards** All of Scandinavia's capitals (and some larger cities such as Göteborg) offer 24- and 48-hour tourist cards, which are well worth the money as the price includes admission to many museums, galleries and tourist attractions, and usually free access to public transport or car-parking.

● **Hostels** Youth hostels in Scandinavia are well worth considering: they tend to be good value, family-orientated and have excellent facilities. Bring your own sheets and towels

to save on rental costs.

● **City Bikes** Getting around Scandinavian cities by bicycle is generally a liberating experience. Borrow bicycles for free in Norway (Bergen, Oslo and Trondheim) and Denmark (Copenhagen) and explore further afield.

● **Food** Self-service buffet breakfasts in hostels and hotels are a great boon to the thrifty traveller. Fill up in the morning; at lunchtime snack on sandwiches or look for the daily special on restaurant menus; many places do "early bird" evening

deals, usually between 5.30pm and 7pm.

● **Nature**
Wild, empty space is Scandinavia's greatest treasure. Get back to nature with a tent and immerse yourself in solitude.

● **Free Festivals** Check what's on and when. Many Scandinavian festivals have free as well as ticketed events: for example, at the Copenhagen Jazz Festival in July, the city streets become a venue.

NORTHERLY NEIGHBOURS

At the top of the map, but no longer aloof, the Scandinavian countries are Europe's best-kept secret

To fly over Scandinavia is to discover a vast, sparsely inhabited, natural landscape of sparkling fjords and rocky mountains, glassy lakes and rushing rivers, dense forests and frozen tundra, extending from temperate Denmark far north to the land of the Sami and including Greenland and the Faroe Islands.

Norway, Denmark, Sweden and Finland are among Europe's most ancient civilisations. Early Norse traders ventured deep into Asia, leaving graphic runic graffiti in their wake, and later, the infamous Vikings pillaged round the coasts of Ireland, Britain and France, establishing a network of Norse kingdoms. They were followed by kings, queens and tsars who schemed and battled. Borders shifted, unions came and went, and by the start of the 20th century four distinct nations emerged, growing into today's modern, highly individualistic countries.

The Nordic reputation for cool reserve has had its day, and visitors receive a warm welcome. But cool design remains: everything from bottle openers to new buildings has the stamp of chic Scandinavian understatement. Copenhagen, Oslo, Stockholm and Helsinki are vibrant capitals with some of the most inspirational museums and art collections in Europe, and Turku was deservedly chosen as a European Capital of Culture in 2011.

An inherent love of nature is deeply rooted within the national psyches. At the slightest excuse Scandinavians will take to the outdoors, on bicycles along Denmark's winding lanes, skiing on floodlit trails around Oslo, escaping to red-painted waterside cottages in Sweden, or plunging from sauna to ice pool in Finland. Arrive in any of the Scandinavian countries in Midsummer and you'll find the locals dancing and feasting around maypoles and bonfires.

Transport and communications are excellent: roads join southerly Denmark with the North Cape, railways penetrate Lapland, ferries ply the fjords and link remote islands, and planes cut journey times. Far from being an isolated northern region, Scandinavia is just a short step from its European neighbours. ❏

PRECEDING PAGES: the forested north of Sweden; a Sami family in their colourful traditional costumes; spectacular display of Northern Lights. **LEFT:** market day at the harbour, Helsinki. **ABOVE LEFT:** classic representation of Vikings. **ABOVE RIGHT:** view of Pulpit Rock and Stavangerfjord.

A WILD LAND

Scandinavia's countryside is cherished by its green-minded inhabitants, a spiritual retreat full of lush berries and wild animals

Stretching from mainland Europe to the North Pole's back yard, Scandinavia's vast territory covers all manner of environments. From well-groomed Danish farmland to Norway's wild and breathtaking fjords; from Sweden's great lakes and islands to bear-filled Finnish forests; from white-sand beaches full of sunbathers to empty oceans drifting with icebergs – there's a Scandinavian habitat to suit every mood.

Country retreats

Scandinavians, many only a few generations away from rural life, have a deep-rooted love of nature. With thousands of square miles of pristine countryside, and an enshrined legal freedom to roam through it at will, it's no wonder that they head for the hills at every opportunity. In Norway, Sweden and Finland, the family *hytte*, *stuga* or *mökki* is not just a holiday cottage, but a place for spiritual rejuvenation.

> Finland's forests contain almost 2.2 billion sq metres (23.6 billion sq ft) of timber – enough to build a 1-metre (3ft) -wide, 15-storey-high stockade around the entire planet.

Berry-picking is a common summer pastime – crowberries, bilberries, lingonberries and precious Arctic brambles and cloudberries appear on kitchen tables, supplemented in autumn by earthy mushrooms.

LEFT: Geirangerfjord, Norway.
RIGHT: traditional Norwegian wooden hut with turf providing the roof covering.

Scandinavians have always integrated home and landscape, from wood-built cottages to turf-roofed houses. Modern architecture uses glass to bring nature inside, and the simple lines of Scandinavian design often echo the curves of a lakeshore, or the pale slant of winter sunlight.

Scandinavian landscapes

Finland was flattened during the Ice Age. As the earth warmed, the melting icesheet left behind low rounded hills and tens of thousands of lakes – an angler's delight and perfect for wild swimmers. "Finland" and "forests" go together like coffee and cake – trees cover 86 percent of the land, and although much of the timber is felled for export, the forests are managed as naturally as possible.

Denmark's countryside was also compressed – Møllehøj in East Jutland is its zenith, a vertiginous 170 metres (560ft) above sea level. Free from trees, 40 percent of Denmark is rich arable farmland, glowing with blossom in spring, and golden harvest fields in late summer. With more than 7,400 km (4,600 miles) of coastline, no point in the country is more than a 45-minute drive from the sea. North Zealand and Jutland are frilled by sandy beaches, which draw countless summer visitors, as do the wonderful 70-million-year-old chalk cliffs at Møns Klint.

Sweden's south, too, is characterised by mild, fertile farmland. But Skåne's rolling fields soon give way to vast lakes and heavy woods. In Dalarna, Lake Siljan was formed not by glacial retreat, but by the catastrophic impact of a 2.5km (1½-mile) -wide meteorite. In the northwest of Sweden, the land rises, Alpine peaks shrug off their tree cover, and huge boulders, glaciers and rushing rivers dominate the scenery.

Composer Edvard Grieg acknowledged a hint of the "trollish" in some of his music, a sound that summons up Norway's mountains, fjords and valleys. Whereas the Ice Age levelled much of Finland, Sweden and Denmark, in Norway

SCANDINAVIAN WILDLIFE

Finland, Norway and Sweden contain an exciting array of big beasts, with the brown bear the undisputed King of the Forest. Finland's national animal once had dozens of euphemistic names, such as "forest grandfather" and "honey-eater", as it was taboo to speak the true name of such a fearsome creature. Orsa Björnpark, in Dalarna, central Sweden, is Europe's biggest bear park; and wild bear-watching tours operate on the Finland–Russia border (*see page 349*).

Lynx live in all three countries, although their nocturnal habits mean that they are rarely seen by visitors. The wolverine, actually part of the weasel family, is the most secretive of all Scandinavia's predators – numbers are still

unknown. Wolves are fighting their way back from extinction across the region. Knobbly-kneed elk can grow to 2 metres (6½ft) tall, and have a dangerous habit of lolloping in front of moving cars. Visitors to the far north will see reindeer, traditionally herded by the Sami. The sharp-eyed might spot lemming and foxes and, in northern Finland, the intriguing Siberian flying squirrel.

Denmark has no big forest predators, but it is good for birdlife, particularly aquatic varieties. Greenland's shores contain (rare) polar bears, lemming, Arctic foxes and hares, reindeer and musk oxen. Anyone taking a boat trip will appreciate the abundant marine life, including millions of seals, 15 whale species, and walruses.

the Scandinavian Mountains run like a rocky spine over 46 percent of the country, from south to northern tip. Glaciers scored great grooved valleys into the rock, which filled with water and became Norway's amazing fjords when the ice retreated.

> The Arctic skies contain other odd light displays besides the aurora borealis. Sundogs, ice pillars, arcs and coronas often appear in high-latitude skies, as ice crystals in the atmosphere cause the sun's light to refract.

Midnight sun

Like Scandinavians, the sun in summer shows no inclination to sleep. From within the Arctic Circle, it appears to observers that the "midnight sun" never sets, but simply travels around the horizon in a circle. The further north you go, the more days of midnight sun there are – in Svalbard, it shines for a steady 126 days. The phenomenon is caused by the tilt of the earth as it orbits the sun. This lopsided angle ensures that the North Pole always faces sunwards in summer… and sits in darkness all winter long.

Northern Lights

As summer ebbs away, the gloom is relieved by the bewitching greens, purples, pinks and reds of the aurora borealis, or Northern Lights, which flicker and pulse across the winter sky. Many a high-latitude tale was born while watching the display: the lights were the Sami, out looking for reindeer, or sparks crackling from a fox's fur as it ran across the sky, or even the spirits of the restless dead.

The scientific explanation is no less astonishing. The lights are caused by streams of charged particles – "solar wind" – that flare into space from our sun. When the wind comes into contact with the earth's magnetic field, it is drawn towards the poles where its electrical charge agitates particles of oxygen and nitrogen in the atmosphere, making them glow. Solar activity follows an 11-year cycle, due to peak in 2011–12. If the forecasts are correct, the light displays during this period will be even more

LEFT: Sweden's rocky coastline and myriad islands provide plenty of opportunity for adventure.
RIGHT: Northern Lights.

spectacular, and witnessed in areas that don't usual experience these mesmeric light displays.

Environmental challenges

Scandinavia is blessed with vast uninhabited landscapes, and a small, environmentally-aware population who recycle, have a passion for bicycles and public transport, and see their countryside as a national asset that must be protected. Their environmental record puts the rest of Europe to shame. Stockholm was designated Europe's first Green Capital in 2010, Sweden plans to be carbon-neutral by 2020, and Norway by 2030. Wind supplies 20 percent of Den-

mark's electricity, and the world's biggest solar power station is on the island of Æro.

There are some headaches. Nitrogen run-off from Sweden's southern farmland contributes to Baltic Sea pollution; in Denmark, overfishing is a serious concern; and in Finland's forests, fertiliser use causes water pollution. The demands of a greedy 21st century are seen most clearly in Greenland, whose melting icecaps and stranded polar bears are shorthand for global warming. In 2010 oil reserves were discovered in Baffin Bay; and Greenland's first aluminium smelter will open in 2014. Denmark and Norway have no nuclear power stations. Finland and Sweden are reassessing theirs following the failure of Japan's Fukushima nuclear plant in 2011. ❏

DECISIVE DATES

EARLY HISTORY: 10,000 BC–AD 800
From 10,000 BC
Hunter-gatherer tribes follow the melting ice northwards, establishing settlements in southern Scandinavia.

1500 BC
Trade routes are forged through the rivers of Eastern Europe to the Danube.

c.500 BC–AD 800
Iron Age Grauballe Man and Tollund Man are buried in peat bogs in Denmark.

c.AD 100
The historian Tacitus mentions the Fenni (the Sami of Finland) in his *Germania* and describes the Sveas who inhabit what is now central Sweden.

c.AD 400
Suomalaiset (Baltic Finns) settle in Finland. Sweden's influence over its "eastern province" begins.

THE VIKING AGE
800–1060
Vikings earn a reputation as sea warriors. Swedish Vikings (Varangians) soon control trade routes to Byzantium.

830
A Benedictine monk, Ansgar (801–65), lands on Björkö in Sweden and founds a church.

861
Vikings sack Paris.

866
Vikings raid and plunder, eventually controlling most of England and Normandy.

940–95
Harald Bluetooth brings Christianity to Denmark; Olav Tryggvason uses force in his attempts to convert the Norwegian Vikings.

1001
Leifur Eiríksson discovers Vinland (America).

1050
Harald Hardrada of Norway founds Oslo.

1066
Defeat in England brings the Viking Age to an end.

MIDDLE AGES *c.*1100–1500
1070
Building of Nidaros Cathedral begins in Norway.

1155
King Erik of Sweden launches a crusade into Finland; further Swedish invasions take place in 1239 and 1293.

1319–43
Inter-Scandinavian royal marriages produce a joint Norwegian–Swedish monarchy.

1362
Finland becomes a province of Sweden.

1397
The Kalmar Union unites the kingdoms of Norway, Denmark and Sweden.

1417
Eric VII of Denmark makes Copenhagen his capital and builds a palace at Helsingør.

WARS AND REFORMATION
1520
Kristian II of Denmark invades Sweden and massacres the nobility in the "Stockholm Bloodbath". Gustav Vasa drives him out and the Kalmar Union is disbanded.

1523
In Sweden, Gustav Vasa ascends the throne, marking the start of the Vasa dynasty (1523–1720), which also holds power in Finland.

1530
The Reformation; the Lutheran faith is introduced.

1536
Norway ceases to be an independent kingdom as the Danes take control.

1548
Mikael Agricola's translation of the Bible forms the basis of the Finnish literary language.

1588–1648
Denmark flourishes under Kristian IV (1577–1648).

1625–57
The Thirty Years War launched by the Danish king, Kristian IV, to check Swedish expansion ends in defeat for Denmark.

1714–41
Russia and Sweden battle over Finland. Under the Treaty of Turku (1743) Russia moves its border westwards.

NINETEENTH CENTURY

1801–14
During the Napoleonic Wars, English fleets twice bombard Copenhagen. Denmark sides with Napoleon and suffers defeat; Norway is ceded to Sweden.

1807–1905
Tsar Alexander I occupies Finland in 1807. In 1899 the composer Jean Sibelius writes his patriotic *Finlandia*, and Finnish resistance grows.

FAR LEFT TOP: Tollund Man. LEFT: King Gustav Vasa of Sweden. ABOVE: Tsar Alexander I. RIGHT: Tarja Halonen, Finland's first female president.

1812
Tsar Alexander makes Helsinki Finland's capital.

1815–1907
In Sweden, Jean-Baptiste Bernadotte, French marshal of Napoleon, succeeds to the throne as Karl XIV Johan (1818–44). The great exodus to the United States takes place.

1864
Denmark and Prussia at war. Denmark loses Schleswig-Holstein.

MODERN TIMES

1905
Referendum in Norway leads to the end of the union with Sweden. The Danish prince Håkon VII is King of Norway.

1906
Finnish women become the first in Europe to win the vote.

1917–19
Finland declares its independence from the Soviet Union, but is plunged into civil war.

1919
The Republic of Finland is born under its first president, K.J. Ståhlberg.

1930s
Sweden and Denmark establish welfare states.

1939–48
Winter War between Finland and the Soviet Union: Finland is forced to cede land and war reparations are severe. Sweden remains neutral in World Wars I and II. Norway proclaims neutrality in World War II, but is attacked by the Germans, who also occupy Denmark.

1949
Denmark becomes a founding member of NATO.

1960s
Norway begins oil exploration.

1986
Olof Palme, Swedish prime minister and international peacemaker, is assassinated.

1973
Denmark joins the EEC (EU).

1995
Finland and Sweden join the EU. Norway votes against joining (1972 and 1994).

2000
Øresund bridge opens between Denmark and Sweden.

2006
Finland's first female president, Tarja Halonen, re-elected.

2009
UN climate change conference held in Copenhagen.

2011
A bomb in Oslo and shooting on Utøya island kill 76 people. The gunman, a right-wing Christian extremist, accuses Norway's Labour government of failing on immigration.

BEGINNINGS

As the ice floes retreated, so the hunter-gatherers moved north, colonising the Nordic lands and giving rise to the Viking Age

For 1.6 million years, Scandinavia languished under an ice-sheet that oozed out of the Jostedalsbreen in Norway, stretched as far as the British Isles and Moscow, and was 3,000 metres (9,800ft) thick. When eventually it melted, nomadic hunters and gatherers went after the plants and animals that surfaced in its wake. Some 12,000 years ago, the peninsula celebrated its final liberation from the crushing weight of the ice by rising like bread in an oven. Unleavened Denmark, however, remained barely above sea level, the land bridge with Norway and Sweden broken.

The first inhabitants

Some of the earliest arrivals in this re-sculptured land brought with them tame dogs, knew how to make leather boats, and kept a well-stocked armoury of bows, arrows, harpoons and spears. Not much else is known about them, so a case has been made for recognising the nomadic Sami as Scandinavia's quasi-aboriginals. Other

Grauballe Man was discovered in a Danish peat bog in 1952. The victim, in his mid-30s, had eaten a meal of wheat porridge before his throat was slashed and his body dumped. Estimated time of death: 300 BC.

schools of thought put them down as comparatively recent arrivals from Siberia.

As for the Finns, the second group of somewhat exceptional Scandinavians, a 19th-century scholar, M.A. Castren, suggested that they and anyone else speaking a Finno-Ugric language, which includes Hungarians, Estonians and the Sami, hailed from Outer Mongolia and could therefore claim kinship with the likes of Genghis Khan. An increasing number of Finns see themselves as indigenous Baltic folk who drifted into their present location between the Bronze Age and the start of the great European migration in the 5th century AD.

The origins of today's Swedes, Norwegians and Danes are also something of a mystery. In the Mesolithic era, shifting tribes of hunter-gatherers lived along the coasts of southern Scandinavia, making seasonal trips inland

LEFT: Viking raiding party sets out across the North Sea, 9th century. RIGHT: Grauballe Man.

to hunt boar and deer in the rich forests that covered the region at the time. These inhabitants consituted one of the last major hunter-gatherer complexes in Stone Age Europe, and it was always assumed that they evolved into today's Scandinavians.

However, in 2009 genetics research conducted at Uppsala University discovered that these hunter-gatherers are not related to modern Scandinavians – in fact, they seem to have vanished entirely from the region around 4,000 years ago. The theory now is that a new influx of people must have settled at the end of the Stone Age – but who they were, nobody knows.

appointed world of horse-drawn carts, ships with curious beaks at either end, weapons and a religion devoted to the worship of the sun and fertility.

Travellers' tales

In 500 BC, a drastic turn in the weather killed off livestock, wrecked agriculture and forced men into trousers instead of belted cloaks. The beginning of the Iron Age in Scandinavia appears to have been filled with great social change and deep unrest – quantities of swords and other items have been found in peat bogs, presumed to have been sacrificed by their

Bronze Age artwork

As there were still no written records in Scandinavia by the Nordic Bronze Age (1800–500 BC), we can only guess at the religion, law, language and culture of the mysterious new settlers. But they have left tantalising glimpses of their lives. Swords, shields, jewellery and musical instruments have been found across Scandinavia. The Trundholm sun chariot appears to be a religious artefact, showing a horse pulling the sun across the sky; and the well-preserved body of the Egtved Girl, found in southern Jutland, gives us a close-up view of a 3,500-year-old person and her possessions. Bronze Age rock carvings, such as those at Tanumshede in Sweden, reveal a well-

desperate owners. Humans, too, have been unearthed from the depths of Denmark's bogs – Tollund Man, Grauballe Man and Elling Woman were all killed and cast into the peaty waters during these troubled centuries.

In the meantime, sun-drenched Athenians were building the Parthenon and, like most Europeans, had no idea whatsoever of Scandinavia until the voyager Pytheas of Marseilles returned a little before 300 BC with tales of a land north of Britain where it was light enough, even at midnight, to pick lice out of a shirt. The local population were barbarians who lived on millet, herbs, roots and fruit because, he noticed, they had hardly any domestic animals, and threshing generally had to be done indoors. Nevertheless, grain fermented with honey produced a giddying drink they enjoyed.

Four centuries later, the Roman historian Tacitus reported significant improvements. The Suiones (Uppland Swedes) had developed a healthy respect for wealth, recognised a king "with an unchallengeable right to obedience", and built powerful sailing ships "unusual in that there is a prow at each end". Augustus and Nero sent expeditions to find out more, and Roman contact may have inspired the Scandinavians to produce their own runic alphabet.

Jordanes, the 6th-century historian of the

Raiding parties

In 789, however, the Scandinavians spoke up for themselves. Three ships of unfamiliar design appeared off the coast of Dorset, southwest England, and the local magistrate ambled down to welcome them. Heavily armed warriors leapt ashore and subjected the hapless man to a fate

> To facilitate carving in wood or stone, the runic alphabet consisted of permutations of straight lines. It was used initially only for names and invocations against evil spirits.

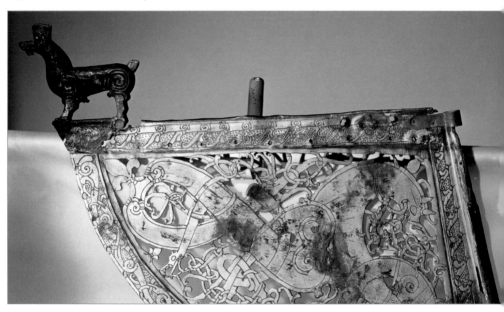

Goths, was the first to identify "Dani" among the local tribes, said to be taller than Germans and ferocious fighters. Procopius, the Byzantine historian, singled out the Sami as people who had neither crops nor wine and wore animal skins held together with sinews. Sami babies, he said, did not touch milk. Put into skin cradles and left dangling from trees while their mothers worked, they tucked into bone marrow. Procopius also described hunters on skis and an excessive enthusiasm for human sacrifice.

LEFT: Bronze Age sun chariot, National Museum of Denmark, Copenhagen.
ABOVE: weather vane from a Viking ship.

known as "kissing the thin lips of the axe". As his head rolled, they filled their ships with whatever caught their fancy, including a number of attractive natives, and were gone. The bemused *Anglo-Saxon Chronicle* could only say that they were apparently "Northmen from Hordaland" (Norwegians from the Bergen area). They, however, called themselves Vikings.

The Vikings returned four years later. As committed pagans, the raiders were unaffected by the sanctity of Christian monasteries stuffed with valuables. Beginning with Lindisfarne in Northumbria, they murdered monks and ransacked coastal monasteries all around the British Isles, repeating the performance every summer.

Around the same time, Swedish counterparts capitalised on the almost uninterrupted navigable grid of lakes and rivers between the Gulf of Finland and the Caspian and Black seas. At the far end lay Constantinople, the richest city on earth and an inexhaustible market for northern products like amber, furs, weapons and European slaves. The Arab traveller and diplomat Ibn Fadlan was impressed by the Swedes' appearance – "perfect physical specimens, tall as date palms, blond and ruddy" – but had reservations about their insistence on exercising seigneurial rights over the merchandise in public and en masse. "A man will have sexual intercourse with slave girls while his companions look on," he said.

On a third contemporary front, Charlemagne's crusade against the heathen Saxons of northwest Germany brought him into contact with their Danish neighbours on the other side of the Eider, whose look he liked even less. As the Danes felt exactly the same way about him and his Franks, they built the Danevirke wall across the Jutland peninsula to keep them at bay and secure the border town of Hedeby. Thus were sown the seeds of the Schleswig-Holstein imbroglio, a territorial dispute of such complexity that even 1,000 years later anyone dragged into it, according to 19th-century British prime minister Lord Palmerston, was in danger of going mad or dying.

Al-Tartushi, another Arab traveller, went to see Hedeby, "a large town at the farthest end of the world ocean." The carcasses of sacrificed animals swung from poles, but the main food was fish "as there is so much of it". Both men and women used eye make-up, he said (not that anyone else ever noticed), and women could unilaterally divorce their husbands whenever they felt like it.

Taken together, these developments across three fronts signalled the start of the "Viking Age" in which they went abroad to conquer most of the British Isles, carve a Norman province out of France, invade Germany, Spain and Italy, settle Iceland and Greenland, discover America, terrorise the Mediterranean, dominate the Baltic region, Poland, Russia and Ukraine, fight for and against Byzantium, attack the Muslim Caliphate in Baghdad, and contribute to the liberation of Jerusalem. Meanwhile, the pack of warring chieftainships and petty kingdoms at home was being shuffled and cut down to form the separate states that exist today.

Trade with Byzantium

Muslim conquests in Europe disrupted traditional trade, encouraging the Swedes to open up alternative routes through Russia. Apparently the Slavs then begged them to take charge of their territory. "Our land is large and fruitful but it lacks order," the message allegedly read. "Come over and rule us." By 900, Swedish influence radiated throughout Eastern Europe from their strongholds at Novgorod and Kiev. The Swedes were soon assimilated under the weight of Slavic numbers, but they left an indelible

VIKING SHIP DESIGN

A Viking's ticket to foreign parts was the latest evolution of the ship design first shown in Bronze Age rock carvings. The prows at either end were the extremities of a keel made out of a single oak. It could twist like a tree in the wind, hence its immense strength. A fighting ship of the type found at Gokstad in Norway was 25 metres (82ft) long, 6 metres (19ft) wide, and carried a crew of 70. Clinker-built, caulked with tarred animal hair or wool, it had a hinged steering oar that swung out of the way so the ships could be aimed at a beach at full speed. An important innovation was the use of sail. Viking ships could cross the North Sea to England in 72 hours.

mark in the name by which they were locally known, Rus.

Polygamy and primogeniture also shaped the Viking Age. Only a tiny proportion of Scandinavia was actually habitable, and farmland could only be subdivided so many times. The whole of a patrimony generally went to the eldest son,

> *In Arthurian romances the Vikings were described as being "wild and savage and had not in them the love of God nor their neighbours".*

foray in 844 opened with a rebuff at La Coruña on Spain's Atlantic coast, improved with the sacking of Lisbon, Cádiz and Seville, and ended with the loss of two ships crammed with gold, silver and prisoners to the Moors.

Terrorising the Mediterranean

Back again in 859 with a fleet of 62 red-sailed ships, Hasting negotiated the Straits of Gibraltar, sacked Algeciras, spent a week in Morocco rounding up "blue men" for subsequent sale in Ireland and then wintered on La Camargue in the Rhône Delta, "causing great annoyance and detriment to the inhabitants". Come spring, he

or rather the eldest surviving son, so Swedish kings with 40 women in their harem, or Norwegian earls with a dozen sons by various wives and concubines, were sure recipes for orgiastic fratricide. Harald Fairhair's ascendancy, *c.*890, went a long way towards defining Norway, but as he stripped and disbanded numerous lesser dynasties, their scions were compelled to try their luck abroad.

To begin with, Viking enterprise abroad was a matter of independent initiative, as epitomised by a certain Hasting. Born in Denmark, his first

---

LEFT: fabulous artefacts are on display at the Viking Ship Museum, Oslo. **ABOVE:** runic script, National Museum, Copenhagen.

was ready for Italy. After looting Pisa, he turned south and came across a city of such marbled magnificence that it could only be Rome.

Hasting dispatched messengers who related that their leader was dying, and his last wish was to be given a Christian burial in hallowed ground. Permission granted, the gates admitted a coffin followed by a long procession of mournful Vikings. As the local bishop was praying over the coffin it flew open and out leapt Hasting himself. The startled bishop was run through with Hasting's sword, and the mourners went off to reduce the city to ashes. Only then did Hasting learn that he had destroyed Luna, not Rome, and felt so cheated that he ordered the massacre of all male prisoners. His next port of call was Alexandria in

Egypt. The campaign closed in 862 with an overland march to sack Pamplona.

England under attack

Three years later, in 865, Hasting appeared at the mouth of the Thames with a new fleet of 80

> *Vikings weren't always victorious. A raid on Córdoba failed, and the emir sent a gift of 200 Vikings' heads to his Moroccan ally. Some of the vanquished Vikings converted to Islam and opened a successful cheese farm in Isla Menor!*

ships just as "a big heathen horde", according to the *Anglo-Saxon Chronicle*, arrived elsewhere in England under Ivar the Boneless. Their immediate mission was to avenge a private grievance, the cruel death of their father Ragnar in a pit full of snakes, but with Hasting's fleet and other Danish private armies dotted around the country, the show took on the appearance of a concerted Danish conquest. The outcome was a Danish kingdom in England and the imposition of a stiff tax, Danegeld.

Ironically, Harald Bluetooth of Denmark (*c.*910–85) was in turn obliged to prostrate himself. His *bête noire* was the crusading Holy Roman Emperor Otto I, a German, who could be appeased only by Harald's submission to Christian baptism. Most of Europe had been Christian for five centuries or more, but Scandinavia was not inclined to abandon paganism. Harald's son and successor, Swein Forkbeard, brushed aside his father's baptism as an aberration. The Norwegian king Olav Tryggvason (*c.*965–1000), a hell-raising pirate from the age of 12, was supposedly convinced by a wise hermit in the Scillies in England, but the methods he then employed to convert his subjects were pure Viking. Sweden remained true to paganism by turning Christian missionaries into martyrs. Sacrifices in the golden temple at Uppsala continued into the late 11th century.

Norman conquest

In France, Vikings who sailed up the Seine and attacked Paris were given 3,000kg (3 tons) of silver by Charles the Bald of France to go away, while his successor Charles the Simple ceded an entire province to Rolf (or "Rollo") the Ganger, a Viking too big to ride any horse. The province became the Duchy of Normandy, and within two centuries it was the springboard for the 1066 Norman conquest of Anglo-Danish England. But if the conquest was a great triumph for Norman arms, it also accelerated the end of the Viking Age.

Harald Hardrada of Norway (1015–66), the "Thunderbolt of the North", had tried to pre-empt William's seizure of England with an invasion of his own, and it was not long before Danish and Norwegian forces attempted to unseat William. But England under the Normans was a tough nut to crack; Normandy itself was no longer open to disgruntled Scandinavians, and Iceland was full. Greenland was the next possibility, and it was from here that Leifur Eiríksson set sail to see if he could find something better in the unknown world to the west. He returned with tales of Vinland, a land of warm sunshine, trees, grass and, as the name implied, grapes. His brother Thorvaldur followed his directions, and on landing in Vinland walked straight into an Indian arrow. The next assessment of the land's potential was by a fearsome woman, Freydís, who murdered most of her party en route. She was not over-impressed: the future America, she thought, was not more than "all right". ❑

LEFT: the Norwegian king and pirate Olav Tryggvason.
RIGHT: Odin, the mythological Norse god of wisdom, war, culture and the dead.

MEDIEVAL THUGS OR MERCHANT TRADERS?

The Vikings plundered their way into the annals of Scandinavian history. But archaeology reveals there's more to these raiders than meets the eye

At first glance the Viking legacy appears to be little more than an impressive catalogue of violence and piracy. Archaeological finds have, however, shed light not only on the way the Vikings lived (everything from the food they ate to the clothing they wore) but also on their burial traditions. Today, the Vikings are recognised for their skills as craftsmen, traders and, of course, sailors.

The Viking longship, essential for both raiding and trading, was also used to bury kings and chieftains. Superb examples can be seen at the Viking ship museums in Roskilde, Denmark, and Oslo, Norway, where textiles, household utensils and other artefacts excavated from the burial mounds around the Oslo Fjord are also on display. In Denmark, Funen's Ladby Ship Museum houses a magnificent burial ship with a dragon's head and tail.

Sites and open-air museums such as those at Birka outside Stockholm (*see right*), and Denmark's Fyrkat and Trelleborg, offer a unique look into the daily lives of the Vikings. Other places of interest include the burial ground at Lindholm Høje, Jutland, and Jelling in Zealand, with its runes and burial mounds, often referred to as Denmark's "birth certificate".

ABOVE: open-air museums offer activities and re-enactments, giving visitors a chance to relive the Viking experience at first hand.

LEFT: the Oseberg ship in Oslo's Viking Ship Museum is thought to be the tomb of a queen buried in 834 with her maidservant and most valued possessions.

ABOVE: the Vikings would commemorate an event or a death on runestones like this one at Lovo Church, Kalmar Lan, Sweden.

THE VIKING SILK ROUTE

This bishop's crosier from Ireland, pictured above, was found at the site of Sweden's first Viking town, Birka. Situated 30km (19 miles) west of Stockholm, Birka was founded towards the end of the 8th century. Archaeological excavations have revealed trade networks stretching east to Byzantium and as far as China. The finds, which include silks from the Far East, Arabic coins and glass beads from the Arabic Caliphate, have challenged the belief that the Viking Age was all murder and mayhem. They point instead to a burgeoning, prosperous society made up of merchants, traders and farmers.

Birka was the first town in Sweden to come into contact with Christianity. But the town was never evangelised, and in some graves Thor's hammer was found alongside a crucifix.

The museum at Birka is open between May and mid-September. Boats leave from outside Stockholm City Hall, at Stadshusbron.

ABOVE: coins entered the region as a result of trading contacts both with Western Europe and the Islamic world. They were valued for their weight and purity, as it was the metal itself which was important, not the coins.

RIGHT: only a handful of Viking helmets have been found, but many carvings show warriors with helmets.

ABOVE AND RIGHT: 11th-century Viking arm ring; harness mount from Gotland, one of a pair known as Odin's Birds, with exaggerated beak and talons.

WAR AND PEACE

From the end of the Viking Age to the dawn of the
20th century, kings battled for supremacy, land changed
hands and unions were made and broken

As the Viking Age drew to a close in the 11th century, the kings of Norway, Sweden and Denmark – "all handsome and big men, of noble looks and well spoken" – met at Konghelle on the Göta River in 1098 to acknowledge one another's legitimacy and to adopt a common policy on robbery and theft, ever the crimes of greatest concern. To seal the pact, King Magnus of Norway – known as "Barelegs" since returning from Scotland sporting a kilt – married Inge of Sweden's daughter Margaret, hence "The Peace Maiden".

Five years later, however, Magnus fulfilled one of his own favourite sayings – "a king stands for his country's honour and glory, not for a long life" – by being killed in action in Ireland. Norway was carved up among his three young sons, undoing the single Norwegian kingdom hammered together by Harald Fairhair, and the prospect of smooth Scandinavian coexistence.

Converting the heathens

Denmark's particular difficulty was not fragmentation but a succession of kings so ineffectual (e.g. "Harald the Hen") that several were simply taken out to sea and drowned. In Sweden, the throne bobbed between two dynasties who routinely murdered the opposing incumbent. Next to these goings-on, the princes of the new power in the land, the Church, looked purposeful. As comfortable in the saddle as the pulpit, Bishop Absalon of Roskilde (1128–1201) personally sorted out "the heathen Wend", a tribe of defiant Baltic pagans whose headquarters were

on Rügen island. Smashing the four-headed god Svantevit, he offered everyone the choice of embracing Christ or dying immediately. The island became part of his booming diocese.

With bishops like Absalon around, ambitious kings were obliged to demonstrate their religious credentials by "taking the Cross" and joining a crusade. Sigurd of Norway, one of Barelegs' sons, went to the Holy Land. Valdemar I (1131–82), a more dashing king than Denmark had seen for some time, fought 28 battles against assorted heathens. His successor Valdemar II concentrated on Estonians, and in spite of a fleet of 1,000 ships was only rescued from one certain defeat by the miraculous apparition

---

LEFT: Gustav Vasa (1523–60), first king of the Vasa dynasty, laid the foundations of the Swedish state.
RIGHT: Kristian II of Denmark (1513–23).

of a red-and-white banner in the heavens. It became Denmark's national flag.

Sweden annexes Finland

Erik I of Sweden did his crusader service among the Finns during the 12th century, marking the start of Sweden's 700-year annexation of Finland

The oldest national flag in the world is a source of pride among Danes. It must never touch the ground and only a pennant version may be flown at night.

modities, and the shipping in between, the Hansa had a goose of pure gold, and it gave them a network of strategic ports and market towns across the continent. But if Scandinavia was sapped by an extortionate exchange rate between fish and grain, it was then poleaxed by the Black Death in 1349. With the population of Norway, for example, cut by more than half, economics reverted to the Stone Age.

One interlude in the slow reconstruction process was the arrival of shoals of herring so dense that fish could be caught with bare hands. Fishing vessels raced from all over Europe until some 40,000 were crammed into the Sound,

and Erik's climb to the status of his country's patron saint. But aggrandisement was all too easily reversed, as occurred in Denmark on Valdemar II's exit. "The crown fell off the head of the Danes," a chronicle wailed, "and they became the laughing stock for all their neighbours through civil wars and mutual destruction."

In Sweden, the saintly Erik I was murdered by the son of the king he had removed, Sverker, leaving Erik's son in no doubt about what was expected of him. He did not disappoint.

Like the Church, German and Dutch Hansa traders recognised the chaotic absence of government as an excellent opportunity. Scandinavia had an abundance of fish but a shortage of grain. By tying up the markets in both com-

temporarily loosening the Hansa's grip on the market. The 14th-century king Valdemar IV of Denmark launched a snap invasion of the Hansa's base at Visby in Gotland and, flushed with success, assumed the title of "King of the Goths". The Hansa were not amused. Throwing the resources of their 77 towns and cities into a military alliance with Sweden, they bounced Valdemar off his Danish throne and invited applications. Margrethe, the young wife of King Håkon VI of Norway, proposed their son Oluf. He was five years old.

A scheming queen

Margrethe, who had married in 1363 at the age of 10 and given birth to Oluf at 17, knew what she was doing. With Denmark under Oluf's little belt and the Norwegian crown bound to follow in due course, she encouraged him to think of himself as "the true heir to Sweden" as well, a presumption that infuriated Albrecht, the reigning king of Sweden.

Nevertheless, Margrethe had to think again when Oluf died at 17. While personally keeping the Danish throne warm, she persuaded the Norwegian nobility to recognise her grandnephew Erik of Pomerania as Oluf's successor. Erik, too, was five at this turning point in his career. Margrethe went behind Albrecht's back to offer the Swedish nobles perpetual rights to

Circle (including Swedish Finland) to the Eider, and west to Greenland, with no money or support from the wary nobility. Margrethe had her hands full nursing the damage caused by Erik's railings against these constraints, and she was addressing the aftermath of a war with Holstein when she collapsed. The Danish nobility wondered aloud whether their interests might be better served by Erik's nephew, Christopher of Bavaria, and the talk in Sweden was of a separate constitution and a fresh crowned head. Meanwhile, Erik retired to Visborg Castle in Gotland and applied himself, privately and very profitably, to the business of piracy.

their property and privileges in exchange for their support against him. Albrecht could take no more. Raising an army of German mercenaries, he demanded satisfaction at Falköping. A chronicler was surprised by the outcome: "God gave an unexpected victory into the hands of a woman."

Margrethe's grand scheme was at last realised at Kalmar in 1397 when Erik, now 14, donned the three crowns of Norway, Denmark and Sweden. "Rash, violent and obstinate", he faced the tall order of running an empire from the Arctic

Gustav Vasa, the enigmatic king portrayed on the Swedish 1,000-krona note, is credited with founding the Swedish state. He's a folkloric hero, yet his brutal behaviour led to armed rebellions in Småland and Dalarna.

Stockholm Bloodbath

After more than one trial separation Denmark and Sweden were together again under the Danish king Kristian II (1481–1559). Anti-Danish feeling was growing apace in Sweden when the Swedish assembly voted to burn the fortress of the Archbishop of Sweden, a pro-Dane, Gustav Trolle. In the event Trolle was merely

LEFT: the Swedish army is defeated by Peter the Great of Russia at the battle of Poltava, 1709.
ABOVE: a depiction of medieval life at Turku Castle.

imprisoned, but in 1520 the Papal Court excommunicated the Swedish regent, Sten Sture the Younger, for this act. Kristian II had the justification he sought for invading Sweden. He invited Sweden's leading nobles to a feast in Stockholm at which he chopped off the heads of 82 of Sweden's finest. This "Stockholm Bloodbath" provoked a rebellion. Kristian was driven out of Sweden and Gustav Vasa, a nobleman whose family had been victims in the massacre, seized power. Thus began a Swedish dynasty of exceptional distinction and durability.

Hounded out of Denmark, Kristian II sought refuge in the Netherlands. Norway's clergy,

the size of the navy, and sending explorers to investigate the possibility of a northwest passage to Asia. He took an avuncular interest in Norway, renaming Oslo after himself ("Kristiania"), but never managed to achieve friendly relations with Sweden, and the two countries inevitably entered the Thirty Years War on opposite sides.

The battling continued, but it was the Swedish King Karl X Gustav who seized an opportunity when the Sound (Øresund) froze over during the winter of 1657. Two cavalry squadrons crossed the ice and a resounding victory cost Denmark all its territory on the Swedish side of the Sound.

staunchly loyal to Rome, made him an offer of the Norwegian throne, which provoked violent intervention by Danish and Hanseatic forces with far-reaching consequences. Kristian spent the rest of his life in Sonderborg Castle, while the Norwegian Church was purged of Roman Catholics to make it Lutheran, and the Norwegian monarchy was abolished. Norway was thereafter a mere province of Denmark. The tripartite Kalmar Union was dead.

Battle on ice

A larger-than-life character, Kristian IV (1577–1648) was on the Danish throne for 52 years, building palaces and towns, turning Copenhagen into an important European capital, trebling

The warrior king

In Karl XII (1682–1718), Sweden seemed to acquire a reincarnation of the Vikings who fought and caroused their way across Russia. Taking over the mantle of the traditional Germanic *Drang nach Osten* (drive to the east), he collided with Peter the Great of Russia.

The Russians eventually got the better of a titanic struggle, putting Karl in the impossible position of trying to rule Sweden from his bolt-hole in Turkey. Finally, he rode home with two companions, a journey of 2,100km (1,300 miles), only to find that in his absence Sweden had been stripped of all his recent gains. His plan to put matters right began and ended with a siege of Frederiksten in southern Norway. The bullet

Sweden typically bribed North African pirates not to attack their ships, but to plunder those of the Norwegians who insisted on sailing under their own colours.

through his head may have been fired by a genuine enemy sniper or a contracted assassin, but in any case Sweden decided to give absolutism a rest and explore constitutional government.

Denmark's first taste of quasi-constitutional government was deferred until the 1770s and even then only materialised in strange circumstances. Kristian VII's increasingly erratic behaviour clearly needed medical attention, a task entrusted to a German doctor, Johann Friederich Struensee. The patient was off his head, Struensee decided, so the best he could do was to run the country himself. And so he did.

In little more than a year, Struensee drew up 1,069 bills introducing freedom of speech and the press, a national budget, the decriminalisation of fornication and adultery, and the abolition of capital punishment for all but the most unspeakable crimes. He could not have envisaged, as he extended his stately role to touch on the void in Queen Caroline Matilde's conjugal life, that he would be dragged out of bed at dawn and charged with just such a crime, one that still carried the supreme penalty. Locked up in Kronborg Castle at Helsingør, his partner in crime was rescued from her fate by an English warship sent by George III, himself showing signs of instability but her brother nonetheless.

The same navy was again under the guns of Kronborg Castle at the outbreak of the Napoleonic War in the early 19th century, in this instance because Denmark had sided with Russia, at that stage Napoleon's ally. While Britain bombarded Copenhagen, Tsar Alexander I occupied Finland, bringing the ages-old Swedish rule initiated by St Erik to a close.

Russia wins Finland

Russia later changed sides and was sitting with the victors when reparations were decided after the Battle of Waterloo (1815). Russia was allowed to keep Finland; Norway was detached

from Denmark and handed to Sweden, albeit not as a colony but as a supposed equal in a union under a common crown.

The king in question was a curious choice: Jean-Baptiste Bernadotte was French and not only a former general of the French Revolution but a key member of Napoleon's staff. If taking the name Karl Johan was meant to help him to blend into his new surroundings, this was offset by his refusal to speak anything but French.

Thus reorganised, the Scandinavian states stepped into the frenzy of romantic nationalism that swept across Europe and inspired phenomenal scientific progress and a flowering of the

THE GREAT EXODUS

The 19th century witnessed a mass exodus of Scandinavians in search of a better life in the New World. "Potatoes, peace and vaccination" were blamed for a population explosion at home which contributed to an outflow of 750,000 Norwegian and one million Swedish emigrants – a quarter of the Swedish population.

The new settlers sent back glowing accounts of their lives in America, and money to support those left behind. These signs of prosperity and other factors such as The United States Homestead Act of 1862, which promised land almost free to settlers who dared to travel west, encouraged others to follow.

LEFT: the Swedish royal palace of Drottningholm, designed in the 17th century by Tessin the Elder.
RIGHT: *Conversation at Drottningholm*, 1779.

arts. In these respects Scandinavia did its bit and more. Sweden was especially strong in the sciences; consider, for one, Linnaeus, the naturalist *(see box, below)*, and Alfred Nobel, the chemist, engineer and inventor of dynamite. Denmark's most notable contributions were the writer Hans Christian Andersen *(see page 149)* and the philosopher Søren Kierkegaard. Norway offered Edvard Grieg (composer), Henrik Ibsen (dramatist) and Edvard Munch (painter), and Finland (pre-Sibelius) contributed the *Kalevala*, an epic which Elias Lönnrot compiled from old ballads and songs to reinvent his country's hitherto elusive past.

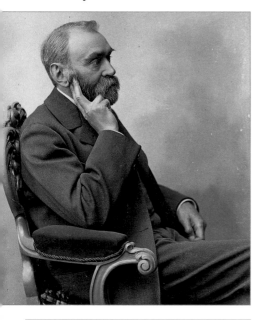

Language became a vexing issue in both Finland and Norway. Mikael Agricola, the Bishop of Turku, had produced a Finnish translation of the Bible as early as 1642, and although Finnish had always been spoken by the majority of

> When Alfred Nobel's brother Ludvig died in 1888, a French newspaper accidentally printed Alfred's obituary, condemning him for his killer invention dynamite. Historians speculate that Alfred rewrote his will, bequeathing his fortune to establish the Nobel Prizes.

the population, it had no official status. The Russians even banned books written in Finnish. In Norway, Old Norse had gone to Iceland with the Viking settlers, while the language in Norway itself had been affected by Danish connections. Pure Danish was used for official business, in literature and by the educated classes. In the 19th century Norwegian nationalists wanted to revert to untainted Norwegian. They concocted a cocktail from Norway's surviving rural dialects called "New Norwegian".

Friends and foes

One 19th-century development was that Swedish, Danish and Norwegian (but not yet Finnish) historians could at last get together for a chat without coming to blows, and in this spirit Swedish and Danish university students took advantage of the atrocious winter of 1838, when the Sound again froze over, to walk across the ice, meet in the middle and improvise odes to Scandinavian solidarity.

If this was reminiscent of Magnus Barelegs and company at Konghelle, the dream was again upset by events in Norway, where the union with Sweden was in trouble. Norway strengthened its border fortifications, and Sweden had its army on alert before a compromise was worked out. The union dissolved in 1905, following a plebiscite that voted overwhelmingly in favour of Norwegian independence. Norway opted for a monarchy rather than a republic, and went shopping for a new king. Scandinavia braced itself for the 20th century. ❑

LINNAEUS, THE PLANTSMAN

Carl Linnaeus (also known as von Linné), the Swedish naturalist who devised the modern classification system for plants and animals, was one of the great scientists of 18th-century Scandinavia. Born in 1707, he studied medicine at the University of Lund and botany at Uppsala. He travelled widely and was a leading figure in the founding of the Swedish Academy of Science. As chair of botany, dietetics and *materia medica* at Uppsala, he pursued his research into nomenclature. His publications included *Systema Naturae* (1735), *Philosophia Botanica* (1750) and *Species Plantarum* (1753). Linnaeus died in 1778. His house and botanical garden can be visited at Uppsala.

LEFT: Alfred Nobel (1833–96), Swedish chemist, inventor of dynamite and founder of the Nobel Prizes.
RIGHT: Sami girls in traditional costume, 1898.

THE MODERN AGE

Two world wars took their toll on the Nordic countries, but by the end of the 20th century they had emerged as sophisticated economic powers

The 20th century dawned with not only the union of Sweden and Norway on the rocks but also the special relationship between Finland and Russia. A new tsar, the ill-fated Nicholas II, did not share his predecessors' fond view of Finland as a separate grand duchy. So while breakaway Norway recruited Håkon VII, né Prince Carl of Denmark, as its first independent king for 600 years, Finland was delivered into the hands of Nikolai Ivanovich Bobrikov, a hard-boiled martinet whose previous assignment had been to knock some sense into Russia's wayward Baltic provinces.

King Håkon accepted the job only after a plebiscite indicated that three-quarters of the Norwegian population wanted him. Bobrikov did not bother with such trifles. Having abolished the Finns' exemption from service in the Russian imperial forces, he was systematically shredding their freedom of speech and other rights when he was met on the staircase to the Senate by Eugen Schauman, a civil servant. Schauman put three bullets into the brute before turning the revolver on himself.

The onset of World War I

Fortunately for Finland, the tsar was too involved in war with Japan and later in the St Petersburg uprising to avenge Bobrikov's murder. Every one of 40 previous wars with Russia had gone badly for the Finns, but they were always ready to try again. The first whiff of World War I saw volunteers flocking to Germany to join a special "Jagar battalion" which

LEFT: flag-waving during the annual National Day celebrations in Norway on 17 May.
RIGHT: evacuated Finnish family, 1939.

duly entered the field against Russia alongside Kaiser Wilhelm's forces.

For their part, the three kings of Scandinavia met at Malmö in Sweden in December 1914 and declared their neutrality. However, putting the proclamation into practice was not so easy. After centuries of anguish over Schleswig-Holstein, Denmark was not Germany's greatest admirer, but it was in no position to defy the Kaiser's orders to mine Danish sea-lanes against the British navy. Conversely, Norway received a warning from Britain that selling fish, iron pyrites or copper to Germany would not be tolerated, and Sweden was blockaded, eventually suffering acute food shortages, for trading too eagerly with Wilhelm. The worst blow, though, was Germany's declaration of unrestricted submarine warfare in 1916. Hundreds of Scandinavian ships and crews commandeered by Britain went to the bottom, with heavy losses.

On Russia's withdrawal from the war after the Bolshevik revolution in 1917, Lenin appealed directly to sympathisers in Scandinavia, particularly Finland. The Finnish Red Guard, about 30,000 strong, accordingly seized government offices in Helsinki and proclaimed a Socialist Workers' Republic. The government's response was to raise a White Guard, including the Jagar battalion, Swedish volunteers and 12,000 Ger-

man troops, under the command of General Baron Gustaf Mannerheim, a former White Russian cavalry officer. The revolution lasted less than four months, but there were 24,000 casualties and a comparable number of Red sympathisers were subsequently executed or left to die in internment camps.

The inter-war years

Consideration was then given to turning Finland into a kingdom with one of Kaiser Wilhelm's sons on the throne, but Germany's defeat in the war turned opinion in favour of a republic under the presidency of Kaarlo Juho Ståhlberg, a local professor of law. The Soviet Union raised no objection to Finland's independence and signed the Treaty of Tartu to that effect, but Finland's fanatical Christian fundamentalists, the Lapua pietists, were determined to clear the nest of vipers. Suspected Communists were kidnapped, beaten and dumped at the Soviet border. The pietists forced the government to ban Communism completely and were arming themselves for a full-scale coup d'état when the army decided enough was enough.

Sweden sailed through the post-war years on a wave of international demand for Swedish steel and ball bearings, Ericsson telephones and Electrolux vacuum cleaners. While also doing well, Norway and Denmark clashed over Greenland and the Arctic islands of Svalbard (Spitzbergen) and Jan Mayen, which raised issues rooted in Viking times. Asked to arbitrate, the international court at The Hague gave Greenland to Denmark, the islands to Norway.

Scandinavia emerged from the second crisis of the inter-war years, the Great Depression, with improved political systems. Small parties with narrow interests – farmers' parties being a prime example – were forced to remove their blinkers and join broader coalitions, the front runners generally calling themselves "Social Democrats".

World War II

As the storm clouds of World War II gathered, Hitler's rise was especially worrying to Denmark because Germany had never formally agreed to the Schleswig-Holstein border after World War I. Accepting his surprising offer of

UNDERCOVER OPERATIONS

The Resistance movement in Denmark and Norway was crucial in undermining the German campaign during World War II. Anders Lassen epitomised the 20,000-strong Danish Resistance. By the time he died aged 24, he had fought in France, Greece, the Balkans and Italy. His commanding officer said, "Anders caused more discomfort to the enemy over five years of war than any other man of his rank and age." Other heroes included the Norwegians who knocked out the heavy water plant at Rjukan *(see page 198)*. Two museums, Frihedsmuseet, Copenhagen, and Norges Hjemmefrontmuseum, Oslo, document the movement's history.

LEFT: World War II poster published during the German occupation of Norway, 1941.
RIGHT: German aircraft on Finland's tundra, 1941.

a non-aggression pact, Denmark nevertheless joined Sweden and Norway in another declaration of neutrality.

Finland was again a special case. When Hitler invaded Poland, Stalin assumed Russia would be next and seized a strip of Finnish territory to strengthen the defences around Leningrad. The 1939 Nazi–Soviet pact removed this threat, but at the same time it allowed Stalin a free hand in Finland, and he ordered an invasion at the end of November that year. Marshal Mannerheim, now in his seventies, came out of retirement to lead Finland in what came to be known as the Winter War.

Finland's wars with Russia

The Finns were outnumbered three to one on the ground, and faced an air force of around 2,500 aircraft – almost 30 times larger than their own. But near-invisible in their white uniforms against driving snow, Finnish troops went into action on skis, employing guerrilla tactics against Russian tanks in temperatures as low as minus 40°C (-40°F). Surprise attacks against frozen, demoralised Soviet troops resulted in some surprising victories: the battle of Suomussalmi is still a textbook example of how small, strategically used forces can defeat a much larger foe. But the odds, ultimately, were against

THE DEMON DRINK

Stringent laws on the purchase of alcohol in Norway and Sweden have been somewhat at odds with the figure these countries have wanted to cut in the modern world. The time-honoured yearning for drink can be blamed on long winter nights, but ancient Scandinavians also drank like fish because their food was preserved with lashings of salt. King Sverre of Norway experimented with prohibition as early as the 12th century. In 1775, however, King Gustav III of Sweden turned the distillation and sale of spirits into a royal monopoly and encouraged his subjects to drink because he needed the money. Against this backdrop, 20th-century prohibitionists had problems. The conundrum in Norway was that France, Spain and Portu-

gal, major consumers of Norwegian fish, had always bartered with wine or brandy. The issue of prohibition led to the downfall of three successive governments in the early 20th century.

Sweden, however, put its faith in the "Bratt Liquor Control System", a certain Dr Ivan Bratt having worked out exactly how much alcohol an individual could consume according to age, physique and other considerations, with the result that it was almost impossible for a married woman to qualify for a single drink in any circumstances. Today, as in Gustav III's time, the sale of wines and spirits in both countries, as well as in Finland, is a state monopoly.

The Royal Line

Monarchy is alive and well in Scandinavia. Sweden, Norway and Denmark all have royal figureheads. Only Finland is a republic

Monarchy could hardly be more entrenched than in Denmark. Queen Margrethe II is the 53rd in an unbroken line of sovereigns spanning more than 1,000 years. Sweden, too, has had more than 60 kings since 980. The present King

Carl Gustaf may be "XVI", but his direct line begins with Jean-Baptiste Bernadotte, the French marshal who became heir apparent in 1810 and Sweden's king in 1818. Norway's royal line ceased when Norway became a Danish province and the monarchy was only restored, after a referendum, following the dissolution in 1905 of the subsequent union with Sweden. The present king, Harald V, is the third of the modern line, the "V" notwithstanding. Finland also considered a monarchy on breaking away from Russia, but chose to become a republic instead.

Nevertheless, not a little craft has gone into keeping the Scandinavian monarchies in good health. When Carl XVI Gustaf ascended the Swedish throne in 1973, the Constitution began with: "The King alone shall govern the realm…" Lest he

got the wrong impression, this was hastily changed to: "All public power in Sweden emanates from the people…" The king decided his own official motto ought to be: "For Sweden – in Keeping with the Times". This was the cue for changing the rules of succession so that they no longer discriminated against daughters. Consequently, next in line is Crown Princess Victoria rather than her younger brother. In 2010, the Swedish royal house had some dramatic highs and lows. Princess Victoria married her beau Daniel Westling in a ceremony that drew crowds of half a million onto Stockholm's streets. But later that year, revelations about Queen Silvia's father's Nazi connections came hot on the heels of a best-selling biography about the king, which contained details of his wild sex life.

Carl Gustaf is also not averse to tearing around in a Ferrari, and was reported to the police in Denmark for doing an alleged 250kph (155mph) on the Copenhagen expressway. In contrast, King Harald loves boats, representing Norway at the Olympic Games, and winning the European Championship in 2005 – right after a heart bypass. Unlike his Swedish counterpart, Harald would not be seen dead in a Ferrari. He uses public transport. Queen Sonja is the daughter of an Oslo shopkeeper and their children went to state schools. Fittingly, the Crown Prince found himself a bachelor flat in an unfashionable part of Oslo, but let the side down, as it were, by sharing it with a waitress, and her three-year-old son by a man who was in prison for drug offences; they are now married and have two children of their own.

If conscientious exercises in non-charisma go down well in Norway, Queen Margrethe could not hope to do the same in Denmark. She has been showered with academic honours from the likes of Cambridge, Oxford and the London School of Economics. While trying unsuccessfully to hide her distinguished output as a painter, writer and designer behind a string of aliases, she has at least persuaded her friends to call her Daisy. Crown Prince Frederik, her heir, is not much better at disguise. Dressing down for a night on the town, he turned out so scruffy that the bar refused to let him in. As a trained soldier, no mean dancer and the leader of a husky-drawn expedition across Greenland, Frederik's status as a dashing bachelor ended in marriage to Australian Mary Donaldson, with whom he now has four children. ❑

LEFT: Queen Sonja of Norway in relaxed mood at Holmenkollen Ski Festival.

the Finns. Surrender came after 105 days, when around a tenth of the country, including the Karelian Isthmus, was ceded to Stalin.

When the Nazi–Soviet pact collapsed in 1941, Germany invaded Russia, and the Finns saw their chance to recover their recent losses, entering into battle against Russia yet again. This round of hostilities lasted until September 1944; Finland did not regain its territories, and was thereafter stigmatised as one of Hitler's allies, although it had never signed a formal military alliance with Germany.

Invasion of Denmark

The German invasion of Denmark and Norway began on 9 April 1940. Some troops crossed the Jutland border into Denmark, others emerged from hiding in German merchant ships in Copenhagen harbour, and paratroops landed at key points around the country. The Danish army was in barracks, the navy was too sur-prised to fire a single shot, and the air force was destroyed on the ground. If nothing else, the Royal Life Guards at Amalienborg Palace in Copenhagen prevented the Germans from capturing King Kristian X just long enough for him to order a surrender.

Denmark remained in theory a sovereign state under German protection, but when the king ignored Hitler's effusive greetings on his birthday in 1942, the pretence was dropped. A new government was expected to jump at Hitler's whim, but it refused to sanction death sentences on members of the increasingly active Resistance movement and made arrangements to smuggle Denmark's endangered Jews to safety in Sweden.

Norway is overrun

In Norway's case, gunners in an old fortress on Oslo Fjord had the satisfaction of sinking the German cruiser *Blücher* on the first day of the invasion, killing around 830 of those on board. While Hitler's local stooge, Vidkun Quisling, the leader of the Fascist National Unity Party, proclaimed himself prime minister, King Håkon and most members of the government escaped to Tromsø in northern Norway and remained there while a combined force of British, French, Polish and Norwegian units recaptured the

RIGHT: the great long-distance runner Paavo Nurmi lights the Olympic flame at the 1952 Helsinki Games.

iron-ore port of Narvik. The sudden collapse of France, however, created a greater demand for the expeditionary force elsewhere. The Allies withdrew, and the king and his entourage were evacuated to England.

Neutral throughout the war, Sweden took in 300,000 refugees. The Swedish Red Cross, led by Count Folke Bernadotte, a nephew of the king, secured the release of 30,000 prisoners of various nationalities from German concentra-tion camps, and the diplomat Raoul Wallen-berg played "Schindler" to Jews in Hungary. But it was also the case that German troops and materials were given permission to cross

Sweden on their way to Norway in 1940 and thereafter when they went on leave. Moreover, Sweden supplied iron ore critical to the Ger-man war machine. These are matters which Norwegians to this day cannot easily forget.

Peacetime recovery

The last stage of the war, with German forces scorching the earth in their retreat from the advancing Soviets, hurt northern Norway but was utterly devastating in Finland. The latter, then, could hardly have been in a worse position to meet Soviet demands for US$600 million in reparations – around half of Finland's annual GDP at the time. Barred by its 1948 treaty with Moscow from accepting Marshall aid, Finland nevertheless beat the 10-year deadline by creating a diversified industrial economy from scratch. Shipbuilding, oil refineries, textiles – the USSR provided a bottomless market for these new industries, and paid for its goods in dirt-cheap oil. Ironically, war reparations transformed Finland into a modern industrial nation – albeit one over which the USSR held great sway.

Recovery from the war in Denmark and Norway was set in motion by the Marshall Plan (1947–51). Neutral Sweden also accepted Marshall aid, and all four Scandinavian countries were caught up in the wave of economic growth that swept through post-war Europe.

The comprehensive "cradle-to-grave" welfare systems came into full being during the 1950s and 1960s. To begin with at least, Scandinavians were happy to live with the high taxes needed to cover their cost, if only because memories of bitterly hard times without a social safety net were still so fresh.

Sweden's international reputation, somewhat damaged by its questionable war role, was given a boost by the selection of diplomat Dag Hammarskjöld as Secretary-General of the UN in 1953. He threw himself into the role, enhancing the reputation of the UN and acting as peace-broker in international disputes from China to Palestine to the Suez Canal. In 1961, Hammarskjöld was killed in a plane crash; he became the first person to be awarded the Nobel Peace Prize posthumously.

The new oil-rich nations...

During the late 1960s and early 70s, the economies of Norway and Denmark were given another welcome leg-up – they struck oil. Denmark had become adept at exploiting niche markets (think Lego, Bang & Olufsen, Carlsberg, and selling streaky bacon to Britain), but this was the first time the country had enjoyed the luxury of natural resources since the 14th-century herring shoals. Ironically, Denmark's North Sea windfall arrived in the middle of its first experiments with wind farms.

Measured against population, the prize in Norway was much bigger and triggered lavish expenditure on road tunnels and other infrastructure investments. By the 1990s, Norway had paid off its entire foreign debt; and in 1995, it began to stash away the cash for a rainy day, creating a sovereign wealth fund with the surplus petroleum money. Oslo began its transformation from quiet town to Europe's fastest-growing city: within 40 years, oil money had created a futuristic harbourside, new financial district and world-class buildings like the Opera House.

...and their oil-free neighbours

Deprived of any share of the North Sea bonanza, Sweden's "Middle Way", a compromise between capitalism and socialism, showed signs of turning into a cul-de-sac. Industry had long been pampered with low taxes while individual tax-payers were bled white, but it still complained loudly about its employees' national insurance contributions, shorter working weeks and longer holidays. By the 1990s, just as Norway was becoming rich as Croesus, recession hit Sweden hard. Swedes were astonished and dismayed when Saab was swallowed by General Motors, Volvo by Ford, and a regiment of other prestigious companies decamped abroad. The government introduced austerity measures, designed to stave off the worst; but interest rates rocketed. Huge public expenditure cuts followed, and in 1994 the Swedish people voted to throw in their lot with the European Union.

Finland too fell into a deep recession, exacerbated by the collapse of the USSR in 1991. Finland gained greater political freedom with the fall of its neighbour, but at the same time the Finnish economy was left floundering – seeking stability, it too joined the EU. But the country went on to experience its second economic miracle since World War II, when amongst other things Nokia recognised the potential of the mobile phone and Porsche decided to build its new Boxster model in Finland.

Assassination shockwaves

Despite Scandinavia's economic ups and downs, an underlying sense of social wellbeing had always prevailed. This was shattered on 28 February 1986, when Sweden's prime minister, Olof Palme, was assassinated in central Stockholm as he and his wife walked home from the

popular Swedish Minister for Foreign Affairs Anna Lindh, widely tipped to be the next prime minister, was knifed while shopping in central Stockholm, and subsequently died of her wounds. Mijailo Mijailović was eventually convicted of her killing: he blamed "voices in his head".

Immigration tensions

From the 1950s onwards, Scandinavia began to receive its first immigrants – "guest workers" from Turkey and the former Yugoslavia, and political refugees from Hungary and the former Czechoslovakia. Initially immigrants received

cinema. Shock and incredulity swept across Scandinavia – increasing when the police failed to find either the murderer or his gun. Palme was a politician of international standing, with strong socialist views that he did not hesitate to express. Conspiracy theories abound, with the KGB, the CIA and the Yugoslavian UDBA variously blamed, but a satisfactory explanation for the assassination has never been found.

Scandinavia was further stunned in 2003 when history appeared to repeat itself. The

LEFT: Dag Hammarskjöld, Secretary-General of the UN. **ABOVE:** Olof Palme, prime minister of Sweden, assassinated in 1986. **ABOVE RIGHT:** Anna Lindh, Minister for Foreign affairs, was also killed.

a warm welcome, but the growing number of foreigners, particularly from Muslim countries, has led to a steady rise in the popularity of mainstream right-wing, anti-immigration political parties across Scandinavia. The past 20 years have also seen an increase in activity by the extreme right wing, apprehensive over jobs and the perceived threat to traditional Nordic culture.

The debate over Muslim immigration and integration reached a head when a Danish newspaper, *Jyllands-Posten*, published cartoons, some of them depicting the Prophet Muhammad, as a way of stimulating debate on the place of Islam within Western democracies. Their publication caused widespread offence across the Muslim world.

Norwegian massacre

Nothing, though, could have prepared the Scandinavian countries for what happened in Norway on 22 July 2011, when Anders Behring Breivik exploded a car bomb near government buildings in Oslo, killing eight people, then travelled to the nearby island of Utøya and gunned down 68 young people attending a Labour Party youth rally.

In his 1,500-page manifesto, "2083 – A European Declaration of Independence", Breivik claimed he had carried out the killings to precipitate a revolution against Islam and multiculturalism.

in 2000, a connection broken by the cataclysmic convulsion at the end of the Ice Age.

And although Scandinavia was hit by the 2008 financial crisis, with sharp rises in inflation and unemployment, signs of recovery are good and there are plenty of ambitious projects in the works. Denmark and Germany are forging closer links with a 32 billion-kroner undersea tunnel across the Fehmarn Strait. In Sweden, the Hallandsås railway tunnel will open in 2012, part of a larger project to create super-efficient train links between Norway, Sweden and Germany. Finland hit the headlines recently when the two largest cruise ships in the world sailed away from their

The massacres led to much soul-searching across the region, shaking as they did the traditional image of the Scandinavian countries as places of tolerance, liberalism and hospitality. In Norway, hundreds of thousands of people expressed their revulsion at the killings by demonstrating their support for democracy and unity. As the prime minister, Jens Stoltenberg, put it, "If one man can show so much hate, think how much love we could show standing together."

Bridge to the future

The new millennium brought change for one of Scandinavia's oldest schisms. The Øresund road and rail bridge rejoined Denmark and Sweden

Turku shipyard in 2009 and 2010 respectively.

Norway insulated itself from economic pain by using its sovereign wealth fund to buy cheap shares – by October 2010, the fund topped 3 trillion kroner (over US$500 billion). A tense standoff with Russia over Arctic territory was resolved in 2010, allowing Norway to begin oil and gas exploration in the Barents Sea and the Arctic Ocean. Today, Norway has the highest GDP per person and the lowest working hours in Scandinavia, pointing to a level of individual wealth and leisure that the rest of us can only dream of. ❑

ABOVE: *Allure of the Seas*, the world's largest cruise ship, with its sister ship, *Oasis of the Seas*. **RIGHT:** Øresund road and rail bridge, completed in 2000.

THE DANES

They're generally warm, witty and welcoming.
But they can also be cool and reserved.
It depends where you meet them

Danes have two reputations in the world, one at home and another abroad. Outside their homeland, Danes are known as warm, curious, friendly, funny, charming. In their modest way, Danish travellers bring on laughs and a sense of pure enjoyment for life. They try not to act too offended when, outside Europe, people ask: "Is Denmark the capital of Sweden?" or "What language do you speak – Dutch?" A short, firm geography lesson is given on the spot, but modesty usually prevents the Dane from pointing out that Denmark is the oldest monarchy in the world, dating from AD 935.

At home, Danes are seen by foreign visitors as distant, sombre, even cold. They keep to themselves. Danes blame this image on the wet, cool climate. "Not much of our social life happens on the pavements or out in front of the home," says Frans Kjær Nielsen, a teacher. "We spend much of our time indoors with our families and friends."

Cosiness prevails

Inside this thin barrier of social contact, Denmark is one of the warmest countries in the world. People are genuine. They speak their minds. They thrive on making life cosy, relaxing and enjoyable – from festive occasions to mundane coffee breaks. This is what Danish *hygge* is all about. *Hygge* (pronounced ***whoo**-guh*) stands for any and every sense of cosiness, and it is found everywhere in Denmark. A good meal has *hygge*, a house can have *hygge*, a story, a walk

in the woods, a meeting at a café, even a person can have *hygge*. Parties for weddings, birthdays, anniversaries and the like have *hygge* at their core. Tables are decorated with flowers and candles and creatively folded napkins. A three-course meal is usually interspersed with songs and speeches, which end in a collective "Hurrah!" Wine flows freely. As the Danish poet and troubadour Benny Andersen wrote in a song well known among Danes: "One must keep the mood wet. I'm drunk and I'm feeling great."

Six hours into such a celebration and filled with spirits, a partygoer has a chance to get up from the table, dance a bit, then fetch some coffee and cookies and sit down again. Later, the

---

PRECEDING PAGES: marching band in Stockholm, Sweden. **LEFT:** jazz on a summer's day at the Riverboat Jazz Festival, Silkeborg, Jutland, Denmark. **RIGHT:** eating alfresco in Copenhagen.

hosts serve the final course, called "get out food", and guests gradually take the hint.

Hygge was born, no doubt, indoors during the grey winter months. From November to February, Danes go to work in darkness and return home in darkness. Warm candlelight fills flats, homes and offices in natural defence. During *Jul* (Christmas), live candles decorate Christmas trees indoors, around which families join hands and sing carols. Local ferries light up the black water with strings of white lights. On New Year's Eve, the Queen gives her annual talk to the nation on television, and fireworks spark and pop, lighting up the midnight sky.

A whiff of spring

By February, winter seems to drag on for ever. In his essay, *Oh! To be Danish*, the author Klaus Rifbjerg writes of this time: "Sure, it can be grim, and now and then we might want to turn our collar up and jump in the river. But then the light suddenly changes and there's a melody in the air, a whiff of spring to come, the smell of the sea and a blackbird singing on a rooftop."

Fields of fluorescent yellow winter rape blossom in May, and the days grow longer. In spring and summer, urban Danes cycle out to their garden houses on the edge of town, and rural Danes collect dead branches and greenery into

EQUALITY FOR ALL

Denmark is an egalitarian society with a high standard of living where, as the Danes themselves say, "Few have too much and fewer have too little." The welfare system gives everyone the same opportunities: free health service, education, support for the elderly and handicapped, unemployment benefits, pensions and more. The system carries a price: goods and services are taxed at 25 percent, and 50–70 percent of income is taxed.

Welfare equality carries through to social mores. Everyone is on first-name terms, the formal address, *De*, being reserved mainly for the Queen. Dress is casual and a tie in the workplace is rare.

huge piles on the beaches and in the countryside. On the evening of 23 June, Midsummer's Eve, those piles of wood are topped with an effigy of a witch and set on fire to drive bad spirits from the land. In July, nearly the whole country goes on holiday for three weeks. Barbecues are lit and bathing suits donned.

By late summer, farmers' tractors haul grain and hay, holding up traffic. Towns hold harvest festivals, children start school and families hunt for mushrooms and berries in the forests. People complain about the diminishing light and increasing rain, and soon temperatures can drop so low the sea freezes solid. So, the Danes light a candle, make some *hygge* with hot cocoa and buns, and look forward to *Jul* again.

A sense of Danish togetherness can be felt in society as well, starting with the generous welfare system *(see box, below left)*. Social benefits are high, workers' unions are strong, and the cooperative spirit prevails. Only four out of 100 Danes do not belong to an association. "We have a joke that if two Danes sit together for

> *More than 100 dialects are spoken in Denmark. Some vary greatly. People in south Jutland are hardly understood by the residents of Copenhagen.*

Being a Dane today therefore involves a great deal of soul-searching on the subjects of tolerance, integration and immigration. The country came under intense criticism in 2005, after the newspaper *Jyllands-Posten* published cartoons that caused offence across the Islamic world. Danes were polarised. Some turned to the far-right, anti-immigration Danish People's Party to represent their hardening attitudes, while others cleaved to their belief in an egalitarian society for all.

The 2008 economic crisis and a consequent spike in unemployment rates did not help the tense immigration question, but the country

five minutes, they will start an association," says Frans Kjær Nielsen.

Danish challenges

But this idyllic-sounding vision of cosiness and cooperation does have its darker side. During the 1980s, a wave of refugees shook up the homogeneity of this little Scandinavian country – threatening, perhaps, that all-important feeling of *hygge*. Denmark was unprepared, and immigration became a huge and emotive domestic issue – and it still is.

LEFT: Denmark is perfect for those who love nature and the great outdoors. **ABOVE:** drinks on the waterfront.

rolled with the punches, and in 2011 it has one of the strongest economies in Europe. The government, however, is still looking around for ways to ease the financial burden. Danes are justly proud of their welfare safety net, and are still happy to pay high taxes to support it, but the system's costs and benefits are another of the country's major preoccupations. In June 2010, the government halved the country's four-year unemployment benefits period to claw back some cash.

The system is still very supportive of women, though. Maternity and paternity leave is generous, the family is all-important in Denmark, and Danish men play a large part in raising their children. ❏

THE NORWEGIANS

Forget the stereotypical image of a cool Scandinavian:
visitors to Norway can be assured of a warm
and friendly welcome

Some say that Norwegians can be cool almost to the point of rudeness when you first meet them. Thomas Hylland Eriksen, Professor of Social Anthropology at the University of Oslo, wants to set that stereotype straight. "Norwegians have a general reputation for being slightly aloof and difficult to approach. While there may be some truth to this, due to late urbanisation and the persistence of rural values, one cannot generalise." It's equally true to say that once you've overcome that initial distance and a Norwegian has got to know you, their warmth and hospitality are unmistakable.

The Norwegian character is complex and sometimes contradictory. Norwegians may be slow in offering their opinions, but when they do their views are forthright. They pride themselves on their internationalism (rather than nationalism), yet can be incredibly inward-looking. They have strong cultural and economic links with the rest of Europe but stubbornly insist on staying outside the European Union. And the enthusiasm of so many Norwegians to participate in commercial whaling often seems to have less to do with its value as an industry, and more to do with a hatred of being told what to do by the international community.

The rugged landscapes, which centuries ago created Norway's geographical isolation, have taught Norwegians to be fiercely independent and self-reliant. This independence was reinforced by the discovery of oil in the 1960s. A strong, stable economy and comprehensive social security system have created a comfort-

able standard of living and cohesive society, where people feel protected if things go wrong. Norwegians have been known to grumble about bad roads and expensive gasoline, but they feel quite secure in their country, where democratic values are upheld and there is little, if any, corruption.

Immigration challenges

Historically, Norway is one of the oldest nations in Europe, if not the oldest. Its people can trace an unbroken line of descent from those who inhabited the area in prehistoric times. During the Viking era, Norway controlled an enormous territory from Russia to the British Isles,

---

LEFT: a warm welcome awaits visitors to Norway.
RIGHT: a Sami woman in traditional dress, decorated with colourful ribbons and exquisite pendants.

and the common European tongue was Old Norse. Yet today's Norway was reconstituted as late as 1905 when the union with Sweden was finally dissolved. The dominance of Old Norse may have gone, but today's Norwegians have regained their pride.

> *Norwegian women have fought for equality for over a century – and appear to be winning. Women are particularly well represented in the political sphere, making up 40 percent of MPs and exactly half of the cabinet.*

World War II, and the Nazi occupation, was a massive shock to the Norwegian psyche. There's still a deep-felt anger against the supposedly neutral Swedes for permitting the transit of German troops into Norway. After the war, the Norwegians realised with some reluctance that strategically they had no choice but to seek the protection of others. So they signed up to NATO, not least as protection against Russia, another unreliable neighbour in the north. But they turned their backs on the European Union. The importance of fishing and farming and the security of the oil revenues meant that economically they preferred to go it alone.

It's too easy, however, to equate this self-reliance with xenophobia. Norwegians don't fear or dislike foreigners, although like their Scandic neighbours, they have experienced an influx of immigrants in recent years. Unfortunately this has given fuel to far-right politicians eager to exploit people's fears of an invading "otherness": but in spite of immigration concerns and far-right rhetoric, Norway is one of the most stable of European countries. Even the 2008 economic crisis had minimal effect thanks to the country's oil wealth, held for the benefit of the whole nation in a sovereign wealth fund (SWF). The SWF now exceeds 3 trillion kroner, and new oil and gas exploration in the Arctic regions look set to fill the piggy bank to bursting.

Home comforts

Hospitality is second nature to a Norwegian, whether he or she lives in Oslo or in the remotest corner of Finnmark. If you're planning to visit people at home be prepared – there's lots of coffee to be drunk and cake to be eaten. Schnapps is also something that gets poured generously. The food will be plentiful and wholesome; your host will expect nothing in return except some appreciative comments about the welcome and any traditional dishes being served.

Thanks to all that oil, and a very generous social security system, there is relatively little poverty in Norway. But nor are they at all ostentatious about their wealth and, especially in rural areas, life can still be very simple.

Small-town life

The more enigmatic aspects of the Norwegian character – including the Nordic gloom that can descend after a drink too many – have been famously scrutinised by Henrik Ibsen. He was brought up in small communities and, during a long exile, turned his critical eye on the experience. One of the themes running through Ibsen's work is the double-edged nature of life in such a community: mutual support in adversity weighed against a suffocating lack of privacy at other times.

The lesser-known, Danish/Norwegian Aksel Sandemose wrote "Ten Commandments for Village Life" in a fictional novel about a town called Jante, the essence being humility bordering on self-abasement. They included: "You must not think that you are worth anything; you must not think that you are better than anyone else; you must not think yourself capable of anything worthwhile; and you must not think that you are in any way exceptional." Scandinavians today are still guided by this fictional Jante law (*janteloven*).

Land of many dialects

Norway's rural nature has compounded one of its thorniest problems – language. The issue has split the country for over a century. Throwing off the Danish-dominated *bokmål* (book language) was crucial to the independence activists of the 19th century. Unfortunately there was no Norwegian alternative on offer, just a variety of often very divergent dialects. Various attempts

Worlds apart

Norway's geography and its sparse population (4.7 million people) have entrenched cultural and economic fragmentation too. Rural lives depended on agriculture, and the land was too poor to support more than a family or two in a single valley. Separated from their neighbours by mountains, which were easier to cross in winter on skis than in summer on foot, they effectively lived in worlds apart. Families managed on their own, a resourcefulness which still runs in the blood.

Whether it's the outdoor life or all the fish in the diet, Norwegians enjoy amazing longev-

were made to bring these together into a truly national language known as *nynorsk* (new Norwegian), but these were never more than a partial success, and even now there are huge regional variations in the spoken tongue.

Most Norwegians speak English extremely well and are more than happy to do so. They realised it was taking national pride too far to deny the pre-eminence of English. Indeed, many an urbanite will claim it's much easier to understand a foreigner speaking English than one of their compatriots speaking a regional dialect.

LEFT: conscripts undergoing winter training in the far north of Norway. **ABOVE:** rural life.

> In February 2008, the remote Spitsbergen Global Seed Bank officially opened. Built to be war- and disaster-proof, it acts as a living library of all known varieties of the world's crops.

ity. They manage to look remarkably healthy all their lives, and the octogenarian grandmother whizzing by on skis is not entirely a myth.

The Swedish king who reluctantly oversaw Norway's independence predicted that bureaucratic incompetence would soon have Norwegians begging to return to the fold. That, of course, never happened, and modern Norway is a strong, successful socialist state. ❏

THE SWEDES

Beneath the cool, sophisticated exterior,
the Swede harbours a deep and heartfelt passion
for nature, tradition and schnapps

Swedes have a reputation for being dry, sombre and painfully serious. It is true that the average Swede is quite quiet and reserved, and that instant gushing friendliness is not commonly witnessed. But contrary to popular opinion, Swedes do have a sense of humour – one that is as elusive as Garbo and as fleeting as a Swedish summer. Swedes may seem calm and collected on the outside, but they're every bit as prone to ribald fits of laughter as the next person, even if they do recover their solemn faces much more quickly. So remember that appearances can be deceptive: underneath that composed exterior, you'll usually find a warm, friendly individual. And once a Swede has decided to let their guard down and befriend you, they will be a friend for life.

Blond and blue-eyed?

When it comes to Sweden, popular misconceptions are rife. Think "Swede", and an image of a blue-eyed blond, no doubt sitting at the wheel of a Volvo, may well spring to mind. But only a proportion of native Swedes fit the old stereotype: Sweden today is a country of growing cultural and social diversity. In 2010, over one million of Sweden's 9.4 million inhabitants were born abroad, the majority in Finland, the former Yugoslavia and Iraq.

However, Sweden's traditionally tolerant outlook has been called into question recently. The high standard of living, strong economy and cradle-to-grave welfare system enjoyed by Swedes has come under increasing pressure, particularly following the 2008 global financial crash. Far-right groups who place the blame on immigrants have made political headway: for the first time, the anti-immigration Sweden

Democrats won 20 of the 349 parliamentary seats – nearly 6 percent of the vote – in the September 2010 elections.

Children of nature

It's no exaggeration to say that Swedes are potty about nature. It's somehow a part of the Swedish soul. They are quick to wax lyrical about the grassy plains of Skåne, expound the virtues of lakeside Dalarna and remind you that theirs is the only true wilderness left in all Europe. Ask any Swede to recount tales of their childhood

ABOVE: a holiday-maker building a raft on the Klarälven River, Varmland. **RIGHT:** traditional images of Sweden; national dress and meatballs.

and they'll dreamily recall summers spent in the country with a noticeable softening of facial expression and a faraway look in their eye.

Nowadays the little red cottage is Sweden's most enduring image, and there's nothing Swedes like better than to take off to their *stuga*, where they can kick off their shoes, swim naked and bond with nature.

Life in Sweden is intrinsically linked to the changing seasons. Swedish winters are famous for their darkness, longevity and Arctic temperatures. But Swedes have learnt how to make the most of it, and winter sports are popular with Swedes of all ages. They eagerly await the spring and the return of sunlight with all the excited anticipation of children at Christmas. Like hibernating animals re-emerging after winter, sun-starved Swedes are wont to stand on street corners, at crossings, in traffic lights, and any other spot with a south-facing aspect, soaking up the first warming rays of spring.

This deep-rooted love of nature means that environmental concerns are a high priority in Sweden. The country plans to wean itself off oil by 2020, and car manufacturers Saab and Volvo have been forerunners in developing vehicles that run on biofuels. Sweden's best restaurants inevitably are part of the international "slow

WINING AND DINING

"Ska vi fika?" ("Shall we have a coffee break?") is a question that induces a warm glow in every Swedish heart; and the answer is always *"Ja!"*. Coffee is vital to Sweden's wellbeing – only Finland consumes more. A snug place in which to drink it is vital, and a piece of cake, most usually a cinnamon bun *(kanelbullar)*, is a non-negotiable accompaniment.

Coffee is one thing, alcohol another. An unyielding state monopoly and steep prices create a faint sense of prohibition. On Friday evenings, stoical Swedes queue at the state's Systembolaget off licences to buy wine or a six-pack. Customs laws changed in 2003, allowing Swedes to bring quantities of alcohol from the EU into the country; but cautious Sweden still sees more harm than good in dereg-

ulating alcohol sales. Yet when the chance to indulge presents itself, Swedes love celebrations… as long as all is done with regard to etiquette. Punctuality is a must, and toasts are made according to strict rules. Impeccable manners only seem to loosen at a crayfish feast, when Swedes will merrily rip off claws with their hands and clash beer glasses in true Viking fashion.

In line with the new Nordic cuisine revolution that has swept across Scandinavia in recent years, Stockholm has seen an incredible restaurant boom. Cosy bistros and sophisticated restaurants (including six with Michelin stars) have sprung up everywhere, placing the city firmly on the gastronomic map.

food" movement, focusing on organic local produce and local culinary culture.

Cosmopolitan citizens of the world

Despite such closeness to the countryside, Sweden is no nation of bumpkins. Its people are a

> Friendships are often sealed over schnapps. Delicately flavoured with fruits or spices, schnapps is a perennial favourite and every Swede can name his or her tipple.

mass destruction in Iraq in 2003) have loomed large on the world stage. According to the Organisation for Economic Co-operation and Development, in 2010 Sweden was the world's most charitable country.

National pride

Swedes have a high opinion of their country and like nothing more than to talk about Sweden itself. This is not to say that Swedes are braggarts: a more humble, self-deprecating tribe you'd be hard pushed to find. But their modesty is merely a thin veil, and all young Swedes are well versed in the achievements

true blend of the provincial *and* the cosmopolitan, every bit at home in the concrete jungle as going barefoot at their place in the country – 85 percent of the country's inhabitants live in an urban area.

Swedes have a reputation for forward thinking, with Sweden deemed to be Europe's most innovative country in 2008. Biotechnology and pharmaceuticals are a major export, and IT companies thrive: one of Skype's two co-founders is Swedish, and the online music service Spotify is a Swedish creation.

Swedes also have a strong international perspective, and many of Sweden's most (in)famous people (Dag Hammarskjöld; Olof Palme; Dr Hans Blix, who led the search for weapons of

of their countrymen, be it Alfred Nobel or August Strindberg. And perhaps this universal satisfaction is not so misplaced: after all, in recent times the rest of the world has come to appreciate various Swedish exports. IKEA sells Swedish homeware in 39 countries, and it is said that one in 10 Europeans was conceived in an IKEA bed! Culturally, Stieg Larsson's thrillers *The Girl with the Dragon Tattoo*, *The Girl Who Played with Fire* and *The Girl Who Kicked the Hornets' Nest* have sold over 50 million copies since the first book was published posthumously in 2005. ❑

ABOVE: glass-blowing in Småland. **RIGHT:** flying the Swedish flag in Fiskebäckskil on the west coast.

THE FINNS

Cool, but not humourless, the innovative Finns have fought hard to preserve their identity and move with the times

Finns are sometimes mistakenly described as being cold, but their demeanour can better be described as calm, modest, even a bit shy. Geographical isolation has created a hardy, self-reliant people who don't feel the need to be overly garrulous. Finns will weigh their words carefully; silences are considered a natural part of conversation, and empty small talk is, frankly, a puzzle. One Finnish proverb advises, "Take a man by his words, take a bull by its horns."

With such respect for speech, it's no surprise that Finns embraced the mobile phone so readily... particularly as it combines communication with an ideal shield from excessive intimacy. Finnish passions find their release not in conversation, but in poetry and music, athletics, football, ice hockey and, oddly, the tango. Practised with Argentinian fervour, the dance has become a national symbol, and festivals and contests are held all over the country.

Sisu is a word synonymous with the Finnish character. Roughly translated it means guts or fortitude, a description which aptly fits the heroic, patriotic and noble warriors of Finland's national epic poem, the Kalevala.

Nordic links

The "typical Finn", should such a person exist, has a genetic combination that is 75 percent identical to that of other Scandinavians, but

25 percent derives from tribes that probably migrated to Finland from east of the Ural Mountains. This more oriental strain accounts for physical traits that set Finns apart from their Nordic neighbours – finely pronounced cheekbones and quite small, slatey-grey or blue eyes. Laplanders tend to be smaller in stature and sturdily built. Karelians are stockier and slightly smaller than people from the west coast, whose ancestors merged with the gargantuan Vikings.

Nature is sacred

All Finns, no matter what their genetic makeup, are heavily influenced by their land of lakes and

LEFT: thick furs protect the Sami against winter cold.
RIGHT: ice hockey, Finland's most popular sport. Champions start training at an early age.

forests. More than 400,000 Finns own a plot of forest, and everyone has the right to roam. Nature is regarded as near-sacred, a place full of mystery as well as one of renewal. The country shuts down for at least a month after Midsummer, when the Finns take to their summer cabins en masse. Fishing, swimming, berry-picking and a host of other outdoor pursuits fill the warm days; most cabins have a sauna, and steambasking followed by a plunge into the nearest cold lake can be seen almost as a ritualistic preparation for the wintry months to follow.

But Finland is becoming more urbanised. Some 80 percent of Finns live on 2 percent of

there has been a broadening of interest in the outside world. Many younger Finns go on to study, work and travel abroad, and Finnish businesses have made serious investments in nearby Estonia over the last 15 years.

Helsinki itself has taken on a more multicul-

> *As a nation, Finns are great lovers of the outdoors and of sport, and some young Finns, following in the footsteps of the great Finnish runner Paavo Nurmi, live for little else but their athletic activities.*

the land. Domestic emigration is accelerating – Finns are moving from small towns to Greater Helsinki, and the big urban centres of Tampere, Turku and Oulu, although many Helsinki business types are relocating to other countries with warmer climates and lower taxes. The much publicised *etätyö* (distance working via the internet) has its attractions, but most people still try to escape to the cities.

Identity and immigration

In the past, Finland has focused much of its energy on the struggle to keep its identity, defending its language against the Russian regime more than 100 years ago and being long dominated by Sweden. In recent years, however,

tural demeanour: an influx of Russian, Eastern European and Somalian immigrants has boosted the city's foreign population to about 5 percent. However, although the numbers are well below the EU average, Finland is experiencing unrest along with these new citizens, perhaps partially explained by the country's historical experiences of foreign influence. A 2010 Gallup poll found that 59 percent of Finns are opposed to further new arrivals, and the right-wing True Finns, who even object to the country's small population of Swedish-speaking Finns, quadrupled their vote in the 2011 elections. The new coalition government is expected to follow a stronger anti-immigration, anti-EU line.

Women and men

At least the battle of the sexes is not a major societal concern. *Sisu*, meaning guts or fortitude, is a word synonymous with the Finnish character, and self-reliance, determination and tenacity are national traits that apply equally to men and women. There has never been a strong feminist movement, because there has never been a need for one. In 1906, Finnish women became the first in the world to gain unrestricted political rights to vote and to stand for election. They were quick to take up the challenge, forming 10 percent of the first Finnish government, and by doing so were directly able

oil money, and tied to the floundering euro (unlike Denmark and Sweden), Finland's GDP fell by 7.5 percent – the sharpest drop since the country's 1918 civil war. But Finland is recovering well, thanks mainly to the solid state of its finances before the crash.

The world may have been taken aback by the scale of the crisis, but the Finns are experts at adjusting themselves to difficult events, gritting their teeth and battling onwards. Adaptation is deep-rooted in the Finnish soul: the big wheel keeps turning, and another year means new opportunities. As the Finns will tell anyone who asks, "The only constant is change." ❏

to influence government policy. Women MPs now make up 42 percent of parliament, and Finland's female president Tarja Halonen was re-elected for a second six-year term in 2006.

Finland today

The 2008 economic crash hit Finland hardest of all the Scandic countries. Its main exports – paper-manufacturing goods and electronics – are sensitive to market fluctuations, and trade with one of its biggest customers, Russia, slowed to a standstill. Without Norway's

LEFT: with the first sign of summer, cafés spill out onto Helsinki's streets and squares.
ABOVE: a Finnish fiddler.

ROMANY GYPSIES

One of the oldest groups in Finland who are not ethnic Finns are the Romany gypsies, whose womenfolk are instantly recognisable by their elaborate embroidered lace blouses and voluminous skirts. Although today most speak only Finnish, few have intermarried, so their dark good looks stand out against fairer Finns.

Most gypsies are no longer nomadic and live instead in houses and flats. Some families still tend to wander, especially in autumn, from one market place to another. Little horse-trading is done these days, however, and the gypsies' appearance at these fairs is little more than a vestige of nostalgia.

THE ACTIVE LIFE

Scandinavians are passionate about nature and the
outdoors. Unfazed by the weather, they hike, ski,
skate, sail, cycle, fish and climb

The people of the Nordic countries are so at
home in their natural surroundings that
they seldom pause to consider how intertwined their daily lives are with the climate, the
seasons, and the amazing and diverse beauty of
the northern landscape.

In spring and summer, the mountains beckon
backpackers to scale their heights, the Swedish
archipelago is dotted with thousands of sailing boats, and serious hikers and day-trippers
wend their way through the Nordic forests.
Danes head for their magnificent beaches
while Swedes, Norwegians, and Finns celebrate
the cool refreshing plunge of the thousands of
lakes that dot the landscape. In recent years,
hordes of Nordic ski enthusiasts have taken to
the open roads and mountain trails.

Winter poses no obstacle to the hardy Scandinavian. They take to their skis to traverse fields
and forests, pull on skates to blaze paths across
icy lakes, fish through the ice and climb frozen
waterfalls just for fun.

Scandinavians often manage to combine a
practical outlook with a sense of adventure and
a sporting spirit – where better to exercise all
three than in the great outdoors?

At the water's edge

Denmark and Sweden offer varied coastlines
and a thriving beach life. There are 8,000km
(5,000 miles) of coastline in Sweden, offering
clean, if often chilly, water to swim in, and rocks
to sun on (but few sandy beaches). The most
spectacular seascape is the Stockholm archi-

pelago, with its 24,000 islands, but nearly as
thrilling are the waves crashing on the rocks of
Bohuslän's archipelago.

The Danes are blessed with sandy beaches.
With more than 7,400km (4,600 miles) of
coastline, the waters surrounding Denmark
are a playground for outdoor activities. Kayaks,
canoes, rowing boats and smaller sailing or
motor craft may be hired at resorts along the
coasts or on the larger lakes. The air is hardly
still in Denmark, and the windsurfing is excellent. Seasoned surfers may prefer the exhilara-
tion of the North Sea, for example the beaches
around Klitmøller; while beginners can try their
hand in the lee of a bay or fjord, or on a lake.

LEFT: Norway, Sweden and Finland offer exciting
opportunities for winter sports enthusiasts.
RIGHT: rafting on the Klarälven River, Sweden.

Norway's fjords can be explored by steamers in summertime. In winter, when the fjords freeze over, families take Sunday "walks" on skates among the rocks and islets. Increased tourism along Finland's lake system is bringing the steamers back into business. There are now regular passenger routes on several of the lake systems, but the oldest and probably the most romantic are those across Saimaa's vast expanse.

Hitting the walking trails

The Nordic region is known for its great open landscapes and is a mecca for hikers and backpackers. Waymarked footpaths are found in scenically outstanding areas (*see box, below opposite*). The Danish countryside offers the most gentle introduction to walkers, with an appealing patchwork of dense forests, coastal dunes, marshes, moors and meticulously manicured farmland. In every type of landscape there are paths or trails that stretch for miles, and a labyrinth of winding country roads.

The greatest proportion of Sweden is virgin country. You can stroll for miles along tracks without seeing another human being. Throughout Sweden, there's an excellent network of waymarked footpaths. Close to Stockholm is the Sörmlandsleden (Sörmland trail),

FREEDOM TO ROAM

The freedom to explore nature is considered a birthright of most Scandinavians, and the politicians have seen fit to put that inheritance into law. Since 1957 Norway has had a *Lov om friluftslivet* (Outdoor Recreations Act), which states succinctly: "At any time of the year, outlying property may be crossed on foot, with consideration and due caution."

In Sweden, the freedom to roam is called *Allemansrätten* (Everyman's Right), and in Finland *Jokamiehenoikeus*. Everyone is permitted to camp anywhere for a night, or to walk, ski or paddle a canoe anywhere, as long as the area is not fenced in or in close proximity to a private home.

with over 1,000km (620 miles) of pathways, starting at Björkhagen underground station. Carefully laid out, the trail offers hikers constantly changing vistas of deep forest, historic sites, lookout points and lakes. It passes several camps where you can eat, rest and buy supplies, with shelters at regular intervals. Sörmlandsleden is an easy hike, but it offers plenty of excitement, with deer, elk, capercaillie, hawks and grouse along the way. For the most exotic views, head for the Kungsleden trail which runs for 450km (280 miles) between Abisko and Hemavan.

ABOVE: admiring the peaks in Jotunheimen, Norway.
RIGHT: brown bears inhabit Finland's wilderness.

Norwegians are quite at home in their wild, unspoilt country, and have a great feeling for its mountains. In Norway, the bulk of the trails and lodges are conveniently in the middle of the triangle bounded by the cities of Oslo, Bergen and Trondheim. A central entry point is Finse, situated above the timber line at 1,200 metres (4,000ft). Finse's main street is the station platform; there are no cars because there are no roads.

Finland also offers pristine wilderness, quaint historical attractions and ample peace and quiet. Some of the country's best hiking is along the Karelian Circle Trek, Finland's longest trekking route, with approximately 1,000km (620 miles) of marked trails. It offers genuine wilderness routes, variety in four different national parks, and the possibility to combine walking with mountain biking, canoeing, fishing or hunting. Bears are rare, but walkers are advised to tie a small bell to their backpack to warn them of their presence. Bed-and-breakfast accommodation is available, as are wilderness huts. Pitching a tent is legal (and free) almost everywhere along this route.

Accessible mountaineering

To the north of Finse lie the Jotunheimen Mountains, literally the "Home of the Giants". Nonetheless, even the loftiest of the Jotunheimen peaks, Galdhøpiggen and Glittertind, which are the highest in Northern Europe, with summits rising more than 2,400 metres (7,900ft), rank low on the international scale of noteworthy mountains where sheer altitude, not challenge, is the main criterion. Though this fact has led to relative anonymity – few Norwegian peaks

appear in the classic mountaineering literature – it does mean that you can ascend the equivalent of the Matterhorn or Mont Blanc without the problems associated with high altitude.

Some of the glaciers that hewed the Norwegian landscape left offspring. One, Jostedalsbreen (Jostedal Glacier), is the largest in

> In Sweden and Norway, the extensive networks of walking and hiking trails are marked by a red "T". Lodges and cabins offer accommodation along the way.

NATIONAL PARKS

The Nordic region has many national parks, each with its own claim to unique native flora and fauna. Denmark's parks are very new – the first opened in 2008 – and contain small but unique environments such as the tidal flats of the Wadden Sea. Parks in the other Scandinavian countries tend to be much bigger, with marked hiking trails. In the more remote parks, you'll often find a chain of mountain stations set a day's walk from one another along way-marked footpaths, providing shelter for walkers. Most are equipped with cooking facilities, a shop and comfortable beds; some have a self-service restaurant and a sauna. They are not hotels, but simple accommodation designed to provide a haven at the end of the day for tired walkers.

Large areas of Norway have been designated as national parks to protect special habitats and support biodiversity. Sweden's 28 national parks cover everything from low-lying marshland to Sarek's trackless mountains and glaciers. For spring flowers and birdsong, head to Dalby Söderskog in Skåne. Store Mosse in Småland is worth a detour for bird-watchers interested in whooper swans, marsh harriers and cranes. Finland's park network is mostly administered by the Forest and Park Service, which controls 37 national parks, including the rugged rift valley of Hiidenporttin Kansallispuisto in Karelia and the Ramsholmen Nature Reserve on the Åland Islands. The organisation rents interesting accommodation in isolated wilderness cottages.

mainland Europe. Jostedalsbreen and its siblings throughout the country are the places to see crampon-shod parties wielding ice axes from spring until autumn. Contact with the ice that shaped their land is currently the Norwegians' fastest-growing wilderness recreation, and many centres now organise specialist courses.

On two wheels

The bicycle is an important mode of transport for Danes and visitors to Denmark alike. Bikes outnumber cars in some city areas, where the streets have bicycle lanes and traffic lights. Denmark has thousands of miles of cycle paths, and bikes may be taken on most trains and ferries. Tourist offices can provide detailed maps of routes. Hærvejen is a bicycle and walking trail that stretches from the German border to Viborg in north-central Jutland. Traders and travellers beat this path a few thousand years ago, and much of it still looks as it did during Viking times. All along the route there are inns, hotels or hostels, as well as shops for provisions.

Cycling is also a popular outdoor sport for Swedes, and there are many well-designed and well-lit routes all over the country. You could spend a week touring the islands of Gotland or Bornholm on a bike. Keen cyclists also head for

TELEMARK SKIING

In the mid-1800s, Sondre Norheim, a young farmer from Morgedal, in the county of Telemark, created a whole new style of skiing. Morgedal is in the mountains, so the ski-makers there sought designs that would perform well in the surrounding rugged terrain, both in everyday winter skiing and for impromptu sporting meetings.

Norheim modified his skis by adding firm bindings, which hold the ski boots to the skis and allow the feet control over them; he also gave them "sidecut", a slight hour-glass profile when seen from above, which enables the skis to run true and turn easily.

Norheim and his friends used the adapted skis to perfect new manoeuvres, including landing from airborne flights off snow-covered rooftops and natural outcrops. Soon they were ready to show off their new skills, and this led to the first ski-jumping contest in 1879. The bent-knee stance with one ski trailing soon became known as the "Telemark".

In modern Telemark skiing, the heel is free to lift up from the ski and turns are steered, with one ski trailing and at an angle to the other. Competitive Telemark ski races are now held on packed slopes, as are Alpine ski races, but true Telemark skiing has spawned the revival of skiathlons, in which competitors must ski jump, ski through a slalom course, and run a cross-country ski race, all on the same pair of skis.

Östergötland, particularly along the banks of the Göta Kanal where the towpaths make ideal cycling tracks. Bikes can be hired at several places along the canal, and the most popular stretch for cyclists is between Berg and Borensberg. For the truly ambitious, there is the Sverigeleden (Sweden Bicycle Route), from Stockholm to Göteborg – a distance of 2,600km (1,600 miles).

Cast your line

One of the most remarkable places to fish is right in the centre of Stockholm, in the fast-moving Strömmen channel which links the fresh water of Lake Mälaren with the Baltic Sea. A clean-up programme has brought salmon and sea trout back to the very heart of the capital.

Big salmon and sea trout can be caught almost anywhere in Sweden – in world-famous waters like the southern Mörrum River, in the large and wild rivers of the north, as well as along the coast when the fish are on their migration. The salmon season varies between rivers, but it usually starts during the summer and continues well into the autumn. The sea trout tend to arrive a little later. Both spinning and fly-fishing can produce good salmon catches, but sturdy tackle is advised.

In Norway the variety of fish and fish products is amazing, and Norwegians look on a proper fresh fish shop as an asset to a community. Norway is a country of fishermen, both commercial and anglers. The long coastline is a mecca for saltwater angling, yet freshwater angling is more popular, and there are a quarter of a million fishable inland lakes and ponds. The most common of around 40 freshwater species are trout and char; in the northernmost parts, and in lakes and ponds at higher elevations, they are the only fish. Grayling and pike are more common in larger lakes and rivers in eastern and central areas.

Ice fishing is a prime wintertime hobby. It's a straightforward form of angling, which requires only a baited hand line or short pole and line, warm clothing and lots of patience.

Winter sports

Long winters, frozen rivers and lakes, and beckoning snow-topped mountains make Sweden,

Norway and Finland a fabulous destination for winter sports enthusiasts. It's possible to participate in all kinds of activities, including snowshoeing, ice climbing and snowmobiling, and many ski areas can provide equipment and organise expeditions. Even in the heart of Scandinavia's cities, winter sports abound: in Stockholm, for example, you can fly round the 14 islands on a pair of ice skates.

Naturally, skiing is the biggest winter sport, whether it's downhill (Alpine), cross-country or Telemark. Downhill skiing in Sweden attracts a growing number of visitors thanks to artificially produced snowfall, a variety of slopes and

a reduced avalanche risk compared to Alpine resorts. Sälen is the largest ski resort in Sweden, and Åre, where the World Cup Ski Championships are held, attracts skiers from all over Europe with hundreds of top-class, superbly groomed pistes served by high-speed lifts and cabins. Half-pipes and snow parks are available for snowboarders.

Norway's six-month long skiing season is a boon to fanatics, and there are resorts scattered up and down the country, from Sirdal in the south to Tromsø way up in the Arctic Circle. Halfway between Oslo and Bergen, Hemsedal is the largest Norwegian ski resort, with 51 downhill slopes, cross-country trails and several excellent terrain parks for snowboarders. Although

LEFT: the wide open spaces of northern Sweden and Finland offer superb wilderness trekking.
RIGHT: the Danes and Swedes are keen cyclists.

Life in Lapland

The indigenous Sami of northern Scandinavia, a hardy semi-nomadic people, can trace their roots back thousands of years

The Sami call themselves "the people of the eight seasons". They are indigenous people who live in Sweden, Norway and Finland's most northerly provinces, and can trace their heritage back more than 8,000 years. They have their

own language, religious traditions and customs. While the life of the Sami has changed in modern times (snowmobiles have become ubiquitous in the last decade), the annual cycle of the reindeer – rutting, herding, separating, slaughtering, calving, marking – continues to shape the Lapland calendar. The winter round-ups are among Europe's most colourful events, resembling scenes from a Wild West film transposed to an Arctic setting. Visitors can enjoy this ancient culture at festivals and ceremonial occasions held throughout the year, where one can sample reindeer delicacies and marvel at Sami handicrafts.

A vivid way to experience the Sami lifestyle and landscape is in spring and summer, when the mountains blossom with heather, globe flowers,

cloudberries and countless other species, inviting the visitor to take to the trails and woods of the many national parks in the Sami regions of Scandinavia. Padjelanta ("the higher mountain" in Sami) is the biggest national park in Sweden. It is one of Sweden's most beautiful areas, with rolling plains, gently rounded mountain massifs, huge lakes such as Vastenjaure and Virihaure, and small streams, which the Lapps call *jokk*. It has always been an important pasture for their reindeer herds.

For golf enthusiasts, nothing can quite top the thrill of golfing under the Midnight Sun in the glorious days of summer, where (depending on latitude and cloud cover) the sun is visible for up to 70 summer days. Anglers will find a true paradise in the primeval wilderness of the north, laced by swift rivers and streams and punctuated by lakes and pools.

To enjoy the wintry wilderness in an entirely different way, try dog-sledging, which is offered by many firms in northern Scandinavia. Drive the dog-sledge yourself or sit back in the vast silence of the mountains and be driven by a team of huskies. Your guide will tell you how to take care of a sledge dog and share bits of trivia, like the fact that in the Inuit language there are 18 different words for snow. Dog-sledging, common in Greenland, is now well established in Sweden and is growing in popularity in Finland's northern wilderness around Muonio.

The Sami winter vistas can also be enjoyed on reindeer sleigh rides and snowshoe treks. Ice climbing is popular, too. Fishing through the ice is common on most lakes and rivers.

To soak up the hard life of the Sami fully, the visitor can stay in the world's largest igloo, the Jukkasjärvi Ice Hotel in Sweden. Each autumn, as the Arctic temperature plummets, Laplanders rebuild this celebrated igloo from thousands of tons of snow and ice. Inside it houses a church, hotel, gallery, golf room, cinema and bar named, appropriately, Absolut Ice. Guests sleep in warm sleeping bags on mattresses of spruce bough and reindeer skins. Temperatures average −4°C (25°F). The hearty fare served from the kitchen and the activities waiting outdoors don't leave guests much time to feel cold. Next morning, the hotel will issue a certificate of survival. It's not quite the same as herding reindeer, but it brings you one step closer to understanding how climate, custom and sheer human persistence have made the Sami what they are today.   ❑

LEFT: a young Sami boy from northern Sweden dressed for winter in a traditional pom-pom hat.

it's only small, the Kvitfjell resort wins kudos for containing the "black diamond" downhill run used in the 1994 Winter Olympics. At Geilo pure adrenalin-seekers can try snowkiting, a hair-raising sport whose stars reach speeds of up to 100kmph (60mph).

> Golf is the fastest-growing sport in Scandinavia, and its popularity has exploded in Denmark in recent years. In Scandinavia's far north enthusiasts like to play golf under the Midnight Sun.

Although Finland has no mountains, it too boasts a good collection of resorts – the biggest is Levi, 170km (105 miles) into the Arctic Circle in Lapland. But the country really comes into its own with cross-country skiing: tens of thousands of kilometres of well-marked trails wind their way through forests, over hills and across frozen lakes.

Adventure activities

Scandinavia makes a thrilling playground for the adventurous in any season, and every year activity companies offer better and better access to the wilderness.

The region's rivers present an exhilarating challenge for white-water rafters: the fast-flowing Gevsjöströmmarna, near Åre, is Sweden's steepest navigable river. In Karelia in Finland, you can work up an appetite by shooting the Ruunaa Rapids on the Lieksanjoki River, before pulling up on the riverbank for a hunter's lunch. Several companies in Norway run rafting trips, including one along the lovely Sjoa River, near Rondane National Park: canyoning and riverboarding are also possible here.

In the winter months, visitors can experience dog-sledging, an ancient form of transport believed to have been around for 4,000 years. Hurtling across packed snow on a dog sledge, pulled by teams of almost-wolves, is truly something out of the ordinary. Wrap up warm, and go for a ride in Greenland, in Norway's Finnmark province, or in Finnish or Swedish Lapland.

RIGHT: the Scandinavian countries are an angler's dream, with numerous lakes, rivers and a varied coastline all offering a good catch.

What the Baltic Sea lacks in tropical reefs, it makes up for in shipwrecks – all well preserved thanks to the low-saline water and an absence of wood-eating worms. Around 40,000 known wrecks lie on its bottom, from Viking vessels to World War II submarines. Diving tourism is just beginning to take off in Sweden and Finland, with several new companies who can lead divers to these sunken treasures.

Europe's unspoilt north contains some of the most fascinating creatures on the planet. Whale-watching is a burgeoning industry, and the north coast of Norway is a prime place to spot orca, minke and sperm whales from May to Septem-

ber. Greenland has even more species to see, including narwhals. Visitors can go on a whale-watching safari in towns such as Nuuk and Kulusuuk, and it's common to see the creatures while walking by the shore or fjord sides.

Sporting heroes

Physical activity is both a pleasure and a serious pursuit to the sporty Scandinavians. Emerging from this broad base of running, jumping, skiing, sailing, puck-thwacking, ball-kicking people come the elite, competitors who enter the many national championships and represent their countries in international sports meetings.

Snowy mountains have naturally given Scandinavians a passionate interest in skiing, and the extended winter season allows them to perfect their sport: unsurprisingly, some of the world's best skiers come from this region. Slalom champion Ingemar Stenmark put Sweden on the international skiing map, and Anja Pärson, the World and Olympic champion skier, has kept the country in the spotlight. In 2007, she became the first person to win World Championship gold medals in all five skiing disciplines.

Norwegian Marit Bjørgen is officially the most successful cross-country sprinter in history, and holds eight World Championship gold medals – the latest won in 2011. Bjørgen also picked up three gold medals at the 2010

THE VASALOPPET

One of the world's greatest skiing competitions takes place in Mora, in the Dalarna region of Sweden. The Vasaloppet, a 90km (56-mile) cross-country skiing race, is the most popular sporting event in the country. It is held every March to commemorate King Gustav Vasa's flight from his enemies in the 16th century. Each year the race includes around 15,000 competitors, who in the past have included the present Swedish king, Carl XVI Gustaf. The first Vasaloppet was run on 19 March 1922. A Vasaloppet victory is regarded as highly as a podium place in the Olympic Games or the World Championships.

Winter Olympics in Vancouver, while fellow cross-country skier Petter Northug brought home two. Aksel Lund Svindal was the world's number one downhill skier in 2007, and fought his way back from major injury to regain the title in 2009.

Traditionally, Norwegians have excelled in sailing and winter sports, but this athletic nation has won international medals in a wide range of events. A personification of national grit and sporting talent was Grete Waitz, who won the New York marathon nine times – an unbeaten world record. She was given a state funeral on her death in 2011.

In Sweden, great players like Björn Borg, Mats Wilander and Stefan Edberg have made Swedish tennis prowess legendary. Denmark shines in rowing and sailing, winning gold medals in four events at the 2008 Beijing Olympics.

The runner Paavo Nurmi (1897–1973) first put Finland on the map in the 1920 Olympics, breaking multiple world records and winning four gold medals. Variously known as the Flying Finn, the Phantom Finn and the Phenomenal Finn, he is remembered for his extraordinary running style, speed and tough character. Another tough cookie, Carina Räihä, became the first Finnish woman to scale Mount Everest in 2010.

These days the Finns maintain a strong presence as world-class rally drivers. Mika Häkkinen, Tommi Mäkinen, Ari Vatanen and Hannu Mikkola may be known only to lovers of motor sports, but probably more non-Finns could name them than could identify Finland's current prime minister.

Ice hockey is one of the most important team sports in Sweden and even more so in Finland. Each country has around 60,000 officially registered federation players, and the countries' national teams constitute two of the International Ice Hockey Federation's "big seven". Around 50 Swedes and 40 Finns play in the North American NHL, including 10-time All-Star Teemu Selänne, also known as the Finnish Flash!

And of course, all the Nordic countries share the European passion for football. Clubs are supported through funds from the football pools and from the sale of players to major European leagues. ❏

LEFT: skiing, both downhill and cross-country, is a national sport in Norway, Sweden and Finland.
RIGHT: hikers enjoy the solitude of the far north.

ART AND CULTURE

Rich in art, music and literature, and pioneers
of modern design, Scandinavians are justifiably
proud of their cultural heritage

The histories of Denmark, Norway, Sweden and Finland have been so intertwined through the centuries that, while each country possesses a unique culture, there are strong similarities, perhaps best seen in design and an overall "feel" for visual expression. A bias towards simplicity pervades, with clean lines, natural materials and a lack of pretence.

Although much of what is considered Scandinavian style is a product of the 20th century (*see page 90*), there is an underlying cultural heritage that complements the modern look. Exceptions exist, such as work commissioned by royalty with French design in mind, but the tastes of the people over the past 200 years make the strongest impression on the visitor.

DENMARK

The rich cultural history of Denmark finds expression in centuries' worth of art and artefacts, including Viking treasures, numerous castles and manor houses, churches (many from the Middle Ages), fortresses, stimulating museums and some of the finest contemporary design in the world.

Denmark's strong literary tradition encompasses sagas and medieval folk songs, the most popular Danish playwright, Ludvig Holberg (1684–1754), the Romantic poet Adam Oehlenschläger (1779–1850) and, in the 19th century, Hans Christian Andersen (1805–75) and Søren Kierkegaard (1813–55). Andersen is probably still the most widely read Danish writer today.

His children's tales – including *The Ugly Duckling*, *The Emperor's New Clothes* and *The Princess and the Pea* – gained him worldwide fame, and are a continuing source for plays, ballets, films, visual arts and bedtime reading. In the 20th century, Karen Blixen (1885–1962), working under the pseudonym Isak Dinesen, gained international recognition for her 1937 memoir of her years in Kenya, *Out of Africa*, which became a Hollywood movie.

The Danish philosopher Søren Kierkegaard, known as the father of existentialism, wrote in the first half of the 19th century. His work made an impact in the mid-20th century when it was translated into German and English.

PRECEDING PAGES: *Midnight* by Sweden's Anders Zorn, 1891. **LEFT:** *The Girl in the Kitchen* by Anna Ancher, 1883–6. **RIGHT:** Karen Blixen, Danish author of *Out of Africa*.

Peter Høeg is Denmark's best-known living author. *Miss Smilla's Feeling for Snow* (1992) is his most famous work, an elegant, absorbing literary thriller which begins in Copenhagen and ends in the icy wastes of Greenland.

Theatre and dance

Plays are still performed on the old stage of Det Kongelige Teater (Royal Theatre) in Copenhagen, founded in 1748; but it has been superseded by a futuristic waterside playhouse, which opened in 2008. In recent years, Copenhagen's arts scene has also been gifted with a purpose-built opera house (Operaen), which houses the

Royal Danish Opera, and the new DR Koncertsalen, where the Royal Danish Orchestra sometimes perform. The Royal Danish Ballet, formed 150 years ago, is one of the most influential worldwide. It has attracted great masters such as August Bournonville (1805–79), creator

> The Killing *(2007), a slow-burn Danish crime drama, follows a single murder investigation over a 20-hour series. Its intelligent script and superb acting have wowed critics and viewers alike.*

of today's "classical ballet" and choreographer of more than 50 productions, including the popular *La Sylphide*.

The big screen

Denmark's Nordisk Film Kompagni, founded in 1906, is the oldest film company still in operation. Carl Theodor Dreyer (1889–1968), who started his career here, directed one of the most influential films of all time, *The Passion of Joan of Arc* (1928). Dreyer died believing his masterpiece had been destroyed in a fire, but the original was rediscovered in 1981 in a Norwegian mental institution.

Today the government-supported Danish Film Institute is the heart of a vibrant Danish film industry. Three films have won the Academy Award for Best Foreign Film: *Babette's Feast* (1986), *Pelle the Conqueror* (1987) and *In a Better World* (2010), directed by Susanne Bier.

Other Danish films have attracted international acclaim, including Lars von Trier's *Dancer in the Dark* and Thomas Vinterberg's *The Celebration*. These directors are signatories (along with Kristian Levring) of the Dogma 95 Manifesto. This set of "chastity" rules – films should be made on location without artificial lighting or sound, using hand-held cameras – was intended as a personal challenge to help reinvigorate the art of filmmaking.

Painting and plastic arts

C.W. Eckersberg (1783–1853) is considered the father of Danish painting. At the end of the 19th century, a group of artists – including P.S. Krøyer (1851–1909) and Michael and Anna Ancher (1859–1935) – based themselves in Skagen at the northernmost tip of Jutland. Known

LOUISIANA MUSEUM OF MODERN ART

Small museum treasures may be found throughout Denmark, but the most complete and satisfying of them all is the Louisiana Museum of Modern Art, situated in a sublime spot in Humlebæk, 35km (22 miles) north of Copenhagen. Louisiana houses a splendid collection of 20th-century art, including pieces by Pablo Picasso, Andy Warhol, Alberto Giacometti and Asger Jorn. It lies on the water's edge, and the extensive sculpture garden, featuring work by Henry Moore and Alexander Calder, that surrounds the unassuming building (much of its space is underground) is backdropped by exquisite coastal scenery and landscaping (www.louisiana.dk).

as the "Skagen painters", they turned away from Impressionism, the favoured French style of the day, and focused on capturing the special northern light within their maritime landscapes.

In the middle of the 20th century, Asger Jorn (1914–73), a member of the CoBrA art movement, created large, bold, brightly coloured paintings. His expressionistic and experimental works on canvas and ceramics played a key role in the development and promotion of modern Danish art.

Olafur Eliasson (1967–) has created some of the 21st century's most innovative installations, which play with light, water and optical

pressed: under Danish rule, Norwegian "dialects" were forbidden for official documents and communications. As a result, Norway's early cultural heritage is identified in rural arts and crafts.

Rustic arts

The country's ancient stave churches represent some of the most distinctive examples of Norwegian artistic production. The rich ornamental carvings on door frames, around windows and on capitals in the interior owe more, stylistically, to the design motifs of the Viking period – dragons, tendrils, leaf patterns – than to Christian iconography. There are 28 stave churches

phenomena – for example, *The Weather Project*, a giant "sun" that illuminated London's Tate Modern in 2004.

NORWAY

After being a world power during the Viking Age, Norway went through various unions with and occupations by Denmark and Sweden until independence in 1905. Over the centuries, "culture" was something the overlords brought with them from foreign capitals…and took away again when they left. Norway's own culture was sup-

in Norway, two of the most striking being the newly restored church at Urnes, which is on the Unesco list, and the Heddal stave church in Telemark, the largest.

Another very "Norwegian" visual expression, from the 18th century, is rustic *rosemaling* or "rose painting", of which there are as many styles as villages. Used to adorn household utensils and interiors, it features organic patterns and flowers, figurative representations and geometric design.

Plays and literature

The re-creation of a national identity began in earnest in the 19th century, inspired by nature, ancient traditions and the heroic Viking sagas of long ago. Henrik Ibsen (1828–1906) wrote many

Cool Looks

Scandinavian design is elegant, light, sparse, shows respect for natural materials, and is made with superb craftsmanship

Say "Scandinavian design" and most people visualise furniture, textiles, glass and domestic ware with pure forms and simple, clean lines. The aesthetic is immediately recognisable, in both Nordic architecture and objects, especially

since the Swedish home-furnishing giant IKEA invaded the world.

Scandinavian architecture and design have their roots in traditional crafts, but are very much a product of the 20th century and the age of Functionalism. Taking off in the 1920s, led by architects and artists such as Le Corbusier in France and Walter Gropius in Germany, Functionalism applies to various movements such as the International Style and Bauhaus. In Scandinavia it has been a source of inspiration since the 1930s.

The move away from ornamentation in favour of clean shapes and lines, allowing for the pure expression of the essence of structures, was more than a mere change in taste. Adherents to this style, which manifested itself in new materials

(tubular metal, steel and glass), also embraced a vision for a new world, one where architecture and design could contribute to the levelling out of injustices in modern society. In Scandinavia, both the aesthetics and the social agenda of the modern, international style were eagerly adopted.

Earlier in the 1900s, Carl and Karin Larsson, taking their cue from the English Arts and Crafts movement, revived an interest in traditional Swedish crafts and craftsmanship. Their home at Sundborn, now a museum of Swedish country style *(see page 281)*, features textiles with simple checked and striped patterns, against a background of sparse wall designs, wooden floors, striped rag runners and furniture brightened with uncomplicated embellishments.

Art Nouveau was an important inspiration. In the hands of Danish designers in the mid-20th century, its fluid decorative lines became part of the quest for a satisfying form that fitted a function, as seen in the chairs of Hans Wegner and Arne Jacobsen from the 1940s and 1950s *(see page 132)*. Designers also began to heed ergonomic research at industrial companies like the car-makers Saab and Volvo.

Today, the adage "form follows function" is taken to a high science in Scandinavia. Aesthetics are fused with efficiency in everything from utensils to welding equipment. Numerous pieces from the early 20th century remain as popular as ever, for example, stools by the Finnish architect and designer Alvar Aalto.

The success of Nordic design has made it a standard far beyond the boundaries of Northern Europe. Smart Scandinavian design is found the world over. Time-tested pieces, such as the Stokke Tripp Trapp chair (1972) by Norwegian Peter Opsvik, are still best-sellers. The multitalented Stefan Lindfors burst onto the scene in the 1980s and since then has created everything from chairs and lamps to prefabricated houses, saunas and sex toys! Much of his crockery and cutlery is sold by the Finnish company Arabia. Other instantly recognisable Finnish designs are Marimekko textiles and Nokia telephones. Swedish glass manufacturers Kosta Boda and Orrefors produce lighting and homeware.

One of the best places to spot up-and-coming talent is Design House Stockholm, which acts as a "publishing house" for around 60 independent designers. ❑

LEFT: Swedish cloud chair, a soft shape that suits tall and short people alike.

plays based on folklore. His best-known works include *Peer Gynt* (1867), to which Edvard Grieg composed the incidental music, *A Doll's House* (1879) and *Hedda Gabler* (1890). Ibsen commented on Norway's relationship with Denmark and Sweden, as well as on the individual's relationship with a society which would have him conform.

> Joik *is a form of singing traditional among the Sami. Composed in response to an event or emotion, it sounds like a yodelling chant.*

Growth of the Soil, which follows the tribulations of a Norwegian peasant family over 20 years, won its author Knut Hamsun (1859–1952) the Nobel Prize for Literature in 1920. His literary power is unquestioned, but his reputation suffered because of his Nazi beliefs – in the middle of World War II, he sent his Nobel medal to Joseph Goebbels as a token of his support. Eight years later, Sigrid Undset (1882–1949) won the prize for her epic trilogy *Kristin Lavransdatter*, whose eponymous heroine lives, loves and dies in a richly reimagined medieval Norway.

More recently, Mrs Pepperpot, an old lady who shrinks at inconvenient moments, is another gutsy female character, and brought children's author Alf Prøysen (1914–70) great success. Her world is still rooted in peasant soil; but over the last 50 years, Norway's obsession with its own past has abated over time, and today's writers embrace contemporary genres and worldwide issues. Jostein Gaarder's philosophical novel *Sophie's World* was translated into 40 languages, and was quickly followed to the top of the international book charts by Åsne Seierstad's controversial bestseller, *The Bookseller of Kabul*, set in Afghanistan. Award-winning author Laars Saabye Christensen is considered one of the original voices in contemporary Nordic fiction – his latest book, *Beatles*, is a darkly comic coming-of-age story set in Oslo.

And "Nordic Noir" is alive and well. Anne Holt's Inspector Hanne Wilhelmsen pursues truth and justice at great personal cost in thrillers such as *1222*. Karin Fossum is hailed as the "Norwegian Queen of Crime": her latest Inspec-

tor Sejer novel, *The Caller*, was translated into English in 2011. And Jo Nesbø reigns supreme with his dry Oslo detective Harry Hole – *The Snowman* and *The Leopard* are his latest white-knuckle page-turners.

From Grieg to Black Metal

Norwegian music also flowered in the early 19th century, mainly influenced by the Royal Swedish Court. The violin virtuoso Ole Bull (1810–80), the "Nordic Paganini", proved a model for musicians and writers alike. The late 1800s became known as the Golden Age of Norwegian music, with such prominent composers

EDVARD MUNCH

Edvard Munch (1863–1944), perhaps Norway's most reproduced artist, is honoured with a museum in Oslo dedicated to his work, as well as an entire floor of the National Gallery. A forerunner of Expressionism, his introspective, symbolist and angst-ridden paintings and prints, such as *The Scream* (1893), *The Kiss* and *The Vampire* (both 1895), verge on the dark side and are a product of Scandinavian themes, artistic developments in France and Germany where he studied, as well as personal idiosyncrasies and obsessions. The Munch Museum will transfer to avant-garde new premises near the Opera House, a work of art themselves, in 2014.

RIGHT: *The Scream* by Edvard Munch, 1893.

as Halfdan Kjerulf (1815–68), Edvard Grieg (1843–1907) and Johan Svendsen (1840–1911). Generally, they incorporated elements of folk music in their work, including Grieg, who fused folk music with Romanticism.

And classical music still thrives in modern Norway: Oslo's incredible submerged Opera House, opened in 2008, is a must-see. Grieg's work forms the kernel of the Bergen International Festival in late May, a major arts festival bursting with music and theatre performances. In recent times, theatre of a different kind has been provided by one of Norway's most unusual musical exports – the thriving black metal

INGMAR BERGMAN

Although Sweden was a cinematic powerhouse in the age of silent films, since the advent of sound it has been a relatively small player, with the exception of exports such as Greta Garbo and Ingrid Bergman, and one of the giants of film and theatre, Ingmar Bergman (1918–2007). Bergman made his breakthrough with *Smiles of a Summer Night* in 1955. Among his most acclaimed films are *The Seventh Seal* (1956), *Wild Strawberries* (1957) and *Cries and Whispers* (1973). *Fanny and Alexander* (1982) was his final film, although he remained active in the theatre until his death. His work offers a very personal perspective on what is Swedish, yet universal.

scene, which courts controversy with its violent lyrics and bloody stage performances.

SWEDEN

As a conqueror rather than one of the conquered, Sweden developed strong cultural traditions, particularly in theatre, music and dance. Diplomatic and commercial links with Europe allowed new ideas to travel into the country. Prosperous Swedish monarchs were patrons of culture, and their private collections became the basis for national art museums.

King Gustav III (1746–92), the "Theatre King", took many of his cues from the royal court of France and patronised drama and the arts. In 1775, construction began on the Kungliga Teatern (Royal Theatre, known today as the Royal Opera), and on the Kungliga Dramatiska Teatern (Royal Dramatic Theatre or *Dramaten*) in 1788. He hired Swedish actors and singers, forming the basis for a tradition of opera and drama performed in Swedish, instead of French or Italian.

The most notable Swedish venue is Drottningholms Slottsteater (Drottningholm Court Theatre), in the grounds of Drottningholm Palace outside Stockholm. Built in 1766 and restored in the mid-20th century, every summer this intimate stage draws spectators from all over the world eager to see Baroque and rococo operas in an intact 18th-century theatre, complete with original backdrops and stage machinery.

Award-winning writers

One of the best-known (at least among Swedes) and still popular writers of the past is Carl Bellman (1740–95), a troubadour, whose lyrics and poems immortalised 18th-century daily life.

Works such as *The Red Room* by August Strindberg (1849–1912) and *Gösta Berlings Saga* by Selma Lagerlöf (1858–1940), two of the country's finest writers, set the foundation for modern Swedish literature. Strindberg, whose personal life was marked by a series of failed marriages, alcoholism and instability, produced books, stories, plays and screenplays that often featured social criticism, satire and emotional angst. The creative output of Lagerlöf, the first woman to win a Nobel Prize in Literature (1909), is distinct from Strindberg, depending more on legend, his-

LEFT: Ingmar Bergman, internationally acclaimed Swedish playwright and film producer.
RIGHT: *Interior at Sundborn*, Sweden, by Carl Larsson.

tory and childhood memories (*Jerusalem*, 1901–2, *The Wonderful Adventures of Nils*, 1906).

Other Swedes have won Nobel Literature prizes, most recently Eyvind Johnson and Harry Martinson, in 1974. A fascinating read, particularly for US visitors with Swedish ancestors, is Vilhelm Moberg's four-volume epic novel, beginning with *The Emigrants*. The book inspired the musical *Kristina from Duvemåla*, written by former ABBA members Benny Andersson and Björn Ulvaeus.

One of the most widely read Swedish writers is Astrid Lindgren, the indefatigable creative mind behind *Pippi Longstocking*, *Emil of Lönneberga*

of Carl Larsson (1853–1919), as well as to the design of his home at Sundborn (*see box, page 281*). Larsson's images are marked by strong outline, subdued colours and a gentle curvilinear quality. Today, however, Swedish visual arts are extraordinarily multifaceted. Artists

> *Based on an international best-selling novel, BAFTA-nominated* Let the Right One In *(2008) is an insightful vampire film, whose young protagonists manage loneliness and love in a snow-covered Stockholm suburb.*

and other free-spirited child heroes, heroines and anti-heroes and heroines. Currently taking the world by storm is Stieg Larsson's posthumously published Millennium trilogy, *The Girl with the Dragon Tattoo*, *The Girl Who Played with Fire* and *The Girl Who Kicked the Hornets' Nest*, which have sold around 50 million copies to date. We can only guess what Astrid Lindgren might have made of Lisbeth Salander, the books' violent, antisocial, computer-hacking heroine – created partly through Stieg Larsson imagining Pippi Longstocking as an adult.

Swedish design

The well-known "Swedish look" is greatly indebted to the graphic work and paintings

such as Ann-Sofi Sidén, Elin Wikström and Carl Michael von Hausswolff work in a variety of media, addressing complex contemporary issues. These trends can be seen at Moderna Museet in Stockholm, which reopened in 1998 in a new building by Rafael Moneo, and at its sister museum in Malmö, inaugurated in late 2009.

FINLAND

What may properly be called "Finnish culture" has existed for only a little over a century. Until the late 19th century, the arts in Finland fell under the influence of the invading powers of Sweden and Russia. Prior to Finnish independence (from Russia) in 1917, talented artists and

> The 19th-century artist Akseli Gallén-Kallela was a seminal figure in Finnish culture whose contribution laid the foundations for contemporary Finnish design.

composers normally studied and worked in Stockholm or St Petersburg.

As for all Nordic countries, innovations from France and Germany preoccupied Finland's artists. Many spent time in Montmartre ateliers, like Albert Edelfelt (1854–1905) and the well-travelled Akseli Gallén-Kallela (1865–1931), who returned to their homeland and gave painterly expression to the growing nationalist spirit. Their influence continued into the 20th century, with rural life and landscapes considered to be the worthiest of Finnish themes.

Musical notes

Jean Sibelius (1865–1957) is still the most notable name in music. Sibelius exemplified 19th-century Romanticism in his compositions, which drew inspiration from Finnish nature, folk music and poetry. His career began while Finland was still under Russian rule, and works such as *Finlandia* (1899; revised 1900) provoked

FINNISH ARCHITECTURE AND DESIGN

One of the more prominent architects of Helsinki is Carl Ludwig Engel (1778–1840) from Germany, who designed much of the capital, including Senate Square and the cathedral, as well as buildings throughout Finland.

The National Romanticism of Armas Lindgren (1874–1929), Herman Gesellius (1874–1916) and Eliel Saarinen (1873–1950) defined Finnish architecture of the late 19th and early 20th centuries, gradually turning from a Gothic look to embrace Art Nouveau.

Alvar Aalto (1898–1976), Finland's most celebrated architect, designed the Finnish pavilion at the New York World's Fair in 1939, gaining international recognition for himself and the unadorned Functionalist style. He designed many build-

ings around the world. In Finland he left his mark on housing, schools, governmental and industrial buildings, theatres and churches. His finest building, Helsinki's Finlandia Hall, was built in 1971 during his "white" period. Alas, critics assailed him for focusing on aesthetics instead of acoustics!

Possibly Aalto's most indelible imprint on the world is from his classic chairs and stools and instantly recognisable curving glass vase (Alvar Aalto Museo, Alvar Aallon katu 7, Jyväskylä; tel: 014 624 809; www.alvaraalto.fi). Industrial designer Yrjö Kukkapuro is known for his timeless furniture designs which are still being produced today by Avarte in leather and steel, and are in the collection of New York's Museum of Modern Art.

such patriotic and nationalistic feelings that they were banned by the Russian authorities. His early symphonies, such as *Kullervo*, used material and motifs from Elias Lönnrot's classic poem *Kalevala*.

A generous funding policy for musicians and musical institutes has spawned a remarkable pool of modern talent. The contemporary classical scene teems with internationally acclaimed figures, snapped up by concert halls, festivals and orchestras across the globe: soprano Karita Mattila graces the stages of the world's major opera houses; Esa-Pekka Salonen is currently the principal conductor of London's Philharmonia Orchestra; and the New York Philharmonic has swiped Magnus Lindberg as its composer in residence until 2012.

At home, the state-of-the-art Helsinki Music Hall (Musiikkikoulu) opened in September 2011, the new residence of the Helsinki Symphony Orchestra, the Finnish Radio Symphony Orchestra and the celebrated Sibelius Academy. Festival fever strikes in summer: the international Savonlinna Opera Festival and Pori Jazz Festival are both held in July.

Rock and heavy metal dominate the modern music scene – bands such as HIM, Nightwish and Eurovision winners Lordi are big in Finland, but less well known abroad. The long-established Ruisrock Festival, held on the island of Ruissalo, and the three-day Provinssirock Festival both attract crowds of tens of thousands, and Helsinki's Tuska Festival is the world's largest heavy-metal festival.

Literary heritage

Until Sweden ceded Finland to Russia in 1809, the Swedish language dominated Finnish culture. All that was to change in 1835 when, after many years of studying and collecting folk poetry, tales and ballads, Elias Lönnrot (1802–84) published his remarkable poem *Kalevala*. The work, a heroic epic on the scale of the *Odyssey* or the *Iliad*, inspired the 19th-century nationalistic surge in writing in Finnish, and is a continuing influence on literature, art and music.

LEFT: the Alvar Aalto Museum, Jyväskylä, celebrates the work of Finland's renowned architect and designer. **RIGHT:** inspired by nature, the composer Jean Sibelius (1865–1957) set the scene for modern music in Finland.

A contemporary of Lönnrot, Aleksis Kivi (1834–72) wrote the first proper Finnish novel, *Seven Brothers*, which celebrated rural life and contributed to a burgeoning national consciousness. The stage performance of Kivi's *Leah* in the late 19th century marked the beginning of Finnish drama. F.E. Sillanpää (1888–1964), the only surviving child of a poor farming couple, took home the country's sole literary Nobel prize (1939) for his depictions of peasant life.

Today, the Moomin books by Tove Jansson are Finland's most famous literary creations, loved by children and adults the world over. Although the contemporary literature scene is

Even the most recalcitrant sopranos come home for the annual Savonlinna Opera Festival. Held in a 500-year-old castle, it is one of the most delightful summer opera festivals in the world.

vibrant – Finland publishes the second-highest number of books per capita in the world – little is translated into English. One exception is the work of Sofi Oksanen, the newest literary voice to gain international attention. Her third novel, *Purge* (2010), has shot to the top of the best-seller lists, and won numerous awards including the European Book Prize and the Nordic Council Literature Prize. ❑

FOOD AND DRINK

Brace yourself for a gastronomic treat: fresh seafood, wild berries and succulent game washed down by fiery aquavit is the order of the day

Magnificent landscapes, clean air and the Baltic and North Seas have created a natural larder from which Scandinavians have helped themselves for centuries. Every home chef makes full use of local fruit, vegetables, grains, fish, meat and game; and the capitals' restaurants have won plaudits and Michelin stars galore for their back-to-basics approach to Nordic cuisine.

Denmark, Sweden, Norway and Finland have their own food cultures, but share gastronomic ground. Seafood is king, and herring is the fish most associated with the region. Marinated, spiced, smoked, fried, salted or baked, it is usually eaten cold and washed down with aquavit. Elk, venison and reindeer are commonly found on menus, and nearly all Scandinavians do a different kind of hunting in autumn – for mushrooms, blueberries and golden cloudberries.

DENMARK

In Denmark, model ships hang in every church, as if to remind parishioners to give thanks for the fruits of the sea. Fish, particularly herring, is still a mainstay, commonly smoked, salted or pickled. Traditional Danish food included lots of pork, butter and dairy products, but Danes today lean towards a lighter, healthier diet, inspired by modern Scandinavian cuisine.

Sandwiches and sausages

Denmark is synonymous with *smørrebrød (see box, page 98)*, for which it seems there are as many toppings as tastebuds. Liver pâté, shrimp,

LEFT: tempting Danish cakes and pastries on display.
RIGHT: *klippfisk* (dried, salted split cod) is a major Norwegian export.

herring, caviar, smoked salmon, roast pork and steak tartare are combined with pickles, jams, remoulade and herbs in a kaleidoscope of culinary deliciousness. Specialist *smørrebrød* restaurants usually open at lunchtime.

Bacon makes up over 5 percent of Denmark's exports, but not all pork products are sent abroad. Danes wisely keep the tastiest for themselves: salami, crackling roast pork and *frikadeller* are national institutions. The last (perfect comfort food) are fried meatballs, usually made from minced pork, served with potato salad and pickled red cabbage. Sausages are popular, with each region having its own speciality – in south Jutland *ølpølse* (beer sausage) is a tasty snack found at the local butcher. Blood sausage, *blødpølse*, appears around Christmas time. The *pølsevogn* (sausage wagon) is a common sight around Danish towns, a cheap place to pick up a lurid *rød pølse* (red hotdog).

Sweet treats

Danish pastry *(wienerbrød)* is famous for a reason. Visit a bakery and try rich, chewy "chocolate snail" pastries, layered cream cakes or a waffle cone filled with ice cream, marshmallow topping and marmalade. Scandinavians have a peculiar love of salty liquorice, found in its strongest form in Denmark!

NORWAY

Norway's long, varied coastline provides ample opportunity for harvesting both "wild" and farm-raised fish. The slow ripening process of everything that grows during the light summer imparts an extraordinary aroma to berries, fruits and vegetables. And animals that graze on the verdant grass provide meat with a distinctive full flavour.

Tasty Norwegian fare

Norway is known for its fish – from cod to monkfish, sea wolf to halibut. Ubiquitous salmon, marinated or smoked, remains a deli-

SMØRREBRØD AND SMÖRGÅSBORD

Danish *smørrebrød* (open sandwiches), eaten daintily with cutlery, are miniature works of art with a near-infinite choice of toppings. Slices of dense rye bread, packed with seeds and grains, serve as the base. It's customary to begin with a herring topping, washed down with cold-as-hailstones aquavit. Next comes a little warmth – perhaps fried fish, lemon and remoulade – then beef slices, pâté or meatballs. Cheese and fruit salad round off the meal.

Norwegian *smørbrød*, Swedish *smörgåsbord* and Finnish *voileipäpöytä* are equally artistic hot-and-cold lunch buffets. Finnish dishes tend to be less sweet, and served with a greater variety of bread.

cacy in this part of the world. Fishballs with new potatoes is a traditional dish, and fishcakes, which can be bought from the fishmonger, make a delicious snack. Whale is found on some restaurant menus.

Autumn is the time to indulge in game such as reindeer, elk or grouse, ideally served with tangy berries and wild mushrooms. Lamb, though not found on many restaurant menus, forms the basis of several treasured Christmas dishes like *farikal* (slowly simmered mutton with cabbage and peppercorns) and *pinnekjott* (which combines salted, dried and smoked lamb). Foreign guests are sceptical of *lutefisk*, another holiday "treat", which translates to cod marinated in lye.

Cheese and fruity desserts

Jarlsberg will be familiar to visitors, but *geitost* (brown goat's cheese) is seldom found outside the country and should be experienced. Usually found at breakfast, it is caramel-coloured and slightly sweet.

Desserts are always popular. Try *bløtkake*, a rich sponge cake topped with strawberries,

> *Danes, Swedes and Norwegians eat sweet, cured gravlax (raw salmon marinaded in salt, sugar and dill) as a lunchtime delicacy.*

There are complex notes in its reindeer, boar and grouse, and a love of "wild larder" ingredients like angelica, caraway and tart red lingonberries.

Husmanskost

Traditional Swedish dishes *(husmanskost)* are often updated for modern palates at the country's best restaurants. Found on the table on Thursdays, *ärtsoppa* is a hearty pea soup served with pork. *Pytt i panna*, a hash of fried diced meat, onions and potatoes, is another speciality. *Kåldolmar* (stuffed cabbage rolls) are said to have been brought back from Turkey by King Karl XII in the 18th century. Alien to foreign

karamellpudding, similar to flan, and fresh waffles served with fresh fruit and whipped cream. Thanks to the cool climate and clean air, plums, pears, berries, and oversized morello cherries are pure indulgence.

SWEDEN

Sweden has access to some of the freshest flavours in Europe, farmed in the mellow climate of the south, or hunted in the unspoilt north. Dishes are generally gentle and unchallenging, but Sweden's cuisine throws up a few surprises.

FAR LEFT: Danish pastries. **LEFT:** Danish open sandwiches *(smørrebrød)*. **ABOVE:** the fish market in Bergen, Norway.

THE NEW NORDIC KITCHEN

In 2004, Scandinavia's finest chefs came together to devise the New Nordic Kitchen manifesto, emphasising slow food, local organic produce and foraged ingredients such as birch juice and Arctic bramble. Behind it lay a healthy appreciation of the Arctic region's long, cool growing season, its abundance of fish and game, and forests and mountainsides full of fungi, wild plants and berries. The manifesto was the start of a staggering regional-cuisine resurgence. Stockholm, Oslo, Helsinki and Copenhagen are the focus of exciting new culinary scenes, exemplified by Denmark's Michelin-starred restaurant Noma, which was named the world's best restaurant in 2010.

tastebuds, sweet gloopy soups such as rosehip or blueberry soup are served hot or cold.

Swedes eat little pork links (*prinskorv*) at a *smörgåsbord* (*see box, page 98*). Another *smörgåsbord* favourite is herring spiced with sandalwood (*matjes*), frequently eaten with boiled

> Crayfish are eaten widely in Finland and Sweden in July and August, when they are boiled, peeled and served at outdoor parties, with plenty of singing and toasting. Guests wear colourful bibs to shield them from crayfish drip.

potatoes and sour cream. In Skåne in southern Sweden, look out for *spettkaka*, a tower-shaped confectionery of sugar, eggs and potato flour baked over an open fire.

Also particular to Sweden is a delicious baked anchovy-potato-cream casserole known as "Jansson's Temptation".

An acquired taste

A summertime favourite in northern Sweden is *surströmming*, Baltic herring, that is salted and "soured" or fermented, then canned. The *surströmming* tin bulges ominously with still-fermenting gases; and when it is opened (*always*

DRINKING IN SCANDINAVIA

Alcohol is expensive in Scandinavia, and the sale of strong beer, wine and spirits in Sweden, Norway and Finland is restricted to state alcohol shops (Systembolaget in Sweden, Vinmonopolet in Norway, Alko in Finland), and licensed bars and restaurants. In contrast, alcohol flows freely in Denmark.

No Scandinavian herring dish is complete without aquavit, literally "water of life". Distilled from potatoes or grain and flavoured with herbs and seasonings (caraway seed, cumin, fennel, dill or St John's wort), ice-cold aquavit warms body and soul. One of the best is Norway's Løiten Linie: part of its maturation involves a sea voyage across the equator and back.

In line with the growing local-food movement, microbreweries have mushroomed all over Scandinavia. At Christmas, out comes the *gløgg* – hot spicy mulled wine, served with gingerbread, cinnamon buns, Danish *æbleskiver* (puff pancakes) or rice pudding.

To gain instant friends in Denmark, Sweden and Norway, lift your drink and say the word for cheers: *"skål"* (pronounced "skoal"). The correct way to *skål* is to look at the person, say the word, lift the glass slightly, drink and look at the person again. At formal occasions, strict rules of etiquette govern the *"skål"*-ing: for example, never drink until your host has given a welcome toast. The Finns usually say *"kippis"* when making a toast.

outdoors), the resulting stench often causes the uninitiated to run for the hills.

FINLAND

Mushrooms, berries, fish, sausages and reindeer are the key elements of Finnish cuisine. In July, look out for thick asparagus and sweet crunchy peas. New potatoes, tiny and tender, are served with fresh, aromatic dill, often as an accompaniment to fresh-salted salmon (*graavilohi*) or herring. Rhubarb is used in puddings, but there's nothing like fresh lingonberries, blueberries, strawberries or Lappish cloudberries with vanilla ice cream.

specialities, best served with creamy mashed potatoes, chanterelles and a tangy berry sauce.

Mushroom magic

Around 500 edible varieties of mushrooms exist in Finland, but only 30 are delicious enough to use in sauces, soups and salads. Signs in Hel-

> In Finland, there are late-night kiosks dispensing polsar *(hot dogs)* to diehard pub crawlers, for sustenance as well as alleviating the next day's hangover.

Fish and game

Finnish waters boast a variety of fish, from famed Baltic herring and pike perch to ubiquitous whitefish and salmon. Salmon soup is often served as a light meal, with dark crusty bread and sweet butter. In Midsummer, the crayfish season arrives, celebrated with rounds of vodka (*viini*, or schnapps) and song. Reindeer, the cow of Lapland, is enjoyed as cutlets, steaks, meatballs, liver, smoked, in stew Karelian-style, or as carpaccio or tartare. Hare, elk, bear, wild duck, snow goose and ptarmigan are other game

FAR LEFT: *smørrebrød* at the Danish Design Centre Café, Copenhagen. **LEFT:** Swedish beer. **ABOVE:** Swedish specialities.

sinki's market warn that some fungi must be boiled for an hour to detoxify!

Konditorei culture

Scandinavians are some of the world's biggest coffee-drinkers. Finns top the chart, consuming an amazing 12kg (26lb) per person each year. The Finns eat *pulla* (wheat buns) with their coffee and indulge in cream cakes topped with strawberries. The Swedish-speaking Finnish population has contributed to the crossover tradition of konditorei culture: elegant tearooms combine a good bakery and assortment of chocolate, and delicate sandwiches and pastries are enjoyed most afternoons by a mix of generations. ❏

PLACES

A detailed guide to the Scandinavian countries,
with principal sites cross-referenced
by number to the maps

Whether you're in a car or coach, on a bicycle, boat or train, on foot or on skis, the Scandinavian countries of Denmark, Norway, Sweden and Finland have an enormous variety of sights and scenery to beguile the visitor.

Denmark is neatly beautiful, with its white-sand beaches, well-groomed farmland, gentle hills and fairytale castles. Chilled-out Copenhagen is a particularly enjoyable capital, with pedestrianised streets, pavement cafés, superb shops and entertainment. Every Danish town has its museum and art gallery, every castle its collection. Remote from the rest of Denmark lie the Faroe Islands, a birdwatchers' paradise, and Greenland, a terrific adventure destination.

Norway is made up of mountains etched with beautiful fjords and dramatic valleys. From the southern beaches, the coastline stretches right into the Arctic Circle, dotted with islands, fishing villages and historic towns like Bergen. Inland, the rugged landscape beckons walkers and skiers. The capital, Oslo, offers every city delight, with forests on its doorstep.

A short drive from Copenhagen brings you to southern Sweden's gentle farmland and sunny islands. At the country's heart lie two vast lakes, Vänern and Vättern, linked by the Göta Kanal, a pleasure-boaters' mecca.

Further north, the folklore province of Dalarna gives way to lakes and forests, winter sports centres and rugged Lapland. Stockholm floats majestically on 14 islands, the most sophisticated of Scandinavia's capitals.

Today, independent Finland has a distinct identity, with remnants of Swedish and Russian influence. The south coast is a summer playground of islands and

beaches, fortresses and painted towns. The "Daughter of the Baltic", Helsinki, is an architecturally fascinating capital. Lakes and forests cover central Finland, while easterly Karelia is a hiker's delight. Lapland, land of the Midnight Sun, attracts anglers, white-water enthusiasts and those in search of true solitude. ❏

PRECEDING PAGES: Finland's snowy beauty in winter; Suitor Waterfall, Geiranger Fjord, Norway; Smogen, on the west coast of Sweden. **LEFT:** windmill in Finland. **ABOVE:** Danish beer. **TOP:** the Universium in Göteborg, Sweden. **ABOVE RIGHT:** getting around the Norwegian coast.

Scandinavia

0 100 km

0 100 miles

N

BARENTS SEA

NORWEGIAN SEA

NORWAY

FINLAND

RUSSIA

Murmansk
Moncegorsk
Apatity
Vardø
Vadsø
Kirkenes
Pedenga
Nordkyn
Honningsvåg
Nordkapp
Hammerfest
Alta
Tromsø
Harstad
Andenes
Narvik
Svolvær
Bodø
Fauske
Mo i Rana
Sandnessjøen
Mosjøen
Steinkjer
Levanger
Inari
Ivalo
Muonio
Kittilä
Sodankylä
Kemijärvi
Kemijoki
Lokan tekojärvi
Rovaniemi
Kiruna
Gällivare
Jokkmokk
Tärnaby
Tärnafräsk
Kebnekaise 2117
Stora Lulevatten
Hornavan
Uddjaure
Kuusamo
Piolärvi
Oulujärvi
Kajaani
Sotkamo
Kuhmo
Nurmes
Lieksa
Kostomuksha
Oulu
Kemi
Tornio
Boden
Luleå
Piteå
Skellefteå
Kokkola

Bottenviken
Perämeri

Arctic Circle

Vesterålen
Lofoten
Vestfjorden

E6 E8 E10 E12 E75 E45 E63 E4 45 81 20 5 8 95 97

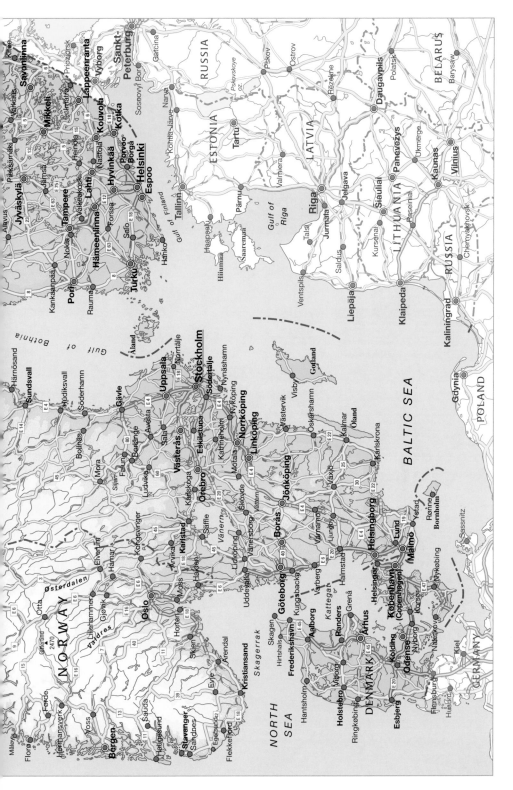

DENMARK

**Small, but perfectly formed, Denmark is a country
of fun-loving, environmentally conscious people**

Hamlet was wrong – there is nothing rotten in the State of Denmark. Yes, winters are dreary, but they're mild with little snow, and summers are sunny, with long hours of daylight. Yes, the tax rate is among the world's highest. But taxes are reinvested to help make this a country "where few have too much and fewer too little".

The world's oldest kingdom packs plenty of international clout. The Vikings are gone, but their descendants are spreading their seed far and wide: Denmark is the biggest supplier of frozen human sperm on the planet. It's also a major purveyor of computer elements and electronic devices, windmills, agricultural products, arts and crafts and skilled professionals.

Denmark is a green nation of cyclists and recyclers. Nine out of 10 Danes own a bicycle, half the country's rubbish is recycled, and windmills provide 20 percent of the country's power needs. Nowhere is very far away. The Jutland peninsula and main Danish islands are linked by a network of spectacular road and railway bridges, which even extends across the Øresund to Sweden. Ferries still play their part, linking islands and crossing the larger lakes, for this is a nation with a strong seafaring past.

Zealand, in the east, holds Scandinavia's liveliest capital city, Copenhagen, and Hamlet's castle, Kronborg at Helsingør (Elsinore). Jutland, in the west, is Denmark's link with mainland Europe. North Jutland's seascapes have captivated artists over the centuries, and its beaches draw summer holidaymakers. East Jutland boasts an intricate lake system, well used for canoeing and water sports, and Århus, Denmark's second city, with its esteemed international arts festival. Funen, sandwiched between Jutland and Zealand, is the "garden of Denmark". Out in the Baltic is Bornholm, Denmark's sunniest holiday spot.

Far to the west and north lie the outposts of the Danish kingdom: the windswept Faroe Islands ("Sheep Islands"), a favourite haunt for birdwatchers, and Greenland, offering adventurous travellers stunning scenery and a pristine natural environment. ❑

LEFT: Amagertorv and the Stork Fountain in Copenhagen's main shopping area.
ABOVE: Bornholm, an island in the Baltic Sea. **ABOVE RIGHT:** Danish glass.

Denmark

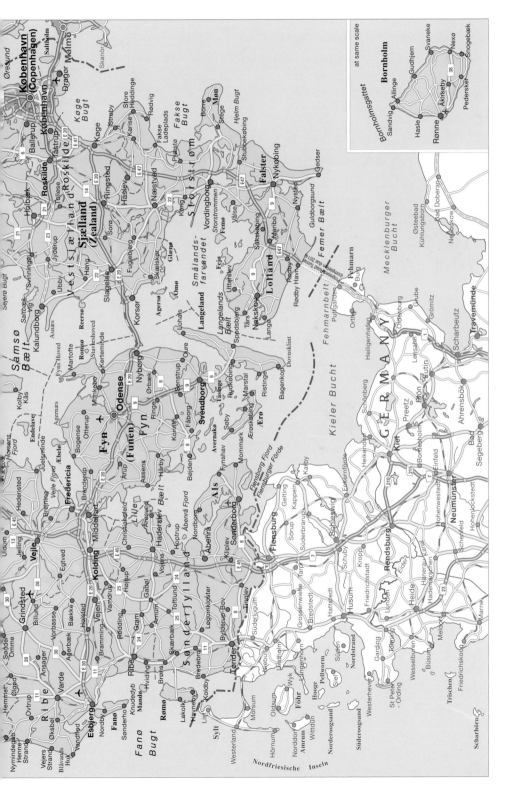

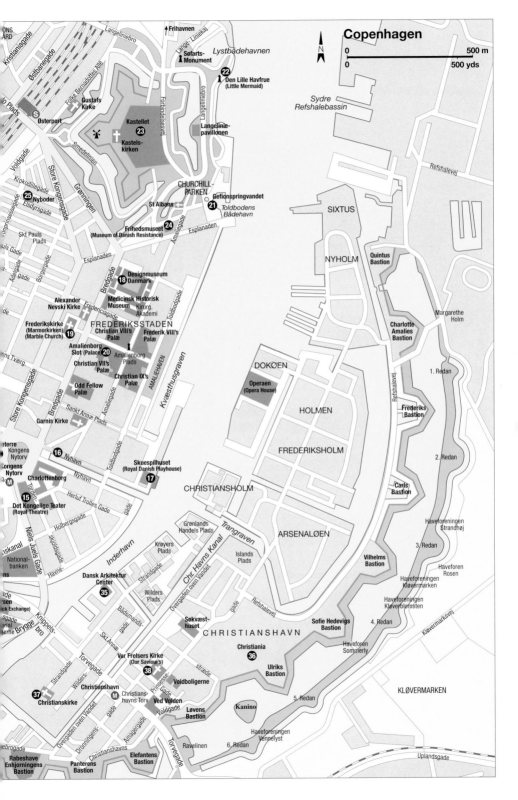

Copenhagen

N

0 — 500 m
0 — 500 yds

Frihavnen

Langelinjebro

Søfarts-Monument

Lystbådehavnen

Den Lille Havfrue
(Little Mermaid) **22**

Langelinie-
pavillonen

ONS
ARD

Kristianiagade

Østbanegade

Folke Bernadottes Allé

Gustafs
Kirke

S Østerport

Kastellet **23**

Kastels-
kirken

Forbindelsesvej

Langelinjebro

Sydre
Refshalebassin

Refshalevej

Voldgade

Krokodillegade

Elsdyrsgade

Nyboder **25**

Grønningen

Store Kongensgade

Smedelinien

CHURCHILL-
PARKEN

St Albans

Gefionspringvandet **21**

Toldbodens
Bådehavn

SIXTUS

Skt Pauls
Plads

Esplanaden

Frihedsmuseet **24**
(Museum of Danish Resistance)

Esplanaden

Amaliegade

NYHOLM

Quintus
Bastion

Adelgade

Borgergade

Bredgade

Designmuseum **18**
Danmark

Alexander
Nevski Kirke

Frederiksgade

Medicinsk Historisk
Museum   Kirurg.
Akademi

Toldbodgade

Margarethe
Holm

Frederikskirke
(Marmorkirken)
(Marble Church) **19**

FREDERIKSSTADEN
Christian VIII's
Palæ

Frederik VIII's
Palæ

Charlotte
Amalies
Bastion

ens Tværg.

Amalienborg
Slot (Palace) **20**

Amalienborg
Plads

Christian VII's
Palæ

AMALIEHAVN

Christian IX's
Palæ

DOKØEN

1. Redan

Store Kongensgade

Bredgade

Odd Fellow
Palæ

Sankt Annæ Plads

Amaliegade

Operaen
(Opera House)

HOLMEN

Refshalevej

Frederiks
Bastion

Garnis Kirke

Kvæsthusgraven

eterre
Kongens
Nytorv

Kongens
Nytorv

M

16 Nyhavn

Charlottenborg

Nyhavn

Toldbodgade

Skuespilhuset
(Royal Danish Playhouse)

17

FREDERIKSHOLM

2. Redan

Carls
Bastion

Det Kongelige Teater
(Royal Theatre) **15**

Holbergsgade

Herluf Trolles Gade

Gade

Skjøldsgade

CHRISTIANSHOLM

CHRISTIANSBORG

skanal

National
banken
ns

Niels Juels Gade

Havne.

Inderhavn

Grønlands
Handels Plads

Trangraven

ARSENALØEN

Haveforeningen
Strandhøj

Krøyers
Plads

Islands
Plads

Vilhelms
Bastion

3. Redan

Haveforen
Rosen

ade
esen
(ck Exchange)

Strandgade

Dansk Arkitektur
Center **35**

Wilders
Plads

Overgaden oven Vandet

Chr. Havns Kanal

Refshalevej

Haveforeningen
Kløvermarken

Kløvermarksvej

Knippels-
bro

sgade
arial
erne Brygge

Bådsmands-
gade

Søkvæst-
huset

CHRISTIANSHAVN

Sofie Hedevigs
Bastion

4. Redan

Haveforeningen
Kløverblomsten

Torvegade

Skt Annæ

Christiania **36**

Haveforen
Sommerly

KLØVERMARKEN

Strandgade

Wilders.

Christianshavn

Vor Frelsers Kirke
(Our Saviour's) **38**

Prinsessegade

stræde

Voldboligerne

Ulriks
Bastion

5. Redan

Christianskirke **37**

Christians-
havns Torv

M

Ved Volden

Voldgade

Løvens
Bastion

Kanino

Amagergade

Overgaden oven Vandet

Drønningens?

Christianshavns

Torvegade

Rabeshave
Enhjorningens
Bastion

Panterens
Bastion

Elefantens
Bastion

Ravelinen

6. Redan

Haveforeningen
Vennelyst

Uplandsgade

ebrogade

COPENHAGEN

Denmark's capital city is the most exuberant in Scandinavia. Pedestrians and cyclists rule, shopping is a pleasure, cultural sights abound, and by night the city buzzes

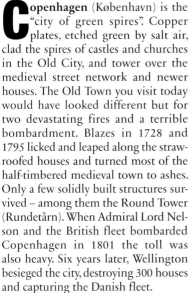

Copenhagen (København) is the "city of green spires". Copper plates, etched green by salt air, clad the spires of castles and churches in the Old City, and tower over the medieval street network and newer houses. The Old Town you visit today would have looked different but for two devastating fires and a terrible bombardment. Blazes in 1728 and 1795 licked and leaped along the straw-roofed houses and turned most of the half-timbered medieval town to ashes. Only a few solidly built structures survived – among them the Round Tower (Rundetårn). When Admiral Lord Nelson and the British fleet bombarded Copenhagen in 1801 the toll was also heavy. Six years later, Wellington besieged the city, destroying 300 houses and capturing the Danish fleet.

Copenhagen is the liveliest – and many claim the most fetching – of the Scandinavian capitals, with things to see and do all the time. With Europe's longest pedestrian mall, this was the first capital to offer the pleasures of ambling through a network of streets free of motor vehicles and exhaust fumes.

A good way to get a first feel of Copenhagen is from the water. Take one of the 60-minute canal boat trips from Kongens Nytorv/Nyhavn or Gammel Strand (tel: 32 96 30 00; mid-Mar–Oct, up to 6 per hour from 9.15am, Nov–mid-Mar 5 per day). If you're the adventurous type you could explore the waterways in a kayak for two hours, starting at Strandgade in Christianshavn. A guide paddles ahead of you (Copenhagen Adventure Tours; tel: 40 50 40 06; www.kajakole.dk).

Rådhuspladsen

City Hall Square (Rådhuspladsen) is the nexus of Copenhagen, grandly lit up at night with its coloured signs, digital news headlines and blinking neon, with the enormous **City Hall ❶** (Rådhuset;

LEFT: on the waterfront in Christianshavn.
RIGHT: meeting for drinks.

TIP

The City of Copenhagen provides 2,500 free bicycles to use within its City Bike zone (bracketed by the three artificial lakes to the west and Stadsgraven moat to the east). All you have to do is deposit a 20DKK coin (about US$4) in one of the 110 City Bike parking places dotted about the city centre, and ride off. The 20DKK is refunded when the cycle is returned (March to end November only).

BELOW: Tivoli Gardens at Halloween.
BELOW: RIGHT: City Hall Square (Rådhuspladsen).

tel: 33 66 25 82; Mon–Fri 8.30am–4.30pm, Sat 10am–1pm; free; tours in English for a charge, 3pm) at its heart. Constructed in the National Romantic style, its inspiration was drawn from medieval Danish and Norwegian architecture with a touch of the palazzo style of northern Italy. The facade and interior are trimmed with historic details from Nordic mythology. For a bird's-eye view of the city's spires and towers, climb the 106-metre (347ft) tower (daily; charge).

Inside the Rådhuset's foyer, look for the entrance to **Jens Olsen's World Clock** (Mon–Fri 8.30am–4.30pm, Sat 10am–1pm; charge). Its star dial mechanism shows the path of the pole star in resettable periods, making it one of the most accurate and complicated clocks in the world. Unsurprisingly, this masterpiece of time-telling took 27 years to build.

Bordering the square to the east on Vester Voldgade are two of Copenhagen's fine traditional hotels. Closest to City Hall is the **Palace Hotel**, one of the few buildings in the *Jugendstil* (Art Nouveau style), and further north, past the square, **Hotel Kong Frederik**,

with the smart and pricey Gastro Pub restaurant.

Between the two hotels is the beginning of Strøget, Europe's longest pedestrianised shopping street, and the kingdoms of wonder that are **Hans Christian Andersen's Wonderful World** and **Ripley's Believe It or Not! Museum** (tel: 33 32 31 31; www.topattractions.dk; mid-June–Aug daily 10am–10pm, Sept–mid-June Sun–Thur 10am–6pm, Fri–Sat 10am–8pm; charge). Forget educational value, and take the family to marvel at animated tableaux of Andersen's most famous stories, or shrunken heads, optical illusions, and a picture of Queen Margrethe carefully constructed from pocket fluff.

On the western side of Rådhuspladsen is Denmark's most visited attraction, the charming **Tivoli Gardens** ❷ (tel: 33 15 10 01; www.tivoli.dk; mid-Apr–late Sept Sun–Thur 11am–10pm, Fri 11am–12.30am, Sat 11am–midnight, also open at Halloween and Christmas; charge). Opened in 1843, the amusement park updates its collection of rides and rollercoasters

regularly while still retaining the air of a pleasure garden from a bygone age. The fair opening in April marks the beginning of summer. It's a Copenhagen institution, attracting visitors of all generations with its old-fashioned side-stalls, aquarium, gardens, cafés, theatres, an open-air stage, its own symphony orchestra, and a concert hall where classical concerts, jazz and musicals are performed. The park has more than 20 restaurants, including the Michelin-starred restaurant Herman.

Art and design

A two-minute walk south of the City Hall on H.C. Andersens Boulevard is the **Dansk Design Centre** ❸ (tel: 33 69 33 69; Mon–Fri 10am–5pm, Wed until 9pm, Sat–Sun 11am–4pm; charge), with ongoing Danish and international exhibitions *(see page 132)*.

Across the road is the **Ny Carlsberg Glyptotek** ❹ (tel: 33 41 81 41; www. glyptoteket.dk; Tue–Sun 11am–5pm; charge). This exquisite museum offers a grand art collection begun by the brewer Carl Jacobsen and maintained by the New Carlsberg Foundation.

There are collections of ancient Egyptian, Greek, Roman and Etruscan sculptures, as well as some French masterpieces from Cézanne, Gauguin and Rodin. The lush, palm-lined indoor Winter Garden has a wonderful café.

Vesterbro

On Bernstorffsgade, across from Tivoli's west entrance, is the **Central Railway Station** (Hovedbanegården). Beyond it to the west lies **Vesterbro**, one of Copenhagen's oldest residential districts, today a multicultural community, vibrant with bizarre shops, exotic restaurants and its red-light boulevard, **Istedgade**. Over the last few years, Vesterbro has been the focus of a whole whirl of stylish new bars, clubs, restaurants and contemporary art galleries, based in **Kødbyen**, the meat-packing district. By day, it is still populated by butchers (although rising rents are forcing many to relocate); by night, it's a place to party.

The **Copenhagen Tourist Office** ❺ lies across the street from Central Station on Bernstorffsgade, near the corner of Vesterbrogade. This travel-

The tall tubes in front of the Moorish-style palace restaurant in Tivoli contain bubbling water. This unusual sculpture was designed by the Danish nuclear physicist Niels Bohr.

BELOW LEFT: guarding Amalienborg Palace.

Historic Trading Post

Although there has been a harbour at Copenhagen since the 8th century, until the Middle Ages it was just a simple trading post called Havn (Harbour), albeit one with an important geographical position. Havn was within easy access of Skåne (Scania), then part of Denmark, across the Sound, and a handy halfway point on the trade route between the growing medieval cities of Roskilde and Lund.

Its fortunes changed dramatically, however, in 1167, when King Valdemar I commanded the local bishop, Absalon of Roskilde, to fortify Havn in order to protect it against Wendic pirates. Absalon built a fortress on the spot where the Parliament building now looms. Copenhagen was on the way to becoming Denmark's biggest and most important town. The fortress became Christiansborg, *borg* meaning castle. Centuries later, it remains the seat of Danish politics, housing the Folketing (Parliament).

During the long reign of Kristian IV (1588–1648), Copenhagen solidified its role as the country's seat of power. This visionary town planner strengthened the city's overseas trade links, enhanced the city's military might with a huge defensive fortification, and made it the country's economic centre by building Børsen, said to be the oldest stock exchange in Europe – a Renaissance structure with a spire of four entwined dragons, steep copper roofs, tiny windows and gables galore.

lers' ganglion has it all: information on sights, cultural activities, transport, eating places and events. A prime source of information is the free magazine *Copenhagen This Week* (www.ctw.dk).

The medieval city

If Rådhuspladsen is the heart of Copenhagen, then **Strøget ❻**, the 1.8km (1-mile) pedestrian shopping street, is the spine. It has endless shops, street vendors, buskers and cellar galleries. Strøget *("stroy-yet")* is where Copenhageners and visitors alike go to shop or just to promenade. The mainstream shops and eateries are on Strøget proper, while the more quirky boutiques, cafés and restaurants are situated on the quieter side streets.

Starting at Rådhuspladsen, Strøget meanders through five streets and four squares before it runs into **Kongens Nytorv** (King's New Square, *see page 124*) the largest square in the Old Town, on which stands an equestrian statue of Kristian V who laid it out in 1670. Good landmarks and meeting places are the squares at **Gammeltorv** (Old Square) and at Strøget's major crossroads, the

crane fountain at **Amagertorv**. Here, another main pedestrian artery, **Købmagergade**, branches off to the north.

Near Gammeltorv, the area behind **Vestergade** is one of the few remaining residential areas in the inner city. Living in the picturesque neoclassical houses is a mixture of old-time Copenhageners, artists and students, and here you find some of the more exotic clothes shops and galleries – try Skt Pedersstræde for starters. **St Peter's Church ❼** (Sankt Petri Kirke), on the corner of Nørregade and Skt Pedersstræde, is the oldest church in Copenhagen, its chancellery built in 1450. Hans Christian Andersen lived at No. 19 Vestergade when, as a young man, he first arrived in Copenhagen from Odense. Another famous Dane, the 19th-century philosopher Søren Kierkegaard, lived in the house on the corner of Nytorv and Frederiksberggade at Gammeltorv.

One block south and running parallel to Strøget is **Kompagnistræde**, with shops specialising in antiques, china and pewter.

Two blocks south, across from the canal on Ny Vestergade, is Denmark's

BELOW: the Winter Garden of Ny Carlsberg Glyptotek.
BELOW RIGHT: there are plenty of bars in the city.

National Museum ❽ (National-museet; tel: 33 13 44 11; www.natmus.dk; Tue–Sun 10am–5pm), the country's most visited museum, which is largely focused on Danish history. It is highly recommended for its newly revamped collections of ancient "bog" finds from the Stone, Bronze and Iron Ages, and includes unique treasures such as the golden Chariot of the Sun, the enigmatic Gundestrup Cauldron and Egtved Girl. A fascinating and well-structured museum that takes days to cover, it also has an interesting section on Danish cultural history.

From Nytorv, continue along Strøget towards Amagertorv. For a close encounter of the rich and sweet, stop at one of Copenhagen's premier confectioners, **Conditori La Glace**, a few stops from Strøget at Skoubogade. Here, cream layer-cakes reign supreme.

The opposite side of Amagertorv is occupied by the shops most often visited by tourists: **Illums Bolighus** ❾, a showcase for superb Danish and international design, and the flagship stores of **Royal Copenhagen Porcelain** and **Georg Jensen** silver.

Latin Quarter

The streets to the north of Amagertorv form the old **Latin Quarter**, featuring the cosy **Greyfriars Square** ❿ (Grå-brødretorv). The cobblestone square is a popular place to enjoy lunch at one of several outdoorsy restaurants, or dinner (Peder Oxe is a local favourite).

The streets just to the north hold **Copenhagen Cathedral** ⓫ (Køben-havns Domkirke) and the main building of the **University of Copenhagen**. The seat of the University Board, beside Nørregade, dates from 1420 and is the oldest building in Copenhagen.

A fun stop for children is the sweet factory on Nørregade 36, **Sømods Bol-cher**, where confectioners make old-fashioned boiled sweets by hand (tel: 33 12 60 46; demonstrations Mon–Fri 9.15am–3pm). **Fiolstræde** is known for its antiquarian bookshops, and **Krystalgade** is the site of Copenhagen's synagogue. Try a sandwich from the busy, bowler-hatted organic butchers, **Slagteren ved Kultorvet** (Coal Square), on the open plaza near the Nørreport subway station, at the top of traffic-free Købmagergade.

TIP

The new City Circle metro line, due to open in 2018, is currently in progress. It will extend Copenhagen's dinky little system with another 15.5km (9½ miles) of track and 17 city-centre stations. You are bound to come across construction sites across the city, or attractions that have closed temporarily due to building work.

BELOW: Gråbrødretorv.

DRINK

For a taste of brewing, visit the famous Carlsberg Brewery and stables, Gamle Carlsberg Vej, Valby, and sample a glass of the best (tel: 33 27 12 82; Tue–Sun 10am–4.30pm; charge).

On Købmagergade itself is one of Copenhagen's most fascinating buildings. The **Round Tower** ⓬ (Rundetårn; tel: 33 73 03 73; late May–late Sept 10am–8pm, late Sept–late May 10am–5pm; charge) was built in 1642 as an observatory, possibly inspired by the work of Denmark's world-renowned astronomer, Tycho Brahe. The viewing platform on the top offers a breathtaking panorama on clear days and nights. The tower stands 36 metres (118ft) high, and to reach the roof one walks up a 209-metre (685ft) spiral ramp. In 1716 Tsar Peter the Great rode a horse to the top while his wife followed in a carriage.

Around the corner off Landemærket is the **Danish Film Institute** ⓭ (Det Danske Filminstitut: tel: 33 74 34 00; www.dfi.dk; performances Tue–Fri 9.30am–10pm, Sat–Sun noon–10pm), home of Cinemateket, which celebrates Denmark's trailblazing successes in cinematography, and shows a programme of Danish and international films.

King's New Square

The last section of Strøget, from the Crane Fountain to Kongens Nytorv, is the home of the exclusive and expensive: fashion shops, furriers and jewellers.

At the end of Strøget, facing **King's New Square** (Kongens Nytorv), stands the grand old hotel of the city, **Hotel D'Angleterre** ⓮. The majestic buildings dominating the square are the **Royal Theatre** ⓯ (Det Kongelige Teater) – the national stage for ballet, opera and drama. The present building was designed in the 1870s, taking the Paris Opera Garnier as its ideal.

Next door is **Charlottenborg**, since 1754 the home of the **Royal Academy of Fine Arts**, where painters, sculptors and architects receive their formal training.

Nyhavn quayside

At the narrow waterway of **Nyhavn** ⓰, a famous landmark from 1673, colourful old wooden schooners line the quay, and the north side is a charming combination of sailors' bars and new restaurants. The south side was always the "nice side", but the north side used to be the "naughty side" where sailors on shore leave would spend their liberty drinking, whoring and getting

BELOW: the colourful quayside at Nyhavn.

tattooed. Times have changed, and gentrified Nyhavn is now one of the most popular and atmospheric spots in town. It's a fine place to wine, dine and socialise, and the opening of the new waterfront **Royal Danish Playhouse** ⓱ (Skuespilhuset) in 2008 has added a cultural element too.

Frederiksstaden

From Nyhavn, Bredgade and its parallel twin, Store Kongensgade, are the main shopping streets of the residential **Frederiksstaden** to the north. The area was planned and built in the 18th century for the well-to-do who wanted stately homes close to the centre.

At Bredgade 68 is **Designmuseum Danmark** ⓲ (tel: 33 18 56 56; www.designmuseum.dk; Tue–Sun 11am–5pm; charge), featuring classic Danish design as well as European and oriental objets. The building (1757) was originally a hospital. Opposite the museum, three domes tower over **Alexander Nevski Russian Orthodox Church**, which was built in 1881 by the Russian government and contains a number of fine icons.

Close by looms the grand copper dome of **Frederikskirke** ⓳ (tel: 33 15 37 63; mid-June–Aug daily 1 and 3pm, Sept–mid-June Sat–Sun only; charge), popularly known as the **Marble Church**. The church was meant to be a majestic rococo monument, designed to rival St Peter's in Rome, but the king, Frederik V, ran out of money and the project was cancelled in 1770. The church was not completed until 1894, and when the project was resumed it was built not in marble but in limestone. The dome was being repaired at the time of writing and was closed to visitors. Once tours resume, join one for a splendid view across the Sound to Sweden. The statues outside the church represent important Danish clergymen and theologians.

Amalienborg Palace ⓴ (Amalienborg Slot), across Bredgade towards the harbour, is the winter residence of the royal family, one of Europe's less assuming royal domiciles, built in the 18th century. One wing of the palace houses the **Amalienborg Museum** (tel: 33 12 21 86; May–Oct daily 10am–4pm, Nov–mid-Dec and Jan–Apr Tue–Sun 11am–4pm; charge), whose reconstructed

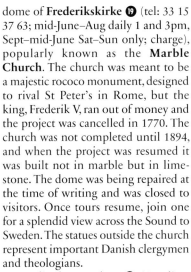

Nyhavn still retains some of the character of bygone days, when it was a haunt for sailors on leave.

LEFT: exhibits at the Designmuseum Danmark.

On Amager Island

Visitors glancing out of the aeroplane window near Copenhagen (Kastrup) airport may be intrigued – or even alarmed – by what appears to be a swirling vortex on Amager island. The spiralling landmark is actually one of many surprising buildings springing up around Copenhagen. On its completion in 2013, it will become the home of Scandinavia's biggest aquarium, The Blue Planet.

For years, Amager was a quiet hinterland, created by some judicious damming and a mass of Copenhagen landfill. Today, it's the scene for some of Denmark's most exciting architecture. A whole "downtown" area, Ørestad, is being created from scratch here: a shining new metro station brings shoppers to one of Denmark's largest malls, and to the beautiful DR Koncerthuset, home of the Danish Symphony Orchestra. Nearby, the Øresund bridge uses the island as a launchpad to curve itself over to Swedish shores.

Islandsbrygge, on the west of Amager, has more to offer the casual visitor, with its wonderful Havneparken (Harbour Park). The water around Copenhagen is clean enough to swim in, and in the park you'll find the harbour baths – five outdoor pools full of happy, splashing people. Even more of a luxury, Amager Strandpark is a beach development on the east, with over 4km (2½ miles) of beaches, an artificial island and a lagoon.

Flame and Citron (2008) is a chilling film noir, directed by Ole Christian Madsen, former member of the Dogme group of Danish filmmakers. Set in 1944 Copenhagen, the plot is based on the real lives of two of Denmark's most famous Resistance fighters and explores the moral complexities of war.

BELOW: at the National Museum for Fine Arts.
BELOW RIGHT: Rosenborg Castle.

rooms contain exhibitions on the monarchy from 1863 to 1972.

The Royal Guard are always on duty, and the changing of the guard at noon every day attracts both children and adults. If the flag is flying, then the Queen is in residence and the full ceremony will take place. The exquisite equestrian statue in the square represents Frederik V and was made by the French sculptor Jacques Saly.

Along the promenade

The other end of the east–west axis through the plaza ends in **Amaliehaven**, a modern park donated to the city by the A.P. Møller shipping company in 1983. Following the promenade to the north, you will find the dazzling fountain, **Gefionspringvandet ㉑**, dedicated to the Nordic goddess Gefion.

At the start of Langelinie is *the* symbol of Copenhagen, **The Little Mermaid ㉒** (Den Lille Havfrue). This bronze statue of the character from the Hans Christian Andersen fairy tale was created by Edvard Eriksen in 1913. Quite bizarrely, she was taken to Shanghai, China, in 2010 to sit in lonely state in the Danish pavilion at the World Expo; but she's now back home.

The quay of Langelinie follows, and Europe's busiest cruise-ship pier is to the north of this at **Frihavnen** (Free Harbour). One of the most architecturally interesting of the newer buildings in this area is **Paustians Hus**, designed by Jørn Utzon, who also designed the Sydney Opera House. Paustian is one of Copenhagen's finest furniture stores; the building also houses a good restaurant.

Return to the city centre via **Kastellet ㉓** (The Citadel), a fortification that has kept its old ramparts intact. Part of the area is still military property.

Churchillparken, a tiny park just south of Kastellet, provides a home for the **Museum of the Danish Resistance ㉔** (Frihedsmuseet; tel: 33 47 39 21; www.natmus.dk; Tue–Sun, May–Sept 10am–5pm, Oct–Apr 10am–3pm; free), which commemorates the Danish resistance fighters of World War II. Apart from acts of sabotage against Nazi occupants, the underground group managed to get 7,000 of Denmark's 8,000 Jews out of the country.

Fine art collections

Continue past Store Kongensgade to visit Denmark's oldest housing development, **Nyboder** ㉕. Construction of the long rows of ochre-coloured houses began in 1631, after Kristian IV addressed the urgent need for housing for Danish Royal Navy personnel. The 616 apartments are still used for staff and retired officers.

Nearby, where Øster Voldgade and Sølvgade meet, is the superb **National Museum for Fine Arts** ㉖ (Statens Museum for Kunst; tel: 33 74 84 94; www.smk.dk; Tue–Sun 10am–5pm, Wed until 8pm; permanent collection free, charge for exhibitions). A new extension houses four storeys of modern art within stunning glass and whitewashed walls. Other Danish and European works are displayed permanently, along with changing international exhibitions.

Behind the museum and across the park is the **Hirschsprungske Collection** ㉗ (Den Hirschsprungske Samling; tel: 35 42 03 36; www.hirschsprung. dk; Wed–Mon 11am–4pm; charge), a fine private collection of 19th-century Danish art assembled by tobacco tycoon Heinrich Hirschsprung – including many of the originals from the Skagen painters *(see page 88)*.

Botanical Gardens and Rosenborg Castle

The **Botanical Gardens** ㉘ (Botanisk Have; tel: 35 32 22 22; summer daily 8.30am–6pm, winter Tue–Sun 8.30am–4pm; free) are just across the street. Visit the rosarium, the perennials and a huge conservatory with tropical and subtropical plants.

One of Copenhagen's most attractive sights is **Rosenborg Castle** ㉙ (Rosenborg Slot; tel: 33 15 32 86; times vary; charge), the fairytale castle across from the Botanical Gardens. King Kristian IV's exquisite palace in Dutch Renaissance style is now a museum, and contains three centuries' worth of royal treasures, as well as the crown jewels. The garden surrounding it, **Kongens Have**, has been a favourite with Copenhageners for centuries.

Castle Island

To the southeast of Strøget and the main shopping area lies **Slotsholmen**

The Little Mermaid (Den Lille Havfrue), sculpted in 1913 by Edvard Eriksen, was modelled on his wife.

BELOW: the ochre-coloured houses of the Nyboder district.

Christiania – the Alternative City

In a beautiful position on Copenhagen's waterfront, Christiania offers a way of life far removed from the bustle of a city

In 1971, a group of alternative thinkers founded Christiania, a 34-hectare (84-acre) "Free City" with woods, dirt roads, workshops, restaurants and funky houses. The hippie enclave in the heart of the city – only 1km (½ mile) from the Parliament buildings – occupies what was previously an abandoned 19th-century military barracks in Christianshavn. The Christianites, about 850 people of all ages, cultures and income levels, have converted barrack blocks, workshops and powder magazines into a place where they can live and work. There are only four rules: no hard drugs, no cars, no gang insignia, no weapons or violence.

From the entrance on, Christiania is a sensory overload. Buildings are painted with rainbows, spiritual figures and politically defiant graffiti. There are barefoot cyclists, their baskets full of vegetables; earthy-smelling organic markets; recycling ware-

houses; workshops and stables. Resident children play in an "organic kindergarten", where modern equipment is replaced with nature. Houses along the leafy path have names such as "The Blue Banana" or "The Pyramid".

Christiania has some of the best restaurants in the city, including SpiseLoppen (The Eating Flea), in the warehouse by the front entrance. In the same building is Loppen, a music club. Månefiskeren (The Moon Fisher), a café in the heart of the collective, serves excellent coffee in a "far-out" atmosphere.

For years, Christiania's unusual social experiment was tolerated, but since 2004 the Danish government has stepped up measures to "normalise" the area. A police crackdown on "Pusher Street", where marijuana was once sold openly, drove the drugs trade underground. In 2006 the government proposed that all buildings should be privately owned, a suggestion fiercely rejected by the Christiania collective. When government workers entered Christiania in 2007 with a police guard and began to demolish a derelict building, tension quickly turned to violent protest, with 59 arrests.

In February 2011, the commune was dealt a blow when the Danish Supreme Court declared that the residents had no legal right to occupy the area. Following the ruling, the right-wing government surprisingly gave residents the chance to buy their spirit-of-Woodstock town for a generous 150m kroner (£18m). It was widely thought that the anti-materialistic inhabitants would reject the offer, and property developers were poised to turn the piece of prime real estate into an affluent suburb. But in a further twist, in May 2011 the residents agreed to stump up the cash.

Barring future surprises, visitors can see Christiania for themselves on an inexpensive walking tour, which leaves at 4pm from the front entrance (July daily, rest of year weekends) – this is the best way to see the Free City and get a broader perspective. Christiania's tourist guide (10DKK) provides a detailed history and self-guided walks. ❑

ABOVE: the streets of Christiania are car-free.
LEFT: murals decorate many of the buildings.

(Castle Island). Surrounded by canals, the island is the seat of the Danish Parliament and government ministries.

Bishop Absalon built a fortress on the islet in 1167. The fortress was replaced by a new castle in 1367 and from 1416 it was the home of the Danish king. In the 1730s King Kristian VI ordered a new palace. This one, a magnificent Baroque building, burned in 1794 and was replaced with another new palace which, ill-fated as it was, burned down in 1884.

The present version of **Christiansborg Palace ③⓪** is around 100 years old and contains Parliament, the prime minister's office, the Supreme Court and the Royal Reception Chambers. The granite facade of this imposing building was made from stones gathered in every parish in the country. The equestrian statue, erected on the Palace Square, depicts King Frederik VII (1843–63).

The public may join conducted tours of the **House of Parliament** (Folketinget; tel: 33 37 55 00; in English, year-round 1pm Sun, also July noon and 2pm Mon–Fri; free). The stately **Royal Reception Chambers**. (tel: 33 92 64 92; May–Sept 10am–5pm, Oct–Apr Tue–Sun 10am–5pm; charge), still used by the royal family, are richly decorated and contain 11 modern gobelin tapestries commissioned for the Queen's 50th birthday.

The **Ruins of Absalon's Old Fortress** (May–Sept daily 10am–5pm, Oct–Apr Tue–Sun 10am–5pm; charge) and the medieval castle are accessible to visitors and make an interesting "underground" visit.

The **Palace Chapel**, inaugurated in 1826, is located to the north of Christiansborg. Behind the chapel is **Thorvaldsens Museum ③①** (tel: 33 32 15 32; Tue–Sun 10am–5pm; charge), which contains the works of Denmark's great sculptor, Bertel Thorvaldsen (1770–1844), who lived and worked in Rome for 40 years.

In front of Christiansborg is the **Ridebanen ③②**, the royal riding grounds from the 1740s bordered by the only surviving buildings from the first Christiansborg. The royal horses are still exercised here, and their stables can be visited on the southeast side of the square – the **Museum of Royal Stables and Coaches** (Kongelige Stalde og Kareter; tel: 33 40 26 76; May–Sept Fri–Sun 2–4pm, Oct–Apr Sat–Sun 2–4pm; charge). Adjacent to the stables, the **Teatermuseet** is one of the oldest court theatres in the world, designed in 1766 by the French architect Nicolas-Henri Jardin (tel: 33 11 51 76; Tue 11am–3pm, Wed 11am–5pm, Thur 11am–3pm, Sat–Sun 1–4pm; charge). The equestrian statue on the riding grounds depicts King Kristian IX, who died in 1906.

East of Christiansborg is another of Copenhagen's best-known buildings, the **Stock Exchange ③③** (Børsen), built in 1619 in Dutch Renaissance style by Kristian IV. Its prominent spire is formed by the entwined tails of four dragons said to protect the building from fire. On the southeast side of the island is the **Royal Library ③④** (Det Kongelige Bibliotek) and its "Black Diamond" – an architectural wonder of

For treasure and trash visit the city's antique and flea markets. Try Israels Plads on Saturday, 8am–3pm, mid-April to September; and Gammel Strand, Friday 7am–6pm and Saturday 8am–4pm, May to September.

BELOW: royal thrones at Christiansborg Palace.

TIP

Visitors to the Carlsberg Brewery Visitor Centre (tel: 33 27 12 82; Tue–Sun 10am–5pm; charge) in the Valby district can learn how the popular lager is made, marvel at the world's largest beer-bottle collection, meet the stocky Jutland horses traditionally used to cart wooden beer barrels, and sample the wares.

old and new. Det Kongelige Bibliotek dates back to 1482 and is the largest library in Scandinavia, with more than 2½ million volumes. The Black Diamond, completed in 1999, is a modern extension in black polished granite perched on the water's edge.

Christianshavn

Cross the harbour via the Knippelsbro bridge to reach **Christianshavn**, one of Copenhagen's oldest and most colourful residential areas. Christianshavn was built on an island in 1617 by Kristian IV and is surrounded by the original star-shaped ramparts. Along the harbour wall, one of the meticulously restored warehouses is well worth a visit, the **Danish Architecture Centre** ❸ (Dansk Arkitektur Center; tel: 32 57 19 30; www.dac.dk; daily 10am–5pm, Wed until 9pm; charge), which features various exhibitions, a bookshop and café.

Until recently a run-down, working-class area and Denmark's largest ship-yard, Christianshavn has changed enormously and now features a mixture of smartly renovated 18th-century

city houses, big apartment blocks, old and new industry, a good deal of the state's administration, laidback café-bars, some of the city's finest restaurants and stunning new architecture. It's a real bohemian mixture, home to all kinds of people, and an area just made for wandering: take a stroll down the streets of Christianshavn and glance into the courtyards of some of the old houses on **Strandgade**, stop for a coffee on **Wildersgade** and then to gaze at **Amagergade 11**, surrounded by old galleries and said to have the finest courtyard in town. On the very bottom edge of Christianshavn is the city's first floating hotel, **CPH Living**.

Christianshavn is also the home of **Christiania** ❸, the hippie-style "free city" (see feature, page 128). The main entrance is on Prinsessegade.

Two of Copenhagen's more notable churches are on Christianshavn. **Christianskirke** ❸ in Strandgade is a rococo building from 1754. It was built as a theatre with boxes, including one for the royal family. The **Church of Our Saviour** ❸ (Vor Frelsers Kirke; tel: 32 54 68 83; July–mid-Sept 11am–7pm, Apr–June and mid-Sept–mid-Nov 11am–4pm) in Prinsessegade attracts the most attention. Built in red brick in 1694, its tall copper-clad tower with a spiralling, external stairway can be seen from all over the city. The tower is open to visitors who are brave enough to climb through a maze of roof timbers and up the 150 gilded steps.

At the northern end of Christianshavn, a cluster of little islands known as **Holmen** were the Danish Royal Navy's base until the 1990s. Some interesting naval architecture remains, such as the 18th-century **Mastekranen**, used for fixing masts onto sailing ships. But the most recent buzz around Holmen was the creation of Copenhagen's immense new **Operaen** (Opera House). Designed by Henning Larsen, the building contains over 1,000 rooms and cost 2.5 billion Danish kroner. ❑

BELOW: Carlsberg Brewery drayman. **RIGHT:** the Opera House.

A FLAIR FOR DESIGN: FUNCTION WITH FORM

When a nation of craftsmen mixed with a late move towards industrialisation in the 1900s, an influential new school of design was born

A chair may be something to sit in, and a lamp may help to light a room, but Danish designers have made these ordinary objects extraordinary. Perhaps their success is linked to the fact that Danish life is so centred around hearth, home and the concept of *hygge* – one's surroundings should always be familiar, functional and beautiful.

Danish design in the 1950s and 60s brought a whole new look to furniture, lighting and homeware, avoiding the hard, geometrical shapes apparent elsewhere in the design world, and imbuing everyday objects with a tactile, organic quality. This iconic look has survived the test of time – Arne Jacobsen's egg chair is a prime example.

Today, the Danes are still at the forefront of design. Old and new companies alike – such as Fredericia Furniture, Gubi and Normann – are keen to promote new designers, revitalising the principles of Danish functionalism and creating tomorrow's classics. Whether in museums, conference rooms or homes, Danish design always brings a sense of elegance to everyday life.

"It always starts with a task," says designer Hans J. Wegner. "I never say to myself, I'm going to make a piece of art. I tell myself, I want to make a good chair". Danish designers "subtract and subtract" unnecessary elements from products and tools to find true function and form, says Jens Bernsen of the Danish Design Centre. "Sometimes these designs even turn out to be beautiful."

ABOVE: the architect Arne Jacobsen designed this stainless steel line of household objects, Cylinda Line, for the company Stelton, and it is now one of the most recognised in Denmark.

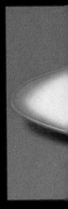

ABOVE: this popular dinner service was designed by Ursula Munch-Petersen for Royal Copenhagen.

LEFT: many of Arne Jacobsen's designs were intended for specific buildings or, in the case of this egg chair, hotel lobbies.

DESIGN IN THE HOME

For all its elegance, Danish design is not something limited to galleries and museums. In Denmark, it is found everywhere – hotels, restaurants, cafés, offices *(pictured above)* and, most importantly, homes. Nearly every Dane, it seems, has some sort of sleek designer lamp hanging over the dinner or coffee table.

For special occasions, such as weddings, birthdays and office receptions, Danes give presents such as arty salad sets, candle holders, salt and pepper grinders, pot holders – even mixing bowls.

"The kitchen drawer is good design's enemy number one," says Erik Bagger, whose wine-serving tools are well known in Denmark. Danish-designed products are meant to be used, however, meaning that Denmark probably has the most stylish contents of kitchen drawers anywhere in the world.

The visually striking sound systems designed by Bang & Olufsen are praised worldwide, and are found in many a Danish home. Even such prosaic items as cupboard handles and other household fittings are given due attention by Danish designers. Organic shapes abound, and recently a certain amount of whimsy has crept in: witness Normann's award-winning grass vase.

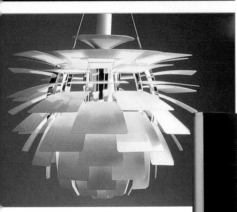

ABOVE: this is the PH lamp; Poul Henningsen saw a light fixture as more than just light – as something to create a sense of space.

LEFT: a grass vase, a quirky take on a typical home accessory from Normann Copenhagen.

LEFT: Bang and Olufsen offers a fine example of contemporary Danish design. The company is well-known for its chic range of electronics.

ZEALAND

Venture north from Copenhagen to Hamlet's castle at Helsingør, or south to the white cliffs of Møn, and discover Zealand, a colourful land rich in culture and tradition

The island of Zealand (Sjælland) is Denmark's largest, yet it is still compact and most of its attractions make ideal day trips from the capital. The area north of Copenhagen makes a classic tour for visitors, with its undulating countryside, beech forests, lakes and good beaches, as well as castles, manor houses, royal hunting lodges, art galleries and museums. The southern and western areas of Zealand have traditionally been entry points for new people and ideas coming from the Continent. This side of the island is an enchanting expanse of rolling hills, woodland and some wonderful seaside scenery.

The Danish Riviera

The coast road from **Copenhagen ①** (København) to Helsingør, officially called Strandvejen, is also known as the "Danish Riviera" for its stylish houses and fine views across the Øresund to Sweden. Small protected harbours shelter working fishing boats and millionaires' yachts alike, and converted marine buildings house fresh fish restaurants.

While it's true that the essence of North Zealand can be glimpsed in a day, it really warrants more time, either by an overnight stop at a charming Danish *kro* (inn) or by taking several day tours from Copenhagen.

From Copenhagen, drive north through fashionable Charlottenlund to

Klampenborg ②. In just 15 minutes you'll come to an ancient deer park, **Klampenborg Dyrhaven** (daily), first mentioned in official documents in 1231. Leave your car and take a horse and carriage through the woods and parkland. Forest walks are indicated by yellow spots painted on trees.

Within the deer park lies the world's oldest funfair, **Bakken** (tel: 39 63 35 44; Apr–late Aug, times vary). **Peter Lieps**'s rustic forest restaurant is where locals go to drink hot chocolate after winter walks. Art-lovers will enjoy the

Main attractions

LOUISIANA MUSEUM FOR MODERN ART
HELSINGØR AND KRONBORG CASTLE
TISVILDE AND LISELEJE BEACHES
VIKINGESKIBSMUSEET, ROSKILDE
ARKEN MODERN ART MUSEUM
CLIFFS OF MØN

LEFT: a girl enjoying the funfair in Bakken.
RIGHT: relaxing on the beach.

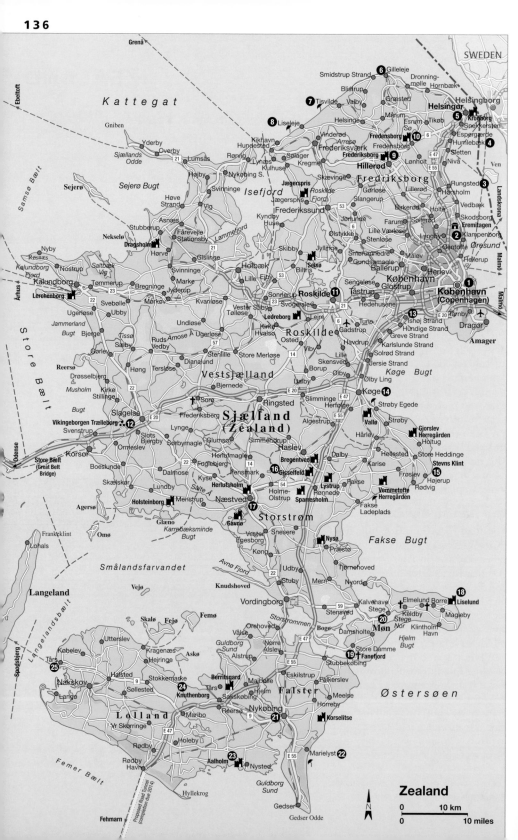

Zealand

0   10 km

0   10 miles

quiet elegance of nearby **Ordrupgaard** (Vilvordevej 110; tel: 39 64 11 83; Tue, Thur, Fri 1–5pm, Wed 1–7pm, Sat–Sun 11am–5pm; charge). Its permanent collection of Danish and French paintings includes works by Matisse and Gauguin. The museum has newly incorporated the home of Finn Juhl, architect and furniture-designer extraordinaire (weekends 11am–5pm).

Karen Blixen's home and the Louisiana Art Museum

A further 12km (7 miles) brings you to **Rungsted ❸**, site of **Rungstedlund** (tel: 45 57 10 57; May–Sept Tue–Sun 10am–5pm, Oct–Apr Wed–Fri 1–4pm, Sat–Sun 11am–4pm; charge), the family home of Karen Blixen, the Danish writer known as Isak Dinesen, author of *Babette's Feast* and *Out of Africa*, which later became acclaimed films, winning one and seven Oscars respectively.

At **Humlebæk ❹**, art-lovers could easily spend an entire day at the **Louisiana Museum for Modern Art** (Louisiana Museum for Moderne Kunst, Gl. Strandvej 13; tel: 49 19 07 19; Tue–Fri 11am–10pm, Sat–Sun 11am–6pm; charge), located in a breathtaking coastal setting overlooking the Øresund. A rich permanent collection, encompassing the work of artists such as Giacometti, Yves Klein, Louise Bourgeois and Picasso, is supplemented by frequent international exhibitions. Various extensions and pavilions stretch into the gardens, their clever designs blurring the distinction between man-made structures and nature *(see box, page 88)*.

Hamlet's Helsingør

Helsingør ❺ is best known for its massive Renaissance-style **Kronborg**, Hamlet's "Castle of Elsinore" (tel: 49 21 30 78; May–Sept daily 10.30am–5pm, Oct and Apr Tue–Sun 11am–4pm, Nov–Mar Tue–Sun 11am–3pm; charge). Originally built by King Eric of Pomerania when he introduced the "Sound Dues" (fees paid to the Danish crown by all ships passing through to the Baltic), Kronborg has been rebuilt several times. It

has provided a backdrop for many productions of Shakespeare's *Hamlet*. Inside, the richly decorated King's and Queen's chambers and the 62-metre (203ft) long Great Hall are worth seeing.

Helsingør is one of Denmark's most historic towns, with entire streets of colour-washed buildings. The 15th-century **Skt Mariæ Kirke** and the **Carmelite Kloster** (Convent) are among the best-preserved Gothic buildings in the world.

The coast road leads on to **Gilleleje ❻**, the most northerly town of Zealand, a small working fishing port. **Adamsens Fisk**, an unpretentious harbourside takeaway, is a great spot for a fish lunch. If the weather is good, you could stop at the sun-worshippers' beaches of **Tisvilde ❼** or **Liseleje ❽**.

Turning back towards Copenhagen, Denmark's National History Museum is at the spectacular Renaissance palace **Frederiksborg ❾** (tel: 48 26 04 39; daily, Apr–Oct 10am–5pm, Nov–Mar 11am–3pm; charge), built between 1605 and 1621 in **Hillerød**. The most notable rooms are the Council Hall, Knights' Hall and the chapel with its

Author Karen Blixen lived at Rungsted.

BELOW: learning to fence at Helsingør castle.

original Compenius organ (1610). Outside is one of the best Baroque gardens in Northern Europe.

Just 9km (5 miles) from Hillerød is the Italianate palace of **Fredensborg** ❿ (guided tours, July daily 1–4.30pm; groups tel: 33 40 31 87). Built in 1722, it is now used by the Danish royal family as a spring and autumn residence. The astonishing 120 hectares (300 acres) of gardens – long, straight 18th-century avenues interspersed with forest and seashore – are open to visitors at all times.

Viking town

A major highlight of Zealand is the town of **Roskilde** ⓫, the island's second-largest town, 20 minutes by train west of Copenhagen. The wonderful **Cathedral** (Domkirke; Apr–Sept Mon–Sat 9am–5pm, Sun 12.30–4pm, Oct–Mar Tue–Sat 10am–4pm, Sun 12.30–4pm; charge), built in 1170, is the burial place of generations of Danish monarchs and a Unesco World Heritage site. The **Viking Ship Museum** (Vikingeskibsmuseet; tel: 46 300 200; www.vikingeskibsmuseet.dk; July–Aug daily 10am–5pm, rest of year 10am–4pm; charge) has

five superbly restored ships (including a dreaded Viking man o' war) found in 1962 at the mouth of Roskildefjord – they were sunk by the 11th-century defenders of Roskilde to block the fjord against enemy attack. Costumed reenactors demonstrate Viking crafts and the restaurant has *mjød* (mead) to quaff.

Vikingeborgen Tælleborg ⓬ (tel: 58 54 95 06; June–Aug Tue–Sun 10am–5pm, Apr–June and Sept–Oct Tue–Thur 10am–4pm; charge), near Slagelse in western Zealand, is an abandoned Viking fortress some 1,000 years old. It was once a huge fortified camp that housed 1,000 Vikings, and one of the houses has been reconstructed.

Southern Zealand

The first stop for modern art enthusiasts south of Copenhagen is the sleek white **Arken Museet for Moderne Kunst** (tel: 43 54 02 22; www.arken.dk; Tue–Sun 10am–5pm, Wed until 9pm; charge) at **Ishøj** ⓭. **Køge** ⓮ is popular for its beaches, crowded with sun-loving Danes. Køge is characterised by half-timbered houses. The oldest, dated 1527, stands at 20 Kirkestræde. **Skt Nikolai Kirke** has one of Denmark's most beautiful town church interiors. Not far from the market is **Hugos Vinkælder**, a historic inn serving old-fashioned draught porter.

The cliffs of **Stevns Klint** ⓯ on the south headland of Køge Bay may not be quite as dramatic as those on the island of Møn, but they are impressive when the sun illuminates them in brilliant hues of white.

Inland, 5km (3 miles) south of the ancient town of **Haslev**, Hans Christian Andersen found inspiration for one of his most famous stories, *The Ugly Duckling*, in **Gisselfeld Slot** ⓰ (grounds and stables daily), a castle built in 1554. **Næstved** ⓱, 10km (6 miles) southwest of Haslev, has been an important trading town for most of its history and has an attractive city centre. About 6km (4 miles) to the southwest is **Gavnø Slot** (tel: 55 70 02 00; Apr–Sept 10am–4pm; charge), set among magnificent gardens on a tiny island linked by road. In the 13th century it was used as a pirates' castle; today it houses Scandinavia's largest privately owned picture collection.

Cliffs of Møn

The island of **Møn** ("The Maid") to the east is linked to Zealand by road bridges. According to legend, its spectacular stretches of luminous white chalk cliffs, topped with beech woods and studded with fossils, became a refuge for the most powerful of Nordic gods, Odin, when Christianity left him homeless. **Geocenter Møns Klint** (tel: 55 86 36 00; www.moensklint.dk; mid-Apr–Oct 10am–5pm, July–Aug until 6pm; charge) explains the area's geology.

Liselund Slot ❶ (tel: 55 81 21 78; May–Sept Wed–Sun 10.30am–3.30pm, by guided tour only; charge) is a thatched mini-chateau, built in 1796. Andersen wrote *The Tinder Box* and *The Little Match Girl* in a summer house on the estate. Møn's churches are noted for their frescoes, particularly those at **Keldby**, **Elmelund** and **Fanefjord** ❶, the last standing on an isolated hill overlooking the narrows of Grønsund.

Beside the church is the longest barrow grave in Denmark, **Grønjægers Høj**. The main town of **Stege** ❷ has medieval ramparts.

Falster and Lolland

The Farø bridges connect Zealand to **Falster**, and the ferry routes to Germany. The main town on the island is **Nykøbing** ❷, noted for the **Czarens Hus** (Tsar's House), where Peter the Great stayed in 1716, which now houses the **Falsters Minder Museum** (tel: 54 84 44 00; Tue–Fri noon–4pm, Sat 10am–1pm; charge) of local history. The area around **Marielyst** ❷, to the southeast, has miles of white sand dunes where families take beach holidays. A choice of bridges links Falster to **Lolland**. The 12th-century castle **Aalholm Slot** ❷ is closed to visitors, but you can visit the **Automobile Museum** (tel: 54 87 19 11; May–Oct 11am–5pm) in its grounds. From Aalholm, the road north runs past lakes to **Knuthenborg** ❷ (tel: 54 78 80 89; May–Oct 10am–6pm; charge), a safari park. In the far west, the **Tårs** ❷ to **Spodsbjerg** crossing connects the island with Langeland and Funen. ❑

TIP

On Midsummer's Eve along the coast north of Copenhagen, beach bonfires and fireworks light the skies and a procession of ships passes through the Øresund, blasting their horns to celebrate the peak of the short Danish summer.

BELOW: farmland landscape, north Zealand.

BORNHOLM

Denmark's Baltic island of Bornholm is
a haven for both artists and holidaymakers,
attracted by its climate, peaceful lifestyle
and natural beauty

Main attractions
HAMMERSHUS
RØNNE
NATURBORNHOLM,
  ÅKIRKEBY
SVANEKE
GUDHJEM
BORNHOLMS KUNSTMUSEUM
MEDIEVAL ROUND CHURCHES
EXPLORING THE ISLAND BY
  BICYCLE

BELOW: a jetty
on the beach in
Bornholm.

Bornholm is "Scandinavia in a nut-shell". Sitting in the middle of the Baltic Sea between Sweden and Poland, this enchanting island features a variety of landscapes typical to different areas of Scandinavia. It is a peaceful place, home to about 42,000 Bornholmers, with no large towns and almost no industry. Visitors have a perfect opportunity to relax, although from early July until the end of August the population swells fourfold with holidaymakers. It is three hours from Copenhagen by train/ferry, and 30 minutes by plane.

Viking strongholds

Bornholm was a maritime centre in the Baltic Sea during the Iron Age. Jewellery, coins and relics from as far away as Rome and the Near East have been discovered on the island, and the scant remains of two forts dating from the Viking period, both known as **Gamleborg**, can be found in **Paradisbakkerne** (The Hills of Paradise) and at **Almindingen Skov**. It is generally believed that Bornholm became a part of the kingdom of Denmark at around that time.

Perched on a huge rocky knoll on the northwest corner of the island are the impressive ruins of **Hammershus** ❶ (tel: 56 48 24 31; daily; free). The castle was built around 1200 to defend the island against attack, and is today Scandinavia's largest castle ruin. At the time the castle was built, Bornholm was owned by the Archbishop of Lund (in what is now southern Sweden, but then part of Denmark); he was openly at war with the kings of Denmark. Strong separatist feelings still exist among some Bornholmers. Their banner is a Danish flag with a green cross instead of the familiar white one.

Around Bornholm

The variety of plant life on Bornholm is astounding. The northern part of the island is extremely rocky and, by radiating heat picked up from the sun, the rocks keep the surface warm enough for figs, grapes, mulberry trees and other plants from Southern Europe to grow well. Sweet cherry trees blossom in June and give a colourful show. Red orchids are common on the banks in the river valleys, and thousands of woodland flowers, especially blue, yellow and white anemones, cover large areas. About 20 percent of Bornholm is woodland: **Almindingen** ❷, in the centre of the island, is Denmark's third-largest forest. **Paradisbakkerne** ❸ is wilder in vegetation than Almindingen and is best enjoyed on foot. Small farms are scattered all over the island.

Rønne ❹, with 14,000 inhabitants, is the largest town on Bornholm, and its harbour is one of the largest provincial ports in Denmark. Some parts of the town have been well preserved, especially in the area just east of **Skt Nikolai Kirke**. The beautiful **Kastellet** (citadel) is on the east side of town; today it is a military museum, **Forsvarsmuseet** (tel: 51 33 00 33; mid-May–Sept Tue–Sat 10am–4pm; charge).

Bornholm has inspired many Danish painters, as well as having produced a few of its own: Oluf Høst is the best known. **Bornholms Museum** (Skt Mortensgade

29; tel: 56 95 07 35; Jan–mid-May and late Oct–Dec Mon–Sat 1–4pm, mid-May–June and Sept–late Oct Mon–Sat 10am–5pm, July–Aug daily 10am–5pm; charge) and its collection of paintings and exhibits from prehistory onwards relating to the island's past is worth visiting. It also includes a charming model of the Bornholm railway.

Åkirkeby ❺ (pop. 2,100) is the main town in the southern part of Bornholm, and the only one of the larger towns situated inland. It was an ecclesiastical centre, and its church, **Åkirke**, was built around 1150 as a chapterhouse in the Archbishopric of Lund. The large tower was extended around 1200, and at the same time it was fortified with walls even heavier than those of Hammershus. It is notable for its sandstone baptismal font depicting the life of Christ in 11 relief carvings; the figures are explained in runic script, and end with the signature of the stonecutter, "Sighraf, master".

Åkirkeby's other attraction is **NaturBornholm** (tel: 56 94 04 00; Apr–Oct 10am–5pm, last admission 4pm; charge), a superb interactive visitor centre that explains the island's

Bornholm is a centre for Danish applied arts and handicrafts. Every village has its silversmiths, wood turners, jewellers, textile artists and more. Potteries and glass-blowing workshops are often open to the public.

BELOW: Hammershus castle ruins.

Bornholm celebrates classical music with a festival from July to mid-August, which attracts music-lovers from around the world.

history, wildlife and geology. The building was designed by Henning Larsen, architect of Copenhagen's Opera House.

The easternmost town in Denmark, **Svaneke ❻**, prospered with the success of its shipping captains. The largest buildings were originally merchants' houses. Today it's the prettiest town on Bornholm, famous for an abundance of **artists' workshops** and its lively **craft market**, from 9am on Wednesdays and Saturdays in summer. North of the town is an old Dutch mill, and nearby an un-traditional water tower, built by the architect Jørn Utzon in 1951.

Cycling downhill is forbidden in **Gudhjem ❼** ("good home"), another very picturesque place, built on steep slopes down to the water. Windmills around the town once provided electricity. Bornholm's most famous artist is celebrated at the **Oluf Høst Museum** (tel: 56 48 50 38; June–Sept 11am–5pm; charge), housed in the painter's former studio. There is an open-air agricultural museum, **Landbrugsmuseet Melstedgård** (tel: 56 48 55 98; July–Aug daily 10am–5pm, mid-May–June and Sept–

BELOW: delicious fresh herrings.

late Oct Sun–Thur 10am–5pm; charge), just southeast of Gudhjem at **Melsted**, complete with horses, pigs and poultry. Northwest of Gudhjem, the excellent **Bornholms Kunstmuseum** (tel: 56 48 43 86; June–Aug 10am–5pm, Apr–May and Sept–Oct Tue–Sun 10am–5pm, reduced hours rest of year; charge) perches on a craggy outcrop above the sea and houses a worthwhile collection of artwork from the Bornholm School, ranging from the 1800s to the present.

Grønbechs Gård (Bornholm Centre of Arts and Crafts; tel: 56 96 18 70; mid-Apr–late Sept daily 10am–5pm; charge), an old merchant's house in **Hasle ❽**, showcases the work of the island's artists and designers, with changing wood, ceramics, jewellery, glass and textile exhibitions.

Christiansø

It's an hour's sail from Gudhjem Harbour to the group of islands known as **Ertholmene**. The largest of these are **Christiansø ❾** and **Frederiksø**. A naval base was constructed here in about 1864, but today only fishermen and their families live on this "fortress

Salmon and Herring

During the summer months, freshly landed herrings are delivered to the island's distinctive white smokehouses. Here they are turned from their original silver colour into the "golden Bornholmers" dearly loved by Danes, which can often be seen drying on stands outside. Elderwood gives them their special taste. The smoked herrings are either eaten warm from the oven or put on black rye bread, sprinkled with salt, chopped chives, onion and radishes, and topped with a raw egg yolk – this typical Danish open sandwich is known as *Sol over Gudhjem* – "Sun over Gudhjem".

Pickled herrings are a lunchtime must. The best spiced herrings are produced on Christiansø. Baltic salmon, said to be the finest edible fish in the world, is normally available, too.

in the sea". It makes an interesting place to visit. The islands are quite rocky, with castle towers, batteries and cannon all serving as reminders of the past. Their isolated setting and car-free environment make them attractive to birdlife, particularly eider ducks, which breed all over the islands.

Round churches

Østerlars Kirke ⑩ just over 4km (2½ miles) southwest from Gudhjem, is the largest of the four medieval "round churches" of Bornholm, which include **Nylars**, **Nyker** and **Olsker**. When the Slavic Wends ravaged the island they were occasionally used as places of refuge, and in the 14th–16th century Hanseatic merchants from northern Germany would move in during the herring season. At Østerlars the enormous support pillars create the impression of a fortress, which was the second purpose of the structure. Inside the church (built around 1150), the vault is painted with fine frescoes of biblical scenes. On the north wall of the oval-shaped choir, stone steps lead to the second storey, where the hollow central pillar has two

entrances. The outer wall has a watchman's gallery. The double altarpiece was painted by the local artist Poul Høm.

If you're here with children, drop in on the nearby **Bornholms Middelaldercenter** (tel: 56 49 83 19; July–mid-Aug Mon–Sat 10am–5pm, May–June and mid-Aug–Sept Mon–Fri 10am–4pm; charge), an activity-packed introduction to the medieval age. The reconstructed town comes alive in summer, with craft demonstrations, performances, a bustling July market, bonfires and booming cannons.

Bornholm by bike

The best way to travel around Bornholm is by bicycle. An extensive network of cycle paths has been established, and it's easy to find houses, hotels and campsites en route. The island's residents often rent rooms or houses to visitors, but remember to book accommodation in advance during the summer months, especially in the southeast part of the island, where the wonderful beaches of **Dueodde ⑪** and **Balka** in particular attract crowds of holidaymakers in high season. ❑

Cycling is the best way to get around Bornholm, and there are plenty of places you can rent bikes from.

BELOW: Gudhjem village, on the north coast.

FUNEN

Bridging the water between Zealand and Jutland is the island of Funen, the "Garden of Denmark", with the buzzing cultural centre of Odense at its heart

Denmark's central island of **Funen** (Fyn in Danish) is known as "the Garden of Denmark" for its natural beauty, flowered gardens, castles and manor houses. Here, too, lies historic Odense, the birthplace of author Hans Christian Andersen *(see page 149)*. South Funen and the island archipelago are a paradise for anglers and yachtsmen.

Funen is linked to Zealand by the mighty Store Bælt bridge and to Jutland by the Lille Bælt bridge, and the E20 runs straight across the island. However, the most satisfying way to appreciate Funen's finer aspects is slowly, by the power of your pedalling feet. There are hundreds of kilometres of marked routes, allowing you to lean your bike beside one of the little white-washed churches to take a look inside, and inhale the scent of the wild flowers that lie beneath roadside rose hedges.

Northeast Funen

Nyborg ❶ is the first Funen town on the eastern coast; before heading north for Kerteminde and the Hindsholm peninsula, take a look at **Nyborg Slot** (tel: 65 31 02 07; Apr–May and Sept–Oct Tue–Sun 10am–3pm, June and Aug until 4pm; charge), which dates from 1170. It was built to defend the country from the Wends of north Germany and, during the Middle Ages, was the meet-ing place for the monarchy, nobility and clergy. However, in 1722, much of Nyborg Slot was demolished to provide building materials for Odense Castle. Part of the original ramparts and moat remain, and the castle has a fine interior of great echoing, empty rooms.

About 15km (9 miles) north, near Kerteminde, are the remains of a Viking chieftain's burial ship at the **Viking Museum** (Vikingemuseet; June–Aug daily 10am–5pm, Mar–May and Sept–Oct Tue–Sun 10am–4pm, Nov–Feb Tue–Sun noon–4pm; charge) at **Ladby ❷**.

Main attractions
VIKING MUSEUM, LADBY
ODENSE
DEN FYNSKE LANDSBY
EGESKOV CASTLE
ÆRØ ISLAND
TICKON SCULPTURE PARK, LANGELAND
LANGELANDSFORT, LANGELAND

LEFT: young visitor at Hans Christian Andersen's house in Odense.
RIGHT: a vintage wooden ship.

Kerteminde ❸ is Funen's foremost fishing village, with old half-timbered houses and a reputation for its stoneware and pottery.

Odense

In the centre of Funen lies quaint but lively **Odense ❹**, Denmark's third-largest city (pop. 190,000). The Gothic cathedral, **Skt Knuds Domkirke**, is one of its most beautiful landmarks. It was named after King Knud (Canute) II, who was murdered in the town in 1086 by his rebellious subjects and later canonised by the Pope. It's adorned with a gilded altarpiece made by Claus Berg in Germany in 1521. In the crypt lie the remains of Skt Knud.

Munkemøllestræde (July–Aug daily 10am–4pm, Sept–June Tue–Sun 11am–3pm; charge), west of the cathedral, is the cobblestone street where the storyteller Hans Christian Andersen grew up in the early 1800s. Northeast of the cathedral is the outstanding **Hans Christian Andersen Museum** (Bangs Boder 29; tel: 65 51 46 01; Sept–June Tue–Sun 10am–4pm, July–Aug daily 9am–5pm; charge). The museum's collection is devoted to the writer's life, with manuscripts and other personal belongings.

Denmark's foremost composer, Carl Nielsen (*see page 149*), spent his early

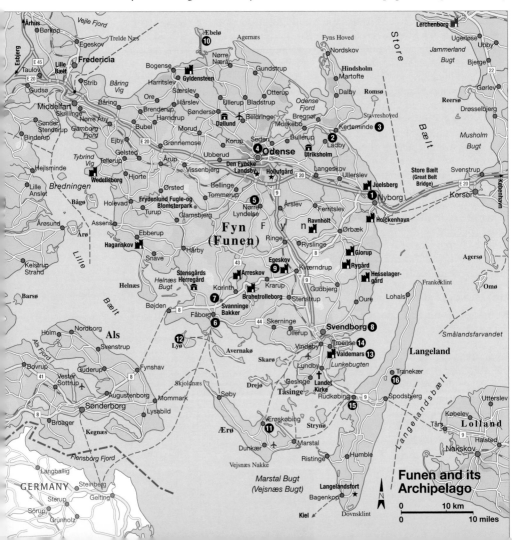

years in the city, and the **Carl Nielsen Museet** (Claus Bergs Gade 11; tel: 65 51 46 01; June–Aug Wed–Sun 11am–3pm, Sept–May Wed–Fri 3–7pm, Sat–Sun 11am–3pm; free) is devoted both to his life and work and to that of his wife, Anne Marie Nielsen, a sculptor. His childhood home can be visited at **Nørre Lyndelse ❺** (tel: 65 51 46 01; May–Sept Tue–Sun 11am–3pm; charge), 15km (9 miles) south of Odense.

Few other cities have a river that is clean enough to offer fishermen sea trout and eel: an accomplishment for a once-polluted industrial centre. Today, the quarter around the old factory buildings at Kongensgade and Vestergade has been revitalised and is a popular destination for leisure-seekers. The former textile mill, **Brandts**, off Vestergade, is now a multipurpose cultural centre, complete with **Museet for Fotokunst** (Museum of Photographic Art); **Kunsthallen** art gallery, featuring a varied programme of exhibitions; **Danmarks Mediemuseum** (Danish Media Museum); and **Tidens Samling** (Time Collection), which follows daily life and fashion since 1900 (all Tue–Wed, Fri–Sun 10am–5pm, Thur noon–9pm; charge), plus cafés, bars and concert halls.

Just south of Odense is a delightful spot, **Den Fynske Landsby** (Funen Village, Sejerskovvej 20; tel: 65 51 46 01; Apr–June and mid-Aug–mid-Oct Tue–Sun 10am–5pm, July–mid-Aug daily 10am–6pm; charge). It contains old farm buildings from different areas, with a vicarage, workshops, a windmill and watermill.

South Funen

Fåborg ❻ on south Funen is a peaceful little town where **Klokketårnet**, Europe's largest carillon, chimes out a hymn four times a day (closed for renovation during 2011). Other low-key attractions include **Fåborg Museum for Fynsk Kunst** (Grønnegade 75; tel: 62 61 06 45; Apr–Oct daily 10am–4pm, Nov–Mar Tue–Sun 11am–3pm; charge), an art gallery featuring the "Funen artists"

(1880–1920), including Peter Hansen, Fritz Syberg and Johannes Larsen, with sculptures by Kai Nielsen.

The heather-covered **Svanninge Bakker ❼**, about 10km (6 miles) north of Fåborg, is a national park. Heading eastwards, **Svendborg ❽** is a beautiful market town and makes a good centre for touring. Along with Fåborg, it is the gateway to the southern islands.

The unmissable **Egeskov Slot ❾** (tel: 62 27 10 16; May–Sept daily 10am–5pm, closes later in summer; charge), 14km (9 miles) north of Svendborg, is one of Denmark's most famous historic sights, a moated castle set in magnificent Baroque and Renaissance gardens. Egeskov means oak forest – legend says that an entire forest of the trees was felled around 1540 to form the piles the castle stands on. The castle and grounds are filled with wonders, including a mysterious *Wooden Man* sculpture, the awesomely detailed doll's house **Titania's Palace**, three **mazes**, a tree-top walk and nine museums, including a **Veteranmuseum** (Veteran Motor Museum), containing a fine collection of vintage cars, aircraft and motor cycles.

Take a ferry to the island of Ærø, where the main town, Ærøskøbing, is filled with cobbled streets and brightly coloured houses.

BELOW: book sale on Funen.

TIP

Whether driving, cycling or walking, follow the "Daisy Routes" marked by a flower sign. These guide you past some of the most beautiful scenery in Funen.

Along the west coast

From Fåborg, turn northwest to explore Funen's west coast. Around 15km (9 miles) north from Assens on the road to **Middelfart**, a broad west-facing bay at **Tybrind Vig** is a site for underwater archaeology. North of Middelfart, dramatic steep cliffs line the shore.

About 3km (2 miles) east of **Bogense** is the castle of **Gyldensteen**, a late Renaissance building with an impressive gatehouse (closed to the public). Here, Karen Blixen (pen name Isak Dinesen), author of *Out of Africa*, wrote some of her books during the German Occupation of Denmark in World War II. From Bogense, you can complete the Funen circle by touring along the sparsely populated north coast to the Hindsholm peninsula and Kerteminde. At low tide you can walk to the island of **Æbelø ⑩**, an unspoilt landscape rich in wildlife.

To the islands

You could spend a lifetime trying to visit all the islands of the Funen archipelago and still miss a few. Only 19 are inhabited permanently, and even the largest hold no more than a few thousand people. You can take day trips aboard wooden sailing ships or longer cruises through the archipelago. This is also an angler's paradise.

From Fåborg, it is a short trip to the most beautiful island of all, **Ærø**. Hire a bike for the short ride from Søby to **Ærøskøbing ⑪**, the main town of cobbled streets and brightly coloured houses, and on to the old naval port of **Marstal**. Cycling is easy, and the roads wind past fertile fields, thatched farmhouses, medieval churches and windmills. From Fåborg, ferries also run to the smaller islands of **Avernakø** and **Lyø ⑫**; both have good inns.

Svendborg is the ferry port for the southern islands. The first island, reached by a narrow bridge, is **Tåsinge**, with some 6,000 inhabitants. **Valdemars Slot ⑬** is one of Denmark's oldest privately owned castles, with a wonderful view over Svendborgsund (tel: 62 22 61 06; June–Aug daily 10am–5pm, May and Sept Tue–Sun 10am–5pm; charge). It was built in 1640 by King Kristian IV for one of his sons, Prince Valdemar Kristian. Most interesting is the castle church, with an excellent restaurant beneath. Beyond the Tea Pavilion, mirrored in its own lake, is a tiny swimming beach beside Lunkebugten Bay. The loveliest village on Tåsinge is **Troense ⑭**. Watching the slim masts of the sailing boats gather in the harbour against a darkening sea is one of the most satisfying pleasures of a Funen summer.

Langeland, literally "long land", is connected to Tåsinge by a bridge. H.C. Ørsted, the discoverer of electromagnetism, was born in the main town of **Rudkøbing ⑮**.

North at **Tranekær ⑯** lies TICKON, a peaceful wooded sculpture park. To the south is fascinating **Langelandsfort** (May–Sept 10am–5pm, Apr and Oct 10am–4pm, last admission one hour before closing; charge), a Cold War listening station with cannons, bunkers, planes and a U-boat. To the south, **Ristinge** and **Bagenkop** both have excellent bathing beaches. ❏

BELOW:
the majestic
Egeskov Castle.

Andersen and Nielsen: Funen's Famous Sons

In the 19th century, two Funen boys, the storyteller Hans Christian Andersen and the composer Carl Nielsen, set off to make their fortunes in the world

Two of Denmark's most noted literary and musical figures, Hans Christian Andersen and Carl Nielsen respectively, were born on the island of Funen. At the height of his fame, the composer Carl Nielsen (1865–1931) told an audience that his mother had always said to him: "Don't forget that Hans Christian Andersen was a poor boy like you." There may have been something in the Funen air that inspired poor boys to rise to fame, but it is more likely that Nielsen was inspired by Andersen, 60 years his senior. Both came from humble homes, both left Odense to seek their fortune in Copenhagen.

Andersen (1805–75) was born in Odense, the son of a shoemaker and a washerwoman, and spent his childhood in a small half-timbered house in Munkemøllestræde, now a museum. Quite apart from his skill as a writer, Andersen had a good singing voice and was a gifted artist. At the age of 14 he set off to Copenhagen to attend the Royal Theatre School. The Theatre Board recognised his skills, and he was found a place at a grammar school in Helsingør.

After school, Andersen travelled widely; *Shadow Picture of a Journey to the Harz Mountains and Saxony* (1831) was the result of his early adventures.

Throughout his life he continued to write poems, novels and plays. His autobiographical novel, *The Improvisatore*, described the rise to fortune of a poor Italian boy. His early fairy tales, including *The Tinder Box* and *The Princess and the Pea* (1835), brought him immortality. In spite of his worldwide fame and extensive travels, Andersen's personal life was a lonely one. In 1840 he met and fell in love with the singer Jenny Lind, "The Swedish Nightingale", but his love was unrequited – she always called him "brother". His fairy tale *The Nightingale* was inspired by her. When he was made an honorary citizen of Odense in 1867, Andersen said it was "an honour greater than I had ever dreamt of".

Carl Nielsen was born in Nørre Lyndelse, where his childhood home is now a museum. His father was a folk musician and Carl played the violin. His earliest compositions, at the age of eight, were two dance tunes. Like Andersen, Nielsen wrote an autobiography, *My Childhood in Funen*. At the Royal Theatre Orchestra in Copenhagen, where Nielsen became second violinist, the Norwegian conductor Johan Svendsen encouraged him to compose. At 25, Nielsen won a fellowship which allowed him to travel, and went to Dresden to steep himself in Wagner's ideas. Nielsen composed two operas: the dark drama *Saul og David*, and a comic opera, *Maskarade*, along with symphonies and choral works, such as *Hymnus Amoris*.   ❑

TOP LEFT AND RIGHT: Hans Christian Andersen and composer Carl Nielsen. **RIGHT:** artefacts at the Hans Christian Andersen House.

JUTLAND

The dune-fringed shores of Jutland have captured the imagination of both painters and holiday-makers, while music-lovers head for Århus, "the world's smallest big city"

J utland (Jylland) is the Danish peninsula that juts up above Germany, the "mainland" in this nation of islands. When Copenhageners talk about the provinces, they usually mean Jutland. Nuggets of Denmark's oldest and richest history – prehistoric bog bodies and Viking runestones – are to be found here, as well as youthful attractions like Legoland. Jutland's rolling hills are crisscrossed with rivers, patched with forests, crusted with castles and edged in fine sandy beaches.

Jutland's capital city

Århus ❶ (pop. 311,000), Denmark's second-largest city, is a lively university town known for its music, theatre, ballet, art and cafés, and its fun Festival Week in early autumn. The pointed spire of the **Cathedral of St Clement** (Domkirken; May–Sept Mon–Sat 9.30am–4pm, rest of year 10am–3pm; charge to tower) is 93 metres (316ft) high and offers a superb view from its belfry. Nearby are the winding, cobblestone streets of the Latin Quarter, with quirky boutiques and trendy cafés and restaurants. **ARoS Århus Art Museum** (Kunstmuseum; tel: 87 30 66 00; Tue, Thur–Sun 10am–5pm, Wed until 10pm; charge) gives an overview of Danish art from the 18th century to the present. The **City Hall** (Rådhus)

was built in 1941 and designed by Arne Jacobsen, one of Denmark's most notable architects and designers.

Den Gamle By (Old Town; tel: 86 12 31 88; all year, times vary; charge) is an open-air, national museum of culture and history, with reconstructions of 75 Danish town buildings – with merchant and artisan houses and workshops, gardens, shops, stalls, streets and alleys.

One of the best museum exhibits in Denmark is the 2,000-year-old Grauballe Man at the **Museum of Prehistory** (Moesgård Museum; tel: 89 42 11

Main attractions
ÅRHUS
GRAUBALLE MAN,
MOESGÅRD MUSEUM
LEGOLAND
RIBE
LINDHOLM HØJE
JELLING STONES
BLÅVANDS HUK
AALBORG
SKAGEN PENINSULA AND THE
GRENEN HEADLAND

LEFT: dappled forest of east Jutland.
RIGHT: the open-air museum in the Old Town of Århus.

Jutland

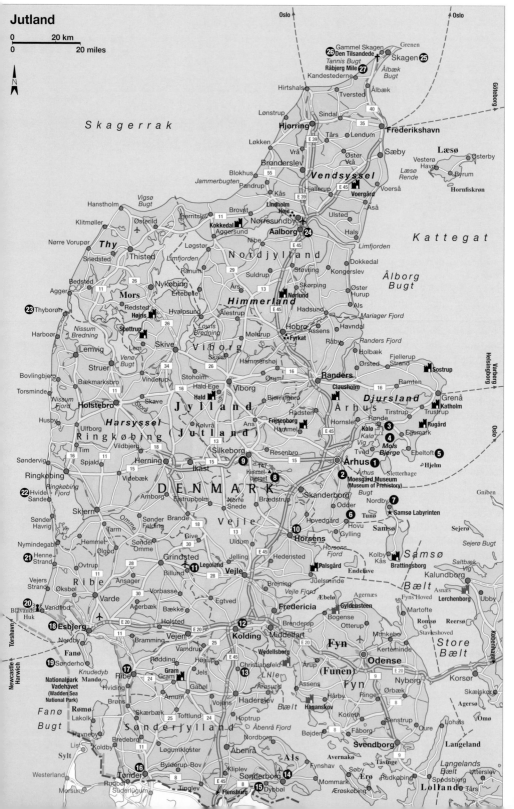

00; Apr–Sept daily 10am–5pm, Oct–Mar Tue–Sun 10am–4pm; charge) at **Moesgård ❷**, 8km (5 miles) south of Århus. To stand centimetres from the twisted body of this Iron Age man, found perfectly preserved in a peat bog in 1952, is a chilling experience.

The ruins of **Kalø Slot ❸**, built in 1313, stand on a small island north of Århus bay, linked to the mainland by a causeway. The nearby hills of **Mols Bjerge ❹**, where Viking relics abound in beautiful nature, are well worth a visit. Several artists have set up shop on the pretty Djursland peninsula.

Samsø island

West of Mols Bjerge is the immaculate town of **Ebeltoft ❺**, with its small, unaltered town hall from 1789. The island of **Samsø** can be seen from here, but it must be reached by ferry from **Hovu ❻**, 25km (15 miles) south of Århus. A haven for artists, farmers and naturelovers alike, Samsø is renowned for its new potatoes and cheese – and wind turbines. The Baltic island is one of the first industrialised places in the world to be entirely energy self-sufficient.

Nordby ❼, on the northern tip, contains a wealth of colourful cross-beam houses, as well as small art galleries. Also worth a visit in Nordby is **Samsø Labyrinten**, the world's largest permanent maze (tel: 86 59 66 59; public holidays and July–mid-Aug daily 11am–5pm; charge). Its 5km (3 miles) of passages wind through a dense fir forest covering 6 hectares (15 acres).

Lake district

A series of lakes snake through forested hills west of Århus, and a fun way to see them is from the paddle steamer MS *Hjejlen* (tel: 86 82 07 66; www.hjejlen.com; May–Sept daily 9am–5pm), which has carried passengers from Ry to Silkeborg since 1861. For a bird's-eye view, climb **Himmelbjerget ❽** (Sky Mountain), at 147 metres (482ft) one of Denmark's highest "mountains". The nearby town of **Silkeborg ❾** features **Museum Jorn** (tel: 86 82 53 88; Apr–

Oct Tue–Sun 10am–5pm, Nov–Mar Tue–Fri noon–4pm, Sat–Sun 10am–5pm; charge), built around the glorious, playful work of the painter Asger Jorn and others from the 20th-century CoBrA group. **Silkeborg Museum** (tel: 86 82 14 99; May–Oct 10am–5pm, Nov–Apr Sat–Sun noon–4pm; charge) houses one of Denmark's best-known bog bodies, Tollund Man.

Further southeast, historical **Horsens ❿** hosts an annual Middle Ages Festival on the last weekend in August, which is highly recommended (www.middelalderfestival.dk). **Billund**, 50km (31 miles) southwest of Horsens, is the home of **Legoland ⓫** (*see right*; tel: 75 33 13 33; Apr–Oct from 10am, closing hours vary; charge).

South Jutland

South Jutland has some of the most patriotic Danes in the country, particularly the generations who remember the area when it was officially part of Germany's Schleswig duchy from 1864 to 1920. **Kolding ⓬** was a border town on the Danish side at the time, and historical sights abound. Of particular

Legoland, a miniature world created from more than 59 million Lego bricks. Lego was developed by Ole Kirk Christiansen and his family in Billund in 1949.

BELOW: the Tollund Man exhibit at Silkeborg Museum.

TIP

South Jutland is known for its meats – particularly salamis and beer sausages. A good place to stop for the local speciality of "marsh sausage" is the Rudbøl Grænsekro, an inn in the village of Rudbøl (southwest of Tønder) that has been serving this delicacy since 1791.

RIGHT: a boat-shaped grave at the Viking burial site of Lindholm Hoje.

interest are the remains of **Koldinghus Slot** (tel: 76 33 81 00; daily 10am–5pm; charge), a castle built in 1268, and **Trapholt** (tel: 76 30 05 30; Tue–Sun 10am–5pm, Wed until 8pm; charge), with a fine collection of modern art.

Driving south 15km (9 miles), the Danish Moravian town of **Christiansfeld ⑬** is famous for its scrumptious honey cakes. Further south, close to the German border, **Sønderborg ⑭** is a striking town on **Als Island**, with a colourful harbour and the mighty **Sønderborg Slot** (tel: 74 42 25 39; May–Sept daily 10am–5pm, Apr and Oct 10am–4pm, Nov–Mar Tue–Sun 1pm–4pm), a fortress built around 1100.

Just to the west, **Dybbøl ⑮** was a key battlefield in the 1864 war with Germany; the Danish army suffered a huge defeat. **Dybbøl Mill**, restored and painted white, is now a national historic park and its Dybbøl Banke history centre (tel: 74 48 90 00; Apr–Oct daily 10am–5pm; charge), dedicated to the battle, is open to the public.

On the western side of south Jutland is **Tønder ⑯**, a lace-making centre in the 17th century, documented in

Tønder Museum (tel: 74 72 89 89; June–Aug daily 10am–5pm, Sept–May closed Mon; charge). Tønder has attractive 17th- and 18th-century houses, many with distinctive painted doorways, and hosts Denmark's biggest **folk festival** at the end of August. At **Møgeltønder**, 3km (2 miles) to the west, the village street is lined with lime trees. **Schackenborg Slot** is home to Prince Joachim (fourth in succession) and his second wife, Princess Marie, who were married in May 2008.

Ribe

Ribe ⑰, built around its 12th-century cathedral, celebrated its 1,300th anniversary in 2010 and ranks high on the list of historic centres in Scandinavia. Its brick and half-timbered houses, courtyards and *kroer* (inns) are much as they were hundreds of years ago. **Ribe Cathedral** (Domkirke; tel: 75 42 06 19; May–Sept Mon–Sat 10am–5pm, Sun noon–4pm, Apr and Oct Mon–Sat 11am–4pm, Sun 11am–4pm, Nov–Mar Mon–Sat 11am–3pm, Sun noon–3pm; church free, charge to tower) stands on the site of one of Denmark's earliest

The Jelling Stones and other Viking Landmarks

Viking sights abound in Jutland. **Lindholm Høje** (tel: 99 31 74 40; Apr–Oct daily 10am–5pm, Nov–Mar Tue–Sun 11am–4pm; charge), just north of Ålborg, is a necropolis with 700 graves, a reconstructed village from the early Iron Age and Viking times, and a museum. Many of the graves have been consructed in the shape of a Viking ship.

Elsewhere, near Hobro, is the Viking fort of **Fyrkat**. Four earth fortifications once enclosed 16 large houses on the site, and one of these longhouses has been reconstructed. Finds from Fyrkat are on display in **Hobro Museum** (tel: 99 82 41 70; May–Sept noon–5pm; charge). On the Mols peninsula near Århus is the **Poskjær Stenhus** barrow, which lies along the road from Agri to Grønfeld.

A memorial referred to as Denmark's "birth certificate" can be found in Jelling. The **Jelling Stones** (Jellingstenene) are covered with runic script that King Harald Bluetooth had carved over 1,000 years ago to proclaim his conversion to Christianity, and to honour his parents, King Gorm the Old and Queen Thyra Danebrod, who were buried in the mounds beside Jelling town church. For a flavour of life in Viking times, re-enactments, including battles and blood oaths, can be experienced at Moesgård, and in Jels in July.

wooden churches, built around AD 860. The "Cat Head Door" was said to be the entrance for the Devil. The choir has been stunningly decorated by CoBrA artist Carl-Henning Petersen, and there are splendid views from the tower.

Ribe continues the medieval tradition of night watchmen. On summer evenings at 8pm and 10pm, the watchman walks around singing the traditional songs that once told the people that all was well and they could sleep soundly.

Around Esbjerg

West Jutland has a sense of space and time different from the rest of the region. In winter, the weather can be rugged, with storms blowing in off a turbulent North Sea. In summer its sandy beaches are popular with holidaymakers. **Esbjerg** ⑱ is the biggest port town on the coast, the main gateway for ferries from Britain. The coastline south of here is part of the **Wadden Sea National Park** (Nationalpark Vadehavet) created in 2010 to preserve important wetlands, rich in bird and animal life. They are home to the spring and autumn **"Black Sun"** phenomenon, when up to one million starlings gather, their flight blotting out the sunset.

A 20-minute ferry ride away from Esbjerg is the island of **Fanø**, a major shipbuilding centre in the 18th and 19th centuries. **Sønderho** ⑲ village in the south of the island has colourful thatch-roofed cottages, an inn and Seamen's Church (1782). The island is characteristic of west Jutland: a superb stretch of white sandy beach, dunes, heath and forest.

Back on the Jutland coast, 30km (19 miles) northwest, is **Blåvands Huk** ⑳ lighthouse, a popular holiday spot with a nature reserve nearby. At the beach during low tide, you'll often see people hunting for nuggets of amber, a golden-coloured petrified tree resin that frequently washes ashore here.

Some 25km (16 miles) to the north, at **Henne Strand** ㉑, the restaurant at **Henne Kirkeby Kro** (tel: 75 25 54 00; Easter–Oct) is one of Denmark's finest.

Northwestern shores

A narrow strip of land runs north from Nymindegab to Søndervig, separating

The night watchman of Ribe, who recounts the town's history in song on his rounds.

BELOW: re-enacting history.

Shell-covered house at Thyborøn.

BELOW: church in the sands in Skagen. **RIGHT:** cyclists explore the lush countryside.

the sea from **Ringkøbing Fjord**, a broad, shallow, saltwater "lake". Driving north towards the fishing village of **Hvide Sande** ㉒, crashing North Sea waves can be heard, but are hidden from view by tall sand dunes. A walk to the top of these dunes is a breathtaking experience.

From here to the northern tip at Skagen, the scenery is similar, broken by several attractive fishing villages and bathing resorts. At **Thyborøn** ㉓, a local has decorated a house with shells, covering all surfaces, inside and out.

Aalborg

At its advantageous location for trade on the Limfjord, **Aalborg** ㉔ – Denmark's fourth-largest city, with a population of 199,000 – is full of historical buildings, castles and Viking monuments. The best-known building in town is the opulent six-storey **Stenhus** (Stone House) on Østerågade, built in 1624 by a merchant, Jens Bang. Bang was annoyed that he had never become a town councillor; on the south facade of Stenhus is a carving of him sticking his tongue out at the town hall across the

street. The tourist information centre (tel: 99 31 75 00) is across the street.

The town's main entertainment artery is **Jomfru Ane Gade**, lined with restaurants and bars in courtyards and half-timbered buildings. For a complete contrast, wander down to the new harbourfront, dominated by the **Utzon Center** – the last project of architect Jørn Utzon before his death in 2008.

In late May, the whole city goes carnival crazy, as 25,000 costumed revellers dance through Aalborg's streets.

Nordic light

Situated on a narrow piece of land with the North Sea on one side and the Baltic on the other, **Skagen** ㉕ has a magical quality. The air shimmers with a certain light that acted as an irresistible lure to the Skagen painters. They made it their home in the late 1800s, with Brøndums Hotel as their rallying ground. Works by Anna and Michael Ancher, P.S. Krøyer and Viggo Johansen can be seen in **Skagens Museum** (tel: 98 44 64 44; May–Aug daily 10am–5pm, Wed until 9pm, Sept–Dec and Feb–Apr Tue–Sun 10am–5pm; charge) and **Ancher's Hus** (Anchers House; tel: 98 44 30 09; May–Sept daily 10am–5pm, Apr and Oct Sat–Thur 11am–3pm, Nov and Feb–Mar Sat 11am–3pm; charge), bought by the Anchers in 1884. A few kilometres southwest is **Gammel Skagen** (Old Skagen), a cosmopolitan resort known for its sun-yellow homes with red-tiled roofs and its gourmet fish restaurants.

Just west of Gammel Skagen, the steeple of the **Sand Covered Church** ㉖ (Den Tilsandede; tel: 98 44 43 71; June–Aug daily 11am–5pm; charge) peeps out of the dunes. To see migrating dunes up close, you need go no further than **Råbjerg Mile** ㉗, 10km (6 miles) south of Skagen. Pushed by the wind and sea, the dunes travel as much as 20 metres (65ft) every year.

For a thrilling experience of nature, go to **Grenen**, 5km (3 miles) north of Skagen, Denmark's northernmost point. At the tip, you can actually see the North and Baltic Seas crash into each other. ❏

GREENLAND

In spring and summer when the ice retreats and the temperature rises, Greenland's spectacular landscape becomes accessible to some of the most adventurous travellers

The world's largest island is a place of stunning natural beauty, dramatic weather and fascinating culture. Greenland (www.greenland.com), like the Faroe Islands, is a former Danish colony, but it's well on its way to full independence, gaining self-government in 2009.

Greenland is like no other place. Its vast Arctic solitude is profound and its silence almost consumes you. Here, where the North Atlantic meets the Arctic Ocean, is the cleanest environment in the world, and measurably the oldest. Where else can you sip a drink cooled by a 1,000-year-old ice cube?

Greenland is called Kalaallit Nunaat (the land of the people) by its own people. They number only about 52,000 (plus an additional 6,300 Danes) in an area of 2,166,000 sq km (836,000 sq miles). The distance north to south is 2,670km (1,655 miles), and the widest part east to west is 1,000km (620 miles). Its closest neighbour is Canada.

More than four-fifths of the country lies under 3km (2 miles) of pack ice; but the southern coastal regions, especially to the west, are green and mild during late spring and summer. Daytime temperatures can climb to a balmy 21°C (70°F) or more, but northerly winds in winter can make the mercury plunge to a bone-cracking –32°C (–25°F). Spring and summer are excellent for hiking, camping and some of the best fishing anywhere.

Greenlanders

Greenlanders are Inuit and live in small towns around the coasts, mainly on the milder western side. Most of these people still earn their livelihoods by fishing and hunting, although oil, gas and aluminium smelting are flagged as future industries. Thanks to its long association with Denmark, Greenland has a modern infrastructure and burgeoning tourist industry.

Main attractions
NUUK
QEQERTARSUAQ (DISKO ISLAND)
ITTOQQORTOORMIIT
DOG-SLEDGING BETWEEN
  SISIMIUT AND KANGERLUSSUAQ
ILULISSAT ICEFJORD
AURORA BOREALIS

LEFT: Greenland coastal settlement.
RIGHT: an Inuit man fishing for halibut.

TIP

Helicopters are an important, often essential, means of transport here. Chopper tours are a breathtakingly beautiful way to travel around Greenland.

The capital is **Nuuk ❶** (Godthåb) on the west coast, the best place to explore the country's human history. The **Greenland National Museum** (tel: 32 26 11; 10am–4pm daily mid-June–mid-Sept, 1–4pm Tue–Sun mid-Sept–mid-June; charge) contains various artefacts, including traditional kayaks and Inuit costumes, plus the fascinating 15th-century Greenland mummies, discovered by hunters in 1972.

Dog-sledging and icebergs

The classic way of touring Greenland is by dog sledge, with the season running from late February to May. You can hire a team and driver for a short sightseeing tour or for a longer journey from many towns in western Greenland, including **Sisimiut ❷**, **Qeqertarsuaq ❸** (Disko Island) and points further north. On the barely populated east coast, you can dog-sledge from **Tasiilaq ❹** and **Ittoqqortoormiit ❺**. Tasiilaq, the largest town in the east, is also a popular summer destination, with its "Valley of Flowers" a beautiful spot for hiking, while the area around Ittoqqortoormiit is famous for its **hot springs**.

A classic, though physically demanding, dog sledge tour is the three-day trip between Sisimiut and **Kangerlussuaq ❻** at Søndre Strømfjord on the west coast, possible from February to April. The route takes you through the vast and beautiful landscapes of mid-Greenland, across frozen lakes and over hilly terrain. You sleep in hunting huts or tents.

Visitors arriving at Kangerlussuaq international airport don't have far to travel to see their first Greenland glacier. An easy day trip from Kangerlussuaq town takes you to **Russells Glacier**, a mere 25km (16 miles) away.

However, one of Greenland's most dazzling sights, near **Ilulissat ❼**, is the Icefjord, a Unesco World Heritage site, which includes the glacier Sermeq Kujalleq – responsible for calving 10 percent of all Greenland's icebergs. There are three marked hiking trails in this protected area; less active types can simply watch the huge icebergs from town as they float out into Disko Bay.

Wildlife and nature

Boat tours along the east and west coasts take you through sparkling seas

BELOW: dog-sledging through the snow.

Greenland

0   200 km
0   200 miles

alive with seals, walruses and whales. You can disembark at harbours and settlements for hiking trips, or dog sledge tours in season. Between ports, you sail past icebergs and glaciers. On land you might see reindeer and musk oxen, and polar bears have been spotted. Birdlife is not abundant in Greenland, but you can encounter Arctic terns, ravens, peregrine falcons and eagles.

A novel way of exploring Greenland's nature is aboard a traditional Inuit vessel – the kayak. Although full-on sea-kayaking here is only for experts, beginners can explore sheltered fjord waters from many towns.

This vast, half-frozen island draws an increasing number of anglers for trout and Arctic char in the lowland lakes, rivers and streams; and Greenland halibut, Norway haddock and cod off the coast. Fishing licences are required.

Among the spectacular natural phenomena in Greenland are the Northern Lights and the Midnight Sun. The aurora borealis occurs all year long but is only visible in a clear night sky in autumn and winter. These ethereal lights can appear as colourful curtains, veins of silk ribbon, or as ghostly souls flying to heaven. In summer, the Midnight Sun keeps the night sky blue.

Ruled by the weather

Some cruise ships include Nuuk on their itineraries; otherwise the only way to travel to Greenland is by air, with direct flights from Copenhagen and Keflavik, Iceland. Once in Greenland, sailing is an option, but schedules are highly dependent on the weather. The same applies to air services. In a climate which changes from hot sun and clear skies to a deluge of rain in a moment, the weather decides whether it's possible to keep to a plan made the day before. Many a visitor has been forced to "overnight" at **Narsarsuaq** ❽ in the south because aircraft couldn't land.

Most towns in Greenland have modern hotels in various categories of comfort. These and the local tourist offices are the best places to book excursions. The more footloose visitor may prefer a hostel, seaman's home or a cabin. Campsites are appearing and tent-roughing is permitted most places, so long as campers observe the rules of nature. ❑

TIP

If you travel to Greenland in summer, it's wise to take shorts, gloves, and everything in between, plus waterproof clothing. Light waterproof hiking boots are the most appropriate footwear.

BELOW: Greenland's icy waters.

A Greenlandic Diet

Traditionally, Greenlandic food is hunted food (seal, whale, reindeer, fish) packed with protein, and eaten frozen, raw, fermented or perhaps boiled over a fire of sticks and smoking heather. The national dish is *svaassat*, seal meat cooked with rice and onions. Another delicacy is *mattak*, pieces of whale skin with a thin layer of blubber.

But "Western" tastebuds won't suffer. Modern Nordic Cuisine has caught on in Greenland, with chefs making full use of the fresh ingredients on their doorstep. Try reindeer venison, honey-roast duck breast, musk-ox steak or Greenlandic lamb cutlets – some of the world's best, and all organic. Greenland's fabulous seafood includes trout, salmon, Atlantic halibut, redfish, whale, bay scallops and world-renowned Greenlandic prawns.

THE FAROE ISLANDS

The fruits of the sea have brought prosperity to the far-flung Faroe Islands. Visitors are attracted by the natural beauty and remarkable birdlife

The remote Faroe Islands lie far to the north of mainland Europe, halfway between Iceland and the Shetland Islands. The sailing distance between this self-governing Danish outpost and Copenhagen is around 1,500km (900 miles). But the trip is worth it: craggy, isolated, raw and alive, the Faroes were voted one of the world's top five island destinations by *National Geographic* magazine.

Although the Faroe islanders are prosperous with a high standard of living, everything is relative. Around 49,000 live on the 17 inhabited islands – a dozen more are home only to the huge colonies of birds. Much of the surface area is virtually bare rock, and only a few areas are habitable. As though to contrast with the muted blues, greens and greys of rocks, sea and hills, modern Faroese favour brightly painted houses. Traditional, living, green turf roofs are becoming popular once more.

Far north as the islands are, the Gulf Stream keeps the climate mild and moist. In the coldest month the average temperature is around 3°C (37°F), although wind chill makes it feel much colder. In the warmest, it reaches only 13°C (55°F). The weather is very changeable; one minute the sun is warm against the back, the next there is driving rain and mist.

The islands' name in Faroese, Føroyar, means "sheep islands" – there are around 20,000 more sheep than people, and lamb is a basic staple. Arable land is extremely limited. Small kitchen gardens have robust plants, leeks, cabbages, carrots. Outside, people hang fish and lamb to dry in the wind.

Tórshavn

The sea is serious business here, and nothing shows that more clearly than **Tórshavn's** ❶ harbour. It is stuffed with boats of all kinds – visiting ships,

Main attractions
TÓRSHAVN
KIRKJUBØUR
VESTMANNA BIRD CLIFFS
SAILING TOUR ABOARD THE
    URÐARDRANGUR
MYKINES ISLAND
FAROESE CULTURAL EVENINGS

LEFT: the turf-roofed church at Saksun set against the green Faroese landscape.
RIGHT: Tórshavn harbour.

The puffin is a Faroese delicacy, caught during the open season in July. The meat has a distinctively tangy flavour.

BELOW: lighthouses are scattered across the islands.

inter-island ferries, sailing boats and other pleasure craft and, most numerous of all, the fishing boats which disgorge their cargoes at one of the big fish processors scattered around the islands' coasts. The fishing fleet is one of the most modern in Europe. Fish products make up 95 percent of the country's export earnings.

The islands' long seafaring history is traced in the **Fornminnissavn** (National Museum; mid-May–mid-Sept Mon–Fri 10am–5pm, Sat–Sun 2–5pm; charge) at Hoyvik, 2km (1¼ miles) north of Tórshavn.

Kirkjubøur

The islands' first substantial settlers came from Norway in the 9th century. Even before that time, an early township had been the centre of life for a group of Irish friars who colonised the islands around the 8th century. The township was **Kirkjubøur ❷**, and today this tiny settlement in the south of Streymoy is the islands' most important historical site. The 14th-century ruins of Magnus Cathedral sit in melancholy splendour by the shore; while

Roykstovan (Smoke Room) is allegedly the oldest wooden structure in continued use in the world, built from logs that were towed from Norway.

In 1380, as Norway came under Danish rule, the islands, too, became part of Denmark and, when the union dissolved in 1814, the Faroes continued as a Danish county. The present system of Home Rule dates from 1948, and the Faroe Islands also send two representatives to the Danish Parliament.

The Western Islands

The Faroe Islands' only airport is on the western island of **Vágar**. Here, the towering faces of the stacks and cliffs are home to thousands of seabirds.

For the seafaring adventurer, boat operators sail from the neighbouring Streymoy village of **Vestmanna**, on an excursion of the islands to view the **Vestmannabjørgini ❸**, or **Enniberg** bird cliffs. The restored sloop *Urðardrangur* takes visitors on a tour of the islands, sailing into fjords and grottoes.

Boat excursions also run to the traffic-free island of **Mykines ❹**, which attracts birdwatchers from around the world.

The hike from pretty Mykines village (the only settlement on the island) to the Mykineshólmur Lighthouse is an exhilarating experience.

Walking and fishing

The Faroe Islands are full of excellent hiking opportunities through stunning terrain. Footpaths crisscross all the islands and were originally the main routes between settlements. Most of the trails are marked by cairns, but some of them are not regularly maintained, and it's imperative to carry a map and compass. The tourist information offices on all the islands provide free maps and arrange guided walks and accommodation.

Anglers may find great challenges in the islands' brooks and lochs, which are rich in trout and salmon. The season extends from 1 May to 31 August. Contact the tourist office in Tórshavn for permits and details (tel: 30 24 25; www.visitfaroeislands.com).

The Northern Islands

Klaksvík ❺, on **Borðoy** island, is the Faroes' second-largest town and an excellent base for exploring the northern islands in all their dramatic, windswept beauty. For an insight into life on the islands, visit the **Norðoya Fornminnissavn** (North Islands Museum; mid-May–mid-Sept daily 1–4pm) in a well-preserved 19th-century merchant's house.

Faroese festivals

The Faroese are proud of the rich culture and traditions of their islands, where the language, costumes and customs are kept very much alive. On festive occasions, such as the national St Olav's Day celebrations at the end of July in Tórshavn, everyone joins in the Faroese chain dance, a slow, hypnotic dance accompanied by chanting and schnapps (*akvavit*) drinking.

In the summer months several islands hold **Faroese Cultural Evenings**, encompassing literature, music, theatre and, of course, chain dancing. From early June to mid-August, the **Summartónar Music Festival**, a celebration of classical and contemporary Faroese music, is staged at venues around the islands. ❏

TIP

For the thirsty, Faroe is not the easiest place to find a drink. Alcoholic beverages are sold only at state-run monopoly stores (*Rúsdrekkasøla Landsins*). Hotels generally have fully stocked bars, as do restaurants.

BELOW: stacking hay Faroese-style.

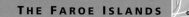

NORWAY

**Breathtaking scenery, historic sights
and modern cities are the big attractions
for the traveller to Norway**

Norway is synonymous with nature: abundant with majestic mountains and mysterious fjords, imposing waterfalls and glaciers, lakes and rivers, and a coastline littered with bays, inlets and thousands of islands. Its landscape is full of contrasts: beautiful and brutal, hospitable and hostile; barren rock submits to soft fertile plains. The Norwegians themselves have adapted rather quickly – the lusty Vikings have turned into global peacemakers. Norway has both urban excitement and rural tranquillity: shopping malls and Mercedes rub shoulders with compass and rucksack; high-technology parallels steadfast tradition. A thriving offshore oil industry has brought prosperity, and, as a consequence, social habits are changing rapidly; however, in a society where the divorce rate is high and cohabitation the norm, the home and family still remain important.

Oslo may be reputed as one of the most expensive cities in the world, but visitors are invited to share the wealth of its cultural and recreational offering. The Norwegian capital boasts a world-class Opera House, a renewed World Cup ski facility, an Intercultural Museum, Human

Rights Communication Center and a diversity of world cuisine. In less than two hours from the city, one can escape to charming hamlets with historic fortresses, open-air museums and manor houses.

Norway is a long, narrow strip of a country, stretching north from mainland Europe far into the Arctic. The ancient capital of Trondheim is 500km (350 miles) from modern Oslo, yet only a quarter of the way up the country's jagged coast. The southern coast is as far from Monaco as it is from the Nordkapp (North Cape), and Norway's northernmost outpost, the islands of Svalbard (Spitsbergen), are hundreds of kilometres further still. With a population of just less than 5 million, Norway has, above all else, space. ❑

PRECEDING PAGES: rocky outline of the Lofoten Islands; Jekteviken and Johannes church, Bergen, against a stormy sky. **LEFT:** Oslo café. **ABOVE LEFT:** Norwegian hats for sale. **ABOVE RIGHT:** look up to see the architectural detail.

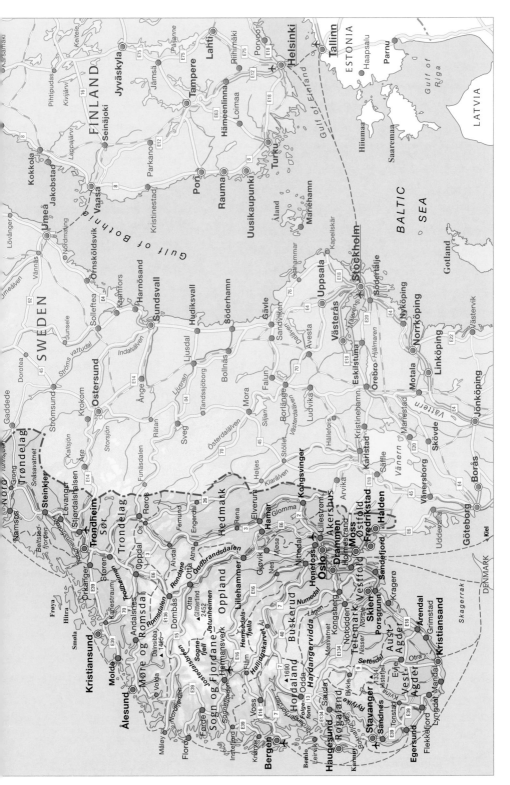

Strømsdammen Lake
Tryvannstårnet
Øvresetertjern
Frogner-setèren

Lillevann
Voksen-kollen
500
Frognerseteren

Skogen
Uttsikten
Voksenkollveien

Sørkedalsveien
Lillevannsveien
Voksenlia
Holmenkollveien

Bogstad camping-plass
Holmenkollen Ski Facility
Holmenkollen kapell

Bogstad Manor
Mältrostveien

Holmenkollen
Midtstuen

Ankerveien
Besserud

Oslo

Det Interasjonale Barnekunstmuseet
Emanuel Vigeland Museum
Frøen

BLINDERN

Borgenveien
Diakonveien
Tårnveien
Thaulows vei

Wilhelm Færdens vei
Kirkeveien

VESTRE GRAVLUND
Borgen

Gydas vei
Suhms gate
Slemdalsveien
Trudvangveien

Fagerborggata

Majorstuen

168

Colosseum senter

Frithjof Nansens vei
Sørkedalsveien
Valkyrie

Sporveismuseet
Misjons-kirken

Aalls gate
Suhms gate
Lyder Sag

Colosseum kino

Sorgenfri-gaten
Majorstuen

Jacob
Hammerstads gate
Ole Vigs gate
Schønings gate

Dovekirk

VIGELANDS-PARKEN

Bogstadveien

Schultz

Industrigata

Majorstuen

MAJORSTUEN

Ole Vigs gate
Vibes gate
Rosenborggata

Monolitten

Frogner stadion

Jacob Aalls gate
Majorstuveien
Gjørstads gate

168

HEGDEHAU

FROGNERPARKEN

St Dominikus

Professor Dahls gate
Industrigata

Oslo Bymuseet

R2

Fuglehauggata

Fearnleys gate

Prof. Dahls gate

HOMANSBYEN

Munthes gate

Briskebyveien
Uranienborgveien
Josefines gate

Hegdehaugsveien

Vigelandmuseet

Kirkeveien

Gydenløves gate

Sundts gate
Holtegata

Oscars gate

Gren

FROGNER

Nordraaks gate
Tidemands gate
Eckersbergs gate

BRISKEBY

Eilert
Sundts gate

Uranienborg

Oscars gate
Uranienborgveien

Kuns
Wer

Solheimgata
Frognerveien

Arno Bergs plass
President Harbitz gate
Skovveien

Camilla Colletts vei

SLOTTSPA

Olav Kyrres plass
Bygdøy allé

Odins
Elisenbergveien

Løvenskiolds gate

Niels Juels gate
Inkognitogata

Ridervolds plass

Det Kongelige (Royal Palac

Bygdøy allé
Drammensveien

Bygdøy allé
Frognerveien

Meltzers gate

Ridervolds gate

DRONNINGS-PARKEN

Frøyas gate
Thomas
Tostrups gate

Frogner
Gimle kino

Gabels gate

Skovveien
Colbjørnsens gate

Drammensveien
Ibsenmuseet

Båthavn

E18

American Lutheran Church

Bygdøy

Mogens Thorsens gate

Niels Juels gate

Universitets-biblioteket

RUSELØKKA

Sophus Lies gate
Stangs gate

Gabels gate

Frognerveien

Solligata
Cort Adelers gate
Huitfeldtsgate
Arbins gate
Løkkeveien

Observatorie-terrasse

Thomas Heftyes gate

Frederik
Stanges gate

Niels Juels gate

Drammensveien

Rikstrygdeverket

SKILLEBEKK

Frammensveien

Munkedamsveien

Parkveien
Observatoriegata
Reichweins gate

Bygdøy

Frognerkilen

Båthavn

Munkedamsveien
Oslotunnelen

AKER BRYGGE

Oscarshall slott

Oscarshallveien

Dronninghavnveien

Båthavn

Fjordshinsveien

Filipstadveien

Ferry port

Kongen

FILIPSTAD

Filipstadkaia

Tjuvholmen

Pipe

Norsk Folkemuseum (Museum of Cultural History)
Mellbydalen
The Holocaust Center

Langviksveien

Dronningen

Filipstadutstikker

Christian Benneches vei

Vikingskipshuset (Viking Ship Museum)

Kon-Tiki Museet
Frammuseet

Oslo

0   500 m
0   500 yds

Langvikbukta
Bygdøynesveien
Lachenveien

Norsk Sjøfartsmuseum (Maritime Museum)

Oslofjord

Denmark, Germany

Hellviktangen Manor, Nesoddtangen

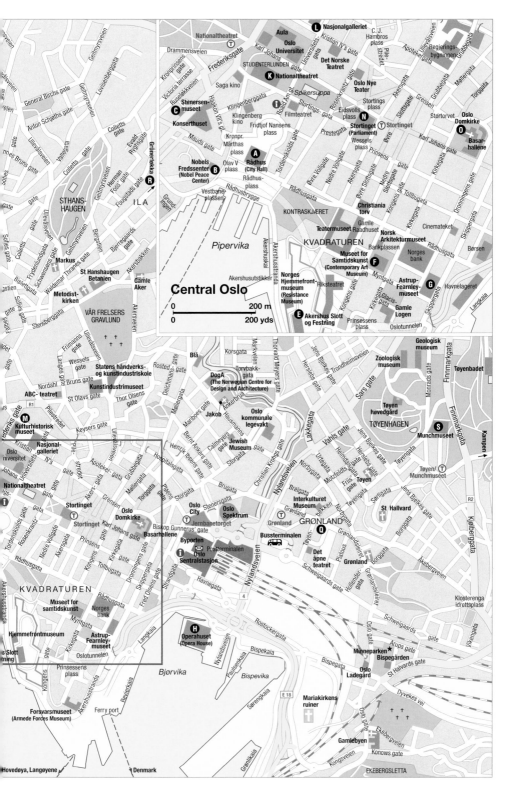

Central Oslo

0 — 200 m
0 — 200 yds

OSLO AND ITS FJORD

Norway's capital offers a lively mix of galleries,
museums, shops, restaurants and nightlife,
with magnificent forests, islands, ski trails
and the beautiful Oslo Fjord close at hand

O slo still ranks as one of the world's most expensive cities, but the "Nordic City of Light" has awakened to the attractions of city fun, and developed into an unexpected metropolis. In 2010 it was the only Scandinavian city to make it into the top 10 city break destinations at the World Travel Awards, the industry's biggest and most prestigious award worldwide. Oslo's cultural rebirth in recent years has been in part conscious, in part a natural outcome of injections of money in the right places. On the back of the oil boom came money for the arts and a flourishing of the arts scene. The new face of Oslo is represented by the magnificent white marble and granite Opera House, at the heart of the newly developing Bjørvika waterfront district.

But in many ways Oslo retains the features of the ideal city of the 19th century. Within easy walking distance (and this is a perfect city for walking in), nestled around the northern tip of the fjord and the central boulevard, Karl Johans gate, are all the accoutrements of a capital – the Royal Palace and its park, Parliament, City Hall, a castle, a cathedral, the National Theatre and excellent museums, the city's biggest draw. The attractions not in this compact grid of streets are just a few stops on the tram or T-Bane (Vigeland

Park, the Munch Museum, the Nordamarka wilderness), while the sights on the Bygdøy peninsula, Oslo's other big draw, are a short ferry ride away.

Waterfront Oslo

The ideal way to arrive in **Oslo ❶** is by boat, for then you get the most complete picture (though arriving by car from the south along the Mosseveien also offers some impressive views). The view from the fjord is dominated by the **City Hall ❹** (Rådhus; tel: 23 46 16 00; May–Aug daily 9am–5pm, Sept–

Main attractions

AKERSHUS CASTLE AND
FORTRESS
OSLO OPERA HOUSE
ROYAL PALACE
IBSEN MUSEUM
NATIONAL GALLERY
VIGELAND PARK AND
MUSEUM
GRØNLAND AND
GRÜNERLØKKA
MUNCH MUSEUM
HOLMENKOLLEN SKI
FACILITY AND SKI JUMP
VIKING SHIP MUSEUM AND OPEN-
AIR FOLK MUSEUM, BYGDØY
PENINSULA

LEFT: showing off a huge catch of plaice.
RIGHT: outdoor café, Aker Brygge.

Akershus Castle (tel: 22 41 25 21) and the University Aula (tel: 22 85 97 11) both stage classical music performances in summer, starting around 7.30pm. Another small concert venue is Den Gamle Logen (Grev Wedels plassen 2; tel: 22 33 44 70), which is closed in summer but stages concerts during the rest of the year.

Apr 9am–4pm; charge May–Aug), a large brick building topped by two square towers which overlooks the busy harbour. The imposing Modernist structure took 20 years to build – it was begun in the 1930s, but with the interruption of war, wasn't completed until the 1950s. The cavernous main hall is decorated with murals of Norwegian history and mythology, and the courtyard is adorned with bronze statues, a fine carved wooden frieze and the swan fountain. Every year on 10 December City Hall hosts the Nobel Peace Prize award ceremony.

On Rådhusplassen is the **Nobel Peace Center** ❸ (Nobels Fredssenter; www.nobelpeacecenter.org; daily 10am–6pm; charge; guided tours in English Sat–Sun, daily in summer), which opened in 2005 on the site of the Vestbane building, a former railway station. Exhibitions staged here focus on former Peace Prize laureates and topics such as war, peace and conflict resolution.

Just north of the Nobel Peace Center, the **Konserthus** (Concert Hall; Munkedamsveien 14; tel: 23 11 31 00), home of the Oslo Philharmonic, holds concerts

most Thursday and Friday nights, except in July. Across the road, the **Stenersen Museum** ❹ (Munkedamsveien 15; Tue–Thur 11am–7pm, Wed and Fri–Sun 11am–5pm) features three private art collections on Norwegian Realism, Modernism and the avant-garde from the 19th and 20th centuries.

The last remnant of Oslo's heavy industry, the Aker Shipyard, closed in 1982. In its place on the western side of the harbour is **Aker Brygge** ❺ (Aker Docks), a vibrant complex of shops, offices and apartments overlooking the fjord. The seafront boardwalk lined with cafés and restaurants is one of Oslo's most popular meeting places and teems with people in the summer months.

The Akershus complex

Across the harbour, with fine views of the fjord, stands the sprawling **Akershus Castle and Fortress** ❻ (Akershus Slott og Festning; castle: May–Aug Mon–Sat 10am–4pm, Sun 12.30–4pm, Sept–Apr, Thur by guided tour only, tour in English at 1pm; bastions and ramparts: 6am–9pm; free entrance to grounds). The major complex was begun in 1300, finished in 1308 and extended through the 17th century. It was built principally to defend the city against attack from Sweden. State events are still held in the beautiful ballrooms and the grounds provide the venue for summer concerts and theatrical performances. The Royal Chapel and Royal Mausoleum are open to the public.

In the fortress, the **Armed Forces Museum** (Forsvarsmuseet; Sept–Apr Tue–Fri 11am–4pm, Sat–Sun 11am–5pm, May–Aug Tue–Fri 10am–5pm, Sat–Sun 11am–5pm, Sept–Mar 11am–3pm Sat–Sun 11am–4pm; free) covers Norwegian military history from the Viking period on, and provides a fascinating insight into Norway's relationship with neighbouring Denmark and Sweden over the centuries.

Just outside the castle, the **Norway Resistance Museum** (Norges Hjemmefrontmuseum; tel: 23 09 31 38; June–Aug Mon–Sat 10am–5pm, Sun 11am–4pm,

BELOW: Oslo Opera House.

closes 4pm rest of year; charge), located at the place where Resistance members were executed by the Gestapo, gives a clear and detailed account (with English labels) of the intense and moving story of occupied Norway.

Bankplassen

Overlooking Bankplassen, an attractive square with fountain and trees, housed in the former Bank of Norway headquarters, is the **Museum of Contemporary Art ❶** (Museet for Samtidskunst; Bankplassen 4; Tue–Fri 11am–5pm, Thur until 7pm, Sat–Sun noon–5pm; free). An extensive collection of post-war Norwegian art is exhibited in its light and spacious environs, along with temporary exhibitions featuring top international artists.

In the nearby **National Museum of Architecture** (Norsk Arkitektur-museet; Bankplassen 3; same hours as Museum of Contemporary Art) exhibitions range from contemporary architecture to historical subjects.

A short walk east of the square, another interesting contemporary art collection can be seen at the **Astrup**

Fearnley Museum of Modern Art ❻ (Dronningens gate 4; tel: 22 93 60 60; Wed–Sun noon–5pm), which focuses on European and American works, with paintings by Francis Bacon and David Hockney, among others.

The Bjørvika Quarter

The stunning new **Opera House ❼** (Operahus; Kirsten Flagstads plassen 1; tel: 21 42 21 21; www.operaen.no; 50-minute guided tours in English, Sat–Sun throughout the year, daily in summer) opened in 2008 at a cost of 4.4 billion kroners (*see box below*). This no-expense-spared building is not just a cultural centre, but an inviting public space which draws visitors in their thousands. The Opera House is to be the cornerstone of a dynamic new residential, cultural and commercial district that is emerging in the old industrial port area of Bjørvika.

Karl Johans gate

All the main city sights are within easy walking distance of Karl Johans gate, central Oslo's main axis, which is pedestrianised through its eastern half

LEFT: alfresco diners.

Oslo Opera House

Sloping like an iceberg into the waves, Norway's dramatic harbourside Opera House opened in 2008 to international acclaim. The modern structure has pride of place on the waterfront, just a five-minute walk from Oslo S (Central) train station, out the south entrance and over the pedestrian bridge. The award-winning design by Norwegian architects Snøhetta is a truly Nordic concoction, built to resemble snow fields and floating ice, with fabulous acoustics. Norway's largest venue for opera and ballet has three stages, with seating for 1,364 in the main auditorium.

The Opera House was deliberately planned so that even non-opera-goers could find something to enjoy. Two sweeping slopes of Italian Carrara marble flank the main bulk of the building, allowing the public to stroll onto the roof, sunbathe, picnic – in short, to claim the building as their own. There is also a gift shop, bar, brasserie and Argent restaurant, for fine dining.

The harbourside location and radical design have lent the Opera House two unusual features. Much of the building is below sea level – orchestra members in the main auditorium actually sit 15 metres (50ft) "underwater". It's also the only opera house in the world to have its own underwater sea defences, a barrier to protect it should the Oslo–Copenhagen car ferry ever drift off course.

BELOW: the National Gallery and Historical Museum.
BELOW RIGHT: guardsman at the Royal Palace.

between the cathedral and Parliament building. Originally designed in 1826 by the royal architect H.D.F. Linstow, it was widened some 50 years later to become Oslo's answer to the Champs Elysées. Its western end merges into the broad avenue leading to the doors of the **Royal Palace** ❶ (Det Kongelige Slott; tel: 81 53 31 33; mid-June–mid-Aug, English guided tours daily, tickets on sale from Mar), the cream-coloured domain of the Norwegian royal family. The palace grounds are a pleasant public park (Slottsparken) that's free to enter. The changing of the guard takes place daily at 1.30pm.

Oslo's chic Westside quarter begins behind the Palace, leading up Byg-doy Allé to the Frogner quarter and Vigelandsparken (*see page 182*), where many 19th-century mansions housing foreign consulates can be found on romantic tree-lined streets.

On the south side of Dronnings-parken, the **Ibsen Museum** ❶ (Henrik Ibsens gate 26; tel: 22 12 35 50; www. ibsenmuseet.no; Tue–Sun noon–3pm; guided tours in English at noon, 1pm and 2pm; charge) incorporates the

apartment once occupied by Henrik Ibsen (1828–1906), Norway's most famous playwright and one of the world's great pioneers of social drama (*see page 89*). A comprehensive exhibition opened here in 2006 to commemorate the centenary of Ibsen's death.

A statue of Ibsen stands in front of the rococo **National Theatre** ❶ (Johanne Dybwads plass 1; tel: 22 00 14 00), which opened its doors in 1899. Norway's largest theatre, it is the venue of the International Ibsen Festival and Contemporary Stage Festival, which are held biennially in alternate years (late Aug–early Sept).

Alongside the National Theatre, opposite the main university building is the **Studenterlunden** (Students Park). In warm weather, this is a popular place for nearby office workers to have an alfresco lunch by the **Spiker-suppa**, a water feature that converts to an outdoor ice-skating rink in winter.

The Great Hall of the University (*Aula*), with its celebrated murals by Edvard Munch, is unfortunately no longer open to the public except for concerts and other special events (*see*

margin tip, page 178). If you have a chance to go there, it is worth it.

The National Gallery and Historical Musem

Just up the road is the splendid **National Gallery** ⓛ (tel: 21 98 00 00; www.nasjonalmuseet.no; Tue–Fri 10am–6pm, Thur until 7pm, Sat–Sun 11am–5pm; free), with a comprehensive collection of 19th-century Norwegian masterpieces, plus some French Impressionist paintings and Russian icons. The main attraction is a version of *Skrik (The Scream)* by Edvard Munch on display with some other of his best-known works, but there are many more lesser-known works to discover like the landscapes of J.C. Dahl and Kitty L. Kieland, and the powerful domestic portraits by Harriet Backer and Christian Krohg. For a more in-depth exploration of Munch's life and work visit the Munch Museum *(see page 183)*.

Behind the National Gallery is the **Historical Museum** ⓜ (Frederiks Gate 2; tel: 22 85 19 00; www.khm.uio.no; mid-May–mid-Sept Tue–Sun 10am–5pm, 11am–4pm the rest of the year; charge).

Dating to 1904, this museum occupies one of Oslo's most elegant Art Nouveau buildings. It covers Norwegian history over 9,000 years, and highlights the Viking Age and medieval times, with Scandinavia's largest collection of Viking gold. There are also displays on indigenous Nordic cultures.

Parliament to Oslo Cathedral

Back on Karl Johans gate, it's a short walk to **Parliament** ⓝ (Stortinget; Akersgate; tel: 23 31 31 80; one-hour guided tours in English on Sat 8 Jan–18 June, Mon–Fri 20 June–19 Aug, 10am, 11.30am and 1pm; free; it is advised to come 15 minutes early). The central building is where sessions are held and dates to 1866.

Further east on the pedestrianised section of Karl Johans gate, just before the main station, is **Oslo Cathedral** ⓞ (Domkirken; daily 10am–5pm). It was consecrated in 1697 after a fire destroyed its predecessor. The ruins of an even earlier cathedral, St Hallvard's, named after Oslo's patron saint, lie to the east of the city at Gamle Oslo,

Tucking into strawberries in the park.

BELOW: National Gallery.

A Green City

Oslo is committed to eco-friendly tourism. It is a "green" city, which means you pay a toll to bring in a car. The centre is easy to get around on foot, and the integrated transport system whisks you in less than half an hour to the hills, forests and fjords. Oslo declared itself a sustainable city a few years back, and has remained committed to backing up the claim. It won the European Sustainable City Award in 2003 for its efforts to reduce greenhouse gases, offer electric car-charging stations and enhance public transportation.

Recently described as "the world's biggest village", it was also honoured by *Reader's Digest* magazine as number 2 on a list of the world's greenest and most liveable cities, following Stockholm.

where the first city stood. Before going into the Domkirke, take a look at the stone relief to the right of the main entrance (*c.*1100). The 1718 tower clock is Norway's oldest. The interior owes its appearance mainly to a restoration completed in 1950, but the original design is typified by the organ front which now surrounds a modern organ. The stained-glass windows are the work of Emanuel Vigeland, and the ceilings were painted by Hugo Louis Mohr, depicting various biblical scenes.

The last stretch of Karl Johans gate leads to **Oslo Central Station** (Sentralstasjon), or Oslo "S," and a more hectic part of town, with shopping centres and city hotels.

Vigeland Sculpture Park

The works of one of Munch's contemporaries, sculptor Gustav Vigeland (1869–1943), dominate the **Vigeland Sculpture Park** **P** (Vigelandsparken; www.vigeland.museum.no; year-round; free) in Frogner Park to the west of the city centre, an extensive display of human life and emotion cast in stone and bronze. The most captivating piece

here is Vigeland's *Monolith*, a swirl of 121 intertwining figures carved from a single block of granite in a moving tribute to the human condition. A 10-minute walk south of the obelisk, at the edge of the park, is the newly renovated **Vigeland Museum** (Nobels Gate 32; tel: 23 49 37 00; charge). This was the artist's atelier and home in the 1920s and is full of sketches, photos, casts and sculptures linked to his work in the the sculpture park. Also within Vigeland Park is the **Oslo City Museum** (Bymuseet; tel: 23 28 41 70; Tue–Sun 11am–4pm; free guided tours Sun at 1.30pm), in the beautiful Frogner Manor House which explores 1,000 years of Oslo's cultural history and urban development.

A few blocks uphill near Slemdal T-Bane station is the **Emanuel Vigeland Museum** (Grimelundsveien 8; tel: 22 14 57 88; Sun noon–4pm; charge). Gustav Vigeland's brother, painter Emanuel Vigeland (1875–1948), was also fascinated by themes of life and death, and used them in the alfresco decoration of a mausoleum, entitled *Vita (Life)*, the museum's main attraction.

Eastern Oslo

Experience Oslo's multicultural environs by heading east of the centre across the Akerselva River to Grønlandsleiret and Smalgangen in **Grønland ○**. Here a wide variety of shops run by immigrants offer everything from exotic textiles and gold to kebabs, spices and saris. The **Grønland Bazaar** (Mon–Fri 10am–8pm, Sat until 6pm), at the corner of Tøyengata and Grønlandsleiret is a delight to all senses.

The newest addition to this lively quarter is the **Intercultural Museum** (Interkulturet Museum; Tøyenbekken 5; tel: 22 05 28 30; Tue–Sun 11am–4pm; guided tours in English on request, Sun 1pm; free). Housed in a converted police station, renamed the Grønland Culture Station, it produces diverse exhibitions on the history of immigration and cultural changes in Norwegian society. Its aim to promote respect for cultural diversity.

Follow Storgata north to explore the neighbourhood of **Grünerløkka ℝ**. Known as the Greenwich Village of Oslo, this former working-class area by the Akerselva River has been transformed in the last decade into a trendy quarter with cafés, restaurants, eclectic galleries and independent shops. Oslo's hippest bars and nightclubs are in the Grønland and Grünerløkka districts.

Southwest of Grünerløkka across the river the **Norwegian Centre for Design and Architecture** (DogA; Hausmanns gate 16; tel: 23 29 28 70; Mon–Fri 10am–5pm, Wed and Thur until 8pm, Sat–Sun noon–5pm; free guided tour every Sun at 2pm) occupies a restored power station next to Jakob's church. The changing exhibitions focus on design and architecture, and there is a shop, café and restaurant.

Housed in a former synagogue (1921), the **Jewish Museum** (Jødisk Museum; Calmeyers gate 15; tel: 22 20 84 00; Tue 10am–3pm, Thur 2–7pm, Sun 11am–4pm; charge) is both a cultural centre and museum tracing the history of Jews in Norway.

The Munch Museum

It's a worthwhile journey to the northeastern suburb of Tøyen to visit the **Munch Museum ○** (tel: 23 49 35 00; www.munch.museum.no; June–Aug daily

Vigeland's Monolith, *a mass of writhing bodies, in the Vigeland Sculpture Park.*

BELOW LEFT: revellers at a bar.
BELOW: at the Munch Museum.

Although Norway gave the word "ski" (meaning "piece of split wood") to the world, the language has no verb equivalent to the act of skiing.

10am–6pm, Sept–May Tue–Fri 10am–4pm, Sat–Sun 11am–5pm, Apr–Sept; charge), dedicated to the life and works of Edvard Munch (1863–1944), the painter and graphic artist who fathered German Expressionism (see box, page 91). The gallery holds thousands of paintings, drawings, photographs and engravings which the artist bequeathed to the city of Oslo. His *Skrik (The Scream)* is Scandinavia's most reproduced work of art, famously stolen in 2004 then recovered two years later. It was actually painted in two versions. The earlier, from 1893, is in the National Gallery of Oslo. What appears to be a somewhat later version hangs here. More important for promoting and spreading the image was the lithographic version from 1895, which is on display in the graphic section. Plans are afoot to transfer the Munch collection to new premises by the Opera House in the burgeoning Bjørvika quarter, in 2014.

Capital sports

High on the hills offering splendid views of the city is the **Holmenkollen Ski Facility ❶** (Kongeveien 5; tel: 22 92 32 00; www.skiforeningen.no; all year; free except during ski meets), which boasts a spectacular new World Cup arena, rebuilt for the 2011 Nordic (Trial) World Ski Championships. This prestigeous winter sport event started in 1892 and is the oldest in the world, drawing huge crowds for 21 different competitions. A few weeks later the Great Ski Jump is held, which also traditionally draws a huge crowd.

The centrepiece of the arena is the impressive **Holmenkollen Ski Jump**, which is part of a complex that includes the world's oldest ski museum and a ski-simulator, where you can experience how it feels to speed down the world's toughest slopes. The **Ski Museum** (tel: 90 01 20 46; 1 June–31 Aug 9am–8pm; Oct–Apr 10am–4pm, May and Sept until 5pm), which is situated within the ski jump, reopened in summer 2010. The exhibition traces 4,000 years of skiing history in Norway, and has added new films which feature downhill racing and ski jumping. Panoramic views of Oslo can be seen from the observation deck on top of the jump tower.

There's a café serving *smørbrød*, and the **Holmenkollen Restaurant** (tel: 22 13 92 00) serves good Norwegian dishes. The walk down to Holmenkollen station takes 10 minutes, and within half an hour you are back in the city.

The Bygdøy peninsula

It's a short ferry ride (or bus journey in winter) from the harbour across the bay to the Bygdøy peninsula. The first stop is Dronningen dock, a 10-minute walk from the **Viking Ship Museum ⓤ** (Vikingskipshus; Huk aveny 35; tel: 22 13 52 80; www.khm.uio.no; May–Sept daily 9am–6pm, Oct–Apr 11am–4pm; charge) featuring one of Oslo's top attractions: a trio of well-preserved Viking longships unearthed in southern Norway.

The **Norwegian Museum of Cultural History ⓥ** (Norsk Folkemuseum; Museumsveien 10; tel: 22 85 16 30; Mon–Fri 11am–3pm, Sat–Sun until 4pm; charge) is a sprawling open-air

BELOW:
Holmenkollen for skiing.

museum with more that 150 historic timber houses from around Norway and a beautifully restored stave church from 1200. Folk music and dancing are often performed in summer.

The pines and waters of Oslo were the training ground for Fridtjof Nansen (1861–1930) and Roald Amundsen (1872–1928), two of the greats of the heroic age of polar exploration. Their ships, *Fram* and *Gjøa*, are preserved in two other museums on the peninsula, the **Fram Museum**  (Bygdøynesveien 36; tel: 23 28 29 50; daily June–Aug 9am–6pm, May and Sept 10am–5pm, Mar–Apr and Oct 10am–4pm, Nov–Feb 10am–3pm; charge) and the **Norwegian Maritime Museum** (Norsk Sjøfarts-museum; Bygdøynesveien 37; tel: 24 11 41 50; mid-May–Aug daily 10am–6pm, Sept–mid-May 10.30am–4pm; charge). Both museums are accessed from the Bygdøynes dock (the next stop after Dronningen dock).

Nearby, the **Kon-Tiki Museum** (Bygdøynesveien 36; tel: 23 08 67 67; Apr, May and Sept daily 10am–5pm, June–Aug 9.30am–5.30pm, Oct–Mar 10.30am–3.30pm; charge) has a fine collection of Easter Island artefacts, as well as detailed displays of the pre-served *Kon-Tiki* and *Ra II* craft used by ethnographic explorer Thor Heyerdahl (1914–2002).

Outwards and southwards

If you stand at a vantage point in Oslo and look south down the fjord, almost everything in view is in Akershus county. Further south, the fjord is flanked on the east by Østfold county and on the west by Vestfold county. Aside from being home to one in three residents of the country, this area plays a key role in contemporary events and history.

In Akershus county, some 67km (42 miles) north of Oslo, lies **Eidsvoll**, a town that grew around the ironworks built in 1624, and closed in 1825; Eidsvoll might have been just another post-industrial town, save for the happenings of the spring of 1814. Following the dissolution of the union with Denmark, 112 representatives convened at the headquarters of the ironworks, then the only convenient large building, to draw up the Norwegian Constitution. **Eidsvoll 1814** (C. Ankersvei; tel: 63

Children will enjoy the old-fashioned candy store and horse and carriage rides at the Norsk Folkemuseum on Bygdøy peninsula (Museumsveien 10; daily; tel: 22 12 37 00).

LEFT: storehouse at the Norwegian Museum of Cultural History.

Oslomarka

Oslo's sporty profile is due in part to the closeness of outdoor recreation. On one side there's the fjord, a broad, sheltered expanse of water ideal for windsurfing and boating. On the other side is a huge woodland recreation area known as **Oslomarka** (Oslo's fields), covering some 1,700 sq km (656 sq miles). Here there are 2,600km (1,600 miles) of ski trails marked with red-painted slashes on trees and rings round sign-poles at trail intersections. The total length of the summertime walking trails is even longer; they are marked in blue, the difference being that red-marked trails can cross lakes and marshes frozen in the winter, while blue-marked trails cannot. Some 110km (68 miles) of these trails are illuminated until 10pm for night skiing, with their trailheads at car parks or underground stations, for ease of after-dark access. All the illuminated trails, as well as some 500km (300 miles) of other trails, are regularly maintained with tracks set by machine. Trail use is free, as cross-country skiing is regarded as part of public recreation. Along the trails, there are some 44 staffed lodges with lounges, cafeterias and toilets; most are open at weekends and during school holidays, and in the winter, some are open in the evening. There are also 16 Alpine ski lift hills and 48 ski jumps. For more information: www.skiforeningen.no

Traditional architecture in Drøbak, south of the capital.

BELOW: Moses with the Ten Commandments, Drobak Church.

92 22 10; May–Aug daily 10am–5pm, Sept–Apr Tue–Fri 10am–3pm, Sat–Sun noon–5pm, Oct–Mar Wed–Fri 10am–3pm, Sat–Sun noon–5pm; charge) is one of Norway's most important cultural monuments. **Eidsvoll Manor** is now a museum to the Constitution and includes the room where the document was signed on 17 May 1814. The country's first railway, built in 1845, connected Oslo and Eidsvoll, and it's now on the E6 highway, the major north–south artery.

Historic provincial cities and towns are scattered throughout Østfold and Vestfold counties. The best way to explore the counties, whether you travel by bus, car or boat, is via **Drøbak** ❸, which has become the Norwegian residence of Santa Claus – there is a shop in the centre (Julehus; daily) with a permanent Christmas exhibition and Santa's own post office. By road, you will pass Vinterbro, at the junction of the E6 and E18 highways, the location of **Tusen Fryd** ❹ (tel: 64 97 66 99; mid-June–mid-Aug daily 10.30am–7pm, early June to 4pm, May, late Aug and Sept weekends only; charge), the country's major amusement park.

Picturesque Drøbak grew out of a fishermen's settlement, and fishing vessels still dock to sell fresh catch on the quayside. Places of interest include the open-air **Heritage Museum** (Follo Museum; tel: 64 93 99 90; late May–mid-Sept Tue–Fri 11am–4pm, Sun 11am–4pm; charge) in Belsjøveien, the **Drøbak Aquarium** (tel: 64 98 87 80; daily June–Aug 10am–7pm, until 4pm the rest of the year; charge), and **Oscarsborg Fort** (Festning) out in the fjord, (guided boat trips from the harbour). Another point of pride is the cross-timbered **Drøbak Church** built in 1776, with an elaborately carved model of a ship inside, a common church decoration in seafaring towns.

Further south, **Fredrikstad** ❺ is a gem among Østfold towns, and Scandinavia's only completely preserved fortress town, dating from 1567. The **Oldtidsveien** (Highway of the Ancients), the 18km (11-mile) stretch of National Highway 110 between Fredrikstad and Skjeberg, has three **Helleristningsfelt** – literally "rock wall carving areas" with Bronze Age

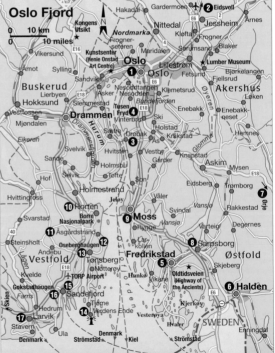

pictographs (free access to grounds).

Halden ❻, south of Skjeberg and close to the Swedish border, is dominated by **Fredriksten Fort** (Festning), a largely intact ruin with many of its buildings serving as small theme museums. In summer, passenger launches travel the **Halden canal** that runs through several sets of massive locks. The **Kanal Museum** (tel: 69 81 10 21; mid-June–mid-Aug Tue–Sun noon–6pm, Sept–Apr times vary; charge) at the locks at **Ørje ❼** displays the implements of canal operations. It also arranges charter tours on the *Engebret Soot*, named after the designer of the canal and now the world's oldest propeller-driven steamship in service.

Throughout Østfold, *Olsok* (St Olav's Day, 29 July) is celebrated with a great show of folk costume, music and dance. One of the best displays is at the **Borgarsyssel Museum** (tel: 69 11 56 50; mid-May–Aug Tue–Fri 10am–4pm, Sat–Sun noon–4pm; charge) in **Sarpsborg ❽**, north of Skjeberg.

Drive back to the E6 which takes you northwards to **Moss ❾** (where you can take the ferry to Horten and the Vestfold), then follow the local road through Moss to reach the small island of **Jeløy**. Visit **Galleri F15** (tel: 69 27 10 33; June–Aug Tue–Fri 11am–7pm; charge), a contemporary art museum in a 19th-century manor house.

Viking Vestfold

The Moss–Horten car ferry connects Østfold and Vestfold in just under an hour. The **Naval Museum** (Marinemuseet; tel: 33 03 33 97; May–Sept daily noon–4pm, Oct–Apr Sun only; free) at **Horten ❿**, home port of Sjøforsvaret (the Royal Norwegian Navy), bulges with maritime history. Horten also has the **Preuss Museum of Photography**, as well as a museum for vintage cars (all year; charge).

To the south lies the heart of eastern Viking country, and **Borre National Park** (all year; free access to grounds), en route to Tønsberg, contains large turf-covered mounds concealing the graves of Viking kings. Keeping to the coastline along Route 311, **Munch's House** (tel: 33 08 21 31; 1 May–31 Jan Sat–Sun 11am–6pm, 1 June–31 Aug 31 Tue–Sun 11am–6pm; charge) at

TIP

For a fun day out for all the family, head for the historic Hadeland Glassworks (Glassverk; www.hadeland glassverk.no) or Blaafarveværket Museum, "The Blue-Colour Works" – a former cobalt mine (www.blaa.no). Both these attractions are set in idyllic locations and can easily be reached by public transport from Oslo's main bus station (www.nettbuss.no).

BELOW: Fredriksten Fort.

TIP

A pleasant way to travel to fjord towns is by boat. Contact any travel agent or Trafikanten at Oslo S station for information on ferry and launch services (tel: 177; www.trafikanten.no).

Åsgårdstrand ⓫ is where the artist lived when in Norway. It was a setting for many of his paintings.

Between Åsgårdstrand and Tønsberg is a burial mound, **Oseberghaugen** ⓬, the most important Viking site yet discovered (all year; grounds free). Oslo's Vikingskipshus *(see page 185)* contains the finds, including the 20-metre (65ft) arch-ended wooden ship. Just south is historic **Tønsberg** ⓭, established in the 9th century. On the 65-metre (200ft) high **Slottsfjellet** are the fortress remains and tower. The main street, **Storgata**, is flanked by Viking graves. These were excavated and incorporated, under glass, into the ground floor of the new library.

The most renowned king to hold court in Tønsberg was Håkon Håkonsson IV (1204–63). The ruins of his court can be seen on **Nordbyen**, a street with historic houses. A more recent native son is Roald Amundsen, the polar explorer. The steamship *Kysten I* (built 1909), moored on Byfjord near the old customs house, operates a three-hour islands tour (July only) out to the skerries and it is a great way to see Norway.

Summer playground

South of Tønsberg, along the eastern side of the fjord, the islands of **Nøtterøy** and **Tjøme**, and the skerries, are fantastic summer hangouts. **World's End** ⓮ (Verdens Ende) is at the end of the chain. The old lighthouse here is a beautifully simple structure made of stone.

On the other side of Tønsbergfjord lies **Sandefjord** ⓯, a whaling town and home to Oslo's second airport. The town centre is compact, and near **Badeparken** are the former spa and the Old Town.

Just outside Sandefjord is another burial site, **Gokstadhaugen** ⓰ (all year; May–Sept guided tours; charge for grounds), in which the *Gokstad* ship, now in Oslo's Viking Ship Museum, was discovered in 1880. The **Vesterøy** peninsula is a supremely peaceful place, ideal for walking, cycling and boating.

Larvik ⓱ was home to two legendary boat-lovers, explorer Thor Heyerdahl and master boatbuilder Colin Archer (1832–1921), designer of the polar ship *Fram*. Archer's first house was at Tollerodden, on the fjord. At Larvik's back is Farris lake, site of the country's only natural mineral-water spring. ❑

BELOW: favourite ways to get around.
RIGHT: Norwegian wood.

SOUTHERN NORWAY

Norway's southern beaches and picturesque seaside towns are a magnet for summer visitors. The west coast is blessed with glorious fjords and the oil-rich city of Stavanger

D raw an upward arc on the map from Oslo in the east to Bergen in the west, and south of it you see the part of Norway where the majority of Norwegians take their home country holidays. They head for their seaside cottages, camp in the forests and by the lakes, or set sail to explore the islands and inlets. In clockwise order starting at Oslo, southern Norway can be divided into the principal regions of **Sørlandet** (southern country), comprising Telemark, Aust-Agder and Vest-Agder counties and their coasts around to about 7 o'clock; **Rogaland** county centred at the city of Stavanger on the west coast; and **Hordaland** county around Bergen.

Sørlandet

Norway's fifth-largest city, lively **Kristiansand ❶** is the unofficial capital of the southern coast. It's a busy summer resort with ferry connections to Denmark. In 1639, King Christian IV of Denmark and Norway selected the site of the city for a fort to control the approaches to the North Sea and the Baltic. You can visit what remains of **Christiansholm Festning** (fortress; tel: 38 07 51 50; 15 May–15 Sept daily 9am–9pm; free), which offers views of the harbour and coast from its stocky ramparts.

One of Norway's most visited attractions is **Kristiansand Dyrepark** (tel:

38 04 97 00; mid-June–mid-Aug daily 10am–7pm, times vary rest of year; charge), 11km (7 miles) east of the city, incorporating a zoo, wilderness park, water park and amusement park.

West of Kristiansand, the seaside resort and former timber town **Mandal ❷** boasts Norway's best sandy beach and a well-preserved centre of cobbled streets and white clapboard houses characteristic of this area. Beyond, the **Lindesnes Fyr** (lighthouse; all year; charge) marks the southernmost point of Norway. The last town before

Main attractions
CHRISTIANSHOLM FORTRESS
MANDAL BEACH
LINDESNES FYR LIGHTHOUSE
TELEMARK MUSEUM AND CANAL CRUISE, SKIEN
HEDDAL STAVE CHURCH
PREIKESTOLEN (PULPIT ROCK)
LAKSESTUDIOET AND RYFYLKE MUSEUM, SAND
OLD STAVANGER AND CATHEDRAL
SKUDENESHAVN, KARMØY
LANGFOSS WATERFALL
HARDANGER FJORD AND FOLK MUSEUM
CABLE CAR UP HANGURFJELL

LEFT: *Boy riding Bear* in the sculpture gardens. **RIGHT:** wooden houses in Kristiansand.

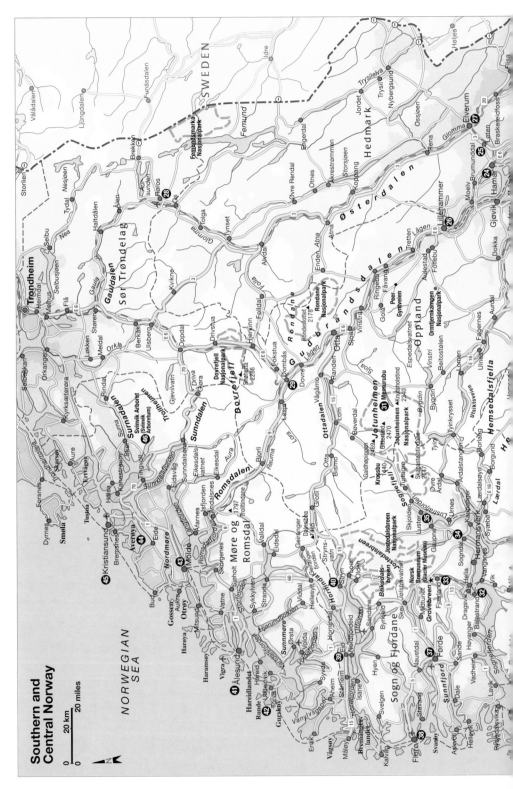

Southern and Central Norway

0   20 km

0   20 miles

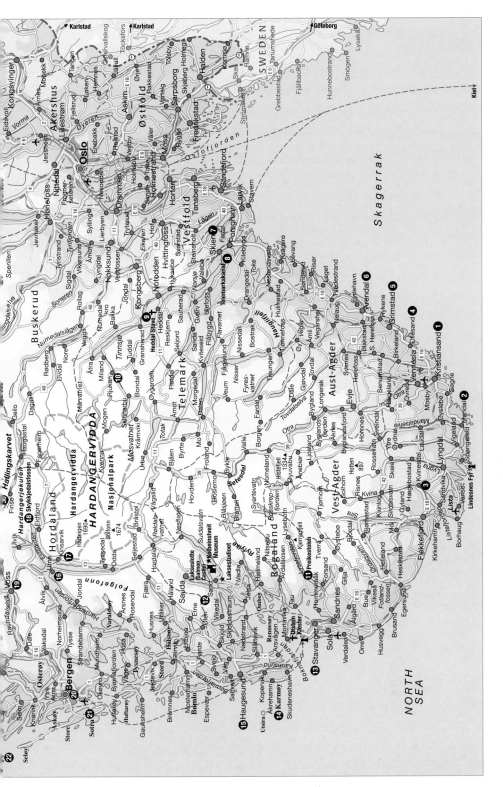

TIP

Express trains speed between Oslo and Kristiansand in 4 hours and 45 minutes, and between Kristiansand and Stavanger in 3 hours and 15 minutes.

Vest-Agder rises to meet Rogaland is the port of **Flekkefjord** and the idyllic island of **Hidra**. The terrain is mountainous, with many splendid waterfalls, especially around **Kvinesdal ❸**.

The Skagerrak coast

East from Kristiansand, the coastline of the Skagerrak strait is made up of islets, skerries and coves. It is relatively protected, but with rocky rather than sandy beaches. The principal centres along the coast, in order, are Lillesand, Grimstad and Arendal. **Lillesand ❹** is a popular holiday town with a lively harbour overlooked by white clapboard houses. Once a major shipbuilding centre, **Grimstad ❺** is now a pretty, laidback town, indelibly associated with Ibsen, who served his apprenticeship to a chemist here. Dating to 1916, the **Ibsen Museum** (Henrik Ibsens gate 14; tel: 37 04 04 90; 5 June–12 Sept Sat 11am–5pm, Sun noon–5pm, 26 June–15 Aug Mon–Sat daily 11am–5pm; charge) is Norway's oldest museum. **Arendal ❻** is one of the liveliest towns on this stretch of coast. It was struck by fire in 1863, and lost the houses on stilts

that had earned it the nickname "Little Venice", but it still enjoys a lovely setting, surrounded by small islands, and features many restored wooden buildings. The **Arendal Town Museum** (Arendal Bymuseum/Kløckers Hus; tel: 37 02 59 25; Tue–Fri 10am–3pm, Sat 10am–2pm; charge) has extensive displays delineating local history, and the **Town Hall** (Rådhus), previously the home of a merchant, is said to be one of the largest wooden buildings ever constructed in Norway.

Telemark

Best known for its stave churches and canal system, the beautiful, rural Telemark region has much else to recommend it, with lakes, mountains, forests and fjords to explore. The regional capital is **Skien ❼**, where Henrik Ibsen (1828–1906) spent his childhood. His home, Venstøp, forms part of the **Telemark Museum** (Brekke Park; tel: 35 54 45 00; mid-May–Aug Mon–Fri noon–5pm, Sat–Sun 11am–5pm; charge). Tulips bloom en masse in the elegant English gardens in summer, which are surrounded by stylish mansions.

BELOW: southerly Mandal's popular bathing beach.

Northwest of Skien lies **Ulefoss**, a village that until the end of the 19th century was a major exporter of ice, which was transported along the waterways of the **Telemark Canal ⑧**, a 105km (65-mile) long waterway linking Skien to Dalen. Blasted out of the rocks over 100 years ago, the canal wends a scenic route through 18 locks. From late May to early September, two venerable passenger launches – the *M/V Victoria* and *M/V Henrik Ibsen* – ply the watercourse on pleasure cruises lasting from 2 to 11 hours (tel: 35 90 00 30; www.telemark skanalen.no or www.visittelemark.com).

The small industrial town of **Notodden** is unremarkable in itself, but just 5km (3 miles) along Route 11 is one of Norway's top attractions, the medieval **Heddal Stave Church ⑨** (tel: 35 01 39 90; 20 May–19 June and 21 Aug–10 Sept 10am–5pm, 20 June–20 Aug 9am–7pm; charge). Considered "a masterpiece in wood", its ornate carvings are rivalled only by the beautiful period rose paintings in the Ramberg room of the nearby **Heddal Bygdetun** (museum; same hours as Stave Church; charge).

About 10km (6 miles) further on, Route 37 branches north past Tinnsjø lake towards **Rjukan ⑩**. The principal attraction here is the former Vemork hydroelectric plant, just west of Rjuken. Dating from 1910 and surrounded by beautiful scenery, it now houses the **Norwegian Industrial Workers Museum** (Norsk Industriarbeidermuseum; tel: 35 09 90 00; Oct–Apr Tue–Fri noon–3pm, Sat–Sun 11am–4pm, May–mid-June and mid-Aug–Sept daily 10am–4pm, mid-June–mid-Aug daily 10am–6pm; charge). The museum details the story of the brave attempts of the Norwegian Resistance to sabotage the plant where heavy water was once produced which the Nazis were using to develop nuclear weapons *(see page 198)*. In 2010, a new exhibition was installed which focuses on the everyday lives of workers from 1950 until the present day.

Rogaland

Though Bergen is known as the capital of fjord country, Rogaland county, centred on the west-coast port of Stavanger, has some of Norway's more spectacular

Whenever a skier performs a Telemark turn, homage is paid to the village of Morgedal in the heart of the Telemark region, considered the cradle of modern skiing. Here, the remarkable skier Sondre Norheim (1825–97) first improved utilitarian skis and ski bindings for greater control in turns. Today, he is regarded as the father of modern downhill skiing.

LEFT: Heddal Stave Church.

Country Afloat

To the world, Norway and seafaring are synonymous. From the age of sail until after World War II, the Norwegian merchant fleet was one of the world's largest, and Norwegian could be heard in ports worldwide.

Norwegians seem happiest when they are in, on or around the sea. Each year, more than a third of the population spend their summer holidays partly or completely in craft that range from small dinghies to motor launches and ocean-going yachts. In all, there are more than 450,000 boats over 4.5 metres (15ft) in length, and an untold number of smaller boats in the country. Most are motor boats, though sailing is popular on the fjords and as a competitive sport.

Geography and topography are the deciding factors. There are thousands of islands, and the fjords and coastal archipelagos are a paradise for competitive and recreational sailors, king and commoner alike. King Olav V (1903–91), the father of present King Harald V, was an accomplished sailor who won a gold medal in sailing in the 1928 Olympic Games in Amsterdam, which made him the world's only Olympic medallist monarch. Norway's first sailing club was founded in 1868 in Tønsberg, since when the nation has been a major force in championship sailing and regattas worldwide.

sights. It also has the country's highest average temperature; in winter there is little snow, and the fertile fields are green for most of the year. The Ryfylke area northeast of Stavanger is true fjord country. It starts with Lysefjord and stretches north past long narrow lakes that once were open fjords, until it reaches Vindafjord, Saudafjord and Suldalsvatn.

Every visitor should try to make the trek to stand on **Preikestolen**  ("Pulpit Rock"), a dramatic table of rock soaring 597 metres (1,958ft) above Lysefjord, and the country's most famous vantage point. It can be reached via a two-hour trail from the Preikestolhytta (hut) along a steep but well-paved path that gives way to steeper, rather soggy terrain, then to thrilling granite slabs and windswept cliffs. There are also buses which link up with ferries, that provide a different perspective from the water below. For more information: www.lysefjordeninfo.no or www.regionstavanger.com.

The sheltered bay north of Stavanger, and outer islands such as Karmøy (see page 199), protect Ryfylke's inshore

BELOW: Lysefjord.

islands from the North Sea. Christianity flourished early here under the protection of the bishops of Stavanger, and the islands are sprinkled with churches, notably the 12th-century **Utstein Kloster** on Mosterøy (see opposite).

The many lighthouses are not only landmarks for islanders and seafarers but make excellent bird-watching sites. The waters around these peaceful islands are well trafficked. Most of the island grocers also provide boat services, and it is easy to hire rowing boats and small craft with outboard engines.

In the northeast highlands of Rogaland, the fjords, lakes and rivers are rich in fish and fine for sailing and canoeing. There are good cross-country skiing tracks in winter and excellent Alpine slopes.

Among the best holiday areas is the Suldal district, stretching from **Sand**  on Sandsfjord, along the Suldalslågen River. At the Sand end of Suldalslågen is **Laksestudioet** (daily 10am–6pm, 21–31 Aug noon–4pm, Sept group booking only; charge), an observation studio built under a waterfall. Also worth a

visit, the **Kolbeinstveit Old Farm-stead Museum** (Ryfylke Museum; tel: 52 79 29 50; www.ryfylkemuseet.no; mid-June–mid-Aug Tue–Sun 11am–5pm, year-round for groups; charge) dates to the 1850s and has recreated traditional farm life in a number of authentically restored buildings.

Stavanger

Stavanger ⑬ is Norway's fourth-largest city and its oil capital. As the once-lucrative fishing industry declined, the city discovered North Sea oilfields in 1965, when the city became the base of oil exploration in the North Sea. Nearly one in ten of its 126,000 inhabitants was born abroad, which is rather ironic since in the 19th and early 20th centuries, Stavanger was the principal port of embarkation for the great waves of Norwegian emigration to the United States: the first 52 emigrants left in 1825, bound for New York on the sloop *Restauration*. Those wishing to trace their roots can contact the **Norwegian Emigration Centre** (Det Norske Utvandrersenteret; tel: 51 53 88 60; Mon–Fri 9am–3pm; charge) for assistance.

The Stavanger *siddis* (colloquialism for a person from Stavanger) claim to be the oldest true Norwegians, tracing their lines to the Battle of Hafrsfjord. This decisive battle that first united the country under King Harald I Hårfagre, *c*.880, took place at a bay just southwest of the city. On the shore is an impressive monument to the event, **Sverd i fjell**, three larger-than-life Viking swords seemingly thrust into bedrock.

The heart of modern Stavanger is the area around **Breiavatnet**, the small lake in the middle of the city, near the Anglo-Norman-style **cathedral**, dating to 1125. Northwest of the cathedral are the winding cobbled streets and old timber houses of **Old (Gamle) Stavanger**. Around 1870, as fishing and shipping were in decline, the fishermen turned their attention to *brisling* (small herring), which were cured and canned in the town and sent as Norwegian "sardines" all over the world. Stavanger thrived on sardines until the 1950s. Today, the **Canning Museum** (tel: 51 52 65 91; mid-June–Aug daily 11am–4pm, Sept–mid-June Tue–Sun; charge), located in the former cannery,

The 12th-century Utstein Kloster on the island of Mosterøy makes a beautiful setting for concerts (tel: 51 72 00 50; mid-Sept–Nov and Mar–mid-May Sun noon–5pm, mid-May–mid-Sept Tue–Sat 10am–4pm, Sun noon–5pm, daily in July; charge).

BELOW LEFT: Pulpit Rock.
BELOW: shopping in Stavanger.

The Heroes of Telemark

The Norwegian Resistance efforts to sabotage Nazi production of the atomic bomb is a tale of bravery and remarkable survival skills

When Germany invaded Norway in 1940, the Norwegian defence forces were no match for Hitler's army and the country was quickly occupied. The Norwegian royal family took refuge in London from where King Harald directed operations by the Norwegian underground to obstruct in any way they could their unwanted Nazi occupiers. The most celebrated act of resistance in Norway during World War II was the sabotage of the Vemork heavy water plant at Rjukan, in Telemark, in February 1943 – successful production of heavy water in the plant could conceivably have aided German development of an atomic bomb. No visitor to Rjukan, dwarfed and darkened by mountains all round, could fail to be awed by the audacity of the saboteurs. Their heroic exploits were made into a Hollywood film in 1965, *The Heroes of Telemark*.

The operation was originally planned for a joint force of Norwegian volunteers and British comman-dos in two towed gliders. It ended disastrously when both gliders and one of the aircraft towing them crashed in bad weather, and the survivors were tortured and executed by the Gestapo.

The next attempt was an all-Norwegian affair. "Gunnerside" was the code name for six men who had been trained in England. They parachuted onto a frozen lake where they joined up with "Swallow", an advance party who had been on the ground since the first failed operation, subsisting for almost four winter months on moss, lichen and a single reindeer. The men skied to the ridge above Rjukan for the perilous descent, up to their waists in snow. Just after midnight, the covering party took up positions while the six-man demolition team cut a chain on the gates and crept forward to the basement of the concrete building where the most vital equipment and the heavy water storage tanks were located. The team broke in, surprising a solitary Norwegian guard who agreed to lead them to vital components, laid their charges and began a rapid withdrawal. They had only gone a few yards when there was what members later variously described as "a cataclysmic explosion" and "a tiny, insignificant pop".

Of the 10 saboteurs, six reached Sweden after a 400km (250-mile) journey on skis in indescribably difficult conditions; the other four remained in Norway. Of the Swallow party, Claus Helberg had the liveliest time. He was chased through the mountains by German soldiers, but escaped. Then he fell over a cliff and broke an arm. The next day he walked into a German patrol but had a good enough story to be taken to a hotel to await treatment. Most of the hotel guests (but not the injured Norwegian) were turned out of their rooms to make way for Reichskommissar Joseph Terboven (the Nazi who ruled Norway). Later, he was bundled along with the remaining guests "into a bus and sent off to the Grini concentration camp". Helberg jumped from the bus. Later, he turned up in Britain, reporting for further duties. ❑

LEFT: Kirk Douglas played a saboteur in the 1965 film *The Heroes of Telemark*.

has recreated an authentic 1920s environment. The interactive **Norwegian Petroleum Museum** (Norsk Oljemuseum; tel: 51 93 93 00; June–Aug daily 10am–7pm, Sept–May daily 10am–4pm, Sun until 6pm; charge) provides an insight into the exploration and production of oil and gas.

The west coast

The sea route to Bergen is a popular way to see the coast. By taking an express boat from Stavanger to Bergen or Haugesund you can drop off at any of the harbour stops and stay a night or a week according to your whim (tel: 177; www.kolumbus.no). **Karmøy** ⑭, the island at the south of the outer islands chain, is big enough to merit its own boat service, which goes to **Skudeneshavn**, an idyllic port with fine sandy beaches at the southern tip. The narrow streets of the Old Town are lined with white wooden houses, dating from the 1800s when the town was a busy herring fishing centre. **St Olafs church at Avaldsnes** is a landmark which dates to 1248; mysterious archaeological remains continue to be discovered here.

The north of the island is linked to the mainland just south of **Haugesund** ⑮, in a region known as "Norway's birthplace". It is the first sizeable coastal town north of Stavanger and has long been a centre for fishing, shipping and farming. Today its harbour is filled with pleasure boats and ringed by 19th-century wooden buildings, lively cafés and modern hotels; the town also hosts the Sildajazz international jazz festival (tel: 52 74 33 70; www.sildajazz.no) and the Norwegian Film Festival (tourist office tel: 52 01 08 30), both in August.

Don't leave town without climbing **Haraldshaugen**, the national monument constructed at the grave of Harald the Fair-Haired in 1872 to celebrate 1,000 years of Norwegian unification. Ten minutes north of the town centre, the impressive structure sits on a high grassy mound overlooking the sea with a spectacular view of the Tonjer light-house. Just south of it is **Krosshaugen**, an early Christian stone cross.

From Haugesund, the scenic E134 highway winds its way northeastwards via the charming hamlets of **Olen** and **Etne** to one of the world's most beautiful waterfalls at **Langfoss**. Have lunch in Etne at the reliable **Fugl Fønix** (www.fuglfonix.no), a unique hotel and restaurant in the heart of the countryside. Route 13, then Route 550 which hugs the western side of the Sør Fjord, lead to **Hardangerfjord** (see below).

Hordaland

Hordaland county includes two of the country's top natural attractions: **Hardangervidda**, Norway's largest national park, whose central mountain plateau is 1,300 metres (4,500ft) above sea level, and **Hardangerfjord**. There are many fine hiking trails, one of which leads past the four giant **Husedalen waterfalls** which run from the Hardanger plateau down to Sørfjord, an arm of the Hardangerfjord. You can stay overnight in nearby Lofthus or Utne.

In days gone by, the fjords provided west Norway's main transport arteries,

Sardines were once the lifeblood of Stavanger.

BELOW:
Langfoss waterfall.

Map on
pages 192–3

*Edvard Grieg used to
visit a small "hytte"
poised on the edge of
Hardangerfjord, near
the village of
Ullensvang, where
with piano and
writing desk at hand,
he would compose
surrounded by the
powerful beauty.*

and **Utne** ⑯ was an important junction between east and west. Its economy once centred on the apple, pear and cherry orchards that still cover the slopes of the Sørfjord; but it was also kept afloat by fishing and its charming painted furniture production, which you can still enjoy at the **Utne Hotel**, founded in 1722, the oldest hotel in Norway. The open-air **Hardanger Folk Museum** (May–Sept daily 10am–4pm, Oct–Apr Mon–Fri 10am–3pm; charge) sums up Hardanger life over the past centuries with historic houses, boats, shops and a school.

A ferry service connects Utne with **Kinsarvik** ⑰ on the east side of Sørfjord, or else Kvanndal, where you can connect with Route 7 to Bergen. Heading northeast on Route 13, you'll find a beautiful stretch of water, Eidfjord. It cuts far into the dramatic landscape that includes the beautiful **Skykkjedalsfossen** ⑱ waterfall.

The Voss district

If you loop back northwest, crossing Eidfjord by ferry and continuing on Route 13, you come to **Voss** ⑲, which lies next to Lake Vangsvatnet in the middle of rich farmland. The Voss district makes full use of its surroundings to attract visitors, who come in summer for fjord excursions, mountain walking, parachuting, hang-gliding and paragliding from **Hangurfjell**, and fishing and watersports on Vangsvatnet. In winter everything changes, and Voss becomes one of the best centres for Alpine and cross-country skiing. At 610 metres (2,000ft) the top station of the Hangurfjell cable car gives one of the best prospects of Voss in its bowl-shaped valley.

Around Bergen and north

From Voss the E16 highway or the train take you to **Bergen** ⑳ *(see page 203)* and its islands. **Askøy** and **Osterøy** islands to the north of the city have their own character, while the long, narrow island of **Sotra** ㉑ to the west shelters Bergen from the North Sea. It is a good base for sea-canoeing in and out of the small offshore islands and rocks and, in good weather, as far as the open sea to combine canoeing with ocean fishing. The area around Bjørnafjord (Bear Fjord) to the south of Bergen is very green and enjoys a particularly mild climate.

Nordhordland is a district of islands north of Bergen that stretches as far as Sognefjord. Fish farming is the economic mainstay here, and the region exports salmon and trout all round the world. There is good sea fishing for cod and coalfish, and rosy-coloured trout inhabit many of the lakes. Diving and sub-aqua fishing are easy in these transparent waters. Oil is a modern, though not conflicting, industry in this area, with the Mongstad refinery illuminated at night.

To the north, the remote island of **Fedje** ㉒ was an important navigation point for many centuries, with two 19th-century lighthouses. Norwegian maritime rules insist that all ships must carry a Norwegian pilot, which here is vital, as tankers serving the Mongstad refinery navigate through the ever-changing waters. ❏

BELOW: traditional Norwegian country wedding. **RIGHT:** beautiful fjord scenery.

BERGEN

With its relaxed atmosphere, stunning setting and vibrant cultural life, Bergen is an appealing mix of the cosmopolitan and the outdoors, with easy access to the western fjords

Standing on a peninsula surrounded by seven mountains, beautiful Bergen is Norway's western capital and gateway to the fjords. Its relaxed atmosphere, stunning setting and vibrant cultural life make it an ideal base for a fjord holiday.

The Gulf Stream blesses Bergen with a benign climate and a harbour that is ice-free year-round. But it also brings rain, some 2,250mm (89 inches), making Bergen the country's wettest city, so be sure to pack an umbrella.

Maritime traditions

With a population of 261,000, Bergen is a major port, with 10km (6 miles) of dockside. Until the railway eastwards over the high mountains to Oslo opened in 1909, Bergen was isolated from the rest of Norway. Scotland by ship was closer than Oslo, England less distant than Copenhagen. As the westernmost city in Scandinavia, Bergen soon became a crossroads of the north and, in the 13th century, the capital of a united Norway. Its favourable location with respect to the other ports of Europe drew Hanseatic tradesmen (merchants from medieval German cities), who established a commercial community at the harbour. Fullriggers plied the port, with peak traffic in 1644, when more than 400 ships docked from Scotland alone.

In July 2014, Bergen will once again be one of the ports welcoming the Tall Ships' Race, a spectacular event with more than 75 large sailing ships from 20 countries participating.

A view from the top

The best place to get a feel for the city and take in its amazing natural setting is on the **Fløibanen funicular** Ⓐ (www.floibanen.no; daily every 10–15 minutes, May–Aug 7.30am until 11.30pm Mon–Fri, from 8 or 9am Sat–Sun; charge), that climbs more than

Main attractions
THE FLØIBANEN FUNICULAR AND ULRIKSBANEN CABLE CAR
THE PASTEL HOUSES OF HANSEATIC BRYGGEN
FISH MARKET
AQUARIUM
CONCERT AT GRIEG HALL
GAMLE BERGEN OPEN-AIR MUSEUM
LAKESIDE ART MUSEUMS
TROLDHAUGEN, EDVARD GRIEG'S HOME
LYSØEN ISLAND AND OLE BULL'S VILLA
HURTIGRUTEN VOYAGE

LEFT: alfresco dining in Bryggen. **RIGHT:** Fløibanen funicular climbing Fløyen.

TIP

Invest in a Bergen Card
from the Tourist
Information Office in
Vågsallmenningen.
Benefits include free
admission or discounts
for museums and free
public transport.

300 metres (1,000ft) in just eight minutes from the city centre to the top of
Fløyen mountain, high above Bergen.
At the summit there is a restaurant,
gift shop, and a fantastic network of
walking paths. Strike out alone or join
the 1½ hour "Walk like a Norwegian"
guided hike through forests, past lakes
and breathtaking views, learning about
history, traditions and legends on the
way. Children can go on a free treasure
hunt (maps available from the ticket
booth at the lower station).

For more breathtaking views of the
city, fjords and islands, the **Ulriksbanen cable car** (May–Sept daily 9am–
9pm, Oct and May 9am–5pm; charge)

goes to the top of Mount Ulriken – at
643 metres (2,109 ft), the highest of the
seven peaks that surround the city. You
can walk for hours on marked trails
while enjoying panoramic views of the
city and surrounding sea.

Bryggen

A walk through the atmospheric
medieval quarter of **Bryggen B** is a
step back in time, to before the Reformation. Many of the Hanseatic buildings remain – a film set in themselves,
meticulously preserved and listed as a
Unesco World Heritage site. Here, too,
are museums, galleries, craft shops,
fashion boutiques and eating places,

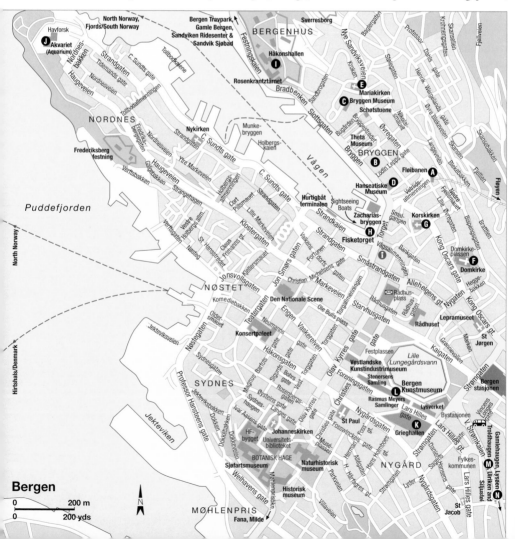

Bergen

interspersed with sailmakers, a freight company and a scrap metal dealer.

The earliest archaeological remains are in **Bryggen Museum ᴄ** (tel: 55 58 80 10; June–Aug daily 10am–5pm, Sept–Apr Mon–Fri 11am–3pm, Sat noon–3pm, Sun noon–4pm; charge). Guides from the museum conduct tours through the rows of Hansa houses and warehouses that line Bryggen. These were built after the great fire of 1702, which destroyed many buildings. A key to understanding the Hanseatic merchants' way of life is to visit the **Hanseatic Museum ᴅ** (tel: 55 54 46 90; June–Aug daily 10am–5pm, Sept–May 11am–2pm, Sun until 4pm; charge), housed in a 1704 trade house complete with original interiors.

Nearby is the oldest building still in use in the city, **St Mary's Church ᴇ** (Mariakirken; closed for renovation until 2015), built in the early 12th century and justly proud of its rich Baroque pulpit. The other medieval churches to survive the periodic fires are **Domkirke ꜰ** (Bergen Cathedral; late June–Aug Mon–Fri 10am–4pm, rest of the year Tue–Fri 11am–12.30pm) and **Korskirken ɢ** (Church of the Holy Cross; Mon–Sat 11am–3pm year-round) both merit a visit.

Torget

To buy fish year-round in the open-air **Fish Market ʜ** (Fisketorget) on the nearby harbour is to walk in and out of a continuous conversation, as animated fishmongers engage in banter. Just opposite is the **Kjøttbasaren,** a restored 1887 meat market with a food hall, fish restaurants, deli and handicraft shops. Both are good places to make a pit stop before taking a pleasant stroll along the harbour.

Bergenhus

Northwest of Bryggen, overlooking the harbour entrance, stands the **Bergen Fortress** (Bergenhus Festning), the grounds of which are a public park. Most of the fortifications date from the 19th century. Most impressive of the

original medieval buildings is **Håkons Hall ɪ** (tel: 55 31 60 67; www.bymuseet. no; mid-May–Aug daily 10am–4pm, Sept–mid-May daily noon–3pm, Thur 3–6pm; charge; guided tours to the Hall and Tower every hour in summer). This imposing Gothic ceremonial hall, built in 1261 for King Håkon Håkonsson, is one of Scandinavia's best examples of medieval secular architecture. The ticket includes entry to the **Rosenkrantz Tower** (Rosenkrantztärnet; tel: 55 31 43 80; same hours), built in the 1560s, which served as a combined governor's residence and fortified tower.

Nordnes peninsula

Across the water, the view from the Nordnes peninsula over the town to the mountain of Fløyen is characterised by the contrast between the green woodland, blue sea and the mainly white-painted wooden houses. At the point of the peninsula (along Carl Sundts Gate) is **Bergen Aquarium ᴊ** (Akvariet; tel: 55 55 71 71; May–Aug daily 9am–7pm, Sept–Apr 10am–6pm, feeding time every hour; charge), one

BELOW: a sign at the Hanseatic Museum.

The summer home of Edvard Grieg (1843–1907) at Troldhaugen.

BELOW: a wooden figure at the Museum of Old Bergen.

of the finest and most extensive collections of marine fauna in Europe. The new shark tunnel which opened in 2010 is a crowd-pleaser, as is feeding time for the seals which takes place every hour from 11am–4pm.

Musical traditions

Most of the time, the city's backdrop is the glacial quiet of the mountains, but music, one is frequently reminded, is very much a part of its heritage. Norway's greatest composer, Edvard Grieg (1843–1907), and virtuoso violinist, Ole Bull, were both Bergeners *(see opposite)*. The **Grieghallen** ⓚ concert hall is renowned as the home of the Bergen Philharmonic Orchestra, founded in 1765, and for the annual Bergen International Music Festival, Norway's oldest such event, held every May–June.

In more recent years, many Bergen rock and indie bands have gathered a pan-European fan base: Ralph Myerz & the Jack Herren Band, Kings of Convenience, Røyksopp, Kurt Nilsen and Sondra Lerche, to name a few. On the more traditional side, the Buekorps brigade is an organisation for 10–20-year-

old boys (and girls, since the 1990s), easily recognised by their natty tunics and tasselled tam-o'-shanter caps. From mid-April until 17 May, the brigades march in formation in the annual Constitution Day parade.

Bergen's art museums

Bergen has several strong art collections, mostly centred on the south side of Lille Lungegårdsvann, an octagonal lake near Grieg Hall, and a focal point for summer festivals. Here the **Bergen Art Museum** ⓛ (Bergen Kunstmuseum; Rasmus Meyers allé 3, 7 and 9; tel: 55 56 80 00; www.kunstmuseene.no; daily 11am–5pm, mid-Sept–mid-May closed Mon; charge) boasts a large collection of fine art in three separate buildings: the **Rasmus Meyers Collection**, specialising in Norwegian masterpieces from the 18th to the early 20th century, including masterpieces by Edvard Munch; the **Lysverket** building, which presents Norwegian and international art from the 15th century to the present; and the **Stenersen Gallery**, which stages interesting contemporary art exhibitions.

Museum of Old Bergen

Set in a pretty park in Sandviken, north of the city centre, **Gamle Bergen** (Nyhavnsveien 4; tel: 55 39 43 00; www. bymuseet.no; 7 May–Aug guided tours daily on the hour 10am–4pm, extra guided tour mid-June–Aug 4–5pm) takes you on a journey back in time to the 18th and 19th centuries. This evocative old town reconstruction comprises some 50 restored and transplanted wooden houses, shops and businesses set on streets and narrow lanes, including a bakery, dentist, photographer's studio, shop and jeweller. It's a family-friendly place with activities for children, entertainments in the open-air theatre and a restaurant. Gamle Bergen is just a 7-minute bus ride (20, 24) from the tourist information office by the harbour (Vågsallmenningen 1; tel: 55 55 22 00).

In between sits the **Bergen Contemporary Art Centre** (Kunsthall, 5 Rasmus Meyers allé; tel: 55 55 93 11; www.kunsthall.no; Tue–Sun noon–5pm, Fri 8–11pm; charge), in a spectacular Modernist building by Ole Landmark, with a buzzing café, bar and nightclub.

Nearby, the **West Norway Museum of Decorative Art** (Vestlandske Kunstindustrimuseum; Nordahl Brunsgate 9; tel: 55 33 66 33; www.kunstmuseene.no; charge) features an art and design collection spanning 500 years, with a focus on furniture, silverware, jewellery, and Ole Bull's famous violin made by Gasparo de Salo in 1562.

South of Bergen

Annual summer concerts attract music-lovers from all over the world to **Troldhaugen**  (tel: 55 92 29 92; May–Sept daily 9am–6pm, Oct–mid-Dec and 5 Jan–Apr Mon–Fri 9am–3pm, Sat–Sun 10am–4pm; charge), the home of Edvard Grieg 8km (5 miles) south of the city. It is said that the composer of *Peer Gynt* was inspired by folk music, but it is clear that nature was his main muse. Take a stroll to the lakefront spot behind his house where he used to fish to take a break from composing. He once said: "My music has the taste of codfish in it."

Not to be missed is the **Fantoft Stave Church** (tel: 55 28 07 10; mid-May–mid-Sept daily 10.30am–6pm; charge), 8km (5 miles) south of the city in Paradis. Built in 1150 in Sogn *(see page 214)*, it was moved to Fantoft in 1883, destroyed by arson in 1992 and completely restored in 1997.

It's a short ferry ride across Lysefjord to the beautiful island of **Lysøen** (Island of Light) and the onion-domed summer residence of composer and violinist Ole Bull (1810–80), who called the villa, built in 1873, his "Little Alhambra". Bull's charismatic personality and musical excellence had a great influence on contemporary artists and musicians who were often guests here. In summer, the old music room resounds to the music Bull played here. Take the passenger ferry from Buena Quay at Lysekloster or arrive by boat from Bergen, on the *M/S Westcruise*, which departs daily from 11am (tel: 56 30 90 77; mid-May–Aug Mon–Sat noon–4pm, Sun 11am–5pm; charge). ❑

Bergen makes a perfect base for exploring the fjords. To experience one of the great sea journeys of the world, join a Hurtigruten cruise, which makes 34 ports of call along the stunning coast between Bergen and Kirkenes near the Russian border (see pages 220–1).

BELOW: National Day celebrations.

THE HEART OF NORWAY

Central Norway encompasses a remarkable landscape, from the shimmering fjords of the west across the peaks, plateaux and valleys that have inspired great writers and composers

The heartland of Norway is the upper part of the southern bulge of the country, extending from above Oslo and Bergen to below Trondheim. The area encompasses the highest mountains in Scandinavia, and freshwater lakes and watercourses abound. To the east there are two long valleys, **Østerdalen** (literally "Easterly Valley") and **Gudbrandsdalen**, orientated roughly parallel to the border with Sweden and knifing through the high interior cordillera to provide the major north–south land transport arteries. In the middle there are the lofty peaks and high plateaus of the Rondane and Jotunheimen ranges, and to the west lies the coast with its fjords and archipelago in waters plied by boats since the land was first settled.

Lake Mjøsa

The glaciers that gouged the fjords also worked the inland and left **Mjøsa ㉓**, a jewel of a lake. Its southern end is at Minnesund just north of Eidsvoll, and its northern tip is at Lillehammer, 101km (63 miles) to the northwest. It's slender – only 15km (9 miles) at its broadest – and like a fjord, deep – up to 449 metres (1,472ft). Around Mjøsa lies some of the best land in the country, and its shores greet undulating countryside with large farms backed by densely forested hills. One of the

best ways to enjoy the lake and its surroundings is a trip on the *Skibladner*, the world's oldest paddle-wheel steamship still in service. In summer, the *Skibladner* carries up to 230 passengers on excursions six days a week; contact any tourist information office in the region or her home port at **Hamar ㉔** for schedules (tel: 61 14 40 80).

Hamar was a medieval centre of Roman Catholicism in Norway and the seat of a bishop. It is still a bishopric, but only ruins remain of its imposing cathedral, now protected

Main attractions
SKIBLADNER STEAMSHIP EXCURSION, HAMAR
LILLEHAMMER
SOGNEFJORD
JOSTEDALSBREEN GLACIER AND GLACIER MUSEUM
KVINFOSS, "LADY'S WATERFALL"
URNES STAVE CHURCH
JOURNEY ON THE FLÅM RAILWAY
BRIKSDALSBREEN GLACIER
ÅLESUND ART NOUVEAU ARCHITECTURE
BIRD WATCHING AT RUNDE
RØROS, UNESCO WORLD HERITAGE SITE

LEFT: fun in the snow – making snow angels.
RIGHT: old and new boats.

There are miles and miles of skiing tracks around Lillehammer.

RIGHT: turf-roofed houses in Røros.

under a spectacular glass structure at **Hedemark Museum and Cathedral Point** (Hedemarks-museet og Dom-kirkeodden; mid-May–mid-Sept Tue–Sun 10am–4pm, July daily until 5pm; charge). In the 19th century Hamar became a railway junction with a loco-motive works. The works are gone, but there's a reminder: the **National Museum of Railway Transport** (Norsk Jernbanemuseum; Strandveien 163; tel: 62 51 31 60; daily 11am–3pm, July–mid-Aug until 5pm; charge), with stations, railway buildings and vintage rolling stock. There are regular excur-sions on a narrow-gauge steam train.

Fertile local lands long ago led to cities and towns producing comes-tibles. Most stimulating, perhaps, is that seven of the country's eight dis-tilleries are located hereabouts. One of them, **Løten Brænderi** (guided tours; charge; tel: 62 59 49 10), at **Løten ㉕**, 13km (8 miles) east of Hamar, is open to the public. A fascinating one-man show (mid-June–Aug Fri–Sun 6pm; charge) recounts the history of the dis-tillery and the production of *akevitt*, the Norwegian liquor made from

potato and caraway seeds. Also worth visiting on the same site is **Løiten Lys** (Mon–Fri 10am–8pm, Sat 10am–6pm, Sun noon–6pm), a candle factory with a display of candles in every conceiv-able shape and size.

Lillehammer

Lillehammer ㉖ is best known in the world of winter sports as the venue of the 1994 Olympic Winter Games. Many of the Olympic facilities still stand, such as the ice event rinks at Hamar and Gjøvik, and luge and bob-sleigh tracks. There's also an Alpine ski area at nearby **Hafjell**, and 500km (300 miles) of cross-country skiing tracks. The cross-country arena now is the finish for the annual trans-mountain Birkebeiner race, one of the world's oldest citizens' races.

For summer visitors, the biggest attraction is the open-air museum, **Maihaugen** (mid-May–Sept daily 10am–5pm, Oct–mid-May Tue–Sun 11am–4pm; charge), with some 185 vintage buildings brought into the 40-hectare (100-acre) site from all over Gudbrandsdalen, including a stave

Røros: Timeless Mining Town

Røros, a Unesco World Heritage site on the E30 north of Alvdal, was until recently the archetypal company town, with life and society revolving around the mining business. Isolated, exposed, nearly 600 metres (2,000ft) above sea level and surrounded by mountains, it owed its existence to copper, which was mined here from 1644 to 1972. Now the inhabitants make their living from sawmills, furniture-making, wool-processing and reindeer meat, as well as tourism. It is a harsh spot; the lowest temperatures in the whole of Norway are often recorded here.

By some miracle Røros escaped the fires that so often laid waste to the wooden buildings in Norwegian towns, and it has retained much of its min-ing town atmosphere. The wealthy folk lived to the east of the river in Bergmannsgate, while the miners had to make do with the area beneath the slagheaps and the smelter. Picturesque log houses remain, while the crooked houses in Slaggveien are particularly interesting. The most notice-able feature is the stone church, "the pride of the mining town", which was dedicated in 1784. Paintings of clergymen and mining officials decorate the interior. The smelter was the focal point of the town and has been restored as a museum. The town is well known for its artists and craftsmen – glass-blowers, woodcarvers, cabinetmakers, potters and painters – and the atmospheric old streets are full of shops selling their wares.

church and two farms. The museum was the life's work of Anders Sandvig. He came to Lillehammer in 1885 suffering from tuberculosis and with a life expectancy of just two years. Whether or not it was his interest in the museum he founded in 1887 which kept him alive, he lived another 65 years.

Housed in a sleek modern building designed by the same architects as the award-winning Oslo Opera House (see page 179), **Lillehammer Art Museum** (tel: 61 05 44 60; July–Aug daily 11am–5pm, Sept–June Tue–Sun until 5pm; charge) pays homage to some of Norway's finest 19th-century painters, from Krohg to Munch. **The Road Transport Museum** (Norsk Vegmuseum; Hunderfossvegen 757; tel: 61 28 52 50; June–Aug daily 10am–6pm, Sept–May Tue–Sun 10am–3pm; free) at **Fåberg**, to the north of Lillehammer on the E6 highway, has everything from horse-drawn sleighs to modern cars.

Østerdalen

To the east of Lake Mjøsa lies **Østerdalen**, carved through the mountains by the Glomma – the country's longest river – stretching 617km (383 miles). The valley carries one of the north–south railway lines, as well as National Highway 3. It starts at **Elverum** ㉗ in the south and continues northwards for 250km (150 miles), becoming broader and more open further north. Just south of **Aursunden**, one of the source lakes for the Glomma River, lies the old copper-mining town of **Røros** ㉘ (see box, opposite), a Unesco World Heritage site.

Gudbrandsdalen

To the west of Østerdalen lies **Gudbrandsdalen**, the country's second-longest valley, cut by the River Lågen flowing south to Lillehammer. Perhaps because mountains surround it, the valley has a long tradition of folk dancing and folk music and is known for its woodcarving and rose painting. For Norwegians everywhere, as well as for curious visitors, Gudbrandsdalen is best remembered as the place where the indigenous Norwegian *geitost* (whey cheese made from goat's milk) was first made in the mid-19th century. The real variety, *ekte geitost*,

The unsung hero of the Gudbrandsdalen Valley is Anne Haav, the budeia (farm maiden) who first made the uniquely Norwegian geitost (goat's cheese) in the 19th century.

BELOW: fun in the snow with trolls.

0 - 4 km

A local hazard for drivers: elk on the road.

BELOW: musk ox in Dovrefjell.

made entirely of goat's milk, is still produced in the valley and elsewhere in the country; it is ubiquitous at all breakfast tables, from humble bed and breakfasts to the best of hotels.

About midway along the valley lies **Dombås 29**, a principal rail and road junction just southwest of the **Dovrefjell** (Dovre Mountains). The Dovre summits are lofty, but even the highest, **Snøhetta**, at 2,286 metres (7,498ft), is lower than the peaks of the Jotunheimen. Yet the Dovre Mountains have a place in the national psyche like no other, embodied in the saying about the strength of the country "United and faithful until Dovre falls".

The Jotunheimen Mountains

South of Dombås is an extensive area of peak and plateau. The Norwegian mountains are made for walking. As explorer Paul Belloni Du Chaillu observed in *Land of the Midnight Sun* (1881): "The difference between the mountains of Switzerland and Norway is this: those of the former are much higher, more bold and pointed, and sharp in the outlines of their thousand forms. On the other hand, the Norwegian mountains have a grave and sombre character, appearing like a gigantic stony wave, with a peak here and there, impressing more by their vastness than their height and ruggedness."

The many hiking trails are marked by red letter Ts painted on rocks and cairns. They meander between *hytte* (lodges), mostly above the timberline, between 950 and 1,600 metres (3,100–5,250ft) above sea level, and the highest summits are around 2,400 metres (7,900ft), hence the lack of mention in mountaineering anthologies, where sheer elevation is the criterion. Therein lies part of the secret: you can enjoy the high-altitude experience without needing high-altitude lungs.

Moreover, in summer you can travel to the heart of the range in only a few steps, by boarding one of the passenger launches that ply the waters of lakes Gjende and Bygdin. In the late 19th century, the composer Edvard Grieg remarked that "when I contemplate the possibility of a future visit to the [Jotunheimen] mountains, I shudder

The *hytte*

The word *hytte*, pronounced "hutta", describes a simple cabin in a tranquil, preferably remote setting in the wilds of nature. In this area the *hytte* is a mountain lodge with comfortable bunk beds (you need only bring a sleeping bag), which usually provides meals for hungry, weary hikers.

Most of these lodges are owned and operated by Den Norske Turistforening (DNT) and its affiliated local organisations, hence the red Ts on rocks and cairns. You need not be a member to stay in a DNT *hytte*, but membership is a good investment, as the price is soon offset by the accumulated discounts on accommodation. You can join DNT at any of the *hytte* or at the head office in Oslo (tel: 40 00 18 68; www.turist foreningen.com).

with joy and expectation, as if it were a matter of hearing Beethoven's 10th Symphony". That attraction was in part why Grieg wrote the incidental music for Henrik Ibsen's play *Peer Gynt*, based on a traditional legend of Gudbrandsdalen, in which braggart Peer leaps astride a reindeer, from a knife ridge into the lake below. The knife ridge and the lake are real: **Besseggen** and **Gjende** in the Jotunheimen, literally "Home of the Giants". The reindeer are equally real, as herds of them still graze here. One reminder of them is the reindeer pattern on the Gjende brand biscuits, sold throughout the country.

Hiking and skiing trails

Accessibility is another allure of these wilderness areas. To the south of the Jotunheimen lies the hamlet of **Finse** ③, the high point at 1,225 metres (4,000ft) on the Oslo–Bergen railway line. Its high street is the station platform; trains are the local traffic, as there are neither cars nor roads. It's a small speck in a seemingly boundless expanse of ice and snow. So remote yet accessible is this place that it was chosen for the filming of the initial sequences of *The Empire Strikes Back*. Finse has the country's largest *hytte* for hikers and skiers, as well as a full-service hotel, as suits its location as the junction between two giant trail networks, north to the **Jotunheimen** and south to **Hardangervidda** (Hardanger plateau). As the crow flies, the trail networks stretch 225km (140 miles) to the north and 100km (60 miles) to the south, and in all have more than 5,000km (3,000 miles) of T-marked hiking trails and, at Easter-time, some 2,000km (1,240 miles) of ski trails, marked by poles in the snow.

To the north and east of the Jotunheimen, on the other side of the Gudbrandsdalen Valley, lies the **Rondane** range, which offers some of the country's finest hiking and cross-country skiing. The trails are less steep, the peaks not as high, the walks not as long and the *hytte* not as numerous as in the Jotunheimen. But the connection to the Gudbrandsdalen legend remains, as there is a Peer Gynt *hytte* here. Moreover, to the south and on the west flank of the valley there is a **Peer**

One of the best views in the region is from Besseggen in the Jotunheimen Mountains, the ridge immortalised by Henrik Ibsen in his play Peer Gynt.

BELOW: hiking through Jotunheimen.

TIP

In summer, guides from the Jostedalsbreen National Park Centre, 20km (12 miles) from Stryn, lead tours and glacier hikes and kayaking explorations to the great Jostedal. The Glacier Bus travels throughout the Sognefjord region and Glacier National Park from mid-June–mid-Sept (tel: 57 68 32 50; www.sognefjord.no).

Gyntveien (Peer Gynt Way) which leads from Gausdal north of Lillehammer to Golå south of Vinstra.

The trails and the *hytte* reflect the Norwegian view of wilderness: it is for everyone. Pristine perhaps is the best word; only the red Ts and an occasional electric power line betray modern times. Little has changed since three English adventurers, with the pseudonyms Skipper, Essau and John, came to the Jotunheimen in the 1880s. Their subsequent book, *Three in Norway by Two of Them*, became one of the classic travelogues of the Victorian age. The remnants of their camp are carefully preserved near **Memurubu** ❶ on Lake Gjende in the Jotunheimen, one of the *hytte* that dot these wilderness areas *(see box page 212)*.

From Sogn to Nordfjord

The county of **Sogn og Fjordane** lies between the coast and the Jotunheimen Mountains. Narrow fingers of water push inland from the main fjords to reach far into the mountains, and waterfalls tumble hundreds of metres into the fjords below. In the past, the terrain

BELOW: the Flåm Valley as seen from the "Norway in a Nutshell" train.

was impassable in winter. Today travel is easier thanks to the network of ferries, tunnels and bridges. The county is easily accessible from Bergen. Indeed, until 1918, it was named Northern Bergen province (Nordre Bergenhus).

The **Sognefjord** is unmatched. On both sides of it small villages cling to the land, each with its atmosphere. **Balestrand** ❷ has been a favourite since the 19th century and has an English church, St Olav's. A narrow side-fjord leads to **Fjærland** ❸, near the two southernmost tongues of the **Jostedalsbreen Glacier**. Nestling at its base is the **Norwegian Glacier Museum** (Norsk Bremuseum and Ulltveit-Moe Climate Centre; tel: 57 69 32 88; Apr, May, Sept and Oct daily 10am–4pm, June–Aug daily 9am–7pm, Nov–Mar on request; charge), where interactive models, displays and films provide an insight into Europe's largest glacier.

Going east from Balestrand, a short crossing takes you to **Hella** and past the glistening arc of **Kvinnfoss** (Lady's Waterfall) close to the main road. At the head of the fjord, **Sogndal** ❹ is the centre for trade and administration. It

swells considerably during term-time because it is also a centre for education, with universities and Norway's oldest folk high school.

In **Luster** ㉟, 25km (15 miles) to the northeast of Sogndal, is the finest of Sogn's many stave churches, **Urnes Stavkirke**. Built around 1130 and believed to be the oldest stave church in Norway, this beautifully preserved church with Viking carvings is now a Unesco World Heritage site (June–Aug daily 10.30am–5.30pm; charge).

The Flåmsbana branch line

Aurlandsvangen, Flåm and Gudvangen lie along the innermost recesses of the fjord, which stretches south from the main fjord like an upside-down "Y". Not to be missed is the mountain railway from Myrdal (on the Bergen line), at 866 metres (2,841 ft) above sea level, to **Flåm** ㊱, which spirals down the steep mountain gorge through 20 tunnels. The 20km (12-mile) train ride is one of Europe's most scenic stretches of railway (www.flaamsbana.no). When disembarking from the train at Flåm, resist the impulse to jump back on and leave the tourists and troll souvenirs behind. Beyond the crowded, ugly harbourside, Flåm with its mountainous backdrop and lovely surroundings of orchards and meadows is worth exploring.

Jølstravatnet

Heading northwest from Balestrand towards **Førde** ㊲ and the coast, you cross a region of many lakes – Jølstravatnet – that penetrate the foothills of the high tops in the east and feed into the fjords in the west. One of the rivers, the Jølstra, said to be one of the best salmon rivers in the area, drops precipitously before reaching Førde on **Førdefjord**. Here is **Sunnfjord Museum** (tel: 57 72 12 20; June–Aug Mon–Fri 10am–4pm, Sat and Sun noon–5pm, July until 6pm weekdays, Sept–May daily 10am–3pm; charge), a collection of 26 historic buildings.

Oddly, **Florø** ㊳, the only community in this large county big enough to be called a town, lies on the remote edge of the sea, but not so odd considering that Norway has always depended on the sea for food, trade and transport. The **Coastal Museum**

The railway from Myrdal to Flåm winds through spectacular mountain scenery. The train ride is part of the "Norway in a Nutshell" journey using a variety of forms of transport to take in some of Norway's best beauty spots (for details, see page 386).

BELOW LEFT: inside Jostedal Glacier. **BELOW:** Balestrand.

Geirangerfjord is located in the Sunnmøre region, in the southernmost part of the county.

RIGHT: young musicans in Molde.

(Sogn og Fjordane Kystmuseet; tel: 57 72 67 82; mid-June–mid-Aug Mon–Fri 11am–6pm, Sat–Sun noon–4pm, mid-Aug–mid-June Mon–Fri 10am–3pm, Sun noon–3pm; charge) in Florø has a fine collection of old boats.

Inland along Nordfjord

Nordfjord is 100km (60 miles) shorter than Sognefjord. With so many side-fjords, lakes and valleys it is easy to get into the mountains or make the journey up **Briksdalsbreen**, one of the most beautiful glaciers in the fjord country. Even better is that you can climb up to the base of the glacier in the two-wheeled farm carriages, *stolk-jaerrer*, pulled by small, sturdy, cream-coloured *fjording* (fjord horses) native to Nordfjord.

The traditional home of the *fjording* is the Eid district, centred around Nordfjordeid, where Nordfjord proper has already divided itself into Eidsfjord and Isefjord. **Eid ㊴**, which is also connected to the coast by Road 15, is known for Firdariket, the seat of the last Viking chief. The town has white-painted buildings, and the church, which dates from 1849, is decorated with beautiful rose painting.

Further along you reach the Inner Nordfjord, where the fjord system ends at Stryn, Loen and Olden, the start of three spectacular valleys stretching up to the northwest edges of the Jostedals-breen. Three tunnels out of the Stryn Valley cut right through the mountain to the renowned **Geirangerfjord** to the north. **Stryn ㊵** is known for summer skiing on the northeast of Strynsvatn, where the ground rises to Tystigbreen.

Ålesund to Kristiansund

Coastal vessels have long called at Ålesund, Molde and Kristiansund on their way to Trondheim and the north. Looking at the coastline, islands and fjord mouths on a map, it is difficult to distinguish where sea and islands end and fjords and mainland begin.

Ålesund ㊶ is Norway's largest fishing town. Yet it is best known for its *Jugendstil* architecture, built in 1904 after fire destroyed its centre. If you arrive here by ferry, which most travellers do, you are pleasantly taken aback

Fjord Formation

Fjords are found in Alaska, Canada, Chile, Greenland, New Zealand, Norway and Scotland. But nowhere are they more prominent than in Norway. A direct line along the coast measures 2,650km (1,645 miles), but the stretch of the entire coastline, including the archipelago, is 57,260km (35,580 miles), a third more than the distance around the earth at the equator. The coast of Norway is more jagged than any other, and Norway can lay claim to giving the word fjord to other languages of the world.

The fjords were formed about 100,000 years ago, during the last Ice Age. Glaciers gouged valleys from the land, to depths that lessened at the coast, where the ice was thinner. When the ice enventually retreated, the sea inundated. So a typical fjord is deepest at its midpoint and far less deep at its mouth: the Sognefjord, for instance, reaches a depth of 1,244 metres (4,080ft), but is only 158 metres (518ft) deep at its mouth.

The fame of these fjords has made them part of the myth of science fiction. In *The Hitchhiker's Guide to the Galaxy*, the venerable planet-builder Slartibartfast recalls: "Doing the coastlines was always my favourite, used to have endless fun doing all the little fiddly bits in fjords… did you ever go to a place… I think it's called Norway?"

by the pastel-hued dwellings embellished with towers, turrets and charming decorative elements: from human faces to docile dragons. Credit for the creative and colourful restoration must go to Kaiser Wilhelm II of Germany, who sent architecture students and four ships laden with supplies and building materials. With help and donations from all over Europe, the people of Ålesund completed the rebuilding of their town within three years.

Until the 1950s, fishing supported Ålesund, and *klippfisk* (traditional Norwegian split dried cod) was its principal export, mainly to the Mediterranean. But as fishing changed so did Ålesund, which added fish processing and aquaculture. Many former warehouses are now offices and restaurants, where you can try one of the more unlikely local specialities such as *bacalao* (Spanish for cod), made from boned *klippfisk*.

There are several attractions worth seeing here: the wonderfully preserved **Aalesunds Art Museum** (tel: 70 12 31 70; Mon–Fri 9am–3pm, in summer until 4pm, Sat 11am–3pm, Sun noon–4pm; charge) features exhibitions on the fire and subsequent rebuilding; in the former Norwegian Bank building next to the Art Nouveau centre, **Art Museum KUBE** (Apotekergate 16; tel: 70 10 49 70; Tue–Sat 11am–4pm, Sun from noon, summer daily 10am–5pm; charge) focuses on art, architecture and design; **Stiftinga Sunnmøre Museum** (tel: 70 17 40 00; Mon–Fri 11am–3pm, Sat June–Aug, Sun noon–4pm; charge) is an open-air attraction which consists of 50 houses and 40 boats that depict life in the seafaring area until the 1900s; the **Atlantic Sea Park** (Atlanterhavsparken; tel: 70 10 70 60; daily, times vary; charge) is one of the largest saltwater aquariums in Northern Europe.

To the southwest of Ålesund is **Runde ⓬**, the island that draws naturalists from around the world, as more than 200 bird species have been recorded here. Take a four-hour tour on one of the boats departing from **Ulsteinvik** daily from June to August. As a bonus, the waters round the island close over myriad wrecks; in 1972, divers found a hoard of gold and silver coins on board the *Akerendam*, a Dutch vessel that sank in 1725.

TIP

Explore the colourful Art Nouveau town of Ålesund: guided walks depart Saturdays at noon from the Tourist Information Office (Rådhus; tel: 70 15 76 00; June–Aug).

BELOW: Ålesund's waterfront.

Fresh strawberries, a treat for passengers on the boats.

Molde **43**, halfway along the coast from Ålesund north to Kristiansund, is part of an archipelago sheltered from the Norwegian Sea; its mild climate, lush vegetation and rose gardens earn it the title "Town of Roses". This modern town was almost entirely rebuilt after German bombing in World War II. It is an excellent base for touring the fjords by boat or car. It is known at home for the might of its football team and for the annual Molde Jazz Festival (mid-July; many free concerts; tel: 71 20 31 50).

From **Bud** on the coast west of Molde, a road leads to the **Atlanterhavsveien** (Atlantic Road) to Kristiansund, over **Averøya 44**, the biggest island in the area. It heads north across the rim of the ocean, so driving seems like a voyage. Archaeologists believe that this was one of the first places to be settled after the last Ice Age, and their finds include remnants of the early Fosna culture that existed around 7000 BC.

Kristiansund

Unlike Ålesund and Molde, **Kristiansund 45** is vulnerably situated on the coast, with weather-beaten rocks pounded by the sea, yet not far inland are grassy areas and small woods. This is the *klippfisk* town, for long the biggest exporter of Norwegian dried cod. A recent census counted just more than 22,000 inhabitants but, because of the centuries-old links with other countries through its sailors and fishermen, and the foreign merchants who settled here, the atmosphere is cosmopolitan. Like most Norwegian towns with "Kristian" in their title, Kristiansund was named after King Christian VI. A good introduction is by *sundbåtene*, the harbour boats that for more than 100 years have linked four of the town's five islands.

Mellemverftet, once one of four shipyards in Vågen, is working again as a centre for preserving the craft of shipbuilding, carefully restoring the beautiful lines of traditional Norwegian boats. **The Nordmore Museum** (tel: 71 58 70 00; mid-June–early-Aug daily noon–5pm; charge) exhibits archaeological finds from the Fosna culture and the history of *klippfisk* processing. Kristiansund's main church was destroyed by bombing in 1940, and the architect named its replacement "Rock Crystal in Roses". Like it or loathe it, you cannot ignore this stark white building known as the **Atlantic Ocean Cathedral** (Atlanterhavskatedralen), which boasts 320 stained-glass panels and a 30-metre (100ft) choir wall.

Trollheimen

Inland, the northern part of Møre og Romsdal county ends in a crisscross of fjords eating into the islands and peninsulas which lead to **Trollheimen**, the "Home of the Trolls", where the mountains reach nearly 1,600 metres (5,000ft). This haunt of climbers and skiers is bounded by two important valleys, Surnadalen and Sunndalen, with between them the tiny Todalfjord. Beside the last is the surprise of the **Svinvik Arboretum 46** (tel: 97 43 37 09; mid-May–Aug Mon–Fri 10am–4pm, Sat–Sun 11am–5pm; charge), beautiful gardens with thousands of rhododendrons, conifers and other plants. ❑

NORWAY'S MOST BEAUTIFUL VOYAGE

The splendid coastal voyage from Bergen to the North Cape and beyond has long been regarded as one of the most beautiful sea journeys in the world

To travel on board the Hurtigruten (literally "swift route") steamships is to partake in a voyage with infinite beauty spots. What began in 1891 as an idea to provide an express shipping service along the rugged Norwegian coast between Trondheim and Hammerfest has evolved into a lucrative form of tourism. Yet part of the charm is watching a working ship going about its business. It is also possible to jump ship while in port and enjoy a unique excursion: to the Nidaros Cathedral or Ålesund's *Jugendstil* quarter, for example. Out of season, it reverts to its traditional role of carrying west-coast Norwegians, who treat it as a bus, for business and pleasure. In season it is extremely popular with retirees from the UK and Europe.

Ports of call

In spring and autumn, the 12-day round trip from Bergen across the Arctic Circle to the Nordkapp (North Cape) and Kirkenes lets you feast on the dramatic seasonal changes. In May, the fjord valleys are brilliantly in bloom, and the hills and the mountains of the north are still covered with snow. The Hurtigruten makes 34 ports of call along this ever-changing coast, some at places no bigger than a handful of houses round a harbour, others at cities such as Trondheim and Tromsø with time ashore to explore.

ABOVE: tranquil Trollfjord: from fjords to open sea, fertile land to barren rock, fishing hamlets to cities, the voyage is a mix of the workaday and the spectacular.

BELOW: a boat rounds a corner of Geirangerfjord, where it's about to get a close-up view of Seven Sisters waterfall. This fjord, in the county of Møre og Romsdal, is one of Norway's most visited.

LEFT: a young Japanese tourist meets a troll in the North Cape.

COMMUNICATIONS REVOLUTION

Over the past century more than 70 ships have served in the Hurtigruten fleet. Before the days of internet and mobile phones, these diverse vessels led a communications revolution, enabling the population and industries along the rugged Norwegian coast to keep in touch in a new way. Previously, it took three weeks in summer or five months in winter to send a letter from Trondheim to Hammerfest; the Coastal Express reduced this time to a few days.

Places such as the Lofoten Islands (pictured above), Trollfjord and the North Cape became accessible to travellers who wanted to see the Midnight Sun. Nature-lovers and birdwatchers are attracted by the scenery and the many bird colonies, which include puffins, kittiwakes and guillemots. Far-flung Tromsø attracts many visitors to its annual film festival. As time went by, ships were built specifically with cold storage and freezer rooms, vehicle roll-on/roll-off capacity and conference facilities, as well as comfortable cabins.

Two companies now run 11 ships, ranging from the grand old M/S *Lofoten* to the M/S *Midnatsol*. They run year-round, and each season offers different landscapes and perspectives.

BOVE: with thousands f islands and skerries, ountains and aciers, the landscape constantly changing nd no two days are ike.

IGHT: steering the ip into harbour.

RIGHT: tourist at the North Cape, where the West Finnmark plateau provides summer grazing for the Sami's reindeer herds.

THE NORTHWEST COAST

North of Trondheim, Norway's religious and cultural capital, lies a beautiful, but often harsh landscape that crosses the Arctic Circle into the land of the Midnight Sun

The northwest coast is where Norway gets thinner, from Trondheim – a large city for its latitude and the gateway to the north – up to Bodø, which lies beyond the Arctic Circle. The land along this narrow conduit is mostly forested, with the benign influence of the Gulf Stream ensuring temperate conditions persist far to the north.

Trondheim ❶ is a pleasant city with clean air, wide streets, low buildings and a compact centre. You get a reminder of the early days by the wharves and narrow streets that run between the wooden buildings. They may date only to the 18th century, but these coloured warehouses echo the architecture of medieval times when fish and timber were the economic mainstays of the city. These days Trondheim has a relatively modest population of 165,000, which swells by nearly a sixth in term-time, as this is a university town, as well as the country's leading hi-tech research centre.

As with all Norwegian cities, the outdoors is close at hand. Trondheim's back garden is Bymarka to the west, where **Gråkallen** (Old Man) at 520 metres (1,700ft) high is a favourite walking and cross-country skiing area. Indeed, outdoor sports are a leading local pastime, and the city has acted as host to the World Nordic Ski Championships.

Nidaros Cathedral

Until the 16th century, Trondheim, known as Nidaros ("mouth of the River Nid"), was the capital of Norway. In 997 the settlers of Nidaros could not have known, but the sheltered site they picked was to become a pivotal city in Europe. In the late 11th century, work started on a major church at Nidaros, erected over the grave of St Olav, the king who brought Christianity to the Vikings (*see page 227*). Apparently the Pope found that fact auspicious, as he appointed an archbishop there and made the bishops

Main attractions
NIDAROS CATHEDRAL AND
NORWEGIAN CROWN JEWELS,
TRONDHEIM
HELL BLUES FESTIVAL
STIKLESTAD
ARCTIC CIRCLE CENTRE

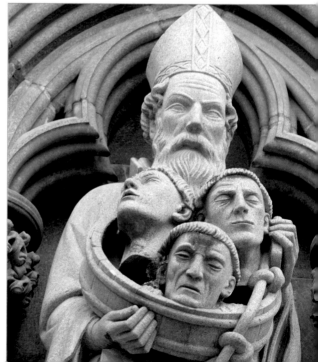

LEFT: a bridge in Trondheim.
RIGHT: the west wall of Nidaros Cathedral.

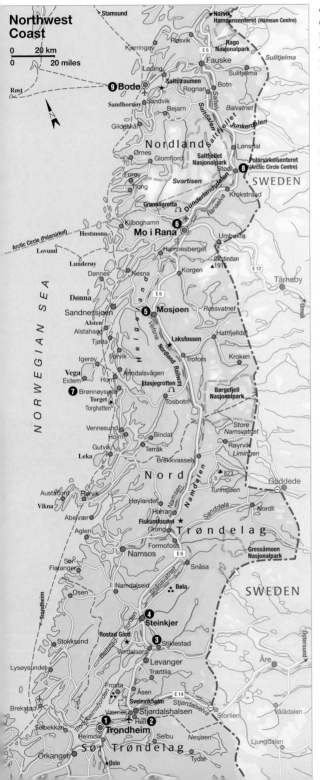

Northwest Coast

0   20 km

0   20 miles

of Greenland, Iceland, the Isle of Man, Orkney and the Faroe Islands, and the bishops in Norway answerable to him. The church became the imposing **Nidaros Cathedral** (Nidarosdomen; 15 June–20 Aug Mon–Fri 9am–3pm, Sat until 6pm, Sun evening mass, opening times vary the rest of the year; charge includes admission to adjacent Archbishop's Palace), Norway's national shrine and the venue for the coronation of Norwegian kings – most recently King Harald V in 1991.

The **Norwegian Crown Jewels** (May–Aug Mon–Fri 9am–6pm, Sat 9am–2pm, Sun 1–4pm, Sept–Apr times vary; charge) may be seen in the cathedral museum, and the regalia for king, queen and crown prince are on display in the **Archbishop's Palace**, next to the cathedral.

City for cyclists

Trondheim has done much to relieve traffic congestion, including implementing a toll ring round the city. Cycling is encouraged on a network of dedicated cycle paths. Yet topography challenges cycling: the flat centre is surrounded by steep hills. So in 1995, the resourceful city built **Trampe**, the world's first bicycle lift, 130 metres (426ft) up Brubakken Hill. The lift operates like a ski tow, and cyclists pay using keycards at the bottom of the hill. Not surprisingly, the annual **Styrkeprøven** (Trial of Strength) trans-mountain bicycle race (June) starts in Trondheim. It finishes 540km (336 miles) south, in Oslo.

Rockheim

The newest addition to the city is **Rockheim** (Brattørkaia 14; tel: 73 60 50 70; www.rockheim.no; Tue–Fri 11am–7pm, Sat–Sun until 6pm; charge), a rock and pop museum housed in an eye-catching modern building just north of the central train station. The permanent exhibition traces Norway's pop music heritage from the 1950s to the present day. Temporary exhibitions focus on aspects of music history

and pop culture. Concerts are held on premises in a hall that seats 350, and there is a restaurant and shop on site.

Hell

Some Norwegian words tempt *double entendre* in English, most notably the name of the village closest to Trondheim's Værnes airport. It's **Hell ❷**. Notwithstanding the derivation of the name from the Old Norse word for cavern, postcards of the railway station at Hell sell astonishingly well. So when in Trondheim, you can indeed go to Hell; it's only 33 minutes east by commuter train. The station here must be one of the most photographed in the country. In September Hell hosts an annual blues festival which attracts international stars and fans to this otherwise quiet settlement.

St Olav's battleground

Many European countries claim histories highlighted by a decisive medieval battle. For Norway, it's the **Battle of Stiklestad** on 29 July 1030, some 36 years before England's momentous Battle of Hastings. Unlike Hastings,

which enabled the winning Normans to conquer the country, at **Stiklestad ❸** it was the loser who ultimately won. The forces of King Canute of Denmark and England were victorious and King Olav Haraldsson of Norway was slain. Olav was later to become a saint *(see page 227)*, and it was his martyrdom that triggered the building of Nidaros Cathedral in Trondheim. Stiklestad, located east of the E6 highway about 100km (60 miles) north of Trondheim, is the venue for the annual St Olav's Play performed every July in an open-air amphitheatre during the 11-day St Olav Festival. A 12th-century church marks the spot where King Olav died, and a the St Olav's Kulturhus (museum) chronicles the events.

Trade and industry

Despite their reputation as marauders, the Vikings were principally farmers and traders who settled and worked the land wherever they went. **Steinkjer ❹**, north of Trondheim, was a trading centre in Viking times, and in 1857 it became an export port for timber and agricultural produce.

Northern road signs appear in Norwegian and Finnish.

BELOW LEFT: Nidaros Cathedral. **BELOW:** Trondheim at night.

The Arctic Circle at 66°N is defined not by temperature, but by light. It is the latitude at which the sun is above the horizon at noon on 21 June. At Bødo, the "Mørketid" (Arctic Night) lasts from 15 to 29 December.

North of Steinkjer, the railway and the E6 highway follow the sheltered Namdalen Valley to **Mosjøen ❺** at the head of the Vefsnfjord and then to **Mo i Rana ❻** at the head of Ranafjord. The word *Mo*, which means sand or gravel flats, is a common place name in Norway. Today the towns support heavy industries, starting in the mid-1950s with the **Norsk Jernverk** (ironworks) at Mo i Rana and **Mosjøen Aluminumverk** (aluminium plant) at Mosjøen. From a business viewpoint, the locations of these industries in small northern towns may be questioned. They are there as part of the government's efforts to provide jobs that keep people in the region. A similar effort is the more recent centralisation of the nine principal government registers at **Brønnøysund ❼**, on the coast south of Mosjøen. If, say, you take out a loan to buy a car anywhere in Norway, the relevant details will be registered at Brønnøysund.

Crossing the Arctic Circle

Most people experience an inexplicable thrill as they cross the **Arctic Circle** (Polarsirkel). Perhaps the reason is celestial: unlike the equator, set by geometry, or the International Date Line, drawn by timekeepers, the Arctic Circle marks the southern boundary of a different sort of world, the Land of the Midnight Sun.

The only building in this landscape is the **Arctic Circle Centre ❽** (Polarsirkelsenteret 66 33" N; tel: 75 12 96 96; 20 May–1 Sept daily 8am–10pm; free). Situated on the Circle, alongside the railway and the E6 highway, the unique architecture has been adapted to the natural surroundings. It has a cafeteria, cinema, gift shop and exhibition hall.

Further north, **Bodø ❾** was founded as a trading centre, in an ill-fated attempt to compete with Bergen. Today the Hurtigruten coastal steamers *(see page 220)* call on their way from Bergen. Bodø also features the world's strongest maelstrom – Saltstraumen – with whirlpools up to 10 metres (30ft) in diameter. It is the northern end of the rail network and a staging post for summer visitors. Some 40km (25 miles) to the north on the coast is the old trading centre at **Kjerringøy** (late Mar–Aug; charge), with 15 preserved buildings, and some typical Nordland boats. ❑

BELOW: a route through the snow.

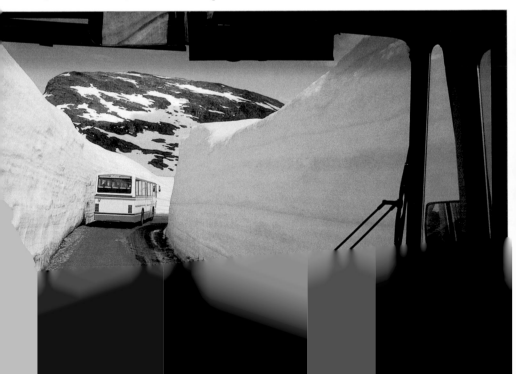

Stiklestad:
the Making of a Saint

The site of the Battle of Stiklestad near Trondheim in 1030 marks a pivotal point in the history of the Norwegian nation and the adoption of Christianity

T he ancient battlefield of Stiklestad, north of Trondheim, is the place that saw the foundation of Norwegian unity and the adoption of the Christian faith. In the 11th century Norway was a country constantly disrupted by disputes between rival chieftains. The ambition of the reigning king, Olav Haraldsson, was a united Norway. He also wanted to create a Christian country with Christian laws and churches and clergy.

He was not the first to attempt this. In the previous century Olav Tryggvason had been converted to Christianity in England. He returned to Norway in 995 with the express purpose of crushing the chieftains and imposing his new-found faith. But Olav Tryggvason's conversion had not swept away all his Viking instincts, and in his zeal he used great cruelty to convert the populace. His chieftains became disenchanted, and Olav was killed in the Battle of Svolder in the year 1000.

Olav Haraldsson ascended the throne in 1015, but like Olav Tryggvason he foolishly made too great a use of the sword to establish Christianity. King Canute of Denmark and England, with his eye on the Norwegian throne, gave support to discontented factions within the country and in 1028

invaded Norway, forcing King Olav to flee to Russia. Undaunted, Olav returned with a few followers, but his support had dwindled. He met his end on 29 July 1030 at the Battle of Stiklestad. Olav's corpse was taken to the then capital, Nidaros, and buried on the banks of the Nidelva River. When the body was disinterred a year later, it showed no signs of corruption: his face was unchanged and his nails and hair had grown. This was taken as a sign of sanctity. Following this revelation, Olav was proclaimed a saint and his body placed in a silver shrine in Nidaros Cathedral. Faith in the holiness of King Olav – St Olav – spread and his shrine became a centre of pilgrimage.

Canute's victory at the Battle of Stiklestad was brief. He ceded power to his son, Svejn, but as rumours of Olav's sanctity grew, popular support for Canute evaporated and Svejn was exiled to Denmark in 1035. Meanwhile, St Olav's son, Magnus, had been in exile in Russia. Norway now invited him to return and accept the crown.

From that time Stiklestad has been a place of pilgrimage. It now has a beautiful open-air theatre, the largest in Scandinavia, and on the anniversary of the battle a cast of 300 actors, dancers and musicians re-enact the events of July 1030 in the annual St Olav Play, which has been staged every year since 1954, drawing some 20,000 tourists to the area. ❏

ABOVE: manuscript recounting the battle.
RIGHT: the annual St Olav Play.

NORWAY'S FAR NORTH

Far removed from the rest of Europe,
Norway's spectacular north extends through
Arctic latitudes from the rugged Lofoten
Islands to the Russian border. Beyond is the
remote archipelago of Svalbard

The far north of Norway, comprising Troms and Finnmark counties and the Lofoten Islands, is unique in the Arctic, thanks to the warming currents of the Gulf Stream. Here lies more than a third of the land of Norway, which one resident in 20 calls home.

The Lofoten Islands

Viewed from the mainland across Vestfjord north of Bodø, the **Lofoten Islands** present an imposing wall of rugged peaks rising from the sea. On the west, these mountains form a mighty shield against the onslaught of Norwegian Sea weather, so most of their habitation is along their east coasts, facing the mainland. **Svolvær ❶**, the main town, has been a trading and fishing centre since the 17th century. Fishing has long been the traditional calling of the islanders, and today *Lofot torsk* (Lofoten cod) remains prized throughout the country. **Kabelvåg**, to the south, is the undisputed fishing capital of northern Norway. Up to 10,000 vessels make for Vestfjord between February and April for the colourful *Lofotfiske*, the annual cod-fishing event. From May to September, it is possible to observe sperm whales, minkes and orcas on a whale safari.

The southernmost of the larger Lofoten Islands, **Moskenesøya** is the most

photographed, perhaps because of the picturesque fishing village of **Reine ❷**. Between Lofotodden, its southern cape, and the islet of Mosken lies **Moskenstraumen ❸**, a 4km (2½-mile) wide, shallow channel. Here tidal currents reach speeds of up to 6 knots in their alternating flow between the Norwegian Sea and Vestfjord, and water always swirls around a submerged rock in the middle of the channel. Sailing here is risky, as Dutch navigators first noted on maps published in 1595 in *Mercator's Atlas*, where the current was called

LEFT: the sunset illuminates a frozen waterfall on the Lofoten Islands. **RIGHT:** stilt houses on the islands.

For panoramic views of Tromsø, take the Fjellheisen cable car 420 metres (1,378ft) above sea level. It even operates until 1am when the Midnight Sun is shining.

"Maelstrom". It is now a synonym for a whirlpool treacherous to navigation and, by extension, turbulent confusion.

Tromsø

Tromsø ❹, "Gateway to the Arctic", has long been a leading city in northern Norway and is now regarded as the region's unofficial capital and the cultural centre of the north. International trade and influence came early, and by the 1860s the women of the town were so stylishly dressed as to cause a visiting tourist to remark that the city seemed to be the "Paris of the North". That nickname persists, and now may apply as well to Tromsø's abundant and varied nightlife, with an average of one seat in an eatery or place of entertainment for every three residents. Though it is in the Arctic, the city enjoys a benign climate. The average midday temperature in January is the same as in Oslo, and summer temperatures are about the same as in Trondheim.

The city is built mostly on an island between the mainland and the larger coastal island of **Kvaløya**. The sheltered location made it an ideal port for commercial operations in Arctic waters as well as the last port of call for polar expeditions. Polar exploration, trapping and seal hunting are the main focus of the **Polar Museum** (tel: 77 62 33 60; mid-June–mid-Aug daily 10am–7pm, Mar–mid-June and mid-Aug–Sept 11am–5pm, Oct–Feb 11am–4pm; charge), situated in a former customs house (1830) in the historic harbour area. The **Tromsø Museum** (Lars Thørings veg 10; tel: 77 64 50 00; June–Aug daily 9am–6pm, Sept–May Mon–Fri 10am–4.30pm, Sat noon–3pm, Sun 11am–4pm; charge) on the university campus has some enlightening exhibits on Sami culture and a mesmerising simulation of the Northern Lights.

Sami and northern Norwegian art is well represented in the permanent collection of the **Art Museum of Northern Norway** (Nordnorsk Kunstmuseum; Sjøgata 1; tel: 77 64 70 20; Mon–Fri 10am–5pm, Sat–Sun from noon; free) housed in a neoclassical building facing Roald Amundsen's Square.

Tromsø's most visited tourist attraction is **Polaria** (tel: 77 75 01 00; daily 18 May–31 Aug 10am–7pm, 1 Sept–17

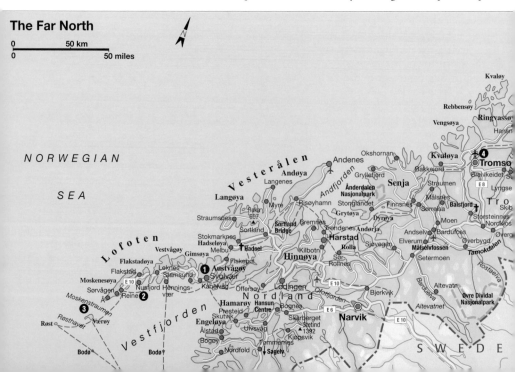

The Far North

0   50 km

0   50 miles

N

May noon–5pm; charge) an Arctic-themed experience centre occupying a distinctive futuristic building. After watching the panoramic film *Svalbard – Arctic Wilderness*, stroll the "Arctic Walkway" to witness elements of Arctic nature, from a snowstorm to the tundra; then observe the local bearded seals in the Aquarium.

Just over the bridge on the mainland, a 25-minute walk from the harbour (or a ride on no. 28 bus) is the striking **Arctic Ocean Cathedral** (Ishavskatedral; tel: 47 68 06 68; June–mid-Aug Mon–Sat 9am–7pm, Sun from 1pm, with services at 11am, 16 Aug–15 Sept daily 3–6pm, 16 Sept–May daily 4–6pm; charge), an impressive modern work by the architect Jan Inge Hovig. Inspired by Arctic landscape, it resembles an elegant iceberg or whale in repose. Midnight Sun concerts are held here in summer (15 May–15 Aug; 11.30pm; charge).

Tromsø is also home to Europe's northernmost brewery, **Macks Olbryggeri** (Storgata 4; tel: 77 62 45 00), established in 1845, where you can sample the famous Arctic ale, Mackøl.

Alta rock carvings

Alta ❺, the largest town in Finnmark, is known among fishermen for having one of the world's best salmon rivers. It is also home to the **Alta Museum, World Heritage Rock Art Centre at Hjemmeluft** (Verdensarvsenter For Bergkunst; Altaveien 19; tel: 41 75 63 30; May–19 June and 24–31 Aug daily 8am–5pm, 20 June–24 Aug until 8pm, 1 Sept–30 Dec and 2 Jan–1 May Mon–Fri 8am–3pm, Sat–Sun 11am–4pm; charge) on the southern outskirts, a collection of rock carvings dating from 4200 to 500 BC. These remarkable "stories in pictures" of people, animals (particularly reindeer), boats and weapons are now a Unesco World Heritage site.

Sami centre

South of Alta on the E93 lies **Kautokeino ❻**, a centre for the Sami, the indigenous people of northern Scandinavia and the Kola peninsula of Russia. The Sami population is conservatively estimated at 70,000, of whom about half live in Norway. Their native languages are related to Finnish, Hungarian and Estonian and have little

After two months of winter darkness, Vardø, Norway's easternmost town, celebrates the return of the sun around 20 January with a gun salute on the first day that the entire disk is visible above the horizon.

A memorial for Roald
Amundsen at the
Tromsø Polar
Museum.

BELOW: the North
Cape – a major
tourist attraction
300 metres
(1,000ft) above the
Arctic Ocean.
RIGHT: Tromsø's
Arctic Ocean
Cathedral.

in common with Norwegian. Traditionally, the Sami have been hunters, fishermen and reindeer herders. Like indigenous minorities elsewhere, the Sami were long suppressed, but now have their own flag and own Parliament, *Sámediggi*, at **Karasjok** ❼.

Northernmost point

Nordkapp ❽ (The North Cape) at 71°10′ 21″N is considered by many to be the most northerly point of mainland Europe. But in fact the tip of **Knivskjelodden**, a low, slim peninsula to the west of Nordkapp, lies 47 seconds of latitude farther north. No matter: the North Cape is the imposing headland that draws visitors from around the world. Wrap up and walk along the cliffs for views from the continent's edge. The tourist complex, **North Cape Hall** (Nordkappallen; tel: 78 47 68 60; Jan–Apr and Apr–early Oct times vary, mid-June–early Aug daily 9am–1am; charge) features a panoramic film about the North Cape through the seasons. The **North Cape Museum** (tel: 78 47 72 00; June–mid-Aug Mon–Sat 10am–7pm, Sun from

noon, mid-Aug–May Mon–Fri noon–4pm; charge), near the Hurtigruten quay in **Honningsvag**, has a variety of displays about the cape and its fishing history, and aspects of everyday life.

North to Svalbard

The **Svalbard** (Spitsbergen) archipelago lies 640km (400 miles) north of the mainland. In 1596, the Dutch navigator Willem Barents, searching for the Northeast Passage, sighted the largest of its four main islands, which he called Spitsbergen (Pointed Peaks). Indeed, the terrain resembles that of the Alps, and Spitsbergen covers an area almost as large as Switzerland. In 1906, John Longyear, an American industrialist, founded the Arctic Coal Company on Spitsbergen. Today, the principal village, **Longyearbyen** (pop. 2,100) is named after him, but only Norway and Russia remain as mine operators.

The climate is relatively mild for the Arctic: midday temperatures at Longyearbyen average –7°C (19°F) in February and 7°C (45°F) in July. But permafrost prevails year-round. In 1998 it made the international news, when Canadian pathologists exhumed the well-preserved corpses of six Svalbard coal miners who had died in the 1918 influenza pandemic, to search for clues that might reveal its origin.

Today, technology is supplanting mining as the main economic activity. The **Svalbard Satellite Station** near Longyearbyen is positioned to download images from all earth observation satellites in polar orbits, and the **Rocket Range** at **Ny-Ålesund** is now instrumental in weather research.

With daily flights (weather permitting) between Tromsø and Longyearbyen, tourism is growing. In summer, the stark mountains around the village are offset by a valley which has meadows spangled with flowers. The polar winter is another matter. The sun does not rise above the horizon, and everything is locked in darkness, lit only by the moon and the multicoloured rays of the Northern Lights. ❑

SWEDEN

From sophisticated Stockholm to mountain
wilderness, Sweden offers the traveller
immense variety

Not so long ago, Sweden was an introverted country perched uneasily on the edge of Western Europe. Many Swedes talked about travelling "to Europe" as if it was on a different continent. All that changed with the country's admission to the European Union in the 1990s and the opening in 2000 of the Öresund bridge between Sweden and Denmark.

The Swedes finally became "good Europeans"; in turn, the outside world began to discover the country's hidden delights. More visitors every year flock to the bustling cultural centres of Stockholm, Göteborg and Malmö, or escape into the rural regions or the vast wilderness areas of Lapland.

Sweden is ideal for those who like the great outdoors and activities such as angling, golf, riding, fell-walking, skiing, sailing or canoeing. Even the capital city, Stockholm, is a place of waterways and green spaces, flanked by thousands of uninhabited islands. The flat, fertile south, including Skåne, was part of Denmark for centuries: a faintly Danish accent persists. South-central Sweden is dominated by the great lakes of Vänern and Vättern, the hub of a vast waterway network. Visitors can sail across the widest part of the country along the Göta Kanal, which links Stockholm to Göteborg.

Sweden's heartland holds Dalarna, a province that guards the country's oldest folk traditions. From here, the lovely Inlandsbanan railway runs north into the Arctic, home to the indigenous Sami, many of whom still herd reindeer across Scandinavia's remote mountains.

Culturally, state-of-the-art museums, well-preserved historical sites like the Viking capital Birka, and the homes of artists such as Carl Larsson, who inspired the clean lines of contemporary Swedish design, are unique attractions. Göteborg's Symphony Orchestra is in the top rank of world orchestras, and Sweden is increasingly admired as a centre of gastronomic excellence.

In winter, visitors are lured by the Northern Lights, the renowned Icehotel… and the magic of a Swedish Christmas, with its traditional markets, brightly decorated streets and St Lucia processions. ❏

PRECEDING PAGES: the smooth rocks of the Bohuslän coast; enjoying a dip outside.
LEFT: wheat fields near Malmö. **ABOVE LEFT:** embroidery from the Nordic Museum, Djurgården. **ABOVE RIGHT:** Drottningsholm Slott, the royal palace, Stockholm.

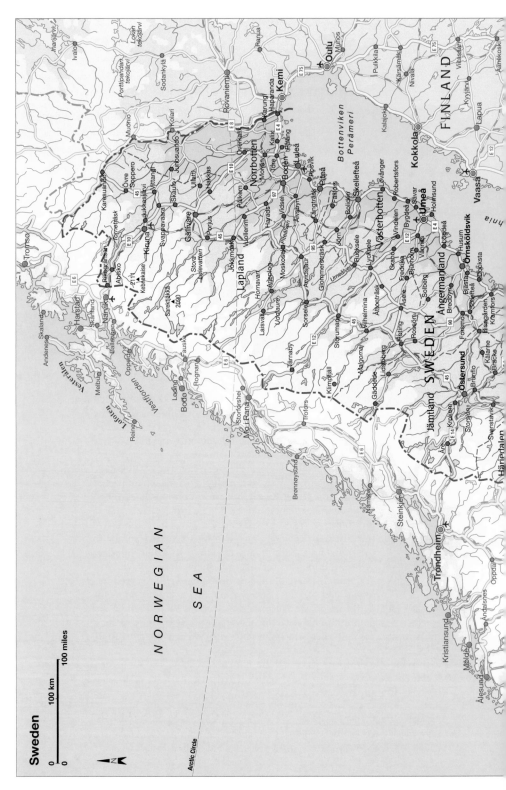

Sweden

0
0   100 km
0   100 miles

Arctic Circle

NORWEGIAN SEA

SWEDEN

FINLAND

Lapland

Norrbotten

Västerbotten

Ångermanland

Jämtland

Härjedalen

Bottenviken
Perämeri

Oulu
Kemi
Kokkola
Vaasa
Umeå
Örnsköldsvik
Östersund
Trondheim
Rovaniemi
Kiruna
Narvik
Bodø
Mo i Rana

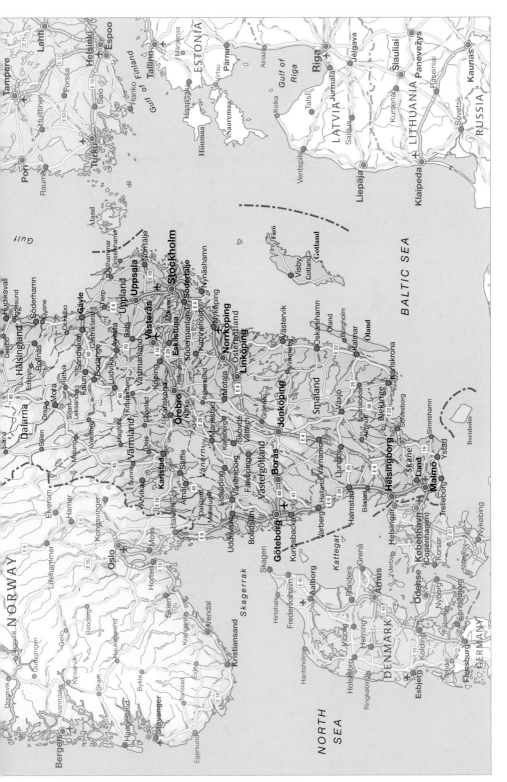

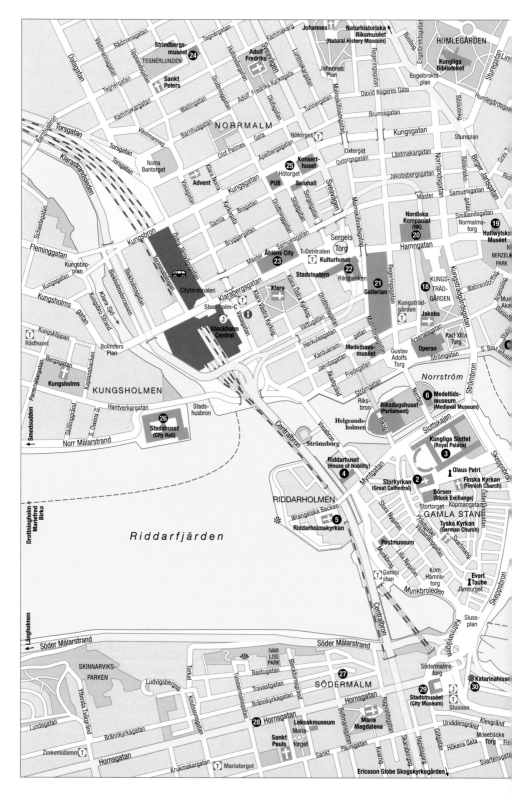

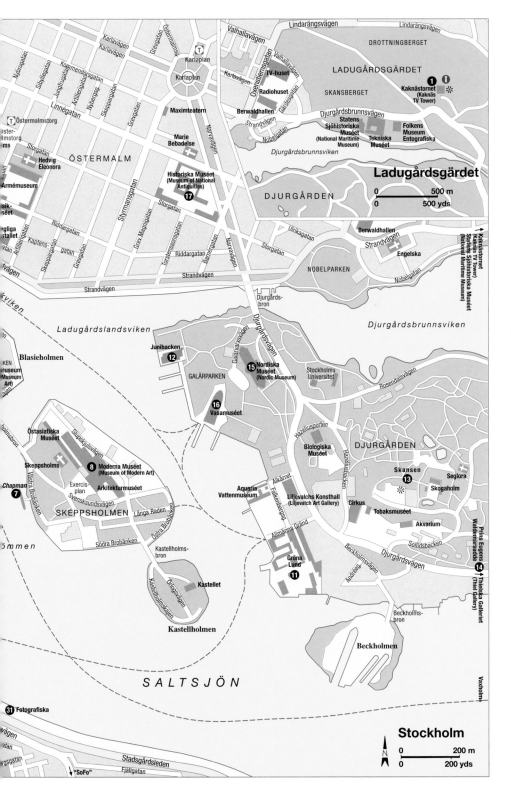

Stockholm

STOCKHOLM

Sweden's capital is a city of islands where palaces and peaceful hideaways line the shores, and where cobbled streets lead to chic shops, cafés and lively cultural attractions

The novelist Selma Lagerlöf called Stockholm "the city that floats on water". Nowhere do you see this more clearly than from the dizzy observation platform on top of the **Kaknäs Television Tower ❶** (Kaknästornet; tel: 08 667 21 80; Mon–Sat 10am–9pm, Sun 10am–6pm; charge), Ladugårdsgärdet, which rises 155 metres (508ft). Below, Stockholm spreads out in a panorama of blue water, the red of the old buildings contrasting with the stark white and glass of the new, and swathes of trees and grass. This pretty low-rise city, designated Europe's first Green Capital in 2010, rests on its 14 islands, for all the world like a raft traveller drifting down a lazy river.

Fresh and salt water are separated by the island of Gamla Stan (Old Town) and the great lock gates of Slussen at the southern end. This island barrier is where Stockholm originated some time before the 13th century. Today, with a population of 2 million in the greater metropolitan area, Stockholm is a modern and sophisticated metropolis, famous for Scandinavian design in furniture, textiles and interiors and a hotbed of innovation in information technology – Europe's Silicon Valley. The city features some of the most exciting cuisine in Europe. Stockholm's nightlife has exploded into an array of young, hip clubs and older, more sedate nightspots. Infusing the old with the new is a speciality of today's vibrant Stockholm.

The Vasa capital

Stockholm's history starts in **Gamla Stan** (Old Town), which still has the character of a medieval city. Its narrow lanes follow the same curves along which the seamen of former times carried their goods. The best place to start a tour is **Stortorget**, the centre of the original city, from which narrow streets fan out in all directions.

LEFT: a hot-air balloon over Gamla Stan.
RIGHT: Stockholm's gorgeous townhouses.

TIP

See more and pay less with a Stockholm Card, available from the Stockholm Tourist Center, Vasagatan 14. It offers free travel, free admission to museums and sights, discounts and a guidebook.

In medieval times, Gamla Stan's Stortorget was a crowded, noisy place of trade, where German merchants, stallholders, craftsmen and young servant girls and boys jostled and shouted. In the cobbled square today, people laze on benches or sit at one of the outdoor cafés, and it is hard to visualise that in 1520 the cobbles ran with blood during the Stockholm Bloodbath. Despite a guarantee of safety, the Danish King Kristian II, known as The Tyrant, murdered 82 people, not only nobles but innocent civilians unlucky enough to have a shop or a business nearby. This gory incident triggered the demise of the Kalmar Union, which had united Sweden with Denmark and Norway. Three years later, Sweden's first heroic king, Gustav Vasa, put an end to the union and made Stockholm his capital.

From the square, it's a short walk to the **Cathedral ❷** (Storkyrkan; tel: 08 723 30 00; year-round daily 9am–4pm, July–Aug Mon–Sat until 6pm, out-of-season guided tours Tue 11am; charge). This awesome Gothic structure is the oldest building in Gamla Stan, in part dating to the 12th century.

RIGHT: the majestic cathedral in Gamla Stan.

It has high vaulted arches and sturdy pillars stripped back to their original red brick. Its most famous statue is *St George and the Dragon*, the largest medieval monument in Scandinavia, a wooden sculpture carved by Bernt Notke in l489, which has retained its original colouring. The cathedral was the setting for the June 2010 royal wedding between Crown Princess Victoria and commoner Daniel Westling: crowds of around half a million lined the streets to watch the procession.

Västerlånggatan is a favourite shopping street for locals and tourists alike. Here and on nearly every other cobbled lane in the Old Town you will find shops, restaurants and cafés to suit every taste. Particularly enjoyable are the cellar restaurants with their musty smell and stone walls. It's easy to imagine the Swedish troubador Evert Taube (1890–1976) raising a beer stein to his compatriots as he composed yet another lyric to the Swedish way of life.

Royal residences

The present **Royal Palace ❸** (Kungliga Slott; tel: 08 402 61 30; mid-May–mid-

Unusual Views of Stockholm

Stockholm is an unusual city, and visitors may well want to explore its delights in an unusual way. There are certainly plenty of opportunities. The city sails along on its 14 islands – join its watery dance by taking to the Riddarfjärden or Saltsjön in a **kayak**, **rowing boat**, **paddle boat** or **canoe**. Djurgårdsbron Sjöcafe (Galärvarvsvägen; tel: 08 660 57 57) is a central hire place, and Kanotcenter Svima Sport (Ekelundsvägen 26; tel: 08 730 22 10; www.svima.se) will also help launch you into the waters.

The **Millenniumtour**, run by the Stadsmuséet, takes thriller-lovers on a walk round Södermalm. Here you can see the sights of Stockholm's trendiest district through the eyes of Lisbeth Salander and Mikael Blomkvist, the characters from Stieg Larsson's wildly popular series.

Vertigo sufferers may pale at the idea of a **rooftop tour** (English tours late Apr–Aug; tel: 08 22 30 05; www.upplevmer.se), but Upplev Mer's ladders and catwalks allow access to the dizzy heights of Riddarholmen, with views over Gamla Stan.

If you're here in winter, you can experience the nearest thing to flying with **tour skating**. Although routes depend on which parts of the archipelago are solidly frozen, tours generally end with a skate through central Stockholm, right past the Stadshus (City Hall). ICEguide (tel: 730 89 47 63; www.iceguide.se) runs a five-hour introduction from January to March.

Sept daily 10am–5pm, mid-Sept–Dec and Jan–mid-May Tue–Sun noon–3pm; charge) was built on the site of the Tre Kronor Palace, which burnt down in 1697, some say not without the help of Nicodemus Tessin the Younger, who had already built a new northern wing and who obviously relished the glory of rebuilding the palace to his Renaissance designs. His father, Nicodemus the Elder, had been architect to the old Tre Kronor Palace, and the grandson, Carl Gustaf, was responsible for supervising the completion of the new palace many years later. The palace comprises 608 rooms. Various suites are open to the public – the stunning Royal Apartments are what most people go to see – and the sprawling palace houses three museums. Lovers of military uniforms and marching can watch the 40-minute Changing of the Guard ceremony in the outer courtyard (May–Aug Mon–Fri 12.15pm, Sun 1.15pm).

For more of Sweden's aristocratic heritage, head for the **House of Nobility** ❹ (Riddarhuset; Mon–Fri 11.30am–12.30pm; charge; tel: 08 723

39 90) on the nearby island of **Riddarholmen**, built in 1641 as a meeting place for the nobles. It is arguably the most beautiful building in Gamla Stan, with two pavilions looking out across the water. Inside, the nobles deliberated in the grandeur of the Main Chamber, watched from above by a painting of Mother Svea, who symbolises Sweden.

On the opposite side of Centralbron is **Riddarholmskyrkan** ❺ (mid-May–mid-Sept 10am–5pm; charge), an iron-spired 13th-century monastery church (the oldest in Stockholm) that serves as the burial place for Sweden's monarchs.

Medieval Museum

The refurbishment of the Swedish **Parliament Building** (Riksdaghus) on Helgeandsholmen to the north of Gamla Stan some years ago led to a remarkable archaeological find and a new museum. When the builders started to excavate the Riksdaghus terrace to form an underground car park, they discovered layer upon layer of the past, including part of the medieval wall and the cellars of an apothecary shop. Stockholm's **Medieval Museum** ❻

A stone cherub inside the Royal Palace.

BELOW LEFT: regal details. **BELOW:** inside the Royal Palace.

One of the gravity-defying rides at the amusement park Grøna Lund.

(Medeltidsmuseum, Strömparterren; tel: 08 508 317 90; www.medeltidsmuseet. stockholm.se; July–Aug daily noon–5pm, Sept–June Tue–Sun noon–5pm), incorporates the old wall and other treasures uncovered during the excavations.

Skeppsholmen

To the east of Gamla Stan lies **Skepps-holmen**. The sleek schooner moored off the island is the 100-year-old *af Chapman* **❼**, now a youth hostel and a café. Also on the island is the spectacular new building of the **Museum of Modern Art ❽** (Moderna Muséet; tel: 08 519 552 00; www.modernamuseet. se; Tue 10am–8pm, Wed–Sun until 6pm; charge), designed by the Spanish architect Rafael Moneo, with a collection of 20th-century art that is considered one of the finest in the world, and includes works by Dalí, Picasso and Magritte among others. Its large restaurant-café is worth visiting for a beautiful panorama of the city skyline. Next door, the **Architecture Museum** (Arkitekturmuseet; tel: 08 587 270 00; same hours; charge) delves into the design aesthetics of Sweden's buildings.

A bridge links Skeppsholmen to the **Blasieholmen** waterfront area, where the sumptuous big building is one of Scandinavia's most famous hotels, the **Grand ❾**. Nearby is the **National Museum of Fine Arts ❿** (Nationalmuseum; Södra Blasieholmshamnen; tel: 08 519 543 00; www.nationalmuseum. se; Tue and Thur 11am–8pm, June–Aug until 5pm, Wed, Fri–Sun 11am–5pm; charge), featuring Sweden's national collection of art, with most of the great masters from 1500–1900. Rembrandt is particularly well represented. In summer, the museum holds concerts in the evening, a lovely setting for music.

Djurgården

From Gamla Stan, it is just 10 minutes by boat across the harbour to the island of **Djurgården**. Once a royal deer park, much of Djurgården is still in its natural state, with paths and woods where you may spot small creatures, both everyday and rare, such as hares and the occasional deer. The island is part of **Ekoparken**, the world's first city national park (*see page 251*). A good way to get around is to

Tourist Information

Stockholm's main Tourist Information Centre (Vasagatan 14; May–mid-Sept Mon–Fri 9am–7pm, Sat 10am–5pm, Sun 10am–4pm; mid-Sept–Apr Mon–Fri 9am–6pm, Sat 10am–5pm, Sun 10am–4pm; tel: 08 508 285 08; www.visitstockholm.com) has moved premises recently, and is now located opposite Stockholm Central railway station.

The centre offers advice, and can book tours, excursions and other entertainment. It also sells the Stockholmskortet (Stockholm Card), which is well worth buying. The card offers free admission to 80 of Stockholm's museums and attractions, and gives the holder free public transport around the city. It is available in 24-/48-/72-/120-hour versions.

You can also pick up the monthly *What's On* magazine here.

hire a bike at the bridge which forms the road entrance (also the place to hire kayaks and rowing boats when the lure of Stockholm's glittering waters proves overwhelming).

As the ferry slides into the Djurgården quay, there is no mistaking that this is an island devoted to enjoyment. On the right is **Gröna Lund** ⑪ (tel: 08 587 501 00; www.gronalund.com; May–mid-Sept, hours vary), an amusement park with 18th-century roots and up-to-the-minute rides, including its seventh rollercoaster, Twister, new for 2011.

Fans of Astrid Lindgren's children's books should not miss **Junibacken** ⑫ (tel: 08 587 230 00; Sept–May Tue–Sun 10am–5pm, June and Aug daily 10am–5pm, July daily 9am–6pm; charge), a children's attraction/theatre dedicated to her eccentric characters. An electrically operated indoor tram, with narration in English, allows the rider to experience *Astrid's World*, floating over miniature scenes from her books with moving figures, lights and sound, as familiar characters suddenly pop out of corners.

Heading south on Djurgården, where the island rises in steps to a hilltop, is **Skansen** ⑬ (tel: 08 442 80 00; July–Aug daily 10am–10pm, May, June and Sept daily 10am–8pm, Mar, Apr and Oct daily 10am–4pm, Nov–Feb Mon–Fri 10am–3pm, Sat–Sun 10am–4pm; charge), the oldest open-air museum in the world. In 1891, Artur Hazelius decided to preserve the fast-disappearing Swedish way of life by collecting traditional buildings. Today there are some 150, including an 18th-century church, still used for services and weddings. In summer, costumed craftspeople meander round the steep cobbled town and demonstrate traditional crafts such as glassblowing in the little workshops. Skansen's **zoo** contains Nordic fauna, such as bears, elk, reindeer, wolves and wild boar; and its **aquarium** holds some distinctly un-Nordic creatures such as monkeys and crocodiles.

While on Djurgården it's worth visiting the lovely former home and collection of the "Painter Prince" **Prins Eugens Waldemarsudde** ⑭ (Prins Eugens väg 6; tel: 08 545 837 00; Tue–Sun 11am–5pm, Thur until 8pm; charge), which overlooks the sea.

Tunnelbanan, Stockholm's metro system, is described as the "world's longest art gallery". Many stations have paintings, sculptures, mosaics and engravings – and all can be seen for the price of a ticket. A free English guide to the artworks in 90 of its stations can be downloaded from the SL website (http://sl.se).

BELOW: winter in the city.

You can see beautiful examples of traditional Swedish arts and crafts at the Nordic Museum.

BELOW: the *Vasa* warship, one of the most important shipwrecks in the world.

On the far side of the island, fans of Nordic art should make time for the **Thielska Galleriet** (tel: 08 662 58 84; noon–4pm; charge): Ernest Thiel was pals with Carl Larsson, Edvard Munch and Bruno Liljefors, and accumulated a fine collection of his friends' work.

If you choose bus instead of boat and enter the island over Djurgårdsbron from Strandvägen, the first museum you come to is the **Nordic Museum** ⓯ (Nordiska Muséet; tel: 08 519 546 00; June–Aug daily 10am–5pm, rest of year Mon–Fri 10am–4pm, Sat–Sun 11am–5pm, Wed until 8pm; charge), which depicts Nordic life from the 16th century. It has peasant costumes, a collection of bridal gowns and the traditional silver and gold crowns worn by Swedish brides, exhibits on Lapland culture, folk art, and more.

To the west of the Nordiska Muséet on the waterfront is the huge, oddly shaped **Vasa Museum** ⓰ (Vasamuséet; Galärvarvet; tel: 08 519 548 00; www.vasamuseet.se; June–Aug daily 8.30am–6pm, Sept–May Thur–Mon 10am–5pm, Wed until 8pm; charge). Inaugurated in 1990, the must-see museum houses the *Vasa* warship, built in the 1620s for the Thirty Years War, on the orders of Sweden's warrior king, Gustav II Adolf. She was a magnificent ship, decorated with 700 sculptures and carvings, but her oak was too solid. In 1628 she sank in Stockholm harbour on her maiden voyage. In 1956 the Swedish marine archaeologist Anders Franzén found her and, in 1961, brought her up from the depths. More than 24,000 objects have been salvaged from the seabed, including skeletons, sails, cannon, clothing, tools, coins, butter, rum and many everyday utensils.

A short walk across the bridge is the spectacular **Guldrummet** (Gold Room), an underground vault featuring more than 3,000 prehistoric gold and silver artefacts, inside the **Museum of National Antiquities** ⓱ (Historiska Muséet; Narvavägen; tel: 08 519 556 00; May–Sept daily 10am–5pm, Oct–Apr Tue, Wed, Fri–Sun 11am–5pm, Thur 11am–8pm; charge).

Kungsträdgården

It's anyone's guess what the Swedish sculptor John Tobias Sergel (1740–1814) might have thought of the huge illuminated obelisk, fountain and square that bear his name, and of the modern city around it. The heart of this business and commercial area is not large, but it sits somewhat uneasily with the rest. From **Sergels Torg** it is hard to miss the five towering office blocks on Sveavägen, which cast their shadow over the other buildings. In the 1960s, Stockholm City Council, like so many others, succumbed to the temptation to knock things down and build concrete and glass high-rise buildings.

The destruction of many fine old buildings continued until it threatened the **King's Garden** ⓲ (Kungsträdgården) with the statue of the warrior king Karl XII on its southern side. At this point the Stockholmers had had enough. Normally placid and biddable, they mustered at the King's Garden, climbed the trees that were in danger of the axe, and swore that if the

trees went so did the people. The City Fathers retreated, and Kungsträdgården survives to soften the edges of the new buildings and harmonise with the older buildings that are left. This is the place to take a leisurely stroll or sit beside the fountains on a summer day and enjoy a coffee at its outdoor café. In summer it is the venue of many outdoor festivals and rock concerts. In winter, part of Kungsträdgården is flooded with water and becomes a popular ice rink, and the restaurant moves indoors.

A short stroll east is the early 20th-century private palace housing one of Stockholm's most unusual museums, the **Hallwyl Collection** ⓭ (Hallwylska Muséet; Hamngatan 4; tel: 08 402 30 99; July–Aug Tue–Sun 10am–4pm, rest of the year Tue, Thur–Sun noon–4pm, Wed noon–7pm; guided tours in English Sat 1.30pm; charge). It's the magpie collection of one person, Countess von Hallwyl, from her ornate piano to china, beautiful furniture and personal knick-knacks.

Just north of the museum on Östermalmstorg, stop to snack at **Östermalmshallen**, a classy deli-style market.

Stockholm's shopping centres

Sweden's equivalent of Harrods or Bloomingdales is **Nordiska Kompaniet (NK)** ⓴, on Hamngatan (just opposite Sweden House), whose rooftop illuminated sign, constantly rotating, is visible from far and wide in the city. NK sells everything from shoes to sporting equipment, men's and women's clothing, glass, pottery and silver, jewellery and perfume; its services range from personal shoppers to post office and travel agency, and multilingual staff are always on hand to assist with changing currency and shipping your purchases back home.

Heading west along Hamngatan, you come to **Gallerian** ㉑, a huge covered shopping arcade that stretches to Jakobsgatan; a block west is Sergels Torg, on whose southern side is **Culture House** ㉒ (Kulturhus; Tue–Sun 11am–7pm), a popular meeting place and venue for lectures and entertainment, and the National Theatre.

Åhléns City ㉓ is on the corner of Sergels Torg and Drottninggatan. It has a similar range and quality to NK, and

BELOW LEFT: Stockholm's favourite store, Nordiska Kompaniet (NK).

Royal Parks and Gardens

Ekoparken is the world's first national city park, a huge set of green lungs that stretch out in a 12km (7-mile) long arch from Djurgården (where the Vasamuséet, Gröna Lund and Skansen are situated) in the south, up to Ulriksdals Slott (castle) in the north. This green swathe is so large you'll need a full day of serious hiking to explore it, by foot during the warmer months or on skis or long-distance skates in the winter. Bus tours to the northerly Haga Royal Park, run by Strömma Turism (www.stromma.se), include a free boat tour on Brunnsviken Lake.

The Ekopark includes three royal parks, Djurgården, Haga and Ulriksdal, with palaces to tour (Ulriksdals Slott, Gustav III's Paviljong, Rosendals Slott). Visit the tropical Fjärilshus (Butterfly House), where hundreds of colourful species land lightly upon your shoulder, the Bergianska (Bergianska Botanical Gardens), which contains the world's largest water lily, and Naturhistoriska Riksmuseet (Museum of Natural History), where you'll also find Sweden's only IMAX cinema.

For a pleasant retreat on northern Djurgården, you'll find Rosendalsträgård (Rosendals Garden), with orchards, flowers and vegetables, garden shops and a café. For many Stockholmers this has become the ideal retreat after a day on Djurgården. For Ekoparken information, call the Stockholm tourist office (tel: 08 508 285 08).

a visit to its supermarket food department is a sightseeing tour in itself.

The third of this trio of huge department stores is **PUB**, on Drottninggatan at Hötorget *(see right)*, a galleria featuring a variety of Swedish and international-brand shops.

Drottninggatan

Drottninggatan (Queen's Street), an old street which leads directly through the Riksdagshus and over the bridge from the Royal Palace, is one of Stockholm's main pedestrian ways. In summer, it is full of casual crowds strolling or sitting at one of the outdoor cafés. .

At its northern end is the excellent **Strindberg Museum** ㉔ (Strindbergsmuséet; Drottninggatan 85; tel: 08 411 53 54; July–Aug Tue–Sun 10am–4pm, rest of year Tue–Sun noon–4pm; charge), housed in the top-floor flat of the **Blåtornet** (Blue Tower) where Sweden's greatest playwright spent his last years and wrote his last epic play, *The Great Highway*, in 1908. Even at the end of his life, Strindberg was astonishingly prolific; he produced some 20 books in his four years in the Blue Tower.

Walking south along Drottninggatan to Kungsgatan, on your left you'll come to **Hötorget** ㉕, with its open-air food stalls and indoor market. This is where Swedes shop for food. Here you can find Swedish delicacies such as elk steak and reindeer and the many varieties of Scandinavian cured herring.

Stadshuset

A city as lovely, unusual and pioneering as Stockholm deserves a fitting symbol. And that symbol is the **Stadshus** ㉖ (City Hall, 1923). Lying across the Stadshubron bridge on the island of Kungsholmen, this city landmark was built in the truest spirit of national romanticism. The building is made from around 8 million decorated bricks, and garnished with spires, domes and minarets of green-tinged copper. One corner of the building rises into a 106-metre (450ft) tower; and at the very pinnacle of the tower shine three golden crowns (Tre Kronor), Sweden's emblem.

Inside this brick behemoth, the Blue Hall, with its sweeping marble staircase and colonnades, is used as the banquet-

ing hall for the Nobel Prize ceremony, held in December each year. After the 1,300 guests have finished dining, they move upstairs to the Stadshus's most jaw-dropping room, the shimmering Golden Hall, where 19 million gold mosaic tiles decorate the walls.

Other notable features include a series of frescoes by Prins Eugens Waldemarsudde – the "Painter Prince" – the 10,000-pipe organ and mechanical figures of St George and the Dragon on the north front of the building, which spring into action at noon and 6pm.

Stadshus is the work of architect Ragnar Östberg, who devoted 12 years of his life to the building. You can admire the interior of his masterpiece by guided tour only. There are usually at least six 45-minute English tours daily (depending on municipal events; charge); it's well worth joining one if you can.

Södermalm: artistic centre

From Gamla Stan, take the Tunnelbanan (underground railway) on a five-minute journey south to Slussen station on **Södermalm** ㉗, commonly referred to as "Söder". Once this was the great working-class area of the city, but today it is the coolest, most bohemian part of Stockholm, popular with local artists and bursting with new cafés, restaurants, boutiques and design shops. There is a concentration of galleries on the steep slope of **Hornsgatan** ㉘, a popular street on which to buy locally made art, glass and ceramics. The inner circle of cool, though, is the **"SoFo"** area (south of Folkungsgagatan), the place to head for cafés and nightlife.

Right next to the Slussen underground station is the **City Museum** ㉙ (Stadsmuséet; Ryssgården; tel: 08 508 316 00; Tue–Sun 11am–5pm, Thur until 8pm; charge), voted Stockholm's best museum in 2007. While Stockholm received virtually no mention until the 13th century, the museum makes it clear that this strategic spot had been inhabited for many centuries. Södermalm forms the backdrop for much of the action in Stieg Larsson's best-selling *The Girl with the Dragon Tattoo* and its follow-ups: the Stadsmuséet runs walking tours that point out pertinent landmarks from the books and films (*see box, page 246*).

Swedish design is world-renowned. Wherever you go in the city, you'll never be far from shops selling crystal, china and ceramics, and the fashions of designers like Fifth Avenue Shoe Repair, Filippa K and Acne Jeans.

BELOW: the gleaming interior of the Stadshus.

Contemporary Swedish crystal design by Bertil Vallien; Blues Sculpture, Four Elements.

After the museum, it would be a pity not to make a quick trip up **Katarina-hissen** ③ (mid-May–Aug 8am–10pm, Sept–mid-May 10am–6pm; charge), a 19th-century lift rebuilt in 1935 that carries you to the heights of Södermalm.

Opened in May 2010, the fabulous **Fotografiska** ③ (Stora Tullhus; Stadsgårdshamnen 22; tel: 08-50 900 500; daily 10am–9pm; charge) exhibition space is currently wowing visitors (if not ABBA fans, whose shelved museum was due to open here!). Fotografiska, housed within the impressive Art-Nouveau Customs House (1906), puts on four major photographic exhibitions per year, and around 20 smaller shows and video installations. Previous exhibitions hosted within its superb spaces have included everything from the portraiture of Annie Leibovitz, to Sandy Skoglund's weird tableaux, to contemporary reportage on conflicts in Guatemala and Rwanda.

Just west of Södermalm, the former prison island **Långholmen** is now a lush green space with its own little **beaches**. And sitting off to the south, like a giant golfball on Stockholm's skyline, the **Ericsson Globe** (tel: 0771 811 000; June–Aug daily 9am–9pm, Sept–May Mon–Fri 10am–7pm, Sat–Sun 9.30am–6pm; charge) is the world's largest spherical building. Since its inauguration in 1989, it has mainly been used as the national ice-hockey arena and as a concert venue, but in February 2010, the new Skyview attraction added another dimension. This highly unusual funicular railway takes visitors up the curving sides of the 130-metre (426ft) high Globe in two glass-sided gondolas.

Woodland Cemetery

A short distance south of the Globe is **Woodland Cemetery** ② (Skogskyrkogården; open 24hrs; guided tours in English July–Sept Sun at 10.30am), in the southern suburb of Enskede. It may sound macabre, but this is another of Stockholm's Unesco World Heritage sites and well worth a visit. Skogskyrkogården is a place of immense calm and beauty, with five striking chapels, and where every curve in every pathway was built with care and purpose. The work of two of Sweden's most

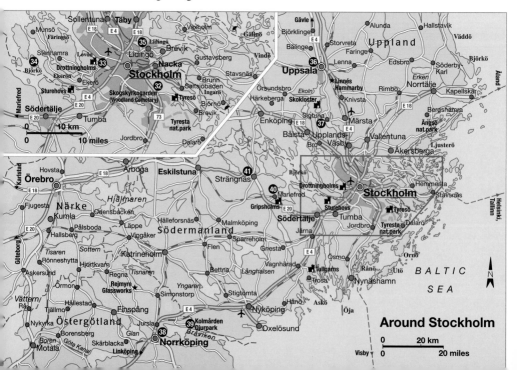

Around Stockholm

0   20 km

0   20 miles

important architects, Gunnar Asplund and Sigurd Lewerentz, this masterpiece of Modernist design took 25 years (1915–40) to create. Greta Garbo is buried here, as is Asplund himself.

The Stockholm archipelago

It is a rare city that has 24,000 islands on its doorstep and 100km (60 miles) of lake at its heart, but this is Stockholm's eternal good fortune. Until the building of the Tunnelbanen, boats were the only means of getting around these vast expanses of water, and today boats are still part of Stockholm life. Boat operators Waxholmsbolaget (www. waxholmsbolaget.se) and Strömma Kanalbolaget (www.stromma.se) transport passengers around the archipelago (see page 258) in a variety of craft, from old coal-fired steamers to modern ferries.

The most popular place to visit in the archipelago is the royal palace, **Drottningholms Slott** ㉝ on Lovön (see page 257), to the west of the city. West of Lovön is **Björkö** ㉞, the site of Sweden's oldest city, **Birka**, now a Unesco World Heritage site. Between AD 790 and 975, Birka was the trad-

ing centre for the 40,000 inhabitants of the rich Mälaren area and the meeting point for traders. This was also where Christianity first came to Sweden, when Ansgar, the Saxon missionary, landed in the 9th century. Almost nothing is left of Birka above ground, but archaeological digs have revealed much of the town's story: **Birka Vikingastaden** (tel: 08 560 514 45; May–Sept 10am–5pm; charge) features the most recent finds, and Viking-based activities in summer add life to the island.

Although it is now easy to get there by underground train (T–Ropsten), in summer it is worthwhile taking the boat to the island suburb of **Lidingö** ㉟, to visit **Millesgården** (tel: 08 446 75 90; mid-May–Sept 11am–5pm, Oct–mid-May Tue–Sun noon–5pm; charge), the summer home of sculptor Carl Milles and his wife, the Austrian painter Olga Granner. Here, Milles patiently reproduced the statues that had made him more famous in his adopted country of the US than in Sweden. His creations seem to defy gravity: they appear to soar and fly, emphasised by their position on terraces carved from the cliffs.

August is the time for a kräftskiva (crayfish party). Under the glow of paper lanterns, Swedes enjoy this beloved shellfish, once plentiful in freshwater lakes, but now imported.

BELOW LEFT: a blacksmith at the Birka Viking museum.
BELOW: interior of the Royal Palace.

There are plenty of outdoor restaurants for alfresco refreshments on Gamla Stan.

BELOW: a house in Valholm.

North of Stockholm

Less than an hour's drive north of Stockholm on the E4 lies **Uppsala 36**, Sweden's ancient capital, seat of one of Europe's greatest universities. This is the birthplace of Ingmar Bergman and the setting for his film *Fanny and Alexander*. The town also has the largest Gothic cathedral to be found in Scandinavia, **Domkyrkan** (May–Sept daily 8am–6pm, Oct–Apr Sun–Fri 8am–6pm, Sat 10am–6pm). Its vaults, from 1435, house the shrine of Saint Erik, a former king and the patron saint of Sweden.

Across the town's lush parks rises **Uppsala Slott**, a fortress from the days of the Vasa dynasty (now a small art gallery; tel: 018-727 24 82). A few minutes north of the town lies **Gamla Uppsala** (Old Uppsala), 5th-century bastion of the Yngling dynasty. The three huge grave mounds of kings Aun, Egil and Adils (described in *Beowulf*) dominate the grave fields beyond the **Gamla Uppsala Museum** (tel: 018 23 93 12; May–Sept daily 10am–4pm, Apr and Oct Mon, Wed, Sat–Sun noon–3pm; charge), which does a good job of explaining the Viking world.

Near Uppsala, where the sea meets the forest, you'll find **Sigtuna 37**, Sweden's oldest town. In the 11th century this was the commercial centre for the Svea and Vandal tribes. Merchant ships from as far away as Asia dropped anchor here; monasteries and abbeys competed with one another in building glorious churches. Today, Sigtuna is a picturesque town with crooked lanes, quaint wooden houses and a miniature town hall. Tant Brun's café on the main pedestrian lane is a lovely place to stop for a cup of strong Swedish coffee and a freshly baked cinnamon bun.

South and west of Stockholm

To the south of Stockholm is **Norrköping 38**, with its tree-lined avenues, outdoor cafés, 19th-century canalscape, trams and elegant architecture. The town's main attraction is **Kolmården Djurpark 39**, Scandinavia's wildlife safari, natural habitat and amusement park supreme (tel: 010 708 7000; May and June daily 10am–5pm, July–mid-Aug 10am–7pm, late Aug 10am–5pm, Sept Sat–Sun 10am–5pm; charge).

Heading west of Stockholm towards Lake Mälaren's bays and inlets, you come to idyllic **Mariefred 40** and the impressive **Gripsholms Slott** (Castle; tel: 0159 101 94; mid-May–mid-Sept daily 10am–4pm, early May and mid-Sept–Nov Sat–Sun noon–3pm; charge), which contains the royal portrait collections and a marvellous theatre from the late 1700s. Best of all is the architecture of this fortress, begun in the 1370s and continually updated. Around the edge of the moat is a collection of runestones carved with serpents, ships and inscriptions. Mariefred is a lazy summer lake town, with cafés and restaurants to suit all tastes, and ferry connections to Stockholm.

Further west around the lakeshore is **Strängnäs 41**, a delightful small town dominated by a magnificent Gothic cathedral. Next to the church at **Boglösa**, 20km (12 miles) north, are hundreds of Bronze Age rock carvings. ❑

A Royal Treat: Drottningholm Palace

Often referred to as Sweden's "mini Versailles", the island palace of Drottningholm with its exquisite gardens and historic theatre is not to be missed

The most popular place to visit in Stockholm's archipelago is Drottningholms Slott (tel: 08 402 62 80; May–Aug daily 10am–4.30pm, Sept 11am–3.30pm, Oct–Apr Sat–Sun noon–3.30pm; charge) on Lovön. Now the main home of the Swedish royal family, the 17th-century palace is a Unesco World Heritage site, surrounded by formal Baroque and rococo gardens of fountains, statues, flowerbeds, box hedges and a variety of trees.

The palace was built for Eleonora, the widow of King Karl X, by the Tessin family of architects headed by Nicodemus the Elder (1615–81). Work began in 1662 and was completed by his son, Nicodemus the Younger.

Although the royal family live at Drottningholm, much of the palace is open to the public. Interior highlights include a magnificent Grand Staircase with *trompe l'œil* paintings by Johan Sylvius, the Baroque Karl X Gallery, Queen Hedwig Eleonora's State Bedroom with its richly painted ceiling, and the library of Queen Louisa Ulrika, who married King Adolf Fredrik in 1744.

In the parkland stands the exotic pagoda roofs and ornamental balconies of the Kina Slott (Chinese Pavilion; tel: 08 402 62 70; May–Aug daily 11am–4-.30pm, Sept daily noon–3.30pm; charge), a birthday present to Queen Louisa Ulrika from her husband. In one of four adjoining pavilions the king had his carpentry workshop. In Kanton, a small village built next to Kina Slott, silkworms that had been introduced perished in the freezing winter, thwarting the court's attempt to produce cheap silk.

The island's greatest treasure is undoubtedly the 18th-century Drottningholms Slottsteater (Court Theatre; tel: 08 759 04 06; May–Sept guided tours only; charge). The theatre was designed for Queen Louisa Ulrika by Carl Fredrik Adelcrantz and opened in 1766. The queen's son, Gustav III, was an actor and playwright who became known as the "Theatre King". He invited French troupes of actors to perform at Drottningholm, and the theatre soon became an influential centre for performing arts. Gustav went on to found Stockholm's Dramatic Theatre and developed a native theatre and opera.

The building fell into disrepair in the 19th century, then in the early 20th century it underwent extensive restoration. Today it is the oldest theatre in the world still using its original backdrops and stage machinery for productions. In summer, the annual opera festival stages works from the time of the theatre's glory days, with the music performed on period instruments – attending one of these performances is a magical experience. ❑

TOP: formal gardens at Drottningholm.
RIGHT: the entrance to the palace.

STEAMING OUT AMONG THE SKERRIES

When summer comes, the Swedes set off by boat to the thousands of idyllic islands that dot the waterways between Stockholm and the Baltic

Every summer thousands of Swedes in boats navigate carefully through waters loaded with the 24,000 islands, rocks and islets of the Stockholm archipelago. The brackish waters start in the centre of Stockholm and extend 80km (50 miles) out into the open Baltic Sea. Close to the mainland, the islands are larger and more lush, the bays and channels wider. Hidden here are idyllic island communities, farmlands and small forests. But as you travel further out, the scenery becomes more rugged, finally ending in sparse windblown islets formed by the last Ice Age.

Island retreats

In the middle of the 19th century affluent Stockholm families began to build their second homes along the shores of the various islands in the archipelago. Over the years, "commoners" had more money and leisure time and soon they, too, sought their way to the archipelago. The combination of wilderness, sea, fresh air and closeness to the city satisfied many leisure needs. Today, Swedes either own their cottages or rent them, and enjoy swimming, fishing, boating, nature walks and socialising with friends.

BELOW: more than 50,000 second homes offering varying degrees of comfort are spread throughout Stockholm's archipelago.

ABOVE: many Swedes learn to sail from a very early age; getting o on the water is almost considered a birthright.

ABOVE: crayfish parties, with much drinking of schnapps and singing of folk songs, are held throughout Sweden to celebrate the summer.

A QUICK GUIDE TO ISLAND-HOPPING

The archipelago can be explored on guided tours from Stockholm's city centre. But if you want to travel like the locals, then buy a *Båtluffarkort* (Inter-skerries card, Skr 420) from the Waxholm boat company (tel: 08 679 58 30; www.waxholmsbolaget.se), which allows you to see as many islands as you can in five days, including:
• Sandön, with its attractive sailing centre village of Sandhamn, sandy beaches and some good restaurants (3 hours by boat from Stockholm).
• Fjäderholmarna, featuring a boat museum, fish-smoking plant, restaurants and crafts shops (20 minutes by boat).
• Vaxholm, with its famous fortress (1 hour by boat).
• Utö, where a 12th-century iron mine is the main attraction, a great place for bike-riding (3½ hours by boat).

RIGHT: there are plenty of ferries to help you get around.

BOVE: Valholm, one the most popular ands in the chipelago.

IGHT: sailing on Lake alaren; such is the portance of water to e Swedes that one ten residents owns boat.

SOUTHERN SWEDEN

Across the Öresund bridge from Denmark, southern Sweden is home to the lively city of Malmö. Castles and Stone Age sites abound, while bathers and birdwatchers head for Öland

Skåne is Sweden's most southerly province, so close to Denmark across the narrow sound that even the accent is faintly Danish. For centuries Swedes and Danes fought over this area, along with the provinces of Halland and Blekinge, until Sweden established its sovereignty in 1658. Since 2000, however, the two countries have been joined by the Öresund road and rail bridge that links Malmö and Copenhagen. The project has prompted a renaissance for southern Sweden as a centre of the Danish–Swedish Öresund region, with a total of 3 million people and one-fifth of the total combined GNP of Sweden and Denmark.

Skåne is often called Sweden's food store because of its rich farmland, mild climate and good fishing. Along the coast the landscape is undulating and lush, and especially spectacular in the southeast corner, Österlen. Inland, there are lakes and three large ridges with lovely walks.

Skåne is renowned for its castles and manor houses. There are said to be 240 in the province, most of which are in private ownership, but it is usually possible to walk round parts of the house and/or gardens such as at **Sofiero ❶**, 4km (2½ miles) north of Helsingborg (tel: 042 14 52 59; daily Apr–Sept 10am–6pm; charge). Built in 1857, Sofiero was used by King Gustav

VI Adolf as his summer palace until his death in 1973. He was a keen botanist, as the gardens show – they were awarded the title of Europe's most beautiful park in 2010.

Malmö: city of the south

Malmö ❷ is Sweden's third city, a lively, multicultural place with a population of about 310,000 and a bubbling restaurant scene. In the 16th century, Malmö competed with Copenhagen to be Scandinavia's leading capital. In those days it was an important port, not

Main attractions
SOFIERO GARDENS
MODERNA MUSÉET, MALMÖ
LUND CATHEDRAL
KARLSKRONA
ÖLAND
UTVANDRARNAS HUS, VÄXJÖ
KALMAR CASTLE
GLASRIKET (GLASS KINGDOM)
GOTLAND AND VISBY

LEFT: gathering for the Midsummer Festival.
RIGHT: the town hall, Malmö.

Sweden leads the world in glass-making. Many of the famous glassworks, such as Kosta Boda, are located in the southeast of the country.

far from rich fishing grounds. Today, the harbour is still busy and many of the old buildings remain. **Malmöhus**, the dominating castle built by King Christian III when Skåne was still part of Denmark, is Scandinavia's oldest remaining Renaissance castle. It houses the **Malmö Museer** (Malmö Museums; tel: 040 34 44 00; June–Aug daily 10am–4pm, Sept–May Mon–Fri 10am–4pm, Sat–Sun noon–4pm; charge), which include the Art Museum, history exhibitions, an aquarium, the Science and Technology/Maritime Museum and the **Kommendants Hus** (Commander's House).

From the same period is **Rådhus** (City Hall; tel: 040 34 34 34; Mon–Fri 8am–4.30pm), which you will find in **Stortorget**, one of the largest squares in Scandinavia. It was built in 1546 in genuine Dutch Renaissance style. In 1860 it was given a facelift with niches, bays, allegorical paintings and colonnades. Northeast from Stortorget is **St Petri Kyrka**, Göran Olsgatan 1, built in the Baltic Gothic style and dating from the 13th century, although its towers were built in the 15th century and

its copper spires in 1890. This elegant cathedral features a beautiful altar area created by sculptors in 1611.

A particularly idyllic place to sit and relax is **Lilla Torg** (Little Square), with its cobblestones, carefully restored houses and 16th-century charm. Through an arch on the south side of the square is Hemanska Gården. Once a merchant's home and trading yard, it now houses the **Form/Design Center** (tel: 040 664 51 50; Tue, Wed and Fri 11am–5pm, Thur until 6pm, Sat–Sun noon–4pm; free), where Swedish industrial design and handicrafts are displayed.

Walking east from Lilla Torg, make sure you don't miss Malmö's exciting new cultural hub, the **Moderna Muséet** (Gasverksgatan 22; tel: 040 685 7937; www.modernamuseet.se/malmo; Wed 11am–9pm, Thur–Sun 11am–6pm; charge), which opened at the end of 2009. This former power station now contains one of the most comprehensive 20th-century art collections in Scandinavia, and hosts changing exhibitions of local and international artists.

Malmö's most impressive modern building is without doubt the **Turn-**

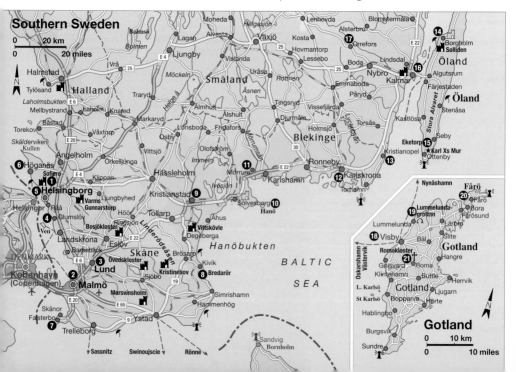

ing Torso, Sweden's tallest building at 190 metres (620ft), designed by Spanish architect Santiago Calatrava. This unique structure, which twists 90° from bottom to top, has revitalised the West Harbour area of the city, now a popular summer dining spot.

Towards Helsingborg

Heading northeast from Malmö, Lund ❸ is a university town with a fine cathedral, **Domkyrkan**, built in the 12th century. Don't miss **Kulturen** (Cultural History Museum; Tegnérplatsen; tel: 046 35 04 00; May–Aug daily 11am–5pm, Sept–Apr Tue–Sun noon–4pm; charge), an open-air museum with dozens of buildings, silver, textiles, ceramics and art. Along with the University of Uppsala, Lund is one of the two ancient Swedish universities. About 30km (19 miles) north along the coast, **Glumslöv** ❹ offers memorable views. From the hill above the church, on a clear day you can see 30 churches and seven towns, including Copenhagen and Helsingør in Denmark.

Helsingborg ❺, 60km (37 miles) north of Malmö, is an interesting town of cobbled streets, dominated by the ruined castle, **Kärnan**. Frequent ferries to Helsingør in Denmark leave from its busy harbour. **Höganäs** ❻, 20km (12 miles) north, is devoted to potters and artists. The large pottery merits a visit.

Along the south coast

Some 40km (25 miles) southwest of Malmö are the summer idylls of **Skanör** and **Falsterbo** ❼. **Skanörs Ljung** is recommended for bird-lovers, particularly in September and October, when a large number of migrating birds gather.

Southeast of Kivik is **Bredarör** ❽, site of the Bronze Age **Kiviksgraven** (King's Grave). Scientists still debate the mysterious markings on the stones, unearthed in 1748, which are different from any others found in the region.

Kristianstad ❾ is the birthplace of the Swedish film industry, which started around 1910. The original studio is intact and is now a museum

where you can watch old films on video (**Filmmuséet**; Östra Storgatan 53; tel: 044 13 57 29; July–mid-Aug Tue–Fri 1–6pm, mid-Aug–June Sun noon–5pm; free). Nearby, **Kristianstad Vattenriket** (Water Kingdom) is a rich wetland on the Helge River, with a diversity of birds, wildlife and plants.

Blekinge is a tiny province with sandy beaches and Sweden's most southerly archipelago. It is excellent for sea fishing. You can enjoy peaceful angling in some of the lakes, or good sport for salmon in the Mörrum River. Canoeing is popular. Driving to Blekinge from Skåne, you first reach **Sölvesborg** ❿, and the ruins of 13th-century **Sölvesborg Castle** (Slott).

Mörrum ⓫, 30km (19 miles) north of Sölvesborg, is noted for its salmon fishing: at **Mörrums Kronolaxfiske** you can see salmon and trout at different stages of their development; fishing fans can cast a line here too (tel: 0454 501 23; Apr–Sept daily 9am–5pm, Oct daily until 4pm; charge).

The biggest town in Blekinge is **Karlskrona** ⓬, a naval centre built in the 17th century, with wide streets and impressive

TIP

Råå, on the outskirts of Helsingborg, is a picturesque fishing village with an excellent inn.

BELOW: Kärnan, the remains of Helsingborg castle.

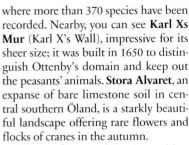

During the late 19th and early 20th centuries, Sweden's population exploded, and many families could no longer eke out a living on the land. So began the years of migration to North America. A popular place to visit is Utvandrarnas Hus (House of the Emigrants; tel: 0470 201 20; www. utvandrarnashus.se/ eng) in Växjö, 70km (43 miles) west of Kalmar, which tells the story of the exodus.

BELOW: limestone formations along the coast at Byrum, Öland.

buildings. In the Björkholmen district you'll find quaint 18th-century cottages built by ships' carpenters. The nearby village of **Kristianopel** is renowned for its smoked herring.

Öland island

The island of **Öland**, off the east coast, is one of the most visited areas of Sweden and, with its diverse landscape and superb beaches, it is a paradise for birdwatchers, nature-lovers and sun-worshippers. Above the main town of **Borgholm** ⑭ rise the huge ruins of **Borgholm Slott** (Castle), a once splendid residence from the 12th century (May–Aug daily 10am–6pm, Apr and Sept until 4pm; charge).

The island has many ancient burial places, and there are remains of 16 fortified dwellings from earlier times. The most interesting is **Eketorp** ⑮ (July–mid-Aug 10am–6pm, June and end of Aug 11am–5pm) in the south, which has been reconstructed and now hums with medieval re-enactors and craftspeople in summer. Sweden's prime bird-watching can be enjoyed at the **Ottenby Bird Station**, on the island's southerly tip,

where more than 370 species have been recorded. Nearby, you can see **Karl Xs Mur** (Karl X's Wall), impressive for its sheer size; it was built in 1650 to distinguish Ottenby's domain and keep out the peasants' animals. **Stora Alvaret**, an expanse of bare limestone soil in central southern Öland, is a starkly beautiful landscape offering rare flowers and flocks of cranes in the autumn.

Kalmar ⑯, one of Sweden's oldest cities, was of great importance in the Swedish–Danish wars. Sweden's best-preserved Renaissance castle, **Kalmar Slott** (tel: 0480 451 490; Apr and Oct Sat–Sun 11am–3.30pm, May–June daily 10am–4pm, July–mid-Aug 10am–6pm, mid-Aug–Sept 10am–4pm; charge), was begun in the 12th century but was completely renovated during the 16th century by the Vasa kings. The castle's coffered ceilings, panelled halls, fresco paintings and magnificent stonework have inspired the Renaissance Festival, held every July, featuring tournament games, market, music and theatre.

Kingdom of glass

Northwest of Kalmar, about 20km (12 miles) is **Orrefors** ⑰, part of Sweden's **Glasriket** (Glass Kingdom). The first glass was melted in Sweden in 1556 but it was not established as an industry until 1742, when **Kosta**, the oldest works, was founded to the west of Orrefors. Today, the Kosta, Orrefors and Åfors glassworks have merged to create one mighty glass-making company: you will find its wares marketed under both the brand names "Kosta Boda" and "Orrefors". Most of the 13 glassworks in the area are open to visitors for demonstrations, and many have shops – for further information, see the Glasriket website www.glasriket.se.

Also look out for *hyttsill* ("glassworks herring") evenings. In bygone times the glassworks were a social centre where locals would gather to bake herring and potatoes in the furnace, with music provided by an accordionist or fiddler. Some glassworks have revived this tradition for visitors. ❑

Gotland: the Sunshine Island

With its medieval towns, sandy beaches and curious rock formations, tranquil Gotland – the largest island in the Baltic – is a favourite holiday spot

Gotland is an island of gaunt rocks, forests, wild flowers, cliffs and sandy beaches, blessed with more hours of sunshine than anywhere else in the country. Swedes naturally flock here for their summer holidays.

Gotland was created over thousands of years as the animals and plants of the ancient Silurian sea slowly sank into the sediment that was to become the limestone platform of modern Gotland. Million-year-old fossils and the island's monumental sea-stacks *(raukar)* can still be found on the coast.

In the Viking Age the island was a busy trading post. **Visby** ⓳, the principal centre of population, later became a prosperous Hanseatic town. Great stone houses were erected, churches were founded and a city wall was built. Today, 3km (2 miles) of the medieval limestone wall remains virtually intact, interspersed with 44 towers and numerous gates. It is now a Unesco World Heritage site.

Limestone has created one of the island's major attractions – the impressive subterranean tunnels and stalactite caves of **Lummelundagrottan** ⓳ (tel: 0498 27 30 50; May–Sept daily; guided tours only; charge), 13km (8 miles) to the north of Visby, which should not be missed. Dress warmly, as it's 8°C (46°F) inside. Above ground, the new Lummelunda Tree Park was due to open in June 2011.

About 50km (30 miles) north of Visby lies **Fårö** ⓴, the "island of sheep". Take a ferry to the island from Fårösund, and enjoy sites such as Gamlehamn, a medieval harbour, and the ruins of a chapel to St Olof. You can also see one of Gotland's most bizarrely shaped *raukar*, "The Camel", and visit the beach of Sundersand. After you have been here a little while, you will begin to understand why Fårö was Ingmar Bergman's favourite place.

Sweden's most primitive horse, the Russ, has lived in the forests of the island from time immemo-

rial. The name Russ comes from the Old Norse *hross*, and it is thought that the horse is a descendant of the wild Tarpan. You can see them, only 123–126cm (46–52 inches) tall, around the island.

Wherever you travel in Gotland, you'll come across at least one of its 92 medieval churches. At **Romakloster** ㉑, in the centre of the island, there is a ruined monastery from the 12th century. There are many other relics of the past, including runic stones and burial mounds. If you reach Gotland's southernmost tip, you'll see some of the most impressive *raukar* on the island. ❑

ABOVE AND RIGHT: Stana Kerlso in Gotland, the perfect getaway island.

SWEDEN'S WEST COAST

From the sandy beaches of Halland to the bustling city of Göteborg and the rocky shores of Bohuslän, the west coast has long been a summer playground for Swedes

The west coast of Sweden, generously dotted with beaches and fishing villages, is 400km (250 miles) of glorious coastline divided in two by the city of Göteborg (Gothenburg). It has been a favourite holiday spot since the early 20th century. The best beaches are in the southern province of Halland. North of Göteborg, in Bohuslän, is a majestic coast of granite rocks and islands.

The E6 connects all the larger cities, but follow the small coastal roads to discover the gems. Starting along the coast in the northwestern corner of the county of Skåne, a number of small towns offer views into the past. **Gamla Viken ❶**, 15km (9 miles) north of Helsingborg on Highway 22, is a picturesque fishing village. **Torekov**, at the tip of the next peninsula, has a seaside golf course and boats to the island of **Hallands Väderö**, where you can spot seals basking offshore.

Halland coast

Halmstad ❷, the largest town in Halland and Sweden's "golf capital", lies on the River Nissan. **Halmstads Slott** (Castle), the provincial governor's residence, was built in the 17th century by the Danish king Kristian IV. In front of the castle is moored the old sail-training vessel *Najaden* (closed for renovation in 2011), built in 1897. Other sights

include **St Nikolai**, a 13th-century church. **Tylösand**, 8km (5 miles) west of Halmstad, is a popular holiday resort with a predominantly sandy beach and two golf courses. There are good beaches at **Östra Strand**, **Ringenäs** and **Haverdalsstrand**.

Falkenberg ❸, 40km (25 miles) north of Halmstad, is on the Ätran, a river famous for its salmon. The old part of the town with its 18th-century wooden houses and cobbled streets is centred on the 14th-century **St Laurenti Church**. There is an old toll

LEFT: holiday cottage on Klädesholmen.
RIGHT: north Bohuslän coast.

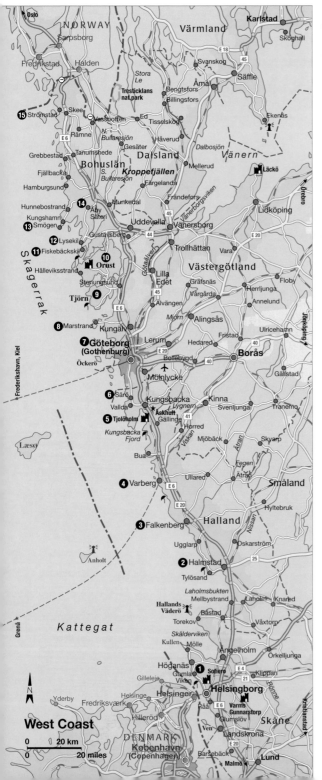

bridge *(tullbron)* from 1756 and Sweden's oldest pottery, **Törngrens Krukmakeri**, run by the Törngren family since 1789 (tel: 0346 103 54; Mon–Fri 9.30am–4.30pm). Good beaches are found at **Olofsby** (north of the town) and **Skrea Strand** (south of the town).

Continue 30km (19 miles) north on the E6 to **Varberg ❹**, a bustling place combining spa, resort, port and commercial centre with a ferry service to Grenå in Denmark. **Varbergs Fästning** (Fortress) stands beside the water and houses a youth hostel, restaurant, apartments and a **museum** (mid-June–mid-Aug 10am–6pm, mid-Aug–mid-June Mon–Fri 10am–4pm, Sat–Sun noon–4pm; charge). Pride of place goes to the Bocksten Man, the only preserved figure in the world wearing a complete costume from the Middle Ages. Reminders of Varberg's late 19th-century development as a spa resort include **Societetshus** (1883), an elaborate wooden pavilion in the park, and the bathing station (1903), a rectangular wooden structure open to the sea, with changing huts and deck chairs round the sides. After a quick plunge in the pool, bathers can relax over coffee and waffles.

North to Särö

Heading 30km (19 miles) north towards **Kungsbacka**, you will pass the most out-of-character building along the entire coast. **Tjolöholm Castle ❺** (tel: 0300 40 46 00; June–Aug daily 11am–4pm, Feb–May and Sept–mid-Nov by guided tour only Sat–Sun noon, 1.30pm and 3pm; charge) was built in the early 20th century in an English Tudor style, with a splendid Art Nouveau interior.

Instead of beaches, a dramatic landscape of rocks, inlets and islands takes over at the little seaside resort of **Särö ❻** (immediately north of Kungsbacka). In the early 19th century Särö was a fashionable resort, popular with the Swedish royal family. It remains in a time warp. You can walk along the Strandpromenaden and through **Särö**

Västerskog, one of the oldest oak woods on the west coast.

Göteborg

Göteborg ❼ (Gothenburg) is the second-largest city in Sweden, with 510,000 inhabitants. Once a gritty industrial seaport, Göteborg has evolved into a sophisticated 21st-century city, with a thriving cultural life (including a growing reputation for world-class cuisine) and beautiful parks (there are reputedly 175 sq metres (1,880 sq ft) of green space per citizen). Dutch architects planned the city in the 17th century for King Gustav II Adolf, and it grew in stature during the 18th century, when the Swedish East India Company began shipping luxury goods from the Orient. Göteborg is still Scandinavia's largest port: the harbour area is its soul and a good place to start your sightseeing.

The bold **Göteborgsoperan** ❹ (Opera House; tel: 031 13 13 00 for bookings, 031 10 80 00 for info) stands on the water just west of the commercial centre. Built in ship-like style in 1994, it is well worth a visit for its architecture alone. Near the Opera is Göteborg's

Maritiman ❸ (Maritime Centre; tel: 031 10 59 50; May–Sept 11am–6pm, Apr and Oct Fri–Sun 11am–4pm; charge), on Packhuskajen. The world's largest floating ship museum, it features 20 ships, including a submarine, destroyer and lightship. Göteborg got its own Ferris wheel, the 60-metre (200ft) high **Wheel of Göteborg** ❹ (June–Aug 11am–9pm, May and Sept Wed–Sun 11am–9pm, Oct–Nov and Feb–Apr Fri–Sun 11am–9pm; charge) in 2010, giving great views of the area.

The heart of Göteborg lies along Östra Hamngatan and Kungsportsavenyn. Start at the northern end of Östra Hamngatan; heading south you will pass **Nordstan**, one of Northern Europe's largest covered shopping centres. Along the intersecting streets of Norra and Södra Hamngatan are dozens of small and inviting boutiques. Cross Stora Hamnkanalen (Great Harbour Canal) and continue south to **Kungsportsplatsen**, where you can pop into the **Göteborgs Turistbyrå** ❹ (Tourist Office; tel: 031 368 42 00 24hr call answering service, 031 61 25 00 hotel booking; call for opening hours).

> **TIP**
>
> A Göteborg City Card gives free parking, unlimited travel on city buses and trams, a boat trip and free admission to many museums and to Liseberg, and is available for 24 or 48 hours.

BELOW: Göteborg's waterfront Opera House.

Take a ride on the wheel of Göteborg for great views of the city.

Across the street is **Saluhallen ⓔ**, a large indoor marketplace (1886–9) stocked with Swedish specialities such as seafood, cheese and meats. This is a good place to enjoy a cup of coffee or a full lunch.

Kungsportsplatsen is also the place to embark on a **Paddan** (Swedish for "toad"), one of the flat-bottomed sightseeing boats that cruise through the old moat, along 17th-century canals, under 20 bridges, out into the harbour and back again (tel: 031 60 96 70; May–Sept, first departure 10.30am).

From Kungsportsplatsen, cross the moat into Kungsportsavenyn – known as "**Avenyn**" ⓕ (The Avenue), a long, wide boulevard lined with trees, restaurants, pubs and cafés. Halfway along the Avenyn, you are just a block away from the **Röhsska Muséet ⓖ** (Vasagatan 37–39; tel: 031 36 83 150; Tue noon–8pm, Wed–Fri noon–5pm, Sat–Sun 11am–5pm; charge), the Swedish museum for design and handicrafts.

At the southern end of the Avenyn is Göteborg's cultural centre, **Götaplatsen**, with the Poseidon fountain by the Swedish sculptor Carl Milles. Götaplat-

sen is flanked by the **Konstmuseum ⓗ** (Art Museum; tel: 031 368 35 00; Tue and Thur 11am–6pm, Wed until 9pm, Fri–Sun until 5pm; charge), with an extensive collection of Scandinavian art, including work by Munch, Zorn, Rembrandt and Pissarro. Also on the square is the **Konserthus ⓘ** (Concert Hall), home of the Göteborg Symphony Orchestra.

Liseberg ⓙ (tel: 031 40 01 00; late Apr–early Sept and Christmas; charge), in the middle of town, is the largest amusement park in Scandinavia, with 37 attractions including 2011's new ride AtmosFear, the highest freefall plummet in Europe.

Also great for families is **Universeum ⓚ** (tel: 031 335 64 50; July–mid-Aug 9am–8pm, mid-Aug–June 10am–6pm; charge), an impressive science and nature centre with shark tunnel and rainforest zone.

For a calmer experience, wander through the picturesque little 18th-century neighbourhood of Haga on the way to the **Botaniska Trädgården ⓛ** (Botanical Gardens) or **Slottsskogen ⓜ**, just two of Göteborg's 20 parks.

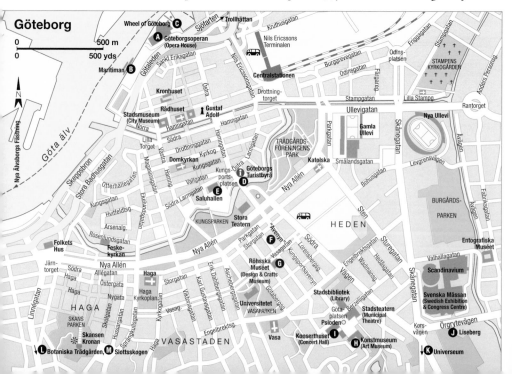

Göteborg

The rugged coast

The province of Bohuslän begins north of Göteborg. To see the coast, head 15km (9 miles) west from Kungälv on route 168 past Tjuvkil, where you can catch a ferry to **Marstrand ❽**, a car-free town and a popular holiday resort and sailing centre. **Carlstens Fästning** (Fortress) dominates the town and offers the best views of the island.

Beyond Marstrand lie the islands of Tjörn and Orust, connected by bridge to the mainland. **Tjörn ❾** is beautiful, with some barren areas inland and a fascinating coastline. A magnificent curved bridge links Tjörn and **Orust ❿**. This island, the third-largest in Sweden, has its quota of fishing villages, including Mollösund, Ellös and Käringön.

Returning to the mainland, take a ferry across the **Gullmarn**, Sweden's only genuine fjord, from **Fiskebäckskil ⓫** to **Lysekil ⓬**. Lysekil comes to life in the summer with boat excursions to the islands and sea fishing trips. **Havets Hus** (sea aquarium; tel: 0523 66 81 61; mid-June–late Aug daily 10am–6pm, late Aug–mid-Nov and mid-Feb–mid-June until 4pm; charge) includes a tunnel aquarium containing rays and sharks.

North of Lysekil on the Sotenäs peninsula, the small harbour of **Smögen ⓭** is a favourite stop for boats. The main attraction is the wooden, waterside boardwalk, where you can shop, stroll and lounge. The other attraction is fresh shrimp. Watch a fish auction and then go round the corner to buy some of the catch.

At **Åby Säteri ⓮**, 17km (11 miles) northeast of Smögen, is **Nordens Ark** (tel: 0523 795 45; daily July–mid-Aug 10am–7pm, May–June and mid-Aug–Sept 10am–5pm, Jan–Apr and Oct–Dec 10am–4pm; charge), a nature park featuring endangered species and old breeds of Nordic farm animals.

Towards Norway

The last town before the Norwegian frontier is **Strömstad ⓯**, a health resort noted for its long hours of sunshine. Strömstad shrimps are considered by the local inhabitants to be in a class of their own, with a distinctive mild flavour. The district has more than a touch of Norwegian about it, having been part of Norway until 1717. ❏

At Vitlycke, near Tanumshede, a small town about 50km (30 miles) north of Göteborg, is Europe's largest collection of Bronze Age rock carvings, and a Unesco World Heritage site. The petroglyphs include detailed depictions of battles, ships, hunting and fishing scenes, and mating couples.

BELOW LEFT: pretty window in Grundsund. **BELOW:** Fiskebäckskil.

SWEDEN'S GREAT LAKES

Two of Europe's largest lakes, Vänern and Vättern, lie at the heart of southern Sweden. In this area of farmland and forests, painted churches, grand castles and literary hideaways abound

Two enormous lakes, Vänern and Vättern, dominate the map of Sweden. The larger of the two is Vänern, a vast stretch of water with an area of 5,585 sq km (2,156 sq miles) and the largest lake in Western Europe. Its western shore embraces two provinces, Dalsland and Värmland.

Dalsland is a province of neat farms and prosperous small towns and villages, with empty roads running through its forests. The greatest attraction here is nature and, thus, the most interesting activities are outdoors: namely, camping, hiking and canoeing. The upland area of **Kroppefjällen ●** is a nature reserve, and one of the best ways to explore the region is to hike along the 15km (9-mile) **Karl XIIs Väg** (Karolinerleden), a historic walking trail; maps can be obtained from the tourist office in **Mellerud** (tel: 0530 189 00).

A local feature is the **Dalslands Kanal**, a network of interconnected lakes and rivers. It was designed by Nils Ericsson and built between 1864 and 1868 to provide better transport for the local ironworks and sawmills. Today, it is popular for sailing and canoeing.

The aqueduct at **Håverud ●**, 14km (9 miles) north of Mellerud, is a dramatic piece of engineering. Made of iron and 33 metres (108ft) long, it carries the canal over the rapids of the River Upperud.

Along the Klarälven

The Värmland region is covered with spruce and pine and crisscrossed with narrow lakes and rivers; the **Klarälven** is among its most beautiful. The river begins turbulently in Norway, where it is called Trysilelva, but gradually becomes broader, winding and sluggish before emptying into Lake Vänern near the province's largest town, **Karlstad ❸**. Highlights of Karlstad include the cathedral (1730), the longest arched stone bridge in Sweden (168 metres/550ft), and a popular park,

Main attractions
HÅVERUD AQUEDUCT
RAFTING ON THE KLARÄLVEN RIVER
NOBEL MUSEUM
ÖREBRO
MARIESTAD
LÄCKÖ CASTLE
TROLLHÄTTAN
CRANE COURTSHIP DANCE, HORNBORGASJÖN
KARLSBORG FORTRESS
BOATING OR CYCLING ALONG THE GÖTA KANAL

LEFT: canoeing on the Klarälven River.
RIGHT: negotiating the Dalslands Kanal.

Mariebergsskogen. The Klarälven was the last Swedish river used for floating logs. The practice ended in 1991, but in **Dyvelsten** ❹, 17km (10 miles) north of Karlstad, the **Flottningsmuseum** (Log Rafting Museum; tel: 054 87 12 26; mid-May–mid-Aug daily 11am–5pm; charge) shows how it was done. You can drift down the gentle Klarälven yourself on a self-assembled raft: contact the Karlstad tourist office (tel: 054 540 24 70) for details.

At **Ransäter** ❺, 40km (25 miles) north of Karlstad on the Klarälven, the **Hembygdsgården** (Heritage Village; tel: 0552 303 43; June–mid-Aug 11am–5pm; charge) includes museums

devoted to mining, forestry, agriculture and rural life, which paint a fascinating picture of the Värmland of yesteryear. Ransäter hosts an annual folk music festival in June and the largest accordion festival in Scandinavia in July.

Nobel laureates and inventors

West of Ransäter, on the eastern shore of Mellan-Fryken, is **Mårbacka** ❻ (tel: 0565 310 27; July–mid-Aug daily 10am–5pm, June and late Aug daily 10am–4pm, May and Sept Sat–Sun 11am–3pm; charge), the manor home of Swedish writer Selma Lagerlöf, the first woman to receive a Nobel Prize for

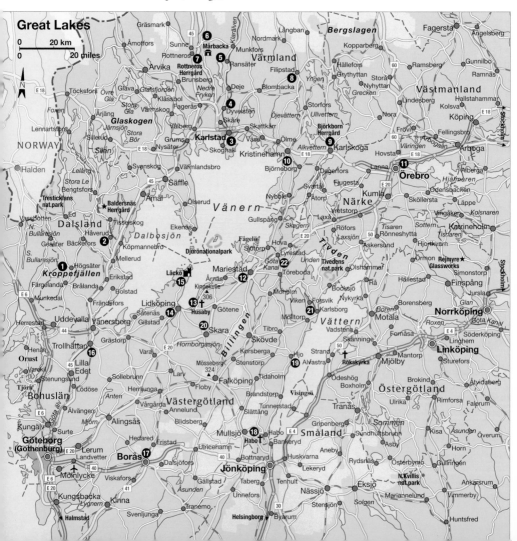

literature, in 1909. Through her books, she made famous the Fryk Valley and lakes. On the western side of the lake is **Rottneros Park ❼** (tel: 0565 602 95; July 10am–6pm, late May–June and Aug–early Sept 10am–4pm; charge), whose elegant manor house appears as Ekeby in Lagerlöf's *The Story of Gösta Berling*. This beautiful park has an arboretum and works by Scandinavian sculptors, including Milles, Eriksson and Vigeland.

North of Lake Vänern, the bedrock is rich in minerals, and this area has long been associated with Sweden's early industrial development. Many Americans make the pilgrimage to **Filipstad ❽**, which has the mausoleum of John Ericsson, the gifted inventor and engineer. **Björkborn Herrgård ❾**, near Karlskoga, was the home of Swedish inventor Alfred Nobel. The manor house is now a museum, **Nobelmuséet** (tel: 08 534 818 18; mid-May–mid-Sept Wed–Mon 10am–6pm, Tue 10am–8pm, mid-Sept–mid-May Wed–Sun 11am–5pm, Tue 11am–8pm; charge). At **Kristinehamn ❿**, 24km (15 miles) west of Karlskoga, a 15-metre (49ft) high sculpture by Picasso is the most striking feature on Lake Vänern.

To the east, in the province of Närke, is **Örebro ⓫**, with a dramatic 17th-century lakeside **castle** (tel: 019 21 21 21; guided tours July–Aug several daily, rest of the year Sat–Sun 1pm; charge).

Between the lakes

The region separating Lake Vänern from Lake Vättern offers rich pickings for the visitor. This is the province of Västergötland. In 1746 the indefatigable Swedish botanist Carolus Linnaeus said: "Truly no one could ever imagine such splendour as in Västergötland who had not seen it for himself."

Heading south along the eastern shore of Vänern, you come to **Mariestad ⓬**, dominated by the spire of the 17th-century Renaissance-style cathedral, one of the few churches of this period remaining in Sweden.

Most Swedes learn in school that the king who first united the Svea and Göta tribes, Olof Skötkonung (994–1022), was baptised in 1008 at Husaby Källa (Husaby Spring) at the southern tip of Kinnekulle. True or not, Husaby is considered to be the cradle of the Swedish state. Next to the spring, 12th-century **Husaby Church ⓭** (tel: 0511 34 31 41; May–Aug Mon–Fri 8am–8pm, Sat–Sun 9am–8pm, Apr and Sept Mon–Fri 8am–4pm, Sat–Sun 9am–4pm) is an imposing three-spired edifice with beautiful ceiling paintings inside.

Nestled into Kinneviken (Kinne Bay), 51km (32 miles) south of Mariestad, is **Lidköping ⓮**, a town founded in 1446 and once renowned for its porcelain. Its most famous company, **Rörstrand** (tel: 0510 823 46; Mon–Fri 10am–7pm, Sat until 4pm, Sun noon–4pm), the maker of the Nobel china, no longer has a factory in Lidköping (its fine china is now manufactured in Hungary and Sri Lanka), but a new Rörstrand museum opened here in 2008, and there is a large factory shop. Lidköping has several fine cafés, including the renowned Garströms Konditori, established in 1859, on the main square.

At Hornborgasjön thousands of cranes can be seen around March and April, often taking part in elaborate courtship rituals, like this dance.

BELOW: fun at Läckö Castle, near Lidköping.

North of Lidköping on the Kållandsö peninsula stands the restored Baroque-style 17th-century **Läckö Slott** ⑮ (tel: 0510 48 46 60; mid-June–Aug 10am–5pm, guided tour only May–mid-June and Sept; charge), one of the most impressive castles in Sweden. In summer it holds cultural exhibitions and is a venue for outdoor concerts.

Trollhättan ⑯, at the southern tip of Lake Vänern, is the hometown of Saab Automobile and has a rich industrial heritage: it's also known as "Trollywood" thanks to its film production! The town has long been famous for the magnificent 32-metre (105ft) falls of the Göta River. Today, the river is diverted to generate electricity and the falls are silent. But during the annual Falls Festival in July it is released to follow the old course, providing an impressive spectacle.

The southern part of Västergötland is still the heartland of Sweden's textile industry, with the focal point at **Borås** ⑰, where there is a **Textilmuséet** (Textile Museum; tel: 033 35 89 50; Tue and Thur 11am–8pm, Wed and Fri–Sun 11am–5pm; charge).

Around Lake Vättern

Lake Vättern covers an area of 1,912 sq km (738 sq miles). Near the southern tip of the lake, on the west side, is the 14th-century timber-built **Habo Kyrka** ⑱ (Church), southwest of Habo village. It features an outstanding painted interior, the work of Johan Christian Peterson and Johan Kinnerus, between 1741 and 1743, illustrating Luther's catechism and biblical scenes.

Travelling north along the lake, stop at the small waterside resort of **Hjo** ⑲ to enjoy freshly smoked whitefish. Then tour the town in a horse-drawn carriage, or cruise on the lake in the 1892 steamer *Trafik*. In summer, Hjo hosts Scandinavia's largest craft festival. **Skara** ⑳, 50km (31 miles) to the west of Hjo, has Sweden's second-oldest cathedral (after Lund), dating from the 11th century. **Skara Sommarland** (tel: 0511 770 300; June 10am–5pm, July 10am–7pm, Aug 10am–6pm; charge), 8km (5 miles) east of Skara on route 49, is a delight for children, with numerous attractions from lunar vehicles to a giant water park.

Around 10km (6 miles) southeast of Skara on route 184 is **Hornborgasjön**, a wildlife area with more than 100 species of birds. This is a stopover for migrating cranes (*see margin on page 275*).

Karlsborg fortress

Karlsborg ㉑, on the western shore of Lake Vättern, 30km (19 miles) north of Hjo, is dominated by its huge fortress (**Fästning**; tel: 0505 173 50; June–Aug daily guided tours; charge). In 1809, when Sweden lost Finland to the Russians, the Swedes decided to build two fortresses to house the government and the treasury. The first, at Karlsborg, was started in 1819 and required 250,000 tons of limestone. It was quarried by prison labour on the eastern side of the lake and ferried across by boat. The castle has walls 2 metres (6½ft) thick with 5km (3 miles) of ramparts, but by the time the building was finished, in 1909, fortresses were out of fashion. The second castle was never built. ❑

BELOW: Karlsborg Fortress.

Crossing Sweden by Canal

One of the most leisurely ways of sampling the country's history is to cruise along the Göta Kanal between Stockholm and Göteborg

Kings and industrialists alike spent centuries pondering how to link inland Sweden's lakes and rivers, from Stockholm on the east coast to Göteborg on the west coast, before Baltzar von Platen succeeded in the early 19th century.

At the time, the country needed this new east–west artery to transport timber, iron and food, and to build up local industry. For 22 years, 58,000 soldiers laboured to build the 190km (118-mile) long **Göta Kanal** ㉒. The canal was designated an "International Historic Civil Engineering Landmark", giving it the same status as the Golden Gate Bridge and the Panama Canal, and in 2007 was officially recognised as Sweden's greatest feat of engineering. Today, there is no commercial traffic on the canal… but there are plenty of pleasure craft!

For the visitor, the classic way is to take a cruise between Stockholm and Göteborg on one of the vintage vessels operated by the Göta Kanal Rederiaktiebolaget (Göta Kanal Steamship Company; tel: 031 806 315; www.stromma.se). The oldest of the three vessels is M/S *Juno*, built in 1874.

The four-day cruise westbound starts from Stockholm, finishing the first day at the village of Trosa. On the second day the boat passes through Mem – where the canal was officially inaugurated in 1832 – before reaching Berg, where there's time to visit the historic monastery church at nearby Vreta, once the richest religious establishment in Sweden.

The route crosses two picturesque lakes, Asplången and Roxen, where there are ospreys and herons during the breeding season. The canal then takes you through 15 locks in 3km (2 miles), lifting you 37 metres (120ft). The next night is spent at Motala, a town founded by Baltzar von Platen.

On the third morning the boat crosses Lake Vättern to Karlsborg, site of a huge fortress, and Forsvik, an old metalworking village and the site of the canal's oldest lock, built in 1813. Here, the boat is often greeted by a local family singing hymns and offering passengers wild flowers. This 100-year-old custom originated as a blessing for passengers as they embarked on the once hazardous crossing of Vättern. In the evening the boat reaches Sjötorp, marking the beginning of Lake Vänern.

At the south side of Lake Vänern, the boat enters the gorge at Trollhättan for the last day of the voyage down the Göta River to Göteborg.

It's all very leisurely, but if you prefer to take a more hands-on approach, how about chartering your own motor boat? It's also possible to hire a canoe and paddle along the waterway – several companies offer a pick-up service so you don't have to retrace your route. For landlubbers, the Göta Kanal is Sweden's most popular cycling path. For all these forms of do-it-yourself transport, see the website www.gotakanal.se.   ❏

ABOVE: M/S *Juno*, the oldest ship on the Gota Kanal.
RIGHT: captain of the ship.

DALARNA

Dalarna is Sweden's folklore province, as famous for its scarlet Dala horses as its music and merrymaking at Midsummer. Winter attracts skiers challenged by championship events

Dalarna represents all that is quintessentially Swedish. With its colourful costumes, centuries-old traditions of music and dance, Midsummer festivals and evocative rural landscape, its folklore and beauty attract an increasing number of visitors each year.

Dalarna is the third-largest tourist site in Sweden, after Stockholm and Göteborg. The culture that gave us the red-painted Dalahäst (Dala horse) and inspired two of Sweden's most beloved artists, Carl Larsson and Anders Zorn, can best be experienced in the twilight of *fäbodar*, the old pasture cottages nestled in the hills, in the company of elderly but amazingly energetic fiddlers.

Musical traditions

Music is one of the most defining characteristics of Dala culture. Music on Lake Siljan (Musik vid Siljan) is a huge annual festival, held in late June/early July, that attracts visitors from all over Sweden and abroad. Distinctly Dala are the *spelmansstämmor*, folk musicians' rallies, particularly the one held each July in **Bingsjö ❶**, 30km (19 miles) east of Rättvik, where fiddlers turn the classic polka into a musical performance that rivals any blues master.

An exotic setting for listening to music is **Dalhalla** (tel: 0248 79 79 50; concert tickets from Siljan Turism, tel: 0248 79 72 00; July–mid-Aug guided tours daily 11am–3pm; charge), a cavernous outdoor concert arena set in the depths of an abandoned limestone quarry near the town of **Rättvik ❷**. The annual summer festivals here feature artists of international standing.

Farm cottages

For a change of pace, the gentle quiet of the region's *fäbodar* offer a taste of back-to-the-land living. These pasture cottages and surrounding buildings, dating from the 15th and 16th centuries, are found all over Sweden but are most

Main attractions
MIDSUMMER CELEBRATIONS
DALHALLA MUSIC FESTIVAL
TRADITIONAL FÄBODAR
(FARM COTTAGES)
FALU COPPER MINE, FALUN
SÄTER
DALA HORSE WORKSHOP,
NUSNÄS
SÄLEN SKI RESORT
VASALOPPET CROSS-COUNTRY
SKI RACE
CARL LARSSON'S HOUSE,
SUNDBORN

LEFT: Hambo dances and folk costumes in Dalarna. **RIGHT:** folk art telephone box.

Mora on Lake Siljan is best known as the home of the Swedish artist Anders Zorn (1860–1920). His house and studio, Zorngården, and the Zornmuséet (both daily) are well worth visiting.

often associated with Dalarna. They constitute a living museum, where cows are milked, butter is churned, *messmör* (a type of goat's cheese) is made, and *tunnbröd* (thin bread) is baked. Many *fäbodar* also sell products or serve food.

One worth visiting is **Ljusbodarnas Fäbod** (tel: 070 640 21 08; mid-summer–early Aug), about 20km (12 miles) south of Leksand on route 70 towards Mockfjärd, where children are encouraged to pet the cows, hens, sheep and pigs.

If trying your own hand at 15th-century farming appeals, **Prästbodarnas Fäbod** (tel: 072 240 67 72; June–Aug daily, book in advance), near Bingsjö, has a variety of native Swedish farm animals, and offers one-day courses in butter-churning, milking and cheese-making. The farming life seems a natural accompaniment to the breathtaking scenery of the province.

At the northern extremity of Dalarna is the deceptively gentle start of the mountain range which marches north, gaining height all the time until it culminates in the snow-topped peaks of the Kebnekaise range in Lapland. Dalarna is a transition zone between the softer

landscapes of southern Sweden and the more dramatic, but harsher north.

Industrial traditions

Dalarna is not exclusively rural. The Bergslagen district has been mined for a millennium, and the whole area is now a Unesco World Heritage site. The most impressive industrial site is the 17th-century **Falu Gruva** (Falu Mine; tel: 023 78 20 30; www.falugruva.se; year-round, phone or see website for times), on the edge of the provincial capital, **Falun ❸**, with machinery, museum and 1½-hour tours into the depths. Copper was extracted here, as were the iron pigments used to colour the iconic Falu Red paint, liberally applied to all Sweden's little red houses.

Hedemora ❹ claims to be the oldest town in Dalarna, with a charter dated 1459; its privileges as a market town go back even further than that, while parts of the church are 13th-century. The locals have devised **Husbyringen**, a 56km (35-mile) "museum trail" which you can take by car through the area northeast of the town to see a number of industrial archaeology sites.

Also worth visiting is **Säter 5**, one of the seven best-preserved wooden towns in Sweden. Compared with Hedemora it is quite an upstart, with a town charter dated 1642. The ravines of the Säter Valley were created at the end of the Ice Age and are of interest for their flora.

Handicrafts

This is the province that inspired the distinctive Dala horse, still being made at the Grannas workshop in **Nusnäs 6** (tel: 0250 372 50; mid-June–mid-Aug Mon–Fri 9am–6pm, Sat–Sun 9am–4pm, mid-Aug–mid-June Mon–Fri 9am–4pm; free), so it is not surprising that the region is known for its abundance of carvers, potters, silversmiths, weavers, painters and bakers. This is a mecca for *hemslöjd* (crafts), all of which have their ancient roots in the farming culture.

At **Sätergläntan 7**, 3km (2 miles) south of Insjön Lake, **Hemslöjdens Gård** (tel: 0247 645 70) offers a wide array of handicrafts as well as week-long courses. At **Nittsjö Keramik** (tel: 0248 171 30; Mon–Fri 9am–6pm, Sat 9am–2pm, June–Aug Sun noon–4pm), 6km (4 miles) north of Rättvik, clay goods

are made following a tradition that goes back over 100 years.

Ski resorts

With plenty of snow from December to April, Dalarna's ski resorts are the principal winter tourist attraction, both for cross-country skiing and downhill (some slopes are illuminated for the dark winter days). **Romme Alpin 8** is Sweden's most visited ski resort outside the proper mountain areas, with some 200,000 visitors annually. Together, **Sälen 9** and Idre, in northwest Dalarna, have almost half of Sweden's ski-lift facilities, and Sälen is famous for being the starting point for the very popular **Vasaloppet** – an 85km (53-mile) cross-country skiing race to **Mora 10** on Lake Siljan.

Nearby, the skiing area at Orsa has an added attraction. **Orsa Björnpark** (July and early Aug 10am–6pm daily; rest of year 10am–3pm daily; admission charge; tel: 0250 462 00; www. orsabjornpark.se) is Europe's largest bear park, and your best chance of seeing large predators (brown bears, polar bears, wolves, lynx, wolverines and even leopards) in natural surroundings. ❏

The Dalahäst (Dala Horse), a more readily recognised Swedish symbol than the nation's flag.

BELOW LEFT:
Lisbeth with a Yellow Tulip, by Carl Larsson.

Carl Larsson: Sweden's Favourite Artist

Carl Larsson (1853–1919) is Sweden's best-loved artist. The greatest source of inspiration for Larsson was the life he shared with his wife Karin, a textile artist, and their children at their home at **Sundborn 11** (by guided tour only: May–Sept daily 10am–5pm, Oct–Apr 11am; charge; tel: 023 600 53).

Carl Larsson was born to a poor family in Stockholm, and during his youth he suffered all the deprivations of poverty, a period he later described as "hell on earth". He was determined to leave those hard times behind him and thus it was no coincidence that he became the artist who would best portray the happy, harmonious Swedish family, bathed in light, colour and joyous celebration of home and hearth. In their wooden farmhouse, where Karin and Carl lived with their eight children, they created the simple interiors that were to influence so much of modern design. Stripped floors strewn with rugs, brightly painted furniture and hand-painted friezes were the key elements.

Larsson's paintings were strongly influenced by the local Dalarna folk-art traditions. In his autobiography, Larsson wrote, "My art: it is just like my home; there is no place there for fine furniture... it is simple, but harmonious. Nothing extravagant... just good, strong work."

CENTRAL SWEDEN

Brilliant blue lakes, rushing rivers, the mysterious outlines of mountains and, above all, the space and silence beckon hikers and anglers to this untouched landscape

ive provinces stretch across central Sweden. In the east are Gästrikland, Hälsingland and Medelpad, which share the long coastline known as Jungfrukusten (Virgin Coast). Further inland come Härjedalen and Jämtland, which stretch west to the Norwegian border, the land of lakes and coniferous or birch forests. Härjedalen marks the beginning of the great northern mountain ranges and the further north you go, the more dramatic the scenery is.

Gästrikland

The small province of Gästrikland has one major town, **Gävle ❶**, in the southeast corner of the region. Gävle was one of Sweden's great shipping towns, and the most treasured exhibit at the local museum, **Länsmuséet** (tel: 026 65 56 00; Tue–Fri 10am–4pm, Wed until 8pm, Sat–Sun noon–4pm; free), is the Björke boat, a rare find from around AD 400. Other exhibits include displays on local industry and handicrafts, plus a surprisingly extensive collection of paintings by notable Swedish artists from the 17th century to the present day, including works by Carl Larsson.

Railway enthusiasts should make a point of visiting the **Sveriges Järnvägsmuseum** (Swedish Railway Museum; tel: 026 144 615; June–Aug daily 10am–

5pm, Sept–May Tue–Sun 10am–4pm; charge) on the outskirts of Gävle. The collection embraces gleaming locomotives from the golden age of steam, including the stately 1874 coach of King Oscar II, and comes up-to-the-minute with an X2000 simulator.

For children, **Furuviksparken** (tel: 026 17 73 00; June and mid-Aug–Sept 10am–5pm, July–mid-Aug until 7pm; charge), 10km (6 miles) south of Gävle, combines extensive zoological gardens with a variety of other attractions, including a theatre and a circus.

Main attractions
SVERIGES JÄRNVÄGSMUSEUM (SWEDISH RAILWAY MUSEUM), GÄVLE
BOAT TRIPS FROM SÖDERHAMN
FISHING IN HÄRJEDALEN
FRÖSÖN
JAMTLI OPEN-AIR MUSEUM
JÄMTLAND HIKING TRAILS
ÅRE SKI RESORT
INLANDSBANAN RAILWAY

LEFT: a family day out. **RIGHT:** lynx, resident of northern Scandinavia.

Grilled herring and potatoes with dill butter is a favourite dish all along the Virgin Coast. At **Bönan**, 10km (6 miles) northeast of Gävle, visit **Engeltofta** to sample the town's famous golden-brown smoked herring, cured over spruce wood – in summer you can catch the boat over from Gävle.

Gästrikland is at the eastern end of the swathe of land which gave Sweden its early mining and smelting industries. On summer Sundays, vintage steam trains ply the 4.5km (2¾ miles) from **Jädraås** ❷, northwest of Gävle, to **Tallås**. The railway is typical of those used to haul minerals or timber, and the coach used by King Oscar II (ruled 1872–1907) when he went hunting bears in Dalarna is still in service.

Follow the E4 north to **Söderhamn** ❸, the starting point for boat trips around the archipelago. Söderhamn was founded in 1620 as an armoury for the Swedish army, and the museum is situated in part of what was the gun and rifle factory. Although a commercial centre, the town has an impressive town hall, plus a church to match and a pleasant riverside park.

Hälsingland

Around 120 years ago, when the timber industry was at its peak, **Hudiksvall** ❹ had a reputation for high living. A reminder of the era is the town's theatre, opened in 1882. Hudiksvall also has a group of the best-preserved 19th-century wooden buildings in Sweden, the **Fiskarstan**.

The interior of Hälsingland province has the best scenery, particularly the Ljusnandalen River Valley, which is laced with lakes along its entire length. West of **Ljusdal** ❺, where the Ljusnan meets the Hennan River, the forests begin.

On the first Sunday in July, **Delsbo** ❻ attracts thousands of visitors for the annual **Delsbostämman**, where folk fiddlers, dancers and costumed actors air the region's traditional culture. Surrounded by dark forests, the **Dellenbygden** area is rural Sweden at its best. It's worth doing a circuit through Friggesund and Hassela and back to the coast, taking in the Dellen lakes area, with its boat and canoe trips, and walking trails.

On the following Saturday, 50km (30 miles) further south, one of Sweden's

best-known dance competitions takes place. At dawn on a July morning, around 600 folk dancers in traditional costumes gather in a meadow in **Hårga** ❼ for the unforgettable festival **Hälsingehambo**, epitomised by the catchy polka *Hårgalåten*. The different stages of the competition are danced in four different locations around Hårgaberget mountain. It's a fitting setting: according to local legend, the devil lured a group of young folk out onto Hårgaberget with his bewitching fiddle music, where they danced themselves to death.

Härjedalen

Together the provinces of Härjedalen and Jämtland are as big as Denmark, but with a population of only 127,000. To the east and southeast are extensive forests with hills, rivers and lakes. The higher mountains begin in Härjedalen. This heartland has four main rivers, the Ångermanälven, Indalsälven, Ljungan and Ljusnan, all well stocked with fish, especially trout and grayling. Perch, pike and whitefish are the most common in the forested regions, but many

tarns have been stocked with trout. It is an anglers' paradise – fishing permits can be bought cheaply nearby or at any local tourist office. The vast tracts of near-uninhabited territory are also home to wildlife such as bears, wolverine, lynx and the ubiquitous elk.

When tourism was in its infancy, Härjedalen was one of the first Swedish provinces to attract skiers, who still return to pit their skills against its varied terrain, and come back in the summer for mountain walking. The scenery is impressive and, north of **Funäsdalen**, not far from the Norwegian border, the province has Sweden's highest road over the **Flatruet plateau**, up to 1,000 metres (3,280ft) high.

At the crossroads of the north–south route, highway 45, and east–west, highway 84, is **Sveg**, a small town but Härjedalen's largest, with a population of around 2,700. **Vemdalen** ❽, 60km (37 miles) northwest, has an eight-sided wooden church with a separate onion-domed bell tower. Beyond the village the road climbs between two mountains, **Vemdalsfjällen**, before entering Jämtland.

Dancers compete at the Hälsingehambo festival in Hårga.

BELOW: a house on Lake Söderhamn.

Jämtland

Jämtland is the biggest province in central Sweden, a huge territory of lakes, rivers and mountains. Its heart is the lake of **Storsjön**, the fifth-largest stretch of inland water in the country, which is reputed to have its own monster, a Swedish version of Scotland's "Nessie". Present-day monster-seekers can take a cruise on the lake in the 1875 steamer *Thomée*.

On the banks of Storsjön is Jämtland's largest town, **Östersund** ⑨, connected by a bridge to the beautiful island of **Frösön**. The island was home to the noted Swedish composer and critic Wilhelm Peterson-Berger (1867–1942). His most popular work, the opera *Arnljot*, is performed every summer on the island as a theatrical, rather than a musical, work. Östersund hosts one of Sweden's biggest international music festivals, Storsjöyran, at the end of July: past artists have included Lady Gaga, B.B. King and Motörhead.

In Östersund, **Jamtli** (tel: 063 15 01 00; late June–late Aug daily 11am–5pm, late Aug–late June Tue–Sun 11am–5pm; charge) is one of the biggest open-air museums in the country, an interesting collection of 18th- and 19th-century buildings including a *shieling* (summer farm), baker's cottage, smithy, and an old inn. The food in the café is recommended.

North of Storsjön, on the north bank of Lake Alsensjön at **Glösa** ⑩, are a number of *hällristningar*, primitive rock carvings.

In western Jämtland, the peaks rise up to nearly 1,800 metres (6,000ft). It is a splendid area for trekking in summer and skiing in winter. Centuries ago, melting ice left many strange and unusual formations, such as the deep canyon between the Drommen and Falkfångarfjället mountains. The region is also rich in waterfalls, such as **Ristafallet** near Hålland, **Storfallet** northwest of Höglekardalen and **Tännforsen**, to the west of **Åre** ⑪.

Åre is a popular winter sports resort with a funicular railway that goes from the town centre partway up the local mountain, Åreskutan, and a cable car that continues almost to the summit. Lakes and mountains on every side make up a superb view. ❑

The Inland Railway

A trip on the Inlandsbanan (Inland Railway) is an enjoyable way of seeing some of Sweden's most dramatic scenery. The route stretches through the Central Heartlands from Mora in Dalarna to Gällivare in Lapland.

The idea of building such a long railway through a harsh and inaccessible landscape was first promoted in 1894, but it was to take another 40 years of hard labour before it was completed. The 1,100km (680-mile) line was finally inaugurated in Jokkmokk in Lapland on 6 August 1937, and a monument was erected to commemorate the event.

Today the train stops along the way so passengers can visit local artists and craftspeople or simply admire the views. Sometimes it has to halt to avoid running into herds of reindeer resting on the track. With luck, passengers may also spot elks or bears.

It is possible to make stopovers along the route and stay for a night or two in local towns and villages to do some walking in the mountains, or just enjoy the magnificent landscape. Various packages are available combining rail travel with hotel accommodation, or trekking. For more information contact Inlandsbanan AB, Box 561, SE-831 27 Östersund, Sweden. Tel: +46 63 19 44 00; fax: +46 63 19 44 06; www.inlandsbanan.se.

NORTHERN SWEDEN

Lapland, land of the Midnight Sun and home to the Sami, offers a richly rewarding experience for the traveller. Fishing villages and holiday islands dot the Bothnian coast

In the search for natural landscapes Lapland, which stretches across northern Sweden and Finland, offers some of the finest, wildest lakes and mountains in Europe; and although distances are great, there are quality roads and a rail link. Anglers are guaranteed excellent river fishing, and sea fishing along the coast of Bottenviken (Gulf of Bothnia), the stretch of water that separates Sweden from Finland. Holidaymakers and sailors gravitate to its sheltered coves and islands.

Highway 45

The best way to absorb the immensity of Swedish Lapland is to take the inland highway 45, from south to north. The first town across the border from Ångermanland is **Dorotea ❶**, at the heart of bear country – the animals sometimes wander into town in search of food. **Vilhelmina ❷**, 100km (60 miles) north on the Ångermanälven River, has a well-preserved church village where travellers can find accommodation in its wooden houses.

West of Vilhelmina is the **Kittelfjäll** mountain region and the border with Norway. To the north lies an important road junction at **Storuman ❸**, where the 45 is bisected by the E12, known as the Blå Vägen (Blue Highway) because it follows a succession of lakes and the Umeälven River on its route from the

east coast. It passes through **Lycksele ❹**, where there is a zoo, **Lycksele Djurpark** (tel: 0950 163 63; June–mid-Sept daily 10am–4pm or 5pm; charge), that has Nordic species including bear, elk, musk ox, wolf and reindeer. From Storuman the E12 continues west through Tärnaby to Mo i Rana in Norway.

The Silver Road

From Slagnäs, on highway 45, a secondary road leads through glorious lakeside scenery to **Arjeplog ❺**, one of Swedish Lapland's most interesting towns.

Main attractions
ARJEPLOG SILVER MUSEUM
LAPPSTADEN
  (SAMI CHURCH VILLAGE)
JOKKMOKK WINTER MARKET
GÄLLIVARE
LAPONIA WORLD HERITAGE AREA
LKAB INFOMINE, KIRUNA
ICE HOTEL, JUKKASJÄRVI
KEBNEKAISE MOUNTAIN
KUNGSLEDEN HIKING TRAIL
HÖGA KUSTEN (HIGH COAST)
UMEÅ
GAMMELSTAD

LEFT: Trappstegforsarna Waterfalls, Lapland.
RIGHT: Sami and reindeer.

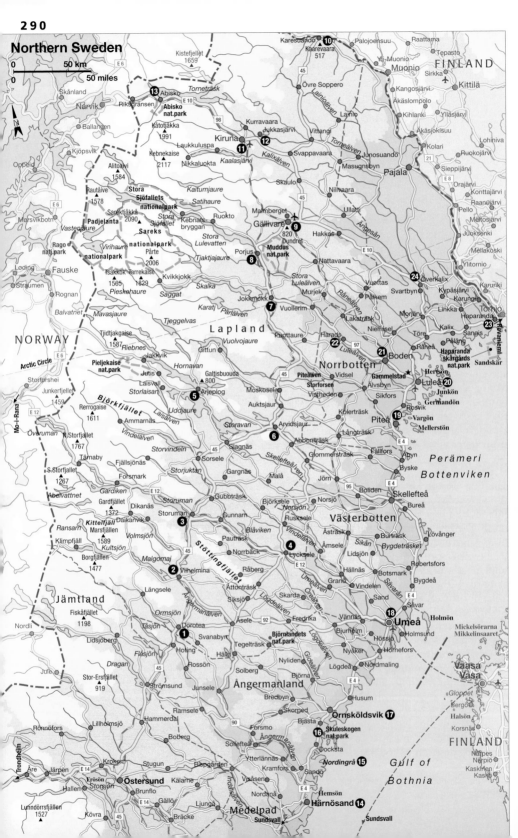

Its **Silvermuséet** (Silver Museum; tel: 0961 145 00; mid-June–mid-Aug daily 9am–6pm, mid-Aug–mid-June Mon–Fri 10am–noon, 1–4pm, Sat 10am–2pm; charge), housed in an old school, provides a fascinating insight into the region's history and the Sami people of Lapland. It owes its existence to Einar Wallqvist, "doctor of the Laplanders", who, besides his medical work, collected cultural objects. He established a museum which today has the finest collection of Sami silver in the world. Arjeplog's church is 17th-century and also worth a visit.

Arjeplog is roughly halfway along highway 95, the Silvervägen (Silver Road) between Skellefteå in the east and Bodø on Norway's west coast. In the 17th century there were silver mines around **Nasafjäll**, and the ore was transported, by reindeer and boat, to the east coast. Not until 1974 did it become an asphalted highway, opening up an area of outstanding beauty. There are magnificent views from Galtisbuouda, 800 metres (2,620ft) high, just north of Arjeplog.

Arvidsjaur ❻, once a trading post, now a junction of roads and railways, has the atmosphere of a frontier town. The major attraction is **Lappstaden** (daily; July guided tours; tel: 0960 175 00), the oldest surviving example of a Sami church village, with *kåtor*, tent-shaped wooden huts, and *härbren*, wooden storehouses. In winter, both Arjeplog and Arvidsjaur are taken over by the motor industry to test products in intense sub-zero temperatures.

Across the Arctic Circle

The **Arctic Circle** is 156km (97 miles) north of Arvidsjaur, and you can buy a certificate to prove you crossed the line at a nearby café. Further north is **Jokkmokk** ❼, the second-largest *kommun* (municipal district) in Sweden, covering an area of 19,425 sq km (7,500 sq miles) with a population of 5,200.

Jokkmokk is a centre for Sami culture, and in summer you can see nomadic Sami here. An annual winter market in February attracts thousands of people, although temperatures can drop to –35°C (–31°F). First held in 1605, the market soon became a meeting place for the Sami and merchants from the coastal communities. Today it is as much a social occasion as an opportunity to trade, and weddings and baptisms often take place. The **Ájtte Fjäll-och Samemuseum** (Swedish Mountain and Sami Museum; tel: 0971 170 70; mid-June–mid-Aug daily 9am–6pm, Feb–mid-June and mid-Aug–Dec Tue–Fri 10am–4pm, Sat 10am–2pm; charge) portrays the local culture as well as the mountain world, placing mankind in a natural, cultural and ecological perspective.

Highway 45 continues through a sparsely populated area to **Porjus** ❽, a major centre for hydroelectric power. To the east of the town is **Muddus National Park** (certain areas are closed during the breeding season, mid-Mar–July; tel: 0971 222 50), home of bear, lynx and wolverine. **Dundret Mountain**, 820 metres (2,690ft) high, northeast of the park, is a bustling ski centre (tel: 0971 145 60) from November to

For those who venture as far as the Arctic Circle, you can get a certificate to prove you've crossed the line.

BELOW:
reindeer herder at winter fair, Jokkmokk.

Huskies are in their element this far north.

RIGHT: Esrange Space Center, a space research facility.

April. In summer, the region abounds with activities – riding, walking, windsurfing, fishing, golf and rafting – contact Gällivare tourist office (tel: 0970 166 60) for details.

To the Finnish frontier

Gällivare ❾ (pop. 18,500), and its twin town, Malmberget, owe their growth to the discovery of iron ore. Gällivare is the end of the railway line, Inlandsbanan (*see box, page 286*), that follows highway 45 north from Östersund. It is a popular tourist route and jumping-off point for treks into the region that include the Padjelanta, Stora Sjöfallet and Sarek national parks, which together with Muddus form the Laponia Unesco World Heritage site. The town has a museum and an 18th-century Sami church. Beyond Gällivare, the 45 joins the E10 and continues north to **Svappavaara**, a former mining centre, and **Karesuando** ❿, on the Finnish frontier. Many place names in Swedish Lapland owe more to Finnish than to Swedish. In Kiruna, for example, a fifth of the population are Finnish immigrants.

The most northerly church in Sweden can be found in Karesuando, which also has the lowest average winter temperatures and Sweden's only tundra. From the top of **Kaarevaara mountain**, 517 metres (1,696ft) high, you can see three countries: Sweden, Finland and Norway.

Kiruna and the Ice Hotel

Beyond Svappavaara, the E10 swings northwest to **Kiruna** ⓫ (pop. 23,000), Sweden's most northerly town. Mining began here in 1900 and is still the main industry. Such is the extent of the underground workings that Kiruna is subsiding, and plans are under way to move the entire town east of its current location. The **LKAB InfoMine** is the world's largest iron-ore mine, with 400km (250 miles) of underground roadways. Tours of the mine can be booked all year round; contact the tourist office (tel: 0980 188 80).

Also visitable through Kiruna tourist office, the **Esrange Space Center** is Europe's only civilian space centre, launching around five to 10 test rockets per year.

Fishing in the Far North

There is nothing quite like fishing against the impressive backdrop of Sweden's mountains. Creeping silently along a riverbank and trying to tempt a shy trout or grayling to the fly is an unforgettable experience. Fishing is well organised in the north. If you are driving along the northeast coast there are plenty of opportunities to fish en route, particularly in the unspoilt Piteälven, Kalixälven and Torneälven rivers; just ask at the nearest tourist office.

Further afield, the Tjuonajokk fishing camp on the Kaitumälven River in northwest Lapland is renowned for its grayling fishing. South from there is the Miekak fishing camp, 100km (60 miles) northwest of Arjeplog (accessible by helicopter from Tjärnberg at Silvervägen, or by snowmobile in winter from Silvervägen), providing arguably the best char fishing in Lapland. At the northernmost extremity of Sweden the fishing centre on Rostojaure Lake is renowned for its char and grayling. It is accessible in summer only by helicopter.

Not surprisingly, transport can be quite expensive, but the cost of fishing permits is relatively low compared with other countries. Permits can be bought at a number of outlets, including tourist offices and some fuel stations. The best month for enthusiasts to go fishing is usually August.

East of Kiruna, **Jukkasjärvi** ⑫ is famous for its **Ice Hotel** (www.icehotel.com), built afresh every winter. Activities in the region include dog-sledging in the snow-covered wilderness and white-water rafting in summer.

The E10 (Nordkalottvägen), from Kiruna via the Norwegian frontier to Narvik, penetrates one of Europe's last wilderness areas. The mountains southwest of the highway can only be reached on foot or by pony, and it is here that **Kebnekaise**, Sweden's highest peak at 2,117 metres (6,945ft), reigns supreme. **Abisko** ⑬, 150km (93 miles) from Kiruna, is a popular base from which to set out along the **Kungsleden** (King's Trail), which enables even inexperienced walkers to see the mountains.

The Bothnian coast

The Bottenviken (Gulf of Bothnia) coastline ranges from polished rock to sand and shingle beaches. Islands form an almost continuous archipelago – a playground for holidaymakers passionate about sailing and the sea. Inland, lakes provide tranquil blue oases in the dense forests.

Starting in the south, the main coastal town of Ångermanland is **Härnösand** ⑭, which is modern except for the town hall, the Domkyrkan (Cathedral) and some 18th-century wooden houses. Overlooking the harbour at Murberget is a large open-air historical museum (Tue–Sun 11am–4pm, Thur until 8pm; free). Slightly inland, the 13th-century church, near **Ytterlännäs** on highway 90, is an antiquarian wonder.

Travelling north on the E4, the Höga Kusten (High Coast) Bridge, modelled partly on San Francisco's Golden Gate Bridge, is an impressive structure, 1.8km (1 mile) long. It marks the start of the most beautiful stretch of coast, the **Höga Kusten**, designated a Unesco World Heritage site. Its towering cliffs are Sweden's highest, created at the end of the last Ice Age when the land, freed from its burden of ice, rose up.

Here you'll find the **Nordingrå peninsula** ⑮, whose bedrock is an intense red *rapakivi* granite. Its scenic treasures include **Omne Bay**, the villages of **Måviken** and **Norrfällsviken**, and the view from the church over Vagsfjärden. **Bönhamn** is a tiny place among the rocks, where **Arnes Sjöbod** is renowned for fresh fish and mashed potatoes and **Mannaminne**, near Häggvik, provides home-baked delicacies, handicrafts and musical evenings. The **Höga Kusten walk**, at 25km (16 miles), starts at Fjordbotten with bathing places at Storsand, Norrfällsviken, Hörsång and Noraström. Between the E4 and the coast lies the majestic **Skuleskogen National Park** ⑯ (all year), noted for its rare birds and mammals.

Örnsköldsvik ⑰, known as Övik, is an industrial town and one of Sweden's leading winter sports areas. The islands offshore include **Ulvön**, with one of the oldest fishermen's chapels in Sweden, **Trysunda**, a favourite with the sailing fraternity, and **Högbonden**, whose former lighthouse is now a cosy clifftop youth hostel, accessible by boat from Bönhamn.

TIP

The mosquitoes are rapacious in summer in northern Sweden, so don't forget to pack insect repellent.

BELOW: the Ice Hotel in Jukkasjärvi.

Sami items hand carved out of reindeer bone; a knife and a box on a string.

BELOW: Hoga Kusten Bridge.
RIGHT: Gammelstad in Luleå.

A new high-speed railway line, opened in 2010, makes **Umeå** ⑱ easily accessible from Stockholm. This young, lively place is gearing up for its stint as European Capital of Culture in 2014. The main attraction here is the open-air museum **Friluftsmuseum Gammlia**, part of the adjacent **Västerbotten Museum** (tel: 090 17 18 00; mid-June–mid-Aug daily 10am–5pm, mid-Aug–mid-June Tue–Fri 10am–4pm, Sat noon–4pm, Sun noon–5pm; charge), which explores local history and contains the oldest ski in the world, which was discovered nearby and is over 5,000 years old.

Continuing north, **Piteå** ⑲ can come as a culture shock. Some 17th-century wooden houses remain, but today it is a centre for timber, paper and pulp industries. Norwegians come in flocks from their calm northern fjords to the large holiday resort of Pite Havsbad.

From Piteå, the road leads northwest through Älvsbyn to Bredsel and **Storforsen**, Europe's longest natural rapids, with an 81-metre (265ft) drop over 5km (3 miles). You can get close to the rushing water via wooden walkways and

bridges; it is an awe-inspiring sight. The hotel nearby offers magnificent views.

Luleå and the Lule Valley

Luleå ⑳ was moved 10km (6 miles) by the king in 1649 and stands now at the mouth of the Luleälven River. The old church town, **Gammelstad**, was left on its original site and is a fascinating place to visit with its 400 red-painted cottages and a 15th-century church, still used on important religious occasions. The town is a Unesco World Heritage site. Beside the original harbour there is an open-air museum, **Friluftsmuséet Hägnan** (tel: 0920 45 38 09; mid-June–mid-Aug daily 11am–5pm; free), which includes a hay shed typical of Norrbotten. The **Norrbottens Museum** (tel: 0920 24 35 02; June–Aug Mon–Fri 10am–4pm, Sat–Sun noon–4pm, Sept–May closed Mon; free) in Hermelin Park provides a picture of the province and has Sami artefacts.

In the 19th century, **Boden** ㉑, 35km (22 miles) inland from Luleå on the Luleälven River, was referred to as "one of the strongest fortresses of Europe – that is to say, in the whole world". Today, Boden is still the largest garrison town in Sweden.

For a complete change of scene, head 45km (28 miles) northwest to the peaceful Lule Valley near **Harads** ㉒, where you'll find some of Sweden's weirdest accommodation. If you've ever wanted to sleep in a bird's nest or have a sauna up a tree, here's your chance.

The eastern frontier

Haparanda ㉓, Sweden's easternmost town, was built opposite Finnish Tornio on the Torneälven River, which forms the border between the two countries. Road 400 goes north along the river on the Swedish side into the Tornedalen Valley to the Kukkolaforsen waterfall. West of the falls, on the Kalixälven River, is **Överkalix** ㉔, with fine views from the top of Brännaberget. At the end of June, this is the place to see the amazing tradition of netting whitefish and salmon. ❏

FINLAND

The serenity of Finland's lakes and forests remain
timeless, but change is always in the air

For a country of just over 5.2 million people, Finland has produced an astonishing number of architects, artists, sculptors, musicians and athletes; the tradition continues. Helsinki was named World Design Capital 2012, a biennial honour given to a city for merits in successful utilisation of design for cultural, social and economic improvement. In 2011, Turku celebrated its role as the European Capital of Culture, hosting an unparalleled year of events featuring two opera premieres in Turku Castle and attracting thousands of visitors. In autumn 2011, Helsinki opened a new Music Centre next to Alvar Aalto's Finlandia Hall, and Helsinki's restaurant scene continues to evolve, with several Michelin-star restaurants and a lively dining out culture.

This drive and tenacity may also explain why the World Economic Forum deemed Finland "the seventh-most competitive country in the world". Sisu is a Finnish word that is synonymous with having guts and being resilient; one Finn described it as pushing open a door that says "pull", but it is the extra ingredient in the Finnish DNA that helps them survive climactic and economic challenges. Long known for its substantial pulp and paper industry, Finland is also considered a worldwide force with

technological innovations: from mobile phones to state-of-the-art medical equipment and progressive internet services. After mobile phones were overtaken in the market by smart phones, Nokia found itself at a critical juncture. In 2010, they began a new partnership with Microsoft, designing and manufacturing new products in Finland.

Finns may work hard, but they also know how to wind down. The endless expanses of untouched landscape soothe the soul of the urban Finn, who escapes to the country at the weekend, and enjoys each season accordingly. The silence of the forests provides reflection, as the sauna provides solace. With fishing, swimming and a small boat in summer, and skis, snowshoes or snowmobile in the winter, Finland remains a paradise for all. ❏

PRECEDING PAGES: Sami life as captured by the Sami artist Alariesto; Helsinki's city centre in winter. **LEFT:** getting around in Finnish style. **ABOVE LEFT:** a classic Finnish scene at Vuorhajärvi Lake, Inari. **TOP:** the best Finnish chefs make the most of Finland's local produce, such as mushrooms and wild berries.

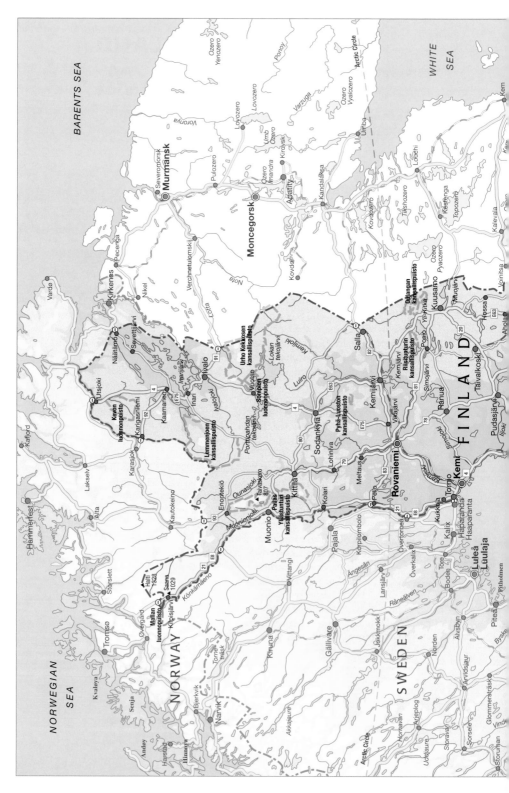

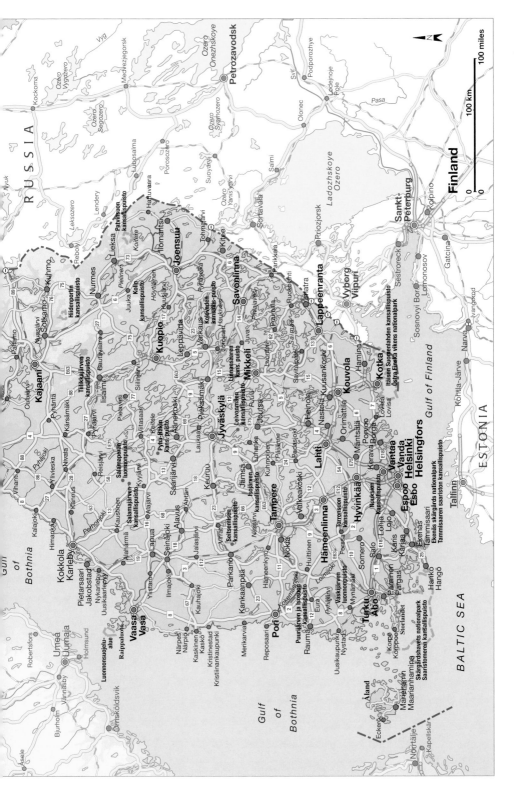

Pukkisaaret

Seurasaarentie

Seurasaarensalmi

MEILAHDEN PUISTO

Paciuksenkatu

Messeniuksenk.

Nordenskiöldinkatu

Mannerheimintie

Olympia-
stadion

KAUP-
PUUT

Stenbäckinkatu

Tavaststjernak.
M. Lybeckink.

Topeliuksenkatu

Urheilunkatu

Talkotie

Paavo Nurmentie

Humallahti

Linnankoskenkatu

Humalistonkatu

Eino Leinon k.

Mäntymäentie

Ulkomuseo
★ (Open-Air Museum)

Rajasaarent.

Mechelininkatu

SIBELIUKSEN
PUISTO

Sibeliuksenk.

❶

㉜

Sibeliusmonumentti

Helsinginkatu

❿

Suomen
Kansallis
(Finnish N
Opera Hou

31
Seurasaari

Rajasaari

TAKA-TÖÖLÖ

Kivelänk.

Mannerheimintie

Kesäk.

Valaskärinkatu

Töölönkatu

Töölö

Pohj.Hesperiankatu

Apollonk.atu

Finlandia
(Finlandia

Mustasaari

Seurasaarenselkä

Taivalluoto

Eteläinen Hesperiankatu

Mechelininkatu

Runeberginkatu

Oksasenk.k.

Caloniuk.k

Tunturik.

Museokatu

Kansallismuseo
(National Museum)

❼

Hakasalmi

Eduskunta
(Parlia
Build

Porsas

Hiekkarannantie

Hietaniemenkatu

Krematorionkatu

Sammonk.

Temppelik.

Nervanderink.

❶❶

Temppeliaukion
kirkko

Luonnontieteellinen museo ❻
(Natural History Museum)

Ourit

HIETANIEMEN
HAUTAUSMAA

Hietaniemenk.atu

Tennispalatsi
(Tennis Palace)

❹

Pieni-Porsas

Lapinlahti

Leppäsuonk.

Pohj. Rautatiekatu

Malminkatu

Fredrikink.

Salo
(S

Kamppi

Länsiväylä

Länsiväylä

Pohjoiskaari

Lapinlahdentie

V.k. Lapinlahdenk.

Lapinlahdenk.

Lastenk.

Eerik.

Kale

SALMISAARI

Ruoholahdenk.

Salmisaar
renranta

Tallberg.
katu

Porkkalankatu

Itämerenkatu

Ruoholahti Ⓜ

Santakatu

Ruohonlahdenk.

Hietalahdenranta

Aleksanterin teatteri
(Aleksander Theatre)

Lönnro

Suomen Valokuvataiteen
museo & Teatterimuseo
(Photography &
Theatre Museums)
❶❹

Tammasaarenlaituri

Kaapeli
(Cable Factory)

Kellosaarenranta

Tammasaarenranta

Selkämerenk.-katu

Hietalahdentori
(Hietalahti Flea
Market) ㉔

Bulevar

Sinebry
Taider

PUNAVU

Kansallisarkisto
(National Archives)

Vironkatu

Jaatäranta

Länsisatamankatu

Laivapojankatu

Hietalahti

Fabianinkatu

Unioninkatu

Snellmaninkatu

Rauhankatu

Ritarikatu

Rauhankatu

Säätytalo
(House of Estates)

Kirkkokatu

Mariankatu

Messiytönkatu

Miettaipojankuja

Lantinen vaihdekuja

Itäinen vaihdekuja

Tarmonk.

Munkkis.k.

Hernesaare

Ⓜ Kaisaniemi

Suomen Pankki
(Bank of Finland)

Kirkkokatu

Tuomiokirkko
(Cathedral)

KRUUNUNHAKA

Hietalahti

Vuorikatu

Yliopiston kirjasto
(University Library)

Yliopistonkatu

Hallituskatu

Ritarihuone
(House of Nobility)

Kluuvikatu

Unioninkatu

Yliopisto
(University)

Regeringsgatan
Senaatintori
(Senate Sq.)

Katariinank.

Aleksanteri II ❶

Valtioneuvoston linna
(Council of State)

Meritullintori

Uspenskin
katedraali
(Uspenski
Cathedral)
㉒

LÄNSISATAMA

Hyläemenpylänk.

Poseidoninkuja

Helsingin Kaupunginmuseo
(Helsinki City Museum) ㉑

Aleksanterinkatu

Kaupungin
matkailutoimisto ❶❻
(Helsinki City
Tourist Office) ❶

Sederholmin Talo ㉚
(Sederholm House)

Bockin talo ㉚
(Bock House)

Kaupungintalo
(City Hall)
❶❽

Presidentinlinna
(Presidential Palace)

Kanavakatu

Länsi-
terminaali

Pohjoisesplanadi

Havis
Amanda

Pohjoisesplanadi

❶J.L. Runeberg
ESPLANADIN
❶❸ PUISTO

❶❺ Kappeli
Restaurant

Kauppatori
(Central
Market Sq.)

❶❼

Obeliski Keisarinnan kivi
(Czarinas Obelisk)

KATAJANOKKA

Kanavakatu

Matalasalmenk.

KAARTINKAUPUNKI

Fabianinkatu

Eteläranta

Vanha Kauppahalli
(Old Market Hall)

Kanava-
terminaali

MUNKKISAARI

P. makasiinikatu

Eteläsatama

0 _____ 200 m
0 _____ 200 yds

Stockholm,
Mariehamn,
Tallinn

Suomenlinna, Korkeasaari

Tallinn

㊱ Pihlajasaari

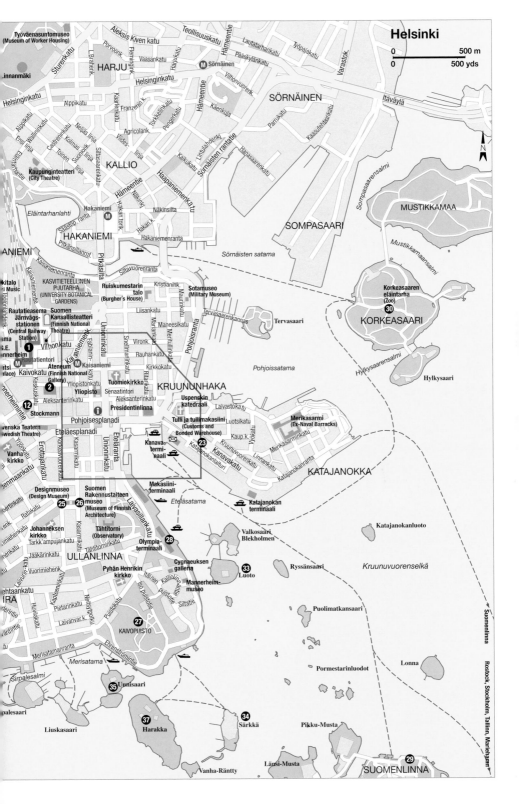

Helsinki

0 — 500 m
0 — 500 yds

N

Työväenasuntomuseo
(Museum of Worker Housing)

Aleksis Kiven katu

Porvoonk.

Fleminginkatu

Vaasankatu

Teollisuuskatu

Lautatarhankatu

Pääskylänkatu

Työpajakatu

Varastok.

M Sörnäinen

Itäväylä

SÖRNÄINEN

Vilhonvuorenk.

Hämeentie

Kaasutehtaankatu

Kuste

HARJU

.innanmäki

Sturenkatu

LBraherik.

Helsinginkatu

Helsinginkatu

Alppikatu

Kaarlenkatu

Franzenin k.

Torkkelinkatu

Pengerkatu

Käenkuja

Parrukatu

Agricolank.

Alppikatu

Wallininkatu

Castreninkatu

Neljäs linja

Kolmas linja

Siltasaarenkatu

Kaikukatu

Lintulahdenkj

Hanasaarenkatu

Sörnäisten rantatie

SOMPASAARI

Sompasaarensalmi

MUSTIKKAMAA

Mustikkamaanaalmi

Ensi linja

Toinen linja

Suomonk.

Viides linja

KALLIO

Haapaniemenkatu

Sörnäisten satama

Kaupunginteatteri
(City Theatre)

Hämeentie

Näkink.

Hakaniemi

Näkinkatu

Näkinsilta

Eläintarhanlahti

M Hakaniemi

Hakak.

Hakan torik

Hakan k.

ANIEMI

Pitkänsillanr.

HAKANIEMI

Hakaniemenranta

Siltavuorenranta

Korkeasaaren
eläintarha
(Zoo)
30

Pitkäsilta

Kasvitieteellinen

Kristianink.

Sotamuseo
(Military Museum)

Maurinkatu

Tervasaarenkannas

Tervasaari

KORKEASAARI

kitalo
l Music

**KASVITIETEELLINEN
PUUTARHA**
(UNIVERSITY BOTANICAL
GARDENS)

Ruiskumestarin
talo
(Burgher's House)

Liisankatu

Hylkysaarensalmi

Rautatieasema
Järnvägs-
stationen
(Central Railway
Station)

Suomen
Kansallisteatteri
(Finnish National
Theatre)

Unioninkatu

Maneesikatu

Pohjoisranta

Pohjoissatama

Hylkysaari

sma
Station)

1
nnerheim

Vilhonkatu

Fabianin.

Vironk.

Shellmaninkatu

Meritullinkatu

atsi
lace)

M Rautatientori

Kaivokatu

Keskuskatu

M Ateneum
(Finnish National
Gallery)

M Kaisaniemi

Rauhankatu

Kirkkokatu

Yliopistonkatu

Tuomiokirkko

KRUUNUNHAKA

2

Yliopisto

Senaatintori

Uspenskin
katedraali

Laivastoka tu

Merikasarmi
(Ex-Naval Barracks)

12

Aleksanterinkatu

Aleksanterinkatu

Luotsikatu

Stockmann

Presidentinlinna

Tulli ja tullimakasiini
(Customs and
Bonded Warehouse)

Kaup.k.

Merikasarminkatu

Pohjoisesplanadi

23

Kanavavuorenkatu

Kruununvuorenkatu

Linnankatu

KATAJANOKKA

venska Teatern
wedish Theatre)

Eteläesplanadi

Kanava-
termi-
naali

Katajanokanlaituri

Kanavakatu

Katajanokanranta

Vanha
kirkko

Erottajankatu

Kasarminkatu

Unioninkatu

Eteläranta

Makasiini-
terminaali

Katajanokan
terminaali

denmaankatu

Designmuseo
(Design Museum)
25

Suomen
Rakennustaiteen
museo
(Museum of Finnish
Architecture)
26

Eteläsatama

Katajanokanluoto

erik.

Ratakatu

Laivasillankatu

imeenkatu

Johanneksen
kirkko

Tähtitorni
(Observatory)

Tarkk'ampujankatu

Tähtitorninkatu

Olympia-
terminaali
28

Valkosaari
Blekholmen

Jääkärinkatu

ULLANLINNA

Pyhän Henrikin
kirkko

Cygnaeuksen
galleria

33
Luoto

Ryssänsaari

Kruunuvuorenselkä

Mannerheim-
museo

Vuorimiehenk.

Kapteeninkatu

IRA

Pietarinkatu

Iso puistotie

Kalliolinnantie

Itäinen

Puistotie

Siltatie

Puolimatkansaari

Laivanvar.k.

27
KAIVOPUISTO

Ehrenströmintie

Lonna

Pormestarinluodot

ehtaankatu

Huvilakatu

Merisatamanranta

Suomenlinna

Merisatama

35 Uunisaari

Sirpalesalmi

37
Harakka

34
Särkkä

Pikku-Musta

palesaari

Liuskasaari

Rostock, Stockholm, Tallinn, Mariehamn

Vanha-Räntty

Länsi-Musta

29
SUOMENLINNA

HELSINKI

An intriguing mix of Swedish and Russian influences combine with an ultramodern architectural stamp to make Finland's unique capital a gem of the northern Baltic

Helsinki

A proud and active member of the EU, Finland's capital city continues to evolve as a lively, cosmopolitan city with its own unique identity, beyond the Swedish and Russian influences of the past.

Flying over Helsinki, one sees nothing but lakes and forests. Arriving in the city centre, one is pleasantly confronted with stately granite buildings and a potpourri of impressive architecture styles: from neoclassical and neo-Renaissance to Art Nouveau, National Romanticism and Functionalism. People bustle along purposefully, stylishly or outrageously dressed, fueled by high-octane doses of *kahvi* (coffee).

After a complex 460-year history, Helsinki has grown from a picturesque village with a harbour to a modern, confident capital where the quality of life has been ranked as among the highest in Europe. It's accessible, surprisingly quiet, and less intense, proceeding at its own steady pace. The "Daughter of the Baltic" has gained her own identity and wears it with pride.

Building a capital

Before gaining independence in 1917, Finland lived through 500 years of Swedish rule, and more than 100 years under the Russians. These diverse influences from the west and then from the east have contributed to Helsinki's char-

acter. Helsinki was founded in 1550 by the Swedish King Gustav Vasa, but the monumental city centre was built in the early 19th century, thanks largely to the talents of the German-born architect Carl Ludwig Engel. Engel's first commission was a new administrative centre, followed by the cathedral, senate building, university and university library. Engel's neoclassical work can also be seen in St Petersburg and Tallinn. At the same time, Helsinki became the seat of a nationalist movement. Native architects such as Eliel

Main attractions

CENTRAL RAILWAY STATION
ATENEUM ART MUSEUM
KIASMA CONTEMPORARY ART MUSEUM
HELSINKI MUSIC CENTRE
TEMPPELIAUKION KIRKKO, "ROCK CHURCH"
CENTRAL MARKET SQUARE AND OLD MARKET HALL
SENATE SQUARE, HELSINKI CATHEDRAL
USPENSKI CATHEDRAL
DESIGN MUSEUM AND DESIGN DISTRICT
SUOMENLINNA FORTRESS

LEFT: monument to Jean Sibelius.
RIGHT: young sailor at the harbour.

Saarinen and Alvar Aalto emerged and, after independence in 1917, Finnish Functionalism replaced Art Nouveau as Helsinki's predominant architectural style *(see page 312)*.

Nothing could completely protect the city from the massive Russian air raids of 1944 – nor from fervent, and not always lovely, post-war reconstruction. But Helsinki's position on the sea soon helped it to regain and then increase its stature, not only as a major port, but also as the important site for shipbuilding and international meetings it is today.

Helsinki Central

Modern Helsinki is a tranquil but still growing city with some 583,000 occupants. The heart of the city pulses around the **Central Railway Station** ❶ (Rautatieasema), a memorable Helsinki landmark, which also contains a metro station and an underground shopping complex. Designed by Eliel Saarinen, who travelled through Europe to study railway stations, and completed in 1919, it links two of Helsinki's most prevalent styles: National Romanticism and Functionalism. The broad entrance is guarded on either side by two giant figures – the work of leading sculptor Emil Wikström (1864–1942) – each holding a globe lantern to light the way for the passengers ebbing and flowing through its doors.

While in the vicinity of the station, take a look at the **Finnish National Theatre** (Suomen Kansallisteatteri) located on the northeastern side of the station, another impressive building in the National Romantic style.

To the southeast of the station in another stately building is the **Ateneum** ❷ (Finnish National Gallery; Kaivokatu 2; tel: 09 1733 6401; www.ateneum.fi; Tue and Fri 10am–6pm, Wed and Thur until 8pm, Sat–Sun 11am–5pm; charge, free Wed after 5pm), built in 1887. The museum's fine collection of Finnish paintings, sculpture and graphic art covers the years 1750 to 1960 and includes works by such prominent Finnish artists as Akseli Gallen-Kallela, Hugo Simberg, and Albert Edelfelt, alongside a small international collection with works by Van Gogh, Munch, Cézanne, Goya and Delacroix. Also worth singling out are

some evocative Finnish landscapes by Pekka Halonen, and the collection of Finnish prints and Japanese woodcuts. The temporary exhibitions throughout the year are impressive, too.

Mannerheimintie

To orientate yourself in Helsinki, just remember that all roads lead to **Mannerheimintie**, the city's main thoroughfare and the longest street in Finland. It was named after Carl Gustav Mannerheim, commander-in-chief of Finnish forces during World War II, and postwar president.

From the railway station turn north into Mannerheimintie and on the right is Finland's most visited museum **Kiasma ❸** (Museum of Contemporary Art; tel: 09 1733 6501; www.kiasma.fi; Tue 10am–5pm, Wed–Fri 10am–8.30pm, Sat–Sun 10am–6pm; charge). This remarkable curvaceous structure with its bright-white, naturally lit interior was designed by American architect Steven Holl as a showcase for contemporary art, which is displayed in a series of rotating exhibitions. Its bar and outdoor terrace are a popular meeting place.

Joining Kiasma to create a triangle of Functionalist architecture are two other cultural institutions: **Lasipalatsi** (Glass Palace) across Mannerheimintie and the former **Tennispalatsi ❹** (Tennis Palace) at the other end of the new Kamppi underground and bus station. Built for the 1940 Helsinki Olympics, the Lasipalatsi building has been rejuvenated to create a Film and Media Centre, designed to "bring the services of modern technology and IT close to people". It incorporates an internet library, television studios, cinema, fine cafés and the Ravintola restaurant, restored to its 1930s glory.

Built in the same period, the Tennispalatsi was used during the 1952 Olympic Games and was extensively renovated to house Finland's largest cinema complex (14 screens) and two museums – a branch of the **City Art Museum** (Helsingin Kaupungin Taidemuseo; tel: 09 3108 7001; Tue–Sun 11am–7pm; charge, free Fri 11am–4pm), used for temporary exhibitions, and the **Museum of Cultures** (tel: 09 40501; www.nba.fi; Tue 11am–8pm, Wed–Sun 11am–6pm; free), which holds ethnographic collections

Skateboarding outside Kiasma.

BELOW: Kiasma, the Museum of Contemporary Art.

Kickbikes in front of Finlandia Hall.

from around the world, with the emphasis on Finno-Ugric peoples.

Opposite Kiasma is the **Parliament Building ❺**, built between 1925 and 1930 and distinguished by an impressive sweep of steps and a facade of 14 columns of grey granite.

Just behind the Parliament Building, the extensively refurbished **Natural History Museum ❻** (Pohjoinen Rautatiekatu 13; tel: 09 1912 8800; www. luomus.fi; Tue, Wed and Fri 9am–4pm, Thur until 6pm, Sat–Sun 10am–4pm; charge) has turned the University of Helsinki's vast zoological collection of animal specimens into engaging exhibits on Finnish flora and fauna.

Museums of History

Statues of former Finnish presidents scatter the area between Parliament and the **National Museum of Finland ❼** (Kansallismuseo; tel: 09 40501; www.nba. fi; Tue–Wed 11am–8pm, Thur–Sun until 6pm; charge), two blocks to the north. It focuses on Finnish history, with interesting displays on life in pre-industrial Finland, and Finnish folk culture. The museum's decoration and the stone bear

by the entrance are by Emil Wikström (*see page 308*), and the frescoes on the foyer ceiling, depicting scenes from Finland's national epic, the *Kalevala*, are by renowned Finnish artist Gallen-Kallela (1865–1931).

Across Mannerheimintie is a branch of the **Helsinki City Museum** (Mannerheimintie 13d; tel: 09 3107 8519; Wed–Sun 11am–5pm, Thur 11am–7pm). Housed in the fine **Hakasalmi Villa** (1843) designed in the Italian neoclassical style, it stages interesting exhibitions on different aspects of the capital's history.

World-class venues

Finlandia Hall ❽ (Mannerheimintie 13; tel: 09 40 241 for information about guided tours; www.finlandiatalo. fi), opposite the National Museum, is undoubtedly the most famous building in Helsinki with its clean lines and Carrara marble exterior, designed by Alvar Aalto. It was long the residence of the Helsinki Philharmonic Orchestra and a venue for various congress events, but that changed radically in September 2011 with the opening of

the long-awaited, overdue and much-debated **Helsinki Music Centre**  (Musiikkitalo; for information, www.musiikkitalo.fi), a state-of-the-art concert hall whose main occupants are the Helsinki Philharmonic and the Finnish Radio Symphony orchestras, and Sibelius Academy, Helsinki's famous musical conservatory.

Continuing north along Mannerheimintie to where Hesperia Park and Töölö Bay come to an end, the contemporary **Finnish National Opera House** ❿ (Helsinginkatu 58; tel: 09 403 021), which opened in 1993, offers an ambitious season with many international performers. In 2011, the Finnish National Opera celebrated its centenary with several world premieres and prominent guest artists.

Nestling, literally, into a small hill west of the Parliament Building behind Mannerheimintie and the winding streets of Töölö, is the ultra-modern Lutheran church, **Temppeliaukion Kirkko,** or "Rock Church" ⓫ (Lutherinkatu 3; tel: 09 2340 5920; mid-June–mid-Sept Mon–Tue, Thur–Fri 10am–8pm, Wed and Sat until 6pm,

Sun noon–6pm), which reopened in 2011 after extensive repair work. It is not only an architectural oddity – built as it is directly into the granite rocks, with inner walls of stone and an impressive copper-covered dome – but it is also the site of many good concerts. A service for English-speakers is held every Sunday at 2pm.

Around Esplanadi

Heading south, back to town on Mannerheimintie, you'll find **Stockmann,** ⓬ Finland's largest department store, which has an excellent food hall on the lower level. Behind it, on Keskuskatu, is Scandinavia's largest bookshop, **Akateeminen Kirjakauppa**, a great place to browse or to take a break in the stylish café designed by Alvar Aalto.

The bookshop faces another Helsinki landmark, **Esplanadi Park and Boulevards** ⓭, which was first laid out in 1831 and runs between Mannerheimintie and South Harbour. In summer its narrow lawns and benches are filled with people relaxing and eating ice creams, while being entertained by buskers. Summer concerts are held on

The Helsinki Festival is a lively international arts festival held every year from mid-August to early September, with a varied programme of classical and world music, circus, dance, theatre, cinema and a whole host of other events (tel: 09 6126 5100; www.helsingin juhlaviikot.fi). A festival highlight is the popular Night of the Arts (held at the end of August), a city-wide cultural celebration that lasts late into the night.

BELOW: Concert in Esplandi Park

Helsinki Card

If you plan on doing lots of sightseeing in and around Helsinki, consider investing in a Helsinki Card, which can be purchased from the City Tourist Office (Tour Shop), Pohjoisesplanadi 19, hotels, sightseeing departure points, Airport Travel Services (at the airport, arrivals area 2b, open 24 hours) and railway station – or online, with a €3 discount.

The card provides free admission to museums and sights, a 1½-hour Audio City Tour, free travel to Suomenlinna Sea Fortress and entry to the main sights, entry to Helsinki Zoo, and free travel on city buses, trams, trains and the metro. It also includes various other discounts and benefits.

The card can be purchased for periods of 24–72 hours; for adults €35–55; for children 7–16 years old, €14–20.

On the Trail of *Jugendstil*

Helsinki offers a wealth of interest for lovers of architecture, especially among its flamboyant Art Nouveau buildings

Helsinki has a wealth of architecture, which can be discovered in different quarters of the city. From Baroque Classicism and neo-Renaissance to neoclassical Empire and Modernist design. However, for the first-time visitor, it is the *Jugend* style which really makes an impression. It was around the turn of the 20th century that a younger generation of architects, inspired by the Arts and Crafts movement, rose in revolt against Classicism and older styles which recreated the past. These included: Lars Sonck (1870–1956), Bertel Jung (1872–1946), and the trio Herman Gesellius (1874–1916), Armas Lindgren (1874–1929) and Eliel Saarinen (1873–1950), who were committed to creating "a more domestic, freer and more authentic world" with their work.

In France, the name of this new style was Art Nouveau, and in Germany *Jugendstil*. It is recognised by its own unique elements which have taken on a more local form in Finland known as National

Romanticism, characterised by visually striking windows, heavy ornamentation, serious figurative components, the use of natural materials like timber and granite, and castle-inspired features like spires and towers.

With its four globe-bearing figures by Emil Wikström and imposing facade, **Helsinki Central Station** *(see page 308)*, designed by Eliel Saarinen, is a memorable example of the National Romantic style. Arrive in good time before your train leaves to look at the striking murals in the Eliel restaurant.

The **National Museum** *(see page 310)* with its spires, distinctive clock tower, carved bear at the entrance also by Wikström and ceiling painting by Akseli Gallen-Kallela, both prominent artists of the period, was jointly designed by Saarinen and his partners Herman Gesellius and Armas Lindgren, who won an architectural competition for the project in 1902. They also created **Hvitträsk**, in Kirkkonummi *(see page 324)*, a stone and log structure in an idyllic lakeside setting on a forested hill, just west of Helsinki. The villa served as their country home and studio until their tumultuous personal relationships ended their collaboration in 1905; it is one of the masterpieces of Finnish architecture. The **National Theatre** *(see page 308)* is another example of their work, as is **Pohjola House** at Aleksanterinkatu 44, former HQ of the Helsinki Telephone Company, now head office of Pohjola Insurance.

Examples of *Jugendstil* architecture can be found all around Helsinki, like Katajanokka (east of Senate Square), Kruununhaka (just to the south) and the stylish Eira neighbourhood, just south of Kaivopuisto Park, known for its splendid **embassy mansions**. Other buildings to look out for include the **hospital** at Laivurinkatu 27, designed by Lars Sonck, Lindahl and Thomé's **Linna Hotel**, Lönnrotinkatu 29, and the **Otava publishing house** at Uudenmaankatu 10.

National Romanticism was not just expressed through architecture, but in the visual arts and classical music (most notably in the Karelia Suite by Sibelius). Architects looked to their national history for inspiration, like Karelia, the province that spans Russia and Finland, of great historic importance, and to the national epic, the *Kalevala*, which is rich in mythology and symbolism.

For dedicated walks and tours of Jugendstil sights, visit www.archtours.com. ❑

LEFT: the National Theatre, a good example of National Romantic style.

the bandstand and come winter, it's the setting for the annual Christmas Fair.

Two boulevards stretch east–west along either side of the park. Nowadays the fine 19th-century buildings along **Pohjoisesplanadi** (North Esplanade) mostly house Finnish design shops, including Marimekko, Arabia and Aarikka.

The **Swedish Theatre** (Svenska Teatern), an elegant semicircular stone building dating from 1866, commands Esplanadi's western head on Mannerheimintie. In front of the theatre, bus no. 20 will take you just five minutes out of town to the **Ruoholahti** area and the **Cable Factor**y (Kaapeli), a lively cultural complex (with café and restaurant), where the **Finnish Museum of Photography** and **Theatre Museum**  are located (Tallberginkatu 1; tel: 09 6866 3621; www.valokuvataiteenmuseo. fi for photography; 0207 96 1670, www. teatterimuseo.fi for theatre; Tue–Sun 11am–6pm; charge).

Heading east through Esplanadi, past the central statue of J.L. Runeberg, Finland's national poet, you come to the historic café-restaurant and former haunt of Sibelius, **Kappeli**  (Eteläesplanadi 1; tel: 09 681 2440). It is a popular meeting place near the harbour with a pleasant outdoor terrace.

The nearby **Helsinki City Tourist Office**  (Pohjoisesplanadi 19; tel 09 3101 3300; www.visithelsinki.fi; mid-May–mid-Sept Mon–Fri 9am–8pm, Sat–Sun 9am–6pm, mid-Sept–mid-May Mon–Fri 9am–6pm, Sat–Sun 10am–4pm) offers tour advice, maps and brochures, and there's a booking desk here too.

In 1999 the **Hotel Kämp**, Pohjoiseplenadi 29, a popular rendezvous in Helsinki at the end of the 19th century, reopened its doors as a luxury hotel. The **Kämp Galleria** is an exclusive shopping complex on the street and lower levels.

Market Square

Across the road from the Kappeli restaurant is the **Havis Amanda Fountain**, which created quite a stir when it was first erected in 1908. The bronze statue of a nubile mermaid represents the city of Helsinki rising from the sea, innocent and naked. Opposite the fountain is the bustling **Central Market Square**  (Kauppatori; Mon–Fri 6.30am–6pm, Sat until 4pm, in summer also Sun 10am–5pm). This is where locals buy their fruits, vegetables, flowers and fish. The small tents serve tasty cinnamon buns or meat pastries and there's a heated coffee tent. Other stalls sell arts and crafts, including Sami handicrafts. Every year in October, the traditional Herring Market is held on the square.

To the south of the square at the 100-year-old, yellow-and-red-brick **Old Market Hall** (Vanha Kauppahalli), you can buy salmon, reindeer cold-cuts, and even Vietnamese *loempia* (egg rolls).

Behind the market are the long blue **City Hall**  designed by Engel in 1833, and **Presidential Palace**, designed in 1818 as a private home and turned into a tsarist palace by Engel in 1843. The Finnish president no longer resides here.

To the cathedral

Another major landmark, **Senate Square**, stands one block north of

The Design Walk is a two-hour expedition that focuses on fashion, furnishing and art along 25 streets of Helsinki's design district. www. designdistrict.fi.

BELOW: Helsinki's fine cathedral, Tuomiokirkko.

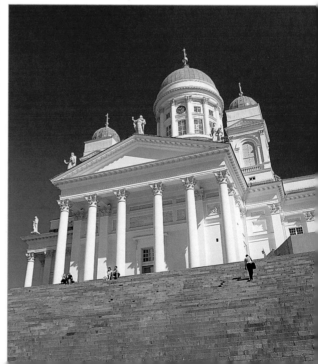

The interior of Russian Orthodox Uspenski Cathedral.

BELOW: Kappeli, a popular meeting place on Esplanadi.

here, on the busy **Aleksanterinkatu** shopping street. Over the centuries the square has remained a very impressive spot, where thousands gathered for the funeral of Jean Sibelius.

Helsinki Cathedral ⓲ (Tuomiokirkko; Mon–Sat 9am–6pm, Sun noon–7pm), at the top of a flight of steep steps on the north side, is a point of pride for Finns, and the exterior – with its five green cupolas, numerous white Corinthian columns and sprinkling of important figurines posing on its roof – is certainly impressive.

At the southeastern corner of the square stands the city's oldest stone building, dating from 1757, the small blue-grey **Sederholm House** ⓴ (Sederholmin Talo; Aleksanterinkatu 16–18; tel: 09 169 3625; Wed, Fri–Sun 11am–5pm, Thur until 7pm), which contains a small museum that evokes 18th-century Helsinki through the life story of its former owner, merchant Johan Sederholm.

For the city's history, head one block south to the **Helsinki City Museum** ⓴ (Sofiankatu 4; tel: 09 3103 6630; Mon–Wed and Fri 9am–5pm, Thur 9am–7pm, Sat–Sun 11am–5pm; free). Here, an exhibition entitled "Helsinki's Horizons" presents the 450-year history of the nation's capital and the events that have shaped it, through three periods: the Swedish era, the Russian era and the era of Finnish independence.

Katajanokka

After exploring Helsinki's centre, venture into one of the surrounding districts, each of which has its own particular character. **Katajanokka** lies on a small promontory sticking out into the sea a few blocks east from Senate Square, connected by two short bridges. The spires and onion-shaped domes of the Russian Orthodox **Uspenski Cathedral** ⓴ (Uspenskin Katedraali), built in 1868, tower above a popular restaurant complex across the street. Helsinki's oldest Russian restaurant (1917), the **Bellevue**, sits at the base of the cathedral, across from Katajanokka Park.

Jugendstil (Art Nouveau) architecture dominates **Luotsikatu** street, just east of the cathedral. Don't miss the charming griffin doorway at No. 5 *(see feature page 312)*.

In recent years, many of the old warehouses have been converted to restaurants, shops and a hotel. The **Customs and Bonded Warehouse** ㉓ (Katajanokkan Laituri 5) from 1900 remains the same, with its imaginative *Jugendstil* architecture.

West of Esplanadi

Head west from Esplanadi along **Bulevardi** and explore the neighbouring streets like Eerikinkatu, Fredrikinkatu and Uudenmaankatu, a fashionable quarter known for its galleries, boutiques, antique bookshops and restaurants. At the end of Bulevardi, past the old Opera House, don't miss the **Hietalahti flea market** ㉔ (Mon–Fri 10am–6pm, Sat 8am–4pm, also Sun 10am–4pm in summer), a popular open-air market in the summer months.

To the south of Bulevardi are the exclusive **Eira** and **Ullanlinna** districts. The **Design Museum** ㉕ (Korkeavuorenkatu 23; tel: 09 622 0540; www.designmuseum.fi; Tue 11am–8pm, Wed–Sun 11am–6pm, summer daily 11am–6pm; charge) provides an overview of modern Finnish style and the roots of its aesthetic, showcasing Finland's leading designers of the 20th and 21st century who transform everyday items – lamps, chairs, glasses, toys – into objects of simple, functional beauty. In the same block is the **Museum of Finnish Architecture** ㉖ (Kasarmikatu 24; tel: 09 8567 5100; www.mfa.fi; Tue and Thur–Fri 10am–4pm, Wed until 8pm, Sat–Sun from 11am; charge), which has an excellent archive of architectural drawings and changing exhibitions focusing on Finnish architectural movements.

The southernmost end of the peninsula is lined by parkland, frequented by joggers, skaters and cyclists. In summer, the city sponsors free concerts in **Kaivopuisto Park** ㉗. Strollers head for refreshment at the **Café Ursula** whose terrace offers a stunning view of the Suomenlinna Castle, or the seafront **Café Carusel**. In winter, when the sea is frozen, you can actually walk out to some of the closer offshore islands. On the eastern point, the grand villas of foreign embassies fill the chic Ullanlinna district. **Olympia Quay** ㉘ (Olympia terminaali) is a mooring place for the huge Silja and Viking liners. The fast ferries that ply the route to medieval Tallin, the Estonian capital, board at the West Terminal (*see box, page 316*).

Suomenlinna

Suomenlinna ㉙ (Fortress of Finland; visitor centre, tel: 09 684 1880; www.suomenlinna.fi) consists of five islands, over which the ruins of a naval fortress and its fortifications are spread. Suomenlinna has played an integral part in Helsinki's life since its construction started in 1748. Listed by Unesco as a World Heritage site, today it is a thriving local artists' community with the restored bastions being used as studios and showrooms. Visitors arrive here year-round by ferry which departs from Market Square every half-hour. They dock on **Iso Mustasaari**, from where a hilly path leads up through **Rantakasarmi** (Jetty Barracks), which houses art exhibitions and the restaurant and microbrewery **Panimo**.

Helsinki has a number of public saunas, but the only wood-heated one is Kotiharjun Sauna, Harjutorinkatu 1 in Kallio (near Sörnäinen metro station; Tue–Fri 2–8pm, Sat 1–7pm; tel: 09 753 1535).

BELOW: Helsinki City Museum.

Taking a break on the harbourside.

RIGHT: café life, central Helsinki.

For information on the island's museums, stop by the **Visitor Centre** (daily; entrance to fortress free, charge to museums; tel: 09 684 1880 for information about guided tours in English). The expansive **Suomenlinna Museum** covers the history of the sea fortress from the 18th century to the present. The castle courtyard, the best-preserved section of the fortress, contains the 1788 sarcophagus of Count Ehrensvärd, commander of the fort, whose former home is now the **Ehrensvärd Museum** with period furniture, arms and lithographs. Other museums include a **Toy Museum, Artillery Museum** and the fascinating **Vesikko** (summer only), a World War II submarine. Try to visit the atmospheric summer restaurant **Walhalla**, where on a clear day it is possible to see Estonia, some 80km (50 miles) away *(see box below)*.

Korkeasaari

In summer, **Helsinki Zoo** ㉚ (Korkeasaari island; tel: 09 3101 615; daily May–Aug 10am–8pm, Oct–Mar until 4pm, Apr and Sept until 6pm; charge) can be reached by boat from Market Square or on bus no. 11 from the Railway Square. The zoo, unsurprisingly, specialises in "cold climate animals", although there's an interesting enclosure of South American species.

Seurasaari

The island of **Seurasaari** ㉛ is eminently atmospheric. A pretty, forested place with a national park (all year), its northeastern side has been made into an **Open-Air Museum** (tel: 04 0509 660; June–Aug daily 11am–5pm; charge) containing wooden buildings from provinces all over Finland from the 17th to 19th centuries.

The island is connected to the Helsinki shore by a wooden footbridge, close to which is the second branch of the **City Art Museum** (Tue–Sun 11am–6.30pm; charge). Take either bus no. 24 from Erottaja (in front of the Swedish Theatre), or cycle along the Meilahti coastal drive which takes you past the lovely **Sibelius Park** ㉜ and its silvery tubular **Sibelius Monument** to the bridge.

Other islands

Less well known are the smaller islands that form a string around Helsinki's southern peninsula. Across the "Olympic Harbour" are **Luoto** ㉝ and **Valkosaari**, restaurant islands with romantic villas. A long pier outside Kaivopuisto offers a boat service to **Särkkä** ㉞, another island with a popular restaurant. **Uunisaari** ㉟ is accessible at the southern end of Neitsytpolku Street. It's a popular recreational island with a beach, sauna and restaurant.

Pihlajasaari ㊱ is Helsinki's favourite island for swimming. It actually comprises two islands, with a sandy beach, café and changing cabins on the larger island's western shore. Helsinki's only nudist beach is on the smaller island. Boats to Pihlajasaari depart in summer every 15 to 30 minutes from outside Café Carusel in Eira.

The former military island of **Harakka** ㊲, south of Kaivopuisto, is now a wildlife reserve. ❏

Ferries to Estonia, Trains to Russia

Across the Gulf of Finland lies the northernmost of the Baltic states, Estonia. Its capital, Tallinn, is 85km (53 miles) from Helsinki and about 130km (80 miles) from St Petersburg. Finns have long taken advantage of Estonia's proximity and relative cheapness, making the ferry crossing in droves. It is easy to see the attraction: Tallinn has the prettiest Old Town in the Baltics, a medieval enclave set on a hillock above its port. Within the fairytale walls and towers and beneath the Gothic spires are winding cobbled lanes, artisan shops, historic buildings, charming cafés and breathtaking vistas – a wonderful contrast to the modern city centre, where a rapidly developing commercial district has redrawn the city's skyline. For information on organised day trips visit www.helsinkiexpert.com; for information on fast boat services visit www.tallink.fi.com (the journey takes 2 hours each way).

For an alternative, land-based excursion across the Russian border take the fast train from Helsinki and St Petersburg. The ultramodern Allegro train takes you on a 3½-hour journey from city centre to city centre. There are four daily services. Border formalities are conducted conveniently during the journey on board the train, and you can also exchange currency during the trip. There is one daily departure from Helsinki to Moscow by the train Tolstoi, www.vr.fi.

THE TRADITIONAL FINNISH SAUNA

An old Finnish proverb says: "First you build the sauna, then you build the house". Even today, there is nothing so uniquely Finnish as a sauna

There are some things along the way which a traveller does not forget – and a real Finnish sauna is one of them. Although its origin is obscure and legend claims that the sauna came to Finland over 2,000 years ago, credit must go to the Karelian people for introducing the sauna to Finnish culture (*see page 347*). Official statistics now estimate that there are over 1.6 million saunas in Finland, not counting those in private houses or summer cottages that dot the shoreline of the country's lakes. The actual figure could easily be over 2 million in a country of over 5 million people.

Business and pleasure

The sauna outgrew its rural roots long ago. Today, be it city or village, you will find public saunas, and it is safe to assume that every new apartment block has a sauna for its tenants. Many companies also have saunas for their employees, most hotels have them for guests, and there is even one in Helsinki's Parliament building.

A Finnish sauna is not a meeting place for sex, as it is in some countries; codes of behaviour are strict, and public saunas are not for both genders at the same time. It is not unusual for board meetings and government cabinet meetings to be held in a sauna – perhaps because it's "not done" to swear or raise one's voice. Titles and position are, they say, left hanging in the changing room along with the clothes.

In 2010, this national institution was honoured with a documentary film *Steam of Life*, that was a big hit on the festival circuit.

ABOVE: the sauna has become an integral part of Finnish life, where friends meet and business deals are struck. A popular seasonal option is to spring into a lake between steam sessions.

ABOVE: an instant sauna in Lapland, put together out of ice blocks. Despite the nudity, a Finnish sauna is a moral place. Generally, saunas are same-sex only; a mixed sauna is usually a family affair.

BELOW: a concert by Finnish artist M A Numminen, performing in Suomenlinna's Naval Academy, the biggest sauna in the country.

LEFT: birch leaves, cut in early summer, are tied up in bundles and used as switches to increase blood circulation.

ABOVE: a couple cooling off after enjoying the heat in the sauna.

ABOVE: in winter, brave souls jump through holes in the ice or roll around in the snow — not recommended practice for people with high blood pressure.

HOW TO TAKE A SAUNA

There is no "right way" to take a sauna – temperature and style vary. The ideal temperature is between 60–80°C (140–175°F), although it can be a cooler 30°C (85°F) on the bottom platform, reserved for children. A common practice is to brush oneself with a wet birch switch, called the *vihta*. This not only gives off a fresh fragrance but increases blood circulation and perspiration.

How long you sit in the sauna is entirely up to you. When you have had enough, you move on to stage two: cooling off. A cold shower is the most common way but, if the sauna is by a lake or the sea, a quick plunge into the cool water is stimulating.

The final stage is to dry off, which should be done naturally, to avoid further perspiration. It is also time for a beer or coffee and a snack to complete the ritual.

BELOW: water thrown over the hot stones creates a dry steam *(löyly)*, which makes the heat tolerable and stimulates perspiration.

SOUTHERN FINLAND

Follow the route of the Nordic kings from west to east across southern Finland, through a gentle landscape of painted villages, ancient castles and an island-studded coast

Helsinki

The route once travelled by Nordic kings and princes to St Petersburg is known as the King's Road; it passes through mainly flat coastal country covered with farmland and dense forest. From Pargas (Parainen), south of **Turku ❶** (Åbo; *see page 329*) at the head of the Turunmaa archipelago chain, through Hanko (Hangö), Ekenäs (Tammisaari), Karis (Karjaa) and further east via Porvoo (Borgå) through a cluster of small villages on the approach to Kotka, you will hear a great deal of Swedish being spoken and read it as the first language on signposts.

Exploring the islands

Richly vegetated but sparsely populated, the archipelago of **Turunmaa ❷** is quieter than the Ålands (*see page 327*) in terms of tourism, and the islands are reached more quickly from the mainland by local bus or car. They are linked by a series of bridges and then ferries, which also service some of the smaller islands that spin off south from the main chain. Many Finnish families have their own islands – the ultimate refuge.

Turunmaa's finest harbour is on the northern spur of **Nagu**. An old wooden house overlooking the marina has been made into a guesthouse-style hotel. Also to be found in Nagu is a

small **Hembygdsmuseum** and the 15th-century **St Olof's Church**.

As you approach **Pargas ❸** (Parainen) from the west or the south you come to **Sattmark**, on the island of Stortervolandet. Here you can lodge in a tiny log cabin that was once a sailor's quarters, or just stop for some refreshment in the charming café (tel: 082 458 7577; www.sattmark.fi).

Continuing east towards Piikkiö, it is worth making a detour to **Kuusisto Castle ❹** (Kuusiston Linna) on the Kuusisto peninsula. This medieval

Main attractions
TURUNMAA ARCHIPELAGO
HANKO HARBOUR AND 19TH-
  CENTURY VILLAS
VOYAGE TO BENGTSKÄR
  LIGHTHOUSE
EKENÄS/TAMMISAARI OLD TOWN
  AND NATIONAL PARK
FISKARS VILLAGE
HVITTRÄSK
GALLEN-KALLELA MUSEUM
PORVOO OLD TOWN
KOTKA MARITIME FESTIVAL
ÅLAND ISLANDS

LEFT: models of ships traditionally grace the windows of Loviisa's wooden houses.
RIGHT: a summer treat.

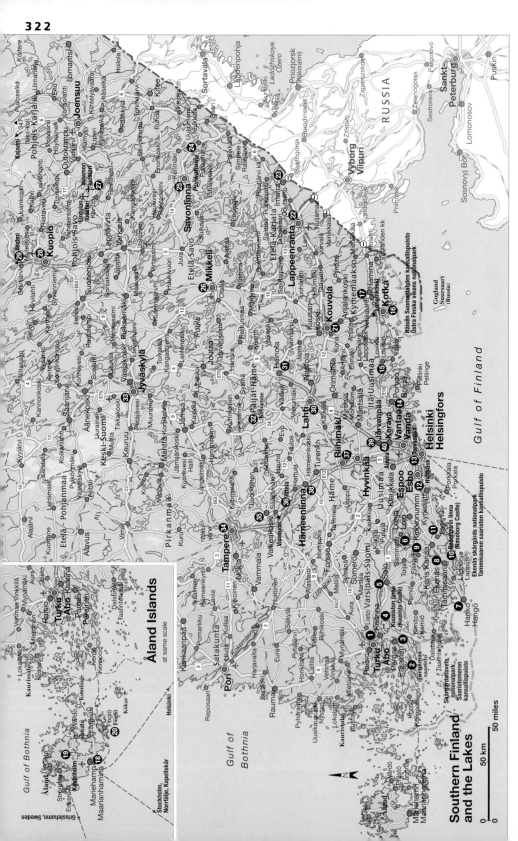

Southern Finland and the Lakes

Åland Islands
at same scale

RUSSIA

Gulf of Finland

Gulf of Bothnia

Helsinki
Helsingfors

Turku
Åbo

Tampere

Kuopio

Joensuu

Savonlinna

Mikkeli

Lappeenranta

Kouvola

Kotka

Lahti

Hämeenlinna

Riihimäki

Hyvinkää

Järvenpää

Kerava

Vantaa
Vanda

Espoo
Esbo

Jyväskylä

Pori

Vyborg
Viipuri

Sankt-
Peterburg

Mariehamn
Maarianhamina

0   50 km
0   50 miles

Stockholm,
Norrtälje, Kapellskär

bishop's castle stood stoutly until Gustav Vasa ordered its demolition in 1528, but enough remains to have encouraged restoration.

Salo and Sammatti

Salo ❺, to the east on the mainland, has a lively market and is set off by a triad of churches – the Lutheran **Uskela** (1832) by C.L. Engel, the Greek Orthodox **Tsasouna** at its foot, and the stunningly modern **Helisnummi Church** about 4km (2½ miles) outside the town. At **Sammatti** ❻, 48km (30 miles) east of Salo, look out for the sign to **Paikkari Cottage** (Paikkarin Torppa), the home of Elias Lönnrot who collected the legends and tales for the *Kalevala (see page 95)*.

The coast: west of Helsinki

Southwest of Salo is **Hanko** ❼ (Hangö), Finland's southernmost town, once a popular spa resort, and now frequented for its annual regatta and its beaches. Hanko is distinguished by an abundance of turreted villas in pastel shades which grace the stretch of beach behind a line of charming white changing huts. These stately homes were built in the late 19th century for the Russian nobility who came for health cures; several offer bed and breakfast accommodation.

The City Hall Gallery and Municipal Library Gallery offer a range of exhibitions. Just a stone's throw away at Villa Orrmanissa you can indulge in freshly baked pastries at **Alan's Cafe**, and browse in the antiquarian bookshop and crafts gallery. There are two fish restaurants on the harbourfront and several in the adjacent renovated warehouses. On 26 August, the annual Night of the Bonfires takes place and launches the Hanko Days Weekend Festival (note that at the end of August hotels and restaurants virtually shut down, however some villas may be hired privately).

In summer, seal safaris take off from the eastern harbour Wed and Fri–Sun at 3pm. Book at the tourist office (tel: 019 2203 411). There are also boat excursions to the adjacent town of Ekenäs (www.marinelines.fi), or to **Bengtskär Lighthouse**, 25km (15 miles) south of Hanko, which make a memorable day's adventure. Built in 1906, the massive stone structure is Scandinavia's tallest lighthouse at 52 metres (170ft) high. The climb to the top of the 252 steps is worth it for the view. There is a café and gift shop, and it is also possible to lodge here.

Ekenäs ❽ (Tammisaari) is the next main coastal stop along the King's Road. It is a finely laid out old town, with 18th- and 19th-century cobbled streets and charming wooden buildings, and is a great place for a stroll. Just to the south is the **Tammisaari National Park**, resplendent with marshes, forests and water birds.

There is an extremely active boating life in and around Ekenäs, and numerous outdoor concerts in summer. The **Knipan** summer restaurant and the steeple of the old granite church (1680) are the town's main landmarks. Visit **Ekenäs Museum** (Porvaristalo, Wasas gata 11; tel: 020-619 3161; summer

Setting off for a sail from the marina at Hanko.

BELOW: the flat landscape of southern Finland is ideal for cycling.

Windmills are a feature of the islands and low-lying districts of the south.

Tue–Sun 11am–5pm; charge) for some local history. Boat tours depart from the North Harbour in July and August.

From Ekenäs, take a detour north to the picturesque village of **Fiskars ❾**, a craft, design and art centre and the original home of Fiskars knives and scissors, founded in 1649. The **Fiskars Museum** (tel: 019 237 013; May–Sept Mon–Fri 11am–5pm, Sat–Sun until 6pm, rest of the year Sat 11am–4pm; charge) portrays the company's history.

A few kilometres east from Ekenäs is **Snappertuna**, a farming village 15km (10 miles) from the late 14th-century castle at **Raasepori ❿**. The outdoor theatre in the Raseborg dale stages dramatic and musical evenings. Further east beyond Snappertuna is **Fagervik ⓫**, the site of a tremendous old manor overlooking an inlet. The nearby fishing village of **Ingå** (Inkoo) has pretty cafés and craft shops.

Hvitträsk and Tarvaspää

Just outside Espoo, **Hvitträsk ⓬** (tel: 09 4050 9630; Wed–Sun 11am–5pm; charge) merits a visit. This *Jugendstil* jewel was designed by Eliel Saarinen

(1901–3) and his colleagues, Herman Gesellius and Armas Lindgren, and for a time served as the architects' communal residence and studio *(see feature on Jugendstil style, page 312)*, and was frequented by the likes of Sibelius, Gallen-Kallela *(see below)* and Gorki. Set on a forested hill by a lake, this fantastic and fanciful creation of timber and granite now functions as a museum with a café that serves local specialities.

A little further west, approaching Helsinki, **Tarvaspää ⓭** was the home of Finland's national artist, Akseli Gallen-Kallela (1865–1931). His *Jugendstil*-inspired studio has been converted into the **Gallen-Kallela Museum** (tel: 09 849 2340; mid-May–Aug daily 11am–6pm, Sept–mid-May Tue–Sat 11am–4pm, Sun 11am–5pm; charge), displaying the artist's paintings, stained glass, tools and objects collected on his travels. There is an outdoor café and nearby walking trails.

Porvoo

East of Helsinki, **Porvoo ⓮** (Borgå) is one of Finland's most important historical towns. The Swedish king

BELOW: the former home of Finland's national poet, J.L. Runeberg, Porvoo.

Magnus Eriksson gave Porvoo a royal charter in 1346; it soon became a busy trading post and, ultimately, it was the place where the Diet of Porvoo (1809) convened to transfer Finland from Swedish to Russian hands. The striking 15th-century **Porvoo Cathedral** (May–Sept Mon–Fri 10am–6pm, Sat 10am–2pm, Sun 2–5pm, Oct–Apr Tue–Sat 10am–2pm, Sun 2–4pm) is where this momentous event took place.

While its rich history made the town important, Porvoo's writers and artists gave it its real character. The former residence of Finland's national poet, **J.L. Runeberg** (Aleksanterinkatu 3; tel: 019 581 330; May–Sept Tue–Sun 10am–4pm, Oct–Apr Wed–Sun; charge) opened to the public as a museum in 1882, and its well-preserved interior contains original antiques, books, manuscripts and memorabilia. The **Walter Runeberg Sculpture Collection** (Aleksanterinkatu 5; tel: 019 582 186; May–Sept Tue–Sun 10am–4pm; charge) has over 100 sculptures by J.L Runeberg's son, a respected sculptor who was commissioned to make statues of his father and Tsar Alexander II.

Porvoo Museum (tel: 019 574 7500; May–Aug Tue–Sat 10am–4pm, Sun 11am–4pm, Sept–Apr Wed–Sun noon–4pm; charge) occupies two buildings (1763) on the cobbled old town square. It focuses on life as lived by a wealthy 18th-century merchant family.

For scenery, the medieval atmosphere of **Old Porvoo** has few rivals: its riverbanks are lined with red-ochre warehouses and pastel-coloured wooden houses. On summer weekdays, guided walking tours of the Old Town start from the town hall on the square at 2pm (tel: 019 520 2316). From mid-May–Sept, the M/S *J.L. Runeberg* operates cruises from Helsinki to Porvoo (tel: 019 524 3331; www.msjlruneberg.fi).

The **Albert Edelfelt Atelier** (June–Aug Tue–Sun 10am–4pm, 15–31 May and 1–15 Sept Tue–Sun 10am–2pm; charge) built in 1883 in Haikko, 6km (4 miles) south of Porvoo, exhibits the oeuvre of one of Finland's finest 19th-century artists.

East of Porvoo, the landscape becomes more rural and less populated. In summer the grassy hillocks bristle with wild flowers. **Loviisa** ⑮ is

Good stopping points on the journey east from Loviisa to Kotka are the excellent sandy beaches of Pyhtää and the holiday island of Kaunissaari, with its interesting fishing village.

BELOW: wooden home typical of southern Finland.

Tsar Alexander III, whose hand-crafted timber fishing lodge at Langinkoski was a gift from the Finnish state.

a pretty coastal town with an esplanade headed by the New Gothic Church. A town museum tells the local history, including the role of the Rosen and Ungern bastions, built in the 18th century to protect the trade route between Vyborg and Turku. Just 10km (6 miles) from the centre of town on an island at the mouth of Loviisa Bay is the **Svartholma** sea fortress, built in 1748.

Kotka

Kotka ⑯ is the next important destination on the King's Road and is one of the most beautifully situated cities in Finland. Here, the fast-flowing Kymi River breaks up into five branches before rushing off into the sea, making for perfect salmon and trout fishing. The local fish species can also be found in the **Kotka Aquarium** (Maretarium; tel: 040 311 0330; Jan–6 Dec daily 10am–5pm, summer until 8pm; charge).

Tourists flock to the modern town of Kotka every July to join in the fun at the largest **maritime festival** in Finland. The pleasant **Sapokka Marina** has a nice park, with a high artificial waterfall. Step aboard a water bus for a tour of the beautiful Kotka archipelago.

The **Kymenlaakso** (Kymi River Valley) extends further inland, where there are forest trails, fishing and whitewater rafting. Enquire for details at the Kotka Tourist Office (Keskuskatu 6, tel: 05 234 4424).

The main attraction at nearby **Langinkoski** is the impressive **Imperial Fishing Lodge Museum** (tel: 044 8050; June–Aug daily 10am–6pm, May 10am–4pm, Sept Sat–Sun 10am–4pm; charge), in a beautiful wooded setting, by the Kymi River, some 5km (3 miles) north of the town centre. This striking two-storey log building was crafted by the Finns for Tsar Alexander III (1845–94), who used it to break his journeys between Helsinki and St Petersburg.

It's another 5km (3 miles) from here to the **Siikakoski rapids**, an ideal spot for fishing, and **Restaurant Munkkisaari**, built on the site of an Orthodox monastery. The restaurant sells fishing licences and has boats and cabins for hire (tel: 05 210 7400).

In summer, **Kärkisaari**, just west of Kotka, makes for a lovely excursion. The long swimming dock leads into the island-filled inlet of the Gulf of Finland. On the adjacent peninsula is **Santalahti**; the crescent-shaped beach has grassy knolls at the edge of a sandy bay.

To the Russian border

Kotka is only 70km (45 miles) from the nearest Russian city, Viipuri (Vyborg), and 270km (170 miles) from St Petersburg; all varieties of Finland–Russia trips can be arranged with the Kotka Tourist Board, but remember to plan overnight trips well in advance so that your visa will be ready.

The streets of the 350-year-old town of **Hamina** ⑰ are laid out in concentric circles and lined with beautiful wooden buildings, small restaurants, cafés and craft shops.

Further east lies **Vaalimaa**, a busy border station with huge supermarkets selling goods to Russians and Finns crossing the frontier.   ❑

Åland Islands: the Ultimate Retreat

To the west of Finland, the Ålands are a perfect island-hopping destination. Catch a ferry, hire a bike and discover this little-known paradise

The Åland Islands (Ahvenanmaa in Finnish) are a collection of granite skerries made up of over 6,000 islands in the Baltic Sea, between the west coast of Finland and the east coast of Sweden. Ålanders have inhabited their islands for thousands of years, and have a strong ethnic culture and a formidable pride in their identity. The population of 28,000 has had its own flag since 1954 (a red cross within a yellow cross against a blue background) and its own postage stamps since 1984. Today, the islands are an autonomous demilitarised zone represented both in the Finnish Parliament and the Nordic Council, with Swedish being the official language. Although part of the EU, Åland remains outside the tax union agreement, so tax-free shopping is available to travellers.

The islands are a paradise for hiking, fishing, golfing, swimming and other watersports, and, because they are mostly flat, are ideally explored by bike. Bicycle ferries (June–Aug) link bike routes between islands. For timetables, visit www.alandstrafiken.aland.fi. You can hire bicycles from the Mariehamn harbours and campsites.

June to August is the ideal time to visit. A high point of the summer are the midsummer celebrations held in almost every village with the traditional raising of the Midsummer pole and dancing.

Take a Viking or Silja Line ferry from Turku, Helsinki, or Stockholm to **Mariehamn** ⓲, the Åland capital, sailing through the maze of skerries en route. There are also Air Åland flights from Helsinki and SAS flights from Stockholm to Mariehamm.

With 11,000 inhabitants in total, Mariehamm is the only town-sized settlement on the archipelago. It is known as "the town of a thousand linden trees" due to its broad tree-lined trees. In the West Harbour, the four-masted museum ship *Pommern*, built in Glasgow in 1904, is worth a visit, as is the nearby Maritime Museum (May, June and Aug daily 9am–5pm, July until 7pm; charge). Other museums in the town focus on Ice and Bronze Age life, photography, hunting, fishing – there's even a museum on the postal service.

Most notable in Åland's northeast is the historic **Kastelholm Castle** ⓳ (May–Sept daily 10am–5pm, July until 6pm; charge), a medieval fortress built in the 14th century; it was once the administrative centre for the islands, and of strategic importance to Swedish control of the Baltic. Badly damaged in a fire in 1745, the castle was massively restored in the 1980s. With the adjacent Jan Karlsgården Open-Air Museum (May–Aug daily; charge), and nearby ruins of the Russian-built fortress Bomarsund, it is a major attraction.

To the southeast of Åland lies the lush island of **Föglö** ⓴, once an important vodka-smuggling destination. Its eastern side is a seabird reserve (the name Föglö means "the place of many birds"). There are scenic hiking trails around Jyddö and Hastersboda, which also offers excellent birdwatching opportunities. Canoeing in the bays and canals of the island is a popular leisure activity.

Hotels, guesthouses, cottages and camping facilities are available throughout Åland. For more information, contact the Åland Tourism Board, Storagatan 8; tel: 018 24 000; www.visitaland.com. ❑

RIGHT: sauna on the water's edge.

TURKU

Ancient and modern coexist in Turku, Finland's former historic capital. Colourful restaurant boats line the river; museums, bars and galleries intermingle in the city centre

In 2011, Turku (Åbo in Swedish) celebrated its role as the European Capital of Culture, jointly with Tallinn in Estonia, hosting an unparalleled year of cultural events which put this "small town with a big soul" in the spotlight. Surrounded by islands, river and sea, Finland's former capital is a town for all seasons. The River Aura divides the modern city in two, and you can cross its five main bridges or take the little ferry (year-round) that still carries pedestrians and bicycles free of charge.

Medieval Turku is Finland's oldest city and yet many of the buildings go back only to the Great Fire of 1827 which destroyed a town then largely made of wood. In 1300, when it acquired a new cathedral, Turku became the spiritual centre of Finland. Around the same time, the solid lines of a castle began to rise near the mouth of the River Aura as the heart of royal power in Finland, where the Swedish governor lived and visiting dignitaries paid their respects.

After the Great Fire, the market and town moved away from the cathedral to the west bank of the Aura, much of it designed and built to the plan of Carl Ludwig Engel. Turku had the first university in Finland, founded by the 17th-century Governor General of Finland, Count Per Brahe.

LEFT: Turku's 14th-century cathedral.
RIGHT: market day in the main square.

Exploring the town

A good place to begin a walking tour of the town is the **Turku Art Museum Ⓐ** (Aurakatu 26; tel: 02 262 7100; www.turuntaidemuseo.fi; Tue–Fri 11am–7pm, Sat–Sun 11am–5pm; charge), an impressive Art Nouveau building which presents works from the Golden Age of Finnish art (1880–1910) by Gallen-Kallela, Victor Westerholm, Pekka Halonen, Albert Edelfelt and others.

Follow Aurakatu to the **Orthodox Cathedral Ⓑ**, built in 1838 on the

Main attractions
TURKU ART MUSEUM
KAUPPAHALLI, 19TH-CENTURY INDOOR MARKET HALL
LUOSTARINMÄKI HANDICRAFTS MUSEUM
TURKU CATHEDRAL
A CONCERT AT THE SIBELIUS MUSEUM
ABO VETUS & ARS NOVA
TURKU CASTLE
CRUISE TO NAANTALI ON S/S UKKOPEKKA
THE "LACE VILLAS" AT RUISSALO

Turku has become known for its unusual bars in the city centre, housed in buildings that have been converted from a pharmacy, bank, schoolhouse, and even a public toilet.

orders of Tsar Nicholas I. The church is next to the bustling market square (Kauppatori) flanked by Sokos and Stockmann department stores. Be sure to visit the 19th-century **Kauppahalli** **G** (Indoor Market Hall), across the street in Eerikinkatu, an ideal spot for a quick lunch or coffee and pastry.

Turning down Aurakatu, the Auransilta (bridge) gives the first view of the numerous restaurant boats moored along the river. Across the bridge is a Turku must-see – the **Luostarinmäki Handicrafts Museum** **D** (tel: 02 262 0350; mid-Apr–mid-Sept daily 10am– 6pm; charge), an authentic open-air museum in the only 18th-century area to survive the Great Fire. Here you can wander down unpaved streets past traditional wooden houses and watch artisans in period costume at work.

Around Old Great Square

Until the Great Fire of 1827, **Old Great Square** (Vanha Suurtori) was the heart of Turku, its adminstrative centre and main market place. Today the square stages the summer Medieval Market and Finland's old-

est Christmas Market. Nearby **Turku Cathedral** **E** (Tuomiokirkko; daily 16 Sept–15 Apr 9am–7pm, 16 Apr–15 Sept until 8pm) maintains a stately presence. Consecrated in 1300, it is the country's national shrine and its most important medieval structure. Outside the cathedral stands a statue of Per Brahe, governor of Finland from 1637, who introduced welfare reforms and founded Finland's first university.

Beyond the museum towards the river, the **Sibelius Museum** **F** (Piispankatu 17; tel: 02 215 4494; Tue– Sun 11am–4pm, extended hours Wed 6–8pm; charge) chronicles the life and times of the great composer, with an interesting collection of instruments housed in a sleek Modernist building. In spring and autumn, evening concerts are held every Wednesday.

On the riverbank south of the Old Great Square stands **Rettig Palace**, built in 1928 for one of Turku's aristocratic families. It now houses the the two-in-one museum **Aboa Vetus & Ars Nova** **G** (Museum of History and Contemporary Art; Itäinen Rantakatu 4–6; tel: 02 0718 1640; www.

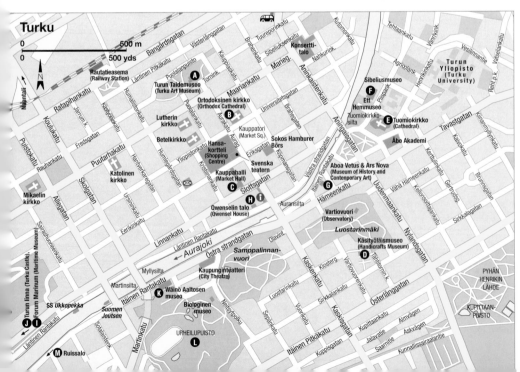

aboavetusarsnova.fi; 29 Mar–18 Sept daily 11am–7pm, Sept–Mar Tue–Sun 11am–7pm; charge), which translates as "Old City, New Art". The museum's contemporary art exhibits are juxtaposed with the excavated remains of medieval Turku (discovered during building works) to great effect, providing insight into Turku both as a historical city and forward-thinking cultural centre.

Along the riverbank

For a riverside tour, return to the north bank and **Qwensel House**, Turku's oldest wooden building (1695), which now houses the **Pharmacy Museum** **H** (Läntinen Rantakatu 13; tel: 02 262 0280; May–Sept Tue–Sun 10am–6pm, rest of the year until 4pm; charge) and a popular courtyard café. Walk past **Mill Bridge** (Myllysilta) to the next bridge, Martinsilta, where the **S/S *Ukkopekka*** is moored. Between June and August, pleasant excursions through the archipelago aboard the steamship run from the quay at the bridge (*see margin tip, right*). Continue on this side of the river as far as Turku Castle (*see below*) and the modern harbour area, with merchant tugs and tankers and Viking and Silja Lines terminals.

On your way to the harbour is the **Maritime Museum** **I** (Forum Marinarum; Linnankatu 74; tel: 02 267 9511; May–Sept daily 11am–7pm, Oct–Apr Tue–Sun 11am–6pm; charge), which documents Turku's shipping history, and a fleet of museum ships moored outside, including the handsome three-masted barque *Sigyn* and the sleek white hull of the sailing ship *Suomen Joutsen* (Swan of Finland) which once plied the ocean between Europe and South America.

The riverside walk culminates at **Turku Castle** **J** (Turun linna; Linnankatu 80; tel: 02 262 0300; 3 May–18 Sept Tue–Sun 10am–6pm, 19 Sept–2 May Tue and Thur–Sun 10am–6pm, Wed noon–8pm; charge), some 3km (2 miles) from the centre. In its labyrinth of rooms, Turku's history from medieval times is relayed.

Heading back towards the centre along the opposite bank you come to the **Wäinö Aaltonen Museum** **K** (Itäinen Rantakatu 38, tel: 02 262 0850; May–mid-Sept Tue–Sun 10am–6pm, rest of the year Wed noon–8pm; charge), exhibiting works by one of Finland's most important sculptors, Wäinö Aaltonen (1894–1966). In **Urheilupuisto** **L**, the surrounding park, the windmill on Samppalinnanmäki is the last of its kind in Turku. Next to it is the running track where the champion long-distance runner and Olympic gold medallist Paavo Nurmi (1897–1973) trained. His statue stands on the Auransilta (bridge).

Ruissalo Island

Boat services depart several times daily for **Ruissalo Island** **M**. An ideal excursion for cyclists, walkers and nature- and beach-lovers. The 19th-century **Villa Roma** is typical of the "lace villas" (so called because of their latticed balconies and windows) built by wealthy merchants, and shows summer exhibitions of top-quality Finnish art. In summer, the island hosts **Ruisrock**, the annual rock festival. ❏

One of the best ways to see the archipelago is on a cruise aboard the steamship S/S Ukkopekka (tel: 02 515 3300; www.ukopekka. fi). The two-hour cruise to Naantali, a charming seaside town north of Turku, is popular in the summer. Children come in droves to visit nearby Moomin World (tel: 02 511 1111; www. muumimaailma.fi), a theme park based on Tove Jansson's Moomintroll stories.

BELOW: boats on the Aura River.

FINLAND'S LAKELAND

A labyrinth of lakes and pine-covered islands extends north from Helsinki. The landscape that was home to Sibelius rewards exploration by lake steamer and canoe

With some 33,000 islands and peninsulas, the Great Lakes of Saimaa and Päijänne in central Finland provide a diverse waterscape of lakes, rivers and canals to form Europe's largest waterway system. This varied landscape owes its beauty to the Ice Age, when glaciers carved out the shape of lakes and ridges. The area attracts thousands of visitors each year yet never appears crowded.

The best approach to the lakes is via industrial **Kouvola ㉑**, about 140km (86 miles) northeast of Helsinki and a junction of road and rail routes into Saimaa. Although not the most interesting town in Finland, Kouvola's Kaunisnurmi quarters house quaint handicraft shops and several museums.

To capture the spirit of Saimaa, ignore the direct routes to Kuopio in the north and head east on route 6 to **Lappeenranta ㉒**, south Karelia's main town. The fortress next to the harbour, in the Linnoitus quarter, was built by the Russians in 1775 and today houses the **South Karelian Museum** (Etelä-Karjalan Museo, Linnoitus; tel: 05 616 2255; June–mid-Aug Mon–Fri 10am–6pm, Sat–Sun 11am–5pm, mid-Aug–May Tue–Sun 11am–5pm; charge). Its permanent "On the Border" exhibition chronicles the history of Lappeenranta and Vyborg, formerly in Karelia but now

just a few miles south in Russia, whose fate was sealed by the 1939–40 Winter War between Russia and Finland. The **Cavalry Museum** (Ratsuväkimuseo; tel: 05 616 2257; June–mid-Aug Mon–Fri 10am–6pm, Sat–Sun 11am–5pm; charge) details the history and distinctive red uniforms of Finland's proud soldiers. Also in Linnoitus is Finland's oldest **Orthodox church** (1785).

Day cruises to Russia operate from Lappeenranta, for which Western visitors do not require visas, although they are obligatory for other visits.

Main attractions
SOUTH KARELIAN MUSEUM, LAPPEENRANTA
IMATRANKOSKI RAPIDS, IMATRA
RETRETTI ARTS CENTRE
ALVAR AALTO MUSEUM AND BUILDINGS
VAPRIIKKI MUSEUM COMPLEX, TAMPERE
TAMPERE CATHEDRAL AND SIMBERG'S WOUNDED ANGEL
POET'S WAY CRUISE ABOARD STEAMSHIP S/S TARJANNE
IITTALA GLASS CENTRE
HÄME CASTLE
JÄRVENPÄÄ'S CULTURE TRAIL AND THE HOMES OF SIBELIUS

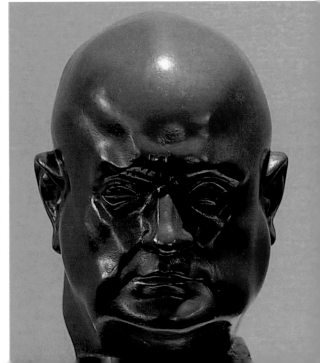

LEFT: peaceful Lakeland waters.
RIGHT: composer Jean Sibelius was born in the town of Hämeenlinna.

The Retretti Arts Centre, Punkaharju, is housed in caverns literally blasted out of the rock to provide a remarkable exhibition space for Finnish art and design, and an atmospheric underground area with a concert hall (www.retretti.fi).

A few miles further east is the industrial city of **Imatra** ㉓, once erroneously described as the "Niagara of Finland", but worth a brief visit to see the impressive **Imatrankoski** (Rapids).

Punkaharju

About 50km (30 miles) north of Imatra, route 6 passes within a few hundred metres of the Russian border. Switching to route 14, you soon come to **Punkaharju** ㉔, one of countless ridges bequeathed to Finland by the last Ice Age. It's around 7km (4 miles) long and in places is just wide enough to carry the road; elsewhere it widens to accommodate magnificent pine and birch woods. **Lusto** – the Finnish Forest Museum (tel: 015 345 100; May and Sept daily 10am–5pm, June–Aug until 7pm, Oct–Apr Tue–Sun 10am–5pm; charge) documents the relationship between the Finns and their forests, past and present. The **Retretti Arts Centre** (tel: 015 775 2200; www.retretti. fi; June–Aug daily 10am–6pm; charge), built into the bedrock on the ridge, has a well-attended annual exhibition, featuring four usually quite differ-

ent, internationally acclaimed artists. Nearby, in Kerimäki, it is possible to visit the world's largest Christian wooden church, built in 1847. In summer, a lake steamer sails between Punkaharju and Savonlinna from Retretti. The two-hour trip is a delightful mini-voyage through the islands. There is also an enjoyable diesel rail tour connecting tourist attractions in this area.

Savonlinna

Savonlinna ㉕ is the most charming of Finland's main lakeland towns and the best base in Saimaa for making trips. The medieval castle of **Olavinlinna** (tel: 015 531 164; tours June–mid-Aug daily 10am–6pm, on opera days in July until 5pm, mid-Aug–May Mon–Fri 10am–4pm, Sat–Sun from 11am; charge), is the site of the annual Opera Festival that takes place throughout July. Its massive granite walls, ramparts and round towers provide a dramatic stage setting. Tickets for, and accommodation during, the festival should be booked well ahead (tel: 015 476 750; www.operafestival.fi).

Near the castle, the museum ship *Salama* – a steam schooner built in 1874, shipwrecked in 1898 and raised from the lake in 1971 – is one of four converted old ships that form the inland navigation section of the **Savonlinna Provincial Museum** (Riihisaari; tel: 044 417 4466; Sept–May Tue–Sun 10am–5pm, June–Aug daily 10am–5pm; charge).

Scenic routes to Kuopio

From Savonlinna to Kuopio by lake steamer is a full day's journey. Road travellers have a choice of continuing west from Savonlinna on routes 14 and 5 to Mikkeli or staying with Saimaa to its northern limits beyond Kuopio.

Mikkeli ㉖, a pleasant provincial capital, is a historic army town. Near Mikkeli, **Visulahti** amusement park has a vintage car exhibition, plastic dinosaurs and waxworks (tel: 015 182 81; park and waxworks year-round, Mon–Sat 9am–5pm, Dinosauria Water

BELOW: the lakes attract windsurfers.

Park and vintage car exhibition early June daily 11am–5pm, late June–mid-Aug daily 11am–7pm; charge).

The recommended scenic route to Kuopio from Savonlinna is via Varkaus on route 464. Then take route 23 heading northeast towards Joensuu in north Karelia, passing by the Orthodox monastery of **Valamon Luostari** ❷ (tel: 017 570 111; www.valamo.fi; Sun–Thur 8am–5pm, Fri–Sat until 9pm) and the nearby convent, **Lintulan Luostari** (tel: 017 563 106; June–Aug daily 9am–6pm). On all three counts of history, culture and scenery, these merit a visit. M/S *Sergei* cruises along the canal between the two in high summer.

The monastery was formed by monks fleeing from Lake Lagoda in 1940, after the Finno-Russian Winter War. There is a fine chapel, completed in 1977, a cafeteria, souvenir shop and a modern hotel.

Kuopio

Kuopio ❷ hosts the International Dance and Music Festival in June. Sights to see include the **Old Kuopio Museum** (Kuopion Kortellimuseo; Kirkkokatu 22; tel: 017 182 625; mid-May–Aug Tue–Sun 10am–5pm, Sept–mid-May Tue–Fri 10am–3pm, Sat–Sun until 4pm; charge). The open-air museum comprises 11 original dwellings complete with authentic furniture, warehouses and even gardens dating from the late 18th–19th centuries.

The **Kuopio Art Museum** (Kuopion Museo; Kauppakatu 35; tel: 017 182 633; Tue–Fri 10am–5pm, Wed until 7pm, Sat–Sun 11am–5pm; charge) exhibits art from the late 19th century to the present day. Nearby at no. 23 is a lovely Art Nouveau castle-like structure which is the shared home of the **Kuopio Museums of Cultural and Natural History** (same telephone and opening hours).

At **Iisalmi** ❷, 80km (50 miles) north of Kuopio on route 5, the **Karelian Orthodox Centre** (Kyllikinkatu 8; tel: 017 816 441; mid-June–mid-Aug Tue–Sat 10am–4pm, rest of the year Mon–Fri same times; charge) displays valuable relics recovered from territory now in Russia. Dine and drink with a view at **Olutmestari** (Savonkatu 18), a popular summer restaurant in the harbour.

The traditional woodsmoke sauna is enjoying something of a revival in Finland, and there are a number of places in the Kuopio region where you can enjoy the real thing. For a truly memorable sauna experience, visit the world's biggest smoke sauna in an atmospheric log-built lodge in Rauhalaht (www.rauhalahti.fi).

BELOW: Olavinlinna, a dramatic setting for opera.

Street-corner kiosks offer everything from culinary delights to fast food.

BELOW: dancers perform at Kuopio's annual festival.

Lake Päijänne

To the west of the region lies Päijänne, Finland's deepest lake and its longest at 119km (74 miles). At the southern and northern ends of the lake system are two of Finland's more substantial towns, Lahti and Jyväskylä respectively, which are linked to the west of Päijänne by one of Europe's main highways, E24, and to the east of it by a network of slower, more attractive routes.

Lahti ⑳, a modern town and winter sports centre, lies 103km (64 miles) north of Helsinki on route 4 (E75). The **Lahden Urheilukeskus** sports centre is the venue for the annual (March) Finlandia Ski Race and the Ski Games. One of its few older buildings is the Art Nouveau **Town Hall** (Kaupungintalo) designed by Eliel Saarinen in 1912. Three blocks north is the market, and two blocks further north, at Kirkkokatu 4, the highly individualistic **Ristinkirkko** (Church of the Cross; mid-May–Aug daily 9.30am–6pm), built in 1978, and the last church in Finland designed by Alvar Aalto. Built in 2000, the award-winning **Sibelius Concert Hall and Congress Centre**

(Ankkurikatu 7) on the Vesijärvi waterfront is made entirely of wood, its design inspired by Finnish forests. The **Lahti Historical Museum** (Lahdenkatu 4; tel: 03 814 4536; Mon–Fri 10am–5pm, Sat–Sun 11am–5pm; charge) exhibits regional ethnographical and cultural history collections in a 19th-century manor house.

From Lahti it's only 35km (21 miles) northeast on Route 4 to the pleasant little town of **Heinola** ㉛. Taking the summer lake route, it's four hours by steamer. The **Jyrängönkoski** (rapids) provide good sport for local canoeists and for fishermen casting for lake and rainbow trout. Rent a rod at the **Siltasaari Fishing Centre** and have your catch smoked to eat on the spot or take it away.

An attractive route to Jyväskylä is along the minor road 314 from Asikkala. This will take you along the **Pulkkilanharju** (Ridge), offering magnificent views en route. Continue via Sysmä and Luhanka, through various waterscapes to rejoin route 9 (E63) at Korpilahti. For the final leg to Jyväskylä you can use the enormous

bridge across Kärkistensalmi, one of Päijänne's many narrow straits.

A beauty spot inside the **Päijänne National Park** is the long, slender island of **Kelvenne** ❷, 60km (37 miles) north of Lahti, with its lakes, lagoons and curious geological formations. You can reach it from the Ravintola Laivaranta camping area at Padasjoki.

Jyväskylä, Alvar Aalto's city

Jyväskylä ❸ is situated on the northern shore of Lake Päijänne. Alvar Aalto grew up here, and there are no fewer than 30 of his buildings around the area, including the university, theatre and the Museum of Central Finland. The **Alvar Aalto Museum** (7 Alvar Aallonkatu; tel: 014 266 7113; www.alvaraalto.fi; Tue–Sun 11am–6pm, July–Aug Tue–Fri 10am–6pm, Sat–Sun from 11am; charge) has a collection of architectural plans, photographs, scale models and furniture designs.

There are a number of winter and summer sports facilities in Jyväskylä, but the town is best known internationally as the venue for the well-attended Neste Rally, Finland's premier motor-racing

event, in August. The Jyväskylä Arts Festival is a major cultural event held in July, always with a different theme.

Tampere

Tampere ❹, Finland's industrial capital and Scandinavia's largest inland city, lies 150km (94 miles) southwest of Jyväskylä. Situated between lakes Näsijärvi and Pyhäjärvi, it is the gateway to southern Finland. Of the 200 lakes in the area, these two are the largest.

Tampere was officially founded in 1779 by King Gustav III of Sweden-Finland and owes its fortunes to the Tammerkoski rapids, which divide the city and first brought power and a booming textile industry to the area. Hence it's description as the "Manchester" or "Pittsburgh" of Finland. It is an appealing city, enjoying a beautiful natural setting that's actually enhanced by the landmarks of its past in the form of brick-built textile mills dotted along the river. A rich cultural heritage, interesting architecture and a thriving arts scene all add to Tampere's appeal.

The historic **Tampere Cathedral** ❹ (Tuomiokirkonkatu 3; daily June–Aug

Many wild berries grow in Finland – bilberries, as seen here, lingonberries and cloudberries are the most popular.

BELOW: a boat is an essential part of Lakeland life.

With over 200 lakes in the area, make sure to take a boat journey from Tampere, either south on the Silverline route, or north on the Poet's Way, or hop on a boat to Viikinsaari to retreat into nature.

10am–5pm, rest of the year 11am–3pm), designed by Lars Sonck and completed in 1907, is one of the finest examples of the National Romantic style in Finland. It contains works by two key artists of the period: an altar fresco of the Resurrection by Magnus Enckell, and Hugo Simberg's masterpiece, *The Wounded Angel*.

West of the cathedral, on the banks of the Tammerkoski River, stands the the old Tampella foundry and linen mill. Built in 1850, it remained productive until the 1990s (though fabric manufature ceased in the 1970s). It was transformed in 1996 into an impressive museum centre and renamed **Vapriikki** Ⓑ (Alaverstaanraitti 5; tel: 03 5656 6966; Tue–Sun 10am–6pm; charge) – the Finnish word for fabric. It features unique exhibitions on the region from archaeology to technology and the natural sciences, and houses a quirky collection of museums to hockey, dolls and even shoes on its extensive premises. There is a café-restaurant and museum shop.Across the river, the old **Finlayson Factory**, built in 1899 (named after the Scot James Finlay-

son who set up the first engineering workshop here) has been converted into a cultural and business centre, with restaurants and bars, computer and technology firms, a polytechnic, a newspaper headquarters... and a **Spy Museum** Ⓒ (Vakoilumuseo; Satakunnankatu 18; tel: 03 212 3007; Sept–May daily 11am–5pm, June–Aug Mon–Sat 10am–4pm, Sun 11am–5pm; charge). This intriguing little museum unlocks some of the secrets and tricks of the espionage trade adopted by Finnish spies during the Cold War.

Another museum worth a look is the **Lenin Museum** Ⓓ (Hämeenpuisto 28; tel: 03 276 8100; www.lenin.fi; Mon–Fri 9am–6pm, Sat–Sun 11am–4pm; charge), housed in the Workers' Hall where Lenin and Stalin met for the first time in 1905. The exhibit focuses on Lenin's life in Tampere before the Russian Revolution.

Among the city's significant modern landmarks is the 20th-century **Kirjasto** Ⓔ (City Library) by husband and wife architects, Reima and Raili Pietilä, the design of which is said to be based on the open wings and spread tail feathers

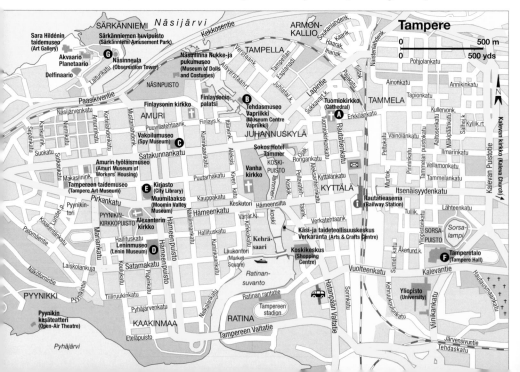

of a wood grouse. In a park on the eastern side of town is another Pietilä design, the stark **Kaleva Church** (Liisanpuisto 1; daily July–Aug 11am–5pm, rest of the year until 3pm). Built in 1966, its most striking feature is the organ with 3,000 pipes shaped like a sail. In Sorsapuisto Park, just east of the station, **Tampere-talo** ❺ (Tampere Hall) is a spectacular concert venue designed in 1990 by Esa Piiroinen and Sakari Aartelo.

At the northern harbour entrance, at the centre of **Särkänniemi Park**, stands the **Näsinneula Observation Tower** ❻ (Mon–Fri 11am–11pm, Sat–Sun noon–11.30pm). At 120 metres (400ft), it is the highest viewpoint in Finland. The park is a favourite place for children with its aquarium, dolphinarium, planetarium, children's zoo and amusement park (tel: 02 0713 0200; www.sarkanniemi.fi; Mon–Fri 11am–7pm, Sat–Sun noon–8pm; charge).

Viikinsaari island

A favourite summer getaway from Tampere is **Viikinsaari island**. Just 3km (2 miles) from the city in Lake Pyhajärvi, it has a nature trail, beach, playground, sauna, sports field, rowing boats and fishing-rod hire. After a full day, visitors usually enjoy a meal at Wanha Kaidesaari, an atmospheric dance pavilion serving Finnish specialities. On Saturday nights, there is traditional dancing with an orchestra. Open June–late Aug; the boat leaves on the hour from Tampere's Laukuntori quay and returns on the half hour. The trip takes 25 minutes.

South of Tampere

From Tampere, the 175km (110-mile) route back to Helsinki passes through the industrial centre of **Valkeakoski** ㉟. In the Middle Ages, it was a hamlet, and later a mining village in the parish of Sääksmäki; but, even then, it had the rapids that meant water power, first to grind corn and then to make paper.

The old **Voipaala Manor** on Rapola Hill was once the home of the sculptor Elias Ilkka and is now where the Valkeakoski Summer Theatre performs. Make your way to **Visavuori** (June–Aug daily 10am–6pm, Sept–Nov Tue–Sun 10am–4pm; charge), the lakeside studio-home complex of one of Finland's best-known

Tampere Library houses "Moomin Valley", an exhibition of the characters from Tove Jansson's popular books.

BELOW: Näsinneula Observation Tower.

"Poet's Way" Cruise

Highly recommended is the "Poet's Way" cruise from Tampere to Ruovesi/Virrat on scenic Lake Nasijarvi. The memorable 8-hour steamboat cruise on the S/S *Tarjanne* was inspired by a journey made over 100 years ago by the Finnish national poet, J.L. Runeberg, and writer Zacharias Topelius, and has now become a tradition for thousands of visitors every summer (www.runoilijantie.fi/eng).

If you don't wish to make the full trip, you can jump ship at Ruovesi (about two-thirds of the way), a picturesque village with handicraft shops and a pleasant café. Nearby is the former summer residence and studio of Akseli Gallen-Kallela, one of Finland's most prominent artists, open in summer. For information, contact Ruoveden Matkailu (Tourist Office; www.ruovesi.fi).

Häme Castle, Hämeenlinna, built by the Swedes in the 13th century.

BELOW: keeping up the glass-making tradition at Iittala.

sculptors, Emil Wikström (1864–1942). It is a fine example of Karelian architecture built in the National Romantic Style. In summer, it is also accessible by Silverline ferry from Tampere or Hämeenlinna (www.runoilijantie.fi.)

Glass-making centres

Of all Finland's glassmakers, **Iittala** ㊱ is the most famous. Beautiful, functional glassware and objets d'art are made at the **Iittala Glass Centre** (tel: 02 0439 6230; May–Aug daily 10am–6pm, Sept–Apr Sat–Sun 10am–5pm; charge), and put on display along with designs by Alvar Aalto, Timo Sarpaneva and other glass artists. Visit the Iittala factory outlet, where seconds are often indistinguishable to the inexpert eye and less than half the price of perfect work.

It's also worth visiting the **Finnish Glass Museum** (Suomen Lasimuseo; tel: 019 758 4108; Mar–Dec Tue–Sun 10am–6pm; charge) in **Riihimäki** ㊲, just off route 3, 35km (26 miles) south of Hämeenlinna. The museum is housed in an authentic glassworks from 1914. Exhibits trace the history of glass-making.

Sibelius country

Continuing south from Iittala, route 57 leads to the lake of Hattula and the **Hattulan Church of the Holy Cross**, one of Finland's best-known and oldest churches, built in 1320. Just off the E12, **Aulanko Forest Park** is ideal for a break, overlooking Lake Aulankojärvi. Jean Sibelius, who was born in nearby **Hämeenlinna** ㊳, is said to have commented on Aulanko: "I was thinking of these scenes from my childhood when I composed *Finlandia*."

Hämeenlinna has two claims to fame: first, the early 13th-century **Häme Castle** (tel: 03 675 6820; June–mid-Aug daily 10am–6pm, mid-Aug–May Mon–Fri 10am–4pm, Sat–Sun 11 from 11am; charge), and, second, that Jean Sibelius was born here in December 1865 in the little timber-board house of the town physician, Christian Gustaf Sibelius, now the **Sibelius Childhood Home** (Hallituskatu 11; tel: 03 621 2755; May–Aug Tue–Sun 10am–4pm, Sept–Apr from noon; charge). The big dining room is used for recitals, and the house is full of memorabilia.

Heading south through Hyvinkää to **Järvenpää** ㊴, you are only 45km (30 miles) from Helsinki. **Lake Tuusula** (Tuusulanjärvi) attracted late 19th-century artists and intellectuals away from their city haunts to build studio-villas on the eastern side. Among them was the portrait painter Eero Järnefelt, noted for his rural and folk scenes, artists Juhani Aho, Pekka Halonen, and Jean Sibelius and his wife Aino.

Ainola ㊵ was the Sibelius home for 53 years (tel: 09 287 322; www.ainola. fi; May–Sept Tue–Sun 10am–5pm; charge). Designed by Lars Sonck in 1904, the original log house in National Romantic style was transformed over the years to accommodate the growing family. It is still furnished as it was in Sibelius's time, with a collection of fine paintings and ceramics by one of the daughters; the drawing room holds the composer's piano. Floral tributes adorn the couple's grave in the garden. ❑

Canoeing the Open Waters

Paddling a canoe on the lakes and rivers of Finland is one of the most pleasurable ways to explore the country

O ne of the more challenging annual events on the European canoeing calendar is the Arctic Circle Race, which takes place every summer north of the Arctic Circle from Kilipsjärvi to Tornio along 537km (334 miles) of the border rivers between Finland and Sweden. Another is the six-day 700km (435-mile) Finlandia Canoe Relay each June, usually through the complex Saimaa system.

With 187,888 lakes (at the last count) and innumerable rivers, it's surprising that canoeing has only become popular in Finland in recent years. There is a growing range of packages whereby you can canoe well-tried routes of varying lengths with the option of hiring equipment, camping or staying in farmhouse accommodation.

A particularly well-tried series of routes forms an overall 350km (217-mile) circuit beginning and ending at Heinola. This needs 10–15 days, but can also be divided into shorter sections. Another, along 320km (200 miles) of the Ounasjoki River in Lapland from Enontekiö to Rovaniemi, features sections of true Arctic wilderness; the rapids are mainly Grade I, but it is possible to portage round the most daunting of these. Yet another follows a 285km (180-mile) lake-and-river route taken by the old tar boats from Kuhmo to Oulu.

If you're attracted to the idea of pioneering across the lakes the possibilities are legion. Any of the 19 road maps which cover the entire country on a scale of of 1:200,000 will be sufficient for general planning, but absolutely essential for more detail are the special inland water charts, for example, for Saimaa on a scale of 1:40,000/1:50,000. It's not until you are in your canoe, however, that navigation problems become clear. From water level one island of rock and pine trees looks like another with few helpful landmarks. You will appreciate those other vital aids to canoeing the Finnish lakes: a compass and a pair of binoculars.

The greatest inconvenience you are likely to encounter is wind. Squalls blow up quickly, and

across these great expanses, waters are soon whipped up into turbulence. Head for shelter at the first sign.

Seek permission to camp whenever possible, since the right to pitch your tent anywhere has been abused by some foreigners and is no longer permitted. Often, of course, there is no one to ask. It is one of the joys of canoeing in Finland that you may travel for days without any sign of humanity, other than a tugboat hauling timber, or a fisherman. ❏

TOP RIGHT: canoeists stop for a well-earned rest.
RIGHT: slalom competitor.

FINLAND'S WEST COAST

The beautiful Bothnian coastline preserves
its rich maritime heritage and its blend
of Finnish-Swedish culture in the islands
and towns along the road to Lapland

The west coast of Finland is a fascinating mixture of past and present: stately churches and old wooden houses, museums and modern industry. With its close proximity to Sweden, Swedish remains the first language for many communities, and some towns have both Swedish and Finnish names.

North of Turku

The first main town north of **Turku** (*see page 329*) on route 8 is **Uusikaupunki** ❶ (Nystad). The **Museum of Culture History** (tel: 02 8451 5447; June–Sept Mon–Fri 10am–5pm, Sat–Sun noon–3pm, the rest of the year noon–5pm; charge) is in the house of F.W. Wahlberg, a former shipowner and tobacco manufacturer. **Myllymäki Windmill Park** is a reminder that many retired sailors became millers and the countryside was once dotted with windmills.

Rauma ❷ is the largest medieval town in Scandinavia, listed as a Unesco World Heritage site with 600 or so wooden buildings painted in traditional pastel shades. Although the dwellings and shops are 18th- and 19th-century buildings, the narrow streets date back to the 16th century.

Pori ❸, some 47km (37 miles) north of Rauma, was founded by Duke Johan of Sweden in 1558. With a population of 140,000 in the region, it is one of Finland's chief export harbours and hosts a popular jazz festival every July. The **City Hall** was built in the style of a Venetian Palace, and more offbeat is the **Jusélius Mausoleum** (May–Aug daily noon–3pm, Sept–Apr Sun only until 2pm; free) at Käppärä Cemetery, built by a Pori businessman in memory of his young daughter.

Satakunta Museum (tel: 02 621 1078; Tue–Sun 11am–6pm, Wed until 8pm; charge), is the largest cultural

Main attractions
MEDIEVAL TOWN OF RAUMA
BRAGE OPEN-AIR MUSEUM IN
 VAASA
RESTORED WOODEN HOUSES IN
 JAKOBSTAD'S OLD TOWN
LUMILINNA SNOW CASTLE
KOSKIKESKUS RAPIDS CENTRE,
 OULU
"CRUISE" ON THE *SAMPO*
 ICEBREAKER

LEFT: sparkling water in the Gulf of Bothnia.
RIGHT: Rauma's Franciscan monastery church.

West Coast

0   50 km

0   50 miles

---

history museum in Finland. The **Pori Art Museum** (Eteläranta; tel: 02 621 1080; Tue–Sun 11am–6pm, Wed until 8pm; charge, free on Wed after 6pm), housed in a converted customs warehouse, features contemporary art.

The peninsula leading from Pori to **Reposaari** is one of Finland's best beach resorts. **Kristinestad ❹** (Kristiinankaupunki), 95km (59 miles) to the north, was founded by the Swedish governor Count Per Brahe in 1649. A master of diplomacy, he gave the town the name of both his wife and Queen Kristina of Sweden-Finland.

Vaasa to Oulu

Vaasa ❺ (Vasa), established in the 14th century, devastated by wars and fire in the past, is today a handsome town with wide, attractively laid-out streets and a large market square. Notable buildings include the Orthodox church, the Court of Appeal (1862) and the Town Hall (1883). Vaasa has many museums: the **Ostrobothnian Museum** (Museokatu 3; tel: 06 325 3800; Tue, Thur and Sun noon–5pm, Wed until 8pm; charge) covers local history and art, the **Terra Nova–Kvarken Nature Centre** invites visitors to experience the sights and sounds of nature and the **Brage Open-Air Museum** (tel: 06 312 7166; June–Aug Tue–Fri 11am–5pm, Sat–Sun noon–4pm; charge) features nine original houses furnished to depict 19th-century peasant tradition. Ala-Härmä has an amusement park with a wooden rollercoaster and a karting circuit named after the Formula 1 driver Mika Salo, who also helped to plan it (signposted from Route 19).

Jakobstad ❻ (Pietarsaari), a reputed shipbuilding centre, produced vessels that opened new trade routes around the world. One of the town's best-known sailing ships, *Jakobstads Wapen*, a 1767 galleon, still makes cruises. Some 300 or so restored wooden houses may be seen in the old part of town.

From Jakobstad to **Kokkola ❼**, take the attractive route called the "road of seven bridges", which runs from island to island across the archipelago. Kokkola's Town Hall was designed by Carl Ludwig Engel, and there is an English park and boathouse commemorating an episode in the Crimean War with the British fleet. On the 230km (140-mile) road north between Kokkola and Oulu, the town of **Kalajoki** ❽ is a popular spot for fishing and sailing.

Oulu ❾ is the largest city in northern Finland, with a population of 140,500. **Turkansaari Open-Air Museum** (tel: 08 5586 7191; mid-May–mid-Aug daily 10am–6pm, mid-Aug–mid-Sept until 4pm; charge) can be found on a small island in the Oulujoki, 14km (8 miles) east of Oulu. It has an interesting collection of Ostrobothnian buildings, including a church, farm buildings and windmills. In town, the **Tietomaa Science Centre** (Nahkatehtaankatu 6; tel: 08 5584 1340; daily 10am–4pm, summer until 6pm; charge) has a wealth of hands-on exhibits. The **Oulu Art Museum** (tel: 08 5584 7450; Tue–Sun 10am–5pm, Fri noon–7pm; charge), in the old industrial district, has exhibitions of contemporary art. Visit **Koskikeskus** (Rapids Centre) on the mouth of the Oulujoki, with a power station, driven by the rapids, and 12 fountains designed by Alvar Aalto.

To the Swedish border

Kemi ❿ is known as the seaport of Lapland, and in winter you can take an excursion on the 1961 icebreaker *Sampo* (www.sampotours.com) – a 4-hour journey through the icefields of the Gulf of Bothnia.

On the border a short distance west is **Tornio** ⓫, near the mouth of the Tornionjoki. The **Aine Art Museum** (tel: 05 0594 6868; Tue–Thur 11am–6pm, Fri–Sun until 3pm; charge) houses a fine collection of Finnish art. For a great view, visit the **Vesitorni** water tower (daily mid-June–mid-Aug 11am–7pm). At the **Green Zone Golf Course** (tel: 016 431 711; June–Oct) on the Finnish–Swedish border, you can play nine holes in Sweden and nine in Finland. It is a rare delight to play a night round in summer, thanks to the Midnight Sun.

A 9-mile (15km) drive north of Tornio off Route E78, **Kukkolankoski** ⓬ are the longest free-flowing rapids in Finland at 3,500 metres (11,485ft).   ❏

Lumilinna *(tel: 016 258 878; late Jan–early Apr daily 10am–7pm; charge) is a sight not to miss. The snow castle, with its dazzling white walls, illuminated towers and ice hotel, is rebuilt every year at Kemi.*

BELOW: tranquil scene on the west coast.

KARELIA AND KUUSAMO

Helsinki

Easterly Karelia with its distinctly Orthodox heritage is the setting for Finland's epic poem *Kalevala*. Traditions abound, the air is pure and the landscape untouched

Main attractions
JOENSUU ART MUSEUM
RUNONLAULAJAN PIRTTI, THE
SINGERS' LODGE
RUAANKOSKI RAPIDS
FERRY DOWN LAKE PIELINEN
TO KOLIN NATIONAL PARK
WILDERNESS WALKS

BELOW: the Karelian Orthodox Cultural Centre (Evakkokeskuksen); many Karelians belong to the Orthodox Church.

K arelia is the general name for the area whose westernmost part is still in Finland and the larger, easternmost part – which was ceded to the Soviet Union as a result of the Treaty of Paris in 1947 – is in Russia. There are many holiday options, including renting a cottage or log cabin by the water or staying in a "working" farmhouse. Depending on the season, one can enjoy a range of water or winter sports, fishing, hiking and berry-picking.

Joensuu ❶, the "capital" of north Karelia, is a lively student town and the starting point for exploration of the surrounding wilderness. The **Carelicum Cultural and Tourism Centre** (Koskikatu 5; tel: 013 267 5222; Mon–Fri 9am–5pm, Sat–Sun 11am–4pm; charge) by the market square has exhibitions on the history and folk culture of this part of Karelia. The nearby **Art Museum** (Taidemuseo, Kirkkokatu 23; tel: 013 267 5388; Tue–Sun 11am–4pm, Wed until 8pm; charge) occupies an imposing neo-Renaissance building (1894), a former schoolhouse, and contains a diverse collection of

art and artefacts from Etruscan pottery, through a fine collection of 19th-century painting to Finnish artworks of the 1950s.

Before turning north, go east to **Ilomantsi ❷**, the oldest inhabited area of north Karelia and a stronghold of the Orthodox Church. Easter is the most impressive festival here, but other colourful events are held throughout the summer. Ilomantsi was one of the main battlegrounds in the war of 1939–45, and the **Fighter's House** on Hattuvaara Hill has exhibitions about that period. Nearby in the village of **Runokylä**, visit **Runonlaulajan Pirtti** (the Singers' Lodge; tel: 013 881 248; June–Aug daily 10am–4pm, July until 6pm; charge) on Parppeinvaara Hill. A cultural centre in a traditional Karelian log building, where the ancient folk poems of the *Kalevala* are sung by women in traditional costume (accompanied by the *kantele*, a zither-like instrument). The **Parppeinpirtti** restaurant (tel: 10 239 9950) on the hill serves traditional Karelian dishes such as *vendace* (tiny fish), cold smoked whitefish, hearty meat casseroles and pies, *pirakka* pastries, and baked cheese with cloudberry jam.

Gateway to the wilderness

Heading north from Joensuu, take route 6 and the eastward fork to route 73 to **Lieksa ❸**, where the **Ruuankoski** (Rapids) must be seen, and possibly experienced, under the supervision of a guide. Lieksa, one of the many forest centres in Finland, is only about 20 years old and has a population of 19,000 in an area larger than London. The **Pielisen Museo** (Pielinen Open-Air Museum; Pappilantie 2; tel: 4010 44151; 15 May–15 Sept daily 10am–6pm, 16 Sept–14 May until 3pm; charge) has 70 buildings, some dating to the 17th century, which document local settlement.

At **Vuonisjärvi ❹**, 29km (18 miles) from the centre, is **Paateri** (tel: 013 543 223; Mar, June–Aug daily 10am–6pm; charge), the former studio of Eeva Ryynänen (1915–2001), a wood sculptor noted for her spectacular Wilderness Church (adjacent).

Lieksa is the gateway to Finland's wilderness. "Never go hiking on your

TIP

Mountain biking is a popular way to explore Karelia. Hire a bike locally, or join a week-long guided trail bike expedition from Lieksa (details from Karelia Expert Tourist Service; tel: 0400 175 323).

LEFT: traditional way of life on a Karelian farm.

Karelia: Soul and Sauna

If Finland has a soul, that soul lives on in Karelia. When Finns have gone to war, it has concerned Karelia. A Karelian theme runs through the music of Sibelius, and his Karelian Suite reaches sublime heights of patriotism.

The Karelians were one of the earliest of the Finnish communities; they are evident in Bronze and Iron Age discoveries. The *Kalevala*, the great epic saga of ancient life in the far north, is really about Karelians. The poem, which in the 18th and 19th centuries became the cornerstone of the struggle for national culture, recounts everyday events and rituals and finally the heroes' joy as they celebrate in song the salvation of the land of Kalevala from its enemies.

True Karelia exists only as a fragment of its former self. The greater part of the region lies east of the Russian border, lost to Finland after the Winter War (1939–40). As a result 400,000 Karelians had to be resettled in the 1940s. Since then, people of Karelian origin can be found in all parts of Finland. They tend to be lively and talkative, in contrast with the more taciturn nature of other Finns.

It is they who are responsible for the sauna. Early Karelians cleared woodland to grow crops and used steam heat to dry their grain. The therapeutic benefits of this heat were later realised, and so the sauna was born in Finland.

own" is the warning motto of this region, whose dense forests are inhabited by bears, wolves, elk and reindeer.

From Lieksa, route 73 leads to the beautiful town of **Nurmes ❺**, its existence first documented in 1556. **Bomba House** (Suojärvenkatu 1; tel: 013 687 2501; mid-June–mid-Aug Wed–Sun 11am–5.30pm, Wed 5pm part-English service in Orthodox prayer hut) is a traditional Karelian log house at Ritoniemi, about 2km (1¼ miles) from the town, surrounded by a "Karelian village" which provides visitors not only with comfortable accommodation, but also with delicious meals of local specialities.

Nurmes is the place to leave the car and take a scenic ride on Finland's largest inland waterway ferry down Lake Pielinen to **Kolin Kansallispuisto ❻** (Kolin National Park). You will be captivated by the same views that inspired some of Finland's greatest painters, as well as the composer Sibelius.

Before reaching the Oulu area, if you opt for route 6 north you could detour to the remote national park **Tiilikkajärven Kansallispuisto ❼**, near Rautavaara. It was established to conserve the uninhabited area of Lake Tiilikka and the surrounding bogs.

Another national park, **Hiidenportin Kansallispuisto ❽**, is southeast of Sotkamo and also best reached from route 6. This is a rugged area with the narrow Hiidenporti Gorge, its rift walls dropping 20 metres (70ft) to the floor. There are well-marked trails and campsites in the park.

Both in and outside the parks you may encounter reindeer. These animals are the main source of income for many people living in the region, and it is very important to take special care on roads when reindeer are around, especially at dusk.

The Finnish frontier

Kuhmo ❾ is a frontier town surrounded by dense forests in the wilderness area of Kainuu. It is known for its annual Kuhmo Chamber Music Festival.

A recreated **Kalevala Village** (tel: 086 520 114 June–Aug daily; charge) in a wooded park on the outskirts of Kuhmo displays numerous local folk traditions, to give modern-day visitors an idea of Finnish culture as it was immortalised in Finland's epic poem *Kalevala*. The **Hotel Kalevala** specialises in regional cuisine (tel: 086 554 100).

A long straight road through some of Finland's darkest forests leads west out of Kuhmo to Sotkamo and then onwards to **Kajaani** , the area's main town, on the eastern edge of Oulujärvi (Lake). Kajaani still has the ruins of the 1604 castle, and its town hall was designed by Carl Ludwig Engel, who was responsible for so much of early Helsinki. The road from Kajaani towards **Oulu** hugs the shores of Oulujärvi, plunging first into thickly wooded hill country. Before entering Oulu, the route goes through **Muhos**, which has the second-oldest church in Finland, dating from 1634.

Kuusamo

The only other main centre in this scantily populated area is **Kuusamo** , sharing 123km (76 miles) of borderline with Russia. The Kuusamo region is marvellous wilderness country, ideal for canoeing and fishing. This is also berry country, with several varieties growing in great profusion on the Arctic tundra. The only snag is the number of mosquitoes: take plenty of protection.

Karhuntassu Tourist Centre (tel: 0306 502 540) provides information on activities, accommodation and most other aspects of the region. In winter, the area is excellent for skiing and snowmobiling. There are two national parks: the larger, **Oulangan Kansallispuisto** , to the north, covers a largely untouched region bordering the Oulanka River. **Karhunkierros**, the most famous walking route in Finland, stretches some 100km (60 miles) through the Oulanka canyon to the **Rukatunturi Fells** . A smaller national park, **Riisitunturi**, lies to the southwest of Oulanka. Moving further north approaching Lapland, the landscape and culture change from the traditions of Karelia to the ancient ways of the Sami people. ❏

BELOW: white-water expedition.

FINNISH LAPLAND

For some travellers, Lapland is the land of the Midnight Sun, a haven for fell-walkers and anglers. For others, it's the land of Father Christmas, reindeer-racing and dog-sledging

Whatever the season, Lapland offers a variety of interesting natural phenomena and cultures, from the mysterious Northern Lights and the dark *Kaamos* (polar night) skies, to the magical contrast of the Midnight Sun and *Ruska* – Lapland's glorious blaze of autumn colour. However you choose to arrive – by air, sea, train or car – be prepared to experience Lapland and the Arctic Circle on foot, whether reindeer-spotting, cross-country skiing, snowmobiling, salmon-fishing, discovering the Sami culture, or simply hiking the rich swampland in search of cloudberries. These activities will only whet your appetite for the delicious Lappish cuisine.

Two main roads bore their way northwards through the province of Lapland (Lappi). Route 4 (E75), sometimes called the Arctic Highway, links Kemi (coming from Oulu) with Rovaniemi before continuing northeastwards into Norway at Utsjoki. The other is Route 21 (E8), which follows the Tornio Valley upstream from Tornio, continuing beside various tributaries that form the border with Sweden, eventually to cross into Norway near Kilpisjärvi.

When exploring this region, the need for proper clothing and equipment cannot be overstressed. Always inform someone where you are heading and when you expect to return: climatic changes are rapid and, for all its mag-nificence, the Arctic wilderness can be a ruthless place. In summer take plenty of mosquito repellent, ideally bought from a local *apteekki* (pharmacy).

Rovaniemi, Lapland's capital

From Kemi, route 4 follows the valley of the Kemijoki for 115km (70 miles) to **Rovaniemi ❶**. The administrative capital of Lapland, on the cusp of the Arctic Circle, is the launching point for most trips into the province. The town has been completely rebuilt since

Main attractions
MIDNIGHT SUN, *KAAMOS*, NORTHERN LIGHTS AND *RUSKA*
LAPPIA HOUSE, THE ARCTIC CENTRE AND KORUNDI HOUSE OF CULTURE, ROVANIEMI
SANTA CLAUS'S WORKSHOP VILLAGE
REINDEER SPOTTING
HIKING IN THE PYHÄ-LUOSTO AND URHO KEKKONEN NATIONAL PARKS
TANKAVAARA GOLD VILLAGE
SIIDA SAMI VILLAGE, INARI
SEVETTIJÄRVI, SKOLT SAMI CULTURE
WESTERN LAPLAND FELL COUNTRY

LEFT: snow travel. **RIGHT:** tending reindeer.

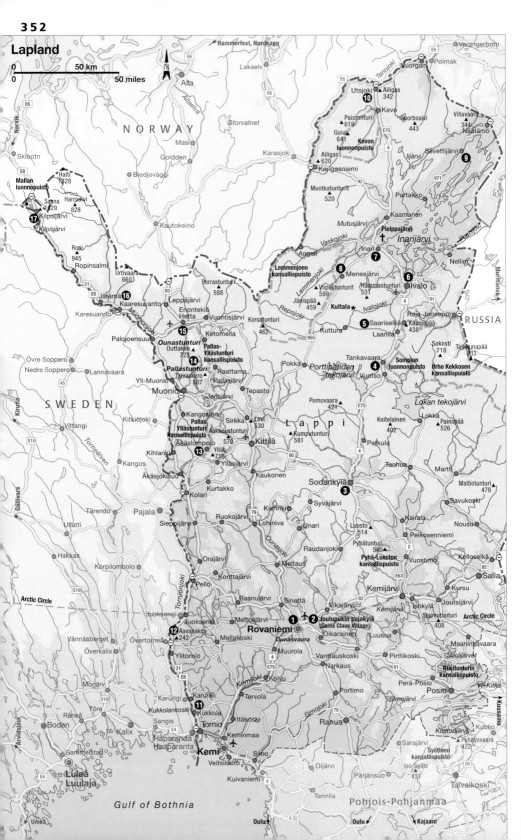

Lapland

0 — 50 km
0 — 50 miles

NORWAY

Hammerfest, Nordkapp

Varangerbotn

E6 Lakselv

E6 Nuorgam Polmak

Alta

Altaelva

Utsjoki **10** Ailigas 342

Storvatnet

Kevo Vuorboaivi
443

Masi

Paistunturi 619

Villavaara 344 **9** Näätämö

Goldden

Guivli 641

Kevon luonnonpuisto

Karasjok

Ailigas 620 Kärigasniemi

Iijärvi Sevettijärvi

Biedjovággi

92 Muotkatunturit 520

971

Partakko

Kautokeino

Vaskojoki

Kaamanen

Mutusjärvi

Pielppajärvi †

Angeli **7** Inari **Inarijärvi**

Mallan luonnonpuisto

Halti 1328

Nellim

Lemmenjoen kansallispuisto

8 Menesjärvi

Pedtsikko

Saana 1029 Harropaivi 828

Vipustunturi 599

Hammastunturi 531

6 Ivalo

Kilpisjärvi

17 Kilpisjärvi

Lemmenjoki

Jänispää 459

Kultala ★

Ivalojoki

Raja-Jooseppi

RUSSIA

Ropi 945 Ropinsalmi

Repojoki

Kuttura

5 Saariselkä Kaunispää 438

Urtivaara 660

Porrastunturi 588

Korsatunturi 462

Kutturu Laanila

Sokosti 718 Talkkunapää 933

Övre Soppero

Järämä **16**

93 Leppäjärvi

Enontekiö Hetta

Tankavaara

4 **Sompion luonnonpuisto**

Urho Kekkosen kansallispuisto

Kaaresuvanto

Vuontisjärvi

Ketomella

Pokka

Porttipahdan tekojärvi

Vuotso

Karesuando

SWEDEN

Muonionjoki

Palojoensuu

15

Outtakka 723

Ounastunturi

Pallas-Yllästunturi kansallispuisto

Raattama

Tepasto

Pomovaara 421

E75

Lokan tekojärvi

Nedre Soppero

Lannavaara

14 **Pallastunturi**

Tarvaskero 807

Pallasjärvi

Jerisjärvi

Lappi

Koitelainen 402

Lokka Painopää 526

Yli-Muonio

Muonio

Kangosjärvi

Pallas Yllästunturi kansallispuisto

Sirkka

Levi 530

Kumputunturi 581

Perkula

Vittangi

Kitkiöjoki

Aakenustunturi

Ylläs 718

13 Äkäslompolo

Kihlanki

570 **Kittilä**

80

Taohua

Martti

Maltiotunturi 478

Kangos

Äkäsjokisuu

Yllasjärvi

Kaukonen

Savukoski

Tärendo

Kolari

Kolari

Kurtakko

Sodankylä **3**

Kierinki

Syväjärvi

Kairala

Nousu

Ullatti

Pajala

Ruokojärvi

79

Lohiniva

Unari

Luosto 514

Pelkosenniemi

Hakkas

Sieppijärvi

Orajärvi

Raudanjoki

Pyhätunturi 540

Pyhä-Luoston kansallispuisto

Vuostimo

Kelloselkä

82

Salla

Korpilombolo

Pello

Konttajärvi

Meltaus

Ounasjoki

E63 Kursu

Arctic Circle

E10

Raanujärvi Sinettä

Vikajärvi 82

Kemijärvi

Isokylä Suomutunturi 408

Arctic Circle

Juoksengi

Juoksenki

Meltosjärvi

1 ↑ **2** **Joulupukin pajakylä (Santa Claus Village)**

Kemijoki

Joutsijärvi

Vännäsberget

Överkalix

12 Aavasaksa 242

Mellakoski

Rovaniemi

Ounasvaara

Oikarainen

Luusua

Maaninkavaara

Övertorneå

Ylitornio

Muurola

Vanttauskoski

Pirttikoski

81

Suolijärvet

Morjärv

21

E8

Karungi

Kemijoki Koivu

E75

Narkaus

Perä-Posio

Riisitunturin kansallispuisto

Yli-Kitka

Kuusamo

Råneå Töre

E10

Karunki

Kukkolankoski

11 Kukkola

Tervola

Portimo

Simojärvi

Posio

Kostonjärvi

Boden

Sangis

E4

Tornio

Itäkoski

Simojoki

78 Rauha

Sarajärvi

Pyhitysvaara 422

Kalix

Haparanda Haaparanta

Keminmaa

Kemi ✈

Simo

Oijärvi

Iso-Syöte

Syötteen kansallispuisto

Luleå Luulaja

Veitsiluoto

Kuivaniemi

Pärjänsuo

20

Talvikoski

E4

Gammelstad

Arvidsjaur

Kuivaniemi

Tannila

Gulf of Bothnia

Pohjois-Pohjanmaa

Umeå

Oulu ✈

Oulu ✈

Kajaani

World War II, following a reconstruction plan drawn up by Alvar Aalto, who also designed the fine **Lappia House** complex on Hallituskatu, containing a theatre, library and congress facilities.

Half underground, the eye-catching **Arktikum** (Pohjoisranta 4; tel: 016 322 3260; June–Aug daily 9am–6pm, Sept–May Tue–Sun 10am–6pm; charge) houses the Arctic Centre and the Provincial Museum of Lapland, which provide a good introduction to Lapland's nature, Sami traditions and Rovaniemi's history. In 2011, the **Rovaniemi Art Museum** (Lapinkävijäntie 4; tel: 016 322 2822; www.korundi.fi; Tue–Sun noon–5pm; charge) reopened within the newly established **Korundi House of Culture**, a former mail-truck depot, and now a state-of-the-art auditorium and home of the Lapland Chamber Orchestra. The Art Museum features contemporary Finnish art.

Two open-air museums in scenic **Pöykkölä**, 3km (2 miles) south of Rovaniemi, give an insight into 19th-century Lapland life and its logging and farming traditions: the **Forestry Museum of Lapland** (tel: 040 536 0080; June–Aug Tue–Sun noon–6pm; charge) has a number of authentic logging cabins, and nearby **Rovaniemi Local History Museum** (Poykkolantie 4; tel: 050 325 2017; June–Aug Tue–Sun noon–18; charge) has more than a dozen original buildings to explore.

Rising up from the confluence of the Ounasjoki and Kemijoki to the south of Rovaniemi are the wooded slopes of **Ounasvaara**, a well-developed skiing area and the site of annual international winter games.

Santa Claus land

About 8km (5 miles) from the town on route 4, soon after the turnoff for Rovaniemi airport, **Joulupukin Pajakylä ❷** (Santa Claus's Workshop Village; tel: 016 356 2096; June–Aug daily 9am–6pm, Sept–May 10am–5pm, Dec–early Jan 9am–7pm; free) straddles the Arctic Circle. Its post office annually handles thousands of letters from chil-

dren. There are shops, a puppet theatre, art exhibitions, a glass factory, a few reindeer and, of course, Santa Claus.

At Syväsenvaara, 5km (3 miles) from Rovaniemi, **Santapark** (tel: 0600 301 203; www.santapark.com; mid-June–mid-Aug Tue–Sat 10am–6pm) has fun rides and attractions for children.

As you travel further north, the predominantly forested landscapes become progressively emptier. However, there are reindeer aplenty and the occasional elk, so do drive slowly; keep your eyes open and your camera handy – they say white reindeer bring good luck.

Sodankylä and the national parks

One of the best fell areas east of route 4 is centred on **Pyhätunturi**, about 135km (84 miles) northeast of Rovaniemi in the **Pyhä-Luosto National Park**, which has 102km (63 miles) of marked hiking trails through pine-forested valleys and deep ravines, past lakes and waterfalls. It is a perfect area for short hikes and day trips. The starting point for most trails is the **Pyhätunturi Visitor Centre** (Kulta-

Rovaniemi lies just 8km (5 miles) south of the Arctic Circle.

BELOW: Santa Claus out for a stroll.

TIP

Ranua, south of Rovaniemi, is the cloudberry capital of Finland. These unusual berries grow on peat bogs and pine marshes and are ripe for picking in July. Taste them at Ranua's cloudberry markets in early August.

keronkatu 22; tel: 020 564 7302; www. luontoon.fi) – signposted on route 4 between Rovaniemi and Sodankylä.

The small town of **Sodankylä** ❸, 130km (80 miles) from Rovaniemi, is a stop-off point en route to the north. It is home of the Midnight Sun Film Festival held each June (www.msfilmfestival.fi).

Northwards, there's little to detain you for the next 100km (60 miles) or so until, a few miles beyond Vuotso, you reach **Tankavaara** ❹. Gold panning has been practised in Lapland for well over a century, and at **Tankavaara Gold Village** (tel: 016 626 158; www. tankavaara.fi) you can pan for gold for a modest fee. There are cabins where you may lodge, and a simple restaurant.

About 40km (25 miles) further north there is more self-catering accommodation, together with modern hotels, centred on the resort town of **Saariselkä** ❺, a popular winter sports centre with good facilities. It is also the base for hiking in the spectacular **Urho-Kekkosnen National Park** (www.luontoon.fi), which offers gentle trails on its western side, and more demanding treks in its eastern wilderness areas by the Russian border.

Ivalo and Inari

Another 23km (14 miles) north is the turning for Ivalo airport, Finland's northernmost. **Ivalo** ❻ is the largest community in northern Lapland. There is an attractive wooden Orthodox church tucked away in the woods, serving the Skolt Sami, a branch of the Sami people who formerly lived in territory ceded to the Soviet Union in 1944. Ivalo's Lutheran church stands near the bridge which carries route 4 over the Ivalojoki; then it's a further 39km (27 miles) to **Inari** ❼, much of it a delightful route along the shores of Inarijärvi (*see below*). Inari village is an excellent base for wilderness exploration; you can lodge at the traditional Hotel Inarin Kultahovi (tel: 016 511 7100; www.hotelkultahovi.fi). Though smaller than Ivalo, Inari is the administrative centre for a vast if sparsely populated area, and a traditional meeting place for colourfully costumed Sami people, especially during the Easter church festivals. If you have a chance to attend a traditional Sami Joik concert, do so.

Inarijärvi is Finland's third-largest lake, covering 1,300 sq km (500 sq

RIGHT: reindeer-sledging is a popular activity.

Sledging

The easiest way to get across Lapland's vast, icy and largely flat landscape has always been on skis or sledges, the latter less exhausting for longer distances. There are many types of sledging, but the most popular and readily associated with northern Finland is the dog sledge. Four or six husky dogs, hardy beasts naturally acclimatised to snow and ice, are harnessed to the front of the sledge, with passengers standing on the back runners. Unlike horses, the huskies are not readily controllable, so keeping the sledge stationary is done with a hook wedged deep in the snow. Once the hook is withdrawn, the dogs lurch forward.

Reindeer-sledging, as epitomised by images of Santa and his sleigh at Christmas, is another method of getting around the icy wilderness, with the advantage that these animals can cover longer and more snowy distances, although they travel more slowly than dogs.

Many centres in Lapland now offer the chance of sledging excursions. Operating near Kuusamo, Spirit of Adventure, for example, offers exhilarating husky safaris or a combination of dog-sledge and snowmobile safaris along the Russian frontier (www.spirit-of-adventure.com). For details of other operators, contact tourist offices in the main towns. Remember, the right equipment is essential: thermals, waterproofs, hats and goggles are necessary to combat the dampness and brightness of the snow.

miles) and is dotted with 3,000 islands, some of them considered sacred according to Sami tradition. Boat trips and sightseeing flights are available during the summer to the holy **Ukko Island**.

Inari's excellent **Siida Sami Museum** (Saamelaismuseo; tel: 0400 898 212; www.samimuseum.fi; June–mid-Sept daily 9am–8pm, mid-Sept–May Tue–Sun 10am–5pm; charge) comprises a modern museum building and an open-air section *(skansen)* with old buildings and equipment illustrating the traditionally nomadic way of life. The Siida building also houses the **Customer Service of Metsähallitus at the Nature Centre Siida**, which assists in hiking plans for those wishing to explore the wilderness. Be sure to leave time to shop at Inari's many fine handicraft shops.

Towards Norway

Route 955 from Inari leads 40km (25 miles) southwest to **Menesjärvi** ❽, a Sami settlement from which one can continue by road then riverboat or on foot up the wild and beautiful **Lemmenjoki Valley** ("river of love") to a remote gold prospectors' camp. From Menesjärvi, route 955 continues across Lapland to join route 79 at Kittilä. Around Inari and north of it, the road passes a number of attractive holiday centres, mostly of the self-catering variety. After 26km (16 miles) you come to Kaamanen, from which a minor road branches northeast 100km (60 miles) to **Sevettijärvi** ❾, the modern main settlement for the Skolt Sami. While there, visit the Sami graveyard, with its unusual turf-covered graves.

A couple of kilometres north of Kaamanen, take the minor road to **Utsjoki** ❿, 94km (58 miles) away on the border with Norway, passing a series of beautiful lakes close to the eastern fringes of the **Kevo Nature Park**. Utsjoki is an important Sami community close to Finland's northernmost point. Its church (1860) is one of the few pre-World War II churches still standing.

The village and road follow the Utsjoki downstream to join with the Tenojoki, a renowned salmon river. As you approach the Norwegian border at **Kirkenes**, the landscape changes dramatically. You can connect with a variety of routes, returning into western Lapland at Kilpisjärvi or Enontekiö.

Western Lapland

Your route through western Lapland is likely to begin at **Tornio**, about 80km (50 miles) south of the Arctic Circle. The earlier stretches of the **Way of the Four Winds** (E8) present a very different face of Lapland from the Arctic Road, for the lower section of the Tornio Valley is much more populated, and served by Finland's northernmost railway branch to Kolari. In its southern stages the road passes through a string of small communities mainly based on agriculture and dairy farming. The Tornionjoki is a good salmon river. Perch, whitefish, grayling, trout and even Arctic char can be found in Lapland's waters. Local travel agencies will organise guided fishing trips complete with gear and permits. At **Kukkola** ⓫ look out for the **Kukkolankoski Rapids**.

Leather goods and "puukko" knives are among the best buys in Lapland.

BELOW: panning for gold, Tankavaara.

Map on page 352

In northern Lapland the sun stays above the horizon from late May to late July. Autumn is known as Ruska, *when the leaves turn explosive shades of red, yellow and orange.*

About 70km (43 miles) north of Tornio, beyond Ylitornio, is the 242-metre (794ft) high **Aavasaksa Hill** ⓬, the most southerly point from which the Midnight Sun can be seen, attracting considerable throngs for Midsummer Eve festivities. A few miles nearer Juoksenki, you cross the Arctic Circle.

Fell country

About 10km (6 miles) north of Kolari, a detour by Route 940 leads to **Akäslompolo** ⓭. This well-equipped tourist resort and skiing centre, on the shores of a small lake, is set among magnificent forested hills and bare-topped fells; the highest is **Ylläs**, at 718 metres (2,355ft), served by chair lifts. A marked trail follows the chain of fells stretching northwards from here, eventually leading in about 150km (90 miles) to the **Pallastunturi** ⓮ fell group (*see below*). It's a glorious trail, with overnight shelter available in wilderness huts.

From Akäslompolo you can continue north along minor roads and in 31km (19 miles) turn left onto route 79. This is the main road from Rovaniemi, providing an alternative approach to west-

ern Lapland. Route 957 to the right is recommended as the best approach to Enontekiö. A further branch left off this route leads to the lonely hotel complex of **Pallastunturi**, magnificently cradled in the lap of five of the 14 fells which make up the Pallastunturi group. From here the choice of fell walks includes the long-distance trail north to Enontekiö.

Enontekiö ⓯, also known as Hetta, sprawls along the northern shore of Ounasjärvi (Lake), looking across to the great rounded shoulders of the Ounastunturi fells. Drop by the pretty wooden church, which has an altar mosaic depicting Sami people.

Soaring mountains

From **Palojoensuu**, route 21 proceeds northwest along the Muonionjoki and Könkämäeno valleys, the scenery becoming even wilder and more barren. At **Järämä** ⓰, 10km (6 miles) further from the tiny settlement of Markkina, German soldiers built fortifications during a standstill in the Lapland War of 1944. Many of these bunkers have been restored and are now open to the public.

South and north of **Ropinsalmi**, the mountains reach ever greater heights; the highest, **Halti**, soars to 1,328 metres (4,357ft) on the Norwegian border at Finland's northwesternmost point. More accessible and distinctive is Saana, at 1,029 metres (3,376ft), above the village and the resort of **Kilpisjärvi** ⓱. Kilpisjärvi is an excellent launching pad for wilderness enthusiasts. The western shore of its lake forms the border with Sweden, and a marked trail which takes about a day and leads to the boundary stone marking the triple junction of Finland, Sweden and Norway. Motor boats take visitors to the **Mallan Luonnonpuisto**, a nature reserve to the north of the lake (entry permit required, details from **Kilpisjärvi Hiking Centre**; tel: 016 537 771). Within the reserve, there is a pleasant 15km (9-mile) trek. The rest of these immense, empty, rugged acres are as free to all as the elements – and as unpredictable. ❏

BELOW: traditional wooden cabin.
RIGHT: Lemmenjoki National Park.

TRAVEL TIPS

SCANDINAVIA

DENMARK · NORWAY · SWEDEN · FINLAND

Denmark A – Z

A HANDY SUMMARY OF PRACTICAL INFORMATION

Activities

Outdoor Sports

Cycling

Cycling is easy and safe in Denmark, with flat terrain, beautiful scenery, plenty of dedicated cycle lanes and a high awareness of cyclists by car drivers. There are 11 long-distance national cycle routes, covering over 4,000km (2,500 miles), and good-quality cycles are available to rent across the country for around DKK45/300 per day/week.

Bornholm is the most popular place for cycling holidays. For cycling in Copenhagen, see the "On Your Bike" section on page 367. Also recommended is the *Walking and Cycling Holidays Denmark* booklet, produced by Visit Denmark, www.visitdenmark.com.

Fishing

Anglers must have fishing permits, which can be obtained at any post office or tourist office, or online at www.fisketegn.dk. Fishing rights in lakes and streams are usually privately owned, but permits can often be hired from the local tourist office.

Golf

There are more than 140 golf courses in Denmark. Guests are welcomed at Danish golf clubs on presentation of a valid membership card from their home club. For more information, contact:
Danish Golf Union
Broendby Station 20
Tel: 21 73 40 00; www.golf.dk

Hiking

There are many beautiful places for hiking in Denmark. Local tourist offices have maps of tested walks and will help you to plan routes. Try walking from Rødvig (just an hour south of Copenhagen) along the lovely wooded chalk cliffs of Stevns to Bøgeskov harbour (22km/13 miles). For more ideas on hiking and walking holidays, maps and guides, go to www.visitdenmark.dk/uk.

Sailing

Boats and yachts are available for hire on a weekly basis. Visitors should ask to see a certificate from the Shipping Inspection Office before hiring a boat. Contact the main tourist office of the region you will be visiting to obtain lists of local boat-hire companies.

Swimming

Aside from Denmark's excellent sandy beaches, there are swimming facilities in most Danish towns as well as several funparks with water slides, etc. for children. Tourist offices have details. Copenhagen has a superb swimming-pool complex with six pools: Vandkulturhuset, DGI-byen, Tietgensgade 65, near the Central Station. Tel: 33 29 81 40.

Admission Charges

Admission to Denmark's museums and galleries ranges from around

Copenhagen Card

We suggest you buy a Copenhagen Card (CPHCARD) at your hotel, the Central Railway Station or the Copenhagen tourist information office. The card gives you free entry to 65 attractions across Copenhagen and north Zealand, free bus/train/metro rides in the same area, and an informative guide. The card is available for periods of 24 and 72 hours.

DKK25 to DKK95. Many museums in Copenhagen offer free entrance on Wednesdays. For free entry to museums outside the capital, contact the local tourist office.

Children

Denmark is a peaceful, safe country with many suitable attractions, such as amusement parks, playgrounds, parks and children's theatres. Many museums have opened children's sections, and music festivals are often arranged so kids can take part. Highlights include:

Copenhagen
Experimentarium (Science Centre)
Tuborg Havnevej 7, Hellerup
Tel: 39 27 33 33
www.experimentarium.dk
A hands-on science museum where you can try more than 300 experiments with sound, light, water, currents and more. With short demonstrations and special exhibits. Mon–Fri 9.30am–5pm, Tue until 9pm, Sat–Sun 11am–5pm.
Marionetteatret
From June to August there are free puppet shows for small children in Kongens Have (the Royal Gardens) near Rosenborg Palace. At 2pm and 3pm, Tue–Sun.
Tivoli
Vesterbrogade 3
Tel: 33 15 10 01
www.tivoli.dk
The amusement park, Tivoli, just across from Central Station, is a delight, with a variety of rides, parades and summer pantomimes. Mid-Apr–late Sept Sun–Thur 11am–11pm, Fri and Sat 11am–midnight.
Zoologisk Have (Zoo)
Roskildevej 32
Tel: 72 20 02 00
www.zoo.dk
There is a special children's zoo here, where children are allowed to pet the animals, watch chickens peck their way out of eggs and ride on ponies. Daily 10am–4pm or 6pm, July until 9pm.

Outside Copenhagen
Bakken
A traditional amusement park in the beautiful Dyrehaven area near Klampenborg. This is also a perfect place for a walk in the countryside. Daily Apr–late Aug, times vary. Tel: 39 63 35 44; www.bakken.dk.
Benneweis Circus
The largest touring circus in Northern Europe. Contact the circus for tour dates. Tel: 40 40 20 20; email: info@benneweis.dk; www.benneweis.dk.

ABOVE: riding high in Tivoli Gardens.

Legoland
The original Legoland, built out of 59 million bricks, with rides and a water playground. Daily Apr–end Oct. Tel: 75 33 13 33; www.legoland.dk.
Lejre Research Centre
Historical-archaeological centre in Zealand with a reconstructed Iron Age village. Children can grind flour, chop wood, paddle log canoes and make Viking bread. May–mid-Sept and 3rd week in Oct. Tel: 46 48 08 78; www.lejre-center.dk.

Climate

Denmark's temperate marine climate keeps the weather mild, with the North Atlantic Drift, part of the Gulf Stream, providing a warming influence. Average rainfall is 610mm (24in) a year. Be prepared for a variable climate. You are most likely to encounter good weather in mid-May to mid-June.

What to Bring
Even if Denmark is experiencing a fine summer, you should still prepare for some cold and rainy days. Bring a swimsuit for those sandy beaches…

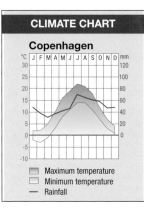

CLIMATE CHART

Copenhagen

☐ Maximum temperature
☐ Minimum temperature
— Rainfall

but bring a sweater and rainwear too.
Danes dress casually: when going out for the evening, men rarely have to put on a suit and tie.

Culture

BILLETnet is an information network where you can reserve tickets and get details on entertainment events. Tel: 70 15 65 65; www.billetnet.dk.
The Danish Arts Agency website lists some of Denmark's larger cultural events: tel: 33 74 45 00; www.danishmusic.info.

Festivals
CPH:PIX – Denmark's biggest international film festival, held in Copenhagen (April)
Roskilde Festival – one of Europe's biggest rock festivals – see box, page 362 (July)
Arhus International Jazz Festival – see box, page 362 (July)
Hamlet Summer – Shakespeare performances, staged in Hamlet's castle at Helsingør (August)
European Medieval Festival – Middle Ages fun and games in Horsens (August)
Culture Night – Copenhageners stay up late to participate in cultural events (October)

Theatre
Most theatre is in Danish, even though the piece may have been written in another language.
Det Kongelige Teater – Skuespilhuset
Sankt Annæ Plads 36
Tel: 33 69 69 69
http://kglteater.dk
The new national playhouse, opened in 2008, stages major plays, ballets and symphonies. Some performances still take place at the 18th-century Old Stage on Kongens Nytorv.

Music Festivals

These are just a few of the music festivals taking place in Denmark every year.

Copenhagen Jazz Festival
For 10 days in July the streets of Copenhagen are filled with the sound of jazz. One of the world's best jazz festivals; www.jazzfestival.dk.

Skanderborg Festival
"Denmark's most beautiful festival", featuring Danish and international acts, is held in August in a beechwood; www.smukfest.dk.

Roskilde Festival
Late June/early July near Roskilde on Zealand. The largest music festival in Denmark and one of the biggest in Europe, featuring major acts from around the world; www.roskilde-festival.dk.

Skagen Festival
In early July at the northernmost tip of Denmark – beautiful windswept Skagen. One of Denmark's largest folk music festivals; www.skagenfestival.dk.

The London Toast Theatre
Kochsvej 18
Tel: 33 22 86 86
www.londontoast.dk
The only English-language theatre in Copenhagen, showing plays of a high standard. It is most famous for its annual Christmas show, the "Crazy Christmas Cabaret", held in Tivoli Gardens.

The Opera House
Ekvipagemestervej 10
Tel: 33 69 69 69
http://kglteater.dk
The impressive new Opera House on the south bank of the river holds major operas.

Wallmans
The Circus Building, Jernbanegade 8
Tel: 33 16 37 00.
www.wallmans.dk
A very popular international dinner show.

Live Music

Copenhagen
Copenhagen Jazz House
Niels Hemmingsensgade 10
Tel: 33 15 47 00
www.jazzhouse.dk
The place for jazz.

Mojo Blues Bar
Løngangstræde 21C
Tel: 33 11 64 53
www.mojo.dk
Live blues every night.

Rust
Guldbergsgade 8
Tel: 35 24 52 00
www.rust.dk
With three floors, this venue hosts upcoming indie bands, and is popular with students.

Vega
Enghavevej 40
Tel: 33 25 70 11
www.vega.dk
Housed in a large 1950s trade union building, this is one of the most popular venues in Copenhagen.

Odense
Jazzhus Dexter
Vindegade 65
Tel: 63 11 27 28
www.dexter.dk
Live jazz. This is Denmark's biggest jazz club.

Odense Koncerthus
Claus Berg Gade 9
Tel: 66 12 13 14
www.odensesymfoni.dk
Classical music.

Odense Theatre
Jernbanegade 21
Tel: 66 12 00 52
www.odenseteater.dk
Theatre and opera performances.

Posten
Østre Stationsvej 35
Tel: 66 13 60 20
www.postenlive.dk
Occasional blues/rock/metal gigs.

Århus
Århus is one of the best places in Denmark for a night out, with a multitude of good restaurants and performance venues. Nightlife is centred around Skolegade.

Fatter Eskil
Skolegade 25
Tel: 86 19 44 11
www.fattereskil.dk
Jazz and blues music, Tuesday to Saturday.

Musikcaféen
Mejlgade 53
Tel: 86 76 03 44
www.musikcafeen.dk
Rock, blues, soul, electronica, folk: music of all kinds.

Musikhus Århus
Thomas Jensens Allé
Tel: 89 40 40 40
www.musikhusetaarhus.dk
The city's main concert hall, with theatre, dance and music performances.

Train
Toldbodgade 6
Tel: 86 13 47 22
www.train.dk
Concert venue and nightclub, hosting several home-grown/international bands each week.

Cinema

All foreign films are shown with their original soundtrack. Local newspapers have the details of what's on where.

Customs Regulations

Danish customs formalities are usually painless and baggage is rarely opened, but it's sensible to observe the duty-free limits and other rules.

Cigarettes, spirits, perfume, cameras and other luxury items are relatively expensive in Denmark. The rules about how much one can bring into Denmark depend on whether or not you are coming from an EU country. Most EU citizens can now carry almost any amount across EU borders, so long as it is for "personal use". If you are coming from outside the EU, you can bring only 1 litre of spirits or 2 litres of wine; 200 cigarettes or 50 cigars or 250g of tobacco; 500g of coffee; 100g of tea; 50g of perfume; 250ml of eau de toilette; and goods/gifts not exceeding DKK1,350 in value. It is wise to check with your local Danish consul if in doubt. The Danish customs and tax authority website is: www.skat.dk.

D isabled Travellers

In Denmark as a whole, a lot of thought is given to the comfort and unhindered access to all parts of society for those with disabilities, including on public transport. For further information contact:
Danske Handicaporganisationer, Kløverprisvej 10b, DK-2650 Hvidovre
Tel: 36 75 17 17
www.handicap.dk
Turistgruppen Vestjylland publishes an excellent disabled travel guide, covering the west Jutland region (www.disabledtravelguide.com).

The Danish Accessibility Association has a growing online database where you can check the accessibility of specific restaurants, museums and tourist attractions (www.godadgang.dk).

Local tourist information offices can provide specific information about facilities in their area.

E mbassies and Consulates

The following embassies and consulates are in Copenhagen.
Canada
Kristen Bernikowsgade 1
Tel: 33 48 32 00
www.denmark.gc.ca
Germany
Stockholmsgade 57

Tel: 35 45 99 00
www.kopenhagen.diplo.de
Ireland
Østbanegade 21
Tel: 35 47 32 00
www.embassyofireland.de
UK
Kastelsvej 40
Tel: 35 44 52 00
http://ukindenmark.fco.gov.uk
US
Daghammarskjölds Allé 24
Tel: 33 41 71 00
http://denmark.usembassy.gov

Emergencies

Police, ambulance, fire 112
International collect calls 80 30
40 00

G ay and Lesbian Travellers

Denmark is one of the most liberal
and gay-friendly countries in the
world. It has had anti-discrimination
laws since 1987, and in 1989 was
the first nation to recognise same-sex
marriages. The age of consent for
homosexuals is 15, the same as for
heterosexuals. Contact LGBT
Denmark for general information:
Nygade 7, 1164 Copenhagen; tel: 33
13 19 48; www.lgbt.dk.

Copenhagen is a very welcoming
city for gay people and has been for
years. Its first gay bar, Centralhjørnet,
opened over 80 years ago and is still
open today. There are smaller gay
scenes in towns such as Aalborg,
Århus and Odense.

Tourist offices in Copenhagen will
provide a list of the latest venues and
events, or visit the comprehensive
website www.copenhagen-gay-life.dk. In
mid-August Copenhagen has an
annual gay pride parade, **Copenhagen
Pride** (www.copenhagenpride.dk), and every
October hosts a **Gay and Lesbian
Film Festival** (www.cglff.dk).

Some of the most popular gay
venues include:
Cosy Bar
Studiestræde 24; tel: 33 12 74 27;
www.myspace.com/cosybar
Masken Bar
Studiestræde 33; tel: 33 91 09 37;
www.maskenbar.dk
Oscar Bar café
Rådhuspladsen 77; tel: 33 12 09 99;
www.oscarbarcafe.dk
For more information see www.out-
and-about.dk or www.gayguide.dk.

H ealth and Medical Care

Standards of hygiene in Scandinavia
are among the highest in the world.

There are no major health hazards
and the tap water is safe to drink.

The Danish medical system will
assist anyone in an emergency;
however, you should take out travel
insurance before you leave. British
nationals should take a European
Health Insurance Card (EHIC), which
you can apply for online (www.ehic.org.
uk), by phone (0845 606 2030), or by
post (form available from any post
office in the UK). You will be charged
for doctors' and dentists' consultations
and prescriptions, but not hospital
treatment. To get a refund, take the
receipts and your EHIC and passport to
the local council. Citizens of other
countries should ensure that they take
out private health insurance before
departing for Denmark.

Medical Services

Health care is generally free in
Denmark. Acute illnesses or accidents
will be treated at the casualty
department of the nearest hospital. To
contact a doctor outside normal
business hours: In Copenhagen tel:
70 13 00 41; Zealand tel: 70 15 07
00; north Jutland tel: 70 15 03 00;
mid-Jutland tel: 70 11 31 31; south
Jutland tel: 70 11 07 07.

Pharmacies

There is a 24-hour pharmacy in every
region, the name and address of
which is posted on the door of every
pharmacy. In Copenhagen: Steno
Apotek, Vesterbrogade 6c; tel: 33 14
82 66.

Dental Services

Dental care is by appointment only.
Check the listings under Tandlæger in
the Yellow Pages. **Tandlægevagten**,
Oslo Plads 14, Copenhagen, tel: 35
38 02 51, is open for personal callers
on an emergency basis daily
8–9.30pm, plus weekends and
holidays 10am–noon.

L anguage

Pronunciation

The old joke says that Danish is not so
much a language as a disease of the
throat, and so it sometimes seems.
Danish has three extra letters – æ, ø,
and å – plus unpronounceable sub-
glottal stops, and myriad dialects and
accents. Here are a few simple rules
of thumb for pronouncing vowels:
a = a, as in bar
å = aw, as in paw
æ = e, as in pear
e = e, as in bed
i = ee, as in sleep
ø = u, as in fur

General

yes/no ja/nej
big/little stor(t)/lille
good/bad god(t)/dårlig(t)
hot/cold varm/kold
much/little meget/lidt
many/few mange/få
and/or og/eller
please/thank you vær så venlig/
tak
I jeg
you (formal) du (De)
he/she han/hun
it den/det
we vi
you (plural, formal) I (De)
they de

Medical

pharmacy (et) apotek
hospital (et) hospital
casualty (en) skadestue
doctor (en) læge

Food and Drink

breakfast morgenmad
lunch (break) frokost (pause)
dinner middag
tea te
coffee kaffe
beer (bottle/draught) øl/fadøl

Getting Around

left venstre
right højre
street (en) gade/vej
bicycle (path) (en) cykel (sti)
car (en) bil
bus/coach (en) bus
train (et) tog
ferry (en) færge
bridge (en) bro
traffic light (et) trafiklys
square (et) torv
north nord
south syd
east øst
west vest

Buying a Ticket

ticket billet
adult voksen
child barn
single enkelt
return retur

Money

How much is it? Hvad koster det?
Can I pay with... Må jeg betale
med...
Please may I have...? Må jeg få...?
the bill regningen
May I have a...? Må jeg få en...?
receipt kvittering
exchange veksle
open åben
closed lukket
value-added tax (VAT) MOMS

Time

good morning godmorgen
good day/evening goddag
goodnight godaften/godnat
today i dag
tomorrow i morgen
yesterday i går
morning formiddag
noon middag
afternoon eftermiddag
evening aften
night nat
What time is it? Hvad er klokken?

Days of the Week

Monday mandag
Tuesday tirsdag
Wednesday onsdag
Thursday torsdag
Friday fredag
Saturday lørdag
Sunday søndag

Numbers

0 nul
1 en/et
2 to
3 tre
4 fire
5 fem
6 seks
7 syv
8 otte
9 ni
10 ti
11 elleve
12 tolv
13 tretten
14 fjorten
15 femten
16 seksten
17 sytten
18 atten
19 nitten
20 tyve
30 tredive
40 fyrre
50 halvtreds
60 tres
70 halvfjerds
80 firs
90 halvfems
100 hundrede

M edia

Newspapers and Magazines

English-language newspapers are widely available at all main train stations and kiosks. Read them free at the Central Library, Krystalgade 15, or Café Europa, Amagertorv 1, Copenhagen.

The English-language weekly *The Copenhagen Post* (www.cphpost.dk) has news, entertainment and restaurant guides (from tourist offices and newsstands). *Copenhagen This Week* (www.ctw.dk), published 10 times per year, offers the most comprehensive listings information.

Books

Many public libraries have books in English, and Copenhagen has bookshops that specialise in foreign literature *(see Shopping, page 365)*.

Television

Most hotels have satellite/cable channels featuring CNN, BBC and MTV in English. In addition, there are often movies in English on the national channels DR1, DR2 and TV2.

Money

Currency and Exchange

Danish krone (crown); plural kroner; marked kr in shops or DKK internationally; split into 100 øre. Notes come in 50, 100, 200, 500 and 1,000 denominations. There is a 50 øre coin (copper-coloured), 1 krone, 2 krone, 5 krone (silver-coloured with a hole in the centre), and 10 and 20 krone (solid gold-coloured coins that are similar-looking, except the 20 krone piece is a little bigger than the 10 krone).

Exchanges are open outside normal business hours at the Copenhagen Central Railway Station, and in the city centre. Forex is open daily 8am–9pm. There are several 24-hour machines near Copenhagen City Hall.

How to Pay

Visa is the most widely accepted credit card, and you can usually pay by MasterCard and American Express in hotels, restaurants and shops. Note that some places will charge a fee if you pay with a foreign credit card. Diners Club is accepted in many restaurants.

Banks and ATMs

Most banks have 24-hour cash machines (ATMs) – look for the word *Kontanten*. You can draw out up to DKK2,000 per day.

Tipping

Service is included in all bills, but in restaurants it is a friendly gesture to pick up the notes but leave the coins. Taxi drivers appreciate it if the fare is rounded up to the nearest DKK5 or 10.

N ightlife

The best clubs are found in Copenhagen, Århus and Odense. Check the local newspapers or call tourist information offices for current listings. *See also Culture, page 361.*

O pening Hours

Offices: 8/9am–4/5pm.
Shops: Mon–Thur 9.30am/10am–5.30pm, Fri until 7pm (8pm in Copenhagen), Sat 9am–noon or 1pm (5pm in Copenhagen). All are closed on Sunday except for bakeries and kiosks, some of which are open around the clock.
Pharmacies: as shops, except Steno Apotek in Copenhagen (across the street from the train station) which opens all hours.
Supermarkets: until 7/8pm, at least in Copenhagen. The one at the railway station opens all hours.
Banks: Mon–Fri 10am–4pm, some Thur until 6pm.
Post offices: Mon–Fri 9am–5pm, Sat 9am–noon.

P ostal Services

The Danish postal service is fast and efficient. A postcard to the UK/US

BELOW: the Copenhagen Opera House.

costs DKK9/11 economy, DKK11/13 priority. Post offices are generally open 9am–5pm on weekdays, and 9am–noon (smaller branches closed) on Saturday. In Copenhagen, the most central **post office**, at the main railway station, opens Mon–Fri 8am–9pm, Sat–Sun 10am–4pm.

Money orders can be collected or dispatched at all post offices during normal business hours.

Public Holidays

1 January New Year's Day
April Maundy Thursday, Good Friday, Easter Day and Easter Monday
May/June Whit Monday, Ascension Day
5 June Constitution Day
24–26 Dec Christmas
31 Dec New Year's Eve
A floating holiday is **Prayer Day** (Store Bededag), which falls on the fourth Friday after Easter. All shops close during holidays.

R eligious Services

The official Church is the Evangelical Lutheran Church of Denmark. Church attendance is low, and many Danes are agnostic or atheist. For details of church serices, ask at the tourist office.

S hopping

What to Buy

Danish design is famous all over the world, especially in kitchenware, furniture and stereo equipment.

Beautiful amber necklaces are to be found in all jewellery stores, along with exquisite replicas of ancient Viking jewellery in silver and gold.

Ceramics and glassware are a tradition in Denmark and, in addition to Royal Copenhagen Porcelain, there are many small ceramic studios scattered throughout the country.

Danish furs are very popular among tourists, and countless shops specialise in traditional and modern knitwear.

Lego bricks originated in Denmark, but most Danish children's toys are made of strong, durable wood with designs and functions that are based on educational principles.

Feather bedding is a Danish speciality, and many stores sell down duvets, eiderdowns, quilts and pillows, and can arrange shipment of bulky items.

Danish pipe makers carve wood and meerschaum pipes with excellent craftsmanship.

ABOVE: Illums Bolighus features the best in Danish design.

Tax-Free Shopping

Part of the reason for the high prices is a value-added tax (called MOMS) of 25 percent, added to all sales and services.

All visitors can avoid making this contribution to the Danish state by having their purchases shipped home directly. Non-EU residents can get a tax refund by shopping in stores that offer a tax-free service – minimum spend is DKK300. See www.global-blue.com for details. (See Customs, page 362, for further details.)

Shopping in Copenhagen

The main shopping in Copenhagen is along the "walking street" Strøget, which is actually four streets that stretch from the Rådhuspladsen for about 1km (⅔ mile) to Kongens Nytorv. Unfortunately, in the last couple of years or so rising rents have forced out many of the characterful small stores and they have been replaced, mainly, by large chain stores. But small stores still remain in the streets parallel and to the side of Strøget, particularly the interesting Strædet.

Amber

Copenhagen is the capital of amber, and in recent years the **House of Amber** (www.houseofamber.com) has consolidated its position as the leading retailer in the city and now has four stores, with the most prominent being at Kongens Nytorv 2 – which also includes the Amber Museum, tel: 33 11 67 00; Nygade 6, tel: 39 55 14 00; Frederiksberggade 34, tel: 33 11 26 44; Langelinie Allé 36, tel: 35 26 36 88.

Books

The following shops all have good selections of foreign-language literature:

Arnold Busck
Købmagergade 49
Tel: 33 73 35 00
Atheneum Academic Books
Norregade 6
Tel: 33 12 69 70
The Book Trader
Skindergade 23
Tel: 33 12 06 69
www.booktrader.dk
Second-hand humanities books.
Politikens Boghallen
Rådhuspladsen 37
Tel: 33 47 25 60
www.boghallen.dk
Two floors of books, with an excellent English-language selection.

Danish Design
Bodum
Østergade 10 (Strøget)
Tel: 33 36 40 80
www.bodum.com
Bodum has lots of outlets in the city, but this is its flagship store.
DZOO, Designer Zoo
Vesterbrogade 137
Tel: 33 24 94 93
www.dzoo.dk
In this part of now fashionable Vesterbrogade, you will find an innovative and interesting collection of clothing, jewellery and houseware.
Illums Bolighus
Amagertorv 10
Tel: 33 14 19 41
www.illumsbolighus.dk
Mouthwatering collections of homeware (if design is your thing), from shining teaspoons to curvy chairs and sofas.

Department Stores
Magasin du Nord
Kongens Nytorv 13
Tel: 33 11 44 33
www.magasin.dk
Once the Hotel du Nord and facing the famous Kongens Nytorv, this is

Denmark's most famous department store and has branches in other cities in the country.

Fashion

Kronprinsensgade is a good place to start looking for designer clothing.

By Malene Birger
Antonigade 10
Tel: 35 43 22 33
www.bymalenebirger.com
Winner of the Best Danish Designer award in 2009, Malene Birger makes contemporary women's clothing and accessories.

Bruuns Bazaar
Kronprinsensgade 8 & 9
Tel: 33 32 19 99
www.bruunsbazaar.dk
A leading men's and women's fashion design shop, with other branches around Europe and in North America.

Munthe plus Simonsen
Grønnegade 10
Tel: 33 32 03 12
www.muntheplussimonsen.dk
A highly fashionable women's store, with a second branch in Århus.

Handicrafts

Danish Crafts
Kongens Nytorv 1E
Tel: 33 12 61 62
www.danishcrafts.dk
An information centre for Danish handicrafts, which organises exhibitions to promote the country's craftsmen and women.

Workshop Copenhagen
Studiestræde 16
Tel: 33 25 27 33
www.workshop-cph.dk
Unique, handmade designs by a collective of 25 artists.

Outdoor Wear

Guns & Gents
Skindergade 31
Tel: 33 91 24 24
www.gunsandgents.dk
Although primarily a hunting shop, this also has the best collection of waterproof and windproof Barbour jackets – often needed in Copenhagen even in summer.

Porcelain

Royal Copenhagen Porcelain
Amagertorv 6
Tel: 33 13 71 81
www.royalcopenhagen.com
Located in a beautiful building on Strøget, this company has been going for over 235 years. This flagship store contains a museum and mini-production line.

Silverwear

Georg Jensen

Amagertorv 4
Tel: 33 11 40 80
www.georgjensen.com
Look no farther than here, on Strøget, for all kinds of beautifully designed silver jewellery.

Stereo Equipment

Bang & Olufsen
Kongens Nytorv 26
Tel: 33 11 14 15
www.bang-olufsen.com
The company's flagship shore, where you can admire their full range of top-quality stereo equipment.

Telephones

Most phone boxes take prepaid telephone cards, available from newsagents, supermarkets, petrol stations, etc.

Danish mobile phones operate on the 900/1800 MHz GSM network – most European phones are compatible, although your phone must be unlocked in order to link up with the network. US phones work on a slightly different frequency, so US visitors will only be able to use their mobile in Denmark if it is a tri-band phone that can switch bands.

If you are likely to be making a lot of phone calls in Denmark, it's worth buying a Danish SIM card, available from mobile phone shops; buy top-ups from newsagents and supermarkets.

To call abroad, dial 00 followed by the country code (44 for the UK, 1 for the US and Canada, 353 for Ireland), then dial the number, omitting any initial 0.

Denmark's country code is **45**. There are no area codes.

Tourist Information

The Danish tourist board can provide helpful information and brochures before you travel:
UK VisitDenmark, 55 Sloane Street, London SW1X 9SY;
email: london@visitdenmark.com; www.visitdenmark.com.
US VisitDenmark, PO Box 4649, Grand Central Station, New York, NY 10163-4649; tel: 212-885 9700; email: info@goscandinavia.com; www.visitdenmark.com.

There is a tourist office in almost every city, with knowledgeable and friendly staff. They can assist in planning a trip, make reservations, or provide directions and leaflets. Some of the main tourist bureaus are:

Copenhagen
Vesterbrogade 4A (across from the Tivoli main entrance)

Tel: 70 22 24 42
www.visitcopenhagen.com

North Zealand
Havnepladsen 3, 3000 Helsingør
Tel: 49 21 13 33.
Email: info@visitnordsjaelland.com
www.visitnordsjaelland.com

Southwest Zealand
Stændertorvet 1, 4000 Roskilde
Tel: 46 31 65 65.
Email: visit@roskilde.dk
www.visitroskilde.com

Bornholms Velkomstcenter
Ndr. Kystvej 3, 3700 Rønne
Tel: 56 95 95 00.
Email: info@bornholm.info
www.bornholminfo.dk

Funen
Rådhus, 5000 Odense C
Tel: 63 75 75 20.
Email: otb@visitodense.com
www.visitodense.com

East Jutland
Banegårdpladsen 20, 8000 Århus C
Tel: 87 31 50 10
Email: info@visitaarhus.com
www.visitaarhus.com

North Jutland
Østerågade 8, 9000 Ålborg
Tel: 99 31 75 00.
Email: awh@aalborg.dk
www.visitaalborg.com

West Jutland
Nytorv 9, 8800 Viborg
Tel: 87 87 88 88
Email: info@visitviborg.dk
www.visitviborg.dk

South Jutland
Torvet 3–5, 6760 Ribe
Tel: 75 42 15 00
Email: info@visitribe.dk
www.visitribe.dk

Greenland
Greenland Tourism, PO Box 1615, Hans Egedesvej 29, DK-3900 Nuuk, Greenland
Tel: 299 34 28 20
Email: info@greenland.com
www.greenland.com

The Faroe Islands
Vagliđ, PO Box 379, FO-110 Tórshavn
Tel: 298 30 24 25.
Email: info@visitfaroeislands.com
www.visitfaroeislands.com

Useful Copenhagen Websites
www.ctw.dk: *Copenhagen This Week*.
www.aok.dk: all about Copenhagen.

www.visitcopenhagen.dk: the Tourist Board site.
www.out-and-about.dk: gay life.

Tour Operators

Copenhagen

To hire an authorised guide to the city, contact:
Meet the Danes
Tel: 23 28 43 47
Email: info@meetthedanes.dk
www.meetthedanes.dk
Copenhagen This Week (www.ctw.dk; available free at most hotels and tourist agencies) has a list of tours.

Transport

Getting There

By Air
Main international airports:
Copenhagen airport (at Kastrup, 8km/5 miles from central Copenhagen) and **Billund airport** in Jutland.
Denmark's national airline is SAS (Scandinavian Airlines System). Cimber Sterling serves many domestic routes, and flies to other Scandinavian cities and 31 airports in Europe. From the UK, British Airways and Flybmi fly daily from London Heathrow, Manchester and Edinburgh. Low-cost operators Norwegian, Cimber Sterling and easyJet fly daily from London airports to Copenhagen or Billund; easyJet flies six times per week from Manchester. Ryanair flies from Stansted to Århus and Billund. Norwegian and Ryanair fly less frequently from Edinburgh.
From the US, SAS, Delta, KLM, Condor and Continental Airlines fly direct to Copenhagen.

From the UK
British Airways Tel: 0844 493 0787
www.ba.com
Cimber Sterling Tel (Denmark): 70 10 12 18
www.cimber.com
easyJet Tel: 0871 244 2366
www.easyjet.com
flybmi Tel: 0905 828 2828
www.flybmi.com
Norwegian Tel: 020 8099 7254
www.norwegian.com
Ryanair Tel: 0871 246 000
www.ryanair.com
SAS Tel: 0871 521 6000
www.flysas.com

From the US
Several airlines fly direct to Copenhagen. An interesting alternative is to fly **Icelandair** (tel: 1-800-223-5500; www.icelandair.com),

On Your Bike

The best way to enjoy the Danish landscape is on a bicycle. You would do best to bring your own bike if you want to tour the country, but for getting around the city, a rented one will do. The local tourist information office can tell you where to pick one up.
• For information on routes and practical advice, contact:
Dansk Cyklistforbund (Danish Association of Cyclists)
Rømersgade 7, 1362 Copenhagen K
Tel: 33 32 31 21; www.dcf.dk
Mon–Fri 10am–5.30pm, Sat 10am–2pm.
• In the centre of Copenhagen you can borrow bikes for free under a scheme operated by City Bikes, from March to November during daylight hours (the bikes have no lights!). You pay DKK20 (inserted into one of the

with a free stopover in Reykjavik, Iceland, before continuing to Copenhagen or other European destinations.
Condor Tel: 1-866 960 7915
www.condor.com
Continental Tel: 1-800 231 0856
www.continental.com
Delta Airlines Tel: 1-800 241 4141
www.delta.com
KLM Tel: 1-800 618 0104
www.klm.com
SAS Tel: 1-800 221 2350
www.flysas.com

By Sea
From Germany
From Germany, Scandlines (www.scandlines.dk) ferries connect Puttgarden and Rødby (Lolland), and Rostock and Gedser. From April to October, Bornholm Ferries (www.bornholmerfaergen.dk) have a route between Sassnitz and Rønne (Bornholm).

From Sweden
HH Ferries (www.hhferries.se) and Scandlines both operate ferries on the busy crossing between Helsingborg and Helsingør (north Zealand). Stena Line (www.stenaline.dk) operates two routes, from Varberg to Grenå (east Jutland), and from Göteborg to Frederikshavn (north Jutland). Bornholm Ferries sail between Rønne (Bornholm) and Ystad.

From Norway
DFDS Seaways (www.dfdsseaways.dk) run from Oslo to Copenhagen. Stena Lines run from Oslo to Frederikshavn (north Jutland). Colour Line (www.color

racks scattered about the inner-city area), refunded when you deliver the bike back to one of the stands.
City Bikes
Tel: 36 16 42 33; www.bycyklen.dk
• In addition, there are plenty of places to rent bikes at reasonable prices. Contact:
Cyklebørs
157 Gothersgade
Tel: 33 14 07 17
www.cykelborsen.dk
Københavns Cykler
Reventlowsgade 11
Tel: 33 33 86 13
www.copenhagen-bikes.dk
• Cycle tours of Copenhagen are also available, for example with:
Copenhagen Tours
Vodroffsvej 55
Tel: 35 43 01 22
www.copenhagen-tours.dk

line.dk) run, from both Larvik and Kristiansand to Hirtshals (north Jutland). Fjord Line (http://fjordline.dk) has express boats between Kristiansand and Hirtshals, and a normal-speed service from both Bergen and Stavanger to Hirtshals.

From the UK
DFDS Seaways ferries run from Harwich to Esbjerg.

By Rail
Trains arrive daily from Germany, Britain (via Eurostar to Brussels) and Sweden.
For trains from Britain:
Tel: 08448 484 064
www.raileurope.co.uk
For train information in Denmark:
Tel: 70 13 14 15
www.rejseplanen.dk

By Coach
Eurolines (tel: 08717 818 181; www.eurolines-travel.com) is the leading operator of scheduled coach services, with coaches from Denmark to various European countries. Their Scandinavian routes run between Oslo, Göteborg, Malmö and Copenhagen, and from Stockholm to Copenhagen.
Go By Bus (www.gobybus.se) and Swebus (http://swebusexpress.com) run similar routes through Scandinavia.

Getting Around
On Arrival
Almost all international flights arrive and depart from Copenhagen Airport, 8km (5 miles) outside the city in

Kastrup. Trains run six times an hour directly from Terminal 3, the international terminal, to Central Station and take 12 minutes.

Intercity express trains run from the airport direct to Helsingør and Bornholm. Trains run between the airport and many major Swedish cities.

The Øresund bridge connects Denmark and Sweden. Starting near Copenhagen airport, you can reach the Swedish city of Malmö in 20–30 minutes, Stockholm in 5 hrs and Gothenburg in 3 hrs 20 minutes. There is a taxi stand next to Terminal 3.

By Air
If you fly you can be on the other side of Denmark in less than an hour. The main domestic operator, Cimber Sterling, has daily flights from Copenhagen to Billund, Bornholm, Karup, Sønderborg, Ålborg and Århus.
Cimber Air
Tel: 70 10 12 18
www.cimber.dk

By Metro
Copenhagen's tiny metro system (www.m.dk) was extended out to Copenhagen airport in 2007. Trains run to the city centre every 4–6 minutes from 5am–midnight Sunday to Wednesday, with a less frequent (every 15–20 minutes) round-the-clock service from Thursday to Saturday.

By Coach (Long-Distance Bus)
Denmark is not a big country, and its local bus network covers most of the country. For details of local buses on Zealand, contact Movia Customer Service; tel: 36 13 14 15; www.moviatrafik.dk; Mon–Fri 7am–9.30pm, Sat–Sun 8am–9.30pm.

Abildskou (http://abildskou.dk) runs "long-distance" coaches from Copenhagen to Jutland. Thinggaard (www.ekspresbus.dk) runs from Frederikshavn to Esbjerg.

The website www.rejseplanen.dk allows you to plan journeys by bus and train.

By Train
There is a very efficient train service linking all major cities and some of the smaller towns.

There is a boat-train link from Copenhagen to Rønne, Bornholm.

For train information, contact the
DSB Customer Centre
Tel: 70 13 14 15; www.dsb.dk

By Car
Rules of the Road
Drive on the right, and always give way at pedestrian crossings and look out for bicycles when turning right. Look

over your left shoulder every time you open the doors on the driver's side – bicycles are everywhere. Overtake on the left only.

Drivers and passengers must wear seat belts, and dipped headlights are required. Using a mobile phone while driving is illegal at all times. Strict drink-driving laws set the legal limit for blood-alcohol content at 0.05 percent – one drink may put you over.

Speed limits
These are standard speed limits, which are enforced:
Built-up areas 50kph (30mph)
Main roads 80kph (50mph)
Motorways 130kph (80mph) or 110kph (70mph)
For a car with a trailer, the limits are 50kph (30mph), 70kph (40mph) and 80kph (50mph) respectively.

Roadside Assistance
In the event of a breakdown, contact your car rental company or your own private insurer.

Car Rental
It pays to shop around. Ask travel agents about special offers, or try the Yellow Pages. **Avis** (tel: 33 26 80 00), **Europcar** (tel: 89 33 11 33), **Budget Rent A Car** (tel: 33 55 05 00), **Hertz** (tel: 33 17 90 00), and **Sixt Rent A Car** (tel: 32 48 11 00) all have offices all around the country. You need a valid driving licence and must be at least 20–25 years old.

By Taxi
Taxis are available at airports, central train and bus stations and in city centres. Pick them up at taxi ranks or flag them down in the street.

Harbour Tours

One of the best ways of seeing Copenhagen is on a boat cruising the main harbour and the canals around Slotsholmen and Christianshavn.
DFDS Canal Tours
Tel: 32 96 30 00; www.canaltours.com
DFDS's 60-minute guided tours are the most popular. Prices are DKK70 (DKK40 for children). They also offer dinner cruises that last two hours and cost about 450DKK.
The Netto Boats
Tel: 32 54 41 02
www.nettobaadene.dk
The open-top Netto Boats also make a 60-minute guided tour of the harbour and the canals, but cost less at DKK40 (DKK15 for children).

Århus Taxi
Tel: 89 48 48 48
Copenhagen Taxi
Tel: 35 35 35 35
Odense Mini-Taxi
Tel: 66 12 27 12

V isas and Passports
A valid passport entitles you to a stay of up to three months. Visas are not required for EU citizens, or those from Canada and the US. Denmark is a member of the Schengen Agreement, whereby citizens of other member states don't need passports to enter Denmark. Other nationalities may need to obtain a visa before arriving. If in doubt, ask at the nearest Danish Embassy or Consulate.

If you arrive from another Scandinavian country, you will often find that passports aren't checked at all. If you intend to stay longer than three months you will have to obtain a resident's permit.

W hat to Read
Complete Hans Christian Andersen Fairy Tales (Gramercy Books). The classic collection of children's tales by Denmark's master storyteller.
A Conspiracy of Decency by Emmy Werner (Westview Press). The story of how Denmark's Jews were saved from the Nazis, based partly on living eyewitness accounts.
Culture Shock! Denmark by M. Strange (Kuperard). A short guide to Denmark's customs and culture.
Miss Smilla's Feeling for Snow by Peter Høeg (Flamingo). A worldwide best-selling novel that spawned a mediocre film.
The Name of This Book is Dogme 95 by Richard Kelly (Faber). Was Denmark's most famous cinematic innovation a genuine breakthrough or just a clever marketing ploy? Includes interviews with all the key figures, including Lars von Trier.
Seven Gothic Tales by Isak Dinesen, aka Karen Blixen (Penguin Classics). Dark, dreamy fairytales for adults from one of Denmark's most enigmatic 20th-century authors.
The Sixth Floor by Robin Reilly (Cassell). Dramatic account of the Danish Resistance in World War II and the tragic consequences of the British RAF raid on the Gestapo's Copenhagen headquarters.
Other Insight Guides
Insight Guides which highlight destinations in this region are *Smart Guide* Copenhagen and *Step by Step* Copenhagen.

A CCOMMODATION

HOTELS AND FAMILY HOLIDAYS

Choosing a Hotel

Danish hotels are not cheap, but have first-class facilities and are very much business-orientated. Around 500 of the country's larger hotels are classified by one to five stars by HORESTA (Danish Hotel, Restaurant and Tourist Employers' Association).

Greenland

In Greenland hotels come into the expensive category and there is not a wide selection of alternatives. Confirm your booking before you go.
Greenland Tourism
Tel: 299 34 28 20
www.greenland.com

Faroe Islands

Apart from a few good-quality hotels in Torshavn, modern facilities are not plentiful. Private houses and youth hostels provide an alternative.

Faroe Islands Tourist Board
Tel: 298 30 24 25
www.visitfaroeislands.com

Information and Reservations

Danish Hotels, www.dkhotellist.com, have a very comprehensive list of hotels and other places to stay.
You can book a hotel at the tourist information office opposite Central Station in Copenhagen (Mon–Fri 9am–4pm, Sat until 2pm; tel: 70 22 24 42), or online: www.visitcopenhagen.com,

Family Holidays

Camping/caravanning

You can hire stationary caravans or huts on many campsites (all high standard), or take your own tent. You will need a Camping Card Scandinavia, which you can buy at the first campsite you stay at, or online before travelling. For a list of sites, ask

Visit Denmark or contact:
Camping Rådet (Danish Camping Board)
Tel: 39 27 88 44
www.campingraadet.dk

Farm Holidays

For details contact:
Landboferie i Danmark
www.bondegaardsferie.dk

Youth Hostels

Denmark has around 100 youth hostels (vandrerhjem). You need to be a member of the Youth Hostel Association in your home country, or get in touch with Danhostel, www.danhostel.dk, for a free catalogue and a list of sites.

Hotel Listings

Hotels are grouped by area, starting with Copenhagen. Within each city or region, they are listed alphabetically.

A C C O M M O D A T I O N   L I S T I N G S

COPENHAGEN

Hotel Alexandra
H.C. Andersens Boulevard 8
Tel: 33 74 44 44

www.hotelalexandra.dk
This design hotel has filled its bedrooms with classic 1940s and 50s Danish Modernist pieces, but without stinting on modern conveniences. **$$–$$$**
Hotel d'Angleterre
Kongens Nytorv 34
Tel: 33 12 00 95
www.dangleterre.dk
Classic hotel in a prime

location. Reopening in 2012 after an all-singing, all-dancing renovation. **$$$**
Axel Hotel Guldsmeden
Helgolandsgade 11
Tel: 33 31 32 66
www.hotelguldsmeden.dk
Axel gained instant plaudits on its opening in 2007. Balinese-style bedrooms create soothing, clean spaces, and the hotel itself

makes every effort to be green and sustainable. **$$**
Bertrams Hotel Guldsmeden
Vesterbrogade 107
Tel: 33 25 04 05
www.hotelguldsmeden.dk
A sister to the Axel, this is a beautiful boutique hotel where all rooms have four-poster beds and balconies. Service is superb. **$$**

ABOVE: the grand facade of the Hotel d'Angleterre.

CabInn City
Mitchellsgade 14
Tel: 33 46 16 16
www.cabinn.com
Functional budget hotel, with free internet and a fantastic central location – only a short walk from the buzzing Tivoli. **$**

Carlton Hotel Guldsmeden
Vesterbrogade 66
Tel: 33 12 15 00
www.hotelguldsmeden.dk
The third of Hotel Guldsmeden's lovely city-centre properties, in a 19th-century building in a popular part of Copenhagen. Rooms have a rustic, French colonial feel. Friendly service. 64 rooms. **$$**

Copenhagen Plaza
Bernstorffsgade 4
Tel: 33 14 92 62
www.profilhotels.se
Commissioned by King Frederik VIII in 1913, this central hotel retains its aristocratic style. It features the famous Library Bar. **$$$**

Danhostel Copenhagen
H.C. Andersens Boulevard 50
Tel: 33 11 85 85
www.danhostel.dk
Europe's largest designer hostel, with a great location right in the centre of town and a few minutes' walk from the Central Station. **$**

First Hotel Sankt Petri
Krystalgade 22
Tel: 33 45 91 00
www.hotelsktpetri.com
This upmarket, modern 5-star hotel sits in the ancient heart of town. The bathrooms are stunning. There is a good restaurant and pretty atrium where live jazz is played. **$$$**

First Hotel Vesterbro
Vesterbrogade 23
Tel: 33 78 80 00
www.firsthotels.dk/vesterbro
Centrally placed in Vesterbrogade. All the rooms are a decent size and look down onto an internal airy atrium where you have breakfast. In days of yore the building housed the local porn cinema. **$$**

Hilton Copenhagen Airport
Ellehammersvej 20
Tel: 32 50 15 01
www.hilton.com
Featuring Scandinavian furnishings and decor, even the smallest rooms here are the largest in Copenhagen. Although it's right next door to Terminal 3, fantastic soundproofing cuts out all aeroplane noise. **$$$**

Hotel Nebo
Istedgade 6-8
Tel: 33 21 12 17
www.nebo.dk
Travellers on a budget can save money at Nebo: rooms are very plain, but it's extremely central and family rooms are available. **$**

Nimb
Bernstorffsgade 5
Tel: 88 70 00 00
www.tivoli.dk
Currently wowing all-comers, the Nimb, based in Tivoli Gardens, is *the* place to stay in Copenhagen. Its Moorish palace exterior houses the city's cosiest boutique hotel. Just 13 rooms, so book well ahead. **$$$**

Radisson Blu Royal Hotel
Hammerichsgade 1
Tel: 33 42 60 00
www.radissonblu.com/royalhotel-copenhagen
In a landmark building overlooking Tivoli Gardens, this hotel was designed by the world-renowned architect Arne Jacobsen in 1960. It now has all modern facilities to complement the innovative Scandinavian design. **$$$**

The Square
Rådhuspladsen 14
Tel: 33 38 12 00
www.thesquarecopenhagen.com
This 3-star minimalist-style hotel – the only one of its class with air conditioning – has a fantastic if noisy location overlooking the Town Hall Square. **$$**

ZEALAND

Helsingør

Comwell Borupgaard
Nørrevej 80, Snekkersten
Tel: 48 38 03 33
www.comwellborupgaard.dk
On the coast 2km (1¼ miles) from Helsingør, this spa hotel has warm, simple rooms, lots of healthy breakfast choices and views of Sweden. **$$$**

Marienlyst Hotel & Casino
N. Strandvej 2
Tel: 49 21 40 00
www.marienlyst.dk
Relaxed hotel complex with views over the sea and Kronborg Castle. **$$$**

Køge

Hotel Hvide Hus
Strandvejen 111
Tel: 56 65 36 90
www.hotelhvidehus.dk
Modern hotel with sea views. **$$$**

Næstved

Hotel Kirstine
Købmagergade 20
Tel: 55 77 47 00
www.hotelkirstine.dk
A charming 17th-century building, cosy and full of character; some rooms need revamping. **$$**

Roskilde

Hotel Prindsen
Algade 13
Tel: 46 30 91 00
www.prindsen.dk
Regal building over 300 years old. Public rooms maintain a princely grandeur; bedrooms are comfortable and modern. **$$$**

Slagelse

Hotel Frederik d.11
Idagårdsvej 3
Tel: 58 53 03 22
www.fr2.dk
A modern red-brick building near Antvorskou ruins. **$$$**

Stege

Tohøjgaard Guesthouse
Rytsebækbej 17, Hjelm
Tel: 55 81 60 67
http://tohoejgaard.com
The loveliest B&B on Møn. The carefully decorated rooms in this peaceful old farmhouse all have sea views. **$**

Tisvildeleje

Strandhotel
Hovedgaden 75
Tel: 48 70 71 19
www.strand-hotel.dk
Young and arty, near the beach. Popular with Danes and tourists in summer. **$$**

Vedbæk

Hotel Marina
Vedbæk Strandvej 391
Tel: 45 89 17 11
www.choicehotels.dk
Modern hotel with newly renovated rooms, overlooking Vedbæk marina and the beach. **$$$**

BORNHOLM

Allinge

Hotel Pepita
Langebjergvej 1 Sandvig
Tel: 56 48 04 51
www.pepita.dk
Cosy family-run hotel in
Sandvig, close to the beach,
composed of a traditional
17th-century half-timbered
house and a modern
annexe. $–$$

Hotel Romantik
Strandvejen 68
Tel: 56 48 03 44
www.hotel-romantik.dk
Found right on the shore at
Sandvig and very
convenient for swimming
and fishing. Most rooms
have views of the Baltic
Sea. Apartments for 2 to 6
people are also available.
$$

Rønne

Det Lille Hotel
Ellekongstæde 2
Tel: 56 90 77 00
www.detlillehotelbornholm.dk
A pleasant, cosy little hotel,
with the feel of a B&B.
Rooms are simply decorated
but clean. Family room
available. A homely choice.
$

Svaneke

Hotel Siemsens Gaard
Havnebryggen 9
Tel: 56 49 61 49
www.siemsens.dk
A lovingly restored 17th-
century merchant's house
at Svaneke harbour, with
magnificent Baltic Sea
views. First-class restaurant.
49 rooms. $$

FUNEN

Odense

Hotel Ansgar
Østre Stationsvej 32
Tel: 66 11 96 93
www.millinghotels.dk
One of the old mission
hotels, with all facilities. 74
rooms. $$
Ansgarhus Motel
Kirkegaards Alle 17–21
Tel: 66 12 88 00
www.ansgarhus.dk
Lying alongside a peaceful
park, an easy walk from
Odense centre. There are
16 welcoming little rooms
here, with the kind of

warmth missing from many
of the city-centre hotels.
Good value. $
Billesgade B&B
Billesgade 9
Tel: 66 13 00 74
A friendly and good-value
little B&B. Small, cheery
rooms, on a quiet street 15
minutes' walk from the
centre. $
City Hotel Odense
Hans Mulesgade 5
Tel: 66 12 12 58
www.cityhotelodense.eu
Moderately priced 3-star
hotel with all modern
comforts. $$

Odense Congress Center
Ørbækvej 350
Tel: 65 56 01 00
www.occ.dk
Comfortable if slightly
spartan; handy for shoppers
visiting the nearby
Rosengårdcentret,
Denmark's biggest
shopping centre. $$
**Radisson Blu H.C.
Andersen Hotel**
Claus Bergs Gade 7
Tel: 66 14 78 00
www.radissonblu.com/hotel-odense
Good, modern hotel in the
old part of town. Conference
facilities. $$$

Ydes Hotel
Hans Tausensgade 11
Tel: 66 12 11 31
www.ydes.dk
Small hotel with small
rooms but friendly service.
English breakfast. $

Svendborg

Hotel Svendborg
Centrumpladsen 1
Tel: 62 21 17 00
www.hotel-svendborg.dk
Large, modern, clean-cut
hotel with many facilities,
right in the centre of town.
$$–$$$

JUTLAND

Ålborg

**Radisson Blu Limfjord
Hotel**
Ved Stranden 14–16
Tel: 98 16 43 33
www.radissonblu.dk/hotel-aalborg
Superbly located hotel in
the centre of Ålborg. Quieter
rooms lie on the waterside.
$$$

Århus

Hotel Guldsmeden Aarhus
Guldsmedgade 40
Tel: 86 13 45 50
www.hotelguldsmeden.dk
In a traditional old building
that was carefully restored
in 1999, this small hotel is
one of the most charming in
Århus. 27 rooms. $$–$$$
Helnan Marselis Hotel
Strandvejen 25

Tel: 86 14 44 11
www.helnan.info
In a superb location looking
over the Kattegat. All rooms
have impeccable sea views.
$$–$$$
Radisson Blu Scandinavia
Margrethepladsen 1
Tel: 86 12 86 65
www.radissonblu.dk/hotel-aarhus
Stylish steel and glass
building, with large,
comfortable rooms. Award-
winning hotel. $$$
Hotel Royal
Store Torv 4
Tel: 86 12 00 11
www.hotelroyal.dk
Beautiful building, more
than 150 years old, but
modernised with a fine
conservatory restaurant.
$$$
Scandic Hotel Plaza Århus
Banegårdspladsen 14

Tel: 87 32 01 00
www.scandichotels.com
Central, with a bar, fitness
centre, Jacuzzi and indoor
parking. $$
Villa Provence
Fredens Torv 10
Tel: 86 18 24 00
www.villaprovence.dk
An oasis of charm and calm
in the heart of the city, near
the bus station, with all
rooms individually designed
in Provençal style. 35
rooms, 4 suites and 2
apartments. $$$

Christiansfeld

Den Gamle Grænsekro
Koldingvej 51
Tel: 75 57 32 18
www.graensekroen.dk
Dating back to 1600, this is
one of Denmark's royally

licensed inns, and only three
families have operated it in
its long and illustrious
history. 26 rooms. $

Esbjerg

Hotel Ansgar
Skolegade 36
Tel: 75 12 82 44
www.hotelansgar.dk
This is a 3-star-rated hotel,
with a very pleasant
ambience, located in the
heart of Esbjerg. 49 rooms.
$$

PRICE CATEGORIES

Price categories are based
on an average double room
including tax, usually with
breakfast:
$ = under DKK1,000
$$ = DKK1,000–1,400
$$$ = over DKK1,400

Hotel Britannia
Torvegade 24
Tel: 75 13 01 11
www.britannia.dk
Found in the centre of town on the Market Square, this modern hotel has 108 spacious rooms decorated in sleek, Scandinavian style. **$$$**

Fanø

Sønderho Kro
Kropladsen 11
Tel: 75 16 40 09
www.sonderhokro.dk
Built in 1722, this is the town's oldest building and

one of Denmark's best-preserved inns. Renowned for its food. 13 old-fashioned rooms. **$$$**

Frederikshavn

Scandic The Reef, Frederikshavn
Tordenskjoldsgade 14
Tel: 98 43 32 33
www.scandichotels.com
Not many hotels have their own wave machine! After a total refurb in 2010, this Scandic hotel is a Caribbean-themed hotel with a fabulous waterpark with slides, waterfalls and

tropical weather – great for families. **$$$**

Hirtshals

Hotel Strandlyst
Strandvejen 20
Tel: 98 97 70 76
www.hotel-strandlyst.dk
Cosy 100-year-old hotel, just 10 minutes from the beach. **$**

Ribe

Hotel Dagmar
Torvet 1
Tel: 75 42 00 33
www.hoteldagmar.dk

The oldest hotel in Denmark (1581) is quaint, although it charges a premium for character. Fine location on the old town square, opposite the cathedral. **$$$**

Vejle

Munkebjerg Hotel
Munkebjergvej 125
Tel: 76 42 85 00
www.munkebjerg.dk
Modern hotel in the middle of forest with marvellous panoramic views. It has three restaurants, a sauna and an indoor heated pool. **$$$**

GREENLAND

Ilulissat

Hotel Arctic
Box 1501
Tel: 299 94 41 53
www.hotel-arctic.gl
Excellent modern hotel with superb views over Disko Bay. Between May and Sept five "igloos" are also available. **$$$**

Narsarsuaq

Hotel Narsarsuaq
The Airport
Tel: 299 66 52 53

www.airporthotels.gl
The modern and well-equipped airport hotel, with 92 rooms, is around 16km (10 miles) from the start of the inland ice. **$$$**

Nuuk

Hotel Hans Egede
Aqqusinersuaq 1–5, Box 1049
Tel: 299 32 42 22
www.hhe.gl
Modern conference hotel with friendly staff. 140 rooms and 10 apartments. **$$$**

Qaanaaq

Hotel Qaanaaq
Box 88
Tel: 299 97 12 34
www.turistqaanaaq.gl
A small (5 double rooms), simple hotel on the remote northwest coast of Greenland. **$**

Sisimiut

Hotel Sisimiut
Aqqusinersuaq 86, Box 70
Tel: 299 86 48 40
www.hotelsisimiut.gl

One of Greenland's best hotels, with 40 well-equipped (for Greenland) rooms. The hotel's restaurant, Nasaasaaq, has a reputation for fine dining, and for its hearty Sunday brunch. **$$$**

• For further information on accommodation options in Greenland contact:
Greenland Tourism
PO Box 1615, Hans Egedesvej 29, Nuuk
Tel: 299 34 28 20
www.greenland.com

THE FAROE ISLANDS

Borðoy, Klaksvík

Hotel Klaksvík
Víkarvegur 38
Tel: 298 45 53 33
www.hotelklaksvik.fo
Family-run hotel with 28 clean rooms – it's worth getting one with a harbour view. Restaurant and generous breakfast buffet. Handy for the ferry. **$$**

Eysturoy, Eiði

Gjáargarður
FO-476
Tel: 298 42 31 71
www.gjaargardur.fo
A turf-roofed guesthouse offering rooms with shared or private bathrooms: finer accommodation in the new extension. Some rooms have fjord views. Restaurant. **$**

Tórshavn

Hotel Føroyar
Oyggjarvegur, PO Box 3303
Tel: 298 31 75 00
www.hotelforoyar.com
Perched on a hillside on the

edge of town, this purpose-built hotel has good service, spacious rooms and splendid panoramic views. **$$$**

Hotel Hafnia
Áarvegur 4–10
Tel: 298 31 32 33
www.hafnia.fo
Clean, comfortable choice by the harbour, with 53 rooms and 4 suites, all with private facilities. **$$$**

Hotel Tórshavn
Tórsgøta 4
Tel: 298 35 00 00
www.hotel.fo
A recently updated hotel (flatscreen TVs, wireless internet) in Tórshavn centre. Smart and comfortable, with

trendy Hvonn Brasserie on the ground floor. **$$–$$$**

Viðoy, Viðareiði

Hotel Norð
Viðareiði
Tel: 298 45 12 44
www.hotelnord.fo
The island's most northerly hotel is a friendly spot; rooms were updated in 2007. A paradise for bird-lovers. **$**

• For further information contact:
Visit Faroe Islands
Tel: 298 30 24 25
Email: info@visitfaroeislands.com
www.visitfaroeislands.com

E ATING OUT

RECOMMENDED RESTAURANTS AND CAFÉS

What to Eat

Within the past couple of decades the Danish kitchen has gone through a quiet revolution, and a new pride in Scandinavian cuisine has taken root. Traditional dishes such as pork and beef are still appreciated, but have been transformed into lighter delicacies for a modern palate. World-class restaurants serving distinctly Scandinavian dishes have popped up all over Copenhagen. However, the food that is most strongly associated with Denmark has not suffered from this New Nordic wave: open sandwiches (smørrebrød) are still most common for lunch. Smørgåsbord is a lunch buffet of cold dishes, where you can pick and choose from a range of Danish specialities. Take advantage of the varieties of fish from the Baltic and North seas. Fowl and game are common, especially in autumn.

Many restaurants offer "a two-course meal of good, Danish food". This is where one finds roast pork, minced beef, meat or fish balls, and other traditional dishes.

Restaurant Listings

Restaurants are grouped by area, starting with Copenhagen. Within each city or region they are listed in alphabetical order.

RESTAURANT LISTINGS

COPENHAGEN

Michelin-Starred Restaurants

Copenhagen has nine Michelin-starred restaurants, including the following:

BELOW: dining out in Copenhagen.

Era Ora
Overgaden Neden Vandet 33B
Tel: 32 54 06 93
www.era-ora.dk
Considered to be the best Italian restaurant in Northern Europe, it also has a wine cellar containing over 72,000 bottles and 450 labels that can be visited by those so interested. **$$$**

Formel B
Vesterbrogade 182
Tel: 33 25 10 66
www.formel-b.dk
Stylish and modern, this restaurant is famous for its French/Danish cuisine. Its six-course menu is one of the country's finest. **$$$**

Noma
Strandgade 93
Tel: 32 96 32 97
www.noma.dk
People come to Denmark just to eat here – bookings taken three months prior to dining. Renowned for its "New Nordic" cuisine and innovative presentation. Received a second star in 2007 and voted World's Best Restaurant in 2010. **$$$**

The Paul
Vesterbrogade 3
Tel: 33 75 07 75
www.thepaul.dk
Opened in 2003 and located in Tivoli; Paul Cunningham only had to wait one year to be awarded a Michelin star. Spacious, open dining areas, and exquisitely prepared and presented cuisine. **$$$**

PRICE CATEGORIES

Price categories are per person for an average two-course meal, excluding drinks but with tax:
$ = under DKK150
$$ = DKK150–300
$$$ = over DKK300

Other Restaurants

Aamanns
Øster Farimagsgade 10
Tel: 35 55 33 44
www.aamanns.dk
Copenhagen folk swear by Aamanns deli/takeaway, where traditional Danish smørrebrød are given a contemporary touch. (Aamanns also have a fine-dining restaurant next door). **$**

Famo
Saxogade 3
Tel: 33 23 22 50
www.famo.dk
Cheerful Italian restaurant with a set four-course seasonal menu. The antipasti in particular are full of rich, authentic flavours. **$$$**

Restaurant Cofoco
Abel Cathrines Gade 7
Tel: 33 13 60 60
www.cofoco.dk

Top-quality French/Danish cuisine at an excellent price. Eat at private tables, or turn it into a shared dining experience and join the sociable long table. **$$**

Restaurant Godt
Gothersgade 38
Tel: 33 15 21 22
www.restaurant-godt.dk
This tiny, cosy family-run restaurant (seats 20) serves finely balanced seasonal menus. Reservations are advised. **$$–$$$**

Restaurant Puk
Vandkunsten 8
Tel: 33 11 14 17
www.restaurantpuk.dk
This basement restaurant serves up perfectly cooked traditional/Bornholm dishes – plankebøf, Danish hash, roast pork – in a homey atmosphere. **$$**

Restaurationen
Møntergade 19
Tel: 33 14 94 95

www.restaurationen.com
With its one fixed Danish-style menu of five courses (changed weekly), this is a Copenhagen favourite. **$$$**

Riz Raz
Store Kannikestræde 19
Tel: 33 32 33 45
Kompagnistræde 20
Tel: 33 15 05 75
www.rizraz.dk
With two locations in Copenhagen, Riz Raz is famed for its ultra-good-value vegetarian buffet, bursting with Mediterranean flavours. Very popular with locals. **$**

Spiseloppen
Christiania
Tel: 32 57 95 58
www.spiseloppen.dk
Featuring an international menu prepared by chefs from around the globe, Spiseloppen is an ever-surprising restaurant at the heart of Christiania. **$$**

Cafés

Bang & Jensen
Istedgade 130, 1650 V
Tel: 33 25 53 18
Popular with the young. **$**

Café Dan Turell
Store Regnegade 3, 1110 K
Tel: 33 14 10 47
www.danturell.dk
Artists frequent this café. **$**

Café Katz
Frederiksholms Kanal 1
Tel: 33 93 33 87
www.cafe-katz.dk
Great waterside location. **$**

Park Café
Østerbrogade 79, 2100 Ø
Tel: 70 333 222
www.parkcafe.dk
Often has live contemporary music. **$**

Zirup
Læderstræde 32
Tel: 33 13 50 60
www.zirup.dk
Perfect place for people-watching. **$$**

ZEALAND

Helsingør

Café Hyacint
Bjerggade 4a
Tel: 49 21 69 70
Stop here for mid-morning coffee, or indulge in one of the excellent Danish lunch platters. **$**

Madam Sprunck
Stengade 48F
Tel: 49 26 48 49
www.madamsprunck.dk
A varied international menu awaits at this atmospheric courtyard restaurant. A popular brunch is also served here. **$$–$$$**

Hillerød

Spisestedet Leonora
Frederiksborg Slot, 3400
Tel: 48 26 75 16
www.leonora.dk
A good lunch choice, particularly on sunny days when the terrace opens. **$$**

Kongens Lyngby

Brede Spisehus
I.C. Modewegsvej. Tel: 45 85 54 57
www.bredespisehus.dk
Danish/French cuisine in wonderful natural setting in a small village just outside Copenhagen. **$$–$$$**

BORNHOLM

Gudhjem

Restaurant Bokulhus
Bokulvej 4
Tel: 56 48 52 97
Modern Danish food using the best local produce. Excellent fish platters. **$$**

Rønne

Di 5 Stâuerna
Strandvejen 116
Tel: 56 90 44 44
www.radissonblu.com/hotel-bornholm
The Radisson Hotel's excellent restaurant with a

perfect sea view. **$$$**

Restaurant Fyrtøjet
Store Torvegade 22
Tel: 56 96 30 12
www.fyrtoejet.dk
A decent choice of fish and meat mains, with lunch and evening buffets. **$$**

Svaneke

Rogeriet I Svaneke
Fiskergade 12
Tel: 56 49 63 24
Wash down smoked eel, salmon and Baltic herring with home-brewed beer. **$$**

FUNEN

Odense

Den Gamle Kro
Overgade 23
Tel: 66 12 14 33
www.dengamlekro.eu
Traditional Danish and

French cuisine in a higgledy-piggledy building (1683): in sunny weather, head for the leafy courtyard. **$$–$$$**

Olivia Brasserie
Vintappersstræde 37
Tel: 66 17 87 44

www.cafeolivia.dk
This smart, welcoming brasserie serves epic brunches, light lunches and a "rustic" evening menu. **$$**

Restaurant under Lindetræet

Ramsherred 2, 5000 Odense
Tel: 66 12 92 86
www.underlindetraet.dk
This lovely old inn serves up mouthwatering Danish/French dishes. Odense's finest. **$$**

JUTLAND

ABOVE: shellfish are always on the menu.

Aabenraa

Krusmølle
Krusmøllevej 10, Feldstedskov
Tel: 74 68 61 72
www.krusmoelle.dk
Linger over coffee and cake
or a light lunch at this café,
which shares an old mill
building with glass and
ceramics workshops. **$$**

Ålborg

Restaurant "Mortens Kro"
Mølleå 4
Tel: 98 12 48 60
www.mortenskro.com
Super-swish gourmet

restaurant, with its own
champagne bar. **$$$**

Arden

Rold Gammel Kro
Hobrovej 11
Tel: 98 56 17 00
www.roldkro.dk
Small lunchtime selection of
smørrebrød and meat/fish/
cheese platters, with meaty
Danish dishes (boar, beef,
pork) at night. **$$$**

Århus

L'Estragon
Klostergade 6

Tel: 86 12 40 66
www.lestragon.dk
Top-class Danish/French
food served in an intimate
setting. **$$$**

Klassisk 65
Jægergårdsgade 65
Tel: 86 13 12 21
This bistro/wine bar offers
fabulously tasty food in a
cosy atmosphere. Excellent
service. Recommended
Sunday brunch. **$$**

Mefisto
Volden 28
Tel: 86 13 18 13
www.mefisto.dk
A smashing little café/
restaurant in the Latin
quarter, Mefisto is open for
coffee, brunch, lunch and
dinner. On Tuesdays there's
a gourmet fish menu,
created from whatever the
fishermen bring in. **$$–$$$**

Pind's Café
Skolegade 11
Tel: 86 12 20 60
www.pindscafe.dk
An Århus institution serving
traditional Danish fare. **$**

Svineriet
Mejlgade 35-Baggården
Tel: 86 12 30 00
www.svineriet.dk
A gastronomic delight, using
local seasonal produce in its
inventive menus. Based in

the laidback Latin quarter.
$$$

Esbjerg

Café Cozmo
Skolegade 18
Tel: 75 12 65 30
www.cafecozmo.dk
This swish café-bar is the
place to grab burgers,
salads, wraps and
pancakes, or an evening
cocktail. **$–$$**

Skagen

Brøndums Hotel
Anchersvej 3
Tel: 98 44 10 55
www.broendums-hotel.dk
Established in 1840. Good-
quality wine and traditional
Danish cuisine. Book
ahead. **$$$**

Viborg

Kafé & Restaurant Arthur
Vestergade 4
Tel: 86 62 21 26
www.restaurant-arthur.dk
An excellent choice: part of
the slow food movement,
Arthur serves classy,
flavour-packed modern
Danish cuisine at
reasonable prices. **$$–$$$**

GREENLAND

Nuuk

Restaurant Charoen Porn
Aqqusinersuaq 3
Tel: 299 32 57 59

Cuisine as far away from the
icebergs as it's possible to
get – here you'll find spicy
flavours from the Far East at
a genuine Thai restaurant.

$–$$

Restaurant Sarfalik
Hotel Hans Egede, 3900
Tel: 299 32 42 22
On the fifth floor of Hotel

Hans Egede, this is another
top-class restaurant serving
traditional Greenland
dishes. With fine views.
$$$

THE FAROE ISLANDS

Tórshavn

Áarstova
Gongin 1
Tel: 298 33 30 00
www.aarstova.fo
Tórshavn's gourmet choice,
with top-quality Faroese and
New Nordic cuisine, with an
emphasis on fish dishes,
served in a wooden house
near the harbour. **$$$**

**Glasstovan at Hotel
Føroyar**
Oyggjarvegur 45
Tel: 298 31 75 00
An upmarket choice with
fine views over Tórshavn,
Glasstovan offers classic
dishes such as lobster
bisque, rack of lamb or
baked salmon – or try the
speciality Faroese platter.
$$$

Restaurant Marco Polo
Sverrisgøta 12
Tel: 298 31 34 30
A well-priced family
restaurant, serving pizzas,
burgers, steaks and fish
mains. **$–$$**

Toscana
Nólsoyar Pálsgøta 13, FO-100
Tel: 298 31 11 09
www.toscana.fo
Exceedingly pleasant Italian

restaurant, with rich dishes
of venison, seafood, meat
and pasta. **$$–$$$**

PRICE CATEGORIES

Price categories are per
person for an average two-
course meal, excluding
drinks but with tax:
$ = under DKK150
$$ = DKK150–300
$$$ = over DKK300

DENMARK

NORWAY

SWEDEN

FINLAND

Norway A – Z

A HANDY SUMMARY OF PRACTICAL INFORMATION

A ctivities

Outdoor Sports

If Norwegians can contrive a sport as an excuse to be outdoors, they'll do it. For a full listing of the range of sports and sports facilities in the Oslo region, see the *Outdoor Activities* pages of the *Oslo Guide* from tourist offices.

Canoeing

Some of the best canoeing and kayaking lakes and rivers are in the Femund area, Østfold, Aust and Vest Agder, Telemark and suburban Oslo. Contact the local tourist office for details.

Cycling

Cycling in Norway is safe and pleasurable, as there is relatively little traffic on many minor roads. But although there are a few cycle routes, it is not an integrated system, so you should still ride with caution. Helmets are advised. Cycling is a particularly good way of exploring the area outside Oslo: bicycles are allowed on most trains and buses for a small charge. Note that cyclists are not permitted to travel through the longer

tunnels (because of car fumes).
For more information, see the Getting Around section, page 388.

Fishing

The fishing is excellent in Norway, whether you're at sea or on a fjord, lake or river. You need a local fishing permit to fish sea char, salmon or sea trout and a national fishing licence for inland fishing in Norway. You can buy a fishing permit at or near to your holiday spot. See the tourist board's *Angling in Norway* for full details.

Glacier Hiking

Glacier hiking is an exhilarating experience, but should be attempted only with an experienced local guide. Several Norwegian tour companies offer guided glacier walks *(breer)*, particularly in the following areas:
Fjord Norway: Hardangerjøkulen, Folgefonna, Buarbre, Bondhusbre, Smørstabbre, Fannaråkbre and Nigardsbre.
Norland Reiseliv: Svartisen and Engenbreen.
Oppland: Styggebre.
Sognefjord: Jostedalsbreen and Fjæland.

For details, contact Glacier Information Centres in western Norway at Jostedalsbreen National Park Centre at Oppstryn (tel: 57 87 72 00), Tourist Office Fjærland (tel: 57 69 32 33) and Breheimsenteret Josterdal (tel: 57 68 32 50).

Golf

Norwegian golf courses are by and large difficult and challenging. Most require either a Green Card or a handicap under 20. Green fees are in line with most European golf courses. Some nine-hole courses offer day fees.
In the Oslo region professional competitions are held at Bogstad, Larvik, Borre and Vestfold golf clubs, but by far the most beautifully situated is the Tyrifjord golf links. For information, contact:
Norges Golfforbund (Golf Federation) Ullevål Stadion, 0840 Oslo; tel: 21 02 91 50; www.golfforbundet.no.

Hiking

The country's extensive mountain ranges and high plains make ideal walking terrain. The most popular areas include the Jotunheim, Rondane and Dovrefjell mountains,

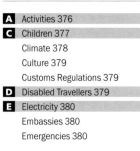

Winter Norway

Norway is often dubbed the "Cradle of Skiing"; but skiing is just one of Norway's winter attractions. There are snowmobile trips to the North Cape, reindeer safaris and dog-sledge races over the plain of Finnmarksvidda.

You can go on horse-drawn sleigh rides, or try your hand at sledging, ice fishing, snow-boarding or ice skating. For details of tour operators who specialise in winter holidays in Norway, see *Specialist Tour Operators on page 383*, or contact the Norwegian Tourist Board, which has a list of holiday agents offering packages.

the Hardangervidda plateau in the Trollheimen district, and the Finnmarksvidda plain. Mountain cabins are open from the end of June until mid-September, plus over the Easter holiday.

The Norwegian Mountain Touring Association (DNT) runs about 300 guided hikes in summer, and glacier walks in winter. Membership includes hut *(hytte)* access. For details:
Norwegian Trekking Association (Den Norske Turistforening)
Youngstorget 1, 0181 Oslo; tel: 22 82 22 82; email: turinfo@dntoslo.no; www.turistforeningen.no.
(See also Norway on Foot, p.389.)

Horse Riding
There are riding centres and hotels all over Norway where you can hire a horse for organised trekking or take lessons. For further details contact tourist offices, or:
Norges Rytterforbund (Riding Federation)
Tel: 21 02 96 50; email: nryf@rytter.no; www.rytter.no.

Husky Safaris
The most thrilling way to explore the northeastern Finnmark region, the heart of the Sami country. Choose from a variety of adventures: drive your own dog team, join a dog-sledge safari, observe the Sami reindeer migration, or enjoy a horse safari. Lodge in authentic log cabins and enjoy the rugged northern landscape.
Sven Engholm's Husky Lodge (B&B), tel: 784 67 166; www.engholm.no.
Direct Adventures, tel: +44 (0)845 155 9625; www.directadventures.co.uk.

Skiing
Even in summer Norwegians take to the slopes (as a rule from June to September), and the sight of people skiing in bikinis and trunks is something to behold.

The main ski resorts are at Lillehammer, Trysil, Geilo, Hemsedal, Voss, Norefjell (the nearest to Oslo) and of course Tryvann, Oslo's Winter Park; all tourist offices can advise on local ski facilities for cross-country and slalom. Also check the Norwegian ski guide on www.skiinfo.no, or www.skiforbundet.no.

Sailing
There are sailing and boating clubs and associations throughout Norway. Without your own boat, sailing of any sort can be expensive, and the closest you may get is a small catamaran or even a windsurfer. In Oslo you can hire equipment from:
SrfSnoSk8
Munkedamsveien 20; tel: 22 83 78 73; email: oslo@srfsnosk8.no or stavanger@srfsnosk8.no.
Norges Seilforbund (Sailing Federation)
Serviceboks 1, Ullevål Stadion, 0840 Oslo; tel: 21 02 90 00; www.sailing.no.

Swimming
Temperatures along the coast and inland reach 25°C (77°F) in summer, and even in the north it can be warm enough to swim. Nude beaches are to be found in Oslo, Moss, Halden, Tønsberg, Larvik, Molde, Ålesund, Bergen, Trondheim and Salten. Most larger hotels have pools, and there are numerous leisure centres throughout Norway.

Watersports
There are several possibilities for waterskiing and windsurfing along the coast, as well as on Norway's numerous lakes.

White-water rafting is available on the following rivers: Sjoaelva in Oppland, Trysilelva in Hedmark and Driva in Sør-Trøndelag.

The Norwegian coast offers good conditions for diving. There are several diving centres along the west coast, particularly in the counties of Møre and Romsdal, and in north Norway.
Norges Dykkeforbund (Diving Federation)
Sognsveien 75L, Serviceboks 1 Ullevål Stadion, N-0480 Oslo; tel: 21 02 97 42; www.ndf.no.
Sjoa Raftingsenter
Varphaugen Gård, 2670 Otta; tel: 47 66 06 80; email: rafting@sjoaraftingsenter.no.

Whale Safaris
In northern Norway between May and September, massive sperm whales can be found in the area around the Lofoten Islands. There are also minkes and orcas, and on some of these "safaris", seals, and various seabirds – puffins and gullemots – can be observed. Despite propaganda that cameras are replacing harpoons, the area remains a prime hunting ground for Norway's still prevalent whaling industry. A few years ago, one of these tours actually witnessed a whale being shot and killed.
Arctic Whale Tours, in Andenes; tel: 76 13 43 00; www.arcticwhaletours.com.
Hvalsafari in Stø; tel: 76 11 56 00; www.whalesafari.com.

C hildren

With its wide open spaces, beaches within easy reach of the city centre and attractions on the Bygdoy peninsula, Oslo is a particularly family-friendly city. Here is a small selection of the many family attractions Norway has to offer:

BELOW: dog-sledging is one of Norway's winter attractions.

ABOVE: the spectacular Northern Lights.

In and around Oslo

International Museum of Children's Art
Lille Frøens vei 4; tel: 22 46 85 73; www.barnekunst.no; July–Aug Tue–Thur, Sun 11am–4pm, Sept–mid-Dec and mid-Jan–June Tue–Thur 9.30am–2pm, Sun 11am–4pm; charge. A unique museum exhibiting children's art from 150 countries.

Horse riding, minigolf and Minizoo
Ekeberg near Ekeberghallen, tel: 22 68 26 69 (summer only).

Puppet Theatre
Frognerveien 67 (next to Vigeland Park); tel: 22 34 86 00. High-quality performances for children aged 4 and above.

Tusenfryd Amusement Park
Ås, Østfold; tel: 64 97 66 99; www.tusenfryd.no. Attractions include: rollercoaster, waterpark, flume ride, carousel and magic carpet. Transport by the TusenFryd Bus from Oslo bus station, every half-hour. June–Aug (May and Sept Sat–Sun).

Youth Information in Oslo
Møllergata 3, Oslo; tel: 24 14 98 20; www.unginfo.oslo.no. Provides information on all subjects for young people. Mon–Fri 11am–5pm, July–Aug 9am–6pm, Thur from 11am.

Around Norway

The Troll Family Park
Near Lillehammer; tel: 61 27 55 30; www.hunderfossen.no. Main attractions are: river rafting, the fairytale castle, the world's largest troll, fairytale cave, racing-car track, high-wire forest course, raft ride and Wax Museum. Mid-June–late August.

Kongeparken
Near Stavanger; tel: 815 22 673; www.kongeparken.no. Over 40 attractions, including "life-sized" model of the Giant Gulliver (85 x 7.5 metres/279 x 25ft), riding tracks, bob track, farm, car track, Wild West City, birds and funfair. Mid-June–late August.

Telemark Sommarland
Bø in Telemark; tel: 35 06 16 00; www.sommarland.no. Norway's biggest water park with various wet and dry attractions, including many waterslides and Magasuget, a 26-metre (80ft) high water chute, Flow Rider, said to be the world's biggest surf wave, and a floating river. Plus live entertainment, pony rides, Wild West City and children's playground. Early June–mid-August.

Kristiansand Dyrepark
Tel: 38 04 97 00; www.dyreparken.no. Norway's largest wildlife park and most visited tourist attraction. The park has a wide range of other attractions: amusement park, waterpark, show and entertainment park. Open all year, times vary.

Climate

Oslo is one of the warmest places in Norway during winter; in January the average 24-hour high is −2°C (28°F) and the low is −7°C (19°F). Bergen is slightly warmer but wetter, and snow rarely lies for long. Up north, sub-zero temperatures reign for months and a good number of roads shut over winter due to long-term snow. February and March are the best skiing months. March, April and early May are the wet spring months, when roads are buckled due to thaws and refreezes; through this period the temperature slowly lifts from about 4°C (39°F) to 16°C (61°F).

Come summertime and the season of the Midnight Sun, Oslo enjoys average temperatures in the low to mid-20s°C (70s°F), while the sunlight-bathed north has a perfect hiking temperature, around 20°C (68°F). October is the time for autumn rains as temperatures dip below 10°C (50°F), then continue their slide towards zero. The first snow arrives mid-October.

What to Bring

You're in for a pleasant surprise if travelling to Norway in summer. As it is influenced by the Gulf Stream, it can get even warmer than some of its southern neighbours. In the south, temperatures above 25°C (77°F) are not unusual. The average temperature for the country as a whole in July, including the far north, is about 16°C (60°F), 22°C (71°F) in Oslo. Bring swimming gear, as the water in most fjords, except northern Norway, is 20°C (68°F) in midsummer.

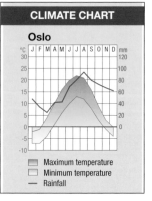

CLIMATE CHART

Oslo

- Maximum temperature
- Minimum temperature
- Rainfall

A first-aid kit is recommended for those who plan to make any trips to remoter parts. And be sure to include medicines for preventing and treating mosquito bites, as from midsummer into early autumn biting insects are rife, especially in Finnmark. If you plan to visit Bergen, pack an umbrella – it may be one of Norway's warmest cities, but it is also its wettest.

Culture

Music and Opera

In summer the arts take to the outdoors in Norway, and classical music and opera are no exception. For Oslo dates, pick up the *What's On in Oslo* guide. The very active Oslo Philharmonic, founded by Edvard Grieg, is conducted by Jukka-Pekka Saraste at the Konserthus, with frequent visits by acclaimed guest conductors and soloists. Den Norske Opera & Ballett (National Opera) stages big productions in its magnificent new waterfront location just east of Akershus.

Akershus Fortress and the Henie Onstad Art Centre (Høvikodden) are two other fine settings for summer concerts, and there are several outdoor jazz, folk, rock, and pop festivals from June to August *(see below)*.

Whether the performers are Norwegian or foreign, the season winter or summer, Norway has a rich and varied musical and operatic life.

Den Norske Opera & Ballett
Kirsten Flagstads pl. 1
Tel: 21 42 21 00
www.operaen.no
Oslo Konserthus
Munkedamsveien 14
Tel: 23 11 31 00
www.oslokonserthus.no

Festivals

Norwegians love a festival, and there are far too many to list them all (consult area guides for festival schedules local to your destination or visit www.norwayfestivals.com).
Here is a small selection:
Holmenkollen Ski Festival – ski-jumping competitions, cross-country races and other events (March).
Sami Easter Festival – a seven-day celebration of Sami culture, from films and concerts to reindeer racing (Easter).
Bergen International Festival – a 15-day arts festival in Norway's culture capital, with a focus on Grieg and Ibsen (May/June).
Norwegian Wood Festival – Norway's top rock festival brings big-

name international artists to the stage, Oslo (June).
Molde International Jazz Festival – attracts some of the best jazz artists in the world (July).

National Day (17 May) and Midsummer's Eve (around 21 June, the longest day) are both celebrated throughout the country with parades, music, feasting and bonfires.

Theatre and Dance

Theatre is booming in Norway, but performances are in Norwegian. Some plays are held in English at Oslo's National Theatre during the International Ibsen Festival and Contemporary Stage Festival, which are held in alternate years (late Aug–early Sept).

Dance has also come into its own. Classical ballet is performed at the Oslo Opera House *(see above)*. Traditional folk dances can be seen in many towns on National Day (17 May).

National Theatret Oslo
Stortingsgate 15
Tel: 22 00 14 73
www.nationaltheatret.no

Cinema

The Norwegians love films, hence the vast number of cinemas; Oslo has around 40 screens, including the impressive wide-screen cinema at the Colosseum in Frogner. First-run and repertory films are always shown in the original language, with Norwegian subtitles. Kiosks, newspapers and local city guides have listings. Booking tickets is recommended for Fridays and Saturdays.

Customs Regulations

The following can be brought into Norway by visitors:
Money Notes and coins (Norwegian and foreign) up to NOK25,000 or equivalent. If you intend to import more, you must fill in a form (available at all entry and exit points) for the Customs Office.
Alcohol Permitted imports for people aged 20 and over include 1 litre of spirits (up to 60 percent vol.) plus 1 litre of fortified wine (up to 22 percent vol.) or 3 litres of wine (if no spirits) and 2 litres of beer, or 5 litres of beer.
Tobacco European residents over the age of 18 may bring 200 cigarettes or 250g of other tobacco goods.
Sweets 1kg (2¼ pounds) duty-free chocolate and sweets.
Meat and dairy products Meat, meat products, cheese and foodstuffs except dog and cat food, totalling 10kg (22 pounds) altogether from EEA

(European Economic Area) countries. From countries outside the EEA, it is prohibited to bring meat, meat products, milk and milk products with you in your luggage.
Sundries Other goods (excluding articles for personal use) may be brought in duty-free up to a value of NOK6,000.
Prohibited goods Narcotics, medicines (except for personal use), poisons, firearms, ammunition and explosives. Note: the mild narcotic leaf khat is illegal in Norway.
Agricultural produce This comes under strict surveillance. If it concerns you, get specific details beforehand.

D isabled Travellers

Visitors in need of assistance should contact Norges handikapforbund, Schweigaards gate 12, 0134 Oslo; tel: 24 10 24 00; www.nhf.no.

Hotel listings in accommodation guides have symbols designating disabled access and toilets. Under the "Oslo for all" section of the VisitOslo website (www.visitoslo.com), wheelchair users and visitors with hearing or visual impairments can search for accommodation, restaurants and attractions that are tailored to accommodate their needs.

The Euro Terra Nova AS, at Prinsensgate 3B, 0152 Oslo, offers brochures on coach tours around Norway especially for wheelchair users. They also provide hotel bookings and hire cars; tel: 22 94 13 50; www.euroterranova.no. Guidebooks for Nordland county (north Norway) can be ordered free of charge from Nordland Reiseliv.

BELOW: a night out at the theatre.

Above: enjoying the water.

The Society for Accessible Travel and Hospitality (SATH) provides information and advice for travellers with disabilities. Their website is: www.sath.org.

E lectricity

220 volts AC, 50 cycles. Plugs have two small round pins, so you may need an adaptor for appliances you bring with you.

Embassies

In Oslo

Canada
Wergelandsveien 7
Tel: 22 99 53 00
www.canada.no
UK
Thomas Heftyes gate 8
Tel: 23 13 27 00
www.britain.no
Honorary Consul in Bergen: Carl Konows gate 34, 5161 Laksevag
Tel: 55 36 78 10
US
Henrik Ibsens gate 48
Tel: 21 30 85 40
www.usa.no

Emergencies

Fire 110
Police 112 (911 from mobile phones)
Ambulance 113
Emergency at sea 120
Medical problems for emergency medical treatment in Oslo (legevakt)
Tel: 22 93 22 93

G ay and Lesbian Travellers

In common with the rest of Scandinavia, Norway has a very relaxed attitude to homosexuality. There is very little open hostility to gays and lesbians in general society

and, partly as a result, the commercial gay scene is relatively small. Tourist offices *(see page 384)* carry details of the main places and events, including the Oslo Gay Pride, known as "Skeive Dager" in Norwegian.

H ealth and Medical Care

There are no major health hazards in Norway. No vaccinations are necessary to enter Norway and the tap water is (generally) good. A degree of common sense is required when travelling in remote areas, especially during the winter. When hiking/skiing in the mountains, always let someone know of your travel intentions, and use guides wherever possible.

Norway has reciprocal treatment agreements with the UK and many other European countries; your own National Insurance should cover you to receive free treatment at public hospitals. EU citizens should obtain the relevant documentation to entitle them to this (for British citizens an EHIC, European Health Insurance Card, is available from post offices or online at www.ehic.org.uk). People from countries without such agreements, and those without an EHIC card, will have to pay a small fee. If you are concerned whether you need extra cover, check in your own country before you go. The EHIC card only covers the basics and does not include the cost of medicine, so it is advisable to take out additional medical insurance. You will need to take out extra cover if you are going skiing or considering any other possibly dangerous sports.

Medical Services

If you are ill or have an accident while you are in Norway and you need to see a doctor, visit the Accident and Emergency (Legevakt) department of the hospital. A full list of doctors can be

found in the Yellow Pages, or ask the hotel for an English-speaking doctor.
Oslo Emergency Medical Centre (Oslo Legevakt)
Storgate 40, Oslo
Tel: 22 93 22 93
Bergen Emergency Hospital (Bergen Legevakt)
Strømskaien 19, Bergen
Tel: 55 56 87 60

Pharmacies

For minor problems, head for a pharmacy, or Apotek *(for opening hours, see page 382)*. Most larger cities have all-night or late-night pharmacies *(see below)*. In other cities enquire at your hotel, or try the emergency number in the phone book under Legevakt (doctor on duty). Where there is a rota of 24-hour pharmacies in a city, a list will usually be posted on the door of each one.
Oslo
Jernbanetorgets Apotek, across from Central Station, Jernbanetorget 4B. Tel: 23 35 81 00. 24 hours.
Bergen
Vitus Apotek Nordstjernen, at Storsenter, Strøm gate 8.
Tel: 55 21 83 84. Mon–Sat 8am–11pm, Sun 10am–11pm.
Stavanger
Loeveapoteket, Olav V's gt 11. Tel: 51 91 08 80. Daily until 11pm.
Trondheim
St Olav Vakt-apotek, Beddingen 4. Tel: 73 88 37 37. Mon–Sat 8.30am–midnight, Sun 10am–midnight.

Dental Services

Emergency dental treatment in Oslo and Bergen, outside regular dentists' office hours, is available from:

Oslo Kommunale Tannlegevakt, Schweigaards gate 6c, 3rd floor (near the Central Railway Station).
Tel: 22 67 30 00. Mon–Fri 8am–11pm, Sat–Sun and holidays 11am–2pm, 8–11pm.
Bergen Tannlegevakt, Vestre Strømkai 19; Tel: 55 56 87 17. Mon–Fri 6–8.30pm, Sat–Sun 3.30–8.30pm.

I nternet

Besides most hotels, free internet access is available at public libraries in Norway. Screen time is limited, and you may need to book a slot in advance. The Oslo Tourist Information Service publishes a list of internet cafés in the capital. These include:
@rctic Internet, Oslo Central Station. Tel: 22 17 19 40. Daily 9am–11pm.
Akers Mic Nettcafe, Akersgata 39,

tel: 22 41 21 90 & **Underworld** (same address), tel: 22 33 38 98.
Qba, Olaf Ryes Plass 4. Tel: 22 35 24 60. Mon–Fri 8am–1am, Sat–Sun 11am–1am.

L anguage

Introduction

Germanic in origin, Norwegian is one of the three Scandinavian languages, and is closely related to Danish and Swedish. There are two official forms of Norwegian, *bokmål* and *nynorsk*. The former reflects Norway's 400 years of Danish domination, while *nynorsk* is built on native Norwegian dialects. The Sami population in north Norway speak a version of Samic, a Uralic language. English is widely understood.

Getting By

Yes *Ja*
No *Nei*
Good morning *God morgen*
Good afternoon *God eftermiddag*
Good evening *God kveld*
Today *I dag*
Tomorrow *I morgen*
Yesterday *I går*
Hello *Hei*
How do you do? *Står det til?*
Goodbye *Adjø/Ha det bra/Hadet*
Thank you *Takk*
How do I get to...? *Hvordan kommer jeg til...?*
Where is...? *Hvor er...?*
What time is it? *Hvor mye er klokken?*
It is (The time is...) *Den er (Klokken er...)*
When? *Når*
Where? *Hvor?*
Could I have your name please? *Hva er navnet?*
My name is... *Mitt navn er...*
Do you have English newspapers? *Har du engelske aviser?*
Do you speak English? *Snakker du engelsk?*
I only speak English *Jeg snakker bare engelsk*
May I help you? *Kan jeg hjelpe deg?*
I do not understand *Jeg forstår ikke*
I do not know *Jeg vet ikke*
It has disappeared *Den har forsvunnet*
aircraft *flymaskin*
car *bil*
train *tog*
ticket *billet*
single/return *en vei/tur-retur*
To rent *Leie*
Free *Ledig*
Room to rent *Rom til leie*
chalet *hytte*
Can we camp here? *Kan vi campe her?*
No camping *Camping forbudt*

Signs and Sights

Right *Høyre*
To the right *Til høyre*
Left *Venstre*
To the left *Til venstre*
Straight on *Rett frem*
phrasebook *parlør*
dictionary *ordbok*
money *penger*
chemist *apotek*
hospital *sykehus*
doctor *lege*
police station *politistasjion*
parking *parkering*
department store *hus/stormagasin*
toilet *toalett/WC*
Gentlemen *Herrer*
Ladies *Damer*
Vacant *Ledig*
Engaged *Opptatt*
Entrance *Inngang*
Exit *Utgang*
No entry *Ingen adgang*
Open *Åpent*
Closed *Stengt*
Push *Skyv*
Pull *Trekk*
No smoking *Røyking forbudt*

Eating Out

breakfast *frokost*
lunch *lunsj*
dinner *middag*
Can I order please? *Kan jeg få bestille?*
Could I have the bill please? *Kan jeg få regningen?*
eat *spise*
drink *drikke*
Cheers! *Skål!*
hot *varm*
cold *kald*

Shopping

grocery store (in countryside) *landhandel*
shop *butikk*
food *mat/kost*
to buy *kjøpe*
sauna *badstue*
off licence/liquor store *vinmonopol*
How much is this? *Hvor mye koster det?*
It costs *Det koster...*
clothes *klær*
overcoat *frakk*
jacket *jakke*
suit *dress*
shoes *sko*
skirt *skjørt*
blouse *bluse*
jersey *genser*

Days of the Week

Sunday *søndag*
Monday *mondag*
Tuesday *tirsdag*
Wednesday *onsdag*
Thursday *torsdag*
Friday *fredag*
Saturday *lørdag*

Numbers

1 *en*
2 *to*
3 *tre*
4 *fire*
5 *fem*
6 *seks*
7 *sju*
8 *åtte*
9 *ni*
10 *ti*
11 *elleve*
12 *tolv*
13 *tretten*
14 *fjorten*
15 *femten*
16 *seksten*
17 *sytten*
18 *åtten*
19 *nitten*
20 *tjue*
40 *forti*
60 *seksti*
80 *åtti*
100 *hundre*
200 *to hundre*
1,000 *tusen*

M edia

Newspapers

Most larger kiosks (like the Narvesen chain) and some bookshops sell English-language newspapers. Norwegian news in English is found on the website of Norway's main newspaper Aftenposten: www. aftenposten.no.

BELOW: celebrating National Day.

Deichmanske Bibliotek, the main public library, is at Arne Garborgs plass 4 in Oslo; you'll find a selection of international papers and periodicals in its reading rooms, as well as free internet access. Mon–Fri 10am–7pm, Sat 10am–4pm.

Bookshops

There are several bookshops in Oslo with English-language sections, including:
Tronsmo
Kristian Augusts gate 19
Tel: 22 99 03 99
A classic indie shop by the university with a great selection of fiction, politics, gay and lesbian literature, and comics.
Litteraturhuset
Wergelandsveien 29
Tel: 22 95 55 30
Plus **Tanum** and **Norli** are quality book chains with many locations.

Radio

On Sundays, Radio Norway (93 FM) broadcasts the news from Norway in English, daily at 5pm. During the winter months BBC radios 1, 2, 3 and 4 can sometimes be received on AM, but reception is often distorted. For local frequencies of the BBC World Service, enquire at the nearest tourist office.

Television

The Norwegian government is the leading broadcaster in Norway which owns and operates the NRK stations. Cable TV is common here and allows you to pick up a variety of channels, including BBC Prime, BBC World, CNN, Swedish TV1 and TV2, Discovery, MTV, French TV5, Eurosport, TV3 and so on, depending on the distributor. Most hotels have pay channels in addition to the above. English films on Norwegian television are subtitled, not dubbed.

Money

The Norwegian krone (NOK) is divided into 100 øre. Notes come in denominations of NOK50, 100, 200, 500 and 1,000, and coins are 50 øre and NOK1, 5, 10 and 20.

You can change currency at post offices, the Oslo S train station, international airports, some hotels and commercial banks. The forex offices have good rates and no fees. It is always useful to carry a certain amount of cash with you in case of emergency.

Credit Cards

Use of credit cards is widespread in Norway, with Eurocard, Visa,

ABOVE: colourful glassware for sale.

MasterCard and American Express the most common. Check with your own credit card company about acceptability and other services.

In most banks you can generally get cash on a debit card or a Visa or MasterCard.

Tipping

Tipping is quite straightforward in Norway. Hotels include a service charge and tipping is generally not expected. Restaurants usually have the service charge included, in which case it's your choice to add anything (5–10 percent is customary). The same applies to taxis. Table service in bars (particularly outdoor tables) requires tipping. With hairdressers a tip isn't quite as customary, but again 5–10 percent would be appropriate. Cloakrooms usually have a fixed fee of about NOK5–10; if not, leave a few krone for the attendant.

Nightlife

Oslo is now vying with Stockholm and Copenhagen to be Scandinavia's nightlife capital. For up-to-date venue listings check the official *Oslo Guide* provided free by Oslo Promotion at www.visitoslo.com. In Bergen, Stavanger, Trondheim and Tromsø nightlife exists to a much lesser extent. But you can guarantee that most large hotels have nightclubs and bars. In small towns, you may be out of luck altogether.

International rock, folk and jazz musicians often include Oslo on European tours.

There are only two things you need to be warned about before a night out: the high cost of drinking, and age restrictions: some clubs have minimum

ages as high as 26 (although 21 and 23 are more common).

Opening Hours

Offices 8 or 9am–4pm; lunch is taken early, 11.30am–12.30pm, or noon–2pm at a restaurant.
Shops Mon–Fri 9am–5pm, Thur until 8pm, Sat from 9am until 1, or until 3pm.
Shopping centres 10am–9pm on weekdays, 9am–6pm on Sat.
Banks Mon–Wed and Fri 8.30am–3.30pm, summer until 3pm, Thur until 5pm.
Pharmacies Mon–Fri 9am–5pm, Saturday mornings and on a rota basis in larger cities.

Postal Services

Post offices in Oslo open Mon–Fri 9am–5pm and Sat 9am–3pm.

Letters and postcards cost the same price to send to the UK and Continental Europe, slightly more to send outside Europe. Post takes 2–3 days to Europe and 7–10 days to North America.

Public Holidays

1 January New Year's Day
March/April Easter: Thursday to Monday inclusive
1 May Labour Day
17 May National Independence Day
May/June Ascension Day
May/June Whit Monday
25 December Christmas Day
26 December 2nd Christmas Day

Religious Services

The Lutheran Church is Norway's state Church, with around 83 percent of the population registered as Lutherans. Oslo has many Lutheran places of worship, including the American Lutheran Church (Fritzners gate 15; tel: 22 44 35 84).

Services are held in English at the American Lutheran church and the Anglican/Episcopalian church (St Edmund's, Møllergate 30; tel: 22 69 22 14).

The Oslo Cathedral (Protestant), Oslo Cathedral (Domkirke Karl Johans gate 11; tel: 23 62 90 1031; daily 10am–4pm); reopened in 2010 after being closed for renovations; concerts are often held Wednesdays.

Shopping

In Oslo, Karl Johansgate, Grensen and Bogstadveien are all major shopping streets. With the exception of Oslo, most Norwegian towns are so compact that your best bet is to window-shop and go into the places that look most appealing.

Look out for *lavpris* (low-price) shops offering discounts. The first Saturday of each month is "Super Saturday", when shops in Oslo open longer and offer special discounts.

What to Buy

Popular souvenirs include knitted jumpers, cardigans, gloves and mittens, pewter, silver jewellery and cutlery, hand-painted wooden objects (like bowls with rose designs), trolls and fjord horses carved out of wood, goat and reindeer skin, enamel jewellery, woven wall designs, furs, handicrafts, glassware and pottery – to name just a few *(see Tax-Free Shopping, below, on how to reclaim tax).*

Department Stores

The major department stores are **Glasmagasinet** and **Steen & Strøm**, both of which have a good selection of most of the above items. **House of Oslo** (Ruseløkkveien 26) specialises in design.

Art

Anyone interested in buying Norwegian art will have ample prospects – from south to north, Norway abounds in galleries, and museum shops are often a good source for interesting items. The reputed Kaare Berntsen is the largest dealer and art gallery in Northern Europe, for modern works as well as fine Norwegian classics, including Munch.

Kaare Berntsen
Munkedamsveien 62a
Tel: 22 99 10 10
www.kaare-berntsen.com

Tax-Free Shopping

Norway is the only Scandinavian country in which visitors from the British Isles can claim VAT refunds. Other residents outside Scandinavia will get the Norwegian Value Added Tax (MOMS) refunded at the airport when leaving the country. Pick up a brochure at the tourist information office, or contact Global Refund Norge; tel: 67 15 60 10; www.global refund.no for details.

In the shop, you pay in full (the amount must be over NOK315 for ordinary goods and NOK285 for food items) and collect a "cheque" for the amount. The tax portion is refunded on the way out of the country from special tax-free representatives (not

customs officers) at airports, ports and frontiers.

T elephones

International dialling code: +47
When calling from Norway to foreign countries, always dial 00 first. Cheapest calling times are outside business hours: 5pm–8am. Extra-cheap international calling cards, such as Eurocity, can be purchased online and from a variety of kiosks (corner shops) in most major towns.

Calls abroad can be made from hotels – with a hefty surcharge – or from phone booths or the main telegraph office at Kongensgate 21 (entrance Prinsensgate), Oslo. You can also send faxes from this office.

Norwegian payphones take 1, 5, 10 and 20 kroner pieces. Phonecards, which can be used in the green phone booths, can be bought in Narvesen kiosks and at post offices. Credit cards are accepted in card phones.

Telephone directories have a page

of instructions in English in the index. When looking up names, remember the vowels æ, ø, and å come at the end of the alphabet, in that order.

Some US phone companies have their own international access numbers, to allow US citizens cheaper calls, as follows:
AT&T 800-19 011
Sprint 800-19 877
WorldPhone 800-19 912

Time Zone

Central European Time, 1 hour ahead of Greenwich Mean Time, 6 hours ahead of Eastern Standard Time. The clock is set forward an hour to summer time at the end of March, and back an hour at the end of September.

Tourist Information

Before You Go

The Norwegian tourist board can provide helpful information and

Specialist Tour Operators in the UK

Activity Holidays

Inntravel
Whitewell Grange, Nr Castle Howard, York YO60 7JU
Tel: 01653 617 949
www.inntravel.co.uk
Scantours
73 Mornington St, London NW1 7QE
Tel: 020 7554 3530
www.hotfrog.co.uk

Arctic Voyages/Dog-sledging/ Whale-Watching

Arctic Experience and Discover the World
8 Bolters Lane, Banstead, Surrey SM7 2AR
Tel: 01737 218 800
www.arctic-experience.co.uk
Arcturus Expeditions
Ninestone, South Zeal, Devon EX20 2PZ
Tel: 01837 840 640
www.arcturusexpeditions.co.uk

Christmas Holidays

Page and Moy
Compass House, Rockingham Road, Market Harborough, Leicestershire LE16 7QD
Tel: 0844 567 6633
www.pageandmoy.com

Norway Specialists

Norsc Holidays
The Court, The Street, Charmouth DT6 6PE

Tel: 01297 560 033
www.norsc.co.uk
Taber Holidays
PO Box 176, Tofts House, Tofts Road, Cleckheaton, West Yorkshire BD19 3WX
Tel: 01274 875 199
www.taberhols.co.uk

Skiing/Walking

Crystal Holidays
King's Place, 12–42 Wood Street, Kingston, Surrey KT1 1JY
Tel: 0871 231 5655
www.crystalholidays.co.uk
Exodus Travel
Grange Mills, Weir Road, London SW12 ONE
Tel: 0845 863 9600
www.exodus.co.uk

Tours

Explore Worldwide
55 Victoria Road, Farnborough, Hampshire GU14 7PA
Tel: 0845 013 1537
www.explore.co.uk
ScanMeridian (Nordic Experience)
39 Crouch Street, Colchester, Essex CO3 3EN
Tel: 01206 708 888
www.nordicexperience.co.uk
Great Rail Journeys
Saviour House, 9 St Saviourgate, York YO1 8NL
Tel: 01904 521 936
www.greatrail.com

brochures before you travel, which can be posted or downloaded from the VisitNorway website:

UK
Innovation Norway
Charles House, 5–11 Lower Regent Street, London SW1Y 4LR
(no walk-in service)
Tel: 020 7389 8800
Email: london@invanor.no
www.visitnorway.com
USA/Canada
Innovation Norway
655 Third Avenue, Suite 1810, New York NY 10017-9111
Tel: 212-885 9700
Email: newyork@innovationnorway.no
www.visitnorway.com

Tourist Offices in Norway

There are about 350 local tourist offices around Norway, as well as 18 regional tourist offices. For general information, including for hotel bookings in Oslo, contact:
The Tourist Information Centre
Fridtjof Nansens Plass 5 (entrance from Roald Amundsens Gate), Oslo
Tel: 24 14 77 00
Email: info@visitoslo.com
www.visitoslo.com

Regional Information
Regional tourist offices are experts in the county they represent. They are not usually open to personal callers, with the exception of the VisitOslo offices, but will supply advice and information in writing or over the phone.

East Norway
Fjell og Fjord Ferie
Gamlevegen 6, N-3550 Gol
Tel: 32 02 99 26
www.eventyrveien.no
Hedmark Reiseliv BA
Grønne Gate 11, N-2317 Hamar
Tel: 62 55 33 20
www.hedmark.com

South Norway
Arendal Turist Kontor
Sam Eydes Plass, Postboks 780 Stoa, 4809 Arendal
Tel: 37 00 55 44
Destinasjon Sørlandet
Rädhus Gate 6, N-4612 Kristiansand
Tel: 38 12 13 14
www.visitsorlandet.com
Telemarkreiser
Nedre Hjelle Gate 18, N-3724 Skien
Tel: 35 90 00 20
www.visittelemark.com

Fjord Norway
Bergen
Slotts Gate 3, 3rd floor,
N-5835 Bergen

ABOVE: farmhouses look out onto Geirangerfjord.

Tel: 55 55 20 00
www.visitbergen.com
Fjord Norge AS
Lodin Leppsgt 2B, N-5003 Bergen
Tel: 55 30 26 40
www.fjordnorway.com
Hordaland Reiseliv
PO Box 416 Marken, N-5828 Bergen
Tel: 55 31 66 00
www.visithordaland.no
Møre og Romsdal Reiselivsråd
Fylkeshuset, N-6404 Molde
Tel: 71 24 50 80
www.visitmr.com
Rogaland Reiseliv
PO Box 130, N-4001 Stavanger
Tel: 51 51 67 88
www.rogfk.no
Sogn and Fjordane Tourist Board
PO Box 370, N-6782 Stryn
Tel: 57 87 40 40
www.sfr.no

Central Norway
Trøndelag Reiseliv AS
PO Box 65, N-7004 Trondheim

Fjord Tours

Whether you are planning a short break or a long holiday, many companies offer tours of the fjord, coastal and mountain scenery. Two of the main ones are:
Fjord Tours
Strømst 4
5015 Bergen
Tel: +47 81 56 82 22
www.fjord-tours.com
Fjord Travel Norway
Østre Nesttunvei 4–6
5221 Nesttun, Bergen
Tel: +47 55 13 13 10
www.fjordtravel.no

Tel: 73 84 24 50
www.trondelag.com
Northern Norway
Finnmark Tourist Board
Kunnskapsparken, NO-9509 Alta
Tel: 78 44 90 60
www.finnmark.com
Nordland Reiseliv AS
PO Box 434, N-8001 Bodø
Tel: 75 54 52 00
www.visitnordland.no
Svalbard Reiseliv
N-9171 Longyearbyen
Tel: 79 02 55 50
www.svalbard.net
Troms Reiseliv
Storgata 17, N-9300 Finnsnes
Tel: 77 85 07 30
www.visittroms.no

Transport

Getting There

By Air
Norway is exceptionally well served by domestic airlines, with about 50 airports and airfields throughout the country. The main international airport is **Oslo airport, Gardermoen**, 45km (28 miles) northeast of Oslo. The main domestic airlines are SAS, Widerøe and Norwegian Air Shuttle. Each offers discount travel passes.

Scandinavian Air Systems (SAS) merged with local Norwegian carrier Braathens. SASBraathens (tel: 05400; www.scandinavian.net) offers daily flights from London Heathrow to Oslo, Bergen and Stavanger. There are also daily flights to Oslo Gardermoen and Oslo Torp from Aberdeen, Belfast, Birmingham, Dublin, Edinburgh, Glasgow, Manchester and Newcastle.

SAS also offers special cheap tickets for flights within Norway, such as Oslo to Bergen for around NOK400 one way.

British Airways (tel: 0844 493 0787 from the UK; www.britishairways.com) runs around six flights daily from London (Heathrow) to Oslo.

Wideroe (tel: 81 52 20 14 or 81 00 12 00; www.wideroe.no) flies to 41 destinations within Norway and has flights to London Heathrow and City, Manchester, Aberdeen, Edinburgh, Newcastle, Copenhagen, Gothenburg and Stockholm. It is based at Oslo Torp airport in Sandefjord, 130km (80 miles) south of Oslo.

Norwegian Air Shuttle (tel: 47 214 90015 (outside of Norway); 815 21 815 (within Norway); www.norwegian.no) operates on a daily basis from eight major airports in Norway, in addition to daily flights from Oslo, Bergen and Trondheim to London Gatwick, Southern Europe and regional routes in northern Norway.

Ryanair operates bargain flights from London Gatwick, Luton or Stansted, Glasgow, Dublin, Newcastle and Liverpool to Oslo Ryge airport at Moss or Oslo Torp airport at Sandefjord. Buses transport visitors into Oslo. For details tel: 0871 246 0000 or visit www.ryanair.com.

For budget travel to Norway it may be easier to book online. Try these booking agents:

www.cheapflights.com offers online bookings from the US.

www.lastminute.com has flights from the UK to Norway.

www.priceline.com allows you to pick your own flights and times or name your own price. Price reductions of up to 30 percent on fares. US only.

www.opodo.co.uk. A fast search engine with instant access to cheap flights from over 400 airlines around the world, as well as accommodation, car hire and holidays.

By Sea

There is currently no ferry service between the UK and Norway. Color Line is the main ferry service linking Oslo to the Continent, with big cruise ferries sailing to Kiel in Germany, and services to the northern tip of Denmark (Hirtshals) from Kristiansand and Larvik. Color Line, PO Box 1422, Vika; N-0115 Oslo; tel: 22 94 42 00; www.colorline.com.

By Rail

Numerous rail services link Norway with the rest of Scandinavia and Europe. From mainland Europe, express trains operate to Copenhagen, where inter-Scandinavian trains connect to Oslo.

There are frequent connections from Copenhagen, Stockholm and Götenborg to Oslo. You can also get to northern Norway from Stockholm, with Trondheim and Narvik the principal destinations. International arrivals and departures are located at Sentralstasjon (Oslo-S).

Getting Around

There is an excellent network of domestic transport services – a necessity in a country so large and often impassable by land. You may have to use more than one means (for example, train and bus or plane and bus), but if you're travelling beyond Oslo you'll find these services indispensable.

Although covering great distances can be expensive, Norway offers transport bargains through special tourist cards like the Fjord Pass, the Bonus Pass (which covers the whole of Scandinavia), plus some of the pan-European programmes like InterRail and Eurail. Within larger cities, tourist passes cover urban transport and give free entry to many museums.

On Arrival

Gardermoen airport is 45km (28 miles) north of Oslo. It is served by the Airport Express Train/Flytoget to Oslo S (the Central Station) every 10–20 minutes and takes 22 minutes. Details at www.flytoget.no; tel: 815 00 777. For about half the price, regional and local trains also connect Oslo and the airport and take about 37 minutes; there is normally a train at least every hour. Note that rail passes are not valid on the Airport Express. See also www.nsb.no.

The airport bus departs six times an hour to and from the Radisson Blu Scandinavia Hotel via Oslo Bustermingl/Clarion Royal Christiania Hotel, Helsfyr and Furuset. It takes 45 minutes. The regular bus No. 344 from the Radisson Blu Scandinavia Hotel via Oslo S departs three times an hour and takes 50 minutes. Buses 332 and 355 also make the journey. Tel: 177 or 22 80 49 71.

The Flybusseksspressen is another option, departing from 120 places around Oslo. Tel: 815 44 444; www.flybussen.no.

If you arrive from London Stansted at **Torp airport** at Sandefjord on the southwest side of the fjord, buses and trains will take up to 2½ hours to reach the capital, depending on traffic conditions.

Bergen Flesland airport is 19km (12 miles) south of the city. The airport bus goes to the Radisson Blu Royal at

Bryggen, via Radisson Blu Hotel Norge and the bus station. There are around three buses per hour and the journey takes between 35 and 45 minutes, depending on traffic. Tel: 177.

A taxi to/from the city is around NOK630 before 5pm, when it increases to around NOK735. Tel: 23 23 23 23.

By Train

Most of **Norwegian State Railways (NSB)** lines run through tourist country, presenting continuous panoramas of unspoilt scenic beauty. The Oslo–Bergen line is hailed as one of the world's most spectacular for its scenery.

There are fast train connections from Oslo to other cities in Norway, with sleeper coaches on all of the overnight expresses. Seat reservations are required on all night and long-distance day trains, as well as on express and high-speed services.

Rail passes make travelling in Norway cheaper. The Norwegian State Railway (NSB) is part of the InterRail, EuroDomino, Eurailpass and Eurail Youthpass system, which offers various discount tickets (including to students). If you live in Europe, the InterRail Norway Pass gives 3, 4, 6 or 8 days' unlimited 1st- or 2nd-class travel within a one-month period. It also offers discounts on some ferry services. See www.interrailnet.com for details. If you live outside Europe, the Eurail Scandinavia Pass entitles you to unlimited second-class travel across Scandinavia, for 4, 5, 6, 8 or 10 days within a two-month period. Buy the pass before you travel from www.scandinavianrail.com.

Norwegian State Railways
NSB Reisesenter, Prinsens Gate 7–9, N-0048 Oslo
Tel: 81 50 08 88
www.nsb.no
NSB provides train information and also operates as a travel bureau across Norway. For information about

Transport Information

For tickets, routes, times and all other queries about public transport, information and booking service, visit the Trafikanten Service Center, by the Oslo Sentralstasjon (at the bottom of the glass tower at the front of the station). Mon–Fri 7am–8pm, Sat–Sun 8am–6pm; Tel: 815 30 555 or 815 001 76.

For information about local trains and transport, including ferries, when in Norway call, 177 8am–11pm.

Norway in a Nutshell

One of the most pleasurable ways of seeing western Norway is to take a **Norway in a Nutshell** journey *(see page 215)*. The trip uses various forms of public transport and takes you from Myrdal to Flåm, Gudvangen and Voss through some of the country's most beautiful scenery. A selection of packages is on offer. Tel: 81 56 82 22; www.norwaynutshell.com.

The railway line from Myrdal to Flåm is a masterpiece of engineering. When you have made the 850-metre (2,800ft) descent you are at the head of one of the longest fjords in the world, Sognefjord, and on the brink of another scenic high.

The trips can be made in either direction and from any of the stations between Oslo and Bergen. **Norway in a Nutshell round trip:** train from Oslo to Myrdal/Flåm, boat to Gudvangen, bus to Voss, train to Oslo.
Norway in a Nutshell one way: train from Oslo to Myrdal/Flåm, boat to Gudvangen, bus to Voss, train to Bergen.

Tickets are sold at the railway stations in Oslo and Bergen or from travel agencies. See www.norway nutshell.com for more details.

old) pay a child's fare. The steamers take cars, and should be booked well in advance. Either contact your local travel agent or:
Hurtigruten
Tel: 81 03 00 00
www.hurtigruten.com
Kystopplevelser (Coastal Experiences)
Tel: 75 54 17 10
www.kystopplevelser.no
Two days in Geirangerfjord. Fly to Ålesund, sail to Geiranger, stay overnight and then return to Oslo. Prices from NOK3,200.

Getting around in Oslo

Public Transport
Buses and Trams
Oslo's bus and tram system is comprehensive and punctual; there are detailed timetables at every stop. Trafikanten (177; www.trafikanten.no) can suggest bus or tram routes to get you where you wish to go. There are night buses on some routes and very early morning buses (starting at 4am), so that public transport is available virtually around the clock. Bergen and Trondheim also have tram systems.

Underground
Oslo's underground is called the T-bane (see map on inside back cover) and is simple to use. There are six lines that converge under the centre of Oslo. A circle line linking the station of Storo with Carl Berners plass was completed in 2006. You can catch any train to any of the far-flung suburbs from any of the stations between Tøyen and Majorstuen. Station entrances are marked with a "T". Trafikanten has route maps. The most scenic route is T-bane 1 up to

---

timetables, ticket prices and bookings, contact Trafikanten, Jernbanetorvet 1, by Oslo S, tel: 81 50 01 76 or 177.

By Road
Most major shipping lines to Norway allow passengers to bring cars. But coming by car increases sea travel costs, and petrol is expensive in Norway.
Norges Automobil Forbund
(NAF or Norwegian Automobile Association)
Østensjøveien 14, 0609 Oslo
In Norway tel: 08 505
From abroad tel: +47 926 08505
www.naf.no
Kongelig Norsk Automobilklub
(KNA or Royal Norwegian Automobile Club)
Cort Adelers Gate 16, 0201 Oslo
Tel: 21 60 49 00
Emergency tel: 800 31 660 (members only)

By Bus
Where the rail network stops, the bus goes further: you can get to practically anywhere you want by bus on an ever-growing number of bus lines. Time Express is a popular one (see www. nettbuss.no). Usually it is not necessary to book in advance; just pay the driver on boarding. nor-way Bussekspress (bus pass) guarantees a seat for all passengers. Children up to the age of 4 travel free, while 4 to 16 years pay 75 percent of the adult price.
nor-way Bussekspress AS, Karl Johans Gate 2, N-0154 Oslo; tel: 81 54 44 44; www.nor-way.no.

Water Transport
Ferries
Ferries are an invaluable means of transport that allow short cuts across fjords to eliminate long road journeys; in built-up areas they are crucial to

commuters, like the Horten-Moss ferry across Oslofjord between Vestfold and Østfold. Ferries to the fjord islands around Oslo leave from the Vippetangen quay near Akershus Castle.

The following company operates the ferries which run between the centre of Oslo and the Bygdøy peninsula:
Bygdøfærgene Skibs
Rådhusbrygge 3, Oslo
Tel: 23 35 68 90
www.boatsightseeing.com

Long-Distance Ships
Hurtigruten, the Norwegian Coastal Express service, is a vital means of water transport for Norwegians, but also a superb way for visitors to see Norway's dramatic coast. In summer, boats leave daily, travelling between Bergen and Kirkenes in 11 days and putting in at 34 ports.
Children (between 4 and 15 years

BELOW: going by boat is the best way to travel.

ABOVE: the Lærdal tunnel, the longest in the world, links Oslo with Bergen.

Frognerseteren. From there enjoy panoramic views back down to Oslo.

Taxis

Taxis are widely available, even in many suburban and rural areas, so you need never risk drink-driving (for which penalties are severe).

No matter where you are in Oslo, telephone 023 23 and your call will be transferred to the nearest taxi rank. Minibuses and taxis (for up to 16 people) can also be booked on tel: 22 38 80 70. Otherwise, you can take a taxi from one of the many taxi ranks scattered around the city or simply hail one.

In Oslo, taxis are more expensive at night or if ordered by phone. At night there are two things to watch out for: when everyone leaves the bars and restaurants late, long queues build up

The Oslo Pass

The **Oslo Pass**, issued for 24, 48 or 72 hours, with half-price for children, is your ticket to unlimited public transport (including city ferries) and free entry to 33 museums and attractions. If you want a card for travel only, there are all kinds of passes available, including a Dagskortet (valid for 24 hours) and Flexikort (eight rides at a discount), plus passes appropriate for longer stays.

The Oslo Pass may be purchased at the Central Railway Station (Oslo S), Trafikanten, Tourist Office, as well as all Narvesen kiosks and hotels, camp sites and tourist offices.

Other cities offer similar tourist travel cards: for example, the **Bergen Card**, a 24-hour or 48-hour pass available from tourist information offices, the railway station, hotels, campsites and the Hurtigruten terminal.

at taxi ranks. This can be extremely uncomfortable in the winter if you are not dressed appropriately. The problem has given rise to a second difficulty: "pirate" taxis. These either cruise up out of the blue or a "dummy" comes and asks you if you want a taxi without queuing. Pirate taxis are a risk, but if you do use one, make sure you agree a price beforehand. They tend to gather at Stortorget, opposite GlassMagasin.

Private Transport
By Car

Norway's roads are extremely good, particularly in view of the treacherous weather conditions encountered in winter. Be prepared for tunnels, though, as some routes have long lengths of road underground.

EU driving licences are valid in Norway, but drivers from other countries must carry an international driving licence. Drive on the right.

Traffic regulations are strictly enforced *(see Rules of the Road, below)*.

Winter Driving

With Norway's winters, you should never assume all roads are passable. Small roads in the north are often closed so the authorities can put all manpower into keeping main roads safe, and even the E6 highway from Oslo to Trondheim has been known to close. If you intend to travel on minor roads, seek a local's advice or phone the 24-hour Road-User Information Centre (tel: 175 in Norway; tel: 08 15 48 991 from abroad) and go prepared for anything. Your car must be equipped with winter tyres.

Snow-Tyre Hire

If you're driving in Norway in winter you can hire the appropriate tyres and snow chains by the week. Ask in any petrol station. In the UK contact:

Snowchains Europroducts
Tel: 01732 884 408
www.snowchains.co.uk

Breakdown and Accidents

The AA and RAC are affiliated to the AIT (Alliance Internationale de Tourisme), so members receive free assistance (with journey planning as well as backup in case of breakdown or accident) from Norway's NAF (Norges Automobilforbund). More comprehensive repairs can be carried out at NAF-contracted garages (for which you will have to pay). NAF also patrols Norway's main roads and mountain passes from mid-June to mid-August. They have emergency phones along the mountain passes.

NAF

Østensjøveien 14, 0609 Oslo
Tel: 08 505
24-hour emergency service (for members of ait clubs), tel: 22 34 16 00/81 00 05 05.

If you are involved in an accident where there are no injuries, telephone **Falck Rescue Service** at 02222 or **Viking Redningstjeneste AS** at 06000. Their offices provide a 24-hour service for all Norway.

In an emergency you can contact **Alarmsentralen** (Air Ambulance), tel: 223 20 11 or UIO (Universitet Oslo), tel: 228 55007

It is not necessary to call the police for minor accidents, but drivers must exchange names and addresses; leaving the scene without doing so is a crime.

Only call the **police** (on **112**) or an **ambulance** (on **113**) if it's a real emergency.

Rules of the Road

It is essential for visitors to Norway to be aware of Norwegian driving regulations, some of which vary significantly from those in the UK and on the Continent. Here are a few tips to help you drive safely, but for further guidance it's worth getting a copy of *Velkommen på norske veier (Welcome to Norwegian Roads)*, which includes an English section and is available at tourist offices.

Speed limits The maximum speed limit is usually 80kph (50mph), though 100kph (62mph) is permitted on some roads (mainly motorways). The limit is reduced to 40kph (24mph) in built-up areas, and even 30kph (18mph) on certain residential roads. On-the-spot fines are given for drivers found speeding (this may be as much as NOK3,500). Speed cameras and radar traps are both used.

Giving way This can be very confusing to the visitor. Roads marked at intervals by yellow diamond signs indicate that you have priority. On all other roads you are required to give way to traffic entering from the right. This is further confused by the fact that some roads have a series of white triangles painted across them at junctions, which mean stop and give way, though as you can imagine these easily become obliterated by snow and ice in the winter.

On roundabouts, priority is from the left. Always give way to trams, buses and taxis. Many roads have a right-hand lane exclusively for buses and taxis.

Drinking and driving You are strongly advised not to drink at all if you anticipate driving within at least eight hours. The current permissible limit is 0.02 per ml, and penalties are severe (imprisonment, a high fine and loss of licence are automatic).

Documentation and equipment You must always have the following with you in your car: driving licence, car registration documents, European accident statement form, insurance policy and a reflective warning triangle. A snow shovel and tow rope are also useful in winter. For regularly updated information in the UK, the AA runs a very good fact line for just a small charge on tel: 0870 600 0371; www.theaa.com.

Lights It is obligatory to drive with dipped headlights on during the daytime, even on the brightest summer day. This rule applies to all vehicles, including motorcycles and mopeds. We recommend you carry spare bulbs. Do not forget that right-hand drive cars require black adhesive triangles (often supplied by ferry companies), or clip-on beam deflectors, so you don't dazzle oncoming drivers.

Seat belts must be worn, both front and back (again, there are on-the-spot fines for failing to comply). Motorcycle and moped drivers and their passengers must wear helmets.

Tyres It is obligatory to use winter tyres from October to April. These are either tyres with studs *(piggdekk)* or specially designed tyres for use in ice and snow. Studded tyres are preferred, but these may soon be prohibited in urban areas for environmental reasons.

Car Hire

Hiring a car in Norway can be expensive, but may be worthwhile if shared between several people. Otherwise, watch for special weekend and summer prices. Most agencies have offices at Gardermoen international airport.

Avis Bilutleie-Liva Bil AS
Billingstadletta 14 (near Oslo)
Tel: 66 77 11 11
www.avis.no

Europcar
Dronning Mauds Gate 10-11
(Entrance from Munkedamsveien)
Tel: 2283 1242
www.europcar.no

Hertz Bilutleie
Holbergs gate 30
Tel: 22 21 0000
www.hertz.no

Cycling

Norway has a series of national cycle routes. Though the terrain can be challenging, the scenery makes the effort worthwhile. If you're tempted to embark on some pedal-powered exploration, there are plenty of bike rental companies around. Cycling is also a good way of exploring many towns and cities. Trondheim is a particularly bike-friendly city – it was the first place to introduce the bicycle lift *(Trampe)*, to help cyclists uphill.

Most ferries will carry bikes free of charge. Buses vary – not all will carry bikes, and of those that do, some charge a nominal fee. NSB trains charge a fee of around 10 percent of the price of your ticket. Note that special cycle trains are laid on during the summer.

Sykkelturisme i Norge

Post Boks 448 Sentrum 0104 Oslo,
Tel: 2200 2500
Email: hns@snd.no
www.bike-norway.com.
Sykkelturisme i Norge – the Institute for Cycle Tourism – was set up in conjunction with the Norwegian Tourist Board to help promote cycling in Norway. It gives details of marked cycle paths throughout the country including the Bergen–Voss, the Rallarvegen and the Lofoten Isles cycle routes, and suggest routes for a variety of skill levels, from gentle rides on relatively easy terrain to challenging expeditions on tough terrain. Its website is full of practical information and inspiration.

The Syklistens Landsforening
Storg. 23D, Pb. 8883 Youngstorget, 0028 Oslo
Tel: 22 47 30 30
Email: post@syklistene.no
www.slf.no
Syklistens Landsforening – the Norwegian Cycling Association – can help plan tours and cycling holidays. They also have a good range of guides (some translated into English) and maps of cycle routes.

Cycle Rental
In Oslo and Bergen, bikes can be

BELOW: cycling is a great way to explore.

hired from hotels, campsites, local tourist offices or sports shops, as well as small cycle-hire shops.

The City Bike campaign is a cycling initiative for short and medium-range transport. It is currently available in four Norwegian cities: Oslo, Bergen, Trondheim and Drammen. To access one of the army of bikes parked at stands throughout the city centres, you need to buy an electronic smartcard from the tourist office. Armed with the card, you can pick up a bike and deposit it back at any one of the many bike stations (over 100 in Oslo) in and around the city centre (www.oslobysykkel.no). In Trondheim, only coins are required.

Vestbanen Bike Rental (next to
tourist office at main railway station) Brynjulf Bulls plass 2, 0250 Oslo Tel: 22 83 52 08

Norway on Foot

Norway is a nation of devout walkers, and walking is one of the most popular outdoor activities at weekends. The law of access to the natural environment, known as "everyman's right", allows you to walk wherever you want in the wilderness such as seashore, forests, mountains and in other non-cultivated regions. This should be done with consideration. Use paths and roads when walking in agricultural and populated areas.

With a network of well-marked trails and welcoming mountain cabins set in magnificent mountain scenery, Norway's national parks (there are 34 national parks on the Norwegian mainland) draw hikers in their thousands (see p.376).

Campers are advised to make use of campsites, though you can, by rights, pitch a tent anywhere in the wilderness, so long as it is situated at least 150 metres/yds from the nearest house or hut. Open fires are prohibited from 15 April to 15 September.

The Norwegian Tourist Board publishes a handbook, *Mountain Hiking in Norway*, which gives suggested itineraries for mountain walks and details of chalets and where to stay.

Den Norske Turistforening,
(Norwegian Trekking Association) Storgata 7, 0101 Oslo Tel: 40 00 18 68 www.turistforening.no. Detailed maps are available from the Norwegian Trekking Association (DNT). Membership gives you rights to

use the association's huts. The map and guidebook selection is excellent: survey maps of Norway are sold; sketch maps are free.

Visas and Passports

A valid passport is all that is necessary for citizens of most countries to enter Norway. Visas are not required. Norway is a member of the Schengen Agreement, allowing citizens of other Schengen countries to enter without passports. If you enter from another Nordic country (Denmark, Finland, Iceland, or Sweden), you won't get an entry stamp. Tourists are generally limited to a three-month visit; it is possible to stay longer, but you must apply for a visa after the initial three months (Scandinavian passport holders are exempt from this requirement), or if you plan to work in Norway.

Animals

Dogs, cats and ferrets from all EU countries except Sweden must have pet passports, ID marking, a valid rabies vaccination and valid blood-test documentation (this does not apply to ferrets). Dogs and cats must also be given approved tapeworm treatment during the week before and the week after they have been brought into the country.

Weights and Measures

Metric. Distances are given in kilometres (km), but Norwegians often refer to a *mil*, which is 10km (thus 10 *mil* = 100km). When talking about land area you will often hear the word *mål*. This old measure of 984.34 sq metres has been rounded up to 1,000 sq metres (or 1 decare).

What to Read

History

Heimskringla (*History of the Kings of Norway*), Snorri Sturluson (University of Texas Press, 1991).
King Harald's Saga (an excerpt from the *Heimskringla*), Snorri Sturluson (Penguin Classics, 1976).
The Real Heroes of Telemark: the True Story of the Secret Mission to Stop Hitler's Atomic Bomb, Ray Mears (Coronet, 2004).

Art and Literature

Knut Hamsun: ***Hunger, Mysteries, Victoria, The Growth of the Soil, Wayfarers***, are excellent novels and available in Penguin Classics, Oxford Classics, Condor Books and other imprints.
Knut Hamsun, Dreamer and Dissenter, Ingar Sletten Kolloen (Yale University Press, 2009).
Henrik Ibsen: ***A Doll's House, Peer Gynt, The Master Builder, Hedda Gabler, The Wild Duck***, among other works available in Oxford World's Classics and other imprints.
Edvard Munch: ***Behind the Scream***, Sue Prideaux (Yale University Press, 2005).
Sigrid Undset: ***Kristin Lavransdatter*** (Penguin Classics). Historical epic by nobel laureate Sigrid Undset.

Arctic Explorers

Scott and Amundsen: Last Place on Earth, Roland Huntford (Abacus, 2000).
The South Pole: An Account of the Norwegian Antarctic Exploration in the Fram, 1910–12, Roald Amundsen (Cooper Square Press, 2001).
Kon Tiki: across the Pacific by Raft, Thor Heyerdahl (Simon and Schuster Press, 1995).
Kon Tiki Expedition (Flamingo, 1996).

A CCOMMODATION

HOTELS, *HYTTE* AND FISHERMEN'S CABINS

When it comes to places to stay, Norway has something to suit every requirement. The range covers hotels from the luxurious to the simple, to bed and breakfasts, guesthouses, cosy self-catering cottages, seaside cabins, mountain lodges, youth hostels and campsites.

Children often go free, provided the child stays in the parents' room. Guesthouses *(pensjonat)* offer lower rates and may have shared baths (the bathroom may be down the hall). A breakfast buffet is almost always included in the room rate.

Norwegian hotels reduce their rates during the outdoor summer holiday period, and often at weekends, when business decreases. This makes May to September attractive when compared with standard rates. Hotel taxes are included in the quoted rates.

The state-run visitors' site, www.visit norway.com, can be a good starting point for tracking down accommodation.

An online hotel-booking service is available at www.hotels-in-norway.com.

Hotel Chains

Some of the major hotel chains are well represented in Norway's cities (Best Western, Choice, Norlandia, Rica, Scandic, Thon, Radisson Blu). Together with several local chains, they offer passes and discount schemes to help reduce the cost of accommodation. These passes, available for sale at participating hotels, usually involve a modest one-time fee (around NOK100) and then entitle the holder to discounted rates, mostly in the summer and at weekends. Some passes also offer a free night of accommodation after the pass holder has logged several nights on the programme.

City Packages

The Oslo Package offers great value for money. It is available at weekends and during the holiday seasons (Easter, summer holidays and Christmas time). The price includes accommodation with breakfast (there are over 40 hotels to choose from in

Oslo), plus the Oslo Card which includes free entrance to many museums and attractions, free inner city transport and numerous discounts. The packages can be booked through the tourist information office in Oslo at Fridtjof Nansens Plass (Mon–Sat 9am–5pm; www.visitoslo.com/hotel-booking) or through a travel agency, but not directly with the hotel.

Chalets *(Hytte)*

There are abundant holiday *hytte* (cabins or chalets) available for rent. These are often situated in more remote locations by the sea or in the heart of the forest, ideal for those in search of nature and tranquillity. They usually house four to six people. If you want to spend just one night in a chalet and then move on, you can stay in one on a campsite without booking ahead. See accommodation guides at www.visitnorway.com, or try the Cultural Heritage Association's website at www.olavsrosa.no/en.

Fishermen's Cabins (Rorbuer)

In the Lofoten Islands in northern Norway, and at numerous places elsewhere along the coast, you can rent a traditional former fisherman's cabin, or *rorbu*. Most of them have been modernised, and some have their own shower and toilet.
Destination Lofoten Tourist Office Tel: 76 06 98 00; www.lofoten.info.

Camping

Norway has more than 1,000 campsites, classified by 1–5 stars,

BELOW: fishermen's cabins *(rorbuer)* in the Lofoten Islands.

Norway's Historic Hotels

Massive investment in historic properties has made it possible for visitors to stay in a wide range of them, while enjoying every modern convenience. Some of these charming fairytale-like structures are in towns and cities, but many are in the mountains and along fjords. Most include dinner and breakfast as part of the room rate. Overnight accommodation for two including dinner and breakfast generally runs

to around NOK2,800, plus drinks. For further information:
De historiske
PO Box 196 Sentrum
5804 Bergen
Tel: 55 31 67 60
www.dehistoriske.no
This is a group of around 30 historic hotels, manor houses or timbered lodges and 14 selected restaurants around Norway, catering to visitors keen on style and good food.

The Great Life Company
Karenslyst allé 11, PO Box 54
Skøyen, 0212 Oslo
Tel: 24 12 62 10
www.thegreatlifecompany.com
Controlled by a ship-owning Oslo family that's made a business out of restoring gracious old lodging establishments. The group consists of around 20 mostly historic inns and restaurants, with a few modern surprises.

depending on the standard and facilities available. The fixed charge per plot is usually NOK80–160, with additional charges per person.

With the Norwegian camping card *(Norsk Campingkort)* you receive a faster checking-in service along with special discount deals. The card is available from participating campsites.

Many campsites have cabins that may be booked in advance. Some are small and basic, but others are large and well equipped. Both close to Oslo, Ekeberg Camping (tel: 22 19 85 68) and Bogstad Camping (tel: 22 51 08 00) – the largest campsite in Norway – also have cabins.

For further information, write to: Norwegian Camping Guide, Essendropsgt. 3, PO Box 5465 Majorstuen, N-0305 Oslo, or visit www.camping.no.

Bed and Breakfasts

British-style bed and breakfasts are catching on in Norway, and they are all of a high standard. You can book at local tourist offices or at Oslo's Central Railway Station, or look out for signs for *Rom* or *Husrom* outside houses as you drive. A guidebook, *The Norway Bed and Breakfast Book*, with listings throughout the country, is available from tourist offices and bookshops in Norway or from:
Scandinavia Connection
26 Woodsford Square, London
W14 8DP
Tel: 020 7602 0657
www.scandinavia-connection.co.uk

Youth and Family Hostels

There are approximately 100 youth hostels in Norway, all of a relatively

high standard. A night's accommodation costs from NOK200, breakfast NOK60–75 for members of the YHA. Further information can be obtained by contacting Hostelling International Norway, or your local YHA office.

Reserving space during the high season is essential.
Norske Vandrerhjem
(Hostelling International Norway), P.B. 53 Grefsen, 0409 Oslo
Tel: 23 12 45 10
www.hihostels.no

Price Categories

Hotels vary in price seasonally and some offer special weekend rates, so be sure to double check the exact price when you book. Breakfast is almost always included in Norwegian hotels.

OSLO

Best Western West Hotell
Skovveien 15
Tel: 22 54 21 60
www.bestwestern.no
This classical-style hotel is located slightly west in the Frogner quarter, behind the Royal Palace. Its French-inspired restaurant is known for its excellent fish dishes. **€€**

Best Western Hotel Bondeheimen
Rosenkrantz gate 8
Tel: 23 21 41 00
www.bondeheimen.com
A large, old-fashioned hotel, dating to 1913, whose name means "farmer's

home". Rooms are tastefully decorated with polished pine features. The inclusive buffet breakfast is top-class. The homely restaurant Kaffistova offers simple, inexpensive meals. Heimen, an authentic handicrafts and souvenir shop, is just off the hotel lobby. **€€**

Hotel Bristol
Kristian IV's gate 7
Tel: 22 82 60 00
www.bristol.no
This exclusive hostelry attracts an international clientele with its ornate lobby and antiques in the bedrooms. **€€€**

Clarion Collection Gabelshus Hotel
Gabels gate 16
Tel: 23 27 65 00
www.gabelshus.no
This quaint, historic gabled hotel, opened in 1912, was recently refurbished under new management and offers modern comforts with antique furnishings. **€€**

Cochs Pensjonat
Parkveien 25
Tel: 23 33 24 00
www.cochspensjonat.no
A friendly relatively low-price alternative with a loyal following, just at the foot of one of Oslo's most popular

shopping streets (Hegdehaugsveien-Bogstadveien) and a block from the park around the Royal Palace. Some rooms have kitchenettes. **€**

Hotel Continental
Stortingsgaten 24–26
Tel: 22 82 40 00
www.hotel-continental.no

PRICE CATEGORIES

Price categories are based on an average double room for two, with breakfast in high season:
$ = under NOK1,100
$$ = NOK1,100–1,700
$$$ = over NOK1,700

Each room in this elegant, luxury hotel across from the National Theatre is individually decorated. The acclaimed Annen Etage restaurant provides haute cuisine, while the Theater Café attracts locals and visitors. €€€

First Hotel Grims Grenka
Kongens gate 5
Tel: 23 10 72 00
www.grimsgrenka.no
This comfortable hotel is located in the old Oslo district of Kvadraturen. All rooms have cool, Modernist decor and kitchenettes. There is a roof terrace with outdoor Jacuzzi with a view of Akershus Castle. €€

First Hotel Millennium
Tollbugata 25
Tel: 21 02 28 00
www.firsthotels.com
The interior of the hotel was designed in the 1930s by Platou, one of Norway's best-known architectural groups. The top floor has 10 rooms with separate large balconies. €€

Frogner House Apartments
Skovveien 8 (head office)
Tel: 930 10 009
www.frognerhouse.no
Once a small hotel, it is now an apartment complex with three locations in the stylish West End. Guests can enjoy a home away from home in the central location with access to shops and

restaurants. Each fully furnished apartment includes a kitchenette, bathroom, cable TV and WiFi; some have a balcony. €€

Grand Hotel
Karl Johans gate 31
Tel: 23 21 20 00
www.grand.no
Situated on Oslo's main thoroughfare since 1874, this exclusive hotel has been the location for many Nobel Prize celebrations and is where visiting heads of state tend to stay when they're in town. There is an entire Ladies' Floor, with specially designed rooms providing every comfort for female travellers. €€€

Holmenkollen Park Hotel Rica
Kongeveien 26
Tel: 22 92 20 00
www.holmenkollenparkhotel.no
This is a lovely traditional Norwegian building dating in part to 1894, with a good fitness and spa centre. It's located near to the Holmenkollen ski jump, 15 minutes by underground train to Stortinget. €€€

Radisson Blu Scandinavia Hotel
Holbergs gate 30
Tel: 23 29 30 00
www.radissonblu.com/scandinaviahotel-oslo
A 5-minute walk from the Royal Palace, this hotel offers all mod cons and a

bus to the airport. The bar, Summit 21, on the 21st floor, gives the best view over the city and Oslo Fjord. €€€

Rica Hotel Bygdøy Allé
Bygdøy allé 53
Tel: 23 08 58 00
www.rica.no
This hotel is located in Oslo's stylish West End (10 minutes by bus from the city centre). Rooms are well furnished and decorated in bright colours, and the service is attentive. €€

Rica Hotel Holberg
Holbergs plassen 1
Tel: 23 15 72 00
www.rica.no
This hotel near the National Museum is close to the shops and Aker Brygge and offers comfortable, minimalist but well-equipped rooms. €€

Scandic Byporten
Jernbanetorget 6
Tel: 23 15 55 00
www.scandic-hotels.no/byporten
You can walk directly from the airport express train to this hotel without going outdoors – it's located in the Central Train Station at the foot of Karl Johan. There's a wide choice of tastefully decorated rooms. €€

Scandic KNA
Parkveien 68
Tel: 23 15 57 00
www.scandic-hotels.no/kna
Located between the Royal

Palace and Aker Brygge, this hotel has 189 rooms with modern facilities, including kids' play area and sauna; 39 rooms have a balcony and an excellent view of the Oslo Fjord. €€

Thon Hotel Gyldenløve
Bogstadveien 20
Tel: 23 33 23 00
www.thonhotels.no/gyldenlove
Comfortable hotel with car park in the heart of the lively Majorstuen shopping district. There are 29 rooms suitable for people with allergies. €€

Thon Hotel Stefan
Rosenkrantz gate 1
Tel: 23 31 55 00
www.thonhotels.no/stefan
Located around the corner from Karl Johan, this 4-star hotel has bright and cheery rooms, suitable both for families and business travellers, and the popular Junsten café/bar. €€

Voksenåsen Hotel
Ullveien 4
Tel: 22 81 15 00
www.voksenaasen.no
Voksenåsen is an upmarket hotel in the wealthy Holmenkollen area, with excellent views of Oslo. It features stylish rooms decorated with antiques, an outdoor swimming pool and a fine collection of modern art. There's also a large, recently refurbished restaurant. €€€

Around Oslo

Oscarsborg Festning
1443 Oscarsborg
Tel: 64 90 40 00
www.oscarsborghotel.no
This historic fortress on an island off Drøbak in the Oslo Fjord is very good value for money and open all year, although arguably most

appealing in the summer months. The ferry service (it's a 5-minute ride) is from Drøbak, a picturesque coastal town in itself. Some rooms have fjord views. $

Radisson Blu Airport Hotel
Oslo Airport Gardermoen
Tel: 63 93 30 00
www.radissonblu.com
If you need to be near Oslo's main airport, then you can't beat this for comfort and convenience. You can walk from baggage claim to this elegant and comfortable hotel in minutes. $$

Hotell Refsnesgods
Godset 5, 1518 Moss
Tel: 69 27 83 00
www.refsnesgods.com
Located right on the Oslo Fjord on the island of Jeløy, about an hour south of Oslo, this is an elegant getaway spot known for its wine cellar and art collection. Several rooms face the beach. $$$

Scandic Asker
Askerveien 61
Tel: 23 15 54 00
www.scandichotels.com
Suburban hotel, completely renovated in 2008, near the

train station and the main motorway into Oslo. $

Thon Hotel Oslofjord
Sandviksveien 184, 1337 Sandvika
Tel: 67 55 66 00
www.thonhotels.no/oslofjord
This large conference hotel on the busy E18 motorway in the western suburb of Sandvika has been part of several chains and is now in the Thon group. It's close to downtown Sandvika, Bærum Kulturhus and IKEA at Slependen, and 10 minutes by car from Oslo centre. Also close to the fjord. $

PRICE CATEGORIES

Price categories are based on an average double room for two, with breakfast in high season:
$ = under NOK1,100
$$ = NOK1,100–1,700
$$$ = over NOK1,700

STAVANGER

Radisson Blu Atlantic Hotel
Olav V's Gate 3
Tel: 51 76 10 00
www.radissonblu.com
High-rise business hotel in the heart of town, overlooking Lake Breiavatnet. Five-minute walk to the harbour and all its restaurants and bars, with discounted room rates in the summer. **$$**

Radisson Blu Royal Hotel
Løkkeveien 26
Tel: 51 76 60 00
www.radissonblu.com
Located behind its sister

property Atlantic, this is a mid-rise luxury hotel most memorable for its themed floors. Swimming pool, sauna and Jacuzzi. **$$–$$$**

Sola Strand Hotel
Axel Lundsveien 27, 4050 Sola
Tel: 51 94 30 00
www.sola-strandhotel.no
"Strand" means "beach" in Norwegian, and this hotel is located on one of the many windswept beaches along the North Sea, about a 20-minute drive from downtown Stavanger. A classic, traditional hotel with modern spa facilities,

restaurant, conference centre and plenty of space to unwind. **$$**

Thon Hotel Maritim
Kongsgaten 32
Tel: 51 85 05 00
www.thonhotels.no/maritim
Tucked into a side-street across from Stavanger's downtown lake, this mid-range hotel offers discounted rates on weekends and in the summer. **€**

Utstein Kloster Hotel
Mosterøyveien 661, 4156 Mosterøy
Tel: 51 72 01 00
www.utsteinklosterhotell.no

Another waterfront hotel, on an island north of Stavanger near the historic Utstein Cloister. It's connected to the mainland, though, by an underwater tunnel. Excellent area for cycling and seeing historic sites. **€€**

Victoria Hotel
Skansegate 1
Tel: 51 86 70 00
www.victoria-hotel.no
Historic, first-class, family-run hotel on the harbour, in the heart of the bar and restaurant district yet somehow quietly removed. **$$**

BERGEN

Augustin Hotel
C. Sundts gate 22
Tel: 55 30 40 00
www.augustin.no
Family-run hotel with comfortable rooms, some with views. Popular cellar bar and restaurant. **€€**

Bergen Travel Hotel
Vestre Torgagate 20A
Tel: 55 59 90 90
www.hotelbergen.com
Plain rooms and apartments with kitchens are available in this central hotel. The interiors are simply furnished in white with polished floorboards. **€€**

Best Western Hotell Hordaheimen
C. Sundts gate 18
Tel: 55 33 50 00
www.hordaheimen.hl.no

One of Bergen's oldest hotels, combining modern design and comfort with the best of Norwegian rural traditions. It's in a scenic central location close to Torgallmenningen and the fish market. The Kaffistova restaurant is an authentic country kitchen. **€€**

Clarion Hotel Admiral
C. Sundts gate 9
Tel: 55 23 64 00
www.admiral.no
This hotel, which has lovely, well-equipped rooms, looks over the harbour to Bryggen. Good restaurant, with terrace. **€€€**

First Hotel Marin
Rosenkrantz gate 8
Tel: 53 05 15 00
www.firsthotels.com

Just minutes from the fish market, Bryggen and the Fløybanen, this tasteful hotel with well-equipped rooms is designed in "maritime" style, with two separate "theme" rooms (princess or pirate) for children. **€€€**

Grand Terminus
Zander Kaaes gate 6
Tel: 55 21 25 00
www.ght.no
This elegant hotel across from the railway station has been a popular stopover for wealthy tourists since 1928. The comfortable rooms are beautifully decorated, and the restaurant serves traditional Norwegian dishes including Bergen specialities. **€€€**

Neptun Hotell Rica Partner
Valkendorfs gate 8
Tel: 55 30 68 00
www.neptun-hotell.no
A central hotel with 124 imaginatively decorated rooms. The 700-plus works of art displayed around the hotel create a unique atmosphere. The Lucillus restaurant serves gourmet French cuisine, while Pascal Mat&Vin is an informal wine bar and bistro. **€€€**

Hotel Park
Harald Harfagres gate 35
Tel: 55 54 44 00
www.parkhotel.no

This delightful, family-run hotel is in the fashionable University quarter close to the city centre. Rooms in the main building are furnished with antiques; those in the newer annexe are more modern, and there is a lovely penthouse apartment. **€€**

Radisson Blu Hotel Norge
Ole Bulls plass 4
Tel: 55 57 30 00
www.radissonbluhotels.com
The Norge completed an extensive renovation in 2007. It has four restaurants, including the Ole Bull which overlooks the city park. There's also a nightclub, indoor pool, fitness centre and a winter garden. **€€€**

Radisson Blu Royal Hotel
Bryggen
Tel: 55 54 30 00
www.radissonbluhotels.com
The Royal is built into several of Bergen's lovely historic wharves on the picturesque waterfront, and its entrance is close to the Bryggen Museum. It offers good

BERGEN CATEGORIES

Price categories are based on an average double room for two, usually with a lavish breakfast:
$ = under NOK800
$$ = NOK800–1,500
$$$ = over NOK1,500

BELOW: the timber buildings at Bergen.

facilities, including WiFi and an indoor pool. €€€
Steens Hotel
Parkveien 22
Tel: 55 30 88 88
www.steenshotel.no
This delightful family-run hotel (21 rooms) dates from 1890, and the style and

atmosphere of the period have been well preserved, including the oak-panelled dining room. Most rooms face a beautiful park. €€
Thon Hotel Bergen Brygge
Bradbenken 3
Tel: 55 30 87 00
www.thonhotels.com/bergenbrygge

This popular, mid-priced hotel has simple, spacious rooms and is located in the heart of Bergen, between the Mariakirken and Håkonshallen. Breakfasts are a real treat here. €€
Thon Hotel Rosenkrantz
Rosenkrantz gate 7

Tel: 55 30 14 00
www.rainbow-hotels.no/rosenkrantz
This hotel is near the harbour and fish market; the upper-floor rooms have the best sea views. Located in an old building, the hotel has been totally modernised. €€

TRONDHEIM

Britannia Hotel
Dronningensgate 5
Tel: 73 800 800
www.britannia.no
A brand-new spa opened here in 2008. Otherwise the Britannia is an old-fashioned, independently owned place, with comfortable rooms and four restaurants. €€€
Clarion Collection Bakeriet
Brattorgata 2
Tel: 73 99 10 00
www.choicehotels.no
Based in an old bakery, this pleasant hotel keeps up

traditions by offering guests freshly baked afternoon waffles. Unusually for Scandinavia, many of the rooms have bath tubs. €€
Grand Olav Clarion Hotel
Kjøpmannsgaten 48
Tel: 73 80 80 80
www.choicehotels.no
Top-class hotel in the heart of Trondheim, close to the concert hall, shops, bars and restaurants. Renovated in 2007. €€€
Quality Hotel Augustin
Kongensgate 26
Tel: 73 54 70 00

www.hotel-augustin.no
Close to the main city square, this huge old brick hotel has 139 comfortable rooms, bar, fitness room, internet access and covered parking. €€
Radisson Blu Royal Garden Hotel
Kjøpmannsgt 73
Tel: 73 80 30 00
www.radissonblu.com
Has 298 well-appointed rooms in a soothing riverfront location, with the city's only indoor swimming pool, plus solarium,

gymnasium, sauna and several good restaurants. Runs an airport bus every 15 minutes. €€
Thon Hotel Gildevangen
Søndre gate 22B
Tel: 73 87 01 30
www.thonhotels.no/gildevangen
In a grand building in the centre of town, near the bus and train stations, and with a stop for the airport shuttle right outside. All the rooms are a good size and decorated to a high standard. Bar; internet access. €€

TROMSØ

Ami Hotel
Skolegata 24
Tel: 77 62 10 00
www.amihotel.no
More B&B than hotel, this is a great-value option for those on a budget. All rooms have fridges, and there's a guest kitchen so you can self-cater. €

Clarion Collection Hotel With
Sjøgata 35–37
Tel: 77 66 42 00
www.clarionhotel.com
This first-class hotel on the waterfront in Tromsø's dock district offers beautiful sea and mountain views. Sauna. €€

Rica Grand Hotel Tromsø
Storgate 44
Tel: 77 75 37 77
www.nordic.no
Close to the centre, with full conference facilities and well-appointed rooms. €€
Quality Hotel Saga
Richard Withs plass 2
Tel: 77 60 70 00

www.qualityinn.com
Established chain hotel in the city centre. €€
Rica Ishavshotel
Fr. Langesgt. 2
Tel: 77 66 64 00
www.rica-hotel.com
First-rate hotel, oozing style with unique quayside location and magnificent views of the cathedral, harbour and mountains. €€€
Scandic Tromsø
Heiloveien 23
Tel: 77 75 50 00
www.scandichotels.no/tromso
Modest hotel in Tromsø suburb close to the airport. Restaurant, kids' playroom, sauna and WiFi. Free bicycle hire for guests. €€

BELOW: the Rica Ishavshotel at Tromsø.

EATING OUT

RECOMMENDED RESTAURANTS AND CAFÉS

What to Eat

Norwegians eat hearty breakfasts, but light lunches; the size of the evening meal *(middag)* depends on the day of the week and the occasion.

With the abundant supply of seafood and what can be gleaned from forest and field, the Norwegian diet has traditionally been healthy and appetising. For those who relish game, the hunting season (early autumn) offers some irresistible temptations: pheasant, grouse, elk and reindeer steaks served with peppercorns and rich wild mushroom sauces. It is also a good time of year to make the most of seafood (with cod considered best in months with an r in them).

Frokost (breakfast) is more or less a variation of the lunch *Kaldtbord*, a spread including breads (try *grovbrød* and *knekkebrød*), sausage, cheese – Norway's national cheese is *geitost*, a caramel-brown goat's-milk cheese (try the piquant *Gudbrandsalsost* variety) – eggs, herrings, *gravlax* (marinated salmon), and coffee and tea.

The lunch version has hot dishes, such as sliced roast meats, meatballs or fish. *Øllebrød* (beef marinated in beer and served inside pitta bread with salad) makes a hearty, inexpensive lunch; an open-faced shrimp or ham sandwich is another staple.

Dinner in a city restaurant can be anything you wish, and many of the new, modern restaurants in Oslo or Bergen could just as easily be found in London or Los Angeles. When dining in more remote places, the menus will invariably be limited by availability. A more traditional menu might include mutton stew or a fish ragout, and boiled potatoes with dill or parsley will often accompany a hot main course.

Drinking Notes

No one talks about a trip to Norway without complaining of the high cost of alcohol. For those who can afford the prices, serving hours are long; in Oslo you can drink spirits until midnight and wine or beer until 3am. Outside Oslo, times are less predictable; a conservative Lutheran culture holds sway in many west-coast areas, rendering some counties virtually dry. But there are exceptions to this: in Oslo, for example, there are some no-alcohol hotel/restaurants and in the "dry" counties it is always possible to find a hotel/restaurant that serves some

form of alcohol.

The Vinmonopolet (state off licences/liquor stores) in cities are open Mon–Fri 10am–6pm and Sat 9am–2pm; they are closed on election days, holidays and the preceding day of a holiday.

Most Norwegians drink beer and/ or wine. Traditional *akevitt*, similar in taste to schnapps, is derived from potato and caraway seeds, and is also a favourite. It can be sipped neat in small glasses at room temperature, or served cold with beer to accompany salty, spicy or pungent dishes.

For dessert, ice cream is a favourite, as is apple pie. In summer there are all kinds of puddings based on the fresh berries that grow profusely in the Norwegian woods.

Outside main meals there are many coffee breaks, often accompanied with fresh pastries, including *bolle* (raisin buns) and *wienerbrød* (lighter pastries laced with fruit or nuts). *Smørbrød* is a snack (called *aftens* when eaten late at night), usually of bread or crackers with butter, cheese and salami or ham.

For more on classic Norwegian food, see page 98.

Where to Eat

There has been a significant increase in what's on offer when you choose to eat out in Norway. Pizza is very popular, and the cynic may even describe it as the Norwegian national dish. Asian food has also become a local favourite, although Indian

restaurants tend to tone down the spices to suit the more delicate Norwegian palate. Continental European dishes have always played a role in Norwegian cuisine (such as Viennese- and French-style dishes), but pride in native foods and an interest in "New Scandinavian" cuisine is prevalent.

At lunchtime many restaurants offer special fixed-price menus. Reasonably priced snacks and simple meals can be enjoyed in museum cafés and such informal establishments as *stovas*, *kros* and *gjæstgiveris*, which may sell alcohol as well as coffee and soft drinks. For an even more casual meal, buy a hot dog *(pølse)*, kebab or a waffle from a kiosk; these stay open late to catch pub-crawlers.

Restaurant Listings

Restaurants are grouped by area starting with Oslo. They are listed alphabetically.

OSLO

Norwegian: Classic and Modern

De Fem Stuer
Holmenkollen Park Hotel
Tel: 22 92 20 00
Elegant dining inside the historic timbered salons of this fairytale-like hotel overlooking the city and fjord. Booking recommended. €€€

Det Gamle Raadhus
Nedre Slotts gate 1
Tel: 22 42 01 07
Housed in the capital's old City Hall from the 1600s, now best known for its *lutefisk* (a pungent Scandinavian speciality of cod marinated in lye) in the months leading up to Christmas. €€

DS Louise
Stranden 3
Tel: 22 83 00 60
Roomy waterfront restaurant in a former mechanical workshop, decorated with ship and shipyard paraphernalia, offering both informal and fine dining. There's an outdoor terrace with great views over Aker Brygge. €€€

Restaurant Eik
Universitetsgata 11
Tel: 22 36 07 10
Arguably the best of Oslo's "menu-based" restaurants, where you select how many courses you want from a carefully planned multi-course meal. Next to Oslo's National Gallery. €€

Ekeberg Restaurant
Kongsveien 15
Tel: 23 24 23 00
Take the No. 18–19 tram to Sjømannsskolen and walk up the hill to this recently restored gem. Knockout view over the city and fjord, with a large outdoor terrace complementing the restaurant inside. €€

Feinschmecker
Balchens gate 5
Tel: 22 12 93 80
The chef of this long-established Michelin-star restaurant favours seasonal specialities like crayfish or cod as well as an à la carte selection of succulent scallops or tender Norwegian lamb. The dessert menu is an absolute must. Old-school fine dining, in the upmarket Frogner area. Closed Sunday. €€€

Fru Hagen
Thorvald Meyers gate 40
Tel: 45 49 19 04
A lively bistro/bakery where the young and the hip come for Thai wok specialities, pastas or burgers. €–€€

Grand Café
Karl Johans gate 31
Tel: 23 21 20 00
Henrik Ibsen's former haunt, known for its murals and stylish surroundings just across from the Parliament. €€

Kaffistova
Rosenkrantz gate 8
Tel: 23 21 41 00
Cafeteria-style place dishing up authentic rural Norwegian food. Fast and filling. €

Lille Herbern Fjordkro
Herbernveien, Lille Herbern
Tel: 22 44 97 00
One of Oslo's most romantic summer destinations for seafood, drinks and all-round ambience. Accessible only by ferry – a 25-minute ride from the Herbern Marina near Aker Brygge. €€–€€€

Maud's
Tollbugate 24
Tel: 22 83 72 28
Old-fashioned Norwegian-style restaurant, named after Norway's first modern queen, the former Princess Maud of England. €€

Solsiden
Sondre Akershus Kai 34
Tel: 22 33 36 30
One of the best seafood restaurants in Oslo, situated right on the harbour under the historic Akershus

ABOVE: enjoying a cold beverage in Oslo.

Fortress. Try the shellfish platter or catch of the day. Summer only. €€

Statholdergaarden
Rådhus gate 11
Tel: 22 41 88 00
Danish chef Bent Stiansen's inventive dishes are impeccably served in the elegant upstairs restaurant of this fine 17th-century townhouse. €€€

Sult
Thorbald Meyers gate 26
Tel: 22 87 04 67
Named after Knut Hamsun's novel *Hunger*, this was one of the first restaurants to pop up in the lively Grünerløkka district. Simple, fresh food dubbed "neo-Norsk". €€

Theatercafeen
Stortings Gate 24–26
Tel: 22 82 40 50
Famed Vienna-style café; classic dishes served with flair, live violin music. A place to see and be seen in Oslo. €€

Euro/Asian

Bambus
Kirkeveien 57
Tel: 22 85 07 00
Blend of Thai, Vietnamese and Japanese food in a stylish setting in the trendy Majorstua neighbourhood. €

Bistro Brocante
Thorvald Meyers gate 40
Tel: 22 35 68 71
A friendly French bistro specialising in seasonal French fare for lunch and dinner. In summers, the terrace is "le happening" spot. €€

Curry & Ketchup
Kirkveien 51
Tel: 22 69 05 22
Inexpensive curries and South Asian vegetarian dishes in the unpretentious Majorstua quarter. €

East Sushi & Noodles
Aker Brygge Bryggetorget 7
Tel: 22 83 63 51
This fast-growing chain of noodle and sushi cafés can be found throughout Oslo. Quick, healthy and delicious food. €–€€

La Rosa Magra
Arbins gate 1
Tel: 22 56 14 00
Excellent Italian food, from small pizzas to full-course meals, located just under the Ibsen Museum. €–€€

Vegeta Verthus
Munkedamsveien 3b
Tel: 221 66 28 65
Hot and cold buffets are prepared for a loyal vegetarian clientele. From soups and salads to casseroles and pizza slices. €

STAVANGER

Charlottenlund
Kongsgaten 45
Tel: 51 91 76 00
Graceful, Norwegian- and French-inspired cuisine served in a former private mansion on the lake in the heart of town. **€€**

Gaffel & Karaffel
Øvre Holmgate 20
Tel: 51 86 41 58
This excellent, unpretentious restaurant offers a seasonal menu, featuring wild salmon and

reindeer among other succulent offerings. Champagne bar. **€€**

N.B. Sørensens Dampskibsexpedition
Skagen 26
Tel: 51 84 38 20
One of the most traditional restaurants in Stavanger, at the marina. The international menu makes full use of fresh Norwegian ingredients. **€€**

Ostehuset
Hospitalgaten 6
Tel: 51 86 4010

Fresh and health-conscious ingredients are a speciality of this "cheese house", which dishes up salads, sandwiches and unique pizzas. **€–€€**

Renaa
Breitorget 6
Tel: 51 55 11 11
The two restaurants (Craig's Kjøkken and Jan's Mat og Vinhus) that occupied this two-storey building were a tough act to follow, but in less than a year, nationally

reputed chef Sven Erik Renaa created his own following for two restaurants of his own: The Matbaren bistro upstairs and the gourmet dining room below. **€€–€€€**

Tango Bar & Kjøkken
Nedre Strandgate 25
Tel: 51 50 1230
Fresh ingredients and excellent preparation have made this jewel by the harbour a real success story. **€€–€€€**

BERGEN

Boha
Vaskerelven
Tel: 55 31 31 60
Proprietors Arve Haga and Per Trygve Bolstad are committed to translating their passion to the fresh, seasonal food they serve. The "pavement" restaurant for alfresco dining is a recent innovation, and the ground-floor Onkel Lauritz bar is a popular meeting place. **€€–€€€**

Bryggeloftet & Stuene
Bryggen 11
Tel: 55 30 20 70
A favourite with tourists, this typical Norwegian restaurant features traditional meals, such as reindeer, fillet of wolf fish, cod, and holiday specialities such as *pinnekjøtt* (salted mutton) and *lutefisk*, the traditional fishy Christmas dish. **$$$**

Café Opera
Engen 18
Tel: 55 23 03 15
Hang out for the hip crowd serving salads, snacks, sandwiches and light traditional Norwegian dishes. Open daily for lunch and dinner. It also operates as a bar and popular club. **$$**

Cornelia
Kjøttbasaren (Bergen Food Hall)
Tel: 55 011 885
Within the old meat market building turned epicurean centre, these two adjacent restaurants – a brasserie and a seafood restaurant – opened in 2010 and are run by Alf Roald Sætre and Odd-Einar Tufteland, whose Cornelius restaurant (25 minutes from Bergen by boat in Mathopen; tel: 56 33 48 80) has long been considered one of Norway's

top addresses. Fresh fish and game in season. **€€–€€€**

Dr Livingstone Travellers Pub and Café
Kong Oscars gate 12
Tel: 55 56 03 12
In an old Bergen homestead dating back to 1702, this is a laidback gastro pub spread across two floors, with an outside dining area. It is centrally situated at the beginning of Bergen's most cosmopolitan street. **$–$$**

Finnegaardstuene
Rosenkrantz gate 6
Tel: 55 55 03 00
Fresh seasonal ingredients – from halibut to venison – are presented in a (13th-century) former Hanseatic warehouse by an inspired culinary team in four separate dining rooms. **€€€**

Fiskekrogen
Fish Market
Tel: 55 55 96 40
Excellent seafood served in an idyllic setting on the wharf. It's hard to get an outdoor table here in summer, but worth the effort. **€€–€€€**

Fløien Folkerestaurant
Top of Fløien funicular
Tel: 55 33 69 99
Good, reasonably priced food with an intoxicating view. Work up an appetite by walking there. **€€**

Mago
Neumanns gate 5 (next to the large cinemaplex)
Tel: 55 96 29 80

Mago means "magician" in Norwegian, but there are no tricks going on in the kitchen which features fresh seasonal ingredients like scallops and lamb. The wine list is one of the best in town. **€€**

Nama Sushi & Noodles
Lodin Lepps gate 2b
Tel: 55 32 20 10
East meets North with top-quality Norwegian seafood prepared Japanese style – sushi, noodles, raw fish, halibut, oysters. **€€–€€€**

Pasta Sentral
Vestre Torggaten 5–7
Tel: 55 96 00 37
A well-priced oasis for pasta, pizza and other Italian specialities, which makes it very popular with students, families and visitors. Try the daily special – for around NOK70 you can get bread, a drink and your main course. Cash only. **€**

Potetkjellern
Kong Oscars gate 1a
Tel: 55 32 00 70
Voted Bergen's Best Restaurant in 2010. Located in an old potato cellar with a comfortable

BELOW: there is always an abundance of fresh ingredients.

PRICE CATEGORIES

Price categories are per person for an average three-course meal, excluding wine:
$ = under NOK280
$$ = NOK280–560
$$$ = over NOK560

atmosphere, it specialises in seasonal specialities from halibut and cod to lamb and reindeer. Excellent wine list. **€€–€€€**

Vagen Fetevare
Kong Oscars gate 10
(no phone)
This retro coffeehouse is an unpretentious oasis of good, cheap chow. The house speciality, known as *blingser*,

is an open sandwich on freshly baked bread with ham, cheese or other tasty toppings. Save room for the chocolate cake or a bowl of their famed hot chocolate. Closed evenings. **€**

Wesselstuen
Ole Bulls plass 6
Tel: 55 55 49 49
Traditional Norwegian fish and stews are served to a

loyal local crowd. Good atmosphere. **€€**

Yang Tse Kiang
Galleriet at Torgallmenningen
Tel: 55 32 88 86
A simple, pleasant Chinese restaurant that offers good-value lunch specials, including classics such as sweet and sour chicken and beef in black-bean sauce, from around NOK90. **€**

Zupperia
Nordahl Bruns gate 9
Tel: 55 55 81 14
A popular "soup kitchen" (even dessert soups are available) within the West Norway Museum of Decorative Art has its own entrance and opening hours (11am until midnight). Sandwiches and salads are also on the menu. **€**

TRONDHEIM

Bari Café and Bar
Munkegata 25
Tel: 73 60 60 24
Bari has an Italian-influenced menu with dishes ranging from lunchtime burgers to more sophisticated fish and meat evening mains. **€€**

Credo Restaurant and Bar
Ørjaveita 4A
Tel: 73 53 03 88
An unconventional gourmet restaurant with no fixed menu, which instead offers a different fish and a meat special each day. The wine cellar is one of Norway's best. **€€**

Eld
Kongens gate 30
Tel: 47 93 10 10
Eld is an old Norwegian word for flame or fire, which is the theme of this spacious restaurant with open kitchen, fireplace and the largest grill in Scandinavia. Launched in 2011, their entrecôte is already legendary. Look out

for the daily 3-course special. **€€–€€€**

Emilies
Erling Skaktes gate 45
Tel: 73 92 96 41
At this intimate, modern restaurant, you can dine on tapas or from a three-course menu with matching wine. **€€**

Grenaderen
Kongsgårdsgata 1
Tel: 73 51 66 80
In an old 16th-century forge with a large terrace. Choose from a traditional menu including fish and reindeer, or go on one of the special buffet days that focus on salads and warm dishes. **€€**

Havfruen Fiskerestaurant
Kjøpmannsgate 7
Tel: 73 87 40 70
Some of the finest Norwegian fish and seafood, plus meat, in a converted riverside warehouse. Trendy bar. **€€**

Palmehaven Restaurant
Dronningensgate 5
Tel: 73 80 08 00
Situated in the stylish Brittania Hotel with Moorish-style garden, this has been a traditional haunt among locals for fine dining and festive occasions since 1918. **€€**

BELOW: Norwegian treats.

To Rom og Kjøkken
Carl Johansgate 5
Tel: 73 56 89 00
Opened in 2005 by two gentleman with a passionate commitment to food and wine. The focus is on using the freshest local ingredients and giving them a Mediterranean twist. **€€€**

TROMSØ

Emmas Drømmekjøkken
Kirkegata 8
Tel: 77 63 77 30
Emma's Dream Kitchen delivers high-quality Norwegian fish, seafood, duck and lamb dishes, pepped with ginger, enriched by truffle sauces, and generally turned into culinary triumphs. The service is excellent and the ambience warm. Just across the street from the cathedral. Reservations advised. **€€€**

Fiskekompaniet
Killengrens Gate
Tel: 77 68 76 00
Just fish and seafood served in a modern, Scandic environment, taken straight from the harbour and prepared in a variety of styles, from traditional to "New Scandinavian". On the town's main shopping street. **€€€**

Peppermøllen Mat og Vinhus
Storgata 42
Tel: 77 68 62 60

The city's oldest, most traditional restaurant features about 160 dishes using mainly Norwegian ingredients, with fish as the headliner. **€€**

Vertshuset Skarven
Strandtorget 1
Tel: 77 60 07 20
Skarven is made up of two adjacent restaurants which attract loyal customers. The old brick building, Arctandria, specialises in fresh fish and shellfish. Smoked and salted seal

meat is a speciality. The yellow wood building, BiffHus, serves several varieties of steak alongside other well-prepared meat dishes. Good value and a cheerful atmosphere. **€€**

PRICE CATEGORIES

Price categories are per person for an average three-course meal, excluding wine:
$ = under NOK280
$$ = NOK280–560
$$$ = over NOK560

Sweden A – Z

A HANDY SUMMARY OF PRACTICAL INFORMATION

A ctivities

Outdoor Sports

Sweden is a health-conscious nation, offering copious sports facilities nationwide. Visitors who wish to centre their holiday around sport can order the brochures *Outdoor Activities, Summer Activities and Winter Activities* from VisitSweden (www.visitsweden.com).

Cycling

There are some pleasant bike trails in Sweden, and bikes are available to rent around the country. Gotland is a cyclists' favourite, as is the scenic towpath alongside the Göta Kanal. For more information contact:
Svenska Cykelförbundet
Idrottens Hus, Fiskartorpsvägen 15A, 114 73 Stockholm
Tel: 08-699 60 00
Email: kansli@scf.se
www.scf.se

Fishing

You can fish in the sea with rod and line free of charge around the Swedish coastline. Fishing is also free from the shores of the five largest lakes: Vänern, Vättern, Mälaren, Hjälmaren and Storsjön; elsewhere a permit is required, available from local tourist information offices. For special conditions regarding permitted equipment, close seasons, minimum size and catch limits, check with tourist offices. Poaching is severely punished. For further information:
Swedish Angling Federation
Svartviksslingan 28, 16739 Bromma
Tel: 08-410 80 600
Email: info@sportfiskarna.se
www.sportfiskarna.se

Golf

Golf is played at more than 300 courses. The best are located in the south, but you can even play a round in the light of the Midnight Sun at several courses inside the Arctic Circle: the world's most northerly golf course is at Bjorkliden. The more popular golf courses can be extremely busy in the summer, so booking is advisable. For information contact:
Svenska Golfförbundet
Box 84, 182 11 Danderyd
Tel: 08-622 15 00
Email: info@sgf.golf.se
www.golf.se

Hiking

In the countryside, serious walkers will find plenty of long-distance paths, including the Kungsleden (King's Trail), which traverses the high peaks of Lapland. The Swedish Tourist Federation (Svenska Turistföreningen) maintains a network of cabins for overnight accommodation and also operates Sweden's youth hostels. For more details contact:
Svenska Turistföreningen
Box 17251, 104 62 Stockholm
Tel: 08-463 21 00
Email: info@stfturist.se
www.svenskaturistforeningen.se
Sweden's National Parks
Valhallavägen 195,
106 48 Stockholm
Tel: 08-698 10 00
www.naturvardsverket.se

Horse Riding

Almost every town has riding stables or a riding school, and more experienced riders can enjoy a pony-trekking safari in the Kebnekaise mountain range. For further information contact:
Svenska Ridsportförbundet
Ridsportenshus, 734 94 Strömsholm
Tel: 0220-456 00

ABOVE: having fun at Astrid Lindgren's World in Småland.

Email: kansliet@ridsport.se
www.ridsport.se

Husky Safaris
Winter tourism is really taking off in Sweden, and one of the most popular icy activities is a husky safari. Long and short trips are available from mid-November to late April; the weather is generally best towards the end of the season.

Sailing
Right on the city's doorstep lie 24,000 islets and skerries which provide some of the most sheltered waters in Europe. No wonder, then, that the Swedes are such keen sailors. Opportunities for sailing adventures abound, with many charter companies running day cruises, or longer, to picturesque islands. **Stockholm Adventures** operate day sails in a historic schooner or luxury yacht (www.stockholmadventures.se).

Skiing
Swedes learn to ski when they are toddlers, so there are plenty of facilities for both downhill and cross-country enthusiasts. The best-known resorts are Åre, which was a close contender for the 1994 Winter Olympics, and Sälen in the province of Dalarna. The skiing season in Riksgränsen in the far north of the country extends into the summer: pistes open from February until late May, and over the Midsummer holiday in June. For more information:
Svenska Skidförbundet
Riksskidstadion
791 19 Falun
Tel: 023-874 40
www.skidor.com

Tennis
The country's tennis facilities are

excellent. There is a wide range of both indoor and outdoor courts for public use throughout Sweden, and tennis is not at all considered an exclusive sport.
Svenska Tennisförbundet (Tennis)
Lidingövägen 75, 115 41 Stockholm
Tel: 08-450 43 10
Email: info@tennis.se
www.tennis.se

Watersports
With almost 100,000 lakes and thousands of kilometres of waterways, Sweden has a lot to offer to watersports devotees, including waterskiing, windsurfing, canoeing and white-water rafting. Dalsland and Värmland are good areas for canoe safaris.

Spectator Sports
Göteborg is probably the most sport-focused town in Sweden, and its Scandinavium is the venue for major tennis, ice hockey and table tennis events. The Ullevi Stadium stages international tournaments in football, athletics and speedway.

Tennis is a favourite spectator sport: the Swedish Open is held at Båstad, on the southwest coast, in mid-July and the Stockholm Open in October.
Horse-racing and trotting are popular in Sweden, with the best-known courses at Stockholm (Täby and Solvalla), Göteborg (Åby) and Malmö (Jägersro). Another important annual international horse show is held at the Göteborg Scandinavium in April.

Admission Charges
Admission to museums, galleries and palaces varies enormously, from free to around 120 kronor. Stockholm and

Göteborg both offer superb tourist cards giving free admission to heaps of attractions and free public transport.

C hildren
Sweden is child-friendly, and Swedes are good at devising excellent attractions for the whole family, like amusement parks such as **Liseberg** (www.liseberg.se) in Göteborg and **Gröna Lund Tivoli** (www.gronalund.com) in Stockholm.

Astrid Lindgren Fantasies
The famous author Astrid Lindgren is a master at creating fantasy characters that appeal to children. Pippi Longstocking, Emil and Karlsson on the Roof are just some of the attractions at Junibacken, a wonderful fairytale house in Stockholm, where characters from many favourite children's books come to life and kids can play, discover and learn. All attractions are indoors, and there's also a restaurant and a bookshop with Sweden's largest selection of children's books.
Junibacken, Galärvarvsvägen, close to Gröna Lund Tivoli, Stockholm
Tel: 08-587 230 00
Email: info@junibacken.se
www.junibacken.se
The author was born in Vimmerby in the province of Småland, where you can also visit Astrid Lindgren's World, another fairytale land with living characters from her books. It is open daily from mid-May until the end of August, plus weekends in September.
Astrid Lindgren's World
Tel: 0492-798 00
Email: info@alv.se
www.alv.se

Skara Sommarland
Scandinavia's largest waterpark is Skara Sommarland at Skara, northeast of Göteborg. As well as water slides, flumes and wave pools, other attractions include a grand prix race track, fairground rides, a railway and three boating lakes.
Tel: 0511-77 03 00; www.sommarland.se.

Zoos
The best-known zoo/safari park is at Kolmården (tel: 011-24 90 00; www.kolmarden.com) near Norrköping. It has lions, giraffes, elephants and so on, as well as Sweden's only dolphinarium. Other zoos of note are Borås zoo, Ölands Djur & Nöjespark near Kalmar, Parken Zoo at Eskilstuna, Furuvik zoo and Skansen in Stockholm.
In a park in Grönklitt (tel: 0250 462 00; www.orsabjornpark.se), Dalarna, brown bears live in their natural forest habitat.

CLIMATE CHART

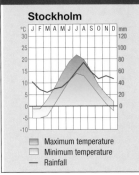

Stockholm

- ▢ Maximum temperature
- ▢ Minimum temperature
- — Rainfall

This park offers a great opportunity to see them and their cubs up close.

Santaworld

Not far from Orsa is Tomteland (Santaworld; tel: 0250 287 70; www.santaworld.se), where children can explore Santa's house, workshop and animals, the elf village, the Snow Queen's Palace... and place orders for Christmas.

Vintage Railways

Sweden has a number of vintage railways, some of which still operate steam locomotives. The longest preserved railway is the 32km (20-mile) narrow-gauge line Lennakatten, running from Uppsala to Lenna, which operates Wednesday, Thursday and weekends in high summer.

Cowboy Capers

An unusual visitor attraction in Småland is **High Chaparral** (tel: 0370-827 00; www.highchaparral.se), a mock Wild West town, complete with cowboys, Indians, bandits and sheriffs.

Climate

In summer Sweden's weather is similar to that in Britain – and just as unpredictable – although in a good year some remarkably high temperatures can be recorded in the Arctic regions. The area round Piteå on the Gulf of Bothnia is known as the Northern Riviera because of its warmth. But in the north, autumn and winter arrive early and spring comes in late May.

Winter can be cold; even in Stockholm, maximum temperatures in the day are likely to remain below freezing in January and February.

What to Bring

Sweden's weather is unpredictable, so plan for any eventuality. In summer, even in the Arctic north, you could have hot sunny days that call for shorts and T-shirts, or it could be one of those summers when the sun never appears and sweaters and rainwear are needed. Winters can be very cold, but this is "dry" cold, which is not uncomfortable. Still, you should take a heavy coat and warm headgear, as well as sturdy footwear for the slushy streets.

Culture

Festivals

Kiruna Snow Festival – a celebration of Sami traditions and snow-sculpting (January).
Vasaloppet – the exalted cross-country ski race, held between Sälen and Mora (March).
Walpurgis Night – across Sweden, parades, singing and bonfires mark the beginning of spring (30 April).
Midsummer's Eve – Sweden's biggest celebration, with more

bonfires, plus maypoles, drinking and dancing (June).
Music vid Siljan – folk and jazz in venues around Lake Siljan (July).
Medieval Week – parades, plays and performances with a medieval feel, held in Visby (August).
Nobel Prize Day – the prestigious prizes are given out at a ceremony in Stockholm (10 December).

Music

The musical scene in Sweden is busiest in the autumn, winter and spring, but there is still a lot going on in summer. In Dalarna, for example, several communities organise traditional music festivals. The town of Borlänge in Dalarna also hosts Sweden's biggest pop and rock festival, Peace & Love, held in late June/early July.

Stockholm, Göteborg and Malmö all have highly regarded orchestras based in the cities' main Konserthus. Each city also has a dedicated modern opera house, offering varied programmes of opera, ballet and musicals. Most concert halls are closed in the month of July.

Theatre

Sweden has a lively theatrical scene in the major cities, but many theatres close during the peak summer months. Performances are usually in Swedish.

Stockholm

The most prestigious theatre is the Royal Dramatic Theatre (Dramaten) on Nybroplan, which contains eight stages. The most unusual one is the Drottningholms Slottsteater at Drottningholms Palace, founded by King Gustav III in 1766. More than 30 sets from the era are still in use today. In summer it stages 17th- and 18th-century operas, attracting music-lovers from around the world.

Current performances are listed in the Stockholm What's On booklet. There is a booth on Norrmalmstorg Square, Biljett Direkt, where you can buy last-minute theatre seats.

Göteborg

The two main theatres are Stadsteatern and Folkteatern; both open from September to May. In summer, the Liseberg amusement park hosts many famous artists.

Malmö

The Stadsteater is a modern building with three stages. Plays are in Swedish, but you can often catch an opera or musical performance.

BELOW: Göteborg Opera House.

Traditional Plays

Several places in Sweden stage traditional plays in summer. For example, Rune Lindström's play *Himlaspelet (The Road to Heaven)* has been performed in Leksand in mid-July since 1949. In Visby, on the island of Gotland, the atmospheric Medieval Week (Medeltidsveckan) in early August features lively parades and theatrical performances.

Cinema

Virtually all foreign films are shown with their original soundtracks and Swedish subtitles (rather than being dubbed). Local newspapers have full details of programmes and times. In Stockholm, cinemas showing first-run international films include Filmstaden Sergel, Filmstaden Söder, Rigoletto and Filmstaden Kista.

The film company SF has a website where you can book your ticket for any cinema around the country; www.sf.se.

Customs Regulations

There are no restrictions on importing/exporting goods for people travelling between Sweden and other EU countries, as long as the goods are for personal use or your family's use and not resale; it is up to the individual customs officer to decide whether quantities of imported alcohol and tobacco products are for personal use or should be considered commercial imports. Visitors travelling to/from non-EU countries can import duty-free 200 cigarettes/100 cigarillos/50 cigars or 250g tobacco, 1 litre of spirits or 2 litres of dessert wine (maximum 22 percent alcohol by volume), 4 litres of wine plus 16 litres of beer.

D isabled Travellers

In line with its enlightened social attitudes, Sweden has long been a pioneer in accommodating travellers with disabilities. Many hotel rooms and facilities are adapted for the needs both of people with mobility problems and those suffering from allergies. New public buildings are all accessible to people with disabilities, and toilets with the handicap symbol can be found almost everywhere.

The "Stay in Sweden" directory (order from www.visitsweden.com) lists hotels with wheelchair access.

In Stockholm, most buses are designed for easy access for people with wheelchairs and pushchairs. Mainline and underground trains have elevators or ramps.

For general information contact:
DHR De Handikappades Riksförbund
Box 43, 123 21 Farsta
Tel: 08-685 80 00
Email: info@dhr.se
www.dhr.se
For wheelchair rental contact:
Contact Hjälpmedelsinstitutet
Tel: 08-620 17 00
Email: registrator@hi.se
www.hi.se

E mbassies and Consulates

Canada
Klarabergsgatan 23, 6th floor
Tel: 08 453 30 00
www.canadaemb.se
Ireland
Hovslagargatan 5
Tel: 08 545 04 040
www.embassyofireland.se
UK
Skarpögatan 6–8
Tel: 08 671 30 00
http://ukinsweden.fco.gov.uk/en
US
Dag Hammarskjölds Väg 31
Tel: 08 783 53 00
www.usemb.se

Emergencies

Police, fire, ambulance 112 (calls are free)

G ay and Lesbian Travellers

Sweden is renowned for its liberal attitudes to sex, and its age of consent is 15 for heterosexuals and gays. But there is nevertheless little open affection between gay couples, and the gay scene is less apparent in Stockholm than in other capitals, with few places for gays only. Södermalm is the most relaxed, gay-friendly area of the city.

QX is a gay/lesbian magazine that offers information about clubs, restaurants, bars and shops mainly in Stockholm, Götenborg, Malmö and Copenhagen. www.qx.se.

H ealth and Medical Care

Precautions

Standards of hygiene in Sweden are among the highest in the world. No inoculations are needed, and tap water is safe to drink.

In the far north of Sweden in high summer, precautions need to be taken against the vicious mosquitoes. In forested areas, wear long socks and use insect repellent to guard against ticks.

Above: lunch is served.

Medical Treatment

Sweden has reciprocal agreements with the UK and other countries, under which visitors are entitled to the same medical treatment as Swedes. To qualify, EU nationals must obtain an European Health Insurance Card (EHIC; available in the UK through post offices and online at www.ehic.org.uk). To see a doctor, take the EHIC and your passport to the nearest hospital clinic ("Akutmottagning" or "Vårdcentral"). With the EHIC, visitors pay a small fee (the same as Swedes); without it, visitors must pay for the actual cost of the treatment. For hospital treatment, inpatient care is usually free, with just a small daily rate payable.

Visitors from outside the EU pay higher clinic consultation fees, although these are modest compared with those charged in North America. Non-EU visitors also pay in full for hospital treatment, so it is important to take out adequate medical insurance coverage before your visit so that you can reclaim the money on your return.

Pharmacies

The larger cities all have a 24-hour pharmacy *(apotek)*. In Stockholm, it is located opposite the Central Railway Station: Apoteket C.W. Scheele, Klarabergsgatan 64; tel: 0771-450 450.

I nternet

Most hotels offer WiFi internet access; cybercafés are easy to find in towns and cities. Ask at the local tourist office for details.

Language

The Alphabet

The Swedish alphabet has 29 letters; the additional three are å, ä and ö, and come after the letter z. To find Mr Åkerblad in the phone book, therefore, look at the end of the listings.

Useful Words and Phrases

Yes *Ja*
No *Nej*
Hello *Hej*
Goodbye *Hejdå*
Thank you *Tack*
Please *Tack/Var så god*
Do you speak English? *talar du engelska?*
I only speak English *jag talar bara engelska*
Good morning *God morgon*
Good afternoon *God eftermiddag*
Good evening *God kväll*
Today *Idag*
Tomorrow *I morgon*
Yesterday *Igår*
How do you do *Goddag*
What time is it? *Hur mycket är klockan?*
It is (the time is) *Den är (klockan är)*
Could I have your name please? *Hur var namnet?*
My name is *Jag heter*
Can I help you? *Kan jag hjälpa till?*
I do not understand *Jag förstår inte*
I do not know *Jag vet inte*

Eating and Drinking

breakfast *frukost*
lunch *lunch*
dinner *middag*
eat *äta*
drink *dricka*
Cheers *Skål!*
off-licence *Systembolaget*
Can I order please? *Får jag beställa?*
Could I have the bill please? *Kan jag få notan?*

Getting Around

aircraft *flygplan*
bus/coach *buss*
car *bil*
parking *parkering, garage*
train *tåg*
How do I get to ...? *Hur kommer jag till ...?*
Where is ...? *Var finns ...?*
Right *Höger*
To the right *Till höger*
Left *Vänster*
To the left *Till vänster*
Straight on *Rakt fram*

Shopping

to buy *att köpa*
department store *varuhus*

food *mat*
grocery store (in countryside) *lanthandel*
handicraft *hemslöjd*
money *pengar*
shop *affär*
clothes *kläder*
overcoat *kappa, överrock*
jacket *jacka*
suit *kostym*
shoes *skor*
skirt *kjol*
jersey *tröja, jumper*
How much is this? *Vad kostar det?*
It costs ... *Det kostar ...*
Do you have English newspapers? *Har du engelska tidningar?*

Health and Security

chemist *apotek*
accident and emergency clinic *akutmottagning/vårdcentral*
hospital *sjukhus*
doctor *doktor*
police station *polisstation*

Miscellaneous

Toilet *Toalett*
Gentlemen *Herrar*
Ladies *Damer*
Vacant *Ledigt*
Engaged *Upptagen*
No smoking *Rökning förbjuden*
Entrance *Ingång*
Exit *Utgång*
No entry *Ingen ingång*
Open *Öppen/Öppet*
Closed *Stängt*

Days of the Week

Monday *måndag*
Tuesday *tisdag*
Wednesday *onsdag*
Thursday *torsdag*
Friday *fredag*
Saturday *lördag*
Sunday *söndag*

Numbers

0 *noll*
1 *en/ett*
2 *två*
3 *tre*
4 *fyra*
5 *fem*
6 *sex*
7 *sju*
8 *åtta*
9 *nio*
10 *tio*
11 *elva*
12 *tolv*
13 *tretton*
14 *fjorton*
15 *femton*
16 *sexton*
17 *sjutton*
18 *arton*

19 *nitton*
20 *tjugo*
21 *tjugoen*
22 *tjugotvå*
30 *trettio*
40 *fyrtio*
50 *femtio*
60 *sextio*
70 *sjuttio*
80 *åttio*
90 *nittio*
100 *hundra*
200 *två hundra*
1,000 *tusen*

Media

Newspapers and Magazines

English-language newspapers are widely available at kiosks in larger cities, usually on the day of publication. Kulturhus (the cultural centre) in Stockholm at Sergels Torg has a good selection of English newspapers and magazines that can be read for free, as does the City Library in Göteborg on the main square, Götaplatsen. For a wide selection of English-language magazines try a Press Stop Store (in Stockholm there's one in the central Gallerian shopping centre, on Hamngatan).

Books

English-language books are widely available. In Stockholm, excellent bookshops include:
Akademibokhandeln, Mäster Samuelsgaten 32 (Scandinavia's largest bookshop); www. akademibokhandeln.se.
Hedengrens Bokhandel, Stureplan 4; www.hedengrens.se.
Sweden Bookshop, Slottsbacken 10 (bookshop selling Swedish Institute publications); www.swedenbookshop.com.
For maps and guides, try **Kartbutiken**, Vasagatan 16; www. kartbutiken.se.

Television

Sweden's state-run STV1 and STV2 show a film most evenings. The commercial channels TV3, TV6, Kanal 5 and Kanal 9 run American chat shows, movies, and comedy and drama series. Plus there are many satellite/cable channels, featuring CNN, BBC and MTV, broadcast in English with subtitles.

Radio

Radio Sweden has a 30-minute English-language broadcast with news and information about Sweden on the P2 network at 3pm Monday to Friday. There is a similar broadcast in the Stockholm area on the P6 FM

89.6 MHz network at 8.30pm Monday to Friday.

A variety of BBC and NPR programmes are also available on channel 89.6 FM.

Money

There is no limit on the import of either Swedish or foreign currency.

Travellers' cheques can be exchanged without difficulty at banks all over Sweden. A foreign exchange service is also provided by post offices with the "PK Exchange" sign. Forex and X-change, bureaux de change with branches in most major towns and airports, usually have better exchange rates than the banks and post offices and don't charge any commission.

Leading credit cards (although some restrictions may apply to American Express) are accepted by most hotels, restaurants and shops throughout the country, and you can also take out cash on these cards at foreign exchange offices and banks.

Currency

Swedish krona (plural kronor), marked ":-" or "kr" or "Skr" in shops, or SEK internationally, and split into 100 öre. The 50-öre coin is no longer legal tender. Coins are 1 krona, 5 and 10 kronor. Notes are 20, 50, 100, 500 and 1,000 kronor.

Swedish coins and banknotes were undergoing a complete rehaul at the time of writing, with lighter coins, new banknote designs, and a new 2-kronor coin and 200-kronor banknote to be introduced in 2014–15.

Tipping

• In hotels and restaurants a service charge is included in the bill and a further tip is not generally expected, although it's usual to round up the bill to the nearest SEK10 or 20 for an evening meal.
• Taxi drivers are usually tipped.
• Cloakrooms at restaurants and clubs charge about SEK15–20.
• Tipping for special services provided by hotel staff is fine but not expected.

Nightlife

Where to Go

There is an active nightlife in the larger cities, but nothing particularly hectic in the smaller communities. Many hotels have bars, nightclubs and sometimes even live dance music. University cities like Uppsala, Lund, Linköping and Umeå have a

busy nightlife, at least for the students.

Skiing resorts like Åre and Sälen are also good for nightlife from December to April, with après-ski bands playing covers of well-known tunes to packed crowds.

Out in the countryside and in smaller towns *dansband* music is popular – Swedish-style country music to which people dance foxtrot and a kind of jive. If you like dancing this could be a fun thing to try and a chance to meet the locals. Dancing may not begin until midnight.

The cost of drinking has fallen a little in recent years, but a night out on the town can still be expensive. The best value is probably at a jazz club, or at one of the piano bars, which offer a quieter and more relaxing environment for a late-night drink.

Nightclubs, Bars and Live Music

Opening Hours

Nightclubs and discos usually close around 3am (sometimes 5am in Stockholm). Unfortunately, numerous nightclubs have long queues outside after 9 or 10pm, even if it's not full inside – an irritating way of showing that the club is popular. Avoid the queue by getting there early, or booking a table and having dinner there (Swedes often combine dining and drinking on a night out), which also means you avoid paying the nightclub entrance fee.

Age Limits

If you're in your early 20s or younger, you may not be able to get into some clubs. Some have remarkably high minimum age limits: the more upmarket nightclubs impose a minimum age of up to 26 for men and 24 for women.

BELOW: keep your cool in the Absolut Ice Bar.

Stockholm

For the most happening clubs and bars, check out www.stockholmtown.com.
Absolut Ice Bar
Vasaplan 4
Tel: 08 505 635 20
www.nordicseahotel.se
A little gimmicky! Nevertheless, you may want to sip a quick cocktail at the world's first permanent ice bar. Its –5°C (23°F) interior is entirely sculpted from Lapland ice – including the glasses. Reservations required.
Akkurat
Hornsgatan 18
Tel: 08 644 00 15
Popular Söder hangout for those who enjoy listening to good blues, rock and soul, played here on Sunday nights. Also has a wide selection of whiskies and beers.
Berns
Berzelii Park 6
Tel: 08 566 322 00
www.berns.se
This entertainment palace at Berzelii Park has been in existence since 1863, but it has never been in better form since Sir Terence Conran redesigned it a few years ago. It now has several stylish bars, including the Berns Bar under crystal chandeliers, the cocktail bar in a sober glass veranda and a cellar bar that attracts the trendy crowd. Its 2.35:1 nightclub opens until 4.30am on Fridays and Saturdays.
Café Opera
Operahus
Tel: 08 676 58 07
www.cafeopera.se
Expensive but ever-popular bar, restaurant and club (which starts around midnight) with a mix of younger people and older regulars. There is an impressive classical architectural interior. Minimum age is 23.

ABOVE: taking part in Midsummer festivities.

Debaser Slussen
Karl Johans Torget 1
Tel: 08 30 56 20
www.debaser.se
Great live metal and rock gigs.
Debaser Medis, in Södermalm, is a
newer venue hosting everything from
world music and hip hop to rock and
pop. Wednesday to Sunday.

Fasching
Kungsgatan 63
Tel: 08 543 829 60
www.fasching.se
This is Stockholm's largest and most
popular jazz club, with restaurant and
nightclub.

Glenn Miller Café
Brunnsgatan 21A
Tel: 08 10 03 22
www.glennmillercafe.com
Small bar and restaurant with nightly
jazz from 8pm.

Hornstull Strand
Hornstull Strand 4
Tel: 08 658 63 50
http://hornstullstrand.se
This laidback restaurant/bar/club
welcomes interesting young bands as
well as some of Sweden's most
famous DJs. Cosy sofas and table-
tennis tables add to the at-home
ambience.

La Habana
Sveavägen 108
Tel: 08 16 64 65
www.lahabana.se
Rum, cigars and salsa are the order of
the day at this fun, rough-and-ready
Cuban place, with live music from
Wednesday to Saturday.

Nada
Åsögatan 140
Tel: 08 644 70 20
Pleasant, cosy bar with DJs spinning
indie-pop tunes.

Och Himlen Därtill
Gotgatan 78
Tel: 08-660 60 68
www.restauranghimlen.se

This super-chic skybar is the place to
sip cocktails and admire spectacular
views of Stockholm from the 26th
floor.

Patricia
Stadsgårdskajen 152
Tel: 08 743 05 70
www.patricia.st
The steamship M/S *Patricia* is now a
party boat, with three floors of bars
and dancing and a great mix of
people. Gay club night on Sundays.

Spy Bar
Birger Jarlsgatan 20
Tel: 08 545 076 55
One of Stockholm's most legendary
nightclubs, Spy Bar is popular with an
intellectual, media-savvy crowd.

Stampen
Stora Nygatan 5
Tel: 08 20 57 93
www.stampen.se
Lively, well-known jazz pub in the Old
Town, with live music from 8pm until
late.

Sturecompagniet
Sturegatan 4
Tel: 08 545 076 01
www.sturecompagniet.se
This massive club, with its dramatic
ballroom entrance, sprawls across
three floors in the city centre, packed
with bars and dance floors.

Göteborg
For the latest on Göteborg's nightlife,
see www.goteborg.com.

Blissresto
Magasinsgatan 3
Tel: 031 13 85 55
www.blissresto.com
This sophisticated tapas restaurant
slides into clubland as evening
becomes night, with DJs and dancing
until late. Perfect cocktails.

Excet
Vasagatan 52
Tel: 031 711 99 11
http://excet.se

One of Göteborg's biggest, this three-
storey nightclub attracts a mixed
crowd with its two dance floors, DJs
and a summer terrace.

Jazzhuset
Erik Dahlbergsgatan 3
Tel: 031 13 35 44
www.jazzhuset.se
There's always live music here.
Various club nights feature different
sounds, from pure jazz to electronica.

Lounge(s)
Kungsportsavenyen 5
Tel: 031 711 15 41
www.lounges.se
Stylish club with themed lounges,
resident DJs and a very sleek casino.

Nefertiti Jazz Club
Hvidfeldtsplatsen 6
Tel: 031 711 40 76
www.nefertiti.se
Running for over 30 years, this
popular place bursts at the seams on
club nights, when happy revellers
dance to jazz, blues, soul, electronic
and world music.

Park Lane
Kungsportsavenyn 36–38
Tel: 031 20 60 58
www.parklane.se
An upmarket nightclub with an
international atmosphere and
clientele of all ages and orientation.
There are three bars, a restaurant, a
casino and live performances.

Push
Kungsportsavenyn 11
Tel: 031 701 80 90
www.push.se
One of Göteborg's newest nightclubs,
set up by Stockholm's
Sturecompagniet crew. The fabulous
interior (Scandinavian-minimalism
with retro-future touches) throbs to
the sounds of mainstream house.
Rooftop terrace.

Trädgår'n
Nya Allén
Tel: 031 10 20 80

Dance Boats

A popular outing – among young
and old as well as conference
parties – is to take the boat from
Stockholm to Finland for a day's
visit to Helsinki or Åbo (Turku). The
round trip takes about 40 hours
and includes one or two nights on
the boat and one day in Helsinki or
Åbo. The boats have several dance
floors, bars and a restaurant to
entertain the captive audience.
Contact Tallink Silja (tel: 08 22 21
40; www.tallinksilja.com) or Viking
Line (tel: 08 452 40 00; www.vikingline.se)
for information.

Restaurant in the centre of the city's botanical garden, with outdoor dining, live performances and weekend nightclub.

Malmö
Lilla Torg (Small Square) is a buzzing area where new restaurants and bars open up all the time.
Brogatan
Brogatan 12
Tel: 040 30 77 17
The place to be seen, this is a popular bar among Malmö's celebrities. In summer, there's a weekend nightclub until 3am.
Club Privé
Malmborgsgatan 7
Tel: 0734 22 59 96
www.clubprive.nu
One of Malmö's biggest clubs, with two dance floors, five bars and big sound systems dedicated to R&B and house.
Crown Nightclub
Amiralsgatan 19
Tel: 040 611 80 88
In this popular club there are different themes for different days of the week, from 1960s music to soul and R&B, or 1980s music/disco.
Etage
Stortorget 6
Tel: 040 23 20 60
Popular place with young people.
Harry's
Södergatan 14
Tel: 040-12 34 90
Bar and disco with a friendly and relaxed atmosphere.
Hipp
Kalendegatan 12
Tel: 040 97 40 30
Beautiful, late 19th-century-style restaurant and bar with club arrangements every Saturday.
Kulturbolaget
Bergsgatan 18
Tel: 040 30 20 11
This big rock-music venue becomes a club on Fridays and Saturdays, featuring rock/pop music and sometimes disco.
Swing Inn
Stadt Hamburgsgatan 2C
Tel: 040 12 22 21
Popular among 30-somethings, the music is soft disco; jacket and tie required. Minimum age limit 28.

O pening Hours

Shops on the whole open 9.30am–6pm on weekdays and until between 1 and 4pm on Saturdays. In larger cities many shops are open on Sundays as well, usually noon–4pm. Shops generally close early the day before a public holiday.

Public Holidays

Sweden has several official holidays:
1 January New Year's Day
6 January Epiphany
March/April Good Friday and Easter Monday
1 May Labour Day
May Ascension (usually second part of the month); Pentecost (10 days after Ascension)
6 June National Day
June Midsummer's Day (around the 24th)
November All Saints' Day (usually at start of the month)
25 and 26 December Christmas
31 December New Year's Eve

Department stores may remain open until 8pm or 9pm and possibly also on Sundays.
Banks Monday–Friday 10am–3pm (6pm in some larger cities), but closed on Saturdays. SEB Exchange at Stockholm Arlanda airport's Terminal 5 arrival hall is open daily 5am–11pm.

P ostal Services

Post offices have been phased out and their services taken over by supermarkets, grocery stores and petrol stations. Stamps (frimärken) are also on sale at Pressbyrån newsstands, bookstalls and stationers' shops. Mailboxes are blue for local letters and yellow for all other destinations.

R eligious Services

The Swedish State Church is in the Lutheran tradition and has churches throughout the country.

Stockholm has the widest range of places of worship, including Catholic churches, a Greek Orthodox church, several synagogues and a mosque.

Protestant services in English are usually held once a week in major cities. Enquire at your hotel for more information.

S hopping
Where to Shop

Sweden is famous the world over for its elegant design, and you will find plenty of good buys in glassware, stainless steel, silver, pottery, ceramics, textiles and leather goods. Department stores such as NK and Åhléns are noted for their high-quality, inexpensive kitchenware.

Glass The best bargains are found in "Glass Country" – Småland, in the southeast – where there are 13 glassworks. Most of the glassworks (including Orrefors, Kosta-Boda, SEA and Skruf) have shops adjoining their factories where you can buy everything from one-off sculptures to cheap factory seconds. Visitors to Stockholm can buy Swedish glass from department stores like NK, or dedicated glass shops such as Crystal Art Centre, Nordiska Kristall or Orrefors Kosta Boda.

Porcelain and Ceramics Sweden is also renowned for its high-quality porcelain, and bargains can be found at the Gustavsberg factory outside Stockholm and at the Rörstrand factory in Lidköping. Höganäs in Skåne has a strong history of ceramics: a factory outlet there sells quality Swedish brands.

Fashion For cheap clothing, try Hennes & Mauritz (H&M), Lindex, JC and KappAhl. The best shopping area is probably Borås, near Göteborg, which is the centre of the Tygriket (Weavers' Country). Knalleland is a large shopping centre in Borås where you can get bargains from the leading direct-mail companies.

The centre of the fur business is Tranås in the province of Småland, where you can usually find bargains.

Tax-Free Shopping

Visitors from outside the EU are entitled to a tax refund of up to 17.5 per cent on purchases of over 200 kronor in shops displaying the Tax Free Shopping sign. For further details, see www.global-blue.com.

Markets

Stockholm has markets at Hötorget, Östermalmstorg and Medborgarplatsen, which are worth a visit, while Göteborg has its "Fish Church", a thriving fish market built in an ecclesiastical style. Göteborg also has a fascinating food market (Saluhallen).

Stockholm's suburbs contain what is claimed to be Northern Europe's largest flea market at Vårberg, 30 minutes on the underground from the city centre. It's open daily, but Saturday and Sunday are the best days to go (a small admission charge applies at weekends).

Factory Outlets

Below are factory outlets selling Swedish and international brand names:

Abecita
Borås
Tel: 033 23 76 05
Ladies' underwear, swimsuits,
dressing gowns.
Freeport Kungsbacka Designer Outlet Village
Kungsparksvägen 80, Kungsbacka
Tel: 0300 57 00 00
www.freeport.se
Designer clothes, toys, home
furnishings in 50 shops.
Ge-Kås
Ullared Tel: 0346 375 00
www.gekas.se
Clothes, kitchenware, food.
Stockholm Quality Outlet
Majorsvägen 2–4, Järfälla
Tel: 08 564 720 31
www.qualityoutlet.com
Outside Stockholm, 50 brand-name
shops.
Visko
Skene
Tel: 0320 322 90
www.visko.se
Shoes and more near Göteborg.

Local Crafts

All over Sweden you can see crafts-
people at work and buy their work at
low prices. In the countryside, look out
for *hemslöjd*, or handicraft centres.
Women's and children's clothes are
especially good buys, as well as furs
and needlework.
Below is a selection of outlets in
Stockholm and Göteborg. The Yellow
Pages website (www.gulasidorna.se; in
Swedish) lists shops in Sweden:
search for *hemslöjd*, *slöjd* or
konsthantverk.
Bohusslöjd
Teatergatan 19, Göteborg
Tel: 031 16 00 72
Kronhusbodarna
Central Göteborg

BELOW: glassware is a popular gift.

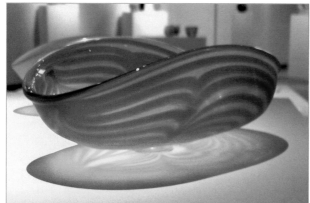

Tel: 031 13 18 00
www.kronhusbodarna.nu
Handicraft centre with glass, ceramic,
chocolate and jewellery workshops.
Svensk Hemslöjd
Norrlandsgatan 20, Stockholm
Tel: 08 23 21 15
www.svenskhemslojd.com
Svensk Slöjd
Nybrogatan 23, Stockholm
Tel: 08 663 66 50
www.svenskslojd.se

Design

For contemporary Swedish (and
international) design, several shops in
Stockholm are worth visiting:
Blås & Knåda
Hornsgatan 26a
Tel: 08 642 77 67
www.blasknada.se
Co-operative selling modern ceramic
and glass items.
Design House Stockholm
Smålandsgatan 11
Tel: 08 509 081 13
www.designhousestockholm.com
Acts as a "publisher" for new talent –
classics in the making, from
candlesticks and clothing to chests of
drawers.
DesignTorget
Kulturhuset, Sergelgången 29
Tel: 08 21 91 50
www.designtorget.se
Homeware and gifts from established
and up-and-coming designers. With
six other outlets in Stockholm,
including at Arlanda airport.
Nordiska Galleriet
Nybrogatan 11
Tel: 08 442 83 60
www.nordiskagalleriet.se
Established in 1913, this is one of the
city's leading interior design stores.
Norrgavel
Birger Jarlsgatan 27

Tel: 08 545 220 50
www.norrgavel.se
Two floors of furniture, ceramics, glass
and textiles.
Malmstenbutiken
Strandvägen 5B
Tel: 08 23 33 80
www.malmsten.se
Selling furniture-maker Carl
Malmsten's designs, alongside work
by designers inspired by him.
R.O.O.M.
PUB, plan 03, Hötorget
Tel: 08 692 50 00
www.room.se
Svenskt Tenn
Strandvägen 5 (temporarily based in
the former Astoria Cinema,
Nybrogatan 15, during store redesign)
Tel: 08 670 16 00
www.svenskttenn.se
Tiny glass vases, jewellery, bright
fabrics, furniture and more.
VIDE
Birger Jarlsgatan 34
Tel: 08 545 480 08
www.videform.se
Homeware and clean-lined furniture
from companies such as G.A.D.

IKEA

After exhorting people the world over
to "chuck out the chintz", the Swedish
behemoth IKEA will probably need no
introduction to readers. The
company's creative headquarters is
based in Älmhult, in Småland – fans
can stay in town at the Värdshuset
IKEA hotel. IKEA stores are found
across Sweden, usually on the
outskirts of towns.

Telephones

Mobile phones are widely used across
Sweden, although you can still find
payphones on the street, at petrol
stations and post offices. Most
payphones no longer take coins –
they operate only with credit cards
(signposted CCC) or a telephone card
(*telia telefonkort*). Telephone cards
are widely available in Pressbyrån,
kiosks, bookstalls, grocery stores and
stationers' shops. As elsewhere, it is
expensive to phone from hotel rooms.
The telephone directory enquiry
service (*see Useful Numbers, below*)
is also expensive.
To call abroad, dial 00 followed by
the country code (44 for the UK, 1 for
the US and Canada, 353 for Ireland,
61 for Australia and 64 for New
Zealand), then dial the number,
omitting any initial 0.
Swedish mobile phones operate on
the 900/1800 MHz GSM network –
most European phones are

compatible, although your phone must be unlocked in order to link up with the network. US phones work on a slightly different frequency, so US visitors should check with their phone company first regarding usability. The cheapest way to use your own mobile phone in Sweden is to buy a Swedish SIM card from a newsagent – ask for a *startpaket*.

To make a call from your mobile phone, dial the area code (e.g. 08 for Stockholm) followed by the number. To ring a friend's (foreign) mobile phone in Sweden you have to dial 00 followed by your friend's country code and area code (omitting the 0), plus the number.

Useful Numbers

Swedish directory enquiries 118 118
International directory enquiries 118 119
International dialling code: +46

Tourist Information

A good starting point for national tourist information is:
VisitSweden
Stortorget 2–4, 831 30 Östersund
Email: info@visitsweden.com
www.visitsweden.com

Local Offices

Sweden has a country-wide network of tourist information offices, or *Turistbyrå*, in more than 300 cities and towns, which can be identified by the international "I" sign. They have multilingual staff, and can supply information about local sightseeing and sporting activities. Some are open during the summer only. About half of the tourist information offices sport a blue-and-yellow (rather than a green) "I" sign: these provide a more comprehensive service, with local *and* national information, and hotel booking service (*rumsförmedling* or *hotellcentral*) that cover the whole country.

A complete list of offices can be obtained from the **FörTur** (Association for Swedish Tourism) website, www. turism.se. The main offices are:

Stockholm
Vasagatan 14
Tel: 08 508 285 08
Email: touristinfo@stockholm.se
www.stockholmtown.com
This is the country's busiest tourist office. Run by the Stockholm Visitors Board, it can book tickets, tours and accommodation for you. It also publishes a monthly *What's On* magazine.

Göteborg
Kungsportsplatsen 2,
SE-411 10 Göteborg
Tel: 031 368 42 00
www.goteborg.com
Gotland
Skeppsbron 4–6, Visby
Tel: 0498 20 17 00
Email: info@gotland.info
www.gotland.info
Lapland
Lars Janssonsgatan 17,
SE-981 31 Kiruna
Tel: 0980 188 80
www.kirunalapland.se
Skåne
Dockplatsen 26, SE-205 25 Malmö
Tel: 040 675 30 01
Email: tourism@skane.se
www.skane.com
Småland
Västra Storgatan 18a,
SE-551 11 Jönköping
Tel: 036 35 12 70
Email: info@visitsmaland.se
www.visitsmaland.se

Tour Operators

The brochure *Your Guide to Sweden* contains a guide to tour operators offering holidays in Sweden. The brochure is available to order or to download from VisitSweden.

A selection of tour operators with interests in Sweden includes:

UK

Best Served Scandinavia
45–49 Brompton Road, London SW3 1DE
Tel: 020 7838 5956
Email: sales@best-served.co.uk
www.best-served.co.uk
Large range of packages, including city breaks, Göta Kanal cruises, cycling holidays and winter safaris.
Discover the World
Arctic House, 8 Bolters Lane, Banstead, Surrey SM7 2AR
Tel: 01737 214 250
Email: travel@discover-the-world.co.uk
www.discover-the-world.co.uk
Specialist in activity holidays, plus self-drive summer holidays and winter breaks to Lapland.
Nordic Experience
39 Crouch Street, Colchester, Essex CO3 3EN
Tel: 01206 708 888
Email: reservations@nordicexperience.co.uk
www.nordicexperience.co.uk
Offers Stockholm breaks, Ice Hotel packages, husky mushing and winter holidays.
Simply Sweden
The Poplars, Bridge Street, Brigg, Lincolnshire DN20 8NQ

Tel: 0845 890 0300
Email: info@simplysweden.co.uk
www.simplysweden.co.uk
Offers tailor-made Swedish holidays including Ice Hotel, city breaks, log cabins, rafting, etc.

US and Canada

There are numerous tour operators in the US, a complete list of which can be obtained from the Scandinavian Tourist Board in New York (see www.goscandinavia.com). The following is just a selection:
Five Stars of Scandinavia
Tel: 1-800 722 41 26
http://5stars-scandinavia.com
Nelson's Scandinavia
Tel: 1-800 542 16 89
www.nelsonsscandinavia.com
Nordic Saga Tours
Tel: 1-800 848 64 49
www.nordicsaga.com

Unique Holidays

Vildmark I Värmland
Tel: 0560-140 40
www.vildmark.se
One-, two-, five- and eight-day cruises on the Klarälven River. Not just any cruise, though: they assist you in building a log raft and provide camping equipment for your journey.

Transport

Getting There

By Air
From the UK and Ireland
Scandinavian Airlines (SAS), Finnair and British Airways operate direct daily flights from London Heathrow to Stockholm Arlanda, and Norwegian Air fly there from London Gatwick. SAS also flies direct to Stockholm from Manchester, and Norwegian Air from Edinburgh. Ryanair also operates flights from London Stansted to Stockholm's Vasterås and Skavsta airports, both about an hour and 20 minutes' drive from the capital (to the northwest and southwest respectively), and also from London Gatwick to Skavsta.

From London, SAS and British Airways fly daily to Göteborg (Gothenburg), as does Ryanair. From Glasgow Prestwick, Ryanair flies daily to Skavsta (Stockholm) and Göteborg. From Birmingham and Liverpool, Ryanair flies several times per week to Skavsta. From Dublin, Ryanair has regular flights to Skavsta and Göteborg. City Airline flies around four times per week from Manchester to Göteborg. Travelling time from the UK is around 2½ hours.

From the US
Services between Stockholm and North America are operated by SAS, Finnair, Iceland Air, and by the US airlines Delta and American.

Airline offices in the UK and Ireland
British Airways, tel: 0844 493 0787; www.ba.com.
City Airline, tel: 0870 220 6835; www.cityairline.com
Finnair, tel: 0870 241 4411; www.finnair.com.
Norwegian Air, tel: 020 8099 7254; www.norwegian.com.
Ryanair, UK, tel: 0871 246 0000; www.ryanair.com.
Dublin, tel: 0818 30 30 30
SAS, tel: 0871 226 7760; www.flysas.com.

Airline offices in the US
Finnair, tel: 1-800 950 50 00; www.finnair.com
Icelandair, tel: 1-800 223 55 00; www.icelandair.com
SAS, tel: 1-800 221 23 50; www.flysas.com.

By Sea
There are no longer any ferries from the UK to Sweden. There are many ferry links from Denmark and Germany to Sweden, as well as from Sweden to Finland.

By Train
The fastest rail route from the UK to Sweden is via the Eurostar service, through the Channel Tunnel from London St Pancras to Brussels, with onward trains to Copenhagen and then connecting services to Sweden.
For further information call:
Eurostar, tel: 08432 186 186; www.eurostar.com
European Rail, tel: 020 7619 1083; www.europeanrail.co.uk.

By Car
With the 16km (10-mile) Öresund bridge connecting Copenhagen with Malmö, you can drive all the way to Sweden from Denmark. The drive from Copenhagen airport to Malmö takes about 45 minutes.

Getting Around
On Arrival
All three of Sweden's major international airports – Stockholm (Arlanda), Göteborg (Landvetter) and Malmö (Sturup) – have excellent links to their respective city centres. From Arlanda, passengers can use the Arlanda Express high-speed train which operates four times an hour to Stockholm Central Station in only 20

ABOVE: travelling by rail is fast and efficient.

minutes. There are also frequent bus services from Arlanda's international and domestic terminals to the City Terminal at Klarabergsgatan above Central Station. In Göteborg and Malmö, coaches operate from the airport to the cities' Central Stations.
A connecting bus meets all Ryanair flights at Vasterås and Skavsta airports and goes directly to the Cityterminalen bus terminal in central Stockholm, taking around 1 hour and 20 minutes from both.
Taxis are always available. Get a price for your destination before getting into the taxi – you are not obliged to take the cab at the head of the taxi rank. At Arlanda airport, the larger taxi companies (Taxi 020, Taxi Kurir or Taxi Stockholm) offer fixed fares for rides into the city centre: these are usually cheaper than a metered taxi ride, particularly during rush hour.

By Air
Air travel is part of everyday life in a country as large as Sweden, and all major cities and towns are linked by an efficient network of services operated mainly by SAS. Stockholm alone has flights to almost 40 places within Sweden.
Cheap flights are available on selected domestic services all year, as well as standby flights for under-25s and special fares for senior citizens. But many of the best deals are during the summer peak season in July, when few business executives are travelling.
Air Passes, sold in conjunction with an international fare, allow up to six flights within Scandinavia at affordable prices. For more information call:

Malmö Aviation, www.malmoaviation.se
SAS, www.flysas.com
Skyways, www.skyways.se

By Train
Swedish State Railways, or SJ (tel: 0771 75 75 75; www.sj.se), operate an efficient electrified network covering the entire country. The route from Trelleborg in the south to Riksgränsen in the far north is reckoned to be the longest continuous stretch of electrified rail line in the world.
Swedish trains run at a high frequency, particularly on the main trunk route linking Stockholm with Göteborg, on which there is an hourly service. The high-speed train X2000 travels at up to 200kph (125mph) and is a good choice if you want to travel long distances; the journey from Göteborg to Stockholm, for example, takes only three hours.

Rail Passes
Swedish State Railways offer a wide range of fares for both business and leisure travellers. Conditions and prices may depend on whether you buy your ticket in Sweden or abroad. A number of discount fares are available, including the following, which must be purchased outside Sweden:
InterRail Sweden Passes offer travellers who live in Europe but outside Sweden unlimited rail travel within Sweden. Check www.interrailnet.com for details.
Eurail Sweden (or Eurail Scandinavia) Passes offer travellers who live outside Europe unlimited rail travel within Sweden (or Scandinavia). Check www.eurail.com for details.
Resplus If you want to combine rail, bus and boat in one ticket, the best way is probably to buy a *Resplus* ticket

that enables you to reach over 3,000 destinations within Sweden. For more information, see www.resplus.se.

To get a *förköpsbiljett* (reduced-rate ticket) in Sweden, you must book 7 days in advance. For more information, prices and bookings call: 0771 75 75 75.

Scenic Train Route

One very beautiful journey to take by train is the Inlandsbanan (Inland Railway), which runs for more than 1,300km (800 miles) down the spine of Sweden from Gällivare, north of the Arctic Circle, to Kristinehamn in the south. You can explore stretches of the route with point-to-point tickets; or purchase the Inlandsbane Kort, a card that is valid for 14 days, allowing you to stop and continue wherever you please within the time limit.

More information is available from Inlandsbanan AB, PO Box 561, S-831 27 Östersund. Tel: 0771 53 53 53, www.inlandsbanan.se.

By Underground

Stockholm is justifiably proud of its underground railway, known as T-banan (the "T" stands for "tunnel" – all stations are identified by the "T" sign). The T-banan is spotless, with 100 stations covering 108km (67 miles).

The commuter trains *(pendeltåg)* take you very quickly to the suburbs of Stockholm as well as down to Nynäshamn, where you can board the ferry to the island of Gotland.

By Bus

Travelling by bus is usually cheap compared to rail, but travelling time is longer. There are weekend-only services on a number of key routes.

An efficient network of express bus services links all major towns and cities, operated mainly by:
Svenska Buss, tel: 0771 67 67 67; www.svenskabuss.se.
Swebus Express, tel: 0771 21 82 18; www.swebus.se.

Stockholm

Stockholm Transit Authority (www.sl.se) is the umbrella organisation that oversees the city's integrated transport system. The same travel tickets are used on the bus, the train and the underground systems. Tickets are used according to which of Stockholm's three transport zones you are travelling in – most visitors to the city will travel within Zone A. You are allowed to travel freely within one zone on the bus, train and underground for an hour on the same ticket.

It is no longer possible to buy tickets on the bus. Most bus stops have ticket machines that take cards and cash. The bus driver stamps your ticket when you board the bus and start your journey.

If you are intending to make several journeys within the city, it is cheaper to buy a set of 10 tickets, a one-, three- or seven-day travel card or the worthwhile *Stockholmskortet* tourist card, which gives free public transport in the Greater Stockholm area for a period of one, two, three or five days.

Göteborg

Göteborg has a superior tram system, as well as a good network of bus routes.

By Boat or Ferry

For a country that boasts about its 96,000 lakes and countless rivers and canals, water transport plays a surprisingly small part in Sweden's public transport system. The main ferry links the Baltic island of Gotland and has services from Nynäshamn and Oskarshamn. For more information check with the local tourist office or call Destination Gotland, tel: 0771 22 33 00; www.destinationgotland.se.

There are also innumerable commuter services in the Stockholm archipelago operated by the famous white boats of the Waxholm Steamship Company. In the summer, visitors can buy a range of discounted tickets which give unlimited travel on the Waxholm boats. For information call: 08 679 58 30; www.waxholmsbolaget.se.

Strömma Kanalbolaget runs cruises in the Stockholm archipelago: www.stromma.se.

By Taxi

Swedish taxis are usually efficient, but rely more on the telephone than being flagged down. In larger cities, a computer system gives instructions to drivers to indicate where the next person is to be picked up.

Fares are steep. There is a minimum charge, and the meter goes on as soon as the taxi arrives at your address. If you are late, the meter starts at the time you ordered the taxi – even a five-minute delay can be costly. The bigger firms accept credit cards. In Stockholm, some companies have a maximum fare for rides within the centre. This is good value when crossing the city or if there are traffic jams.

By Bicycle

Many of Sweden's towns are ideal for exploring by bike, with good cycle lanes. Cycling holidays are also popular in Sweden. The Sweden Trail *(Sverigeleden)* is the largest network of cycle paths, linking a great number of tourist centres and ports. Cykelspåret follows the entire Swedish coastline. And a particularly scenic and popular ride for cyclists is alongside the Göta Kanal.

Bikes can be hired in most places; just enquire at the local tourist office. Costs are per day or per week.

On Foot
Sightseeing

All three of Sweden's largest cities, Stockholm, Malmö and Göteborg, are compact enough to sightsee on foot. They are pedestrian-friendly to the extent that they have traffic lights that motorists actually observe; conversely, Swedish pedestrians are disciplined, and respect red lights even when there is not a car in sight.

BELOW: the Øresund bridge links Denmark and Sweden.

Hitchhiking
This is officially discouraged, and in any case finding a lift can be difficult in the holiday season, when every Swedish car seems to be packed with children, baggage and camping gear.

Driving
Main Routes
Sweden's roads are uncrowded, with toll-free motorways covering more than 1,400km (870 miles), trunk roads some 80,500km (50,000 miles), and then there are thousands of kilometres of often picturesque byroads.

Rules of the Road
• Traffic gives way to approaching traffic from the right, unless signs indicate otherwise, and gives way to traffic already on a roundabout.
• Everyone must wear seat belts.
• Headlights are obligatory both day and night.
• Drivers are not required to call the police after accidents but must exchange names and addresses. If you do not stop at all you may be liable to a fine or imprisonment.
• Sweden's drink-drive laws are strictly enforced, with spot checks, heavy fines, loss of licences and even prison sentences imposed. The blood/alcohol limit is 0.02, which equates to less than a can of beer.
• Drivers must stop at pedestrian crossings when a person is crossing or indicates an intention to cross.
• Swedes often forget to indicate when changing lanes, so be careful.

Speed Limits
Motorways 110kph (70mph)
Dual carriageways 90kph (55mph)
Unsigned roads 70kph (43mph)
Built-up areas 50kph (31mph), or 30kph (19mph) around school areas.
Over the last few years, municipalities have been given more freedom to set new speed limits to suit local road conditions better, so you may also see speed-limit signs for 30, 40, 60, 80, 100 and 120kph.

Car Hire
All the major companies have desks at the airports.

Stockholm
Avis, Klarabergsviadukten 86 and Arlanda airport; tel: 0770 82 00 82; www.avis.se.
Budget, Klarabergsviadukten 86 and Arlanda airport; tel: 0770 11 00 12; www.budget.se.
Europcar, near Hotel Sheraton, Vasagatan 4 and Arlanda airport; tel:

ABOVE: be prepared for all weathers.

08 462 48 00; www.europcar.se.
Hertz, Vasagatan 26 and Arlanda airport; tel: 0771 21 12 12; www.hertz.se.

V isas and Passports
A valid passport entitles EU and North American visitors to stay for up to three months, and visas are not normally required. Immigration rarely causes problems in Sweden. If you arrive from another Scandinavian country, passports aren't usually checked at all. If you intend to stay longer than three months you will need to obtain a resident's permit, which you can do once you are in Sweden.

W hat to Read
Good books on Sweden are few and far between, but the best source of information on publications in English is the Swedish Institute, which itself publishes a good range of guides, available through its website.
Svenska Institutet
Slottsbacken 10, Box 7434, SE-103 91 Stockholm.
Tel: 08 453 78 00
Fax: 08 20 72 48
www.si.se (also search under Sweden bookshop; www.swedenbookshop.com)

History
A History of the Swedish People by Vilhelm Moberg Vols I & II (University of Minnesota Press). Iconoclastic view of Sweden's history by one of the country's greatest authors.
Sweden: The Nation's History by Franklin D. Scott (Southern Illinois University Press). Swedish history from its beginnings.

Swedish History in Outline by Jörgen Welbull (Swedish Institute).
The Vikings, Lords of the Seas by Yves Cohat (Thames & Hudson). History of the Vikings, with excellent colour photography.

Architecture
The Complete Guide to Architecture in Stockholm (Arkitektur Forlag AB). A guide to over 400 of the city's buildings, plus detailed maps.
Great Royal Palaces of Sweden by Göran Alm (M.T. Train/Scala Books). A dozen castles, palaces and pavilions belonging to Swedish royalty over the past 500 years.
See also the bookshop on the Swedish architecture website www.arkitektur.se.

Art and Design
Carl and Karin Larsson: Creators of the Swedish Style by Michael Snodin and Elisabet Stavenow-Hidemark (eds). A profile of two of Sweden's most influential designers.
A History of Swedish Art by Mereth Lindgren, Louise Lyberg, Birgitta Sandström and Anna Greta Wahlberg (Bokförlaget Signum). A bird's-eye view of Swedish painting, sculpture and architecture.
The Swedish Room by Lars Sjöberg and Ursula Sjöberg (Frances Lincoln Limited). Some of Sweden's most classic interiors.

Food
The Swedish Kitchen: a Culinary Journey by Lennart Hagerfors (Norstedts). A cookbook by one of the best-known chefs in Sweden, with 198 modern Swedish recipes.
The Swedish Table by Helene Henderson (University of Minnesota Press). A native Swede updates traditional dishes to suit a more modern palate.

Fiction
The Girl with the Dragon Tattoo, *The Girl Who Played with Fire* and *The Girl Who Kicked the Hornets' Nest* by Stieg Larsson. Larsson's best-selling Millennium trilogy is currently taking the world by storm, and Hollywood film versions are out.
The Wonderful Adventures of Nils and *The Further Adventures of Nils* by Selma Lagerlöv. Captivating stories about a boy who flies around Sweden on a goose, have made Lagerlöv one of the nation's most popular children's authors.

A CCOMMODATION

HOTELS, BED & BREAKFASTS AND CAMPING

Choosing a Hotel

Swedish hotels are of a uniformly high standard, and can be expensive. However, hotel rates do come down on weekdays in high summer when the expense-account business travellers are on holiday. Scandic and Sweden Hotels are the country's leading multiples. Away from the big cities, there are plenty of privately owned hotels with the individuality lacking in chains. Visit www.hotelsin sweden.net for details on hotels in most towns and cities.

You can book accommodation in Stockholm online through the tourist information office website www.visit stockholm.com.

Discounts

All the hotel groups run discount schemes during summer. Stockholm, Göteborg and Malmö also offer special discount packages at weekends year-round and daily in summer. These often include free public transport and free admission to visitor attractions.

Nationwide Chains

Big international hotel chains have made little impact. Accommodation is dominated by Scandinavian chains such as Scandic or Sweden Hotels.
Best Western Hotels
Skytteholmsvägen 2, Box 28,
SE-171 11 Solna
Tel: 08 566 293 70
www.bestwestern.se
Elite Hotels
Hälsingegatan 30, Box 21034,
SE-100 31 Stockholm
Tel: 0771-788 789
www.elite.se

First Hotels
Tel: 020 41 11 11
www.firsthotels.com
Nordic Choice Hotels
Master Samuelsgaten 42, Box 7620,
SE-103 94 Stockholm
Tel: 0771 666 700
www.choicehotels.se
Scandic Hotels
Sveavägen 167, Box 6197,
SE-102 33 Stockholm
Tel: 08 51 75 17 20
www.scandichotels.com
Sweden Hotels
Lilla Bommen 6, SE-411 04 Göteborg
Tel: 0771 777 800
Email: info@swedenhotels.se
www.swedenhotels.se

Bed and Breakfasts

The bed and breakfast system is becoming more popular. Look for the *Rum* sign (it means "room" and does not include breakfast). Ask at local tourist offices if any *rum* accommodation is available. Prices are very reasonable. There are also many working farms across Sweden offering self-catering and B&B accommodation (www.bopalantgard.org).

Youth Hostels

Sweden has 320 inexpensive youth hostels *(vandrarhem)*, from mansion houses and castles to renovated ships like the 100-year-old *af Chapman* in Stockholm harbour, and modern purpose-built hostels. These are mainly in southern and central Sweden. There are also plenty of youth hostels in the Stockholm archipelago. Most have two- and four-bed rooms or family rooms.

Camping

There are more than 1,000 campsites in Sweden, many in pretty locations and generally of a high standard. Most open from early June to the end of August. Rates are claimed to be among the cheapest in Europe. You can also rent camping chalets and cottages, cabins and mountain huts, caravans and motor homes.

Around 500 campsites are affiliated to Sveriges-Camping och Stugföretagare Riksorganisation (SCR): for fast check-in and check-out plus insurance while at these sites, you should get the Camping Card Scandinavia. This costs around 140Skr, and you can apply for it before you leave for Sweden, or buy it at any SCR campsite. The card is available (allow one month for delivery) from:
SCR, Mässens Gata 10, PO Box 5079, SE-402 22 Göteborg. Or visit the very useful www.camping.se.

Hotel Listings

Hotels are grouped by area, starting with Stockholm. Within each city or region, they are listed alphabetically.

Hotels have self-catering facilities, but meals or snacks are provided in some. There is often use of a washing machine. Most hostels will charge extra for bed linen, so bring your own sheets and towels. Always book ahead in the summer.
For details:
Svenska Turistföreningen (STF)
Tel: 08 463 21 00
www.stfturist.se

ACCOMMODATION LISTINGS

STOCKHOLM

Acapulco Hotell
Bjurholmsplan 23
Tel: 08 702 33 00
www.acapulco-hotell.se
The Acapulco is a decent, comfortable no-frills option in the trendy bohemian Södermalm area. Its apartment-style rooms have little kitchens, complete with kettle, utensils and microwave. **$$**

Adlon Hotell
Vasagatan 42
Tel: 08 402 65 00
www.adlon.se
Rooms are on the small side, but this is great value for a central location. **$$**

Af Chapman & Skeppsholmen
Flaggmansvägen 8
Tel: 08 463 22 66
www.stfchapman.com
A youth hostel situated in a landmark 1888 ship with spectacular views of the Gamla Stan (Old Town). Af Chapman has 136 beds plus a 152-bed building facing the ship's gangway. The café has a terrific view. **$**

Hotel Bentleys
Drottninggatan 77
Tel: 08 14 13 95
www.bentleys.se
Found at the top, and quieter, end of this famous shopping street, this mid-size hotel had a makeover in 2010 and is looking super-spruce. It's worth paying for one of the superior new rooms. **$$$**

Berns Hotel
Näckströmsgatan 8
Tel: 08 566 322 00
www.berns.se
Historic but ultra-modernised hotel and "salons" in the heart of town close to shopping and nightlife. Many rooms were being renovated in early 2011, and the hotel has recently introduced some unusual "extras" to purchase from the minibar... **$$$**

Birger Jarl Hotel
Tulegatan 8
Tel: 08 674 18 00
www.birgerjarl.se
All rooms here are in light, airy Swedish style, but the best have been individually created so visitors can stay in a room surrounded by the work of their favourite Swedish designer! Just a short walk from the centre of town. **$$$**

City Backpackers
Upplandsgatan 2A
Tel: 08 20 69 20
www.citybackpackers.se
A busy central hostel with excellent facilities, including free bike hire. Ideal location, although can get noisy at weekends. **$**

Hotell Diplomat
Strandvägen 7C
Tel: 08 459 68 00
www.diplomathotel.com
Beautiful waterside location on the city's most exclusive street. **$$$**

First Hotel Reisen
Skeppsbron 9
Tel: 08 22 32 60
www.firsthotels.se
With origins from the 18th century, this hotel has a classical ambience. It is really made by its waterfront location, near to the Royal Palace and perfect for exploring the Old Town. **$$$**

Grand Hôtel Stockholm
S. Blasieholmshamnen 8
Tel: 08 679 35 00
www.grandhotel.se
A rare 5-star hotel, with an unparalleled view of the waterfont and Royal Palace. Its restaurants Matbaren and Matsalen at Mathias Dahlgren have one and two Michelin stars respectively. **$$$**

Hotel Hellsten
Luntmakargatan 68
T–el: 08 661 86 00
www.hellsten.se
Situated in what is fast becoming a trendy area, only a few minutes from the town centre. Stylish rooms at a reasonable cost, and with very helpful staff. **$$**

Hilton Stockholm Slussen
Guldgränd 8
Tel: 08 517 353 00
www.hilton.com
A very impressive modern hotel with spectacular views over the water to Gamla Stan and the Town Hall. **$$$**

Hotel J
Ellensviksvägen 1
Nacka Strand
Tel: 08 601 30 00
www.hotelj.com
Decorated in contemporary marine style, reminiscent of the boathouses in New England. The city centre is 15 minutes away by boat or car. Currently being expanded from 45 to 158 rooms – we hope it maintains its delightfully restful ambience. **$$–$$$**

Lord Nelson Hotel
Västerlånggatan 22
Tel: 08 506 401 20
www.lordnelsonhotel.se
Sweden's narrowest hotel at only 6 metres (20ft) wide! What it lacks in size, it makes up for in charm, with an authentic nautical theme and friendly staff. In a popular location in Gamla Stan. **$$**

Mälardrottningen
Riddarholmen
Tel: 08 545 187 80
www.malardrottningen.se
This is your one and only chance to sleep on a 1920s luxury yacht that was once owned by the American Woolworths heiress Barbara Hutton, now divided into tiny guest cabins and moored against Riddarholmen. **$$**

Radisson Blu Strand Hotel
Nybrokajen 9
Tel: 08 506 640 00
www.radissonblu.com/strandhotel-stockholm
Featuring a modern interior within a classical-style building, with views across the water to the impressive Strandvägen street. **$$–$$$**

Rex Hotel
Luntmakargatan 73
Tel: 08 16 00 40
www.rexhotel.se
In a building dating from 1866, this is just across from its sister-hotel the Hellsten and shares much of its character and charm. **$$**

NORWAY

SWEDEN

BELOW: the comfortable rooms at Hotel J.

PRICE CATEGORIES

Price categories are based on an average double room for two, including tax, usually with breakfast:
$ = under 1,300Skr
$$ = 1,300–2,200Skr
$$$ = over 2,200Skr

FINLAND

Rica Hotel Gamla Stan
Lilla Nygatan 25
Tel: 08 72 37 250
www.rica-hotels.com/gamlastan
Rooms here are decorated in charming 18th-century style. The hotel is situated perfectly for Old Town exploration, and there's a great breakfast choice that will set you up for the day. **$$**

Sheraton Stockholm Hotel and Towers
Tegelbacken 6
Tel: 08 412 34 00
www.sheraton.com/stockholm
Found between Central Station and Gamla Stan, this has the largest rooms in town and fabulous views of Lake Mälaren, the Town Hall and the Old Town. **$$$**

Tre Små Rum Hotel
Högbergsgatan 81
Tel: 08 641 23 71
www.tresmarum.se
Simple but very good-value B&B in the trendy suburb of Södermalm. **$**

Victory Hotel
Lilla Nygatan 5
Tel: 08 506 400 00
www.victoryhotel.se
In the heart of Gamla Stan, this has a maritime ambience reflecting the war vessel it is named after and has a great deal of character. **$$$**

Around Stockholm

Mariefred

Gripsholms Värdshus and Hotel
Kyrkogatan 1
Tel: 0159 347 50
www.gripsholms-vardshus.se
A 400-year old inn across the road from Gripsholms Castle. Its romantic rooms are full of antiques. **$$–$$$**

Norrköping

Elite Grand Hotel
Tyska Torget 2
Tel: 011 36 41 00
www.elite.se
First-class early 20th-century hotel by the Motala River, by the Town Hall, in the centre of town. **$$–$$$**

Sigtuna

Sigtuna Stadshotell
Stora Nygatan 3
Tel: 08 592 501 00
www.sigtunastadshotell.se
A renovated, early 20th-century hotel in the heart of this historic town. **$$$**

Uppsala

Park Inn Uppsala
Storgatan 30
Tel: 018 68 11 00
www.parkinn.com/hotel-uppsala
A good-quality, good-value modern business hotel, handy for exploring town. **$$**

SOUTHERN SWEDEN

Helsingborg

Best Western Hotel Helsingborg
Stortorget 20
Tel: 042 37 18 00
http://hotelhelsingborg.se
In the centre of town, right at the foot of the medieval Kärnan tower, this is one of Helsingborg's most pleasant hotels. **$$**

Kalmar

First Hotel Witt
Södra Långgatan 42
Tel: 0480 15250
www.firsthotels.com
It has seen better days, but Kalmar's oldest hotel has history: it has hosted many famous personalities and is where the popular dish "Biff à la Lindstöm" originated. **$$**

Slottshotellet
Slottsvagen 7
Tel: 0480 882 60
www.slottshotellet.se
In Kalmar's Old Town, the main building has a romantic and old-fashioned atmosphere; the (cheaper) annexe rooms are more run-of-the-mill. Opposite the park and castle. **$–$$**

Malmö

Hotell Baltzar
Baltzarsgatan 45
Tel: 040 66 55 700
www.baltzarhotel.se
Turn-of-the-20th-century building, centrally located on a pedestrianised street. **$$**

Elite Hotel Savoy
Norra Vallgatan 62
Tel: 040 664 48 00
www.elite.se
Opposite the train station. Has a restaurant, a French-style brasserie, and a pub, The Bishop's Arms, with a large selection of beers. **$$**

Hilton Malmö City
Triangeln 2
Tel: 040 693 47 00
www.hilton.com
A modern high-rise glass building – try to get as high a room as you can for great views over Malmö. The new Triangeln railway station, completed in December 2010, is just begind the hotel. **$$$**

Mayfair Hotel Tunneln
Adelgatan 4
Tel: 040-10 1620
www.mayfairtunneln.com
This charming and cosy old hotel in the centre of town makes the most of its historical premises, right down to the great breakfast spread in the medieval cellars. **$$**

Best Western Hotel Noble House
Per Weijersgatan 6
Tel: 040 664 30 00
www.hotelnoblehouse.se
Right in the centre, close to shops and restaurants. **$$**

Best Western Hotel Royal
Norra Vallgatan 94
Tel: 040 664 25 00
www.bwhotelroyal.se
Small hotel, recently acquired by Best Western, in an old building close to shops, station and ferries. In summer, breakfast is served in the garden. **$$**

Öland

Halltorps Gästgiveri
Landsvägen Halltorp 105
92 Borgholm
Tel: 0485 850 00
www.halltorpsgastgiveri.se
An agreeable country house just outside Borgholm, with a lovely restaurant, two saunas, an outdoor Jacuzzi and charming rooms, some on split levels. **$$–$$$**

Växjö

Elite Stadshotellet
Kungsgatan 6
Tel: 04 70 134 00
www.elite.se
One of the best options in Växjö. The airport bus stops right outside. **$$**

Visby

Clarion Hotel Wisby
Strandgatan 6
Tel: 0498 25 75 00
www.wisbyhotell.se
A central old tavern turned into a stylish hotel, just a 15-minute walk from the harbour. Steam room, sauna and indoor pool located in the medieval cellar. Relax in the Winter Garden bar. **$$$**

Medeltidshotellet
Norra Kyrkogatan 3–7
Tel: 0498 291 230
www.medeltidshotellet.se
This is a pricey option, but the Medieval Hotel certainly stands out for its chic, individually designed rooms, all with their own "story" and all imbued with medieval character. **$$$**

Tofta Strandpensionat
Solbacksvägen 19
Tel: 0498 29 70 60
www.toftastrand.se
Basic but pleasant boarding house plus self-catering chalets. Excellent location right on the beach 20km (12 miles) from Visby. Bikes for hire, tennis and badminton. **$–$$**

Ystad

Ystads Saltsjöbad
Saltsjöbadsvägen 15
Tel: 0411 13 630
www.ystadssaltsjobad.se
Spa hotel with panoramic Baltic view. Relaxing accommodation. **$$**

WEST COAST

Göteborg

Best Western Hotel Eggers
Drottningtorget
Tel: 031 333 44 40
www.hoteleggers.se
Historic 19th-century railway hotel with individually furnished rooms. By the station and near the city centre. **$$–$$$**

Elite Park Avenue Hotel
Kungsportsavenyn 36–38
Tel: 031 727 10 00
www.elite.se
Historical hotel with newly renovated rooms, ideally situated for those intending to make the most of Göteborg's nightlife. **$$–$$$**

First Hotel G
Nils Ericsonsplatsen 4
Tel: 031 63 72 00
www.firsthotels.com
Spacious rooms and a surprisingly pleasant and peaceful feel, particularly considering the hotel is right above the main railway station! Functional design combined with modern technology. **$$**

Novotel Göteborg
Klippan 1
Tel: 031 720 22 00
www.novotel.se
About 20 minutes' tram or ferry ride out of the city centre, this former brewery has lovely river views and good public transport links. **$$**

Hotel Lorensberg
Berzeliigatan 15
Tel: 031 81 06 00
www.hotel-lorensberg.se
Family-run hotel with beautiful mural paintings, close to Götaplatsen, Avenyn and Liseberg amusement park. **$$**

Pensionat
Gamla Lillhagsvägen 127B,
SE-422 49
Tel: 031 55 39 81
www.st-jorgen.nu
Charming and small in rural setting within easy reach of the centre. **$**

Hotel Riverton
Stora Badhusgatan 26
Tel: 031 750 10 00
www.riverton.se
On the eastern edge of the city, towards the Maritiman Museum, rooms here are decorated in contemporary

Scandinavian style. Many have fabulous harbour views. **$$$**

Scandic Crown
Polhemsplatsen 3
Tel: 031 75 15 100
www.scandichotels.com
Handy for the train station and city centre, the Crown has light, tasteful rooms, great views from the upper balconies, and one of the best breakfast spreads in town. **$$**

St Jörgens Hotell & Vanilj Hotell
Kyrkogatan 38
Tel: 031 71 16 220
www.hotelvanilj.se
A pleasant little hotel with old-fashioned charm, on a quiet street yet handy for the city centre. Close to the cathedral. **$–$$**

Halmstad

Clarion Collection Hotel Norre Park
Norra vägen 7
Tel: 035 218 555
www.norrepark.se
A first-class hotel with a parkside location and relaxing atmosphere. Good-

value room prices include a breakfast and an evening buffet. **$$**

Hotel Continental
Kungsgatan 5
Tel: 035 17 63 00
www.continental-halmstad.com
Stylish, comfortable and with excellent service, this lovely Art Nouveau hotel lies on a quiet street a mere 10 minutes' walk from the centre. **$$**

Marstrand

Grand Hotel Marstrand
Rådhusgatan 2
Tel: 0303 603 22
www.grandmarstrand.se
Attractive late 19th-century hotel – once the summer residence of King Oscar II. Located by the water. **$$$**

Villa Maritime Marstrand
Hamnen
Tel: 0303 610 25
www.villa-maritime.se
Self-caterers may appreciate these apartments with kitchenettes, located on the harbour and close to golf courses, sailing and other activities. **$$**

GREAT LAKES

Borås

First Hotel Grand
Hallbergsplatsen 2
Tel: 033 799 00 00
www.firsthotelgrand.se
First-class and modern, with bar and nightclub. A range of entertainment including dance bands and DJs. **$$**

Karlsborg

Kanalhotellet
Storgatan 94
Tel: 0505 121 30

PRICE CATEGORIES

Price categories are based on an average double room for two, including tax, usually with breakfast:
$ = under 1,300Skr
$$ = 1,300–2,200Skr
$$$ = over 2,200Skr

www.kanalhotellet.se
A charming 19th-century hotel built in "Swiss" style – book early to bag a room with a terrace or balcony overlooking the canal. **$**

Karlstad

Clarion Collection Hotel Drott
Jarnvagsgatan 1
Tel: 054 10 10 10
www.drotthotel.se
Hotel Drott is a congenial modern hotel in the town centre. The free evening buffet makes prices here very reasonable indeed. **$$**

Lidköping

Stadt Lidköping
Gamla Stadens Torg 1, SE-531 32
Tel: 0510 220 85

www.stadtlidkoping.se
Decent hotel with a fine waterfront location. Close to Läckö Castle and Röstrand porcelain factory. **$$**

Motala

Hotel M
Kungsgatan 1
Tel: 0141 21 66 60
www.hotelm.se
Marine-style hotel, newly renovated, close to golf courses. **$$**

Örebro

Elite Stora Hotellet
Drottninggatan 1
Tel: 019 15 69 00
www.elite.se
A historic hotel, built in 1858, centrally ocated near Örebro Castle by the Svartå

River, the art gallery and concert hall. Stylish, comfortable rooms. Popular restaurant. **$$**

Söderköping

Hotel Söderköpings Brunn
Skönbergagatan 35
Tel: 0121 109 00
www.soderkopingsbrunn.se
Traditional spa hotel situated in a park. An outdoor pool opens in summer, and you can rent bicycles and canoes, or enjoy a boat trip on the Göta Kanal. **$$**

Villa Linnéa
Nybrogata 1
Tel: 0121 218 10
www.villalinnea.se
A peaceful B&B which practically dips its toes into the Göta Kanal. **$**

DALARNA

Falun

First Hotel Grand
Trotzgatan 9–11
Tel: 023 79 48 80
www.firsthotels.se
Dalarna's biggest hotel, located in the town centre, complete with indoor pool, spa, sauna and gym. **$$**

Mora

Mora Hotell
Strandgatan 12
Tel: 0250 59 26 50
www.morahotell.se
Modern hotel in the centre close to Lake Siljan, the Zorn Museum, and the finishing line of the famous cross-country ski race, the *Vasaloppet*, plus a number of restaurants to choose from in the area. **$$**

Tällberg

Hotell Klockargården
Siljansvägen 6
Tel: 0247 502 60
www.klockargarden.com
Traditional timber houses built around a peaceful courtyard, with an Arts and Crafts yard nearby. Lovely gardens and superb views of Lake Siljan. The in-house restaurant serves traditional food made with local produce. **$–$$**

CENTRAL SWEDEN

Åre

Åre Ski Lodge
Trondheimsleden 44
Tel: 0647 510 29
www.areskilodge.se
This hostel is a cheap option with comfortable rooms and good facilities including sauna and kitchen. **$**

Hotel Diplomat Åregården
Tel: 0647 178 00
www.diplomathotel.com
On the main square, just a short stride from the ski lifts, with super-cosy public areas for après-ski relaxation. Spa, swimming pool and sauna. Apartments are also available. **$$–$$$**

Sundsvall

Elite Hotel Knaust
Storgatan 13
Tel: 060 60 80 000
www.elite.se
The impressive historical interior – like the grand sweeping staircase, high ceilings and stucco work – of this century-old building has been gracefully melded with modern comfort and stylish contemporary touches. Rooms are charming if on the small side, but the buffet breakfast is generous. Gastro-pub-style food is served in the popular restaurant. Good quality-price ratio. **$$**

NORTHERN SWEDEN

Arvidsjaur

Laponia Hotel
Storgatan 45
Tel: 0960 555 00
www.hotell-laponia.se
Modern hotel which can arrange a wealth of summer and winter activities, such as rafting, dog sledging, golf and "Lappland Olympics". **$$**

Haparanda

Haparanda Stadshotell
Torget 7
Tel: 0922 614 90
www.haparandastadshotell.se
Early 20th-century hotel in the town centre. The restaurant's specialities include reindeer, elk and grouse. **$$**

Kiruna

Hotel Rallaren
Bangårdsvägen 4
Tel: 0980-611 26
www.hotelrallaren.se
Choose between Rallaren's standard hotel rooms or one of their traditional Sami dwellings in the garden. Outdoor hot tub and sauna. **$$–$$$**

Hotell Vinterpalatset
Järnvägsgatan 18
Tel: 0980 677 70
www.vinterpalatset.se
Small, privately owned hotel built in 1904 and renovated into a modern hotel with all facilities. Excellent breakfast buffet, featuring local produce such as salmon. **$$**

Piteå

Piteå Stadshotell
Olof Palmes Gata 1
Tel: 0911 23 40 00
www.piteastadshotell.com
Restored late 19th-century hotel located in the centre of town. 102 rooms and a variety of dining options. **$$**

ABOVE: enjoying an alfresco lunch.

Riksgränsen

Riksgränsen
Riksgränsvågen 15
Tel: 0980 400 80
www.riksgransen.nu
Rooms and self-catering, a short distance from all the skiing facilities and opportunities for hiking nearby in summer. Breakfast included. **$$**

Umeå

Comfort Hotel Winn
Skolgatan 64
Tel: 090 71 11 00
www.comfortinn.com
Comfortable, friendly and central, Hotel Winn also has spruce, modern facilities, a well-equipped gym... and free hotdogs on weekday evenings! **$$**

DENMARK

E ATING OUT

RECOMMENDED RESTAURANTS AND CAFÉS

NORWAY

Choosing a Restaurant

Sweden, once known as the land of *husmanskost* (homely fare), is currently enjoying a culinary renaissance, thanks to a new generation of chefs who know how to give a sophisticated twist to classic Swedish dishes such as reindeer, elk, lingonberries, salmon and herring.

Eating out has become increasingly popular, but can seem expensive, particularly if you drink a lot of wine or beer. Stockholm has more than 700 restaurants covering at least 30 national cuisines: six of them flaunt Michelin stars. Göteborg is particularly good for seafood, and with five Michelin-starred restaurants, is another of Europe's top culinary destinations. Malmö claims to have more restaurants per head than any other Swedish city.

For the latest top-notch restaurants, consult *The White Guide* (www.whiteguide.se; in Swedish only), the bible to fine dining in Sweden.

For travellers on a tight budget there is no shortage of inexpensive places to eat. Look for the *dagens rätt* (dish of the day), a lunch that usually includes bread, a simple salad and a soft drink for around 75Skr. And fast-food outlets are everywhere. The ubiquitous *korvkiosk* sells grilled chicken, sausages, hamburgers and *tunnbrödsrulle* (a parcel of mashed potato, sausage and ketchup or mustard wrapped in soft bread).

The Swedes generally eat early. Restaurants start serving lunch at about 11am, and some small hotels, particularly in country areas, serve evening meals around 6pm. In the cities you can eat much later. Many of the top restaurants in Stockholm close in July for staff holidays.

Restaurant Listings

Below is a selection of restaurants around the country. Restaurants are grouped by area with Stockholm first, and are listed alphabetically.

What to Drink

There is no difficulty in ordering a drink with your meal, although the stronger Class III beer *(starköl)* may not be available in restaurants and bars until noon. However, alcohol is expensive in Sweden due to high taxes.

You can buy strong alcohol only through branches of the State-controlled monopoly Systembolaget, generally open Mon–Fri 10am–6pm and Sat 10am–1pm (closes early the day before a public holiday).

The minimum age for buying alcohol is 20; you may be asked for proof of your age if you are in your early 20s.

Some bars and cafés advertise a reduced-price happy hour. This may be at any time of the day, but is worth finding as it can bring the cost of half a litre of lager down to half the price charged in nightclubs.

For more on eating and drinking in Sweden, see Food and Drink, page 97.

SWEDEN

STOCKHOLM

Den Gyldene Freden
Österlånggatan 51
Tel: 08 24 97 60
www.gyldenefreden.se
Dating from 1722, and with an atmosphere almost unchanged since then, this is the classical restaurant in Stockholm where you'll

combine excellent cuisine with a historical environment. **$$$**
Eriks Bakficka
Fredrikshovsgatan 4
Tel: 08 66 01 599
www.eriks.se
A longstanding and reliable restaurant, Bakficka serves

traditional Swedish dishes. **$$$**
Esperanto
Kungstensgatan 2
Tel: 08 696 23 23
www.esperantorestaurant.se
Another of Stockholm's fabulous restaurants, Esperanto gained its first

PRICE CATEGORIES

Price categories are per person for an average three-course meal, excluding drinks but with tax:
$ = under 300Skr
$$ = 300–500Skr
$$$ = over 500Skr

FINLAND

Michelin star in 2007, and tables have been among the city's most wanted ever since. Two tasting menus are on offer. **$$$**

F12
Fredsgatan 12
Tel: 08 24 80 52
www.f12.se
The splendid F12 flaunts a Michelin star, and is one of the best gastronomic experiences in Sweden, but such remarkable culinary flair comes at a hefty price. **$$$**

Gondolen
Stadsgården 6
Tel: 08 641 70 90
www.eriks.se
Highly recommended. Eating here is a real Stockholm experience. Offers excellent traditional Swedish cuisine with a great view over the city. Those on a tighter budget can enjoy the same view at the bar. A Stockholm institution. **$$$**

Hermans
Fjallgatan 23
Tel: 08 643 94 80
www.hermans.se
One for vegetarian visitors – and those who love beautiful views. There's no menu here: Hermans serves all-you-can-eat organic veggie buffets at lunchtime and in the evening. Come hungry. Garden for eating alfresco in summer. **$**

BELOW: delicious dishes at Mathias Dahlgren.

Indian Garden
Heleneborgsgatan 15
Tel: 08 849 498
Warm, cosy and welcoming, and with an ever-present crowd that testifies to the quality of its curries and baltis. **$$**

Järnet Matsal and Bar
Österlänggatan 34–36
Tel: 08 10 71 37
www.jarnet.nu
With a delightful corner location and outside tables in summer, this combination of bar and restaurant has much charm and good, reasonably priced dishes. **$$**

Mathias Dahlgren
Grand Hotel, Södra Blasieholmshamnen 6
Tel: 08 679 35 84
www.mathiasdahlgren.com
The eponymous masterchef uses the best Swedish ingredients to create elegant, unusual, melt-in-the-mouth dishes in his two restaurants at the Grand Hotel. Matbaren has one Michelin star; Matsalen has two. Superb. **$$$**

Operakällaren
Operan (Royal Opera House)
Tel: 08 676 58 01
www.operakallaren.se
Arguably Stockholm's best-known restaurant and worth visiting for the fantastic decor alone. The lovely Opera Bar also serves food,

in a slightly more low-key setting. **$$$**

Pelikan
Blekingegatan 40
Tel: 08 556 09 090
www.pelikan.se
A Stockholm institution, this bar-restaurant has been going for well over a century. Food is traditional Swedish (meatballs, veal schnitzel, and classic appetiser "SOS" or "*smör, ost, sill*" – butter, cheese and herring), all served in a high-ceilinged hall. **$$**

Pontus by the Sea
Tullhus 2, Skeppsbron
Tel: 08 20 20 95
www.pontusfrithiof.com
Found in the old Gamla Stan Bryggeri, and on the quayside of Skeppsbron, this has a more light-hearted Mediterranean flavour and ambience than its more established sister-restaurant, Pontus!, at Brunnsgatan 1. **$$**

Sturehof
Stureplan 2
Tel: 08 440 57 30
Super-trendy spot serving stylish Swedish food, with the emphasis on seafood. Has a popular bar and live music. **$$–$$$**

Cafés

Café Blå Porten
Djurgårdsvägen 64
Tel: 08 663 87 59
Unpretentious café with good cakes and a light food menu.

Café String
Nytorgsgatan 38
Tel: 08 714 85 14
Café with hip 1950s and 60s decor that is all for sale.

Chokladkoppen
Stortorget 20
Tel: 08 20 31 70
A small and cosy café, with outdoor seating in one of the best people-watching spots in Stockholm.

Fåfängan
Klockestapelsbacken 3
Tel: 08-642 99 00
A visit here is essential in the summer if you can manage the long, steep walk up – the view over Stockholm is fantastic.

Flickorna Helin Voltaire
Rosendalsvägen 14, Djurgården
Tel: 08 664 51 08
Housed in a twisty, fairytale-castle building on Djurgården, this is the place for coffee and delicious cake after a visit to the Vasa Museum.

Konditori Sturekatten
Riddargatan 4
Tel: 08 611 16 12
Classic, cosy café, worth a visit for the old-fashioned decor alone. Home-baked bread and pastries are on offer.

Rosendals Trädgård
Rosendalsterassen 12
Tel: 08 545 812 70
This café within the garden by Rosendal Palace, on Djurgården, attracts hordes of visitors in fine weather for its home-baked goodies, fresh from the bakery's wood-fired oven.

Taxinge Slottscafé
Nykvarn
Tel: 0159 701 14
Located a 45-minute drive south of Stockholm (or a four-hour weekend steamboat ride for the more romantically inclined), this beautiful castle's café features a buffet of around 60 different cakes and buns.

Around Stockholm

Mariefred

Gripsholms Värdshus & Hotel
Kyrkoplan 1
Tel: 0159 347 50
www.gripsholms-vardshus.se
Sweden's oldest inn has a first-class restaurant that specialises in local produce, international cooking as well as fine wines. **$$–$$$**

Norrköping

Fiskmagasinet
Skolgatan 1b
Tel: 011 13 45 60
www.fiskmagasinet.se
This stylish place, with rustic wooden floors and creamy seating, specialises in melt-in-the-mouth fish dishes – everything from pickled herring to fresh lobster. **$$–$$$**

SOUTHERN SWEDEN

Helsingborg

Pålsjö Krog
Drottninggatan 151
Tel: 042 149 730
www.palsjokrog.com
For beautifully presented
Swedish dishes. **$$**

Kalmar

Calmar Hamnkrog
Skeppsbrogatan 30
Tel: 0480 41 10 20
www.calmarhamnkrog.se
Gourmet restaurant with a
sea view. **$$**

Malmö

Brogatan
Brogatan 12

Tel: 040 30 77 17
Popular among the famous.
Organic Swedish food and
live music. **$$–$$$**
Restaurang Johan P
Landbygatan 5
Tel: 040 97 18 18
www.johanp.nu
A rather stark, white-tiled
setting, but Johan P is
considered the best place in
Malmö for fish dishes. **$$**
Salt & Brygga
Sundspromenaden 7
Tel: 040 611 59 40
www.saltobrygga.se
A little way out of the centre,
close to the Turning Torso,
this eco-conscious
restaurant uses local
organic produce wherever
possible in its deeply tasty

dishes. **$$–$$$**
Skeppsbron 2
Börshuset
Tel: 040 30 62 02
www.skeppsbron2.com
Modern and inventive
cuisine in a building
overlooking the sea. **$$**

Visby

Bakfickan
Stora Torget 1
Tel: 0498 27 18 07
www.bakfickan-visby.nu
Gotland's only seafood
restaurant. Warm, cosy
atmosphere serving
excellent dishes. **$–$$**
Donners Brunn
Donners Plats
Tel: 0498 27 10 90

www.donnersbrunn.nu
Friendly gourmet restaurant
with the "Best Lamb Chef"
in Sweden. **$$$**
Isola Bella
Södra Kyrkogatan 20
Tel: 0498 21 87 87
www.isolabella.se
An airy Italian restaurant
with a long pizza menu.
Friendly service. **$$**
Värdshuset Lindgården
Strandgatan 26
Tel: 0498 21 87 00
www.lindgarden.com
A particularly charming
restaurant for a summer
evening, thanks to the lovely
garden. The gourmet
Gotland menu features
regional specialities, such
as roast lamb. **$$$**

WEST COAST

Göteborg

Café Husaren
Haga Nygata 28
Tel: 031 136 378
A classic café with a
beautiful 19th-century glass
roof. Serves the world's
largest cinnamon buns!
La Cucina Italiana
Skånegatan 33
Tel: 031 16 63 07
A high-end Italian restaurant
with an underlying gourmet
concept. **$$–$$$**
Fiskekrogen
Lilla Torget 1
Tel: 031 10 10 05
www.fiskekrogen.com

Best fish restaurant in town;
exciting wines at good
prices. **$$$**
Heaven 23
Hotel Gothia Towers, Mässansgata
Tel: 031 75 08 805
www.heaven23.se
Excellent food, with city
views to match. The king-
size shrimp sandwich is
their best-seller. **$$–$$$**
M2 – Magnus & Magnus
Magasinsgatan 8
Tel: 031 13 30 00
www.magnusmagnus.se
An intimate restaurant: the
candlelit courtyard is a
favourite summer eating
place. Good value for such

high-quality food. **$$–$$$**
Trädgår'n
Nya Allén
Tel: 031 10 20 80
www.tradgarn.se
Exotic award-winning
international restaurant.
Also has live music
performances. **$$$**
Tvåkanten
Kungsportsavenyn 27
Tel: 031 18 21 15
www.tvakanten.se
Traditional Swedish dishes
are given the contemporary
treatment at this classy
restaurant. The Sunday
roast dinner is particularly
good value. **$$$**

Halmstad

Pio & Company
Storgatan 37
Tel: 035 21 06 69
www.pio.se
Italian dishes and
traditional Swedish food,
planked steak a classic. **$$**

Tanumshede

Tanums Gestgifveri
Apoteksvägen 7
Tel: 0525 290 10
www.tanumsgestgifveri.com
Traditional Swedish food.
Fish and oysters feature
high on the menu. **$$$**

GREAT LAKES AND DALARNA

Dalarna

Värdshuset Dala Floda
Badvägen 6, Dala Floda
(40km/25 miles from Borlänge)
Tel: 0241 220 50
www.dalafloda-vardshus.se
Excellent, well-known inn/
restaurant, serving perfect
summer meals using home-
grown ingredients. Best
experienced as part of a
half- or full-board package.
$$–$$$

Falun

Banken Två Rum & Kök
Åsgatan 41
Tel: 023 711 911
www.bankenfalun.se
This elegant, award-winning
restaurant with Art Nouveau
interior, close to the main
square, is Falun's best.
Serves traditional Swedish
and gourmet food.
Impeccable service.
$$–$$$

Jönköping

Mäster Gudmunds Källare
Kapellgatan 2
Tel: 036 10 06 40
www.mastergudmund.se
Atmospheric medieval
cellar-restaurant, focusing
on simple home cooking at
a decent price. **$$**
Restaurang Hemma
Smedjegatan 36
Tel: 036 10 01 15
www.restauranghemma.se

Jönköping's best restaurant,
serving well-rounded, high-
class meals without being
overly fussy. Vegetarians are
well catered for. **$$–$$$**

PRICE CATEGORIES

Price categories are per
person for an average three-
course meal, excluding
drinks but with tax:
$ = under 300Skr
$$ = 300–500Skr
$$$ = over 500Skr

Karlstad

Lilla Martina Bar & Bistro
Hamngatan 22
Tel: 054 18 65 00
www.lillamartina.se
A tiny restaurant with a short-but-sweet menu that shows off the kitchen's French-inspired dishes. $$–$$$

Tiffanys
Västra Torggatan 19
Tel: 054 15 33 83
Stylish restaurant specialising in local fish and game. $$–$$$

Leksand

Åkerblads Hotell & Gästgiveri
Sjögattu 2, Tällberg (13km/8 miles from Leksand)
Tel: 0247 508 00
www.akerblads.se
Romantic lakeside hotel serving everything from morning coffee and cakes to a seven-course tasting menu. Traditional Swedish fare (with the odd surprise!) and a good-value weekend *smörgåsbord*. $$–$$$

Söderköping

Romantik Hotel Söderköpings Brunn
Skönbergagatan 35
Tel: 0121 109 00
www.soderkopingsbrunn.se
Fine Swedish cooking, serving very traditional dishes – pea soup, meatballs, venison. $$$

Vadstena

Restaurang Munkklostret
Lasarettsgatan 5
Tel: 0143 315 30

www.klosterhotel.se
Part of a medieval monastery, set into green parkland close to Lake Vättern. The atmospheric hotel restaurant serves gourmet meals made from local organic produce. With a lovely summer terrace. $$$

Vadstena Valven
Storgatan 18
Tel: 0143 123 40
www.valven.se
In a medieval vaulted cellar, Valven serves excellent food using local ingredients. $$

CENTRAL SWEDEN

Åre

Villa Tottebo
Parkvägen 1
Tel: 0647 506 20
www.villatottebo.se
Pleasant restaurant serving mostly local products, with succulent reindeer a speciality. $$$

Östersund

Brunkullans Krog
Postgränd 5
Tel: 063 10 14 54

A beguiling little bar-restaurant with some good traditional dishes. $$

Innefickan Restaurant and Bar
Postgränd 11
Tel: 063 12 90 99
www.innefickan.se
Former warehouse, now turned into a successful bar and restaurant serving Swedish and Mediterranean-influenced food. $$–$$$

Mikado
Grytan, Brunflo
Tel: 063 209 08

www.mikadosweden.com
Beautifully presented Japanese food created by chef Tsukasa Takeuchi. $$–$$$

Sundsvall

7 Kryddor
Trädgårdsgatan 25
Tel: 060-61 50 80
www.7kryddor.com
For a touch of spice, head to this Turkish restaurant. The barbecued meat dishes are recommended; also good

for vegetarian meze. $$

Restaurang Mezoyo
Nybrogatan 16
Tel: 060 15 15 54
www.mezoyo.se
Deeply tasty Mediterranean dishes. On fine evenings, the summer terrace is the place to dine. $$–$$$

Saffran
Nybrogatan 25
Tel: 060 17 11 07
Small, cosy Spanish restaurant with tapas bar. Very reasonable prices and a varied menu. $–$$

NORTHERN SWEDEN

Jukkasjärvi

Jukkasjärvi Wärdshus
Marknadsvägen 63
Tel: 0980 668 00
www.icehotel.com
The excellent Ice Hotel restaurant specialises in local produce such as reindeer, grouse, char and cloudberries. The cheaper Homestead restaurant is just down the road. $$$

Kiruna

Restaurang Rallaren
Bangårdsvägen 4
Tel: 0980 611 26
www.hotelrallaren.se
For traditional Sami bread (*gahkku*) and dishes made with traditional Lapp ingredients. $–$$

Luleå

Cafe Tallkotten
Luleå Stadshotel, Storgatan 15
Tel: 0920 27 40 20
www.tallkotten.se
Busy hotel restaurant with an Italian menu. $$$

Margaretas Värdshus
Lulevägen 2, Gammelstad
Tel: 0920 25 42 90
www.margaretasvardshus.se
Picturesque inn, close to the church, with a restaurant, serving local specialities. $$

Tärnaby

Sånninggården Restaurang & Pensionat
Klippen, Hemavan (25km/15 miles from Tärnaby)
Tel: 0954 330 00
www.sanninggarden.com

Beautifully located restaurant, specialising in local game and poultry. The special wild menu (featuring elk, grouse, beaver, boar and reindeer) must be booked three days ahead. $$–$$$

Umeå

Rex Bar & Grill
Rådhustorget
Tel: 090 70 60 50
www.rexbar.com
Trendy, stylish bar and restaurant mixing local produce with inspiration from the Med. Inside the Town Hall. $–$$$

Restaurant Sävargården
Gammlia
Tel: 090 77 02 22
www.savargarden.se

Patronised by royalty, Sävargården is open at lunchtimes only, when you can choose between a grand buffet spread or several set menus. $–$$

Sjöbris
Kajen 10
Tel: 090 77 71 23
Enjoy the *sjöbris* (sea breeze) on board this summer fishing-boat restaurant, and a light meal or buffet spread. Live blues on Thursdays. $–$$

PRICE CATEGORIES

Price categories are per person for an average three-course meal, excluding drinks but with tax:
$ = under 300Skr
$$ = 300–500Skr
$$$ = over 500Skr

Finland A – Z

A HANDY SUMMARY OF PRACTICAL INFORMATION

A ctivities

Outdoor Sports

Finland is known as a sporting nation, and has won more Olympic medals per head than any other country. Devotion to training is constant; it is not unusual on a hot summer's day to see squadrons of muscular youths out on roller-skis to make sure they do not lose their touch for the coming winter.

Canoeing

Canoeing is popular in the Lakelands region. Canoe and kayak rental (in the Vuosaari district, near Helsinki) is possible from:

The Viva/Vuosaari Paddling Centre
Conference Hotel Rantapuisto, Ramsinniementie 14, 00980 Helsinki. Tel: 0503 768 585
www.seakayakfinland.com

Cycling

Bicycling is big in Finland. The countryside is ideal for cyclists, dead flat on the west coast leading to gently rolling hill areas. For more information on off-road biking contact:
Mountain Bike Club Finland, Myllypurontie 1, 00920 Helsinki; tel: 09 454 6466. 13 excellent cycling

maps cover the country: see www. mtbct@net.fi.

Hiking

Thanks to its pristine forests and lakes, and freedom to roam policy, Finland offers wonderful hiking and backpacking opportunities. Finland's national parks are all designated hiking areas. For more information on destinations and facilities visit www.outdoors.fi.

Husky Safaris

Explore Lapland's wilderness in traditional style on a husky-drawn sled, or a reindeer sleigh, or opt for the more contemporary mode of transport and explore on a snowmobile. For more information and suggestions for winter adventures, visit www.laplandfinland.com.

Sailing

With its tens of thousands of lakes, and 4,830km (3,000 miles) of coastline, summer sailing opportunities abound in Finland, though the season is short. The most important sailing area is the Åland archipelago, the largest island group in the Baltic. Most harbours have

guest marinas where one can dock for reasonable overnight fees.

Skiing

Finns are particularly famous as cross-country runners and skiers, as well as ski-jumpers. You'll find facilities for any of these sports excellent; in most major urban areas there are maps of the non-auto paths set aside for such pastimes. Ask for the *Ulkoilukartta* (outdoor map) from tourist boards or www.ski.fi.

BELOW: welcome to Moomin World.

One can ski cross-country anywhere in Finland, but Lapland is a favourite spot for this very Nordic sport, as well as for downhill skiing (try to avoid school holiday weeks). Unlike Norway and even Sweden, Finland has very little in the way of mountains, except in the far north, where the Lappish hills, the highest over 1,400 metres (4,000ft), are called *tunturi*.

There are many participant cross-country ski events as well; information is available from **Finnish Ski Trek Association (Suomen Latu)**, Radiokatu 20, 00240 Helsinki; tel: 09 348 12544; www.suomenlatu.fi.

Other Sports
For information on any sport in Finland, please contact **Finnish Sports Federation (Suomen Urheilu ja Liikunta)**, Radiokatu 20, 7th floor, 00240 Helsinki; tel: 09 3481 21; www.slu.fi.

Spectator Sports
There is a near endless list of spectator sports in Finland, but a shortlist of the most popular must include ski-jumping, regatta sailing and ice hockey.

Summer
One of the biggest sailing events of the year is the Hanko Regatta, which takes place in early July off Finland's south coast. Kotka also sponsors a yearly Tall Ships event. The biggest inland sailing regatta is on Lake Päijänne, also in July. Details are available from the **Finnish Sailing Federation**, Westendinkatu 7, Espoo; tel: 0207 964 200; www.sailing.org.

Before mid-June is the annual **Finlandia Canoe Relay**, held in the large Lakeland region – the venue changes annually, and it is geared for exercise and good fun rather than competition. It lasts six days and covers over 545km (350 miles), with day and night action. See www.suomimeloo.fi for details.

Winter
Lahti, about 105km (65 miles) north of Helsinki, is the best place to watch ski-jumping.

For winter spectator sports, the **Finlandia Ski Race** (Hiihto) in mid-February is one of the top events. This 60km (37-mile) event attracts the best Finnish skiers and has ample spectator opportunities: www.finlandiahiihto.fi.

Children

Attractions
Heureka, the Finnish Science Centre (in Tikkurila, 15 minutes by train from downtown Helsinki), has exhibitions, a planetarium/cinema and hands-on experiments, and opens daily year-round. Tel: 09 85799; www.heureka.fi.

Moomin World, theme park based on the popular Moomin characters created by Tove Jansson. Situated 16km (10 miles) from Turku; daily year-round. Tel: 02 511 1111; www.muumimaailma.fi.

There are several good spots in the Lakeland region:

The Snow Centre, Messilä, in Hollola near Lahti, features many supervised activities, including pony riding and (in winter) skiing. Tel: 03 860 11; www.messila.fi.

The Musta and Valkea Ratsu Dollshouse and Puppet Theatre is north from Hollola, towards Hartola, on route 52 (signposted), 19230 Onkiniemi. Tel: 03 718 6959.

Santa Claus's Village, Rovaniemi, near the Arctic Circle. Rumour has it Santa stops off here when travelling from his secret hideaway. Daily year-round. Tel: 016 356 2096; www.santaclausvillage.info.

Åland Islands Check out the amusement park by the west harbour, Pommern Ship Museum at the west harbour, and Lilla Holmen Bird Park on the east harbour.

In Finland, almost every hotel has a list of English-speaking babysitters who can look after children.

Climate

Finland has cold winters and fairly warm summers. In July, the south has similar temperatures to southern England, with less rain and more sunshine. The hottest months are July–Aug, when temperatures average 18°C (65°F); the coldest are Jan–Feb, averaging –4°C (25°F). In south and central Finland snow settles at the start of Dec and melts mid–late Apr (or May in the forests). In the north snow comes about five weeks earlier and ends about three weeks later.

What to Bring
The best advice on packing for Finland is to bring layers of clothes, no matter what the season. While it is famous for icy winters – when gloves, long underwear, hats, woollen tights and socks, and several layers of cotton topped by wool and something waterproof are recommended – Finland is less known for its very sunny temperate summers. As a result, sun block and a sunhat are as essential at these times as warm clothes are in the winter. When travelling to northern Finland in summer, bring a strong mosquito repellent, although local brands seem to work better.

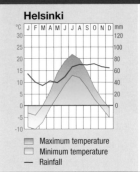

Culture

Museums
Art and design dominate the museum scene, with the greatest variety of venues in Helsinki. Most museums close on Monday. Be prepared that many museums also close for public holidays.

Classical Music and Opera
Most larger cities have a steady itinerary of concerts throughout the year, but music festivals abound in Finland in summer, and many of these are staged in stunning settings. The most famous of these are held in July: the **Savonlinna Opera Festival** at Olavinlinna Castle in eastern Finland (www.operafestival.fi), and the **Kuhmo Chamber Music Festival**, also in eastern Finland (www.Kuhmofestival.fi).

In September 2011, the brand new **Helsinki Music Centre** (Musiikkitalo) opened its impressive new residence for the Helsinki Radio Symphony and Helsinki Philharmonic orchestras, and the Sibelius Academy (www.musiikkitalo.fi). The National Opera House (Oopera and ballet), which opened in 1993, is just down the road.

Helsinki Events
The **Helsinki Festival** (Juhlaviikot) begins at the end of August and extends into the first week of September. It features broad-ranging programmes with artists from Finland and abroad, set at different venues around the city. It is kicked off (around 26 Aug) with the city-wide Night of the Arts, which goes on late into the morning around town at all sorts of venues, from museums and art galleries to nightclubs and parks. Information from: Festival Office (at

Lasipalatsi), Mannerheimintie 22–24, tel: 09 6126 5100; www.helsinginjuhlaviikot.fi.

Try the weekday evening series of concerts at the unique Church in the Rock (Temppeliaukio) in Töölö, Helsinki.

Turku Events

Turku is a lively musical city, and 2011 was even more exceptional when it reigned as European Capital of Culture, jointly with Tallinn. One can enjoy performances by the Turku City Orchestra, a weekly concert series in the Sibelius Museum, as well as events in the cathedral and the castle.

The **Turku Music Festival** (Konserttitalo; Aninkaistenkatu 9; tel: 02 262 0814; www.tmj.fi), held in mid-August, is the oldest in Finland. It hosts world premiere performances of operas, traditional symphonies and chamber music events, as well as more intimate jazz programmes with top international artists.

Tampere Events

Tampere has always had its share of music. Since 1975 the city has held an international choir festival each year, and the **Tampere Biennale** (Tullikamarinaukio 2; tel: 03 5656 6172), started in 1986, is a festival of new Finnish music, arranged in cooperation with the Association of Finnish Composers.

Since the opening of the grand Tampere Hall and Congress Centre in 1990, attendance has soared, as well as its reputation for excellent acoustics and world-class musical events. Tampere holds numerous concerts in its cathedral, churches and halls.

Jazz, Rock and Folk

The most famous of Finland's jazz festivals is **PoriJazz** (tel: 02 626 2200; www.porijazz.fi).

In Tampere there is an annual jazz festival called Jazz Happening. For information on dates and concerts, contact **Tampere Jazz Happening**; tel: 5656 6172; www.tamperemusicfestivals.fi/jazz.

Joensuu, once known for its annual song festival, now hosts **Ilosaari**, a 3-day rock concert event in mid-July that attracts top Finnish and international bands, and around 25,000 delirious fans: www.ilosaarirock.fi.

There is also **Ruisrock** on the island of Ruissalo in Turku, Finland's oldest and highly popular rock festival (see page 331).

Traditional music remains popular, and the **Kaustinen Folk Music Festival** in western Finland is one the oldest and largest of Nordic festivals, held mid-July. www.kaustinen.net/english.

Theatre

Helsinki

The **Savoy Theatre** has been a fixture in Helsinki since 1937. Situated in a stately Functionalist building that seats 700, it was once Finland's largest cinema, until it was converted to a concert hall in 1987. These days you can see top international artists in music, dance and theatre performances. **Finnish National Theatre** and **Svenska Teatern** in Helsinki both enjoy long traditions of performance in, respectively, Finnish and Swedish. The buildings themselves are worth peeking into, or at least enjoy the outdoor terrace of the Svenska Teatern where Esplanadi meets Mannerheimintie.

Tampere

Tampere rivals Helsinki for year-round theatrical events but, again, the difficulty is language. One exception is the **Pyynikki Summer Theatre** (Reservations essential; tel: 03 216 0300), where you can see original and imaginative plays from mid-June to mid-August, with synopses in English. This is particularly worthwhile if you want to enjoy the setting at the edge of Lake Pyhäjärvi and its amazing revolving auditorium which turns 360 degrees. The **Tampere Theatre Festival** (tel: 03 222 8536; www.teatterikesa.fi) in August includes many international companies which produce plays in their own languages. The **Tampere Fringe Festival** takes place at the same time, with its own offbeat programme.

Turku

Plays performed are of a high standard but rarely in languages other than Finnish or Swedish. In winter, there is the Turku City Theatre on the bank of the River Aura and the Swedish Theatre on the corner of the market place – the oldest theatre in Finland still in use. Summer festivals sometimes offer an English-speaking production.

Cinema

Finns do not dub foreign films, and you can enjoy as good a selection of movies here as in any other European city of moderate size.

Helsinki has two big cinema complexes, the 10-screen **Kinopalatsi** at Kaisaniemenkatu 2 and the 14-screen **Finnkino** at Tennispalatsi. These feature mainly Finnish films with some US blockbusters and attract a younger, noisy crowd who like to use their phones during the film. There are several smaller art-house cinemas around the city centre, which show a wider range of independent and quality mainstream titles. Film director Aki Kaurismaki owns **Kino-Andorra** (Eerikinkatu 11), which attracts an eclectic group of film buffs who come for new and old classics. Next door at No. 15 is **Orion**, which operates as both film archive and cinema. **The Forum** (Mannerheimintie 16) shows British and American films; **Bio-Rex** (Mannerheimintie 22–24) features classic films; **Maxim** (Kluuivkatu 1) shows art-house/mainstream, and **Bristol** (Mikonkatu 8) mainstream.

Film showings begin early and run until 9pm (and up to 11pm). Listings are available at the Tourist Board. Seats are reserved at the time you buy the tickets, and box offices usually open 30–45 minutes before show time but at some cinemas may be purchased even earlier.

BELOW: the Pori Jazz Festival at Tampere.

ABOVE: there is usually a pharmacy open late in larger towns.

Tampere has a cinema centre, **Finnkino Plevna**, in the Finlayson area (Itäinen katu 4).

In Turku, **Kinopalatsi** is opposite the Market Square at Kauppiaskatu 11 and usually has something in English. There is a multi-screen theatre in the Hansa Shopping Centre on Eerikinkatu.

Customs Regulations

The following items may be brought into Finland.

Cigarettes/Tobacco

Visitors over 17 years of age from non-EU countries or travelling from the new Eastern European member states may bring in 200 cigarettes, 50 cigars or 250g (1–2lb) of tobacco products duty-free.

Alcohol

Visitors from non-EU countries aged 20 or over can bring in 16 litres of beer, 2 litres of other mild alcohol (drinks containing not more than 22 percent by volume of alcohol) and 1 litre of strong alcohol (spirits). For visitors of 18–19 years of age, the quantity limit is the same, but must not include strong alcohol.

D isabled Travellers

For disabled people, travelling should not pose tremendous problems in Finland. Most newer buildings have access for disabled people, in terms of ramps and lifts. Check the *Finland Hotel* guide which indicates by symbols which hotels have access and facilities for disabled people. With careful planning, transport should also go smoothly; when ordering a taxi, specify your needs (wheelchair is *pyörätuoli*). The Helsinki metro is

accessible for wheelchair users, but other forms of public transport may be a bit more problematic, although some city buses "kneel", making it easier to board. If you have queries related to disabled travel in Finland, contact:
Rullaten ry
Pajutie 7C, 02770 Espoo
Tel: 050 579 5335
www.rullaten.fi

E mbassies and Consulates

Australian Consulate
Museokatu 25B, Helsinki
Tel: 09 4777 6640
Canada
Pohjoisesplanadi 25b, Helsinki
Tel: 09 228 530
Irish
Erottajankatu 7A, Helsinki
Tel: 09 646 006
UK
Itäinen Puistotie 17, Helsinki
Tel: 09 2286 5100
US
Itäinen Puistotie 14b, Helsinki
Tel: 09 6162 5800

Emergencies

Ambulance, rescue services, fire department and police: 112
Police: 10022

G ay and Lesbian Travellers

Finns have a tolerant attitude to gay and lesbian travellers, and the image of the notorious fetish artist Tom of Finland has become internationally iconic. Helsinki's scene has picked up in recent years, and there was even a leather convention held a few years ago. Pick up the *Gay Guide* from the main tourist office. For general information, contact SETA, a non-governmental gay rights organisation.

Mannerheimintie 170 A5; tel: 09 681 2580; www.seta.fi.
(See listings for bars and nightclubs under Helsinki.)

H ealth and Medical Care

You'll have little to worry about healthwise in Finland. However, you may have an uncomfortable time with the mosquitoes in northern and central parts in July and August. Ask your GP about appropriate mosquito treatment before you go and enquire at chemists in Finland about the most effective repellent.

Finland's medical facilities have an excellent reputation worldwide. The country has reciprocal health arrangements with other EU members, so visitors are entitled to the same treatment as Finns. British nationals should take a European Health Insurance Card (EHIC), which you can apply for online (www.ehic.org.uk), by phone (0845 606 2030) or by post (form available from any post office in the UK).

Hospitals

If you need medical treatment, almost any health clinic *(terveysasema)* or hospital *(sairaala)* will treat you for a nominal fee or will bill your insurance firm. All doctors speak English. Casualty is generally called *Ensiapu*. Visitors needing hospital care in Helsinki should contact the following.
For surgery and medicine:
Meilahti Hospital, Haartmaninkatu 4, Helsinki. Tel: 09 4711 112 for all emergencies, or the 24-medical advice hotline 09 100 23.
For serious accidents:
Töölö Hospital, Topeliuksenkatu 5, Helsinki. Tel: 09 471 87383.
For 24-hour private medical care:
Mehiläinen, 3rd floor, Runeberginkatu 47a, Helsinki. Tel: 010 414 0444.

Pharmacies

A pharmacy is called *apteekki*. There is at least one open late at night in larger towns. In Helsinki, the Yliopiston Apteekki at Mannerheimintie 96 is open 24 hours a day.

Dentists

Haartman Hospital treats dental emergencies 24 hours a day. Haartmaninkatu 4, Bldg 12. Tel: 09 310 4999. Emergencies in working hours: Dentarium, Mikaelsgatan 8 Helsinki. Tel: 09 622 1533.
Out-of-hours emergencies:
Oral, 2nd Floor, Erottajankatu 5A, Helsinki. Tel: 010 400 3000.

Internet

Finland is one of the most "wired" countries in the world. In 2010 the government introduced a law guaranteeing broadband access to every person living in Finland, including those in secluded, sparsely populated regions. Service is very reliable. Internet cafés include:

Helsinki: **Kohtaamispaikka@**, Lasipalatsi, Mannerheimintie 22–24, or **mbar** at same address.

Netcup Cafés can be found in Stockmann department stores throughout Finland, and at most libraries.

Language
Getting By

Good morning Hyvää huomenta
Good day Hyvää päivää
Good evening Hyvää iltaa
Today Tänään
Tomorrow Huomenna
Yesterday Eilen
Hello Terve or hei
How do you do? Kuinka voit
Goodbye Näkemiin or hei hei
Yes Kyllä or joo
No Ei
Thank you Kiitos
How much does this cost? Paljonko tämä maksaa?
It costs... Se maksaa...
How do I get to..? Miten pääsen..?
Where is...? Missä on...?
Right Oikealla
To the right Oikealle
Left Vasemmalla
To the left Vasemmalle
Straight on Suoraan
What time is it? Paljonko kello on?
It is (the time is) Kello on
Could I have your name? Saisinko nimesi?
My name is... Nimeni on...
Do you speak English? Puhutko englantia?
I only speak English Puhun vain englantia
Can I help you? Voinko auttaa sinua?
I do not understand En ymmärrä
I do not know En tiedä

Eating Out

breakfast aamiainen
lunch lounas
dinner illallinen
eat syödä
drink juoda
I would like to order... Haluaisin tilata
Could I have the bill? Saisko laskun?
Could I have the key? Saisko avaimen?
Toilet Vessa
Gentlemen Miehet (Swedish: Herrar)

Ladies Naiset (Swedish: Damer)
Vacant Vapaa
Engaged Varattu
Entrance Sisäänkäynti
Exit Uloskääynti
No entry Pääsy kielletty
Open Avoinna, Auki
Closed Suljettu, Kiinni
Push Työnnä
Pull Vedä

Days of the Week

Monday Maanantai
Tuesday Tiistai
Wednesday Keskiviikko
Thursday Torstai
Friday Perjantai
Saturday Launantai
Sunday Sunnuntai

Useful Words

chemist apteekki
hospital sairaala
doctor lääkäri
police station poliisilaitos
parking paikoitus
phrasebook turistien sanakirja
dictionary sanakirja
car auto
bus, coach bussi, linja-auto
train juna
aircraft lentokone
Cheers Kippis (Swedish: skål)
To rent Vuokrata
For sale Myytävänä
Free, no charge Ilmainen
Room to rent Vuokrattavana huone

Media
Newspapers and Books

With the exception of the *International Herald Tribune*, which arrives on the afternoon of its publication date, you'll have to wait a day and a half for English-language newspapers to get to Helsinki. Foreign papers are sold at Helsinki Railway Station and

Akateeminen Kirjakauppa (Academic Bookstore) at Keskuskatu 1 (tel: 09 121 41; www.akateeminen.com), where you can also get books in English, and at the larger hotels in other cities, as well as at main airports.

The Helsinki Times is a weekly English-language newspaper, presenting news about Finland, and sold at various news kiosks. *Helsinki Sanomat*, the daily newspaper, has English pages on its website, with current events and pertinent information about Finland, www.hs.fi/eng.

Tourist Publications

Helsinki This Week, free from the tourist office at Vantaa airport and most hotels, is an English-language guide to cultural and tourist events in the capital, also online: www.helsinki expert.fi.

City in English is a free city guide published each year in June that is targeted at young adults and distributed at Tourist Information and most hotels.

SixDegrees is a free monthly magazine in English with events, trends and current affairs, also online: www.6d.fi.

We Are Helsinki is a free English-language city guide published six times a year that highlights restaurants and fashion, and is distributed at Tourist Information and shops.

Radio and Television

For news in English, you can tune in to the Finnish national broadcasters' YLE Capital FM (97.5 FM) in most of southern Finland. This broadcasts hours of programmes in Spanish, French and Russian, but mainly English, using American, Canadian, Australian and South African stations

BELOW: the Hartwall Arena in Helsinki.

as well as the BBC and Ireland's RTE. The news in English is broadcast daily on YLE Radio 1 (87.9 FM in the Helsinki region) daily at 3.55pm. For up-to-date schedules, contact YLE on 09 14801. YLE 1 also broadcasts news in English on weekdays at 7.30am, and the BBC's World Service and other English language channels are usually available in hotels.

Money

Finland's unit of currency is the euro. Notes are available in 500, 200, 100, 50, 20, 10 and 5 euros and coins in 2 and 1 euros, 50, 20, 10, 5, 2, and 1 cents. Shops do not have to accept 2 and 1 cent coins.

How to Pay

Credit cards MasterCard, Visa, Diner's Club and American Express are accepted in most establishments in main cities.

ATMs marked "Otto" give local currency if you have a card with an international PIN number (Visa, Cirrus, plus, MasterCard and so on).

Nightlife

Pubs, Bars and Clubs

Pub-crawling remains popular, and there are several clubs that attract the best pop bands. Increasing numbers of international stars make a stop at the Hartwall Arena (www.hartwall-areena.com) in Helsinki on their world tours.

The minimum age for drinking alcohol is 18, but some clubs have an age limit of 21. Entrance fees vary.

Helsinki
Ahjo Wine Bar & Night Club
Bulevardi 2/4; tel: 20 770 4700.
Terminally hip and ultra-modern bar and club.
Corona Bar
Eerikinkatu 11; tel: 09 7517 5611.
Attracts a young hip crowd who come to talk, drink beer, eat toasted sandwiches and play pool.
Highlight
Frederikinkatu 42; tel: 010 766 3780.
A nightclub for young people built in an old church.
Lost and Found
Annankatu 6; tel: 09 680 1010.
This popular "hetero-friendly" gay club stays open until 4am, and remains a longstanding favourite after everywhere else has shut down.
Storyville
Museokatu 8; tel: 09 408 007.
A cosy jazz club to have a late drink. In the summer, the terrace is the place to be. Cover charge.

Tavastia
Urho Kekkosenkatu 4; tel: 09 7746 74 20.
This University-owned club attracts some of Helsinki's best live music.
Teatteri
Pohjoisesplanadi 2; tel: 09 6128 5000.
Located in the Swedish Theatre complex, the Klubi nightclub attracts stylish 30- and 40-somethings.
The Tiger
Urho Kekkosenkatu 1A; tel: (0) 20 7759 350.
Considered the number one nightclub in Helsinki for 20-somethings and their admirers, it is immense and absolutely in tune.
Torni
Yrjönkatu 26; tel: 09 4336 6340.
The exclusive Ateljee bar on the 13th floor is famous for its great views over Helsinki, which are included in the price of the drinks.
Zetor
Mannerheimintie 3–5, Kaivopiha; tel: 010 766 4450.
This "tractor-style" pub has to be seen to be believed. Experience the surrealism of the Finnish countryside.

Tampere
Nightlife is very evident on the main street, **Hämeenkatu**. Bar-hopping is easy, although more "traditional" pubs are elsewhere, such as **Salhojankadun Pub** on Salhojankatu and **Ohranjyvä** at Näsilinnankatu 15. Locally brewed beer is available at **Plevna** (Itäinenkatu 8) and **Wanha Posti** (Hämeenkatu 13A).

Turku
Old Bank
Aurakatu 3; tel: 02 274 5700; www.oldbank.fi.
This pub serves more varieties of beer than any other in town.
Panimoravintola Koulu
Eerikinkatu 18; tel: 02 274 5757; www.panimoravintolakoulu.fi

Public Holidays

1 January New Year's Day
6 January Epiphany
March/April Good Friday, Easter Sunday
1 May May Day
May/June Ascension Day
May/June Whitsun
end of June Midsummer's Eve and Day
early November All Saints' Day
6 December Independence Day
24–26 December Christmas Eve and Day, Boxing Day

This former school has a brewery, and the classrooms are now pubs or restaurants.
Uusi Apteekki
Kaskenkatu 1; tel: 02 250 2595; www.uusiapteekki.fi.
Literally "new pharmacy", this pub is set in one from the past.

Opening Hours

Shops Generally open from Monday to Saturday, except for small food stores, which are allowed to stay open on Sunday. In larger cities, hours are 9am–5pm, with late-night opening on Thursday. In Helsinki, many open until 9pm on weekdays and 6pm on Saturday. Larger food stores usually open 9am–8pm weekdays and 9am–4pm on Saturday. The only late shops are in the tunnel under the Helsinki Railway Station: open weekdays 10am–10pm and weekends noon–10pm.
Banks Mon–Fri 9.15am–4.15pm; bureaux de change open a bit later. The one at the airport opens daily 6am–10pm.

Postal Services

Post offices are usually open 9am–5pm weekdays. Services include stamps, registered mail and poste restante. Helsinki's main post office is at Elielinaukio 2, tel: 200 71000, opposite the railway square. Mon–Fri 7am–9pm, Sat–Sun 10am–6pm.

Religious Services

The Lutheran Church is the state Church of Finland, with 82 percent of Finns counted as Lutherans. There is a small Greek Orthodox population, and just two Catholic churches in Finland. In Helsinki, services in English are held at the Temppeliaukio church (Church in the Rock) on Lutherinkatu; there are both Lutheran and ecumenical services here. There is also one synagogue and one mosque in Helsinki, for those of Jewish or Muslim faith.

Shopping

What to Buy

Finnish Design
Helsinki was named World Design Capital 2012, and you can discover the Design District via a "Design Walk" organised by the tourist office. Esplanadi is a compact version of the Champs Elysées, and is the mecca for Finnish design on both sides of its tree-lined park that stretches from Mannerheimintie to the harbour.

Choose from jewellery, woodwork, clothing, glass or kitchenware. **Lapponia Aarikka** and **Kalevala Koru** jewellery are particularly Finnish, the first being a mainly contemporary collection and the second a collection based on designs from the Finnish epic poem *Kalevala*, rendered in silver, gold and brass. Aarikka also supplies some fine woodwork products, including chopping boards, Christmas decorations, toys and wooden jewellery. **Iittala** is known for its stunning glass, dining and cooking utensils, and the most impressive ceramic work is produced by **Arabia**, one of the older Finnish firms. Its factory and museum (Hämeentie 135; tel: 204 39 5357; Tue–Fri noon–6pm, Sat–Sun 10am–4pm; charge) are just a 20-minute tram ride from Helsinki centre. There is an outlet on the premises for Arabia, Pentik, iittala and Finlayson products (outlet hours are Mon–Fri 10am–8pm, Sat–Sun until 4pm).

Marimekko is the quintessential Finnish clothing designer, with its typical brightly coloured fabrics for men, women and children, as well as more elegant clothing for women and textiles for home use. These popular Finnish brands can be found both in their own stores and department stores in most Finnish towns of any size, including several shops on both the Pohjoisesplanadi and Eteläesplanadi in Helsinki.

Other Finnish designers along the block are **Vuokko, Annikki Karvanen** and shoe designer **Pertti Palmroth**. There are also stylish furniture showrooms like **Artek**, as well as home furnishing shops. For functional and distinctive souvenirs of contemporary Finnish design – from stylish wool felt hats to candlestick holders – be sure to visit the **Design Forum in Helsinki** (Erottajankatu 7; tel: 09 622 08132; www.designforum.fi).

Department Stores

The king of department stores in Finland is **Stockmann**, which is found in most Finnish cities like Helsinki, Turku, Tampere and Rovaniemi. Stockmann also owns **Akateeminen Kirjakauppa** (Academic Bookstore), Finland's best-known bookstore, which sells international periodicals. Another good department store to look out for throughout Finland is **Sokos**, and like Stockmann, it is known for its excellent food hall.

Shopping Areas

Helsinki

The city centre has several shopping centres like **Kamppi, Aleksi 13,** **Forum** and **Kämp Galleria**: from basic to upmarket. There are also many local and international boutiques in various neighbourhoods, like Ullanlinna along Korkeovuorenkatu or west of Mannerheimintie on Frederikinkatu and Uudenmaankatu. There are several market squares that sell both fresh food and a range of other consumer goods, from second-hand clothes and records to designer jewellery, Sami mittens and fur hats.

Kauppatori (at the harbour) is the main market, followed by **Hietalaniemi Flea Market** (on the west end of Bulevardi) and the indoor **Hakaniemmi market hall** (with its unique Marimekko outlet) that is frequented by locals. Markets have extended hours in summer and are open until about 8pm. In the weeks leading up to Christmas, there are many markets and fairs around the city centre selling handicrafts, decorations and seasonal treats.

Turku

In the Turku city centre, at Yliopistonkatu 25, you will find **Pentik**, which is famous for ceramics, and **Aarikka** (No. 27), for handmade wooden crafts and decorations. For crafts, look into **Sylvi Salonen**, specialising in linens and decorative crafts at Yliopistonkatu 26. Markets are generally open daily except Sunday. Turku's open-air market features flowers, fish, fruit, vegetables and some crafts. The indoor market hall offers all that and more, including bread, cheese, coffee, tea, spices, snacks and many handicrafts.

Tampere

The **Tampere Market Hall**, at Hämeenkatu 19, is open Mon–Fri 8am–6pm, Sat 8am–3pm.

The **Kehräsaari Shopping Centre**, Laukontori 1, is situated in a converted spinning factory dating to 1897. **Pirkanmaa Arts & Crafts Shop**, Hatanpään valtatie 4, and **Finlayson** textile outlet, Kuninkaankatu 4.

Telephones

International dialling code: 358 Finland is a world leader in telecommunications, with a highly sophisticated, deregulated phone system. Public call boxes and phonecards are soon to be obsolete (on sale for the moment at most kiosks and tourist offices). The best way to call overseas cheaply is at certain internet cafés in main cities.

Hotels usually add a surcharge for calls made from your room. In Helsinki, there are internet call centres at Vuorikatu 8 (Mon–Fri 10am–9pm, Sat 11am–9pm, Sun noon–9pm) and Hämeentie 23 (Mon, Thur, Sat 11am–6pm, Tue, Wed and Fri until 9pm).

Callers from outside Finland should dial the international code, then the country code (358) followed by the area code, omitting the initial zero (0).

Mobile Phones

Finland is the home of Nokia and has the world's highest ownership of mobile (cell) phones – more than 80 percent of Finns own one. There are several operators; two major ones are Radiolinja and Sonera.

Tourist Information

Before You Go

Australia Embassy (supplies tourist information) 12 Darwin Avenue, Yarralumla, ACT 2600 Tel: 02 6273 3800 www.finland.org.au **UK/Ireland** Finnish Tourist Board PO Box 33213, London W6 8JX Tel: 020 8600 5680 (UK) or 01 407 3362 (Ireland) www.visitfinland.com/uk **US/Canada** Finnish Tourist Board PO Box 4649, Grand Central Station, New York NY 10163-4649 Tel: 212 885 9700 or 800-fin-info (North America) www.visitfinland.com/us

In Finland

Finland has over 50 main tourist information offices, marked with an "i", as well as many summer tourist offices. The following are the main tourist offices, but a full list can be obtained at www.visitfinland.com: **Finnish Tourist Board** (correspondence only) PO Box 625, 00101 Helsinki; tel: 010 605 8000; www.visitfinland.com. **Helsinki City Tourist Office** Pohjoisesplanadi 19, 00100 Helsinki; tel: 09 3101 3300; www.visithelsinki.fi. **Rovaniemi Tourist Information** Sampo Shopping Centre, Maakuntakatu 29–31, 96200 Rovaniemi; tel: 016 346 270; www.visitrovaniemi.fi. **Tampere City Tourist Office** Railway Station, Rautatienkatu 25A, 33100 Tampere; tel: 03 56 56 6800; www.gotampere.fi.

DENMARK

NORWAY

SWEDEN

FINLAND

Turku Touring
Aurakatu 4, 20100 Turku; tel: 02 262
7444; www.turkutouring.com.

Transport

Getting There

By Air

Finnair is the national carrier of
Finland and operates international
and national routes. Both Finnair (www.
finnair.com) and British Airways (www.ba.
com) connect London and Helsinki
with daily flights. Finnair (and many
other airlines, including Lufthansa,
Blue 1 and SAS Scandinavian Airlines)
fly direct between Helsinki and most
European capitals.

Finnair also links with several
North American cities, including New
York. You may be able to find value-
for-money package fares and charter
flights from New York or London, but
they are rare; watch newspaper
advertisements for offers.

From Helsinki, Finnair and Blue 1
(www.blue1.com) fly numerous domestic
routes to more than 20 cities,
including several to north Finland
airports, and have cross-country
flights between some of them. Budget
airline Ryanair (www.ryanair.com) flies
between Tampere and London, Riga,
Frankfurt and Dublin. Flights to
Mariehamn from Helsinki and
Stockholm are operated by Air Åland /
Next Jet; www.airaland.com.

Finnair also operates flights to
Tallinn and Saarema in Estonia.

By Sea

You can travel to Finland by boat from
Sweden, Estonia and Germany. **Silja
Line** and **Viking Line** have daily routes
between Stockholm and Helsinki,
which are very popular with locals for
the duty-free shopping. These ferries
are luxurious with restaurants, saunas,
swimming pools, tax-free shops and
children's playrooms. **Tallink** now has
a super-fast direct link between
Helsinki and Rostock, Germany.

There are plenty of services to
choose from for a trip between Helsinki
and Tallinn. For a fast trip **TallinkSilja**
operates a year-round Shuttle Star
service to Tallinn which takes only two
hours; there are restaurants, a
business lounge with wifi connections
and television, and duty-free shopping.
Eckerö Lines' M/S *Nordlandia* makes
the trip in three hours. SuperSeaCat
has suspended operations, and now
only **Linda Line**'s hydrofoil is running
catamaran voyages from Helsinki to
Tallinn, in 1½ hours during the ice-free
period. These fast boats are
dependent on weather conditions,

whereas the bigger boats also manage
in rough weather.

It's less expensive to travel by ferry
from Stockholm to Turku or Naantali
in western Finland, and then overland
to Helsinki rather than by direct ship
to Helsinki. Viking provides very cheap
bus tickets for the overland trip; the
ferry ticket is also cheaper as the
voyage is shorter. One can also travel
to Finland's Åland Islands by boat
from Stockholm or Turku – Viking has
a daily service to Mariehamn. Also, RG
Line operates a cargo boat between
Vaasa and Umeå.

Eckerö Line (West Terminal)
Tel: +358 6000 4300 (€1.64 per min)
www.eckeroline.fi
Linda Line (South Terminal)
Tel: 0600 066 8970 (€1.64 per min)
www.lindaline.fi
RG Line (Satama Terminal Vaasa)
Tel: +358 (0)207 716 810 (Finland) or
+46 (0)90 185 200 (Sweden)
TallinkSilja Line (West Terminal)
Tel: 0600 174 522
www.tallinksilja.com
Viking Line (Katajanokka Terminal)
Tel: 09 12351 (Finland) or 08 452
4000 (Sweden)
www.vikingline.fi

By Rail

It's a long haul to Finland from just
about anywhere by rail, because you
inevitably finish the long rail trip north
with a 15-hour journey by boat and
train from Stockholm to Helsinki.
From Britain, the handiest route is
from Harwich to the Hook of Holland,
overland to Copenhagen, then the
connecting train to Stockholm and
boat/boat and train to Helsinki. Total
travel time is about 45 hours. This is
cheaper than an Apex flight only if you
get a special fare rail ticket; residents
of Nordic countries now qualify for
InterRail tickets regardless of age.

Getting Around

On Arrival

Finland's main international airport,
Helsinki-Vantaa, is connected by
Finnair Bus or the Yellow Line shared
taxi (fixed fares to any destination
within Helsinki city centre); fares are
less on the Finnair bus, which leaves
every 20 minutes with connections to
Helsinki Railway Station.

By Air

Finnair and Blue 1 both operate
domestic flight services. Fares are
relatively inexpensive; in July, fares
are very cheap. It is a good idea to fly
if, for example, you want to get to
Lapland from the south without
spending days on the road. Discounts

are available for groups, families and
senior citizens.

By Rail

The Finnish rail network is limited, but
service is adequate in most cases and
very good between major points like
Turku and Helsinki. Rail travel to north
Finland requires completion by bus as
Finnish rail lines only run as far as
Rovaniemi and Kemijärvi (in winter to
Kolari). Finnrail passes are available for
3-day, 5-day and 10-day periods; first-
class passes are also available. From
June to August, a special Lomapassi
(Holiday Pass) costs about 3139 for
adults and entitles you to 3 travel days
in a month. More information on family
tickets, group tickets and other types of
discount is available online at www.vr.fi/
heo/eng, or contact:
VR Ltd (Finnish Railways)
Vilhonkatu 13
Tel: 09 307 2092
www.vr.fi/en

Water Transport

Ferries and passenger boats in Finland
play a strong role where international
destinations are concerned, but there
are some lakeland ferry routes worth
pursuing. There are the Silverline and
Poet's Way, which begin in Tampere
and cover much of the western
lakelands, tours in the Päijänne region
and over Finland's largest lake,
Saimaa, in the east. Many other
operators run trips on the lakes; for
more information, contact the central
or regional tourist boards (see above).

Helsinki's only real commuter
island is Suomenlinna, with ferries
travelling back and forth roughly every
half-hour (schedule depends on
season). Most of these ferries are part
of the public transport network of
Helsinki. Other Helsinki islands closer
to the coast are connected by road.
Lake Päijänne Cruises
Tel: 010 421 7800
Roll Risteilyt
Tel: 017-266 2466
Silverline and Poet's Way
Tel: 010 422 5600

Bus and Coach

Finland is greatly dependent on buses
for transporting the bulk of its
passenger traffic. There are coach
services on 90 percent of Finland's
public roads (40,000 long-distance
departures a day) which also cover the
areas that trains don't, particularly in
the north and in smaller places
throughout the country. The head
office for long-distance bus traffic is
Matkahuolto, Lauttasaarentie 8,
00200 Helsinki; tel: 09-682 701.

Timetable enquiries can be made at the National Timetable Service, tel: 02000 4000 (31.71 per minute plus local telephone charges), or online at www.matkahuolto.info.

There is no penalty for buying a ticket on the coach, but you cannot get group discounts (for three adults or more on trips over 80km/50 miles) from the coach ticket seller. Senior citizens and full-time students (university and lower) are also eligible for discounts, but must purchase, for €5, a coach card entitling them to this discount – at least 30 percent. Bring a photo, ID and international ISIC student card. Accompanied children under four travel free.

ABOVE: Finland is perfect cycling country.

Driving

Finland's roads are not too plagued by traffic, although they do get very busy between the capital and the countryside on Fridays and Sundays during the summer. There are few multi-lane motorways. Most are two-lane only. Pay attention to road signs showing elk and reindeer zones. Collisions with these animals are usually serious. Use caution at all hours, but especially at dusk when elk are most active. For winter driving, studded tyres should ideally be used from November to March and are strongly recommended throughout December at all times.

Rules of the Road

Drive on the right, overtake on the left. All cars must use their lights outside built-up areas. Elsewhere, lights must be used at dusk or at night or in bad weather (UK cars must sweep their lights right). Wearing of seat belts is also compulsory.

Traffic coming from the right has right of way. Exceptions are on roads marked by a triangle sign; if this is facing you, you must give right of way; similarly, if you are on a very major thoroughfare it is likely that the feed-in streets will have triangles, giving you the right of way. On roundabouts (rotaries), the first vehicle to reach the roundabout has right of way.

Speed limits are signposted, and range from 30kmph (18mph) in school zones to 100kmph (62mph) on motorways.

Taxis

Finnish taxis run throughout the country, with fares starting at around €4.50. Helsinki city centre and the centres of other large cities, as well as most major airports, bus and railway stations, have taxi stands. Otherwise local telephone books list the number of the nearest dispatcher (under *Taksi* in the White Pages). Finding the closest one is worthwhile, especially in Helsinki, as taxis charge from embarkation point (plus an order fee). You can also hail a cab on the street, but this is a rarer way of getting a taxi in Finland than those mentioned above.

Bicycles

Finland is a good cycling country with its well-engineered cycle paths and gently rolling landscape. In Helsinki in summer, there's a free city bike scheme. For better-quality bicycles, try Greenbike rental shop (Bulevardi 32; tel: 050 550 1020). You can rent bikes from the harbours of Mariehamn in the Åland Islands (a popular summer cycling destination).

The Finnish Youth Hostel Association also offers planned route tours at good-value prices (which can also include accommodation). Also ask the Finnish Tourist Board *(see page 427)* about other firms that run planned cycling tours in the country. **Finnish Youth Hostel Association** Yrjönkatu 38B, 00100 Helsinki Tel: 09 694 0377,www.srmnet.org

Hitchhiking

Thumbing is still a time-honoured way to get a cheap ride in Finland, but you may have to wait a long time to get picked up, particularly at weekends and in the furthest reaches of Lapland where traffic can be pretty thin. Hitchhiking is prohibited on motorways; the smaller secondary routes are a better bet. As with any country in the world, however, safety can never be guaranteed on the road, and this mode of transport is not recommended.

V isas and Passports

Citizens of most Western countries do not need to obtain visas to travel to Finland; a valid passport will suffice. As Finland is a member of the Schengen countries, UK citizens may enter the country with a valid ID card.

W hat to Read

Facts about Finland (Otava). This book provides the most comprehensive coverage of Finland's history and culture, by a range of Finnish authors. *Finnish Design: A Concise History*, Pekka Korvenmaa (Cirrus, 2010) *Portraying Finland: Facts and Insights* (Otava, 2005).

Send Us Your Thoughts

We do our best to ensure the information in our books is as accurate and up-to-date as possible. The books are updated on a regular basis using local contacts, who painstakingly add, amend and correct as required. However, some details (such as telephone numbers and opening times) are liable to change, and we are ultimately reliant on our readers to put us in the picture.

We welcome your feedback, especially your experience of using the book "on the road". Maybe we recommended a hotel that you liked (or another that you didn't), or you came across a great bar or new attraction we missed.

We will acknowledge all contributions, and we'll offer an Insight Guide to the best letters received.

Please write to us at:
Insight Guides
PO Box 7910
London SE1 1WE
Or email us at:
insight@apaguide.co.uk

A CCOMMODATION

HOTELS

Choosing a Hotel

Hotels throughout Finland are clean and well equipped, though expensive. One can find bargains at the chain hotels (generally up to 60 percent of standard prices) at weekends, and in summer when they lose their business and conference trade. A generous buffet breakfast is often included in the rate. There are also elegant historic villas which now operate as hostelries.

Budget accommodation includes youth and family hostels, farmhouses, guesthouses, family villages, camping and various forms of self-catering. During the summer holidays, some student residences become Summer Hotels, opening on 1 June.

Local tourist offices and booking centres will provide up-to-date prices, including details of weekend and summer discounts. General information on accommodation is available from the Finnish Tourist Board in your home country, or from the head office in Helsinki (see *Tourist Information, page 427*). Or Helsinki has its own booking centre at the railway station:

Hotel Booking Centre
Central Railway Station
Tel: 09 2288 1400
www.helsinkiexpert.com
For details of youth hostels:
The Finnish Youth Hostel Association
Yrjönkatu 38B 15
Tel: 09 565 7150
www.hostellit.fi

Hotel Chains

Finland has many large hotel chains of its own, as well as foreign ones. Scandic, Sokos and Cumulus offer fairly comfortable standard services in most big towns.

Discount Schemes

When travelling around the country between June and August, you can enrol in the Travel & Stay Cheque scheme (which has replaced Finncheque), run by Sokos, the biggest hotel chain in Finland, with over 40 hotels to choose from. A double/twin room costs €84 (depending on availability). Cheques are valued at €42 and can be purchased via certain travel agents; www.travelandstaycheque.com.

Hotel Listings

Hotels are grouped by area, starting with Helsinki. Within each city or region, they are listed alphabetically.

ACCOMMODATION LISTINGS

HELSINKI

Academica
Hietaniemenkatu 14
Tel: 09 1311 4334
www.hostelacademica.fi
Basic summer hostel providing modern rooms with their own bath and kitchen facilities. Family rooms available. Sauna and swimming pool. €
Eurohostel
Linnankatu 9
Tel: 09 622 0470

www.eurohostel.eu
Located on Katajanokka Island by the ferry terminals, this no-frills hostel has 135 rooms in two categories, with bathroom facilities for men and women: including kitchen, laundry, sauna and café. €
Hotel Fabian
Fabianinkatu 7
Tel: 09 6128 2000
www.hotelfabian.fi

A modern boutique hotel which opened in 2010; the Style rooms on the upper floors feature splendid rooftop views. €€
Hotel Glo Kluuvi
Kluuvikatu 4
Tel: 010 3444 400
www.hotelglo.fi
Another new contemporary hotel, where the rooms go from large to XL and beyond. Under the same

operation as its posh neighbour Hotel Kämp; there is also a Hotel Glo at Helsinki airport and one in Espoo. €€
Hotel Haven
Unioninkatu 17
Tel: 09 681 930
www.hotelhaven.fi
Choose from Comfort, Style or Lux rooms, unless you wish to splash out on a suite. Excellent breakfast

ABOVE: the sheer luxury of Klaus K.

served in the lower courtyard. €€–€€€

Hotel Kämp
Pohjoisesplanadi 29
Tel: 09 576 111
www.hotelkamp.fi
The top hotel in town with a rich history, rubber duckies in the luxury bathtubs, and a VIP clientele. €€–€€€

Klaus K
Bulevardi 2–4
Tel: 020 770 4700
www.klauskhotel.com
A hip boutique hotel in central Helsinki inspired by the Finnish epic *Kalevala*, with themed rooms depending on your mood. Excellent sauna and spa facilities. €€

Hotel Linna
Lönnrotinkatu 29
Tel: 010 3444 100
www.palacekamp.fi
A Finnish Jugendstil castle dating to 1903 in one of the most fashionable areas of Helsinki. The 48 refurbished rooms are located in the rear of the historic area. Restaurant, sauna and parking garage. €€

THE SOUTH

Hanko

Pensionat Garbo
Esplanaadi 84
Tel: 040 542 1732
www.pensionat-garbo.com
Located in Hanko town, not at the seaside, this bed and breakfast is like a Hollywood museum – each themed room features a star from the silver screen. Great value. They also have a log cabin to rent 15km (9 miles) from the town centre. €

Villa Maija
Appelgrenintie 7
Tel: (0) 50 505 2013
www.villamaija.fi
The 19th-century Villa Maija actually consists of three pastel-coloured houses around the same courtyard. All rooms have bath facilities and TV. The rooms facing the sea have verandas or glass balconies. €–€€

Kotka

Santalahti
Santalahdentie 150
Tel: 05 260 5055
www.santalahti.fi
This unique holiday resort offers log villas and cottages (with sauna) by the sea and surrounding pine forests. €–€€

Naantali

Naantali Spa Hotel
Tel: 02 445 5100
www.naantalispa.fi
In a charming seaside town near Turku, this unique spa complex offers a variety of luxury accommodation: from the Sunborn yacht to the Suite or Spa Hotel. Nearby is the Naantali Family Hostel (Opintie 3), which offers budget rates with access to spa and breakfast facilities. €–€€

Turku

Best Western Hotel Seaport
Toinen Poikkikatu 2
(Passenger Harbour)
Tel: 02 283 3000
www.hotelseaport.fi
By the castle, a 19th-century warehouse with red-brick facade in original neo-Gothic style with beautiful wooden beams. €€

Centro Hotel
Yliopistonkatu 12
Tel: 02 211 8100
www.centrohotel.com
Just around the corner from the market place, the 62 comfortable rooms include all the amenities. For a few euros more, you can book a mini-suite. €

Omenahotelli
Humalistonkatu 7
Tel: 0600 18018
www.omenahotels.com
A new concept budget hotel with straightforward, no-frills accommodation and no reception desk; in a building designed by Alvar Aalto. Central, but peaceful. €

Park Hotel
Rauhankatu 1
Tel: 02 273 2555
www.parkhotelturku.fi
Each of the 21 well-furnished rooms in this elegant *Jugendstil* villa (1902) are all different, some with a park view. €

Radisson Blu Marina Palace
Linnankatu 32
Tel: 020 12 34 710
www.radissonblu.com
Reopened, refurbished and under new management rooms are modern and some have river views. Sauna department, gym, beauty salon and heated indoor parking. €€–€€€

LAKELAND

Imatra

Rantasipi Imatran Valtionhotelli
Torkkelinkatu 2
Tel: 05 625 2000
www.rantasipi.fi
Landmark Art Nouveau castle with luxurious modern spa facilities, next to the Vuoksi River and Imatra Rapids. Excellent
Linnasali restaurant on site. €–€€

Jyväskylä

Hotelli Yöpuu
Yliopistonkatu 23
Tel: 014 333 900
www.hotelliyopuu.fi
Each of the 16 rooms in this romantic historic building has a different theme, and
one of the suites has a private sauna. The elegant restaurant Pöllöwaari serves excellent lunches and dinners. €€

Kuopio

Spa Hotel Rauhalahti
Katiskaniementie 8
Tel: 030 608 3100
www.rauhalahti.com
This fine spa hotel has family rooms and includes a wing with budget apartments, or you can opt

PRICE CATEGORIES

Price categories are based on an average double room, including tax, with breakfast:
€ = under €155
€€ = €155–225
€€€ = over €225

for an apartment with sauna facing the forest. Indoor and outdoor pools, plus children's pools. A good choice for families. €–€€

Lappeenranta

Scandic Hotel Patria
Kauppakatu 21
Tel: 05 677 511
www.scandichotels.com
Modern hotel situated close to the harbour and fortress area; 130 rooms, restaurants and saunas. Some rooms have balconies and views over Lake Saimaa. €

Punkaharju

Fontana Punkaharjun Valtionhotelli
Harjutie 596
Tel: 020 752 9800

www.fontana.fi
There are 24 rooms in this wooden Russian-style pair of buildings which exude atmosphere. In the beautiful Punkaharju Ridge area. €–€€

Savonlinna

Fontana Spa Hotel Casino
Kylpylaitoksentie 7
Tel: 015 739 5430
www.spahotelcasino.eng
Most of the 80 rooms in this island complex have a balcony with a view. Cheap hostel beds in summer. €–€€
Perhehotelli Hospitz
Linnankatu 20
Tel: 015 515 661
www.hospitz.com
Cosy, family-run hotel. Very popular and often fully booked in summer. €

ABOVE: fly fishing in calm waters.

Tampere

Kauppi
Kalevan puistotie 2
Tel: 02 253 5353
www.hotelli-kauppi.fi
Just east of the centre, this hotel is popular with families. The large rooms include a fridge and microwave, and

there is parking, a swimming pool and two saunas. €–€€
Hotel Victoria
Itsenäisyydenkatu 1
Tel: 03 242 5111
www.hotellivictoria.fi
Simple rooms and friendly staff. Breakfast is included, and there is a swimming pool and sauna. €

WEST COAST

Oulu

Holiday Club Oulun Eden
Holstinsalmentie 29
Tel: 08 5544 103
www.holidayclubspahotels.com
Indoor pools, water slides, luxury spa and steam rooms

at a seaside location. Good restaurant. €€

Rauma

Hotel Vanha Rauma
Vanhankirkonkatu 26
Tel: 02 8376 2200

www.hotelvanharauma.fi
In the centre of old Rauma in a renovated Art Deco warehouse. Well-equipped, comfortable rooms. €€
Kemi
The SnowCastle of Kemi
Tel: 016 258 878

www.snowcastle.net
The magical SnowHotel opens from January to mid-April. Snug Arctic sleeping bags hold the cold at bay. An unforgettable experience. Book well in advance. €€

KARELIA

Joensuu

Finnhostel Joensuu
Kalevankatu 8
Tel: 013 267 5076
www.islo.fi
Located in the city centre with 24 self-contained, newly renovated single, double and triple rooms.

The Sportti restaurant serves breakfast and lunch weekdays. €

Kuusamo

Sokos Hotel Kuusamo
Kirkkotie 23
Tel: 020 1234 693
www.sokoshotels.fi

Pleasant rooms, near town and close to the Ruka ski slopes and wilderness. Saunas and swimming pool. €

Nurmes

Bomba Holiday Club
Tuulentie 10

Tel: 020 1234 908
www.holidayclubspahotels.com
This historic hotel (and Karelian village) on the shore of Lake Pielinen offers spa treatments, various activities, and is a good destination for families. Sample Karelian cooking. €€

LAPLAND

Rovaniemi

Guesthouse Borealis
Asemieskatu 1
Tel: 016 34 20 130
www.guesthouseborealis.com
Friendly B&B close to the station. There are single,

double and triple rooms, all with own bathroom, one with cooking facilities and sauna; plus an apartment for seven people. €
Rantasipi Pohjanhovi
Pohjanpuistikko 2
Tel: 016 33 711

www.hotelworld.fi
Legendary riverside hotel with swimming pool, nightclub and casino. Located in a scenic location on the banks of the Kemijoki waterfront with lovely river views. €€

E ATING OUT

RECOMMENDED RESTAURANTS

What to Eat

Finnish cuisine has broadened and improved enormously in recent years. Tradition was that Finns would eat a large hot lunch, then a smaller cold meal in the evening. Only businessmen dined out, and it was usually white fish, boiled potatoes and mushrooms. Happily that has radically changed in the last decade, as Helsinki has become more cosmopolitan and now boasts a myriad of gourmet establishments and cosmopolitan restaurants, from Turkish to Thai. The best Russian cuisine outside of Russia continues to be found in Helsinki. Enjoy the seasonal cuisine: crayfish in summer, game (reindeer and elk) in autumn. *For more on eating and drinking in Finland, see Food and Drink chapter.*

Where to Eat

In the past, it was difficult to get a really cheap meal in Finland, but you can find places where you will definitely get value for money. Fixed-price lunches are often very good deals and are usually advertised on boards outside restaurants. Many serve an extensive buffet including tea or coffee for a low price.

The Sokos and Stockmann department stores have excellent food halls; otherwise, for snacks there are more and more cafés sprouting up that supply sandwiches, quiche, soups and salads at reasonable prices. In Helsinki, the Market Square (Kauppatori) has all kinds of delicious cheap eats. Museum cafés are usually reliable places to go for delicious, reasonably priced fare.

Drinking Notes

Alcohol remains expensive in Finland due to high taxes.
Beer The Finnish *tuoppi* is slightly smaller than the British pint. If you do not specify, you will usually be served a *keskiolut* (3.5 percent alcohol). The strongest beer is number 4 (*nelosolut*, 4.5 percent) and the weakest number 1 (*ykkösolut*, just over 1 percent).
Wine is imported and very costly. Alko, the state alcohol monopoly, continues to keep prices high and opening hours still limited at its outlets.

Restaurant Listings

Restaurants are listed in alphabetical order by region, with the most expensive first.

RESTAURANT LISTINGS

HELSINKI

Bellevue
Rahapajankatu 3
Tel: 09 179 560
Superb cuisine in Helsinki's oldest (established in 1917) and most refined Russian restaurant, in the shadow of the Uspenski Orthodox Cathedral. Try the blinis with herring caviar or the borscht, then move on to the filet of beef with barley or a classic chicken Kiev.
€€€

Chez Dominique
Rikhardinkatu 4
Tel: 09 612 7393
A gourmet temple near Esplanadi Park, with two Michelin stars, owned by Hans Välimäki, probably Finland's most famous chef. Chez Dominique is renowned for inventive cuisine such as seared foie gras with a white port and golden raisin sauce. Menu changes weekly. €€€

G.W. Sundmans
Eteläranta 16
Tel: 09 6128 5400
Situated in a 19th-century Empire-style building designed by Engel, this elegant restaurant serves light, seasonal dishes, and the extensive wine list includes some surprisingly inexpensive wines. For a more casual atmosphere and less pricy menu, dine at the

Krog , a gastro pub on the ground floor of the same premises. Close to Market Square.
€€–€€€

PRICE CATEGORIES

Price categories are per person for an average three-course meal, excluding drinks but with tax:
€ = under €20
€€ = €20–40
€€€ = over €40

DENMARK

NORWAY

SWEDEN

FINLAND

Juuri
Korkeavuorenkatu 27
Tel: 09 635 732
This intimate bistro opened in 2009 and is constantly packed, so book ahead. They serve an assortment of *sapas* (Finnish tapas!), and the fish of the day is a good choice. €€

Karljohan
Yrjönkatu 21
Tel: 09 612 1121
Traditional Finnish dishes at good prices which attract locals who come for their daily lunch specials. Fish of the day a good choice here too. €–€€

Kellarikrouvi & Fabian
Pohkoinen Makasiinikatu 6
Tel: 09 6128 5100.
Savvy locals come to dine in this unpretentious vaulted cellar for reasonably priced, seasonal Finnish food. Upstairs the weekly lunch buffet is very popular. €–€€

Lappi
Annankatu 22
Tel: 09 645 550
An authentic Lapland experience is a bonus when sampling anything made of reindeer, tasty fish, salted fungi and exotic berries. Try the Lappish plate to savour

a full range of northern specialities. €€

Restaurant Klippan
Luoto Island
Tel: 09 633 408
The red roof of this distinguished wooden villa is easily reached on the island of Luoto, in the South Harbour. It is a summer restaurant, only open from May to September. The chef is a passionate fisherman and a fanatic for seasonal ingredients. Lunch on Sunday. The shuttle boat leaves from Olympia terminaali by the Peace statue. €€

Sandeep
Lönnrotinkatu 22
Tel: 09 685 6206
Tandoori and vegetarian Indian dishes in a cosy ambience. €€

Savoy
Eteläesplanadi 14
Tel: 09 6128 5300
The ultimate Finnish dining experience since 1937, with a timeless interior by Alvar Aalto. It was a favourite of Marshall Mannerheim, whose *vorschmack* (a spicy meat dish) remains on the menu. Reserve a table on the terrace for a drop-dead view. €€€

THE SOUTH

Turku

Summer in Turku is not complete without a session in one of the dozen boat restaurants on the River Aurajoki, but proceed carefully, as the food doesn't always live up to the surroundings.

Blanko
Aurakatu 1
Tel: 02 233 3966
This oasis of cool serves simple fusion cooking in a unique vaulted environment. It has a disco on Friday and Saturday evenings. €–€€

Fontana
Aurakatu 1
Tel: 02 250 1444
An Art Nouveau café in a prime location serving up simple fare that attracts students, young mums, hip grannies and amorous couples. €

Herman
Läntinen Rantakatu 37
Tel: 02 230 3333
Brewery-restaurant in an Empire structure along the waterfront serving a popular inexpensive lunch buffet on its ground level, while upstairs more refined food is offered. €–€€€

Hiivari
Käsityöläiskatu 5
Tel: 02 231 4008
A popular "hole in the wall" that is loved by locals for its bohemian atmosphere and excellent home cooking. Try the Baltic herring and garlic potatoes. €–€€

Pinella
Itäinen Rantakatu
Tel: 02 445 4200
Finland's oldest restaurant reopened in 2011 after restoration of its historic premises. Enjoy contemporary cuisine in a classic ambience or on the riverside terrace in summer.

Start with an aperitif at the new cocktail and champagne bar. €€–€€€

Pizzeria Dennis
Linnankatu 17
Tel: 02 469 1191
Tasty and authentic pizzas, good toppings. €

Viking Restaurant Harald
Auragatan 3
Tel: 044 766 8204
A themed restaurant that serves up hearty game, fish and vegetarian fare on rustic earthenware. Start with the salmon or red beet soup, then let your costumed server advise you. €€

LAKELAND

BELOW: a platter of mixed fish.

Kuopio

Musta Lammas
Satamakatu 4
Tel: 017 5810 458
This pleasant restaurant specialises in fresh seasonal dishes like pike perch, reindeer, and the lamb you will see in its logo. Start off with blinis and salmon roe as an appetiser. €€

Vapaasatama Sampo
Kauppakatu 13
Tel: 017 261 4677
Informal atmosphere, serving excellent fish. €€

Wanha Satama
Matkustaja-Satama
Tel: 017 197 304
Rustic and lively; located by the passenger harbour. Serves tasty *muikku* (whitefish) with garlic and mashed potatoes. €

Savonlinna

Savonlinna market *(kauppatori)* is a busy and popular place to indulge in a snack from one of the many tempting food stalls. Prices are steep during the Opera Festival, but the market is also at its liveliest then.

Majakka
Satamakatu 11
Tel: 015 531 456
A popular place near the market, serving fish and hearty Finnish dishes. **€€**

Olutravintola Sillansuu
Verkkosaarenkatu 1
Tel: 015 531 451
Popular pub near Market Bridge. **€€**

Tampere

Astor
Aleksis Kivenkatu 26
Tel: 010 321 1600
Live piano music every night. Try the fillets of Baltic herring in mustard sauce. **€€€**

Eetvartti
Sumeliuksenkatu 16
Tel: 020 123 4633
Run by the Pirkanmaa Hotel and Restaurant School. High-quality food cooked by the students. **€–€€**

Näsinneula
Särkänniemi Adventure Park & Tower
Tel: 0207 130 234
Revolving restaurant high in the Näsinneula Observation Tower, where you dine 168 metres (635ft) above the scenic landscape of Tampere. **€€€**

Plevna
Itäinenkatu 8
Tel: 03 260 1200
Lively pub/café specialising in steaks and sausages. Beers are brewed on the premises. **€**

WEST COAST

Oulu

Pannu
Kauppurienkatu 12
Tel: 020 792 8 200
Located next to the Stockmann department store, this popular, well-priced pit stop is busy for lunch and dinner. There's a large pizza selection, but standard Finnish specialities such as wild boar and fresh fish also appear on the menu. **€**

Ravintola Matala
Rantakatu 6
Tel: 08 333 013
Oulu's finest restaurant is located on the shoreline at Market Square. Start off with the blinis and house smoked salmon or roe. Main courses include fresh fish and game in season. Separate vegetarian choice, and a four-course "surprise" menu. Excellent service, good wine list, but pricey. **€€–€€€**

Pori

Raatihuoneen Kellari
Hallituskatu 9
Tel: 02 633 4804
First-class establishment serving Finnish-style meat and fish dishes. Located in the basement of the old Town Hall. **€€–€€€**

Vaasa

Gustav Wasa
Raastuvankatu 24
Tel: 050 466 3208
Cellar restaurant serving excellent meat portions and some fish. The rustic dining hall used to be a coal-storing cellar. **€€€**

Strampen
Rantakatu 6
Tel: 041 451 4512
A summer-only pavilion restaurant, with a fine terrace for people-watching. Good selection of evening dishes and lighter lunches. **€€–€€€**

LAPLAND

Rovaniemi

Fransmanni
Sokos Vaakuna Hotel, Koskikatu 4
Tel: 020 1234 695
Rather pricey, but excellent food. A good place to try Lappish specialities, such as reindeer filet and cloudberry liqueur. If you are on a budget or travelling with children, try the other in-house restaurant, Amarillo, known for tasty Tex-Mex dining, as well as pastas and salads. **€–€€€**

Manza
Ruokasenkatu 2
Tel: 016 319 616
Located in the centre of town, this popular lunch destination attracts locals who come for the extensive buffet, with soup, salads and warm dishes. Good value. **€–€€**

Restaurant Nili
Valtakatu 20
Tel: 0400 369 669
Nili is a snug place, decorated with Lappish woodcarvings and furs. It offers traditional Lapp food – Arctic char, pike perch, reindeer and bear, served with seasonal accompaniments. **€€€**

Restaurant Sky Ounasvaara
Juhannuskalliontie 2
Tel: 016 323 400
For startling beautiful views, head for this panoramic restaurant 3km (2 miles) outside town in the Hotel Sky Ounasvaara. There's a selection of classy international dishes, or try local treats from the Lapp menu. **€€€**

BELOW: smoked fish is a Baltic delicacy.

Saariselkä

Ravintola Pirkon Pirtti
Honkapolku 2
Tel: 016 668 050
Popular restaurant serving reindeer and game dishes, and pizzas for the less adventurous. Also on the menu is marinated fillet of elk, and crispy fried char. Round off the meal with Arctic cloudberry sorbet. Closes in summer. **€€–€€€**

PRICE CATEGORIES

Price categories are per person for an average three-course meal, excluding drinks but with tax:
€ = under €20
€€ = €20–40
€€€ = over €40

436

ART AND PHOTO CREDITS

Peter Adams 166/167
AKG London 26B/T, 27T, 30, 34, 35, 39, 40, 42, 44, 48, 49, 84/85, 86, 87, 91, 92, 137T, 149TL, 198T
Alamy 212, 276, 281, 419
B & C Alexander 2/3, 5B, 70, 80, 162, 163, 165, 199T, 207, 219, 228, 283, 314T
Goran Assner/Goteburg.com 109R
AWL Images 210
Eva Backlund/ Lidkoping.com 275
Ny Carlsberg Glyptotek 122L
Alain Proust/Cephas 98R
Jamsa Finlandia/City of Helsinki Tourist Board 310
Niklas Sjöblom/City of Helsink T Bureau 298/299
S Somerma/City of Helsinki Tourist Board 309T, 312
Paul Williams City of Helsinki Tourist Board 315
Sylvia Cordaiy 83, 158, 215, 317
Erik Cornelius/SKM 38
Jan Dago 144, 150
Courtesy Design House Stockholm 90
Fritz Dressler 341T
Kasper Dudzik 409
Bruno Ehrs 143T
Christian Erichsen 139
Mary Evans 21B, 28
Richard K Evans 209
Fotolia 164T
Robert Fried 1, 41, 327, 340
Getty Images 27B, 29, 52
APA Glyn Genin 6BR, 7ML/MR, 11B, 22, 31, 33, 104/105, 153T, 168/169, 170, 171B/T, 177, 178, 179, 180L/R, 181, 182, 183T, 185, 187, 188L/R, 189, 190, 191, 195, 196, 197L/R/T, 201, 202, 203, 205, 206/T, 212T, 214, 216L/R, 217, 218/T, 223, 225L/R, 229, 230T, 232/T, 233, 376, 380, 390, 393, 421
Dick Gillberg/Goteborg Tourist Office 270T
Robert Harding 8ML, 9BR, 74, 235/234, 257T, 266, 267, 287
APA David Hall 109L
Dave G Hauser 262T, 325, 354, 355T
APA Rudy Hemmingsen 9TR, 59, 60L/R, 88, 89, 120R, 121, 123, 124, 125, 126L, 127, 128B/T, 129, 131, 138, 361, 364, 365
Esa Hiltula 71, 341, 342, 345
APA Jim Holmes 320, 321, 323T, 324/T, 326/T, 332, 333, 334, 336T, 337, 339/T, 340T, 343, 346, 347, 349, 350, 351, 355, 356, 357
Image Bank Sweden 11T, 46, 50, 68, 261, 279, 400
Fedrik Broman/Imagebank Sweden 291T
Kjell Holmner/Image Bank Sweden 401
Kalle Kirstil/Imagebank Sweden 265T
Bo Lind/Imagebank Sweden 289
Henrik Trygg/Image Bank Sweden 82, 282, 292T, 411

Innovation Norge 12BR, 17/18, 181T, 183L, 208, 210T, 211, 215L/R
Nancy Bundt/Innovation Norge 379, 381, 382,
Pal Bugge/Innovation Norge 23, 388
Johan Berge/Innovation Norge 65
Nancy Bundt/Innovation Norge 184, 185T, 397
Per Eide/Innovation Norge 384
Frithjof Fure/Innovation Norge 386, 390
Anders Gjengeda/Innovation Norge 213
Christian Houge/Innovation Norge 62,97
Jens Henrik Nybo/Innovation Norge 99
Bjorn Jorgensen/Innovation Norge 378
Casper Tybjerg/Innovation Norge 377
Johan Wildhagen/Innovation Norge 63, 81, 218/219
Innovation Sweden 15/16
Istockphoto 294T
Jack Jackson 127T
Micahel Jenner 72, 249, 257B, 307, 306, 316T, 336
Ingmar Jrnberg/Goteborg Opera 269
M. Kapanen/Alvar Aalto Museum 94
Jouko Kononen 7TR
Statens Konstmuseer (SKM) 93
Bob Krist 112, 130, 125, 155, 252
Ake Lindman/Architecture Museum 248
Lebrecht Collection 95 149TR
Leonardo 413, 418
APA Julian Love 5T, 8T, 24R, 55, 56/57, 66, 67R, 69, 75, 100L/R, 106/107, 142, 238, 239T, 238, 239T, 244, 245, 246, 247L/R/T, 248T, 250, 251, 252T, 253, 255L/R, 256/T, 271L/R, 272, 277/T, 280, 395, 399,412, 416, 417
Lyle Lawson 296/297
Buddy Mays 329, 331
National Museum of Finland 43, 47, 51, 310
Nordic Photo 286, 292, 293, 295
Nordiska Museet 45, 53L, 239B, 250T
Richard Nowitz 186T
Martin Nyman 410
PA Photos, 53R
Erhard Pansegrau 143,
Nicolai Perjesi/Copenhagen Photo Gallery 61
Photolibrary 4B, 6BL, 7b, 8BL/BR, 8MR, 9TL, 67L, 113L, 135, 140, 154, 159, 160, 164, 227T, 263, 264, 273, 278, 288, 291, 294, 359
Barry Pringle 148
Hans Klüche 226
Rex Features 345T
Royal Caribbean 54
Saippuakauppias 9BL
Isabel Schultz 275T
APA Jeroen Snijders 155T, 156/T
Henrik Stenberg/Copenhagen Photo Gallery 119
Superstock 199,
Erik Lindvall/ Swedish Tourist Board 24L
Miriam Preis/ Swedish Tourist Board 101

Nigel Tisdall 225T,
Topfoto 194
Tourism Denmark 96,
Magnus Skogl/Tourist Board Sweden 398
Sindre Wimberger 209
APA Gregory Wrona 3B, 7MB, 7TL, 108, 309, 311, 313, 323, 328, 321T, 335, 421, 430
courtesy Bertil Vallien 254
Visit Copenhagen 4T, 113R, 118, 120L, 122R, 360, 369, 370, 373/T
Visit Denmark 9M, 12T, 58, 134, 137, 141, 151, 153, 157, 375
Cees van Roeden/Visit Denmark 79, 145, 147T, 149
Karsten Bidstrup/Visit Finland 10T
JN Lanthiez/Visit Finland 78
V Poroajelu/Visit Finland 300
Jon Sparks/Visit Finland 20
M Tervonen/Visit Finland 432, 433
Visit Finland 73, 77, 102/103, 301L/R, 308, 313, 335T, 337T, 353
Visit Norway 76, 176
N Bundt/Visit Norway 98L
B Jorgenson/Visit Norway 6M/T, 18/19
T Rakke/Visitnorway 10B, 25, 389, 396
C Tybjerg/Visit Norway 21T
Bo Lind/Visit Sweden 405

PHOTO FEATURES

36/37: Istockphoto 36/37, 36R, 37BL, APA Rudy Hemminsen 37BL, APA Gly Genin 36BL, Werner Forman Archive 37BR/M

132/133: All Photography Danish Design Centre except: Visit Denmark 132BL, Visit Copenhagen 133BR/T

220/221: All Photography APA Glyn Genin

258/259: Henrik Trygg/Imagebank Sweden 258/259, 258M, 259TR, APA julian Love 258B, 259BL/M, Conny Fridh/Imagebank Sweden 259BR

318/319: Visitfinland.com 318/319, 318M, City of Helsinki 318BM, 319BL, APA Gregory Wrona 319BR, Istockphoto 319M

Map Production: original cartography Gar Bowes Design and Geodata, updated by APA Cartography Department

© APA Publications (UK) Ltd 2012

Production: Tynan Dean, Linton Donaldson and Rebeka Ellam

INDEX

Main references are in bold type

D

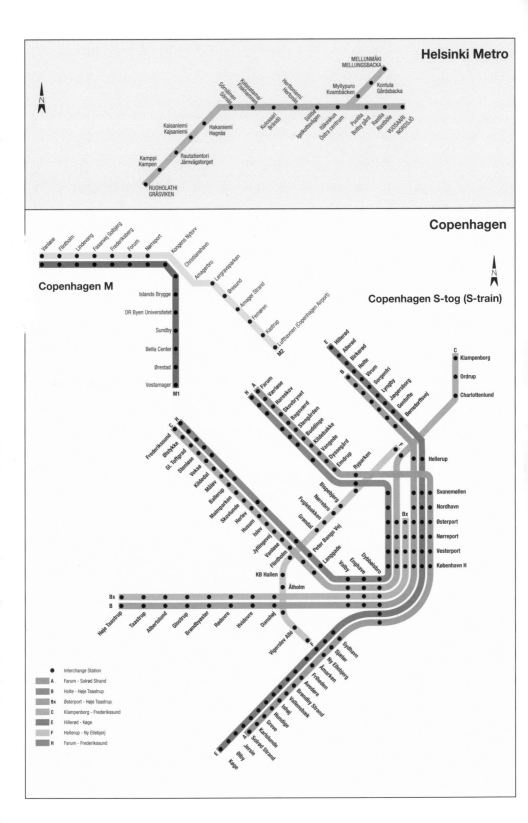

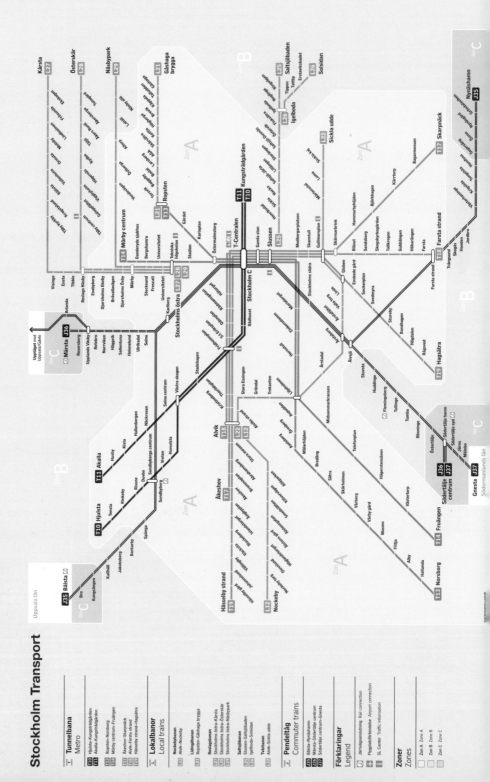

Stockholm Transport